Applied Software Product Line Engineering

Applied Software Product Line Engineering

Edited by
Kyo C. Kang
Vijayan Sugumaran
Sooyong Park

CRC Press
Taylor & Francis Group
Boca Raton   London   New York

CRC Press is an imprint of the
Taylor & Francis Group, an **informa** business
AN AUERBACH BOOK

Auerbach Publications
Taylor & Francis Group
6000 Broken Sound Parkway NW, Suite 300
Boca Raton, FL 33487-2742

© 2010 by Taylor and Francis Group, LLC
Auerbach Publications is an imprint of Taylor & Francis Group, an Informa business

No claim to original U.S. Government works

Printed in the United States of America on acid-free paper
10 9 8 7 6 5 4 3 2 1

International Standard Book Number: 978-1-4200-6841-2 (Hardback)

Library of Congress Cataloging-in-Publication Data

Applied software product line engineering / Kyo C. Kang, Vijayan Sugumaran, Sooyong Park.
    p. cm.
Includes bibliographical references and index.
ISBN 978-1-4200-6841-2 (hardcover : alk. paper)
    1. Software product line engineering. 2. Computer software--Development--Management. 3. Computer software--Reusability. I. Kang, Kyo C. II. Sugumaran, Vijayan, 1960- III. Park, Sooyong.

QA76.76.D47A693 2010
005--dc22
                                         2009040320

Visit the Taylor & Francis Web site at
http://www.taylorandfrancis.com

and the Auerbach Web site at
http://www.auerbach-publications.com

Contents

Contributors

Chapter 1 Software Product Line Engineering: Overview and Future Directions

Kyo C. Kang received his PhD from the University of Michigan in 1982. Since then he has worked as a visiting professor at the University of Michigan and as a member of the technical staff at Bell Communications Research and AT&T Bell Laboratories before joining the Software Engineering Institute, Carnegie Mellon University, as a senior member in 1987. He is currently a professor at the Pohang University of Science and Technology (POSTECH) in Korea. He served as director of the Software Engineering Center at Korea Information Technology Promotion Agency (KIPA) from 2001 to 2003. Dr. Kang also served as general chair for the 8th International Conference on Software Reuse (ICSR) held in Madrid, Spain in 2004 and general chair for the 11th International Product Line Conference (SPLC 2007) held in Kyoto, Japan in September 2007. His areas of research include software reuse and product line engineering, requirements engineering, and computer-aided software engineering.

Vijayan Sugumaran is professor of management information systems in the Department of Decision and Information Sciences at Oakland University, Rochester, Michigan. He also has joint appointment (2010–2013) with the Department of Service Systems Management and Engineering, Sogang University, Seoul, South Korea. His research interests are in the areas of software product line engineering, ontologies and semantic Web, intelligent agent and multi-agent systems, and service science. He has published more than 130 articles in journals, conferences, and books. He has edited seven books and two journal special issues. One special issue is the December 2006 issue of *Communications of the ACM*, focusing on software product line engineering. His most recent publications have appeared in *Information Systems Research, ACM Transactions on Database Systems, IEEE Transactions on Engineering Management, Communications of the ACM, Healthcare Management Science,* and *Data and Knowledge Engineering.* Dr. Sugumaran is the editor-in-chief of the *International Journal of Intelligent Information Technologies* and also serves on the editorial board of eight other journals. He was the program co-chair for the 13th International Conference on Applications of Natural Language to Information Systems (NLDB 2008). In addition, he has served as the chair of the Intelligent Agent and Multi-Agent Systems mini-track for Americas Conference on Information Systems (AMCIS 1999–2009) and the Intelligent Information Systems track for the Information Resources Management Association International Conference (IRMA 2001, 2002, 2005–2007). He served as chair of the E-Commerce track for Decision Science Institute's Annual Conference, 2004. He is the information technology coordinator for the Decision Sciences Institute and regularly serves as a program committee member for numerous national and international conferences.

Sooyong Park is professor of the Computer Science Department and director of the Defense Software Research Center at Sogang University, Seoul, Korea. He received his Bachelor of Engineering degree in computer science from Sogang University in 1986, the Master of Science degree in computer science from Florida State University in 1988, and a PhD in information technology with a major in software engineering from George Mason University, Fairfax, Virginia, in 1995. From 1996 to 1998 he served as a senior software Engineer at TRW ISC. He is actively involved in academic activities including serving as a steering committee member of the Asian-Pacific Software Engineering Conference, guest editor of *CACM* Dec. 2006 software product line issue, and program chair of the International Workshop on Future Software Technology and the International Workshop on Dynamic Software Product Line. He is currently a member of editorial board of the *Industrial Management and Data Systems Journal* and the *Journal of Computer Information Systems*. He is also a founding member of the Korea Defense Software Association and a steering committee member of the Korean Software Engineering Society. His research interests include requirements engineering, service-oriented architecture, self-managed software, and software product line engineering.

Chapter 2   A Roadmap for Software Product Line Adoption

Dr. Lawrence G. Jones is a senior member of the technical staff in the Research, Technology and Systems Solutions Program at the Software Engineering Institute (SEI) of Carnegie Mellon University with more than 39 years experience in software development, management, and education. Dr. Jones served in the U.S. Air Force and is the former chair of the Computer Science Department at the Air Force Academy. He is the chair of the ABET Accreditation Council, past chair of the ABET Computing Accreditation Commission, a senior member of the IEEE and the ACM, and secretary/treasurer of the Computing Sciences Accreditation Board.

Linda M. Northrop is currently director of the Research, Technology, and Systems Solution Program at the Software Engineering Institute, where she leads the work in architecture-centric engineering, software product lines, systems of systems, and ultra-large-scale systems. She is coauthor of the book *Software Product Lines: Practices and Patterns* and led the research group on ULS systems that resulted in the book, *Ultra-Large-Scale Systems: The Software Challenge of the Future.* Before joining the SEI, she was associated with both the U.S. Air Force Academy and the State University of New York as professor of computer science, and with both Eastman Kodak and IBM as a software engineer.

Dr. Paul C. Clements is a senior member of the technical staff at Carnegie Mellon University's Software Engineering Institute, where he has worked since 1994 leading or coleading projects in software product line engineering and software architecture documentation and analysis. He is the coauthor of five books covering areas of software architecture, software product lines, and software engineering. In addition, he has authored dozens of papers in software engineering, reflecting his long-standing interest in the design and specification of challenging software systems.

Dr. John D. McGregor is an associate professor of computer science at Clemson University, a visiting scientist at the Software Engineering Institute, and a partner in Luminary Software, a software engineering consulting firm. His research interests include software product lines, model-driven development, and component-base software engineering. He is interested in strategic issues in software engineering and writes a bimonthly column for JOT titled "Strategic Software Engineering." His latest book is *A Practical Guide to Testing Object-Oriented Software* (Addison-Wesley 2001).

Chapter 3   New Methods behind a New Generation of Software Product Line Successes

Charles W. Krueger, PhD, is the founder and CEO of BigLever Software, a leading provider of software product line engineering (SPLE) frameworks, tools, and services. He is a thought leader in the SPLE field and has helped establish the industry's most acclaimed SPLE practices. A noted author and speaker, Dr. Krueger has cochaired the International Conference on Software Reuse, is instrumental in international SPLE conferences, and moderates the SoftwareProductLines.com Web site. Dr. Krueger received his PhD in computer science from Carnegie Mellon University.

Chapter 4   Evaluating Product Family Development Using the Balanced Scorecard Approach

Jong Woo Kim received his MS degree in computer information systems from Georgia State University in 2004. He is currently working toward the PhD degree in computer information systems at Georgia State University. His current research interests include ontology, software engineering, Web services, and cognitive theory. His research papers appeared in *IEEE Transactions on Engineering Management,*

Software Process Improvement and Practice, and in proceedings of international conferences such as the HICSS and AMCIS.

Kannan Mohan is an associate professor of computer information systems at Baruch College, City University of New York. He received his PhD in CIS from Georgia State University in 2003. His research interests include managing software product family development, providing traceability support for systems development, knowledge integration, and agile development methodologies. Dr. Mohan's work has appeared in journals such as *Decision Support Systems, Communications of the ACM, Information & Management*, and *Communications of the AIS*.

Balasubramaniam Ramesh is the Board of Advisors professor of computer information systems at Georgia State University. His research interests include supporting complex organizational processes such as requirements management, agile software development, and business process management with decision-support and knowledge-management systems and methods. His research has appeared in leading journals, including the *IEEE Transactions on Software Engineering, MIS Quarterly, Journal of the AIS, Annals of Software Engineering, Communications of the ACM, Requirements Engineering Journal, Decision Support Systems, Information Systems Journal, IEEE Computer, IEEE Software, IEEE Internet Computing, IEEE IT Professional*, and *IEEE Intelligent Systems*. His work has been funded by leading government and private industry sources including the National Science Foundation, Defense Advance Projects Agency, Office of Naval Research, Army Research Laboratory, and Accenture and has been incorporated in several computer-aided software engineering tools.

Chapter 5 Product Management for Software Product Lines: An Overview

Georg Herzwurm has held the chair for business administration and information systems, especially business software, at the University of Stuttgart, Germany since 2003. He holds a Masters degree and PhD in business administration from the University of Cologne and spent three years as a professor at the Technical University of Dresden. His research focuses on product development, software product management, as well as the development and use of integrated business software. In 2000 he received the International Akao Prize for outstanding contributions to the further development and support of the method Quality Function Deployment (QFD). Georg is a cofounder and speaker of the board of the German OFD Institute.

Andreas Helferich holds a Masters degree in business administration from the University of Stuttgart, Germany, and a Masters degree in management information systems from the University of Missouri at St. Louis, Missouri. Andreas is senior researcher and lecturer at Georg Herzwurm's department at the University of

Stuttgart and is currently working on his PhD thesis on software mass customization. Besides his university career, he has been working as a consultant in a number of projects in different industries, mainly evaluating and implementing information systems.

Dr. Klaus Schmid holds a professorship in software engineering at the University of Hildesheim, Germany. He has been active in requirements engineering and product line engineering since the mid-1990s. Over time he has been involved in numerous research and industrial projects. His specific interests are in value-based product line engineering and the engineering of adaptive systems. He has authored numerous refereed papers on these subjects and was responsible for several workshops and tutorials at international conferences in this area. He received a diploma degree and a PhD in computer science from the University of Kaiserslautern, Germany.

Chapter 6   A Systems Product Line Approach

Magnus Eriksson is a systems engineering specialist at BAE Systems Hägglunds AB in Sweden. Magnus received his MS, Eng.Lic., and PhD from Umeå University in Sweden. His main research interests are in the areas of modular product platforms, software product line development, and systems engineering. Dr. Eriksson was the 2006 INCOSE Brian Mar Award recipient.

Jürgen Börstler is an associate professor in software engineering at Umeå University, Umeå, Sweden. He has a Masters in computer science with economics as a subsidiary subject from Saarland University, Germany, and a PhD in computer science from Aachen University of Technology, Germany. His main research interests are in the areas of object-oriented software development, requirements management, software product lines, and educational issues in computer science.

Kjell Borg is currently R&D project manager at BAE Systems Hägglunds AB and has more than 20 years of experience in software engineering and research. He holds a BS in mathematics and a Ph.Lic. in computer science. Mr. Borg has experience in the fields of usability design, requirements engineering, software engineering, quality management, embedded systems, project management, and systems engineering. He has business experience in the areas of defense, telecom, transport, and process industry.

Chapter 7   The Adoption of Software Product Lines to Develop Autonomic Pervasive Systems

Carlos Cetina is a PhD candidate in the Research Centre for Software Production Methods. His research interests include model-driven engineering, software product lines, and autonomic computing. Mr. Cetina received an MS in computer engineering from the Universidad Politécnica de Valencia, Spain.

Joan Fons is an assistant professor in the Department of Information Systems and Computation (DISC) at the Universidad Politécnica de Valencia, Spain. His research is involved in the fields of model-driven development, pervasive computing, Web engineering, and SW development for mobile devices. He received his PhD from the Universidad Politécnica de Valencia in 2008. Dr. Fons has been published in several well-known scientific journals, book chapters, and international conferences. He is currently part of the scientific advisory board of the MOSKitt Open Source CASE Tool (http://www.moskitt.org) and the gvSIG Mobile Project (http://www.gvsig.org).

Vicente Pelechano is an associate professor in the Department of Information Systems and Computation (DISC) at the Universidad Politécnica de Valencia, Spain. His research interests are model-driven development, ubiquitous computing, and ambient intelligence, Web engineering, and human-computer interaction. He received his PhD from the Universidad Politécnica de Valencia in 2001. Dr. Pelechano is the head of the Ambient Intelligence and Web Technology Research Group in the ProS Research Center at the UPV. He has published in several well-known scientific journals, book chapters, and international conferences and is currently leading the technical supervision of the MOSKitt Open Source CASE Tool (http://www.moskitt.org).

Chapter 8 Development of a Software Product Line for Validation Environments

Belén Magro is a senior engineer in the Research & Development Department at Dimetronic Signals of Madrid, Spain, which is part of the Invensys Rail Systems Group. Dimetronic is a company leader in the application of advanced technologies and train control systems in the railway-signaling sector. Dr. Magro received her PhD in computer science from the Technical University of Madrid (UPM). Her research interests are software engineering, software product line engineering, acceptance testing environments, and system and software testing processes and tools. Her interest is also focused on managing strict procedures and disciplines that ensure the safety and quality of the software developed. In 1996, she worked in the software development of the new Automatic Train Protection (ATP) System for the so-called Mediterranean Corridor. This RENFE (Spanish National Railway Network) line is between La Encina (Albacete) and Barcelona Sants, passing through Valencia, Castellón, and Tarragona. In 2003, she worked in the software development of ERTMS/ETCS (European Rail Traffic Management System) onboard train equipment for a pilot line in Albacete. Now she is working on software development for a contract for the supply of ERTMS/ETCS on-board equipment for 94 trains of the Madrid commuter network.

Juan Garbajosa is a professor at the Informatics School of the Technical University of Madrid (UPM), Spain. He is the leader of the Systems and Software Technology Research Group (SYST) at UPM. One of the activities in which he is currently involved deals with the evolution of software tools to support more agile though rigorous processes for critical software intensive systems. He is also active in standardization activities. He has been coeditor of several standards related to software tools and currently is the convener of ISO/IEC JTC1 SC7 WG20, Software and Systems Bodies of Knowledge and Professionalization. He has coauthored multiple articles in journals and conferences, and has been involved in many conferences as program committee member or chair. Before joining the university, he spent more than 15 years serving in the aerospace industry, national and local government, with different responsibilities related to software systems development and administration. His research interests include tools for testing, validation, monitoring and operation of complex systems, software product and process models, and quality standards and innovation.

Jennifer Pérez is an associate professor at the Informatics School of the Technical University of Madrid (UPM), Spain. She received her PhD in computer science from Polytechnic University of Valencia, Spain in 2006, where she was part of the Software Engineering and Information Systems (ISSI) Group of the Department of Information Systems and Computation (DSIC). She had a research professional training grant funded by the Spanish government to conduct her thesis work in software engineering and declarative programming. Since 2001, Dr. Pérez has participated in several national projects related to software engineering and software architectures. She was also the project manager of the "PRISMA: Model compiler of aspect-oriented component-based software architectures" Microsoft Research Cambridge Project. Now she is a member of the Systems & Software Technology Group of the Technical University of Madrid (UPM) and she is collaborating with the ISSI Research Group (for software engineering) on several projects and networks. She is the author of several journal articles and numerous national and international articles in conferences related to software engineering and software architectures. She has also been a reviewer of several conferences and workshops. She was PC member and posters chair of the First European Conference on Software Architecture, ECSA 2007. Her research interests are focused on software architectures, service-oriented architectures, component-based software development, aspect-oriented software development, software product lines, model compilers, and software evolution.

Chapter 9 Building a Family of Compilers

Matthias Blume is an assistant professor at Toyota Technical Institute at Chicago (TTI-C). He received his degree in mathematics from Humboldt-Universität zu Berlin in Germany, and his MA and PhD from Princeton. He spent two years as a

JSPS fellow at Kyoto University in Japan and later joined Lucent Bell Labs. While at TTI-C he has held part-time and visiting appointments at the University of Chicago. His research interests are in programming language design and implementation, focusing on compiler optimization and compilation management. Dr. Blume has participated in several projects implementing domain-specific languages, for example for network processors, and high-level languages such as Standard ML.

Wonseok Chae is a PhD candidate at Toyota Technological Institute at Chicago. He received an MS and a BS in computer science and engineering from the Pohang University of Science and Technology. While he worked for Lucent Bell Labs Korea, he developed wireless switching systems. He also served as a provisional software process assessor. His current research interests are in the design and implementation of advanced programming languages. Mr. Chae also exploits emerging software engineering principles and practices, including software product line engineering.

Chapter 10   Formal Verification and Software Product Lines

Tomoji Kishi is a professor at Waseda University, Tokyo, Japan. His research interests include software design, software architecture, software product lines, and embedded systems. He received a BS and an MS in information science at Kyoto University and a PhD in information science from the JAIST. He has engaged in research, development, and consultation on software engineering in industry before entering JAIST.

Natsuko Noda is a researcher at Common Platform Software Research Laboratories, NEC Corporation, Japan. Her research interests include software design, software architecture, software product lines, aspect-oriented technologies, and embedded systems. Dr. Noda received a BS and an MS in mathematics from the Tokyo Woman's Christian University and a PhD in information science from the Japan Advanced Institute of Science and Technology.

Chapter 11   Multiple-View Requirements Models for Software Product Line Engineering

Hassan Gomaa is chair and professor in the Department of Computer Science at George Mason University, Fairfax, Virginia. He received his PhD in computer science from Imperial College of Science and Technology, London. He has published more than 150 technical papers and three textbooks. His latest textbook, entitled *Designing Software Product Lines with UML*, was published by Addison Wesley in 2005. His research has been funded by several organizations including the National Science Foundation, NASA, and DARPA. He has taught in-depth courses on software design in North America, Europe, Japan, and Korea.

Erika Mir Olimpiew is an application designer at CSC in Chantilly, Virginia, and also an adjunct professor for George Mason University in Fairfax, Virginia. Dr. Olimpiew received her PhD in information technology from George Mason University in May 2008. Her research interests are in the areas of software design, software testing and analysis, and software product lines.

Chapter 12: Managing Flexibility and Variability: A Road to Competitive Advantage

Wim Codenie is a program coordinator of software engineering at Sirris, the collective center of the Belgian technology industry. He graduated from the Free University of Brussels in 1988, where he was involved in research on object-oriented frameworks and self-reflection in object-oriented programming languages. He has a strong ICT background and currently advises companies about improving their software product development capabilities. His specific interests include product variability, agile software development, and innovation management in software development. He has set up several research initiatives at the national and European level on these topics.

Nicolás González-Deleito joined the Software Engineering Group of Sirris in September 2007. He is mainly working on the VariBru Project. This project researches the topic of product variability in software product development and aims to help software-intensive product builders in selecting and executing an appropriate variability approach. Before joining Sirris, he was a postdoctoral teaching assistant at the Université Libre de Bruxelles, where his research focused on cryptography and computer security, particularly in fair-exchange protocols.

Jeroen Deleu is a director and member of the executive board of Sirris, the collective centre of the Belgian technology industry. He holds degrees in science as well as business administration and originated the Software Engineering Group at Sirris. He has a broad research background as well as industrial experience in the domains of hardware and software product development, business process reengineering, collaborative engineering, configuration management, and product life-cycle management. His current activities are oriented toward technology transfer and innovation strategy for software-intensive product builders. In that context, he is also involved in several international initiatives concerning the introduction of open business models and agility in organizations.

Vladimir Blagojević started his career helping R&D teams transition toward professional software-intensive product-development organizations, focusing on testing and product quality and on the application of agile development. Blagojević joined Sirris in 2006 and helped shape the software engineering group, building up relevant knowledge and advisory services and starting research initiatives. His focus is in developing new solutions for risk management of product failures in hardware/ software codesign, and his interests lie in agile and flexible product development, the application of social technologies for innovation support, and other software product-development challenges.

Pasi Kuvaja is an assistant professor in the Department of Information Processing Science, University of Oulu, Oulu, Finland. His research interests include software quality, software product quality, software process, software process assessment and improvement, empirical software engineering, embedded systems development, software product development in global context, agile software development approaches, and innovative requirements management. He is one of the developers of the European Software Process Assessment and Improvement Methodology (BOOTSTRAP) and served as a co-product manager of process improvement guide development in the SPICE Project. Pasi has been actively cooperating with European industry and was previously partner manager and work package leader in many European research projects (BOOTSTRAP, Profes, Moose, Merlin) and serves currently in the same role in EUREKA/ITEA2/Flexi and ITEI projects. He has published a couple of textbooks and about 60 articles in the field of software engineering.

Jouni Similä is a full professor of software engineering in the Department of Information Processing Science, University of Oulu, Oulu, Finland. His present research interests include software process assessment and improvement, empirical software engineering, product road mapping, requirements engineering, and open innovation. He has authored more than 70 publications in the information systems and software engineering fields. Prior to assuming an academic position, he worked in the software industry for nearly 20 years.

Chapter 13 Feature-Oriented Analysis and Design for Dynamically Reconfigurable Product Lines

Jaejoon Lee has been a lecturer in the Computing Department of Lancaster University, UK, since January 2008. Before coming to Lancaster, he worked as a scientist and project manager at Fraunhofer IESE in Kaiserslautern, Germany, from October 2005 to December 2007. He also worked as an associate researcher at the R&D Centre of LG Electronics in South Korea from July 1993 to February 2000. He holds a PhD in computer science and engineering; an MS in computer and communications engineering, both from POSTECH in South Korea; and a BS in mathematics from Sogang University in South Korea.

Dirk Muthig manages the Software Development Division at the Fraunhofer Institute for Experimental Software Engineering (IESE), Kaiserslautern, Germany. He has been involved in the definition of the Fraunhofer PULSE™ (Product Line Software and System Engineering) method since the very beginning in 1998. Dr. Muthig has been responsible for all research and technology transfer activities at IESE in the areas of software and system architectures, as well as product lines, since 2002. He received a diploma, as well as a PhD, from the Computer Science Department of the University of Kaiserslautern, Germany.

Chapter 14 Separating Application and Security Concerns in Modeling Software Product Lines

Michael E. Shin is an associate professor in the Department of Computer Science at Texas Tech University, Lubbock, Texas. He received his PhD in information technology from George Mason University, Fairfax, Virginia. He previously worked at the Electronics and Telecommunications Research Institute (ETRI), Daejeon, Korea. His research area is self-healing systems, secure software engineering, and software product lines. His research has been funded by NASA and ETRI.

Hassan Gomaa is chair and professor in the Department of Computer Science at George Mason University, Fairfax, Virginia. He received his PhD in computer science from Imperial College of Science and Technology, London. He has published more than 150 technical papers and three textbooks. His latest textbook, entitled *Designing Software Product Lines with UML*, was published by Addison Wesley in 2005. His research has been funded by several organizations, including the National Science Foundation, NASA, and DARPA. He has taught several in-depth industrial courses on software design in North America, Europe, Japan, and Korea.

Chapter 15 Architecture as Language

Markus Voelter works as an independent researcher, consultant, and coach for itemis AG in Stuttgart, Germany. His focus is on software architecture, model-driven software development, and domain-specific languages as well as on product line engineering. His experience is based on projects small to large, in enterprise as well as in embedded systems. Markus also regularly writes (articles, patterns, books) and speaks (training sessions, conferences) on those subjects. He is the editor of the Software Engineering Radio podcast.

Chapter 16 Management and Financial Controls of a Software Product Line Adoption

Yoshihiro Matsumoto is an adviser at the Advanced Software Technology and Mechatronics (ASTEM) Research Institute of Kyoto. He received his Dr.Eng. degree from the University of Tokyo. He was a principal engineer at Toshiba Corporation from 1954 to 1989, a professor at Kyoto University, Osaka Institute of Technology, and Musashi Institute of Technology from 1989 to 2002. His accomplishments while he was in Toshiba included the development of the software factory at Fuchu, Tokyo. Dr. Matsumoto's has become widely known through his many papers. His Web site is www5d.biglobe.ne.jp/~y-h-m/index.html. He is an IEEE Life Fellow.

Chapter 17 Efficient Scoping with CaVE: A Case Study

Isabel John is a scientist and project leader at the Fraunhofer Institute for Experimental Software Engineering (IESE) in Kaiserslautern, Germany. She is responsible for product line introduction projects in industrial contexts and performs product line technology transfer to software development companies. For almost 10 years, she has worked in research and industrial projects in the context of software product lines, scoping, and product line requirements engineering. Her work focuses on product line analysis, scoping, and information retrieval for product lines. She has given several presentations and tutorials on product line engineering at software engineering conferences and in industrial contexts.

Jens Knodel is a scientist at the Fraunhofer Institute for Experimental Software Engineering (IESE) in Kaiserslautern, Germany. As an applied researcher in the Department of Product Line Architectures, he works in several industrial and research projects in the context of product line engineering and software architectures. His main research interests are architecture compliance checking, software evolution, and architecture reconstruction.

Torsten Schulz is responsible for the product management of all product lines at IBS AG. IBS produces software solutions for production, quality, and traceability management for several branches, with a focus on automotive and electronics. For more than 16 years, he has worked for IBS, starting as a programmer, then becoming a project manager. He was R&D manager responsible for the complete product development at IBS for more than 10 years. For the past three years, he has been responsible for the Product Management Group.

Chapter 18 Model-Driven Aspect-Oriented Product Line Engineering: An Industrial Case Study

Markus Voelter works as an independent researcher, consultant, and coach for itemis AG in Stuttgart, Germany. His focus is on software architecture, model-driven software development, and domain-specific languages as well as on product line engineering. His experience is based on projects small to large, in enterprise as well as in embedded systems. Voelter also regularly writes (articles, patterns, books) and speaks (training sessions, conferences) on those subjects. He is the editor of the Software Engineering Radio podcast.

Christa Schwanninger is a senior research scientist at Siemens AG. She consults Siemens business units in software architecture and product line engineering and conducts industrial research in new and promising areas of software engineering. Schwanninger has worked as a researcher and consultant for software architecture topics for more than 12 years. She was actively involved in the development of systems for the telecommunication, automotive, automation, and medical engineering domain. Currently her focus is on aspect-oriented development, architecture evaluation, and product line engineering. Schwanninger has given tutorials and presentations on aspect-oriented software development, patterns, and product lines within Siemens and externally at conferences such as AOSD, OOP, and OOPSLA.

Iris Groher is a postdoctoral researcher at the Institute for Systems Engineering and Automation at the Johannes Kepler University Linz, Austria. Prior to that, Dr. Groher worked at Siemens AG, Corporate Technology, in Germany, for four years. She received her doctoral degree from the Johannes Kepler University Linz in 2008. Her fields of interest include aspect-oriented software development, model-driven software development, and software product line engineering. She has given presentations and organized workshops at conferences such as AOSD, SPLC, ECOOP, and GPCE.

Chapter 19 Evaluation of Design Options in Embedded Automotive Product Lines

Håkan Gustavsson has been working with vehicle electronic systems integration and architecture since 2002 at Scania CV AB in Södertälje, Sweden. He is currently employed as an industrial PhD student within the Electrical Systems Predevelopment Section at Scania. He received his BS in electrical engineering at the Royal Institute of Technology in 2002 after completing his studies with a final year at Fachhochschule Zentralschweiz, Lucerne, Switzerland. His research area is systems engineering of vehicle electronics. He is currently studying methods to analyze and improve the decisions made during the early phases of E/E-system development. His licentiate thesis on this topic was presented in 2008.

Jakob Axelsson received an MS from Linköping University in 1993 and a PhD in 1997 for a thesis on hardware/software codesign of real-time systems. He is currently with the Volvo Car Corporation in Göteborg, Sweden, where he is program manager for research and advanced engineering for electrical and electronic systems. Dr. Axelsson is also an adjunct professor in software and systems engineering at Mälardalen University in Västerås. Axelsson's research is mainly in the area of complex technical systems, with a focus on methods and tools to handle the early phases of product development. In particular, he researches embedded systems and automotive applications, but other products are also of interest.

Chapter 20   Product Line in the Business Process Management Domain

Marcelo Fantinato is an assistant professor in the School of Arts, Sciences and Humanities, University of São Paulo (USP), Brazil. He earned a PhD in computer science (2007) and an ME (2002) at the University of Campinas (Unicamp), Brazil. He has worked in the software industry as a software testing specialist at the CPqD Foundation in Campinas, Brazil (2001–2006) and as a specialist in research and development at Motorola in Jaguariúna, Brazil (2006–2008). His main research interests are business process management, service-oriented computing, electronic contracts, software product line, and software testing.

Itana Maria de Souza Gimenes is a professor of software engineering at the State University of Maringá, Paraná, Brazil. She has conducted postdoctoral research at the School of Computer Science, University of Waterloo, ON, Canada (2005). She received a PhD in computer science at the University of York, Department of Computer Science, UK (1992). Dr. Gimenes served as president of the Brazilian Computer Society Committee of Software Engineering from 2007 to 2008 and 1998 to 1999 (CEES-SBC). She has also led several research projects, including international cooperation with the European Community. Current research interests include software architecture, software product line, component-based development, workflow management systems, and business process management.

Maria Beatriz Felgar de Toledo is an associate professor at the Institute of Computing, State University of Campiñas (UNICAMP), Brazil. She received her MS in computer science from UNICAMP and her PhD from Lancaster University, UK (1992). She is a member of the SOCOLNET and has organized Brazilian workshops on business process management. Her main research interests are advanced transaction models, business process management systems, knowledge-base systems for clinical research, and cultural heritage.

ORGANIZATIONAL AND MANAGERIAL ISSUES

Chapter 1

Software Product Line Engineering: Overview and Future Directions

Kyo C. Kang
Pohang University of Science and Technology, Korea

Vijayan Sugumaran
Oakland University, Rochester, MI
Sogang University, Seoul, Korea

Sooyong Park
Sogang University, Seoul, Korea

Contents

1.1 Introduction

In this Internet age, the time taken to design and develop software applications has been considerably reduced, and there is increasing pressure for organizations to explore ways to diversify and deliver their products in a timely and efficient manner. Over the last decade, the software product line has emerged as one of the most promising software development paradigms for drastically increasing the productivity of IT-related industries, enabling them to handle the diversity of the global market and reduce time to market (Sugumaran, Park, and Kang, 2006). The idea behind the product line concept is for organizations to develop a product family from reusable core assets rather than from scratch. The product line approach is receiving increased attention, specifically as software engineers or developers are forced to develop software more quickly and economically.

The basic premise in product line engineering is that most software systems are not new. Rather, software systems in an application domain share more commonalities than uniqueness, and most organizations build software systems in a particular domain, repeatedly releasing product variants by adding new features. This insight can be leveraged to improve the software development process. A systematic approach, known as product line engineering, has been developed to build product variants using product line assets including common architectures and components. These architectures and components are built with variation points based on the commonalities and variabilities of the products in the application domain.

To identify and describe the right functionality for reusable implementation is a key challenge within the product line approach. In order to address the challenge, the key requirements for developing future products, which drive the product line and especially make products different, should be identified (Gomaa and Shin, 2007). Thus, a thorough requirements analysis for the product line must be performed, where particularly common and variant requirements are systematically identified and described. Furthermore, the requirements, and commonality, and variability identified must satisfy an organization's high-level business goals.

1.2 History

Software reuse involves generating new designs by combining high-level specifications and existing component artifacts. A number of tools and techniques have been developed over the years to provide support for reuse-based software design. The idea of software reuse has been applied and practiced since programming began. Reuse as a distinct field of study in software engineering, however, is often traced to McIlroy's paper (McIlroy, 1969), which proposed the idea of "mass produced software components" as the basis for application development. Later, David Parnas (1972; 1979) developed the information-hiding principle and the idea of program families, which became the engineering foundation for reusable component development and reuse-based application development. Neighbors (1989) introduced the concepts of domain and domain analysis, and provided the first systematic approach to domain engineering, known as Draco. Soon after, major research endeavors on software reuse and domain engineering followed (Atkinson et al. 2002; Frakes, Prieto-Diaz, and Fox, 1998; Gomaa, 2004; Kang, Lee, and Donohoe, 2002). The Software Engineering Institute (SEI) refined the concept of domain engineering further and developed a framework for reuse-based development of a family of closely related applications and called it "product line" engineering (Clements and Northrop, 2002). The framework includes management aspects as well as technical aspects of asset and product development.

Figure 1.1 shows the reuse history from code reuse to software product line approach through design reuse such as design patterns and architectural patterns/ styles. Important ideas emerging from this period include systematic reuse, design principles such as the three C's model, module interconnection languages, commonality/variability analysis, component-based software engineering, variation points, generative programming, and various approaches to domain specific generators. Recently, the concept of dynamic software product lines with runtime variability has been introduced to employ dynamism and support dynamic changes in product line engineering.

The origin of software product line engineering can be traced as far back as 1977 as a case of industrial practice in Japan. At that point in time, it was known

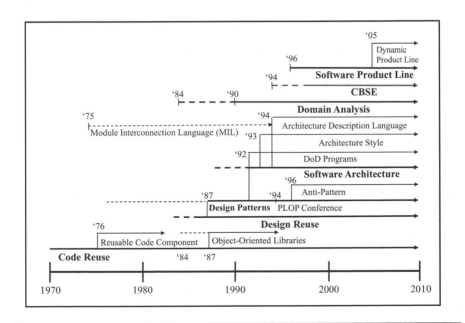

Figure 1.1 Reuse history.

as the Toshiba Software Factory, where concepts similar to the current product line approach were applied in the development of a family of power generators (Matsumoto, 1987). This may be the first industrial case reported in the literature. Since then, a product line approach has been widely and successfully applied to build various product lines in different domains, ranging from avionics to medical devices to information systems, in different organizations, ranging from small to large organizations. Now, owing to government- or European community–sponsored large-scale research projects on software reuse, including ARES, PRAISE, ESAPS, CAFÉ, and FAMILIES projects (http://www.esi.es/en/Projects/Cafe/cafe.html), many successful cases of product line engineering in various industries have been reported in the Product Line Hall of Fame (http://www.sei.cmu.edu/productlines/plp_hof. html). Consistently, noticeable achievements in terms of shortening time to market, reducing cost, and improving qualities of a product have been accomplished.

There are several areas of research that are currently under way in software product line engineering. Some of these areas are the development of asset libraries, methods and tools, software architectures, componentry, generators and generative programming, product line configuration management, measurement and experimentation, and business and organizational issues. In particular, management of variation—so-called variability management in product line engineering—has become more important recently. In addition, the product line engineering process, production planning, formal analysis of feature models, and product line testing are considered a critical part of product line engineering. Application development framework technologies such as .NET, EJB, and Service Oriented Architecture are also areas of active research. Application of, or integration with, other technology areas such as Aspect-Oriented development and agent technologies are also being explored.

Use of software product line engineering approaches in the industry is on the rise. While advanced techniques are central to successful adoption of product line engineering, technical issues have deep and complex interactions with other nontechnical areas, including business and organizational issues. These areas are highlighted in the following section.

1.3 Organizational, Process, and Technical Issues

There is general agreement in the software industry that product line engineering technology will bring profound changes in systems development and delivery (Pohl, Bockle, and van der Linden, 2005). The ultimate goal of product line engineering is to improve the productivity of product development and the quality of products and services that a company provides. Increasing the level of reuse may not necessarily reduce the overall development cost due to asset development and management costs. When and how reusable assets are developed and used in product development will affect the effectiveness of product line–based product development. To maximize reuse profits, then, organizational, process, and technical aspects need to be considered.

1.3.1 Organizational Aspects

Organizational dynamics has a major impact on software development and reuse. As the development process changes, the culture of the organization has to also undergo a corresponding change in order for it to be successful. There are two types of organizational approaches to establishing a product line engineering program that are commonly observed in corporate environments: centralized and distributed asset development (Frakes and Kang, 2005).

The centralized approach typically has an organizational unit dedicated to developing, distributing, maintaining, and, often, training reusable assets for product development projects. The organization has the product line–wide product and engineering vision and core expertise that can be shared among the projects. As this approach often requires pulling experts away from product development projects, it can only be successful where there is a strong commitment from the upper management.

In contrast to the centralized approach, the distributed approach is implemented collaboratively by projects in the same product line, and asset development and support responsibilities are distributed among projects. Although there is less overhead as asset development costs are distributed among projects, it may be difficult to coordinate asset development responsibilities if there is no common vision for the reuse program. Also, there must be a convincing cost-benefit model to solicit active participation. There is a danger in that projects may be willing to use others' contributions but are reluctant to make their own investment for others.

1.3.2 Process Aspects

Institutionalizing a software product line engineering paradigm within an organization requires a systematic transition. Implementing such an initiative in a corporate environment requires a major decision on when and where capital investment is to be made. There are three process models that are often used in adopting a software product line program: proactive, reactive, and extractive models (Frakes and Kang 2005; Krueger 2002).

With the proactive model, an organization makes an up-front investment to develop core assets for the product line, and products are developed using these assets. Although this approach can be effective for product lines in a mature and stable domain where product features can be predicted, it requires a large up-front investment.

On the other hand, if the initial cost is a barrier, the reactive model may be appropriate where reusable assets are developed as needed when reuse opportunities arise. This approach may work well in a domain where product features cannot be predicted in advance. Although this approach does not require a large up-front investment, the cost for reengineering and retrofitting existing products with reusable assets can be high without a well-thought-out common architectural basis.

Another approach proposed by Krueger (2002), called the extractive model, stays in between the proactive and reactive approaches. The extractive approach reuses one or more existing software products for the product line's initial baseline. This approach can be effective for an organization that has accumulated development experiences and artifacts in a domain but wants to quickly transition from conventional to software product line engineering.

1.3.3 Technical Aspects

Successful implementation of the product line engineering approach to software construction has to deal with several technical issues. Though there are many issues from a technical perspective, they can be grouped into three broad categories: core asset development, product development, and run-time dynamism.

For core asset development, scoping and analyzing the domain of the product family is essential. Feature-oriented domain analysis is an approach used for this task. Identification and definition of common features and variation points are the main focus. Managing differences among products of a product line, i.e., variability management, is an important aspect.

In the second category, namely, product development, derivation of new products from core assets, especially product line architecture, is an important activity. It includes selecting appropriate parts, extending the architecture, and resolving conflicts between functionalities as well as quality attributes. New requirements from customers, changes in technology, and future needs pose considerable challenges. Evolution in a product line is complex and needs more attention compared with traditional software development, since most assets are utilized by products within the product line. Particular attention must be paid to unexpected and undesirable interactions between integrated components, known as the feature interaction problem, that may result in a catastrophe. Also, testing, traceability, and quality issues need to be handled carefully.

In the third category, namely, run-time dynamism, the system should be able to handle unexpected conditions at runtime. Due to dynamic changes in the execution environment or various user requests that are not anticipated during development time, software needs to adapt its own behavior or compose different assets during runtime. Thus, the design of a software product line should be able to accommodate dynamic changes by utilizing predefined runtime binding information or self-managing capability. Recently, in order to employ dynamism and provide support for dynamic changes in product line engineering, the concept of dynamic software product line (Kim, Jeong, and Park, 2005; Kim, Park, and Sugumaran, 2006; Hallsteinsen et al. 2008; Andersson and Bosch 2005) has been introduced. A dynamic software product line is defined as a product line that produces software capable of adapting to fluctuations in user needs and available resources (Hallsteinsen et al. 2008). The dynamic product line makes it possible to dynamically support runtime changes such as evolving user needs (i.e., functional and quality requirements) and changing environments. This is accomplished by reconfiguring a product dynamically to produce new products within the product line during execution through dynamic reconfiguration or recomposition. In terms of variability, a dynamic product line binds variation points at runtime, initially when software is launched and then during operation, to adapt to changes in the environment (Hallsteinsen et al. 2008).

1.4 Future Research Directions

While significant research has been carried out in software product line engineering, there are still a number of outstanding issues that have to be resolved. For example, product lines with over thousands of features have been reported recently, and complexity management has become an issue in such product lines. When a family of products is derived from a common asset base and when these products and assets evolve over time, the complexity of managing products and assets increases an order of magnitude compared with managing versions of a single product. Management of a large number of features and complex dependencies between them, asset variants and variation points associated with these features, and product configurations require considerable further research.

A related issue is the integration of components that support a specific set of features with unanticipated consequences. When systems are configured from components that have been tested and used previously, it has been argued that they would be more reliable. However, when asset components are integrated, unexpected behaviors that cannot be predicted from the behavior of the individual components used can emerge, which may result in disastrous consequences. This is generally known as a feature interaction problem. Techniques for uncovering feature interactions among components are needed, especially for systems requiring a high level of safety and reliability.

Product instantiation from the product line architecture is a nontrivial task and requires a lot of domain knowledge. Intelligent tools and techniques are needed to successfully create specific products from the overall product line. When there are a large number of components, with their variants and variation points, and when there are complex dependencies among them, then product derivation from this asset base is a very complex and difficult task (Kastner, Apel, and Kuhlemann 2008). Future research should include developing knowledge-based approaches and tools for product derivation.

The design of adaptable systems is receiving a lot of attention within the software engineering community. In a similar vein, run-time dynamism is an emerging area of research in product line engineering. Computing environments such as service-oriented architecture and ubiquitous computing present new challenges. In particular, modern computing and network environments demand a high degree of adaptability from their software systems. Product architectures and components must be configured autonomously while systems are running in these environments, requiring the embedment of software engineering knowledge in the deployed systems. With these new environments, the focus of software engineering shifts from static development-time engineering to dynamic runtime engineering. This is the scenario where the dynamic product line approach would be relevant. Such an approach could be one way to build self-adaptive (Oreizy et al. 1999), self-healing systems (Garlen et al. 2004), i.e., software systems that can change their own behavior in their operating environment and thus adapt at runtime to the changing environment.

If the software industry is to successfully adopt the product line engineering approach, the technical as well as the nontechnical issues must be addressed adequately. While some of the issues have been resolved satisfactorily, much work is yet to be done to facilitate the widespread adoption and diffusion of software product line engineering across the globe. Some of the areas that require immediate attention are product line-based organizational structure, key practice areas and process models, and empirical research on return on investment. This book has provided a forum for some of the leading researchers in software product line engineering across the world to discuss the current state of the art and the specific approaches they are developing to improve software development.

1.5 Organization of the Book

This book is organized into four parts. The first part contains a number of chapters that discuss organizational and managerial issues related to software product line engineering. The second part consists of five chapters that explicate the methodologies and processes used in creating software product lines. Some of the technical issues related to managing software product lines are discussed in the third part. The fourth part includes chapters that highlight industry experience and provides case studies of software product lines that have been established in various application domains. The following paragraphs provide a quick summary of the salient aspects and contributions of each chapter in the four aforementioned parts.

Part One of the book contains five chapters. In Chapter 1, Kang et al. provide a quick overview of the history of software reuse and software product line engineering (SPLE) and the organizational, process, and technical issues related to establishing a software product line. In Chapter 2, Jones et al. discuss the adoption of the software product line approach in organizations and provide a roadmap. They argue that a combination of technical and business activities needs to occur and that an organization has to establish its product line context before developing code and establish real production capability before attempting to operate the product line. Combining the Adoption Factory pattern with a technology-change model, like the IDEAL^SM model, allows an organization to effectively manage the organizational changes along the way. In Chapter 3, Krueger describes some of the best methods from the industry's most recent software product line successes. He points out that the benefits of product lines go beyond product creation, including lower costs for product maintenance and evolution, lowering the overall complexity of product development, increasing the scalability of product line portfolios, and enabling organizations to create products with orders-of-magnitude less time, cost, and effort. In Chapter 4, Kim et al. demonstrate the use of a balanced scorecard as an instrument to drive the process of product-family engineering and how it can be used to align strategic objectives with the development approach. Since a significant upfront investment is involved in adopting product-family development, they argue that it is important to evaluate the impact of this approach on the strategic goals of the organization. In Chapter 5, Helferich et al. discuss the various tasks associated with software product management and explain the additional challenges for product management for software product lines. Based on this, they present a toolbox that can serve as a first step toward an integrated method for product management within software product lines. The toolbox contains established methods from strategic planning, strategic and tactical marketing, scoping, and value management.

Part Two of the book deals with the process aspects of software product lines and the methodologies used to establish them. In Chapter 6, Eriksson et al. describe PLUSS+ (product line use case modeling for systems and software engineering), a use case–driven approach to systems product lines. PLUSS+ extends traditional systems engineering by incorporating ideas from software product line engineering. It has been developed, refined, and evaluated during several years of application within the Swedish defense industry. In Chapter 7, Cetina et al. propose the adoption of the software product line (SPL) paradigm to develop autonomic pervasive systems in a methodological fashion. They argue that pervasive systems can achieve autonomic behavior by introducing SPL variability both at design and runtime. They present the extensions to the production operation of SPLs in order to transfer variability models from the SPL design to the SPL products. In addition to the selected features at design time, the final product will contain some "extra" features. These features are disabled initially but they can be enabled in a product reconfiguration. In Chapter 8, Magro et al. present their experience in applying the product line approach to develop domain specific validation environments for acceptance testing. This chapter describes the architecture of reference that has been defined and its variability points. It presents the application of the product line to two real case studies: a digital TV decoder and a networked slot machines system. These case studies have been presented emphasizing how the variability points have been derived to support the particularities of each product. Chapter 9 by Chae and Blume discusses the development of a family of compilers for a series of experimental languages that the authors have designed. They show the engineering activities for a family of compilers from product line analysis through product line architecture design to product line component design. They also show how to build specific compilers from core assets resulting from the previous activities and how to take advantage of modern programming language technology to organize this task. In Chapter 10, Kishi and Noda postulate that the time taken for both the derivation and verification of products in a product line should be reduced. To achieve that, they propose a systematic method to verify products based on formal verification techniques. Their approach makes formal verification more widely usable for embedded software development.

Part Three of the book delves into some of the technical aspects of software product line engineering. One essential aspect of the product line approach is effective requirements and variability management. In Chapter 11, Gomaa and Olimpiew discuss multiple-view requirements models for software product line engineering. They describe how a feature-oriented approach can be used to relate features to variability in multiple-view requirements models of an SPL. They distinguish between coarse-grained and fine-grained functional variability in these models. In Chapter 12, Codenie et al. discuss how to manage flexibility and variability in software product lines. They present a decision framework that assists companies to reason about the static perspective of flexibility and variability (i.e., how to interpret both challenges in the applied development model) and the dynamic perspective (i.e., how to deal with changes in the development model). Chapter 13, by Lee and Muthig, integrates SPL techniques and guidelines that addressed the core issues of dynamic product reconfiguration and shows how these pieces fit together to construct a reuse infrastructure. Their approach consists of two phases: The first phase is a feature analysis that enriches feature models by feature-binding units (FBUs). An FBU is thereby defined as a set of features whose variability aspects are strongly related to each other. The second phase takes the analysis results to guide the design of a product line. Chapter 14, by Shin and Gomaa, describes how to model software product lines by modeling application requirements and designs separately from security requirements and designs using the Unified Modeling Language (UML) notation. By careful separation of concerns, the security requirements are captured in security use cases and encapsulated in security objects separately from the application requirements and objects. In the design, security concerns are modeled in security components separately from the application components as well. This approach reduces system complexity caused by mixing security requirements with business application requirements, with the goal of making complex software product lines more maintainable. In Chapter 15, Völter argues that, as one develops an SPL architecture, one should create a language that allows one to describe systems based on this architecture. This makes the architecture tangible and provides an unambiguous description of the architectural building blocks as well as the concrete system while still staying away from technology decisions (which then can be made consciously in a separate step). Based on this language, one can also describe variants in the context of a product line.

Part Four of the book is devoted to industry experiences and case studies. In Chapter 16, Matsumoto summarizes the practices actually applied in the Toshiba Software Factory, in which a series of product lines for the domain of electric power generation, EPG-SPL, has been developed and adopted since 1962. Based on this experience, this chapter provides a window into the financial aspects of SPL, and presents a guide useful for the management and control of SPL adoption. In Chapter 17, John et al. present an industrial case study of the CaVE approach (commonality and variability extraction) that is discussed in the literature. This case study shows that the CaVE approach is applicable in the context of large industrial companies and demonstrates the completeness and correctness of the results produced with the approach. In Chapter 18, Groher et al. discuss a model-driven aspect-oriented SPLE approach that provides concepts and tools to facilitate variability implementation, management, and tracing from requirements modeling to implementation of product lines. They also present an industrial case study conducted at Siemens AG that shows how their approach effectively supports the development of a product line during domain engineering and a systematic product derivation during application engineering. In Chapter 19, Gustavsson and Axelsson discuss an evaluation process for practitioners using Real Options theory that enables analysis of both economic and engineering factors within a software product line. This approach presents the possibility to put an economic value on system adaptability and could therefore support the design decisions in the early phases. Finally, Chapter 20 describes the use of product line in the business process management domain. Fantinato et al. describe a feature-based approach to support Web services (WS) contract negotiation and establishment. This approach includes a meta-model for WS-contracts representation, a mechanism for mapping WS-contracts to business process, and a support toolkit to enable this process automation.

References

Andersson, J., and J. Bosch. 2005. Development and use of dynamic product line architectures. *IEE Proceedings-Software Engineering* 152 (1): 15–28.

Atkinson, C., J. Bayer, C. Bunse, E. Kamsties, O. Laitenberger, R. Laqua, D. Muthig, B. Peach, J. Wust, and J. Zettel. 2002. *Component-based product line engineering with UML*. Edinburgh: Addison-Wesley.

Clements, P., and L. Northrop. 2002. *Software product lines*. Edinburgh: Addison-Wesley.

Frakes, W., R. Prieto-Diaz, and C. Fox. 1998. DARE: Domain analysis and reuse environment. *Annals of Software Engineering* 5:125–141.

Frakes, W. B., and K. C. Kang. 2005. Software reuse research: Status and future. *IEEE Transactions on Software Engineering* 31 (7): 529–536.

Garlan, D., S.-W. Cheng, A.-C. Huang, B. Schmerl, and P. Steenkiste. 2004. Rainbow: Architecture-based self-adaptation with reusable infrastructure. *IEEE Computer* 37 (10): 46–54.

Gomaa, H. 2004. *Designing software product lines with UML: From use cases to pattern-based software architectures*. Boston, MA: Addison-Wesley.

Gomaa, H., and M. E. Shin. 2007. Automated software product line engineering and product derivation. In *Proceedings of the 40th Hawaii international conference on system sciences*, 285–294. Washington, DC: IEEE Computer Society.

Hallsteinsen, S., M. Hinchey, S. Park, and K. Schmid. 2008. Dynamic software product lines. *IEEE Computer* 41 (4): 93–95.

Kang, K. C., J. Lee, and P. Donohoe. 2002. Feature-oriented product line engineering. *IEEE Software* 19 (4): 58–65.

Kastner, C., S. Apel, and M. Kuhlemann. 2008. Granularity in software product lines. In *Proceedings of the 30th international conference on software engineering*, 311–320. New York: ACM Press.

Kim, M., J. Jeong, and S. Park. 2005. From product lines to self-managed systems: An architecture-based runtime reconfiguration framework. In *Proceedings of design and evolution of autonomic application software (DEAS 2005)*, 66–72. New York: ACM Press.

Kim, M., S. Park, and V. Sugumaran. 2006. Toward dynamic software product lines. Paper presented at 37th Decision Sciences Institute annual conference, San Antonio, TX, Nov. 18–21, 28161–28166.

Krueger, C. 2002. Eliminating the adoption barrier. *IEEE Software* 19 (4): 29–31.

Matsumoto, Y. 1987. A software factory: An overall approach to software production. In *Tutorial on software reusability*, ed. P. Freeman, 155–178. Washington, DC: Computer Society Press.

McIlroy, M. 1969. Mass produced software components: Software engineering concepts and techniques. In *Proceedings of NATO conference on software engineering*, ed. P. Naur, B. Randell, and J. N. Buxton, 88–98. New York: Petrocelli/Charter.

Neighbors, J. M. 1989. Draco: A method for engineering reusable software systems. ACM Frontier Series. In *Software reusability*, vol. 1, *Concepts and models*, 295–319. New York: Addison-Wesley.

Oreizy, P., M. M. Gorlick, R. N. Taylor, D. Heimbigner, G. Johnson, N. Medvidovic, A. Quilici, D. S. Rosenblum, and A. L. Wolf. 1999. An architecture-based approach to self-adaptive software. *IEEE Intelligent Systems* 14 (3): 54–62.

Pohl, K., G. Bockle, and F. van der Linden. 2005. *Software product line engineering: Foundations, principles, and techniques*. New York: Springer.

Sugumaran, V., S. Park, and K. C. Kang. 2006. Software product line engineering. *Communications of the ACM* 49 (12): 28–32.

Chapter 2

A Roadmap for Software Product Line Adoption

Lawrence G. Jones
Software Engineering Institute, Carnegie Mellon University, Colorado Springs, CO

Linda M. Northrop and Paul C. Clements
Software Engineering Institute, Carnegie Mellon University, Pittsburgh, PA

John D. McGregor
Clemson University, SC

Contents

2.1 Introduction

You've read about organizations that use the software product line approach to turn out new products in a matter of days or weeks, evolving them as a single family, whereas it takes your company months or years. As you start to think about what it would take to transform your company from a piecework operation to a smoothly running software factory, the complexity of the change starts to sink in. To really change the way your company produces software, you'll have to make business, technical, organizational, procedural, financial, and personnel changes. You can't make them all at once—no organization can tolerate such a major upheaval and still keep turning out products. You can't make the changes piecemeal, either, or you'll never achieve your goal. And, practically speaking, a false start will be expensive, undermine customer confidence, and have a damaging impact on your employees' morale. "How," you wonder, "can I get there from here?"

A roadmap to product line adoption that lays out the necessary decisions and actions would be invaluable in helping you to visualize where you are in the process and identify the necessary coordination points among the various activities. In principle and in practice, a generic product line adoption roadmap has appeal. Organizations could follow a proven path, adapt it to their own needs, and do so in an incremental, manageable way that reduces risks. Such a generic product line adoption roadmap should contain the fundamental milestones in any product line adoption effort and their dependencies. Such a roadmap is presented in this chapter.

A software product line organization embodies a core asset development function and a product development function, all orchestrated by a management function. These three functions are mutually supportive, providing inputs and feedback to each other. Core assets—the artifacts common across the family of products—are maintained as common resources for the entire software product line. They are customizable in predefined ways to fit the needs of individual products. Core assets include plans, requirements, designs, documentation, and tests, as well as code. Product creation produces feedback about the quality and usefulness of the core assets in addition to producing products. The choice of products to be built in the product line is a management decision based on the capabilities provided by the existing core assets and the needs of the market. This decision is accompanied by the necessary managerial oversight to ensure that the core assets are truly useful in developing the products and that those products are built by faithfully using them.

The practices needed to successfully field a software product line are fairly well known; *Framework for Software Product Line Practice* (Northrop and Clements 2007), published by the Software Engineering Institute (SEI), describes 29 of them. These are practices familiar to any software development activity but that take on a different flavor when it comes to software product lines. For example, configuration management is a standard software development practice, but it takes on additional complexity in a software product line setting—versions of products must now be tied to versions of the core assets used to build them.

Knowing the practices is one thing; applying them smoothly in concert with each other is another. Product line practice *patterns* show how practice areas can be combined and coordinated to accomplish useful outcomes, such as setting up the organization's core asset development function (Clements and Northrop, 2002). One of these patterns, *Adoption Factory*, maps out the broad coordination among the many practices needed to initiate (i.e., adopt) the software product line development strategy. The SEI Adoption Factory pattern serves as a roadmap for product line adoption and is the subject of this chapter.

2.2 Product Line Practice Patterns

Product line practice patterns:

- Address recurring software product line problems that arise in specific situations and present solutions to them
- Document existing, well-proven software product line experience
- Identify and specify abstractions that are broader in scope than single practice areas
- Provide an additional common vocabulary and insight into software product lines
- Are a means of documenting new and ongoing software product line efforts
- Help manage the complexity inherent in software product line approaches that can be combined to build complex product line solutions

In short, the patterns show how practice areas can be combined and coordinated to accomplish useful outcomes, such as setting up the organization's core asset development function. Patterns have been useful in many disciplines and

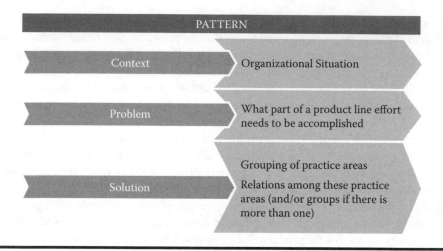

Figure 2.1 Context-problem-solution schema of a pattern.

popularized, especially among software developers, in the form of software design patterns (Gamma 1995) and software architecture patterns (Bruckhaus et al. 1996), which have both become part of the mainstream software developers' vocabulary. Whereas a design pattern organizes software elements, a product line practice pattern organizes the product line activities of an organization.

Product line practice patterns are described using a common template and follow the general context-problem-solution schema illustrated in Figure 2.1.

2.2.1 A Pattern for the Entire Product Line Organization

One pattern, the *Factory* pattern, describes the entire product line organization— for any organization. It solves the general problem: What does an organization look like if it has product line capability? The Factory pattern describes fielding a product line as accomplishing the following six tasks:

1. Deciding what products to include in the product line
2. Preparing the organization for a product line approach
3. Designing and providing the core assets that will be used to construct the products in the product line
4. Building and using the production infrastructure (necessary plans, processes, and tools)
5. Building products from the core assets in a prescribed way
6. Monitoring the product line effort, keeping a pulse on the product line operations, and applying course corrections as necessary to keep the organization on course

Table 2.1   Subpatterns in the Factory Pattern

Subpattern	Description
What to build	Yields the set of products to be included in the product line along with an associated business case
Cold start	Prepares the organization for its first product line operation
Each asset	Provides individual core assets and their attached processes
Product parts	Supplies the core assets from which products will be built
Assembly line	Provides the production infrastructure
Product builder	Yields the individual products in the product line
In motion	Keeps the product line organization running
Monitor	Keeps watch on the organization and responds with any needed changes

Other patterns exist that provide solutions for accomplishing these six tasks. Accordingly, the solution part of the Factory pattern consists of the subpatterns described in Table 2.1. Figure 2.2 illustrates the dynamic structure of the Factory pattern.

The Factory pattern is a blueprint for a "divide and conquer" strategy that is not immediately intuitive to organizations on the threshold of a product line effort or, for that matter, those in the throes of carrying out a software product line approach. The three subpatterns along the bottom row indicate an organization's

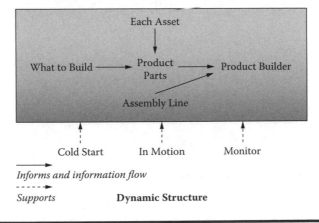

Figure 2.2   Dynamic structure of the Factory pattern.

status. The Cold Start subpattern is used when the product line has not been initiated. The In Motion subpattern builds on practices established during application of the Cold Start subpattern. The Monitor subpattern is used when the product line is operating and needs to be optimized. As such, the Factory pattern has proven to be very useful to organizations. However, it still lacks a bit of horsepower in providing the guidance—the roadmap—that most organizations need to successfully adopt a product line approach.

2.2.2 Making the Factory Pattern into a Roadmap: The Adoption Factory Pattern

While the Factory pattern meets most of the criteria for a useful roadmap, some modifications were necessary to make it work well as an adoption roadmap.

For one, organizations that lack the discipline to define and follow processes, even lightweight or agile ones, need to address that deficiency early in their adoption path. So it was important to add the "Process Discipline" practice area (from the SEI *Framework for Software Product Line Practice*) as a separate element to the Factory pattern.

For another, as a roadmap, the Factory pattern was also lacking perspectives on timing and focus areas and a detailed mapping to practice areas. To make it useful as an adoption roadmap, a number of different perspectives or views were created. Four of those views are described below. The result is the Adoption Factory pattern (Northrop 2004), a variant of the Factory pattern. The dynamic structure of Adoption Factory pattern is shown in Figure 2.3.

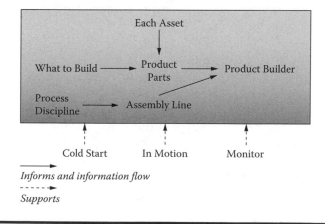

Figure 2.3 Dynamic structure of Adoption Factory pattern.

2.2.3 Four Views of the Adoption Factory Pattern

2.2.3.1 Phases View

An adopting organization progresses through three broad phases, from start-up activities in the first phase to product production in the third phase. Three columns superimposed on the dynamic structure of the Adoption Factory pattern, as shown in Figure 2.4, designate the following temporal phases of product line adoption:

1. **Establish Context:** involves paving the way for product line adoption by determining the scope and associated business case, ensuring the necessary process capability and discipline, and performing the organizational management tasks that support product line initiation. The What to Build and Cold Start patterns and the "Process Discipline" practice area are in this phase.
2. **Establish Production Capability:** involves developing the core asset base and the production infrastructure, and effectively managing those efforts at project and cross-project levels. The Each Asset, Product Parts, Assembly Line, and In Motion patterns are in this phase.
3. **Operate Product Line:** involves using the core asset base to efficiently build products and effectively monitoring and improving the product line operation. The Product Builder and Monitor patterns are in this phase.

Even though the phases represent a temporal ordering of adoption activities, there will of course be iteration. Though the emphasis of effort will shift as an orga-

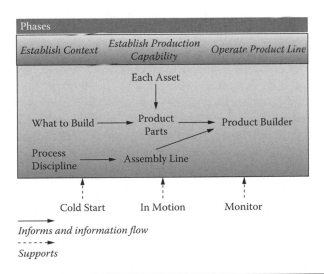

Figure 2.4 Temporal phases of product line adoption.

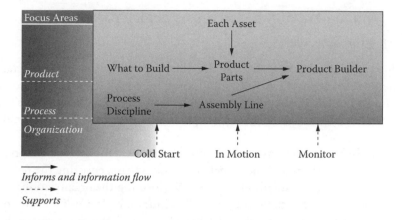

Figure 2.5   Focus areas for certain patterns and practices.

nization moves from an earlier to a later phase, many of the earlier phase's activities will continue, usually on a much smaller scale.

2.2.3.2 Focus Areas View

Three rows superimposed on the dynamic structure of the Adoption Factory pattern, as shown in Figure 2.5, designate the following focus areas for certain patterns and practices:

1. **Product:** involves those activities for defining and developing products and their common assets. The What to Build, Each Asset, Product Parts, and Product Builder patterns make up the product focus area.
2. **Process:** involves the underlying processes and production infrastructure necessary to adopt a product line approach. The "Process Discipline" practice area and the Assembly Line pattern constitute the process focus area.
3. **Organization:** involves the management practices and activities necessary to adopt a product line approach and operate a software product line. The Cold Start, In Motion, and Monitor patterns make up the organization focus area.

2.2.3.3 Phases and Focus Areas View

It is especially useful to view the Adoption Factory pattern's phases and focus areas simultaneously. Figure 2.6 provides this perspective with horizontal focus area delineations and vertical phase delineations.

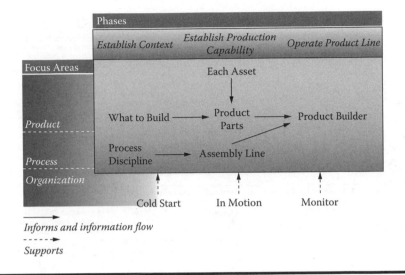

Figure 2.6 Phases and focus areas view.

2.2.3.4 Practice Areas View

Another useful view of the Adoption Factory pattern "unwinds" each of the subpatterns into the practice areas they comprise. This is necessary for detailed product line adoption planning; it lets managers see what practice areas they will need to focus on during particular phases. Figure 2.7 shows the Adoption Factory pattern and its constituent practice areas elaborated in a view that also shows the focus areas and adoption phases.

Some practice areas appear in multiple phases; they will be carried out differently, depending on the phase and overall objective of the associated pattern. For example, the "Architecture Definition" practice area occurs in both the Establish Production Capability Phase and the Operate Product Line Phase. In the former, it comes from the Product Parts pattern and is concerned with defining a product line architecture for use across all products. In the latter, it comes from the Product Builder pattern and is concerned with using the product line architecture to instantiate product architectures.

2.2.4 Mastering the Practice Areas in a Continuous Way

Using these and other views, an organization can plan to master the necessary practice areas in a continuous way that begins at the phase where each practice area first appears. The Adoption Factory pattern very naturally aligns with a proactive product line approach, where core assets are built before any of the products in the product line. However, it also applies in a reactive approach (where one or more products are built before the core asset base is established [Krueger 2001]), or a

	Establish Context	Eatablish Production Capability	Operate Product Line
Product	• Marketing Analysis • Understanding Relevant Domains • Technology Forecasting • Building a Business Case • Scoping	• Requirements Engineering • Architecture Definition • Architecture Evaluation • Mining Existing Assets • Component Development • Using Externally Available Software • Software System Integration • Testing	• Requirements Engineering • Architecture Definition • Architecture Evaluation • Mining Existing Assets • Component Development • Using Externally Available Software • Software System Integration • Testing
Process	• Process Discipline	• Make/Buy/Mine/Commission • Configureation Management • Tool Support • Measurement and Tracking • Technical Planning • Technical Risk Management	
Organization	• Launching and Institutionalizing • Funding • Structuring the Organization • Operations • Organizational Planning • Customer Interface Management • Organizational Risk Management • Developing an Acquisition Strategy • Training	• Launching and Institutionalizing • Funding • Structuring the Organization • Operations • Organizational Planning • Customer Interface Management • Organizational Risk Management • Developing an Acquistion Strategy • Training	• Measurement and Tracking • Technical Risk Management • Organization Risk Management • Customer Interface Management • Organizational Planning

Figure 2.7 Adoption Factory pattern and its constituent practice areas elaborated in a view that also shows the focus areas and adoption phases.

combination of proactive and reactive, or an incremental approach to either. In a reactive approach, the Establish Context Phase happens implicitly when the first product or products are built as single systems and then in a more deliberate way once the decision is made to extract or reengineer a core asset base from a product or products. The Establish Production Capability Phase involves the extracting or reengineering of the production plan (covered under the Product Parts pattern or its Plowed Field variant pattern) and the development of the plan (covered under the Assembly Line pattern).

Using the Adoption Factory pattern as a roadmap lets the manager answer the question "What do I need to focus on next?" by charting and applying practices following the "informs" relationships among the areas. But unlike a path through, say, a state machine, any position merely indicates heightened emphasis. All the subpatterns remain in play throughout because they indicate practices that must eventually be part of the product line approach. For example, the "Scoping" practice area (which is part of the What to Build pattern) is central to the Establish Context Phase and must begin early in the product line effort, though it continues throughout the rest of the product line adoption process (and life cycle). However, the "Component Development" practice area in the Product Parts pattern—though it's certainly important to the product line effort—can begin later in the adoption process. The organization should address other practice areas in a similar fashion, always bearing in mind that there is no barricade between the phases. Rather, because of the inherent iteration in the product line process, there will always be some backward influence on earlier phases.

Even with a generic adoption roadmap, there is still some work to be done. Like any generic artifact, the roadmap is missing details—those necessary for any specific organization to use the pattern as a path to product line adoption. An organization should, with prudent organizational insight, instantiate and customize the roadmap to meet its needs. The two case studies later in this chapter will illustrate this point. An organization, knowing its own strengths, challenges, and timeline for adoption, should also look across the phase horizon and, where it makes sense, begin to prepare early for those activities presenting the greatest challenges. For example, if an organization will rely heavily on legacy assets, it should begin the inventorying part of the "Mining Existing Assets" practice area during the Establish Context Phase in conjunction with scoping. If an organization unwittingly dove into the Establish Production Capability Phase by starting with architecture definition, it will want to plan to backfill sufficiently with practice areas of the Establish Context Phase to ensure that the architecture is targeting a set of products that makes business sense.

2.2.5 Adoption Factory Pattern and Technology Change

It's useful to view software product line adoption as a special case of a technology-change project, which it is. It helps organizations adopt a new technology or new way of doing business. Technology change is a well-studied area, with useful models that can help smooth the transition of the organization to the new state. This section discusses one of the more well-known models, applied to software product line adoption.

All technology-change projects should involve assessing the current state, identifying the desired state, and bridging the gulf between the two. Successful technology change requires vision, skills, incentives, resources, and a plan for implementing the change.

Technology-change experts recommend establishing a technology-change project that is charged with the transformation. A technology-change project for product lines may involve

- changing the way people think about system building
- instituting new practices and procedures
- designing new organizational interfaces (both internal and external)
- reorganizing the staff

Organizations often use technology-change models to guide their technology-change efforts. One such model is the IDEAL[SM] model (McFeeley 1996). Iterative change is often called for both as a means of risk reduction and to guard against the "change shock" that can occur if too much change is imposed too quickly.

As illustrated in Figure 2.8, the IDEAL model has five stages that can be repeatedly applied until the rollout is complete:

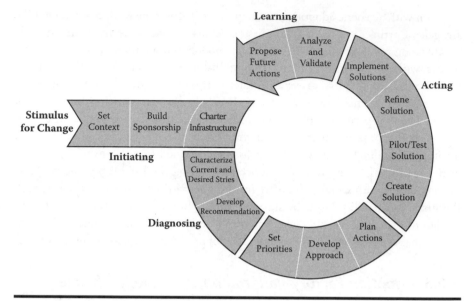

Figure 2.8 Five stages of the IDEAL model.

1. Initiating: getting ready to institute the change project
2. Diagnosing: assessing the current state
3. Establishing: planning the next increment of change toward the desired state
4. Acting: executing the plan
5. Learning: learning lessons from the current iteration and revising the approach for the next

The IDEAL model, as informed by the Adoption Factory, can guide incremental introduction of product line practice within an organization. The rollout strategy might incrementally install

- a complete set of product line practices in portions of the organization
- a limited set of product line practices throughout the organization

or some combination of the above. The Adoption Factory pattern can be used in conjunction with the IDEAL model as follows:

- **Initiating:** Use the Adoption Factory pattern as an easily understood adoption vocabulary that can be shared across an organization and that marks organizational progress. Use the completion of phases or focus areas as product line adoption goals. Use the associated roles to guide staffing and management.

- **Diagnosing:** Use the Adoption Factory pattern to gauge which phase of the adoption process an organization is in and to benchmark its activities by measuring them against the practice areas in that phase.
- **Establishing:** Use the incremental nature of the Adoption Factory pattern to structure a Product Line Adoption Plan. Use the subpatterns and their associated practice areas as the basis of subservient action plans.
- **Acting:** Follow the plans that are based on the Adoption Factory pattern. Apply the practice areas in the organization focus area to steer and manage the activities.
- **Learning:** Collect data and lessons learned in each phase of the Adoption Factory pattern as specified by the "Data Collection, Metrics, and Tracking" practice area of the monitor subpattern. Analyze results against established goals. In addition, modify artifacts, processes, and organizational structures to reflect lessons learned and to take advantage of potential optimizations.

Each IDEAL stage may be executed with more or less rigor, depending on the iteration cycle. For example, a rigorous diagnostic like the Product Line Technical Probe (Clements and Northrop, 2002) may provide sufficient Diagnosing guidance for more than one cycle and, thus, the Diagnosing stage could be abbreviated in a subsequent iteration.

2.3 Two Case Studies

To illustrate the previous points we present two case studies. While neither represents an actual company, both are based on real experience. Both illustrate the combined use of the Adoption Factory pattern and the IDEAL model, but the first case study puts more emphasis on the use of Adoption Factory, while the second emphasizes the use of the IDEAL model to guide iterative rollout of product line capability.

2.3.1 Case Study 1

LMN, Inc., is a small company that until now has been a custom software shop working for a variety of customers. The founder of LMN now has an idea for a personal assistant environment (PAE) that provides unusual but widely desired features. For example, the e-mailer would use natural language techniques to scan outgoing messages for mentions of an attachment and would check that an attachment exists in the e-mail before sending the mail. The environment would provide a basic infrastructure into which individual utilities could be plugged. The infrastructure would include:

- a data model based on an Ecore-compatible meta-model that predefines elements that would be expected to be present in the PAE

- a database service for use by the utilities
- a basic set of filters that can be extended to translate data
- a configurable user interface

LMN is staffed by a core of experienced software development professionals who are supported by a cadre of young, inexperienced, but enthusiastic computer science graduates. The vice president (VP) in charge of product development is forward-looking and has read a special issue of a software engineering journal in which the software product line strategy was described. He believes that the vision for the PAE fits this approach. Since this will be a new line of business for which no expectations have yet been set, the VP decides that a proactive approach paid for by R&D funds is the best approach to adoption. This initial effort will create the infrastructure and four utilities, including the e-mailer and a spell-checker that searches for the typical typing mistakes made by the specific user.

The VP appointed an experienced development manager as the product line manager (PLM). This manager has been recognized as the best manager in the company because of his on-time delivery of products, but he recognizes that he has never managed such a major change in both how products are developed and the number of products over which he will have control. He is looking for help in planning this change. As a developer, the PLM used design patterns and has found them to be a good way to succinctly organize descriptions of what to do and why. When he became a manager he found help in some of the organizational patterns. He went searching for patterns related to software product lines.

The PLM found help in a technical report about the Adoption Factory pattern from SEI. That report described the development issues and provided an adoption roadmap using the IDEAL model for managing change. The PLM sees from the Adoption Factory pattern that LMN is embarking on a Cold Start effort, having never applied the software product line strategy before. Related to this, LMN needs to consider What to Build in its product line and ensure that it possesses sufficient process discipline to manage the larger context of a product line.

The VP and PLM agree that a proactive approach can allow the organization to focus first on core assets and then on products, but many things still have to be considered, virtually simultaneously, before a robust set of core assets can be designed. The Cold Start pattern specifies a number of the practices that are needed. The VP asked the VP of business operations to designate a businessperson to work with the PLM on organizational issues such as funding, operations, and personnel issues. The PLM brings in several technical people to help with determining the product set using the What to Build pattern. With all these people becoming involved, the PLM decides to pause and lay out the actions defined by the Adoption Factory on the framework provided by the IDEAL model. A summary is shown in Table 2.2.

With this overall plan in place, the organization progresses through the IDEAL phases.

- **Initiating:** The VP has chartered an initial organization with a clearly identified focus, an identified source of funding, and a single designated leader. The entire company has been enlisted from the founder, who is happy to get her pet project done, to the development community, by virtue of the appointment of a respected manager with development experience. The PLM is staffing the product line organization beginning with planning support.

Even with the promise of funding, the PLM must estimate costs and schedules and have those approved by the VP. As a first step, the team decided on a rough scope of the products that would be in the product line, based on the What to Build pattern. A set of broad requirements was defined to support the scope. They chose the SIMPLE economic modeling approach (Böckle et al. 2004) as the basis for making cost estimates of the product line. The team constructed cost formulas for each of the practice areas involved in their adoption effort, and thus felt they were able to make reasonable estimates. The estimates were updated later as more specific data became available.

Table 2.2 Summary of Actions

IDEAL Phase	Actions
Initiating	Obtain sufficient executive support
	Obtain initial funding
	Identify initial scope of the product line for the purposes of order-of-magnitude schedule and cost estimates
Diagnosing	Evaluate the capabilities of the organization relative to the 29 product line practice areas
	Capture baseline productivity data from nonproduct line projects in LMN
Establishing	Develop the concept of how the product line organization will operate
	Develop the production plan for how core assets will be turned into products
Acting	Product teams use the core assets to build products
	Core asset team supports product building by maintaining the assets
	Collect performance data to be compared against the company baseline
Leveraging	VP and PLM review data to determine the impact of the product line strategy

The PLM is concerned about only having one pass through the IDEAL phases, but he believes that taking the proactive approach will make that easier. By first concentrating on the core assets and then on product building, the core assets will have a conceptual integrity that is hard to achieve piecemeal. Also, by creating the core assets before building products, the core asset developers will have more time to assist the product builders and respond to change requests rapidly.

■ **Diagnosing:** The PLM decided to focus on two areas in the diagnostic phase. He was concerned that, as a former custom development shop, a culture of rapid response with no consideration of future projects would limit the amount of reuse achieved. He wants to understand how the existing development process must change in order to adequately support reuse. His second area of concern is whether the current management process is adequate to allocate resources and moderate competing demands among multiple projects. As a manager, the PLM knows that he has been able to focus on a single project in the past. He wants to understand what is needed for the product line organization to be ready to coordinate the production of multiple products.

The results of the two diagnoses were very similar. Both diagnoses identified the software architecture as a critical core asset for mitigating the risks the PLM had identified. Both diagnoses also identified the commonality/variability analysis as a critical core asset. The PLM decided to give particular attention to these assets.

The PLM decided to establish separate core asset and product teams. Strategic reuse is critical to the success of a product line but very different from the culture at LMN. Having one team that can focus on that effort seems to be an easier transition than everyone focusing on reuse for part of their time.

■ **Establishing:** The Adoption Factory pattern is divided into three stages: Establish Context, Establish the Production Capability, and Operate the product line. The organization had already begun to establish the context during the Initiating phase by setting a preliminary scope and reaching agreements with executives about funding. The PLM identified leaders for the core asset and product teams and chartered the teams.

The core asset team lead reached agreement with a consulting firm to provide architecture support to the product line organization. The firm will have primary responsibility for developing the architecture but will also mentor two LMN employees in architecture practices. The firm has previous product line experience and may be able to advise LMN on other practices as well.

The core asset team, with a few of the product builders, began work immediately to define the requirements. This analysis activity gave a sharper definition to the products in the product line. The SIMPLE model was refined to reflect this new information.

The leads of the core asset and product-development teams form a committee to develop the production plan. The plan describes how products are built from core assets. In order to develop the plan, the group will have to develop a production strategy and a production method that will determine how the core assets are created.

A training curriculum was developed that balanced concepts and skills. The initial training was intended to give everyone an understanding of basic product line concepts and practices. When the production method was fully defined, training was initiated to acquaint personnel with their roles and responsibilities in the new product line processes.

■ **Acting:** LMN, Inc., initiated development of some assets even as other practices were being planned. The practices in the What to Build pattern had been applied early to define the scope of the product line. This definition was used to revise the cost estimates made previously. The interaction between the scope-definition effort and cost estimation led the PLM to agree to add another utility to the organization's charter.

The high-priority commonality and variability analysis was conducted, and the results were fed into the software architecture definition activity. The architecture effort was central to a number of development, and even management, activities. The architecture provided the core asset team with direction on what to build, and it guided management to further refine estimates.

When a significant number of core assets were completed, the production capability was ready to operate. The first product team was launched. The product builders who had participated in building core assets provided a rapid introduction for the others. Defects and missing features were fed back to the core asset team through a bug-reporting system that will eventually also allow users of the products to request additional features.

The product line organization met most of its expectations, including building five utilities and the infrastructure piece. Most important, the PLM believes that the company now has a production capability that can produce additional products rapidly.

■ **Leveraging:** The staff of the product line organization learned a number of lessons that will help the next product line organization:
  - The software architecture, which was not formerly a part of their development process, was critical to their success. The two budding architects will handle much of their future architecture needs.
  - The product line personnel have gained maturity in balancing the long-term view of reuse over several products and the short-term focus on a single component that is then used across those products.

■ The adoption of a new development strategy touches everyone and how they do their work, but sufficient planning mitigates the risks of change.

2.3.2 Case Study 2: An Iterative Rollout

Our next hypothetical company, RMH Enterprises, is a medium-sized company whose main business is to provide subway ticket dispensers in a handful of U.S. cities. Its main offices are in Boulder, Colorado, with four distributed sites, each with its own software team located near the customers to respond to their unique needs. RMH is a prime example of a company that began selling hardware and found that it increasingly relied on software for functionality.

In looking to expand market, RMH managers decided to sell their subway applications outside the United States and to move into systems to dispense train tickets for international markets. Furthermore, they saw an opportunity to expand into dispensers that have nothing to do with transportation, such as theater and concert tickets. All these applications have to

- accept cash (or tokens) and return change
- accept credit cards (confirming the validity of the transaction over a network)
- dispense tickets with different formats

and they have to do this in a matter of seconds.

While looking toward this expansion, the company's management already saw the negative effects of a "clone and own" approach to software reuse for the different customers. They realized the distributed, largely independent organizational structures, operating as separate profit centers, and their current rewards system did not encourage sharing. The remote sites were rewarded for customer response and not for contributing to overall RMH cost savings. Furthermore, the autonomy and "whatever the customer wants" culture at the sites led to different software support environments and inconsistent process discipline, especially when compared with the highly disciplined approach of the central software team at headquarters.

RMH decided to adopt the product line strategy to remedy these problems, and became savvy in how to use the Adoption Factory pattern and the IDEAL model as a basis for their product line adoption strategy. Three iterations through the IDEAL model were deemed appropriate to build incremental capability as explained below. Their adoption approach using these two models is shown in Figure 2.9.

The three IDEAL cycles taken together constitute a sketch of the overall adoption plan. The major goals for each cycle were:

- Cycle 1: Reconcile organizational structures and processes across sites while getting started on some key product line engineering practices, including an initial product line scope definition.
- Cycle 2: Establish the product line production capability for the initial scope of products and test its operation on a small scale.

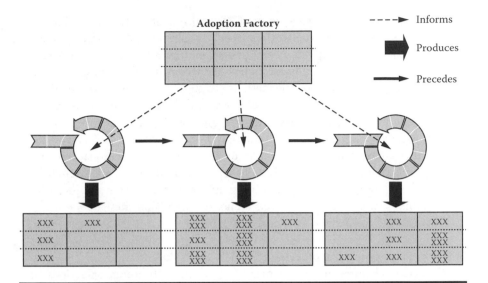

Figure 2.9 Approach to using the Adoption Factory pattern and the IDEAL model in Case Study 2.

■ Cycle 3: Establish product line operations for the initial scope across the organization.

Each IDEAL cycle guides the incremental change but is informed by the Adoption Factory pattern on product line practices. As depicted in the Adoption Factory icons along the bottom, each IDEAL cycle produces a more complete or more mature implementation of the practice areas in the Adoption Factory across the organization. The actual plan will be fairly explicit for the first iteration, but will have less detail for subsequent iterations, to be updated as experience is gained. It is possible that additional iterations may be added to cover a larger scope of products for the product line. By standard company practice, RMH managers typically plan in detail only for 6–12 months ahead, but update their plans monthly so that they are realistic and viable.

2.3.3 Iteration 1: Overview

The initial IDEAL iteration was planned in response to the special challenges of a distributed workforce with different degrees of process discipline and different software development environments. The initial plan for this iteration called for two strategies operating in parallel: an "organizational leveling" strategy, and a "preparing for initial operations" strategy.

For the *Initiating Phase* of this iteration, RMH managers committed to sponsor the effort, form a steering committee to guide and review progress, and allocate appropriate personnel and resources for the iteration. This included resources to conduct appropriate diagnostics, to establish and execute action plans based on the diagnostic results, and to plan the subsequent iterations. Additionally, specific desired outcomes for this iteration were defined with measures to track progress.

The *Diagnosing Phase* of this iteration actually consists of two distinct diagnoses, each with their own recommendations. To support the "organizational leveling" strategy, a "tools and processes" diagnosis will be conducted across the sites to determine the state of process discipline and development environments. To support part of the "preparing for initial operations" strategy, a "structures" diagnosis will be conducted of the suitability of the current organizational structures, funding, operations, and reward system to support a product line approach. (Other aspects of this strategy include determining the product line scope and preparing a product line architecture; these aspects do not require diagnostics.)

The *Establishing Phase* will produce a plan to

- Institute appropriate processes and tools across sites
- Institute changes to the organizational structure, funding, operations, and reward system
- Develop a product line scope and associated business case
- Develop an initial product line architecture to support the envisioned scope

Based on their experience achieving SEI Capability Maturity Model Integration (CMMI) process Maturity Level 2, RMH managers know that instituting process change at the sites will take time. Hence, they have planned for the parallel execution of their two strategies so that the organization will be ready to move out once all sites have a common process and tool basis for operations.

The *Acting Phase* will execute and track this plan, while the *Leveraging Phase* will be to consolidate lessons learned and polish the results as necessary.

2.3.4 Iteration 1: Results

The "tools and processes" diagnostic confirmed that there were different degrees of process discipline and different tools environments in use at all sites. The diagnostic produced a profile of the sites according to the Level 2 of the SEI Capability Maturity Model Integration (CMMI) Process Areas, plus some additional process areas that RMH has identified as important to its operations. The experience in moving to CMMI Maturity Level 2 provided valuable experience in avoiding false starts, so they set a goal of harmonizing the sites with repeatable processes in configuration management, requirements management, project planning and tracking, and product release. Specifics of the software development processes were not determined to be as critical, but having defined handoff interfaces among teams was determined to be important. While a catalogue of existing tools was produced, the diagnostic team recognized that a "process first" approach was appropriate and recommended deferring decisions on tool support until the processes were established.

The Steering Group approved the recommendations, and a planning group was formed to produce an action plan to institute the process improvements, followed by establishing tool support for the processes and development environments.

Meanwhile, the "structures" diagnostic confirmed what intuition told the managers: The current organizational structures, funding, operations, and reward systems in fact would work counter to a product line approach. Various options were discussed, and eventually the top-level managers agreed that some painful changes would be necessary.

The complete autonomy of the sites would have to go. This change of control would also address a key disincentive to strategic reuse inherent in their current cost-accounting approach. A product line manager, acting as an executive agent, would be appointed who would report directly to a vice president given line responsibility over core asset development and all product development. Site managers would work with the vice president to address customer interface issues, but the core asset group at headquarters would now receive a portion of customer-generated revenues. Sites would no longer be given funding to pursue an independent "clone and own" approach. Significant customer and "people" challenges awaited the management team, but the way ahead was clear. Since the cut-over would not need to happen until sometime after the "organizational leveling" strategy was complete, the managers decided to plan incremental changes to lessen the organizational stress at any one time.

As these efforts were proceeding, there was additional work following the practices of the "What to Build" pattern. The scope and associated business case would be produced to provide a basis for developing the product line architecture. The time required to execute the "organizational leveling" strategy allowed for a careful and deliberate approach and reconsideration of the plan as the situation changed.

2.3.5 Subsequent Iterations

Execution of the strategies in the first iteration went well. True to their management practices, RMH managers were following their plans and revising them frequently. Whereas they had initially planned for the second iteration to establish a general product production capability, with the third iteration to actually build the products, a new opportunity arose in the form of an upgrade for an existing customer's system.

The managers engaged in a replanning activity and changed their approach to the second iteration. This iteration would now focus on a complete pilot implementation of product line practices for this customer. The approach would use "lightweight" implementations of certain product line practices, with the idea of making them more robust on a subsequent iteration that encompassed a larger portion of the RMH product portfolio. Of course, lessons learned would be incorporated, and replanning would take place again if the situation warranted.

2.4 Summary

There is still a pervading assumption that product lines involve a new technical approach only. Most product line adopters vastly underestimate the management commitment and involvement required to succeed. Organizations new to product lines typically suffer from inappropriate organizational structures and processes, lack of training, insufficient and inappropriate resources, and lack of carefully constructed plans for product line adoption. Engineering organizations tend to jump right into architecture and component development activities without defining scope or a business case. Frustration and wasted effort result.

Our work with product line adopters across multiple domains bears this out. We have seen cases of product line adoption failure where our roadmap would have provided essential guidance (Donohoe, Jones, and Northop 2005) as well as cases where organizations have greatly benefited from the Adoption Factory pattern (Fritsch and Ferber 2005; Morton and Tharp 2005).

The Adoption Factory pattern maps out the combination of technical and business activities that need to occur; it properly orients an organization to establish its product line context *before* developing code and to establish real production capability *before* attempting to operate the product line. Combining the Adoption Factory pattern with a technology change model, like the IDEAL model, allows an organization to effectively manage the organizational changes along the way.

Note

Capability Maturity Model and CMMI are registered in the U.S. Patent and Trademark Office by Carnegie Mellon University. Framework for Software Product Line Practice and IDEAL are service marks of Carnegie Mellon University.

References

Böckle, Günter, Paul Clements, John D. McGregor, Dirk Muthig, and Klaus Schmid. 2004. Calculating ROI for software product lines. *IEEE Software* 21 (3): 23–31. http://ieeexplore.ieee.org/iel5/52/28793/01293069.pdf.

Bruckhaus, Tilmann, Nazim H. Madhavji, Ingrid Janssen, and John Henshaw. 1996. The impact of tools on software productivity. *IEEE Software* 13 (5): 29–38. http://ieeexplore.ieee.org/iel5/52/11391/00536456.pdf?arnumber=536456.

Clements, Paul, and Linda Northrop. 2002. *Software product lines: Practices and patterns.* Boston, MA: Addison-Wesley Publishers.

Donohoe, Patrick, Larry Jones, and Linda Northop. 2005. Examining product line readiness: Experiences with the SEI product line technical probe. Paper read at 9th international software product line conference, 26–29 September 2005, Rennes, France.

Fritsch, Claudia, and Stefan Ferber. 2005. The right start: Applying the what to build pattern. Paper read at 9th international software product line conference, September 26–29, Rennes, France.

Gamma, Erich. 1995. *Design patterns: Elements of reusable object-oriented software*. Reading, MA: Addison-Wesley.

Krueger, Charles W. 2001. Easing the transition to software mass customization. Paper read at 4th international workshop on software product family engineering, October, Bilbao, Spain.

McFeeley, Robert. 1996. IDEAL: A user's guide for software process improvement. Software Engineering Institute, Carnegie Mellon University, Pittsburgh. http://www.sei.cmu.edu/pub/documents/96.reports/pdf/hb001.96.pdf.

Morton, Callum, and Herb Tharp. 2005. SPL adoption at NCR. Paper read at 9th international software product line conference, September 26–29, Rennes, France.

Northrop, Linda. 2004. Software product line adoption roadmap. Software Engineering Institute, Carnegie Mellon University, Pittsburgh. http://www.sei.cmu.edu/pub/documents/04.reports/pdf/04tr022.pdf.

Northrop, Linda, and Paul Clements. 2007. A framework for software product line practice, Version 5.0. Software Engineering Institute, Carnegie Mellon University, Pittsburgh. http://www.sei.cmu.edu/productlines/framework.html.

Chapter 3

New Methods behind a New Generation of Software Product Line Successes

Charles W. Krueger

BigLever Software, Austin, TX

Contents

3.1 Introduction

The first generation of software product line case studies—from the 1980s and 1990s—described patterns of software development behavior that were characterized a posteriori (after the fact) as *software product line development*. Although these pioneering efforts were all motivated to improve productivity through software reuse, they were each independently discovering a special pattern of reuse that we now recognize as software product line development (Clements and Northrop 2001).

These unintentional occurrences of software product line practice are still recurring in the industry today. What is more interesting, however, is the current generation of *intentional* software product line initiatives, where organizations adopt, with forethought, the best practices discovered from the practical experiences of their predecessors. These cases provide insights about a new generation of software product line methods and the benefits that they offer over the first generation.

In this chapter, we describe three of the new methods that have provided some of the most significant advances to software product line practice:

1. **Software mass customization:** The dichotomy of domain engineering (DE) and application engineering (AE) introduces dissonance and inefficiency in software development. The *software mass customization* methodology utilizes abstraction and automation to eliminate application engineering and thereby the negative effects of the DE/AE dichotomy.
2. **Minimally invasive transitions:** The cost, time, and effort required for organizations to adopt early generation software product line methods is disruptive and prohibitive. *Minimally invasive transition* methods enable rapid adoption of product line practice with low disruption, low cost, and rapid return on investment.
3. **Bounded combinatorics:** Combinatorics in feature models, requirements, architecture, implementation variation points, and test coverage can easily exceed the number of atoms in the universe, which leads to complexity, errors,

and poor testability. New methods for *bounded combinatorics* utilize abstraction, modularity, encapsulation, composition, hierarchy, and constraints to reduce combinatorics from geometric, exponential, and astronomical to simple, linear, and tractable.

3.2 Software Mass Customization

"Application Engineering Considered Harmful"

Software mass customization is a software product line development methodology distinguished by its predominant focus on domain engineering of reusable software assets and the use of fully automated production to virtually eliminate manual application engineering of the individual products. A key characteristic of this approach is the synchronous evolution of all products in the product line in conjunction with the maintenance and evolution of the reusable software assets. Software mass customization utilizes a combination of formal abstraction and automation to enable more effective reuse and higher overall software product line development efficiency compared with earlier methods that relied heavily on manual application engineering.

Analogous to the *mass customization* methodology prevalent in manufacturing today, software mass customization takes advantage of a collection of "parts" capable of being automatically composed and configured in different ways. Each product in the product line is manufactured by an automated production facility capable of composing and configuring the parts based on an abstract and formal *feature model* characterization of the product (Krueger 2001).

The motivations behind the software mass customization methodology are both economic and pragmatic. Compared with the first generation software product line development methods, software mass customization is easier to adopt, has greater similarity to conventional software development, is less disruptive to organizational structures and processes, and offers greater and faster returns on investment. Furthermore, it reduces product creation and evolution to a commodity, so that adding new products to a product line can be trivial.

3.2.1 Sans Application Engineering

At the risk of abusing a well-worn computer science cliché, this section might best be entitled "application engineering considered harmful." Application engineering, which is product-specific development, constituted a significant part of early software product line development theory, but has proved to be problematic in practice. One of the key contributions of software mass customization is to eliminate application engineering and the negative impact it has on software product line development.

The first generation of software product line methods emphasized a clear dichotomy between the activities of domain engineering and those of application engineering. The role of domain engineers was to create core software assets "for reuse," and the role of application engineers was to use the core assets to create products "with reuse." This was a logical extension of component-based software reuse, though in this case the components were designed for a particular application domain and with a particular software architecture in mind.

With application engineering, an individual product is created by configuring and composing the reusable *core assets*. Configuration is the instantiation of predefined variation *within* a core asset, either via automated mechanisms such as template instantiation and #ifdefs, or via manual techniques such as writing code to fill out function stubs. Composition is the development of "glue code" and application logic *around* the core assets. Application engineers are typically guided by a written *production plan* on how to perform the configuration and composition in a way that is consistent with the product line architecture.

At first glance, all seems well. Products are created with much less effort due to reuse of core assets, including the production plan and product line architecture. If the engineering effort for each product ended with its creation, then all would indeed be well. However, most software product lines must be maintained and must evolve over time, and this is where the problems with application engineering arise. These problems can best be characterized by the dichotomy that exists between core assets and product-specific software as the entire product line evolves over time.

The first problem is that product-specific software in each product is just that—product-specific. It is one-of-a-kind software that often requires a team of engineers dedicated to the product to create it, understand it, maintain it, and evolve it. This takes us back to the problems of conventional software development approaches, such as clone-and-own, where there is a strong linear relationship between increasing the number of products in the product line portfolio and increasing the number of engineers required to support the product line.

Because the product-specific software exists in the context of each individual product and its associated application engineering team, this software cannot be easily reused. It is likely that a significant amount of similar software will be independently developed across the different products, but the potential for reuse of emerging abstractions will go unnoticed because of the isolated application engineering teams and the independent, diverging product software branches.

The second problem is that application engineering creates a unique and isolated context in which the core assets are reused. This makes it difficult to enhance, maintain, or refactor the core assets in nontrivial ways. Any syntactic or semantic changes to the interfaces or architectural structure of the core assets have to be merged into the product-specific software in each and every one of the products in the product line. This can be very error prone and very costly, both in terms of time and effort. The effect of this high cost of evolution is to stifle innovation and evolution for the product line. Also, significant upfront effort is required to create immutable and pristine product line architectures and reusable assets so that evolution and maintenance is minimized.

The third problem is that the hard delineation between domain engineering and application engineering creates hard structural boundaries in the software and in the organization. Reusable abstractions that emerge during application engineering go unnoticed by the domain engineering team, since it is outside of their purview. Neither domain engineers nor application engineers can see valuable opportunities for refactoring that may exist across the boundary between core assets and product-specific software.

The fourth problem is that the organizational delineation between domain engineering teams and application engineering teams creates cultural dissonance and political tension within a development community. This organizational dichotomy within the development community is very different from conventional organizational structures, so it can be difficult to initially partition the team. The dichotomy creates a new cultural "us-versus-them" tension. All of the technical software development problems described earlier were due to the challenges at the domain engineering and application engineering interface, which by human nature leads to an acrimonious and unproductive relationship when problems arise. Which side is causing problems? Which side is responsible for fixing problems? Organizational dissonance, of course, decreases the overall efficiency and effectiveness.

A common question in early generation software product line approaches was what percentage of effort should be spent on domain engineering and what percentage of effort should be spent on application engineering. Figure 3.1 illustrates this question. By plotting the accumulated overall cost of developing some number of products in a product line (six products in this example), the green "slider" on the x-axis shows the y-axis cost for any given ratio of DE to AE. Given the cost plots for Product #1 through Product #6 in this figure, it is most advantageous to shift the balance as close as possible to 100% domain engineering. But are the cost plots in Figure 3.1 realistic, and is it possible for a software product line methodology to be predominantly focused on domain engineering?

The software mass customization methodology is an affirmative answer to both of these questions. The negative effects of the DE/AE dichotomy and those of manual application engineering are avoided by shifting the balance away from manual application engineering and focusing entirely on domain engineering and fully automated production using technology called software product line *configurators*.

3.2.2 Software Product Line Configurators

Software product line configurators are a class of technology that enables software mass customization—software product line development based on automated product instantiation rather than manual application engineering. As shown in Figure 3.2, configurators take two types of input—core software assets and product

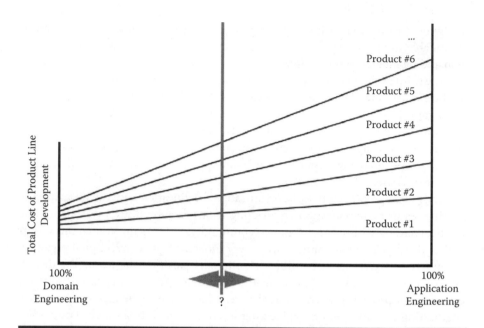

Figure 3.1 Optimal balance of domain engineering and application engineering?

models—in order to automatically create product instances. The core software assets are the common and varying software assets for the product line, such as requirements, architecture and design, source code, test cases, and product documentation. The product models are concise abstractions that characterize the different product instances in the product line, expressed in terms of a *feature model*—the feature profile of the products. BigLever Software *Gears* is an example of a commercial software product line configurator (BigLever Software 2008).

The predominant development effort with configurators is domain engineering of the core assets. There is a relatively small effort that goes into the product models, which essentially replaces the manual application engineering effort that dominates in the DE/AE dichotomy.

With configurators, the product models are a level of abstraction over the core assets. At first glance, this appears similar to the use of abstraction in conventional source code compilers, software generators, or model-driven development compilers. However, configurators work more by composition and configuration of conventional assets rather than generation, transformation, or translation of one representation of software into another representation.

Configurators illustrate the analogy between the practice of mass customization in manufacturing and the practice of software mass customization. In manufacturing, parts that are specially engineered with variations are composed and

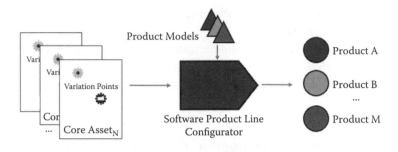

Figure 3.2   Software product line configurator.

configured by an automated factory, based on a feature profile for the product instance under manufacture.

In contrast to the four problems outlined earlier in the DE/AE dichotomy, software mass customization with configurators provides a simpler, more efficient, and more scalable solution.

- Since all software exists within a consolidated collection of core assets, everything is a candidate for reuse. This is true even for product-specific assets that start out as unique to one product. Since the core assets are all within a single context, it is much easier to observe emerging abstractions and to refactor the assets, including requirements, architecture, source code, and test cases.
- Since all development is focused on core asset development, teams are organized around the different assets. This organizational structure looks very similar with 2 products or with 200 products, making for a scalable solution. This eliminates the strong linear relationship between the number of products and staff size that we observed with the DE/AE dichotomy.
- Evolution of the core assets and products is synonymous. For example, a change in the core assets can be followed by automated reinstantiation of all products to reflect that change. No manual merging and reintegration is required.
- Organizational structures are similar to conventional software development, where teams are organized around subsystems. With software product line development, developers need to introduce and manage the variation within core assets, but this is also familiar to any developer who has used primitive variation management techniques such as #ifdefs.

With software mass customization, there is very little overhead to adding a new product to a product line. New products are commodities rather than the subject of a major long-term development and maintenance commitment. If the existing core assets are sufficient to support a new product, then all that is needed is a new product model. If the existing core assets are not sufficient, then the core assets are extended with first-class development on the core assets, not as one-off glue code in a product-specific code branch.

Although the software mass customization model is a simpler and more familiar methodology than the DE/AE dichotomy, there are two new techniques that need to be addressed: *developing the intangible product* and *variation management in space and time*.

3.2.3 Developing the Intangible Product

With the software mass customization methodology, where automated configurators replace manual application engineering, products only become tangible after the automated production step. Under this model, there are no longer tangible teams of application engineers organized around tangible products. And yet, the need remains to have organized and tangible product release plans and to deliver products according to tangible release schedules. How do you manage the domain engineering of the core assets so that release schedules for individual products can be met?

The key to managing product releases is synchronizing the release of features and capabilities in core assets with the product release schedules. In order to release a product at a given point in time, the core assets used in the composition and configuration of that product must meet or exceed the required functionality and the required quality for that product release.

Figure 3.3 illustrates an example of the synchronized release of core assets and products to meet different product release requirements. Time is represented across the top horizontal axis, increasing from left to right, with each baseline (Baseline 1 through Baseline M) occurring on monthly intervals. In between the baselines are weekly and daily synchronization points—such as daily automated builds and weekly integration tests—to manage the evolution and convergence.

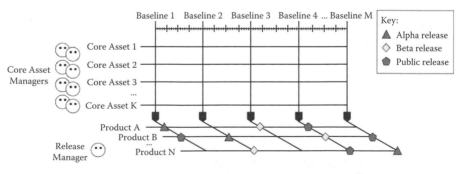

Figure 3.3   Synchronizing the release clocks for core assets and products.

Across the bottom of the figure are the product release schedules for each of the products, A through N. Over time, each product is scheduled to cycle through quality validation levels, which in this example are alpha (triangles) for initial validation, beta (diamonds) for preliminary release, and general availability (GA, pentagons) for final release. Note that these product release points are synchronized on the major release baselines (Baseline 1 through Baseline M).

Product managers in this scenario are not managing tangible teams of application engineers to meet their release schedules. They must manage schedules by coordinating and negotiating with product line architects and core asset managers to make sure that the core assets meet or exceed the required functionality and quality on specific baselines.

From the perspective of the core asset teams (Core Asset 1 through Core Asset K), their release schedules are driven by the consolidated requirements and schedules from all of the products. For the software mass customization methodology to work efficiently and effectively, it is essential to have effective architectural planning, coordination, and synchronization at this level. The product managers and architects represent the interests of the product release schedules in order to provide the core asset development managers with well-defined and realistic core asset release requirements.

A "release" in this methodology is a baseline of the core assets. As shown in Figure 3.3, it is not essential that all products be supported on each baseline, or that all products be released at the same quality state (alpha, beta, general availability). However, there is an advantage to synchronize the release of multiple products on one baseline. You can amortize the release overhead, such as testing and documentation, by clustering multiple product releases on a single baseline.

3.2.4 Variation Management in Time and Space

Core assets and product models evolve over time under the software mass customization methodology, just like conventional software development. Conventional configuration management and component baseline management can be used to manage this *variation in time*.

Different from conventional one-of-a-kind software development, variations within the domain space of the product line must also be managed. At any fixed point in time, such as a core asset baseline, it is the core asset variation points, product models, and configurators that manage this *variation in space*.

Figure 3.4 illustrates the distinction between variation in time and variation in space. In the top portion of the figure, core assets and product models are evolving over time, with the baseline representing stable and compatible releases of the core assets. In the bottom of the figure, the configurator takes core assets and product models from a given baseline and instantiates the different products within the domain space of the product line.

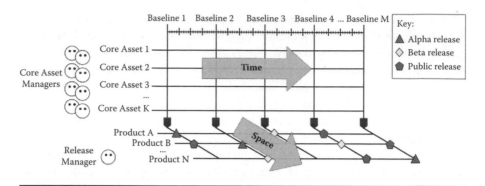

Figure 3.4   Software variation in time and space.

This clean separation of concerns between variation in time and variation in space, which is manifest in the software mass customization methodology, ensures that software product line development is familiar and requires the least amount of disruption when transitioning to a software product line approach. More details on this separation of concerns can be found in Krueger (2002).

3.2.5 *Impact of the Software Mass Customization Methodology*

Software mass customization offers one of the most efficient forms of software reuse possible, according to the taxonomy in Krueger (1992). The *cognitive distance* between a product concept and the specification of that product in a feature model is very small, typically measured in developer-minutes or developer-hours. Configurator technology fully automates product instantiation from the feature model specification for a product. Furthermore, configurators can reuse legacy assets and core assets developed using conventional technology and techniques, so creating the core assets for a product line utilizes the conventional skills of existing development teams.

The impact of this methodology is that products in a product line become commodities. The cost of adding and maintaining a new product in a product line portfolio is almost trivial, making it possible to scale portfolios to include orders-of-magnitude more products than is possible under early generation methods that rely on manual application engineering and the labor-intensive AE/DE dichotomy.

3.3 Minimally Invasive Transitions

"Work Like a Surgeon, Not Like a Coroner"

The software product line development methodology of *minimally invasive transitions* is distinguished by its focus minimizing the cost, time, and effort required for organizations to adopt software product line practice. A key characteristic of this methodology is the minimal disruption of ongoing production schedules during the transition from conventional product-centric development practice. Minimally invasive transitions take advantage of existing software assets and rely on incremental adoption strategies to enable transitions in two orders-of-magnitude less effort than that experienced using earlier methods that relied on upfront, top-down reengineering of significant portions of software assets, processes, and organizational structures (Buhrdorf, Churchett, and Krueger 2003; Hetrick, Krueger, and Moore 2005).

The term *minimally invasive transitions* is intended to invoke the analogy to medical procedures in which problems are surgically corrected with minimal degrees of disruption and negative side effects to the patient. In both cases—medical and software—excessive and extraneous disruption can be very detrimental to the patient.

The motivation behind minimally invasive transitions is to address one of the primary impediments to widespread use of early generation software product line development methods—an imposing and oftentimes a prohibitive adoption barrier. Figure 3.5 illustrates the cost and effort required to build and maintain a software product line under three different product line development methodologies: conventional product-centric development, early generation software product line methodologies, and minimally invasive transition methods. The graph shows the rate of increasing cost and effort as more products are added to the product line portfolio (the slope of the lines), the up-front investment required to adopt the product line practice (the vertical-axis intercept), and the return-on-investment (ROI) points relative to conventional product-centric approaches.

Comparing the product-centric to the early generation software product line methods would suggest an easy business case to justify adopting a software product

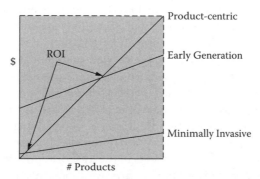

Figure 3.5   Up-front investment and ROI to build and maintain a software product line under three different product line development methodologies.

line approach. However, as part of the business case, resources for the upfront investment have to be allocated. The problem is not so much the money as it is the human resources. Diverting the existing expert engineering resources from product development to software product line transition inevitably means that production schedules are disrupted. In a classic early generation software product line approach, Cummins diverted nine contiguous months of its overall development effort into a software product line transition effort (Clements and Northrop 2001). For most product-development companies, this level of disruption to ongoing production schedules cannot be tolerated. It would kill many companies before return on investment was ever achieved.

In contrast, the graph for minimally invasive transitions illustrates that the benefits of software product line methods can be achieved with a much smaller, nondisruptive transition investment and with much faster ROI. Two primary techniques are employed for this methodology. The first is carefully assessing how to reuse as much as possible of an organization's existing assets, processes, infrastructure, and organizational structures. The second is finding an incremental transition approach that will enable a small upfront investment that will offer immediate and incremental ROI. The excess returns from the initial incremental step can be reinvested to fuel the next incremental step—then repeat as needed.

3.3.1 Minimize the Distance to a Better Product Line Practice

Most product development organizations in today's markets create a portfolio of products—a product line—rather than just a single product. Thus, for software development teams, the idea of creating software for a product line is not new, since they are most likely already doing that.

What is new are some of the "true" software product line development methods, tools, and techniques that make product line development easier and more efficient. Although they may already have innovative solutions in place, organizations considering a transition to software product line practice have often reached the practical limit in some areas of their existing practice. They are looking to new software product development methods that provide better solutions in those areas.

By nature, engineers prefer to reengineer new solutions from a greenfield rather than a brownfield, but that is often ruled out by the business case. Reengineering a product line approach from scratch is too expensive and causes too much disruption to ongoing production schedules. What often makes the most sense is a more surgical approach that fixes the biggest problems while reusing as much as possible from the current approach. In other words, find the shortest path and best ROI that achieves the required improvements in the least disruptive way. Referring back to our medical analogy, this minimally invasive approach is for the benefit of the patient rather than the surgeon.

For example, with software mass customization configurators, it is possible to reuse most of the legacy software assets, with just enough refactoring to allow for composition and configuration by the configurators. The existing architecture and infrastructure is often sufficient with little or no modification. The initial feature model and initial variation points in the consolidated core assets do not need to be elegant, as long as they accurately instantiate product instances. In a stable software product line practice, feature models and variation points are typically undergoing continuous evolution and refactoring, so the initial version of these can be refined later.

To minimize disruption in organizational structures, follow the advice from Section 3.2 and don't introduce new and unfamiliar organizational structures such as the dichotomy of domain engineering and application engineering groups.

In terms of product line *scope*, the shortest path to a live product line deployment is to take the minimalist approach. Initially the core assets should support the products that need to be deployed in the near term. Then a reactive style of scoping can be utilized to evolve the core assets and production line as business demands dictate (Clements and Krueger 2002).

3.3.2 It's Just Like Single-System Development, Except...

Early generation software product line case studies made software product line development look very different from convention single-system software development. New generation case studies have shown that there really doesn't need to be that much difference. For organizations using minimally invasive transitions, the before-and-after pictures look very similar.

It is useful to view software product line development as being just like single-system development except for a few distinct differences. For example, referring back to Figure 3.2 on the software mass customization methodology, the core assets can be viewed as the "single system" that is created and maintained by the development organization. The core assets evolve in a familiar way under configuration management, as illustrated in Figure 3.4. The software product line configurator is analogous to a requirements management tool that instantiates a set of requirements, or a source code compiler. Even the fact that multiple products can be automatically produced from the core assets is not unfamiliar to a software developer that has used #ifdefs, generics, or templates.

Engineers that we speak to from the new generation success stories reinforce this point of view. They tell us that they don't see much difference in their job after making the transition to software product line practice. As they develop their core assets, they now have to deal with variation points and multiple instantiations of the core asset, but the pressures to deliver on schedule and the output of their effort appears to be very familiar.

In fact, because of this perception of "business as usual," the core asset developers are often surprised when they see the global improvements in productivity, time to market, and quality following their transition to product line practice. Thus, it is important for management to provide good feedback about the improvement metrics so that developers can get a strong sense of accomplishment for their new software product line development efforts.

The development role that often perceives the biggest difference between conventional methods and the new software product line methods is that of the project manager. Previously they probably managed product-specific development teams, requirements, and schedules. Now they are managing either core asset development teams or product delivery schedules for intangible products. Referring back to Figure 3.3, the separation and coordination of product delivery schedules and core asset development is relatively unique to software product line development.

3.3.3 Regression Red Flags

Because the before and after pictures can look quite similar with minimally invasive transitions, it can be difficult to remain true to the new software product line principles and not slip into old habits. How can you tell when you inadvertently regress into the familiar old ways of conventional engineering?

The best indicator is when you detect any focus on tangible products rather than intangible products. It is a red warning flag if developers are focused on specific products rather than features and capabilities in the core assets. Examples of regression red flags include:

- References to products in core asset source code
- Product names in core asset file names or directory names
- Product-specific branches in configuration management
- Product development teams working across multiple core assets

3.3.4 Incremental Return on Incremental Investment

Early generation software product line methods suggested that a large upfront investment was required in order to gain the even larger benefits of software product line practice. However, with minimally invasive transition techniques, it is also possible to achieve the same results by making a series of smaller incremental investments. By staging an incremental transition, small incremental investments very quickly yield much larger incremental returns. These returns—in effort, time, and money—can then be partially or fully reinvested to fuel the next incremental steps in the transition. Furthermore, the efficiency and effectiveness of the development organization constantly improves throughout the transition, meaning that development organizations do not need to "take a hit" to reap the benefits of software product line practice.

For example, Engenio Information Technologies achieved a return on investment after an incremental investment of only 4 developer-months of effort. In contrast, the conventional wisdom from first generation software product line methods predicted that the investment for Engenio would be 900 to 1350 developer-months, or 200 to 300 times greater than that actually experienced (Hetrick, Krueger, and Moore 2005).

There are, of course, many different facets to consider within a software development organization when making an incremental transition to software product lines. For example, Clements and Northrop (2001) characterize 29 key practice areas that may be impacted by a software product line approach. Any or all of these might be considered in an incremental transition.

Engenio chose to incrementally address, in sequence, those facets that represented the primary inefficiencies and bottlenecks in their development organization. By eliminating the inefficiencies and bottlenecks in the most critical facet, the next most critical product line problem in the sequence was exposed and targeted for the next increment (Hetrick, Krueger, and Moore 2005).

3.3.5 Impact of Minimally Invasive Transition Methodology

The minimally invasive transition methodology eliminates the highly disruptive and investment-prohibitive adoption barrier exhibited by early generation methods, thereby removing one of the long-standing impediments to the widespread use of software product line approaches. Techniques for reusing as much as possible and changing as little as possible when an organization transitions to product line practice imply that minimal rework is required and that developers and managers stay in a familiar environment. Techniques for incremental return on incremental investment imply that a chain reaction can be started with just a little up-front investment in time and effort, resulting in ongoing returns that dominate the ongoing investments. Minimally invasive transitions are possible with two orders-of-magnitude less upfront investment and nearly immediate return on investment.

3.4 Bounded Combinatorics

"As a practical limitation, the number of possible products in your
  product line should be less than the number of atoms in the
  universe."

The methodology of bounded combinatorics focuses on constraining, eliminating, or avoiding the combinatoric complexity in software product lines. The combinatoric complexity, presented by the multitude of product line variations within core assets and feature models, imposes limitations on the degree of benefits that can be gained and the overall scalability of a product line approach. Bounded combinatorics overcomes the limitations present in early generation product line methods, opening new frontiers in product line practice.

Some simple math illustrates the problem. In product lines with complex domains, companies have reported feature models with over 1000 feature variations (Steger 2004). Note, however, that the combinatorics of only 216 simple Boolean features is comparable to the estimated 10^{65} number of atoms in the entire universe. With only 33 Boolean features, the combinatorics is comparable to the human population of our planet. Clearly, the full combinatoric complexity of 1000 varying features is not necessary in any product line. Clearly, there is great benefit to methods that bound the astronomical combinatorics and bring them in line with the relatively small number of products needed from any product line.

The limitations imposed by combinatoric complexity in a product line are most prominent in the area of testing and quality assurance. Without highly constrained combinatorics, the testing and validation of all of the possible feature combinations is computationally and humanly intractable (SPLiT Workshop 2005).

A combination of new and standard software engineering techniques is applied in innovative ways to form the bounded combinatorics methodology. Abstraction, modularity, scoping, aspects, composition, and hierarchy are applied to feature modeling, product line architectures, and core assets.

3.4.1 Modularity, Encapsulation, and Aspects

The large, monolithic feature models characteristic of early generation product line approaches are like large global variables. Any feature can impact any core asset, and any core asset may be impacted by any feature. This has all of the software engineering comprehension drawbacks as global variables in conventional programming languages, so the bounded combinatorics methodology utilizes the same modularity and encapsulation techniques that are utilized to eliminate the use of global variables in programming languages.

Modularity is applied to partition the feature model into smaller models. The criterion for partitioning is to localize each feature within the smallest scope that it needs to have an influence. For example, some features may only impact a single core asset component and should be encapsulated in a feature model partition for that component. Some features may impact all of the core asset components within a single subsystem, and therefore these should be encapsulated in a feature model partition for that subsystem. Some features may be aspect-oriented and need to cut across multiple core assets, so these should be encapsulated into an aspect-oriented feature model partition and "imported" into the scope of the core asset components or subsystems that need them.

By partitioning the feature model, we limit the impact of each feature to the smallest scope that it needs to impact: subsystem, component, or aspect. Furthermore, this partitioning allows us to apply encapsulation to further hide much of the combinatoric complexity inside of a feature model partition. For example, in BigLever Software *Gears*, we added a new abstraction called a *feature profile* to express which feature combinations within a partition are valid for use in the configuration and composition of the core asset components, subsystems, and aspects (BigLever Software 2008).

For example, imagine a feature model for a core asset component that has five independent variant features, each with four possible values. The full combinatorics for this feature model says that there are 4^5, or 1024, different ways of instantiating the core asset component. However, we may only need 8 of these for our current product line. By declaring the 8 feature profiles for the feature model partition, we are specifying that only these 8 possible configurations are "exported" and valid for use. This means that the remaining 1016 possible feature combinations are not exposed to the outside and therefore do not need to be developed, tested, or validated for use. This encapsulation of feature combinations has reduced the combinatoric complexity by a factor of 128 for this one core asset.

This example is typical of real-world scenarios in product line practice. The geometric and exponential combinatorics present in feature model partitions can be drastically bounded to a linear list of "interesting" feature profiles.

3.4.2 Composition and Hierarchy

Another useful abstraction for bounding combinatorics in a software product line is the *composition*. A composition is a subsystem that is composed of core asset components and other compositions. In other words, a software product line can be represented as a tree of compositions and components, where the components are the leaves of the tree and the compositions are the internal nodes of the tree.

Figure 3.6 illustrates the composition hierarchy in BigLever Software *Gears*. Module 1 through Module 4 are the core asset components at the leaves of the hierarchy. Mixin 1 and Mixin 2 encapsulate the cross-cutting aspect-oriented concerns. Matrix 1 through Matrix 3 are the compositions that represent the subsystems in the software product line.

The role of the composition is twofold: (1) to encapsulate a feature model partition for the subsystem represented by the composition (as described in Section 3.4.1), and (2) to encapsulate a list of *composition profiles* that express the subset of valid combinations of the child components and nested compositions (BigLever Software 2008).

For example, imagine a subsystem composition with four children—two components and two nested compositions—where the two components each declare 8 valid feature profiles and the two nested compositions each declare 8 valid composition profiles. The full combinatorics for the composition of these children says that there are 8^4, or 4096, possible compositions. However, most of these compositions are uninteresting, and we may only need 16 for our current product line. By declaring 16 *composition profiles* for this composition, we are saying that we don't care about the other 4080 possible compositions, so we don't need to develop, test,

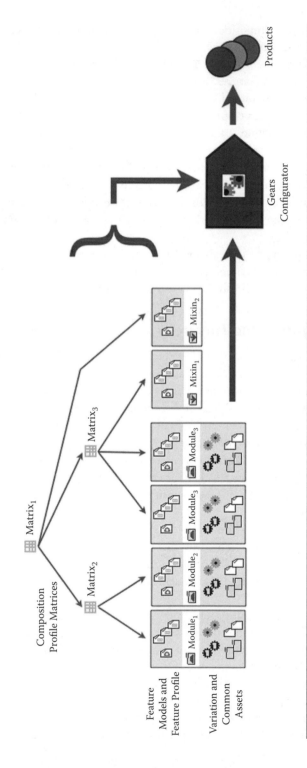

Figure 3.6   Modularity, encapsulation, aspects, composition, and hierarchy in BigLever Software *Gears*.

or validate those compositions. We have reduced the combinatorics by a factor of 256 at this level in the composition hierarchy.

The combined use of feature model partitioning, feature profiles, and composition profiles makes it possible to take the astronomical geometric and exponential feature combinatorics present in a monolith feature model and reduce it to a manageable linear number of configurations and compositions at each level in the composition hierarchy, including the root level that represents a complete product line.

The bounded combinatorics methodology adds two new abstraction layers over the early generation methods. In those early methods, the feature model served as an abstraction layer over the low-level variation points in the core assets. With bounded combinatorics, the feature profile adds an additional layer of abstraction over the feature model, describing valid configurations of core asset components. The composition profile adds a final layer of abstraction over the feature profiles to describe valid compositions of feature profiles and other composition profiles.

One final note of interest with compositions is that each composition can be treated as a smaller, independent product line, nested within the context of the larger product line. This view has many powerful implications. The first is that the composition hierarchy is really a nested product line hierarchy. The second is that each nested product line can be used and reused in multiple different product lines, extending the notion of reusing common components in *product populations* (van Ommering 2002). Third, decomposing a large product line into a collection of smaller product lines makes it easier to allocate smaller development teams to each of the smaller nested product lines. Fourth, the smaller nested product lines offer another opportunity for making incremental, minimally invasive transitions into product line practice.

3.4.3 Controlling the Product Line Scope

A common tendency when engineers are creating reusable software is to overgeneralize. It seems obvious that when you make a piece of software reusable, you should make it as generally reusable as possible. However, with overgenerality comes unnecessary cost, effort, and combinatoric complexity.

With software product line methods, it is important to pay special attention to this detrimental tendency, since the entire product line is built out of reusable core assets. Early generation software product line methods sometimes prescribed generalizing core assets to satisfy predicted products on a five-year horizon. However, Salion, Inc., and BigLever Software illustrated that it can be more effective to be more agile and to generalize the core assets and product line architecture on a much shorter horizon—in their case between three to six months (Buhrdorf, Churchett, and Krueger 2003).

The distinction between very long-range scoping and very short-range scoping has been termed *proactive* versus *reactive* product line scoping (Clements and

Krueger 2002). Proactive is akin to the waterfall methods in conventional software development, and reactive is akin to agile methods. This is really a spectrum rather than a Boolean choice in software product lines. The choice on this spectrum is driven by business cases, the product marketing group, and market conditions.

Mistakes on either end of the spectrum—either being too proactive or too reactive—can be very expensive. You can make architecture mistakes that are difficult to refactor if you are too shortsighted. You may invest in a lot of throwaway development effort if you are overconfident in your crystal ball and your long-term predictions fail. In general, you will want to be more proactive with analysis and architecture while being more reactive with the development of core assets.

Software mass customization and minimally invasive transition methods both shift the balance toward the reactive end of the spectrum. This lowers the overall combinatoric complexity of product line development.

3.4.4 Controlling Entropy

As with conventional software, product line assets can fall victim to *software entropy*, the gradual onset of disarray, degradation of structure, and loss of clarity that occurs in software as it is maintained and evolves over time. One of the most unanticipated and celebrated benefits of the software mass customization methodology is that it is not only possible to control entropy, but also straightforward to reverse it.

In early generation software product line methods, the multiple branches of product development with application engineering and the AE/DE dichotomy created a situation that was highly susceptible to entropy and divergence in the code base. In contrast, the singular development focus on the consolidated collection of core assets with software mass customization is ideally structured for controlling entropy. It is straightforward to monitor reuse ratios and catch degradations before they take hold. It is easy for architects and developers to identify and refactor emerging abstractions within and among the explicit variation points in the core assets.

Applying the refactoring methods of agile development to its core assets, Salion watched the total lines of source code in its core asset base shrink by 30%, even as the number of products and the number of features in its product line increased by 400%. This innovative work is described by Krueger and Churchett (2002).

3.4.5 Impact of Bounded Combinatorics Methodology

Combinatoric complexity in early generation software product line methods created hard limits on the scalability and testability of a product line. Most commercial product lines have feature model, architecture, and variation-point combinatorics that vastly exceed the number of atoms in the universe. Bounded combinatorics methods utilize a combination of abstractions and modularity—such as feature model partitions, feature profiles, hierarchical product line compositions, and composition profiles—to reduce these combinators by tens or even hundreds of orders of magnitude. This in turn extends the limits of what is possible in the scalability and testability of a product line by orders of magnitude.

3.5 Conclusions

The first generation of software product line methods extended software engineering efficiency and effectiveness for a portfolio of products to unprecedented levels. After pushing these methods to their limits and better understanding what those limits were, the next generation of software product line methodologies offer another big step forward. Three important new methodologies described in this chapter are software mass customization, minimally invasive transitions, and bounded combinatorics.

Software mass customization capitalizes on configurator technology to automate the configuration and composition of core assets into products. This methodology allows us to eliminate one of the biggest inefficiencies of the first generation approaches manual application engineering. The benefit of this methodology is that the cost of adding and maintaining new products to a portfolio reaches the commodity level. Product line portfolios can be scaled to much larger levels than previously possible. The entire product line can evolve with a comparable level of effort as evolving an individual product. Commercial experience using this methodology shows that order-of-magnitude improvements are possible in each of these areas.

The minimally invasive transition methodology eliminates one of the longstanding impediments to the widespread use of first generation software product line approaches: the adoption barrier. There are two primary parts to this method. The first is to reuse as much as possible and change as little as possible from the current approach in the organization making the transition. This means that rework is minimized and that things remain familiar to developers and managers. The second is to make incremental transitions in such a way that each incremental step offers larger incremental benefits. Incremental return on incremental investment means that a chain reaction starts with just a little investment of time and effort. The ongoing returns are continually larger than the ongoing investments, which eliminates the huge upfront adoption barrier of the early generation methods.

The bounded combinatorics methodology pushes the complexity barrier many orders of magnitude beyond what was possible in the first generation methods. Utilizing modularity and two additional abstraction layers on top of the feature model abstraction, the astronomical geometric and exponential combinatorics of early generation methods can be bounded to small and simple linear combinatorics.

In combination, these new methods offer companies tactical benefits that are large enough to open a new realm of strategic and competitive advantages over conventional development and first generation product line practice methods.

References

BigLever Software. 2008. BigLever Software Gears data sheet. http://www.biglever.com/extras/Gears_data_sheet.pdf.

Buhrdorf, R., D. Churchett, and C. Krueger. 2003. Salion's experience with a reactive software product line approach. In *Proceedings of the 5th international workshop on product family engineering*, ed. F. van der Linden, 317–322. Heidelberg: Springer-Verlag.

Clements, P., and C. Krueger. 2002. Being proactive pays off: Eliminating the adoption barrier. *IEEE Software, Special Issue of Software Product Lines* 19 (4): 28–31.

Clements, Paul, and Linda Northrop. 2001. *Software product lines: Practice and patterns*. Reading, MA: Addison-Wesley.

Hetrick, W., C. Krueger, and J. Moore. 2005. Incremental return on incremental investment: Engenio's transition to software product line practice. In *Proceedings of the 9th international software product line conference, experience track*. http://www.biglever.com/extras/Engenio_BigLever.pdf.

Krueger, C. 1992. Software reuse. *ACM Computing Surveys* 24 (2): 131–183.

Krueger, C. 2001. Easing the transition to software mass customization. In *Proceedings of the 4th international workshop on product family engineering*, ed. F. van der Linden, 282–293. Heidelberg: Springer-Verlag.

Krueger, C. 2002. Variation management for software product lines. In *Proceedings of the 2nd international conference on software product lines* (SPLC 2), ed. G. Chastek, 37–48. Heidelberg: Springer-Verlag.

Krueger, C., and D. Churchett. 2002. Eliciting abstractions from a software product line. In *Proceedings of the OOPSLA 2002 PLEES international workshop on product line engineering*, 43–47. http://www.plees.info/Plees02/plees02-dokumente/Proceedings-iese-056_02.pdf.

SPLiT Workshop. 2005. *Proceedings of the 2005 software product line testing workshop*. http://www.biglever.com/split2005/Presentations/SPLiT2005_Proceedings.pdf.

Steger, Mirjam, et al. 2004. Introducing PLA at Bosch Gasoline Systems. In *Proceedings of software product lines third international conference*, ed. R. Nord, 34–50. Heidelberg: Springer-Verlag.

van Ommering, Rob. 2002. Widening the scope of software product lines: From variation to composition. In *Software product lines 2nd international conference*, ed. G. Chastek, 328–347. Heidelberg: Springer-Verlag.

Chapter 4

Evaluating Product Family Development Using the Balanced Scorecard Approach

Jong Woo Kim
Georgia State University, Atlanta, GA

Kannan Mohan
Baruch College, New York, NY

Balasubramaniam Ramesh
Georgia State University, Atlanta, GA

Contents

4.1 Introduction

Organizations that focus on developing software products and services that target large market bases are beginning to realize the potential of family-based engineering approaches. Product-family engineering (PFE) approaches have been met with remarkable success in the manufacturing industry, with examples ranging from Sony to Black & Decker, Honda to Airbus, etc. Past research and practice have emphasized the importance of applying family-based engineering techniques to engineering software products as well (Meyer and Lehnerd 1997). Product-family engineering increases reuse levels to around 80% due to a planned approach to reuse rather than an opportunistic approach. Cummins Inc., an organization that develops electronic control units for automobiles, claims that it uses about 20 software builds that are used in about 1000 different engines (Clements and Northrop 2002). Time to market is also shortened remarkably. Cummins Inc. claims that it can bring a new product to the test bench in one week compared with the one year it used to take when using a single-system development approach.

These advantages come at the expense of initial investment and the time required to launch the first set of products. Organizations resorting to a product-family engineering approach spend a considerable amount of time in up-front planning of the product platform. In some organizations, this resulted in shutting down production for a few months. The need for considerable commitment and upfront investment highlights the importance of a careful evaluation of the factors that should be considered before resorting to a family-based approach (Table 4.1). Since the investments in product-family development may result in potential future payoffs that are not easily quantifiable in terms of financial results, applying only

Table 4.1 Factors That Dictate the Use of Family-Based Approach to Software Development

Factor	Explanation
Market diversity	Platform-based development is suitable for moderate market diversity (Krishnan and Gupta 2001)
Market conditions	Competition, demand, and supply-side uncertainties might demand quick derivation of products from platform(s) (Krishnan and Gupta 2001)
Product characteristics	Impact of product platform on the performance constraints on different product members (Simpson, Seepersad, and Mistree 2001)
Maintenance needs	Maintenance of common aspects across products might pose a problem (Mohan and Ramesh 2006)

traditional financial metrics might not be appropriate to justify these investments. In this research, we propose the use of the balanced scorecard (BSC) approach to justify investments in product-family engineering. Using this approach, we illustrate how stakeholders who are responsible for selecting an appropriate software development approach can justify the selection of a product-family engineering approach by aligning the objectives of PFE methodology with the strategic objectives of an organization.

4.2 Background

4.2.1 Product Family Engineering

A product family is defined as a group of related products that share common features, components, or subsystems and satisfy a variety of markets. In broader terms, a family is a set of items that have common aspects and predicted variabilities (Weiss and Lai 1999). A software product family is a set of software-intensive systems that share a common, managed set of features that satisfy the specific needs of a particular market segment or mission. A product family has predicted variations that are introduced by tailoring the core assets using variation mechanisms (Clements and Northrop 2002; Northrop 2002). Some of the common examples of product families include the diagramming tool, Visio, which has a graphics engine and shape-management system as the core assets, while different diagramming palettes addressing various market segments constitute variations, and Cummins Engine Inc.'s family of over 1000 electronically controlled engine types. Examples of physical product families include the following: Airbus A-318, A-319, A-320, and A-321 share a lot of production commonalities; 85% of Sony's Walkman units are produced from minor rearrangements of the existing features and cosmetic redesigns (Simpson 1998). In manufacturing industries, the product-family engineering approach is also commonly referred to as platform-based development, which involves development of a product platform from which various products are derived. The platform encompasses the most common functionalities across the products in the family.

Product-family engineering aims at the systematic development of a set of similar systems by understanding and controlling their common and distinguishing characteristics (Weiss and Lai 1999). It is significantly different from conventional systems-development approaches, which focus on developing systems in isolation of one another. Though there may be considerable reuse of components in the conventional approach, they focus primarily on ad hoc, opportunistic reuse of small pieces of code, whereas, in product-family development, the focus is on planned reuse. The core assets that can be used across multiple products are developed in a planned fashion. Such planned reuse of core assets across multiple products results in significant cost savings. For example, let us consider CelciusTech Systems AB, a Swedish naval defense contractor, which develops shipboard command-and-control systems for navies of different countries. CelciusTech successfully uses product-family engineering as the methodology to develop its shipboard control systems (Bronsword and Clements 1996) and reports realizing significant advantages from the use of product-family engineering vs. traditional development approaches. It claims that software accounts for only 20% of the total system costs when a family-based approach was used compared with 65% of total costs when not using a product-family approach. Cost, schedule, and performance predictability are some other advantages enjoyed by CelciusTech. It is well recognized that these advantages come at the expense of initial time and capital required to initiate the product-family approach at CelciusTech.

A common rule of thumb found in past literature is that a product-family approach will pay off only after the development of the product platform and an initial set of products in the family. Past literature also claims that there is a significant reduction in costs associated with managing the evolution of the products when a product-family approach is followed. However, such cost savings depend on many critical factors like number of products in the product family, commonality across these products, organizational costs involved in adopting a product family, and the nature of evolution of the family. While most of the literature on platform-based product development discusses the advantages of using product platforms, limited attention has been focused on the parameters that should be considered before choosing a platform-based approach (Krishnan and Gupta 2001). Several factors that dictate the choice of development approach have been discussed in the past in the context of physical product development. Table 4.1 summarizes the factors that are associated with the choice of a platform-based approach. It has been recognized that platform-based development might not be the best approach for every product development effort (Krishnan and Gupta 2001). However, there has been a paucity of research focusing on factors that impact the selection of a product-family engineering approach to develop software products.

While considering the use of product-family engineering for software products, certain aspects that are peculiar to software require additional attention. These include the following:

1. **Maintenance:** Software maintenance is significantly different from that of physical products, especially when considering a platform-based approach. Advantages in using a platform-based approach are even more significant for software products due to the fact that any change in the platform can be relatively easily propagated to all the family members. This can be largely attributed to the differences in distribution of changes to users and the differences in the version management approach that can be used during the development of software product families.

2. **Production process:** Low or near-zero marginal costs of software production amplify the cost savings of the platform-based approach. The same factors that dictate the selection of a platform-based approach for physical products may not apply to software development due to the reduced impact of design decisions on production ramp-up, when compared with physical products.

3. **Nature of variety:** Unlike in physical product families, variety in software product families is largely based on functional characteristics rather than nonfunctional ones. For example, while it is common to find two physical products that perform the same functions but at different levels of reliability or performance, most variations in software products are based on functional aspects. There could certainly be exceptions, for example, software products with different levels of scalability.

While product-family engineering has been widely and successfully used in the manufacturing industry, the above differences highlight some challenges in adopting this approach for software products. There has been little attention paid to understanding the drivers of a product-family approach and their impact on the outcomes. Recent research has advocated the linking of product development strategy to the strategic objectives of the organization (Slaughter et al. 2006). Therefore, we propose the use of balanced scorecards that have been used in the past as the instrumentation for measuring performance drivers and their outcomes for a strategy. Here, we demonstrate the use of balanced scorecards in understanding the outcomes of choosing a family-based approach to software development.

4.2.2 Balanced Scorecard

Balanced scorecard has been developed as a means to measure corporate performance based on the premise that the performance of all new strategic initiatives cannot be measured by traditional measures (Kaplan and Norton 1996a). Balanced scorecard paves the way to examine whether a firm's strategic objectives are translated into a set of performance measures. Kaplan and Norton (1992), the pioneers of the balanced scorecard, tout this as a management system and a comprehensive framework that can motivate breakthrough improvements in critical areas like product, process, customer, and market development (Kaplan and Norton 1993). The balanced scorecard is comprised of performance measures from four different perspectives: financial, customer, innovation and learning, and internal business. Balanced scorecards play a critical role especially when companies are attempting to execute improvement programs like process reengineering and total quality. Balanced scorecards provide the much-needed integrated set of performance measures to gauge the success of these programs.

The decision to adopt a product-family engineering approach is crucial because of the nature of upfront investments it demands. It often results in a significant improvement in time to market and the cost of producing additional products as part of the family. Prior research, examining the return on investment of a software product-family approach (Boeckle et al. 2004), emphasizes that a family-based approach can result in significant economic benefits. Typically, family-based approaches are used by organizations that are either considering the development of a set of products to address a particular market segment or those that already have a set of products in a particular market and are planning to consolidate the development of these products as a product family, exploiting the common aspects across these products. To organizations that are used to developing products in isolation, this entails a significant change in processes within the organization.

Balanced scorecards have been demonstrated as most successful when used to drive such processes of change (Kaplan and Norton 1993). Also, a product-family approach might not always result in an immediate and substantial reduction in costs when compared with a single-system development approach. But, over a long period of time, substantial costs savings might be obtained by reduction in sustainment costs (Cohen 2001). This indicates that myopic assessments of the value of a product-family approach might not reveal its actual benefits. A more holistic picture considering a balance of financial and other process-oriented metrics becomes necessary to establish the business case for a product-family approach. Here, we demonstrate the use of a balanced scorecard as an instrument to drive the process of product-family engineering and how it can be used to align strategic objectives with the development approach.

4.3 Balanced Scorecard Approach: Aligning Product Family Engineering Approach with Business Strategy

Today's organizations need metrics linked to their strategic objectives that will foster positive future results and accurately monitor past performance. BSC can help organizations select effective performance metrics that will drive organizational strategy. These metrics can be created by focusing on the four perspectives provided by the BSC approach. These four perspectives include (a) learning and growth, (b) internal business, (c) customer, and (d) financial perspective. Performance metrics developed under these four perspectives can help organizations identify what actions to take in order to achieve strategic objectives.

BSC is a method to communicate strategies to stakeholders in/outside of organizations. BSC enables managers to take a balanced approach in handling all related areas to achieve strategic objectives in concert rather than in isolation, as shown in Figure 4.1. BSC supports not only four areas of perspectives, but also encompasses the relationships among them. For this purpose, BSC encourages organizations to draw a set of cause-and-effect relationships diagram to visualize the relationships among them. This diagram allows managers to better coordinate outside stakeholders and communicate their roles in PFE.

4.3.1 Learning and Growth (Innovation) Perspective

This perspective focuses on the ways organizations improve their learning capabilities to achieve innovation and growth. Prior literature emphasizes learning and new products as essential for the long-term profitability and survivability of organizations (Kalakota and Robinson 2003). This has several implications for PFE. Learning and growth can be achieved through the analysis of existing products to identify commonality and variability across these products, resulting in a clearer understanding of the plausibility of a bottom-up product-family engineering approach as opposed to a top-down approach.

Commonality and variability management are the foundations upon which organizations can achieve the goal of product-family engineering. Variability management includes identifying, representing, incorporating, and using variations. It also involves managing the evolution of dependencies across variations. Commonality management involves identifying the common features across a set of products in a market segment. These two processes are considerably knowledge intensive. Effective management of knowledge across these process areas is essential for implementing an effective software product-family approach.

Knowledge sharing through active collaboration is a prerequisite for effective variability management, as variations could span multiple product variants managed by different application-engineering or product-derivation teams (Huang and

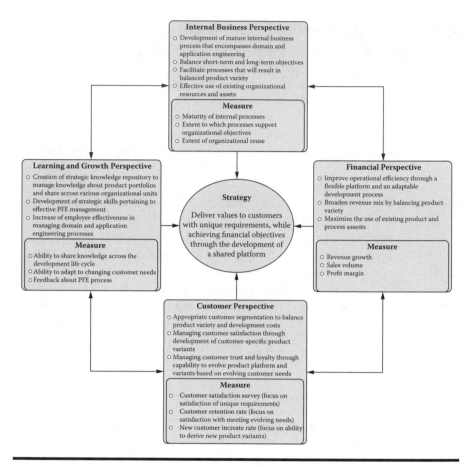

Figure 4.1 Balanced scorecard.

Hu 2004). In other words, variability management requires collaboration across different organizational units that focus on deriving product variants that satisfy different customer-specific requirements (Bosch et al. 2001). To enable effective knowledge sharing, organizations may need to implement standard and formal knowledge-sharing processes. Effective knowledge sharing is likely to result in increased organizational learning and growth in PFE organizations.

Also, organizational agility can be improved by facilitating learning and growth. The ability to quickly react to changing customer and market needs is crucial to the competitiveness of organizations. To sustain agility in PFE environments, organizations need to develop a flexible product platform from which product variants can be derived quickly.

The measures developed with this perspective can potentially serve as enablers of other perspectives in BSC (Niven 2002) . For instance, employee motivation that may result from the innovative skills and tools used for sustainable improvements for PFE are key elements for process improvements, customer satisfaction, and financial benefits.

4.3.2 Internal Business Perspective

This perspective focuses on the identification and improvement of the critical internal business processes in which the organization must excel. PFE entails the development and use of mature internal business processes that encompass domain and application engineering. It assumes that improved business processes provide increased customer value through the development of end products that are customized to meet their unique needs, thereby increasing financial returns. The internal business perspective should incorporate both short-term and long-term operational cycles. The short-term performance measurement system focuses on the processes of creating today's products and services to increase today's customers' satisfaction and to achieve short-term financial objectives. However, long-term financial success depends on the ability to keep creating new products meeting the emerging requirements of current and future clients. Organizations using PFE can balance these objectives by balancing product variety. It should be noted that PFE can result in significant financial benefits only with a flexible product platform, the development of which may require significant up-front investment. To balance their long-term and short-term objectives, organizations need to develop a balanced PFE approach so that they can deliver an initial set of products quickly and further develop the platform for increased product variety.

Managers need to recognize that their actions and their impact on outcome measures are interdependent. Therefore, care must be taken to plan and evaluate each action in relation to other possible actions that may be taken. For example, the goal of achieving a 3% cost reduction (a financial goal), may be achieved through a variety of internal processes or productivity improvements such as improved management of variation points or speeding up delivery cycles.

Process improvements at software PFE organizations can be categorized into two dimensions: engineering process improvements and business process improvements (Keyes 2005). The former refers to engineering process improvements internal to software development organization, and the latter are visible to end users and senior management. The capability maturity model (CMM) can be used for the improvements of engineering and business processes (Keyes 2005). Software quality metrics developed by BSC in accordance with CMM can help achieve strategic goals of PFE projects (Solano et al. 2003).

4.3.3 Customer Perspective

This perspective focuses on customer expectations from organizations using the PFE approach. In competitive environments, software development organizations need to recognize the importance of the customer-value proposition. To ensure value addition for customers, organizations should identify the customer and market segments in which they compete and address the needs that are unique to the market as well as to specific customers. Customer concerns can be categorized into four dimensions: time, quality, performance and service, and cost (Kaplan and Norton 1992). Customers in various market segments may have different preferences along these four dimensions. Organizations adopting a PFE approach should find an optimal balance among these dimensions that address customer needs in their particular market segment. Detailed metrics to cover various aspects of both internal and external customer perspectives should be developed. Fine-grained customer segmentation might lead to increased product variety and thereby will result in higher costs. Therefore, balancing the number of products that satisfy diverse requirements from a variety of customers with the cost of development is critical to PFE organizations.

To achieve a balance between product variety and development cost, organizations should use several measures in the customer-perspective dimension. These include customer satisfaction (with how uniquely the products address their needs), customer retention (with a focus on the ability to evolve product variants based on evolving customer needs), new customer acquisition (based on the ability to develop additional product variants from the same product platform satisfying new customers' unique needs), customer profitability (with a focus on the cost of extensions to the platform and the cost of product derivation from the platform), and market and account share in target segments (Kaplan and Norton 1996a). If these variables are to be measured effectively, the organization must establish appropriate communication mechanisms across departments, especially across marketing/sales and product development (Mair 2002). These internal departments are to be considered internal customers who are to be managed by an internal business perspective.

4.3.4 Financial Perspective

The previous three perspectives contribute to the improvement of the organization's financial bottom line. Typical financial goals can be categorized into three groups: rapid growth, sustain, and harvest (Kaplan and Norton 1996b), according to their business strategy.

Organizations with the financial goal of rapid growth may engage in incremental development of product families. While they have to make a significant investment in developing a flexible product platform and capabilities shared by product variants, they are also acutely aware of the need to quickly deliver the initial set of products. Building a product platform and the capability for product derivation require investment in areas such as process design, infrastructure, and customer relationship management. The main objective in this growth phase is to grow sales in new markets and attract new customers. Organizations need to carefully identify and evaluate the investments required for a product-family approach.

The initial cost of managing the complexity of product-family products might be higher than expected.

Organizations in the sustain stage focus on earning large returns on their investment in a product-family approach. With an established product platform, these organizations focus on the evolution of platform so that variations that were not foreseen during the development of the platform can be incorporated during this stage so that increased product variety can be facilitated. Organizations maintain or gradually increase their existing market share by continuously developing their ability to increase the range of product variants with high quality.

Organizations in the mature phase focus on harvesting the investments made in the two previous stages. They have significant expertise in managing the platform and variations in the product family. Without any additional significant investment on improving the platform, the focus becomes quick derivation of product variants by leveraging the product platform to satisfy a wide variety of customers. The main financial objective in this phase is to maximize dividends of prior investment on the PFE approach.

4.3.5 Cause-and-Effect Relationships across Four Perspectives

The identification of four perspectives and related measures is not sufficient to achieve full benefits from the balanced scorecard approach. The BSC is more than just a collection of critical indicators or key success factors organized into four perspectives. To get the full benefits of the BSC approach, organizations should identify and leverage cause-and-effect relationships among objectives and measures that are consistent and mutually reinforcing (Kaplan and Norton 1996b).

Cause-and-effect linkages outline the specific path PFE organizations will follow to achieve their strategy. Without these connections, developed measures may seem as an ad hoc collection of unrelated measures. PFE organizations can better understand the impact of BSC by examining each of its component parts and the links among them.

Visualization of the relationships shown in Figure 4.2 is crucial to identifying the various causal links. It shows how the different variables are interrelated with each other, encompassing the four different perspectives. This map ensures that all elements are consistent and comprehensive in executing strategies. It also helps organizations communicate across organizational boundaries. The cause-and-effect linkages can tell the story of the organization's strategy. Stories can engage and captivate employees and can be a major contributor to learning. The use of storytelling allows organizations to articulate the specific assumptions contained in the strategy map. This storytelling document makes the nature of all cause-and-effect linkages clear and understandable to anyone reviewing the map.

Figure 4.2 shows a prototypical story on how PFE can help an organization achieve its various goals. PFE results in significant reuse across members of the family and also requires establishment of mature processes. This results in a better

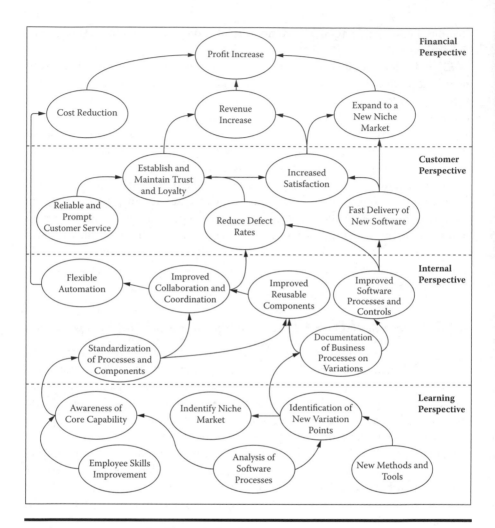

Figure 4.2 Cause-and-effect relationships across the four BSC perspectives.

product portfolio that is more attuned to customer needs, resulting in improved customer satisfaction. This will in turn attract new customers. All these factors finally contribute to better financial performance.

4.4 Discussion

Implementing BSC requires significant changes in the organization, especially requiring alignment of the operations with the organizational strategy. The key elements for strategy-focused organizations have been identified as executive leadership, strategy as a continual process, organizational alignment, and links between strategy and operational tasks (Mair 2002). In this section, we introduce and discuss a phase-based approach to implementing the BSC approach to help organizations become strategy focused. We also discuss the benefits of an integrated approach to product development that is supported by the BSC approach.

In this section, we adapt the integrated methodological framework for BSC implementation proposed by Papalexandris, Ioannou, and Prastacos (2004) and Papalexandris et al. (2005). This methodology consists of the six phases shown in Table 4.2.

4.4.1 Phase 1: Prepare the Project

A team embarking on a BSC effort should examine three critical issues: (a) Who do we want to be? (b) How will we get there, and what goals do we have to achieve? and (c) What do we have to measure? (van der Zee and de Jong 1999). Implementing a BSC may start with a careful examination of the status and possible future of the PFE organization. The important elements that require careful consideration in such an examination include strategy, sponsorship, need, support of key managers, scope, data, and resources. Vision statements can be created by answering the three questions above.

Top management support is crucial for success of the BSC approach in PFE, especially because of the significant up-front investment. The PFE approach requires a broad understanding and coordination across many sectors of organizations. Therefore, management with extensive experience and insight has to lead the BSC effort, which aims at organizing these efforts under overarching strategies. Managers who have the responsibility for just a single department do not have the authority and responsibility to orchestrate the complex processes required to manage the BSC effort.

4.4.2 Phase 2: Understand the Vision and the Strategy

The vision statements created in Phase 1 need to be clarified through workshops and interviews across multiple sectors of the organization. During this phase, visions and strategies should be well communicated, adjusted, and shared by employees of all levels. The resulting visions and strategies should receive an approval from the management. The project should be accomplished through an effort of a special group composed of executive sponsor, champion, and work-group members. An effective communication plan plays a key role in reducing resistance to change and encouraging participation and enthusiasm.

4.4.3 Phase 3: Identify the Strategic Priorities and Objectives

Objectives and goals to be achieved through PFE should be identified and prioritized according to BSC perspectives. Depending on the situation, organizations

Table 4.2 Implementing BSC

Phases	Tasks
1. Prepare the project	• Envisioning, scoping, and planning for the project: This involves product line scoping, identifying broadly the extent of coverage by the product family
	• Avoid resistance to change and to secure commitment: This involves top management commitment to the PFE approach and addressing challenges in implementing process changes from single-system development to PFE
	• Assemble a project team with sufficient knowledge of PFE and commitment
2. Understand the vision and the strategy	• Conduct workshops and interviews to clarify the vision and the strategy of PFE
	• Report outcomes to the management committee
3. Identify the strategic priorities and objectives	• Identify and prioritize the strategic objectives and goals of PFE
	• Design the strategic map entailing strategic objectives and the cause and effect
4. Select performance measures	• Gather, rank, and select performance measures based on the performance drivers and outcomes; these measures may be considerably different for PFE from those for single-system development
	• Establish ways of measurement
	• Establish a performance-measurement owner
5. Operationalize the project	• Fine-tune a goal/target and management process for each objective
	• Establish a budget
	• Determine a measurement frequency
6. Implement and roll out the project	• Roll out the project
	• Prepare a periodic reevaluation plan

can create a different set of BSC perspectives and a strategic map that identifies the causes and effects of the various elements of BSC.

Stories on how the elements at the strategic map lead to organizational strategies should be developed and shared within the PFE organization. They should be rich and interesting enough to captivate the employees. Compelling and interesting stories can enable employees to see the whole picture, find their roles, and commit themselves to BSC.

The links between strategy and operational tasks should be established. Employees should know how their work is linked to organizational strategies. This can be achieved through regular training and ensuring that employees understand the significance of the BSC.

4.4.4 Phase 4: Select Performance Measures

Performance measures for each BSC perspective should be developed. The measures should be quantifiable, linked to the organization's strategies, and easy to understand. Most BSC organizations use about 20–25 measures for high-level organizational scorecards. Before the measures are finalized, they should be reviewed and validated by both management and employees. Therefore, participation from all employees should be encouraged.

Linking rewards to performance becomes essential to motivate employees to commit themselves to the BSC approach. Organizations should carefully plan and design an incentive system for BSC, whether it be monetary or nonmonetary. Linking performance measures to compensation involves careful consideration of the appropriate BSC perspectives, performance targets, and the timing of the implementation. For example, initial scorecard measures may need to be adjusted in the first year of the BSC approach. It would be prudent to create links between scorecard measures and compensation.

4.4.5 Phase 5: Operationalize the Project

Organizations should embed BSC within their management systems. This requires *BSC cascading*, which refers to the process of fine-tuning BSC at each and every level of the PFE organizations. All employees can be linked to the goals of the BSC approach by BSC cascading. A reward and recognition system should be developed to foster performance improvements from all employees. Everyone in the organization should understand the operational and strategic importance of BSC objectives and measures. Employees also should know how their personal BSC affects the organizational BSC. A budget to implement the BSC should be established. For example, the profit generated from BSC can be allocated for rewards based on measurement scores.

PFE organizations should be willing to change organizational structures and policies to reflect strategies developed by the BSC approach. For example, PFE often results in a separation of activities across different organizational units that may serve different product derivations for various customers. If the strategy is to respond to changes in the market rapidly, PFE organizations may need to consider colocation and collaboration of the staff located in geographically distributed areas.

4.4.6 Phase 6: Implement and Roll Out the Project

Selecting an efficient and effective software solution to support BSC is crucial for successful BSC implementation in PFE organizations. Organizations should carefully evaluate issues on configuration, reporting and analysis tools, maintenance, security, and vendor support. BSC software should not be a burden; rather, it should be a facilitator of BSC.

PFE organizations should develop a plan to regularly evaluate strategies and measures. PFE organizations that aim to satisfy clients with diverse requirements should keep a close eye on the market and adjust the BSC to match the market environment. In PFE, the core assets developed need to be flexible enough to meet the constantly changing needs and the dynamics of the competitive market (Clements and Northrop 2002). PFE organizations have to constantly evaluate their strategies and the status of the market to ensure that their product portfolio follows the demands from their target market segment and that the portfolio has evolved sufficiently to address the changing needs of the market. When PFE organizations' strategies are misaligned with the market, they cannot reap the benefits of the BSC approach. Therefore, the strategies and metrics of BSC for PFE organizations should be regularly reevaluated and realigned. PFE organizations engaging in BSC implementation should also be careful not to add additional layers of bureaucracy, thus making the process of change slow (Riva and Del Rosso 2003).

In summary, implementing BSC in a PFE organization involves careful consideration of several factors and appropriate consideration of characteristics of development processes that are specific to PFE.

4.5 Conclusion

The primary contribution of this chapter is that it demonstrates how the balanced scorecard (BSC) approach can be used by IT managers as a technique for maximizing strategic value in organizations that are considering the use of a PFE approach. It highlights various benefits that can be achieved as well as the issues that need to be addressed while implementing a PFE approach to product development. The approach proposed here may be extended linking it to SWOT analysis (strengths, weaknesses, opportunities, and threats) and quality function deployment (QFD) as recommended by Lee and Sai On Ko (2000) to systematically identify various measures in these different perspectives. This proposed framework identifies several dimensions along with strategic negotiations among stakeholders that must be conducted. Such negotiations may be conducted with the use of negotiation support system tools.

References

Boeckle, Guenter, Paul Clements, John D. McGregor, Dirk Muthig, and Klaus Schmid. 2004. Calculating ROI for software product lines. *IEEE Software* 21 (3): 23–31.

Bosch, J., G. Florijn, D. Greefhorst, J. Kuusela, H. Obbink, and K. Pohl. 2001. Variability issues in software product lines. In *Proceedings of the fourth international workshop on product family engineering* (PFE-4), 13–21. Lecture Notes in Computer Science, vol. 2290. Berlin/Heidelberg: Springer.

Bronsword, Linda, and Paul Clements. 1996. A case study in successful product line development. Software Engineering Institute, Carnegie Mellon University, Pittsburgh.

Clements, Paul, and Linda Northrop. 2002. *Software product lines: Practices and patterns*. SEI Series in Software Engineering. Upper Saddle River, NJ: Addison-Wesley.

Cohen, S. 2001. *Case study: Building and communicating a business case for a DoD product line*. Software Engineering Institute, Carnegie Mellon University, Pittsburgh.

Huang, C. Derrick, and Qing Hu. 2004. Integrating Web services with competitive strategies: The balanced scorecard approach. *Communications of the Association for Information Systems* 13:57–80.

Kalakota, Ravi, and Marcia Robinson. 2003. *Services blueprint: Roadmap for execution*. New York: Addison-Wesley.

Kaplan, Robert, and David Norton. 1992. The balanced scorecard: Measures that drive performance. *Harvard Business Review* 70 (1): 71–79.

———. 1993. Putting the balanced scorecard to work. *Harvard Business Review* 71 (5): 134–140.

———. 1996a. Linking balanced scorecard to strategy. *California Management Review* 39 (1): 53–79.

———. 1996b. Using the balanced scorecard as a strategic management system. *Harvard Business Review* 74 (1): 75–85.

Keyes, J. 2005. *Implementing the IT balanced scorecard: Aligning IT with corporate strategy*. Boca Raton, FL: Auerbach Publications.

Krishnan, V., and Saurabh Gupta. 2001. Appropriateness and impact of platform-based product development. *Management Science* 47 (1): 52–68.

Lee, S., and Andrew Sai On Ko. 2000. Building balanced scorecard with SWOT analysis, and implementing Sun Tzu's "The Art of Business Management Strategies" on QFD methodology. *Managerial Auditing Journal* 15 (1/2): 68–76.

Mair, Steven. 2002. A balanced scorecard for a small software group. *IEEE Software* 19 (6): 21–27.

Meyer, M. H., and A. P. Lehnerd. 1997. *The power of product platforms: Building value and cost leadership*. New York: Free Press.

Mohan, K., and B. Ramesh. 2006. Change management patterns in software product lines. *Communications of the ACM* 49 (12): 68–72.

Niven, P. R. 2002. *Balanced scorecard step by step: Maximizing performance and maintaining results*. New York: Wiley.

Northrop, L. M. 2002. Sei's software product line tenets. *IEEE Software* 19 (4): 32–40.

Papalexandris, A., G. Ioannou, and G. P. Prastacos. 2004. Implementing the balanced scorecard in Greece: A software firm's experience. *Long Range Planning* 37 (4): 351–366.

Papalexandris, A., G. Ioannou, G. Prastacos, and K. Eric Soderquist. 2005. An integrated methodology for putting the balanced scorecard into action. *European Management Journal* 23 (2): 214–227.

Riva, C., and C. Del Rosso. 2003. Experiences with software product family evolution. In *Proceedings of the 6th international workshop on principles of software evolution*, 161. Washington, DC: IEEE Computer Society.

Simpson, T. W. 1998. A concept exploration method for product family design. PhD dissertation, Georgia Institute of Technology.

Simpson, T. W., C. C. Seepersad, and F. Mistree. 2001. Balancing commonality and performance within the concurrent design of multiple products in a product family. *Concurrent Engineering: Research and Applications (CERA)* 9 (3): 177–190.

Slaughter, S. A., L. Levine, B. Ramesh, J. Pries-Heje, and R. Baskerville. 2006. Aligning software processes with strategy. *MIS Quarterly* 30 (4): 891–918.

Solano, J., M. P. De Ovalles, T. Rojas, A. G. Padua, and L. M. Morales. 2003. Integration of systemic quality and the balanced scorecard. *Information Systems Management* 20 (1): 66–81.

van der Zee, J. T. M., and B. de Jong. 1999. Alignment is not enough: Integrating business and information technology management with the balanced business scorecard. *Journal of Management Information Systems* 16 (2): 137–156.

Weiss, D. M., and C. T. R. Lai. 1999. *Software product line engineering: A family-based software development process*. Reading, MA: Addison-Wesley.

Chapter 5

Product Management for Software Product Lines: An Overview

Andreas Helferich
University of Stuttgart, Germany

Klaus Schmid
University of Hildesheim, Germany

Georg Herzwurm
University of Stuttgart, Germany

Contents

5.1 Introduction

Software product management is an issue that has gained significant attention in industrial practice, but little research has addressed this area. This is especially the case for software product lines, where the use of a common product line infrastructure creates additional challenges. These challenges mainly result from the additional complexity involved in developing, maintaining, and evolving the common product line infrastructure and the products derived from that infrastructure. But, as we argued in a previous work (Helferich, Schmid, and Herzwurm 2006a), the different perspectives that marketing and software development have on product lines also lead to problems. The remainder of this chapter is structured as follows: In Section 5.2 we explain how the marketing perspective and the (software) engineering perspective on product lines relate to each other and how mismatches between these product lines can create problems. In Section 5.3 we give an overview of the literature on software product management, and use Herzwurm and Pietsch's (2008) list of tasks associated with software product management as a reference to describe the additional challenges for product management in a software product line context. In Section 5.4 we outline a toolset for product management for software product lines that combines existing methods. Since most of them were not developed with software product lines in mind, some alterations will be necessary. While we have not applied the full toolset in practice yet, we have applied parts of it and can also point out problems that are likely to occur when applying the full set.

5.2 Two Perspectives on Software Product Lines

5.2.1 The Marketing Perspective

The marketing perspective on a product line focuses on the usage of the products targeting the same or a similar market segment. Kotler and Keller define a product line as "a group of products that are closely related because they perform a similar function, are sold to the same customer groups, are marketed through the same outlets or channels, or fall within given price ranges. A product line may be composed of different brands or a single family brand or individual brand that has been line extended" (Kotler and Keller 2006, p. 381). Line extension refers to the extension of a product and its associated brand to a product line, i.e., a brand that was created for one product is used for a product line that is created around the "core" product. An example of this is the WISO product line of small information systems in the area of personal finance and/or finance for small companies: The name is based on a popular German TV program called WISO that provides financial advice; the programs have names like WISO SteuerOffice (WISO tax office) or WISO Sparbuch (WISO savings account) and are sold in supermarkets, etc. But even though they are marketed as one product line under the brand WISO, the products are developed individually, even by different companies, and only marketed as part of the same product line. We will also term the product line defined from a marketing perspective as the *marketed product line* (Helferich, Schmid, and Herzwurm 2006b).

5.2.2 The Engineering Perspective

From a software engineering point of view, a product line consists of a number of products that are engineered together, so as to share parts of their implementation. This perspective does not focus on addressing a market, but on generating advantages for software development. We will relate to the product line defined from this perspective also as the *engineered product line* (Helferich, Schmid, and Herzwurm 2006b). This is also expressed by the term *product line engineering* (Pohl, Böckle, and Van der Linden 2005). A core concept of product line engineering is taking advantage of commonalities among software systems to make their development more efficient.

5.2.3 Relationship between Both Perspectives

Obviously, these two perspectives are not identical; therefore, the engineered product line and the marketed product line need not be identical. This in itself is not a problem; still, in many cases, all products developed as part of the same engineered product line will be part of the same marketed product line and vice versa. But in some cases, it is preferable to deviate from this course of action. As an example, an off-the-shelf product developed by a third party might be sold as part of the marketed product line. So why would the company offering the product line purchase an off-the-shelf product instead of developing an additional variant of the engineered product line? Frequently this occurs if the definition of the product line does not conform to the technical attributes of these systems. This can happen if systems for radically different platforms are required, like Web-based and desktop applications.

In this case it is sometimes easier to customize an external product's functionality than to adapt the own system (and so the product line infrastructure) to the other operating system. Another important case is where the variant to be developed is significantly closer to the product line of another company, so that the development is much more economical for them. Generally this possibility is only used if the (sub-)market segment targeted by this product is not of central importance to the company. Another option is in the area of mergers and acquisitions, if the market segment covered by these third-party products is or will be of strategic importance. Figure 5.1 displays the possible relationships between both perspectives.

In some cases, the difference between the engineered and the marketed product line is not based on an explicit decision, but rather due to the fact that, in most companies, the marketed product line is defined by the marketing department well before development is started. This might lead to the situation where the reuse potential for a hypothetical product would be very large, but the product is not developed as part of the engineered product line, since it was originally not planned to be developed as such. In a previous study (Helferich, Schmid, and Herzwurm 2006b), we discussed these cases and their reasons in more detail.

Either way, a number of problems result from these differences, as seen in the following list (the list is not meant to be exhaustive; rather, it is just to illustrate the problem):

■ The core assets and the different members of the product line have potentially very complex mutual interdependencies in terms of resources (e.g., people or source code) needed.

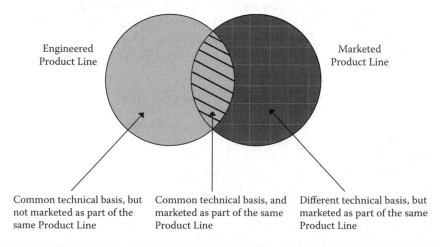

Figure 5.1 Relationship between marketed and engineered product line.
(Helferich, Schmid, Herzwurm, 2006c, p. 240. With permission.)

■ The different customer segments targeted with the different products in the product line might ask for features that, if implemented, would lead to the different products becoming too different from each other, i.e., reducing the scope of the product line infrastructure (core assets).

■ Release planning: release cycles of the core assets and the various members of the product line are not independent from each other, resulting in a number of problems. Irfan Ullah and Ruhe (2006) name the following:

1. Managing delays in the development of core assets due to conflicting requirements of products so that they do not affect product development
2. Evolving core assets with competing requirements of various products
3. Synchronizing different product cycles
4. Allocating resources across product teams
5. Improving quality, productivity, and time-to-market goals while maximizing stakeholders' satisfaction
6. Moving excess resources across product development teams to increase resource utilization
7. Quickly reacting to opportunities for new product development based on existing core assets

So, obviously the common infrastructure, on which all members of the product line are based, results in a complex interaction between the marketing perspective and the engineering perspective on a software product line. If this interaction is adequately considered, this can strongly leverage product management; otherwise, it can become a threat to the success of the entire product line. We argue that product management is the function that needs to ensure that these considerations are not neglected. Therefore, we will explain our understanding of software product management and the additional challenges for product management for software product lines in the next section.

5.3 Software Product Management in the Literature

Literature on software product management is scarce, and where it exists, it often is geared toward practitioners (Dver 2003; Condon 2002). Some research papers exist, but they focus on a small subset of the topic (Irfan Ullah and Ruhe 2006), represent experiences from a single company (Ebert 2007), or try to put software product management in context but describe software product management and its tasks and responsibilities rather superficially (Weerd et al. 2006).

Herzwurm and Pietsch (2008) analyzed literature from both general product management and software product management, discussed software product management with practitioners in numerous seminars, and compiled a comprehensive list of tasks (Table 5.1).

Table 5.1 Tasks Associated with Software Product Management

Area	Tasks
Development	Requirements management
	Test management
	Internal client for development
	Change management
	Configuration management
Project management	Program/multiproject management
	Management of projects
	Project execution
Marketing	Strategic marketing
	Product positioning
	Marketing mix
Organization	Process management , especially product management processes
	Organizational structure
	Knowledge management
Professional services	Service and support
Economic analyses	Cost/benefit analysis
	Effort estimation
	Cost accounting and pricing

Source: Translated and modified from Herzwurm and Pietsch 2008, p. 49. With permission.

Obviously, this extensive list of tasks should not be understood as a list of duties that every product manager must perform. To the contrary, many of these should be performed by the respective departments (marketing, sales, software development, etc.), but product management has to ensure that they are performed in a coordinated manner (Herzwurm and Pietsch 2008, 56). In many of these tasks, product management provides input or is responsible only for bringing people together.

The exact assignment of these tasks to the various functions (product management, marketing, development) depends on a company's business model and other characteristics such as company size, the software domain, etc. (Herzwurm and

Pietsch 2008, 48). The resulting division of labor is not arbitrary; rather, four types of product managers can be identified, each with a coherent set of functions and a specific focus (Herzwurm and Pietsch 2008, 60). Figure 5.2 shows the pyramid of product management functions (with each layer building upon the lower layers, but also providing direction to the fulfillment of the lower layers) and the four different types of product managers.

The product manager of type 1 is focused on requirements management, but also fulfills a few critical functions in the area of product positioning. Building on this, the product manager of type 2 actually focuses on the product as a whole. Therefore, he or she is concerned not only with requirements management, but also with product positioning and, to a limited degree, with product definition. Product definition is the core responsibility of product manager type 3: while this type can usually delegate supporting activities to product managers of type 1 or 2, he or she actually plans and controls the product definition and positioning processes. While this type is involved in economic analyses, these are the main focus of product manager type 4. Product calculation, revenue estimations, and pricing are the main responsibility of product manager type 4. Additionally, he or she is responsible for ensuring that corporate goals and strategies are reflected in the product strategy, e.g., in the product portfolio as a whole and the definition of single product lines and products. As mentioned before, the division of labor between product

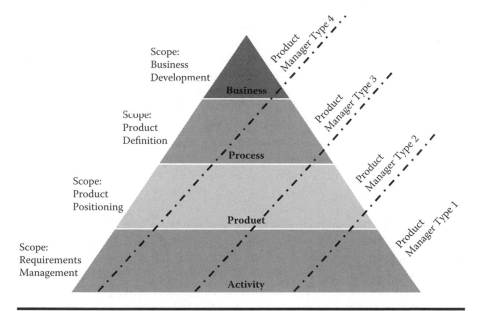

Figure 5.2 The product management pyramid and the different types of product managers. (Translated from Herzwurm and Pietsch 2008, p. 60. With permission.)

management and other functions depends on the company and its environment; therefore, in some companies, it is necessary to have a product manager type 4, while in others this would not necessarily be beneficial.

In the following discussion we introduce a detailed list of the tasks and responsibilities as a basis for outlining the specific challenges associated with product management for software product lines (cf. Table 5.1).

The *development* area contains tasks related to the actual development of software products: requirements management, test management, change management, configuration management, and finally the task of being an internal client for development. While the latter is somewhat special, the former four tasks are well-established support processes in software engineering. However, in the development of a software product line, the complexity resulting from dealing with a number of products instead of a single product and the use of the two-life-cycle model (domain engineering and application engineering) makes these tasks even more difficult. In change management, for example, every change request must be analyzed with respect to its effects on all products sharing the same product line infrastructure (engineering perspective). Additionally, change requests must be evaluated with respect to their impact on the brand (marketing perspective). For example, adding certain features to a product targeting lower market segments might cannibalize sales of products targeting the upper market segments. Since a product line architecture provides for easy changes in some parts (envisioned variability) but difficult changes in other parts (where variability was considered out of scope), some change requests will have to be denied, as they would require very costly changes to the architecture while offering only limited advantage to the customers (or significant advantage only to a small subset of the customers). In its mild form, being the internal client for the development is one of the core tasks of every product manager, since it is his or her responsibility to make the needs and wishes of the customers heard within the company. In its extreme, where the product manager is also the project sponsor and responsible for the budget, it is an indicator for the existence of a product manager type 4.

Program or multiproject management, management of projects, and project execution together form the *project management* area. Following Herzwurm and Pietsch (2008), we separate the management of projects from project execution, arguing that the tasks involved are quite different. The management (in its most literal sense) involves decision making (frequently in coordination with a steering committee), whereas project execution deals with the operative tasks such as preparing reports, updating project schedules, etc. The project schedule is to a large degree determined by the main software development process, for which various models such as the Rational Unified Process or Extreme Programming exist. Again, coordinating the various products belonging to the product line, from either the marketing or the engineering perspective, is an additional challenge compared with traditional software development. Coordinating the development of numerous assets—many of which are used in a number of products, possibly with different release dates, and maybe including off-the-shelf components or complete products that are developed externally—is definitely a complex task.

The *marketing* area consists of strategic marketing, product positioning, and the so-called marketing mix. Strategic marketing deals with the definition of the markets that a company wants to compete in and the products to be offered (Kotler and Keller 2006). Therefore, potential markets are analyzed with regard to market demographics, market needs and trends, as well as competitors and their products. Based on this analysis, a first definition of the products to be offered, the customer segments to be targeted by these products, and the characteristics of the products are developed (product or value positioning). Figure 5.3 shows the value-delivery process that is prevalent in modern industries where customers face an abundance of choices. As the figure shows, tactical marketing is closely related to strategic marketing.

Based on the decisions made in strategic marketing, during tactical marketing the so-called marketing mix is defined (Kotler and Keller 2006). The marketing mix, also known as "the four P's," is a combination of product, price, place [distribution], and promotion activities that are applied to a particular target market. Basically, various actions in each of the four areas ("P's") are combined (mixed, therefore the name *marketing mix*) to generate an optimal, positive, and desired response in the target market. Magrath (1986) complemented the four P's with personnel, process management, and physical evidence, arguing that these areas also need to be taken into account when marketing services.

Obviously, the marketing perspective on the product line is in the focus of all marketing considerations. But reciprocal effects between the marketing perspective and the engineering perspective must also be taken into account. For example, scoping can lead to the discovery of similarities among products, which in turn lead to products being profitable that were previously considered unprofitable (and therefore were not planned to be offered). Additionally, pricing must take into account the value assigned to the product by the customers, but also the prices of all related products, i.e., all products that are members of the same product line. Otherwise, side effects on products developed based on the same product line infrastructure—but marketed as part of a different product line—may endanger the profitability of these products. The reuse of artifacts such as requirements specifications and marketing brochures, as well as common pricing considerations across the product line, can lead to significant cost savings compared with single-system development.

In the *organization* area, the relevant tasks are process management, organizational structure, and knowledge management. While process management has long been in the focus of total quality management initiatives in general as well as software-specific initiatives such as Capability Maturity Model Integrated (CMMI) and SPICE, product management processes are not necessarily as well managed as those in the core software engineering areas. Closely related to process management is the organizational structure. We are mainly interested in the

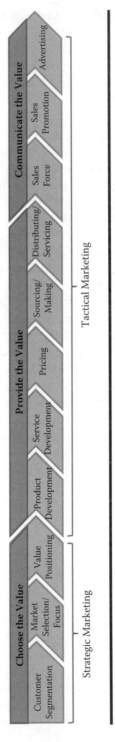

Figure 5.3 The value delivery process. (From Lanning and Michaels 1988. With permission.)

organizational positioning of the product management function. Similarly to the organization of software product line engineering in general (van der Linden, Schmid, and Rommes 2007, 59), product management for software product lines can be organized in several ways. We agree with Herzwurm and Pietsch (2008, 48) that this positioning has to be aligned with the corporate structure and strategy as well as the overall product portfolio of the company. In any case, clear responsibilities for product management are necessary, and the product management function has to make sure that the interdependencies between the two perspectives on a product line are taken into account. Moreover, product line engineering makes it necessary that not only the individual products are represented by product management functions, but also the product line as a whole.

The *professional services* area consists of the task service and support. In the last couple of years, information technology (IT) service management has received growing interest that led to the rise of ITIL (information technology infrastructure library) as the de facto standard and ISO 20000 as the international standard (ITIL 2007). The significance of service and support for software product management lies in the enormous potential that feedback about common problems and wishes voiced by users can have for the development of new products or new releases of existing products (as exemplified by the ITIL problem management process). For software product lines, the complexity created by a number of products based on a common product line infrastructure or marketed as part of the same product line—and with all these products possibly existing in several release levels—makes this task more challenging. Also included in the ITIL definition of service and support (ITIL 2007), but frequently organized differently, are trainings and consulting services such as customization. Organizing trainings and compiling training material is also more complex in a product line setting. Participants in these trainings either need to be separated (separate trainings for each product) or participants need to learn about commonalities and varieties between the different members of the product line. Consulting services, e.g., customizing the members of product lines, require educating the customers about envisioned variability and sometimes denying customization requests (as already discussed under the task of change management).

The *economic analyses* area contains the tasks of cost/benefit analysis, effort estimation, and cost accounting and pricing. These are described in detail in Section 5.4.5.

Because product management for software product lines is not entirely new and different—even though it is more complex and facing additional challenges compared with "traditional" software product management—building upon and combining existing methods seems appropriate. This also enables one to take advantage of the experience gained using the existing methods. Therefore, in the next section, we will outline which existing methods can be used and how they relate to each other.

5.4 A Toolbox for Product Management for Software Product Lines

The methods and tools used to perform the tasks explained in the previous section are as diverse as the tasks themselves. Many of them have been used for years; however, most of them target only one of the tasks. But combined, they provide a good toolbox for product management for software product lines. Irrespective of the methods and tools used, the "secret" of successful product management for software product lines lies primarily in the effective coordination of the parties involved. Insofar, we agree with Ebert (2007, 859), who refers to product management for single systems: "Therefore we underline that these three roles of product manager, marketing manager and (technical or contract) project manager must build a multifunctional core team fully accountable for the success of a product."

Most companies already have a strategic planning process in place, and this will in many cases already be linked with the strategic and tactical marketing process. Companies that offer software product lines should also have a scoping process in place. However, the close interaction between scoping and marketing and, in a number of cases, the use of value management methods is, to our knowledge, frequently still lacking in practice. While we decided to use specific methods as building blocks within this model, we don't argue that every company should use exactly these methods. To the contrary, where a company has equivalent processes in place that fit the company's needs, these should be kept in place. We chose these methods because we consider them suitable for most companies offering software product lines and because they complement each other pretty well, thus providing good coverage of the product management tasks.

Figure 5.4 shows the software product management pyramid and the position of the methods in the pyramid. The main order in which these methods are used (and also the flow of information as well as the level of detail) is top-down, i.e., from the strategic planning methods such as scenario analysis, real options, or Porter's five forces analysis (Porter 1979) all the way to technical scoping (and later on to modeling, architecting, and implementation methods). Yet, the interdependencies between marketing and engineering perspectives result in the need to backtrack every now and then in order to reevaluate the decisions made before in the light of the information gained in subsequent steps. As each level in the pyramid represents a variety of tasks, more than one method per level is usually needed. Additionally, a number of methods cannot be allocated to one level only, but rather help fulfilling tasks belonging to more than one layer.

The methods, which will be explained in more detail in the remainder of this section, are connected as follows:

- Market-oriented strategic planning methods such as Porter's five forces, real options, and qualitative scenarios can be used to guide the definition of the product line strategy.

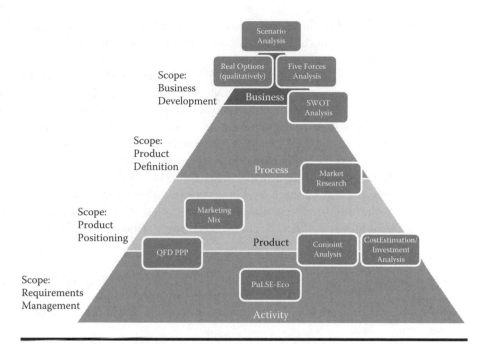

Figure 5.4 The methods and their position in the software product management pyramid. (Translated and extended from Herzwurm and Pietsch 2008, p. 60. With permission.)

- Strategic marketing methods such as SWOT (strengths, weaknesses, opportunities, threats) analysis and market research help to define the markets to compete in, the customer segments that are to be addressed, and the products to be developed in order to address these customer segments.
- The application of the marketing mix supports the company in delivering value to the customers.
- Scoping methods are at the heart of product management for software product lines:
  - QFD-PPP (quality function deployment–product portfolio planning) can be used to derive a first definition of the products to be offered as well as commonalities and variabilities on a conceptual level, i.e., in terms of features and quality characteristics as seen from a marketing perspective.
  - PuLSE™ (Product Line Software Engineering) can be used to define the scope of the product line and the products in more detail. PuLSE-Eco focuses on technical reuse decisions and reflects the engineering perspective, specifically taking risks (primarily development risks, but also marketing risks) into consideration.

- To ensure the profitability of the product line as a whole and of each member of the product line, both the cost side and the revenue side need to be taken into account.
- Cost estimation and investment analysis: SIMPLE (structured intuitive model for product line economics) (Clements, McGregor, Cohen, 2005) can be used as a framework for calculating the costs involved in developing assets and may be extended with real options and/or Monte Carlo simulation, potentially quantifying the narrative scenarios developed during strategic planning. Additionally, PuLSE-Eco contains an investment analysis component.
  - Conjoint analysis can provide input for QFD-PPP and PuLSE-Eco (namely the size of the customer segments and the expected costs) to make the trade-offs regarding the number of products to be offered, make-or-buy of products or components, and potentially even branding decisions.

Once these methods are applied, the product line development process continues, starting with domain analysis. To explain the process in more detail, we will discuss the methods next and highlight the most important interdependencies among them.

5.4.1 Strategic Planning and Strategic Marketing Methods

Several aspects crucial to product management are not part of the product management process itself, but must be decided externally. Decisions about the general strategy and the business model of the company must be made, and the markets that the company wants to compete in must be selected. Additionally, decisions about customer segments and value positioning must be made. Numerous methods have been developed to support making these decisions in the literature on strategic planning and marketing, some of which will be briefly presented in the remainder of this section. Explaining them all in detail is beyond the scope of this chapter; therefore, a number of references are given so that the interested reader can read up on the methods.

The market-based view on strategic management argues that a company must select "the right market," which will then allow the company to achieve long-term profitability. Porter's five competitive forces (threat of entry of new competitors, bargaining power of customers, the threat of substitute products, the bargaining power of suppliers, and the intensity of competitive rivalry) (Porter 1979), real option theory (Copeland and Antikarov 2001), or scenario analysis can be used to analyze a chosen market and—building upon this—define the product line strategy.

Concerning real options, we recommend real options as a means to structure thinking and aid creativity in developing scenarios by trying to find examples for the different kinds of real options. We consider actually calculating the value of real options (for example with the Black-Scholes-model [Black and Scholes 1973]) as problematic, as the calculation is quite volatile with respect to variations in the input parameters, since neither product line revenue nor product line costs can be estimated very accurately. Using real options to structure thinking, one can use the kinds of real options identified by Amram and Kulatilaka (1999): timing options, growth options, staging options, exit options, flexibility options, operating options, and learning options, stressing that, in reality, an option seldom occurs in isolation, but rather as part of a complex bundle. For example, developing a product line and the underlying product line infrastructure creates an option to introduce additional products quite easily. This option can at the same time be a timing option (the decision to offer a specific product can be delayed until later, giving the company time to evaluate the market further), a growth option (developing the product line infrastructure enables the company to offer a large number of additional products at lower costs in case the first products are received positively by the market), a staging option (if the product line infrastructure is developed iteratively, developing the later iterations/stages can be cancelled if market demand is lower than expected), and a learning option (if the experience of the company in the scope of the product line is limited, it can learn from the development of the first iteration of the infrastructure and the products built upon this iteration).

Scenario analysis is another useful method in cases where one has a number of strategic options and where a large number of (often external) factors that are hard to predict influence the decisions. The literature on strategic management recommends the use of concrete, narrative, and internally consistent scenarios over scenarios with assigned probabilities (Schoemaker 1995). In agreement with the literature, e.g., Schoemaker (1993), we think that both kinds of scenarios can complement each other: Since many of the factors influencing the external market potential are very hard to evaluate quantitatively, especially at this stage, and since there is a multitude of variables that can be varied, it seems appropriate to use qualitative scenarios in the beginning. Based on these scenarios, Monte Carlo simulations and sensitivity analysis can be used to analyze the scenarios in detail by varying selected variables.

5.4.2 *Tactical Marketing Methods*

Once the company has chosen the market to compete in and the customer segments to be served and has also decided upon the rough characteristics that the product line and its members shall have, tactical marketing is required to provide more detail: Decisions about product features, promotion, merchandising, pricing, sales channels, and service must be made. These are usually subsumed under the term *marketing mix* (Kotler and Keller 2006). Of the four P's (product, price, place, and promotion), the existing literature on software product lines deals mainly with the product, but even there, elements of warranties, guarantees, and support are not covered. Pricing, distribution, and promotion are also hardly covered. The exclusion of these aspects does by no means indicate that these aspects are not important; to the contrary, they are important, but also quite complex, as we will briefly illustrate. Unfortunately, the literature on software marketing in general is also quite scarce, and where it exists, it frequently applies methods from consumer goods marketing, while marketing for many software products (e.g., enterprise resource planning [ERP] systems or control systems for airplanes, power plants, etc.) has much more in common with industrial goods marketing. While it is not feasible to go into detail here, we will briefly highlight the challenges in pricing, distribution, and promotion for software product lines.

In addition to the large number of decisions involved in pricing regular products (e.g., volume discounts, promotional prices, skimming vs. penetration prices [Kotler and Keller 2006]), pricing for software products adds the problem that the costs of a standard software product are nearly independent of the number of copies sold (Cusumano 2004; Messerschmitt and Szyperski 2003), but rather depend mainly on the cost of developing (and later maintaining) a software product (or a major release thereof), rendering cost-plus pricing not applicable. For a software product line, an additional problem lies in distributing the costs of the common product line infrastructure to the products that are part of the product line: Should this cost be allocated on a by-use basis (e.g., X dollars for each common asset used), proportional to the number of licenses that the company plans to sell, or distributed evenly over the number of products? One approach to answering these questions is to base the price on the value that the software offers to the customer. The value can be measured using conjoint analysis, which will be presented in Section 5.4.5.

Distribution of software products depends on the software product itself: Embedded software is distributed in combination with the physical product (with the potential of distributing updates over the Internet). Computer games, operating systems, and other kinds of products that are relatively simple to understand are either distributed via stores or over the Internet. ERP (enterprise resource planning) systems and similar types of complex information systems are distributed using direct sales and consultants (i.e., bundling the software with additional services such as customizing). For these software products, the company producing the software often uses a partnership model. For example, SAP, one of the market-leaders in ERP systems, owes its success to a large degree to the great number of SAP consultants that are not SAP employees, but employees of IT consulting firms such as Accenture, Cap Gemini, or EDS. Using the same distribution channel for all products belonging to a product line can significantly lower distribution costs (especially the per-unit costs of setting up the channel).

Promotion is also scarcely dealt with in software product line literature, even though it has important consequences for product management in general as well as in a product line context. Promotion deals with the various methods of promoting a product, brand, or company and includes advertising, sales promotion, publicity, personal selling, and branding. As we explained in a previous work (Helferich,

Schmid, and Herzwurm 2006b), branding issues can lead to some products of a software product line (SPL) being sold under a different brand in order to increase total sales.

While these aspects must be decided upon before performing detailed scoping and making trade-offs regarding the exact number of the products to be offered as part of the product line (as well as the respective features), they should also be carefully reevaluated after completing the process. One result of the product management process might be that some customer segments that initially seemed unattractive might actually be very attractive due to unexpected technical similarities that make offering products for these segments easy and cost-effective.

5.4.3 Market-Oriented Scoping: Quality Function Deployment–Product Portfolio Planning (QFD-PPP)

Scoping deals with planning and bounding the scope of a product line. Therefore, three levels of scoping can be differentiated (Schmid 2003):

1. **Product portfolio scoping:** Deals with the definition of the products to be developed, i.e., definition of which and how many products shall be developed and the functionality each shall have.
2. **Domain scoping:** Has the task of bounding the domains (i.e., coherent clusters of functionality) relevant to the product line.
3. **Asset scoping:** Aims at identifying the particular (implementation) components that are to be developed for reuse.

Product portfolio scoping is mainly driven by marketing considerations (Schmid 2002) and can be implemented by QFD-PPP, while domain and asset scoping focus on technical aspects and can be implemented by PuLSE-Eco, which is described in the next section.

While PuLSE-Eco explicitly excludes product portfolio scoping (Schmid 2003), QFD-PPP (Helferich, Herzwurm, and Schockert 2005, 2006) tries to fill this gap. QFD-PPP (quality function deployment–product portfolio planning) is based on QFD, a well-known product development and quality management method that has been successfully applied in many industries all over the world (Akao 1990). Chan and Wu (2002) provide an excellent overview of QFD, its history, and its applications based on a database of 650 publications on QFD.

When used for software, QFD is primarily used for requirements engineering (Herzwurm, Schockert, and Pietsch 2003). Research on requirements engineering indicates that customers have big difficulties expressing their expectations before using the final product because software is immaterial in nature (Nuseibeh and Easterbrook 2000). This is especially true for innovative products where customers can't base their expectations on previous products. Thus, simple market surveys are not sufficient; rather, it is important to get a deep understanding of customer needs and cross-check with technological opportunities (Aasland, Blankenburg, and Reitan 2000). QFD is very well suited for this, since it relies heavily on a project team consisting of representatives of all departments (development, quality management, marketing, sales, help desk, etc.), customer representatives, and a moderator who is an expert in QFD (Herzwurm, Schockert, and Mellis 2000). As Herzwurm, Schockert, and Pietsch (2003) note, "QFD provides a systematic but more informal way of communication between customers and developers" compared with traditional ways of formalizing and specifying product requirements.

QFD-PPP extends QFD insofar as QFD is capable only of planning single products, while QFD-PPP is specifically designed to support companies planning to offer multiple products based on a common product line infrastructure (Helferich, Herzwurm, and Schockert 2005). At the heart of QFD (and QFD-PPP) is the use of matrices that are used in sequences to base all decisions on the actual customer requirements. For a physical product, this sequence can span product planning, component planning, process planning, and production planning, so that the importance of a small step in the production of a product can be traced to the customer requirements that are fulfilled by performing this step correctly (Hauser and Clausing 1988). For the development of a software product, traceability is an important issue in software development, but in many cases even more important is setting prioritized development goals based on the most important customer requirements (Herzwurm, Schockert, and Mellis 2000). This is due to the fact that the production process for software is basically a duplication process and that implementation is largely determined by the system design, especially the system architecture. Additionally, a distinction between a product function and its quality element must be made: A product function is a functional characteristic (often called a "feature"), while a quality element is a nonfunctional characteristic such as reliability or usability.

Building upon input from marketing—a first rough definition of the customer segments that are targeted and the products that are to be offered—customer representatives are invited to participate in the product definition process over the course of several meetings. These meetings are used to gather customer requirements, evaluate possible product functions, quantify quality elements, and prioritize the development effort. In order to prioritize the product functions, the customer requirements are weighed (e.g., using the analytic hierarchy process [Saaty 2001]) and put in relationship with (a) product functions (so-called software house of quality) and (b) quality elements.

Giving the developers the possibility of introducing possible product functions and having the customers evaluate these solutions with regard to their contribution to fulfilling customer requirements allows for the identification of so-called exciting factors in the Kano model (Kano et al. 1984), i.e., product functions that the customers themselves would not have come up with, but that have a very strong positive impact on customer satisfaction.

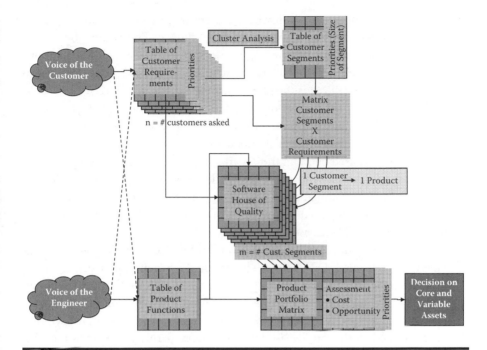

Figure 5.5 The QFD-PPP process. (From Helferich, Herzwurm, and Schockert 2005, p. 169. With permission.)

The last step—and the primary difference between QFD-PPP and other QFD approaches—consists of planning the candidate products (one for each customer segment) in more detail. The so-called product portfolio matrix is used to compare the products with each other, and based on an assessment of the costs and potential revenue involved in offering a product, the products are defined. QFD-PPP does not prescribe the use of a specific model to assess costs and revenues; instead, any model from the marketing and/or software economics literature can be used. In the section on value management (Section 5.4.5), we will describe some models that can be used here.

Figure 5.5 provides an overview of QFD-PPP. Once QFD-PPP is completed, a first description of the products to be offered, their features, the most important competing products (including their strengths and weaknesses), and the customer segments that are targeted with the products is available. In the case that some products already exist, an additional analysis of the strengths and weaknesses of the existing products (measured via customer satisfaction) is available.

5.4.4 Technical Product Line Scoping: PuLSE-Eco

PuLSE™ (product line software engineering) is a well-developed methodology developed at Fraunhofer IESE that consists of a number of modules. The goal of

PuLSE is "the conception and deployment of software product lines within a large variety of enterprise contexts" (Bayer et al. 1999). PuLSE-Eco is the module that deals with scoping, but excludes product portfolio scoping. Instead, product portfolio scoping is explicitly treated as input (Schmid 2003). Still, an activity called product line mapping (PLM) is the first of three components of PuLSE-Eco. PLM is a technical activity, not a decision-making activity (Schmid 2003). It aims at providing a standardized input for the further steps in decision making, due to the large range of different forms in which product line information is usually available in an organization. Based on input from marketing, an interview-based approach is followed to develop a first version of the so-called product map or product feature matrix (Schmid 2002; John et al. 2006). Additionally, PLM product release plans or genealogy charts provide a quick overview of current and future members of the product line and possible release dates.

As the next step, the second component of PuLSE-Eco, domain potential analysis (DPA), is performed. DPA aims at identifying the benefits and risks associated with the various domains forming the product line. More specifically, DPA allows decomposing and individually assessing the technical domains of a product line, thereby also supporting decisions on the incremental introduction of product lines (Schmid and John 2002). Similar to software process maturity assessments, it consists of the three phases: preparation, execution, and analysis. During preparation, the assessment is being set up, i.e., interviewees are selected, and appointments for the interviews are made. PLM can also be seen as a part of the preparations. The execution consists mainly of the interviews with the relevant experts, a primary analysis, and a discussion of the preliminary results that leads to additional feedback.

While the domains that are to be assessed are by their nature product line-specific, a fixed assessment framework exists nonetheless (Schmid and John 2002). Table 5.2 shows the nine evaluation dimensions that are either viability dimensions (focusing on the chances and risks associated with any attempt at introducing a product line approach) or benefit dimensions (focusing on the potential benefits associated with the introduction of a product line approach) (Schmid 2002). Every dimension consists of a number of attributes that again consist of a number of indicators.

Major results of the assessment are (Schmid and John 2002; John et al. 2006):

■ The product line is evaluated with respect to the applicability of the product line approach in this case.
■ The product line is broken down into technical domains (already done in PLM).
■ Each domain is rated along several dimensions describing its reuse capability.
■ Every domain is evaluated in detail.
■ Actions for mitigating or controlling risks are proposed.

Table 5.2 The Evaluation Dimensions

Viability Dimension	Benefit Dimensions
Maturity	Market potential: external
Stability	Market potential: internal
Resource constraints	Commonality and variability
Organizational constraints	Coupling and cohesion
	Existing assets

Source: Schmid 2002. With permission (© IEEE 2002).

■ Recommendations for focusing and planning the product line are generated (answering the question on which domains to focus while developing the product line).

This leads directly to the final component of PuLSE-Eco: reuse infrastructure scoping (RIS). This component aims at deciding which assets to develop for reuse and which to develop as system specific (Schmid 2002). To this end, RIS builds on the results of the previous components, namely the hierarchical list of domains and features (developed in PLM) and the domains selected for reuse (in DPA). Building upon these, an economic model is applied (DeBaud and Schmid 1999). As demonstrated in detail by Schmid (2003), an economic model should ideally characterize all of the economically relevant factors and their interrelations. Besides the costs of developing assets (system-specific or for reuse), the economic benefits also have to be included in the evaluation. The benefits include, but are not limited to:

■ Reduction of development effort/costs
  – Per product
  – Total (for all products)
■ Reduction of time to market
■ Reduction of maintenance costs
■ Improved flexibility of development
■ Quality improvement
■ Unification of systems (usability, total cost of ownership)
■ Reduction of certification costs
■ Improved adaptability of systems
■ Ability to deal with labor shortage
■ Improved management of internal knowledge
■ Reduction of expert load

Typically, one or up to three of the aforementioned benefits is the dominant motivation in an organization.

Additionally, the time value of money (due to inflation and risks, receiving 1 Euro today is better than receiving 1 Euro in 2 years; vice versa for costs) and risks involved in the process (development risks, market risks, or technological risks) as well as the so-called product line selection problem (Green and Krieger 1985) should be included. While product portfolio scoping requires dealing with the product line selection problem (Schmid 2003), PuLSE-Eco does not include product portfolio scoping. Therefore the economic models used for decision making do not deal with the product portfolio selection problem in detail. The economic models available in the software product line literature and the approaches toward solving the product line selection problem are covered in the following sections.

5.4.5 Economic Models for Cost Estimation and Investment Analysis

Companies offer products or services to make money, and one promise of software product lines is to make this easier (by reducing development effort, increasing software quality, and enabling companies to offer more products). To quantify the economic aspect of a software product line, costs and revenue must be taken into account. This can be done by calculating both costs and revenue and comparing them. This comparison should be done before development starts in order to determine which products will be profitable before they are developed. This is important so that the company can refrain from offering unprofitable products. Unfortunately, neither predicting software development costs nor predicting revenues is easy, but we will describe some methods that can be used to estimate both. Also, after developing and selling the product line and its members for a while, the actual costs and revenues can be compared. This enables the company to redirect its investments in an appropriate manner.

We will start with the methods focusing on the costs in this section, while the methods dealing with the (potential) revenues are discussed in the next section. On the cost side, a number of economic models for software reuse in general or software product line engineering exist, among them COCOMO II (Boehm 2000), COPLIMO (Boehm et al. 2004), or other models described in the literature (Böckle et al. 2004; Clements, McGregor, and Cohen 2005; Poulin 1997). Some of these are product line specific (Boehm et al. 2004; Böckle et al. 2004; Clements, McGregor, and Cohen 2005); others have the advantage of being well established with a large knowledge base on customization factors (Boehm 2000); some target a focused problem (Poulin 1997); and others provide more of a generic framework where other methods can be plugged in (Clements, McGregor, and Cohen 2005). Still, all basically follow the same idea: The combined cost of (a) developing the product line infrastructure and (b) developing a number of products based on this infrastructure is estimated and compared to the cost of developing the products independently. If the latter is higher than the former, developing the product line saves money and is therefore beneficial.

Unfortunately, these models do not take risks, the time value of money, or the value of options associated with developing a product line into account. Therefore, some authors have proposed integrating more advanced methods from the accounting and finance literature, e.g.:

> Monte Carlo simulation (Ganesan, Muthig, and Yoshimura 2006)
> NPV and scenario-thinking Wesselius (Wesselius 2006)
> Real options used quantitatively (Geppert and Roessler 2001)

As is true for our toolbox in general, integration of the different models and methods is still lacking and needs further research. Additionally, the vulnerability of some of the methods toward variations in the input parameters creates problems when applying them: If a 5% variation in an input parameter that can only be guessed (e.g., percentage of assets that can be reused among all products) completely changes the result of the calculation, acceptance of the figures calculated with these methods is in danger.

5.4.6 Heuristic Models for Product Line Selection and Benefit Estimation

Since revenue is based on the number of products sold and their respective prices, pricing must be taken into account when estimating product line profitability. There has been significant effort in marketing science concerning pricing in general, but also software pricing. Additionally, in a product line context, the number of products to be offered as part of a product line can be optimized with regard to the company's profits (seller's welfare) or alternatively with regard to the buyer's welfare. Determining the optimal number of products and their characteristics including price, taking into account cannibalization, timing of market introductions, and reactions of the competitors is one of the most complex problems known to marketing science. Since it can be easily demonstrated that these problems are NP-complete, the use of heuristic models is appropriate. Over the last 30 years, marketing science has developed a wealth of models based on either multidimensional scaling (MDS) or conjoint analysis (Green and Krieger 1985; Green and Srinivasan 1978), including those presented in the literature (Dobson and Kalish 1993; Li and Azarm 2002; Moorthy 1984; Kohli and Sukumar 1990). While MDS-based models compare complete products by determining the benefit assigned by (potential) customers, conjoint-analysis-based models can be used to determine the benefit assigned to components of a product or complete products. Conjoint-analysis-based models are also dominant in answering these questions for product lines (instead of single products). Therefore, we include only conjoint-analysis-based models in our set of recommended methods.

Simply speaking, conjoint analysis is used in market research to determine how (potential) customers value different product attributes that make up an individual product or service. Its focus is on determining buyers' preferences for product attribute levels (including price) and the benefits that the buyers expect to receive from the attributes (Green and Krieger 1991). To this end, a controlled set of potential products or services is shown to (potential) customers, and by analyzing how they make preferences between these products, the implicit valuation of the individual elements making up the product or service can be determined (Green and Krieger 1991). For example, by offering the (potential) customers pairs of two different cell phones with attributes such as price, screen size, battery (talk time and standby time), and so on, and varying the levels of the attributes (e.g., a phone with 2.5-inch TFT [thin-film transistor] screen, 4 hours of talk time for 200€ vs. a phone with 3-inch TFT screen, 3 hours of talk time for 250€), one can actually determine the value ascribed to a 2.5-inch TFT screen. The number of potential products increases exponentially with the number of attributes and their levels. Therefore, limiting the number of combinations to be included in the process is advantageous: Building upon the results of conjoint analysis, the application of QFD-PPP can vastly reduce the number of combinations that must be included, and at the same time conjoint analysis can help deciding whether to offer the same product to more than one of the customer segments identified with QFD-PPP.

Conjoint analysis is frequently used in conjunction with target costing. This combination allows the company to base the price of a product on the price that customers are willing to pay for the product. In the traditional cost-plus pricing method, materials, labor, and overhead costs are measured, and a desired profit is added to determine the selling price. Target costing, on the other hand, involves setting a target cost by subtracting the desired profit margin from a competitive market price (Cooper and Slagmulder 1999). The competitive market price for the whole product, but also for relevant components, can be determined using conjoint analysis, as described previously. The integration of target costing, conjoint analysis, and QFD has been successfully performed before (Gustafsson 1996).

5.5 Conclusion/Outlook

Product management for software product lines is a complex and not yet sufficiently researched issue. While we started increasing awareness for this problem before (Helferich, Schmid, and Herzwurm 2006a), the contribution of this chapter lies in describing product management for software product lines in more detail. Using Herzwurm and Pietsch's (2008) list of tasks as reference, we described which tasks must be taken into account and coordinated by product management for software product lines to be successful. Building upon this, we outlined a toolbox consisting of existing methods that can be used as a first step toward building an integrated method (or method set) for product management for software product lines.

Further research is necessary in a number of areas, including exact and reliable cost estimates, the application of conjoint analysis for software product lines, industrial application of QFD-PPP, and, last but not least, the application of the toolset in industrial practice.

References

Aasland, Knut, Detlef Blankenburg, and J. Reitan. 2000. Customer and market input for product program development. Paper presented at *Proceedings of 6th international symposium on QFD*, Novi Sad, Serbia.

Akao, Yoji. 1990. *Quality function deployment: Integrating customer requirements into product design*. Cambridge, MA: Productivity Press.

Amram, Martha, and Nalin Kulatilaka. 1999. Disciplined decisions: Aligning strategy with the financial markets. *Harvard Business Review* 77 (1): 91–104.

Bayer, Joachim, Oliver Flege, Peter Knauber, et al. 1999. PuLSE: A methodology to develop software product lines. In *Proceedings of the 1999 symposium on software reusability* (SSR '99), 122–131. New York: ACM Press.

Black, Fischer, and Myron Scholes. 1973. The pricing of options and corporate liabilities. *Journal of Political Economy* 81 (3): 637.

Boehm, Barry W. 2000. *Software cost estimation with COCOMO II*. Upper Saddle River, NJ: Prentice Hall PTR.

Boehm, Barry, A. Winsor Brown, Ray Madachy, and Ye Yang. 2004. A software product line life cycle cost estimation model. In *Proceedings of the 2004 international symposium on empirical software engineering*, 156–164. Washington, DC: IEEE Computer Society.

Böckle, Günther, Paul Clements, John D. McGregor, Dirk Muthig, and Klaus Schmid. 2004. Calculating ROI for software product lines. *IEEE Software* 21 (3): 23–31.

Chan, Lai-Kow, and Ming-Lu Wu. 2002. Quality function deployment: A literature review. *European Journal of Operational Research* 143:463–497.

Clements, Paul C., John D. McGregor, and Sholom G. Cohen. 2005. *The structured intuitive model for product line economics (SIMPLE)*. Technical report CMU/SEI-2005-TR-003. Software Engineering Institute, Carnegie Mellon University, Pittsburgh. http://www.sei.cmu.edu/publications/documents/05.reports/05tr003.html.

Condon, Dan. 2002. *Software product management*. Boston, MA: Aspatore.

Copeland, Tom, and Vladimir Antikarov. 2001. *Real options*. New York: Texere.

Cooper, R., and R. Slagmulder. 1999. Develop profitable new products with target costing. *Sloan Management Review* 40 (4): 22–33.

Cusumano, Michael A. 2004. *The business of software*. New York: Free Press.

DeBaud, J.-M., and K. Schmid. 1999. A systematic approach to derive the scope of software product lines. In *Proceedings of the international conference on software engineering* (ICSE'21), 34–43. Washington, DC: IEEE Computer Society.

Dobson, Gregory, and Shlomo Kalish. 1993. Heuristics for pricing and positioning a product line using conjoint and cost data. *Management Science* 39 (2): 160–175.

Dver, Alyssa S. 2003. *Software product management essentials*. Tampa, FL: Anclote Press.

Ebert, Christof. 2007. The impacts of software product management. *Journal of Systems and Software* 80 (6): 850–861.

Ganesan, D., D. Muthig, and K. Yoshimura. 2006. Predicting return-on-investment for product line generations. In *Proceedings of the 10th international software product line conference*, 13–22. Washington, DC: IEEE Computer Society.

Geppert, Birgit, and F. Roessler. 2001. Combining product line engineering with options thinking. Paper presented at international workshop on product line engineering: The early steps: Planning, modeling, and managing (PLEES '01), Erfurt, Germany.

Green, Paul E., and Abba M. Krieger. 1985. Models and heuristics for product line selection. *Marketing Science* 4 (1): 1–19.

Green, Paul E., and Abba M. Krieger. 1991. Segmenting markets with conjoint analysis. *Journal of Marketing* 55:20–31.

Green, Paul E., and V. Srinivasan. 1978. Conjoint analysis in consumer research: Issues and outlook. *Journal of Consumer Research* 5 (2): 103–123.

Gustafsson, A. 1996. Customer focused product development by conjoint analysis and QFD. PhD thesis, University of Linköping, Sweden.

Hauser, John R., and Don Clausing. 1988. The house of quality. *Harvard Business Review* 66 (3): 63–73.

Helferich, Andreas, Georg Herzwurm, and Sixten Schockert. 2005. QFD-PPP: Product line portfolio planning using quality function deployment. *Lecture Notes in Computer Science* 3714:162–173.

Helferich, Andreas, Klaus Schmid, and Georg Herzwurm. 2006a. Product management for software product lines: An unsolved problem? *Communications of the ACM* 49 (12): 66–67.

Helferich, Andreas, Klaus Schmid, and Georg Herzwurm. 2006b. Reconciling marketed and engineered software product lines. In *Proceedings of the 10th international software product line conference*, 23–27. Washington, DC: IEEE Computer Society.

Helferich, Andreas, Klaus Schmid and Georg Herzwurm. 2006c. Softwareproduktlinien für Anwendungssysteme: eine Analyse aus Techniksicht und Marktsicht. Proceedings of Multikonferenz Wirtschaftsinformatik 2006, Volume 2, Berlin, p. 237–248. *International mass customization meeting (IMCM'06) & international conference on economic, technical and organizational aspects of product configuration systems* (PETO'06), 217–232, Hamburg, Germany.

Herzwurm, Georg, and Wolfram Pietsch. 2008. *Management von IT-Produkten*. Heidelberg: dpunkt.

Herzwurm, Georg, Sixten Schockert, and Werner Mellis. 2000. *Joint requirements engineering: QFD for rapid customer focused software and Internet development*. Braunschweig, Germany: Vieweg.

Herzwurm, Georg, Sixten Schockert, and Wolfram Pietsch. 2003. QFD for customer-focused requirements engineering. In *Proceedings of the 11th IEEE international conference on requirements engineering*, 330–338. Washington, DC: IEEE Computer Society.

Irfan Ullah, Muhammad, and Guenther Ruhe. 2006. Toward comprehensive release planning for software product lines. In *Proceedings of the international workshop on software product management*, 51–56. Washington, DC: IEEE Computer Society.

ITIL. 2007. *The official introduction to the ITIL service lifecycle.* London: Office of Government Commerce.

John, I., J. Knodel, T. Lehner, and D. Muthig. 2006. A practical guide to product line scoping. In *Proceedings of the 10th international conference on software product line*, 3–12. Washington, DC: IEEE Computer Society.

Kano, Noriaki, N. Seraku, F. Tsuji, and S. Takahashi. 1984. Attractive quality and must-be quality. *Hinshitsu (Quality, The Journal of the Japanese Society for Quality Control)* 14 (2): 39–48.

Kohli, Rajeev, and R. Sukumar. 1990. Heuristics for product line design using conjoint analysis. *Management Science* 36 (12): 1464–1478.

Kotler, Philip, and Kevin Lane Keller. 2006. *Marketing management.* Upper Saddle River, NJ: Pearson/Prentice Hall.

Lanning, Michael J., and Edward G. Michaels. 1988. *Business is a value delivery system.* McKinsey staff paper no. 41 (June). McKinsey & Company, London.

Li, H., and Sh. Azarm. 2002. An approach for product line design selection under uncertainty and competition. *Journal of Mechanical Design* 124 (3): 385–392.

Magrath, A. J. 1986. When marketing services, 4 Ps are not enough. *Business Horizons* 29 (3): 44–50.

Messerschmitt, David G., and Clemens Szyperski. 2003. *Software ecosystem: Understanding an indispensable technology and industry.* Cambridge, MA: MIT Press.

Moorthy, K. Sridhar. 1984. Market segmentation, self-selection, and product line design. *Marketing Science* 3 (4): 288–307.

Nuseibeh, Bashar, and Steve Easterbrook. 2000. Requirements engineering: A roadmap. In *Proceedings of the conference on the future of software engineering*, 35–46. New York: ACM Press.

Pohl, Klaus, Günter Böckle, and Frank van der Linden. 2005. *Software product line engineering.* Berlin: Springer.

Porter, Michael E. 1979. How competitive forces shape strategy. *Harvard Business Review* 57 (2): 137–145.

Poulin, Jeffrey S. 1997. The economics of product line development. *Journal of Applied Software Technology* 3 (1): 20–34.

Saaty, Thomas L. 2001. *Decision making for leaders: The analytic hierarchy process for decisions in a complex world.* Pittsburgh: RWS Publishing.

Schmid, Klaus. 2002. A comprehensive product line scoping approach and its validation. In *Proceedings of the 22nd international conference on software engineering*, 593–603. New York: ACM Press.

Schmid, Klaus. 2003. *Planning software reuse: A disciplined scoping approach for software product lines.* Stuttgart: Fraunhofer-IRB-Verlag.

Schmid, Klaus, and Isabel John. 2002. Developing, validating and evolving an approach to product line benefit and risk assessment. In *Proceedings of the 28th Euromicro conference*, 272–283. Washington, DC: IEEE Computer Society.

Schoemaker, Paul J. H. 1993. Multiple scenario development: Its conceptual and behavioral foundation. *Strategic Management Journal* 14 (3): 193–213.

Schoemaker, Paul J. H. 1995. Scenario planning: A tool for strategic thinking. *Sloan Management Review* 36 (2): 25–40.

van der Linden, Frank, Klaus Schmid, and Eelco Rommes. 2007. *Software product lines in action: The best industrial practice in product line*. Berlin: Springer.

Weerd, Inge van de, Sjaak Brinkkemper, Richard Nieuwenhuis, Johan Versendaal, and Lex Bijlsma. 2006. Towards a reference framework for software product management. In *Proceedings of 14th IEEE international conference*, 319–322. Minneapolis/St. Paul: IEEE Computer Society.

Wesselius, Jacco. 2006. Strategic scenario-based valuation of product line roadmaps. In *Software product lines: Research issues in engineering and management*, ed. Timo Käkölä and Juan Carlos Duenas, 53–90. New York: Springer-Verlag.

METHODOLOGIES AND PROCESSES

Chapter 6

A Systems Product Line Approach

Magnus Eriksson

BAE Systems Hägglunds AB, Örnsköldsvik, Sweden
Umeå University, Sweden

Jürgen Börstler

Umeå University, Sweden

Kjell Borg

BAE Systems Hägglunds AB, Örnsköldsvik, Sweden

Contents

109

6.1 Introduction

Systems engineering is an approach to manage complexity and change and thereby reduce the risk associated with development or modification of complex systems, including hardware, software, and people (INCOSE 2006). It is an interdisciplinary approach involving both technical and nontechnical aspects. Systems engineering communicates a shared vision of a system being developed that is typically not captured by either hardware or software engineers. Traditionally, hardware engineers develop physical views of a (tangible) system, and software engineers develop functional views of (intangible) code. Systems engineering integrates perspectives and disciplines and "considers both the business and the technical needs of all customers with the goal of providing a quality product that meets the user needs" (INCOSE 2004b).

This chapter describes PLUSS+ (product line use case modeling for systems and software engineering), a use case–driven approach to systems product lines. PLUSS+ extends traditional systems engineering by incorporating ideas from software product line engineering. Although there are many similarities between systems engineering and software engineering, there are also important differences. For example, the most important output of software engineering is high-quality executable code, while in systems engineering, the key outputs are requirements and (systems) architecture documents as well as various management and valida- tion plans. A problem with traditional systems engineering approaches is their lack of support for achieving high levels of reuse between projects. PLUSS+ has been developed, refined, and evaluated during several years of application within the Swedish defense industry (Eriksson, Börstler, and Borg 2005, 2006, 2008; Eriksson et al. 2006).

The remainder of this chapter is structured as follows: Section 6.2 provides a brief overview of some of the main systems engineering activities related to the approach presented here. Section 6.3 introduces our systems product line approach PLUSS+, and Section 6.4 introduces the major modeling techniques used by the approach. Sections 6.5 and 6.6 present the two major engineering activities of the approach. Section 6.7 discusses lessons learned from industrial application of the approach.

6.2 Systems Engineering

Systems engineering focuses on stakeholder needs and the required functionality early in the development cycle to synthesize an overall system design that captures those requirements from a total life-cycle perspective (see Figure 6.1). Systems engi- neering is an iterative process that employs the following common-sense strategy (INCOSE 2004a):

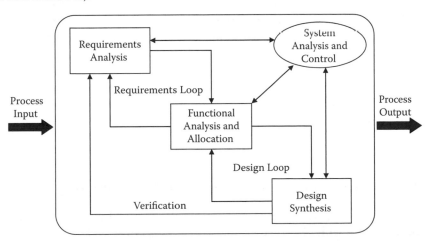

Figure 6.1   High-level overview of the systems engineering process. (From DoD 2001.)

■ Understand the problem before you try to solve it.
■ Do not jump to a design decision; examine alternative solutions.
■ Verify that the design solution is acceptable before proceeding to the next (sub)problem.

The purpose of the *requirements analysis* activity is transforming stakeholder requirements into a technical description of the system that is free of implementation bias (INCOSE 2006). This description should include both functional system requirements and constraints. The description typically takes the form of a natural-language system requirements specification, but any other type of description (e.g., drawings) promoting easy communication is also possible. A major difference between stakeholder requirements and system requirements is that the former are written in the "voice of the stakeholder," while the latter are typically expressed in terms of system functions and required performance or quality to support verification.

The purpose of the *functional analysis and allocation* activity is to clearly describe and refine the system functionality, divide functions into subfunctions, and allocate them appropriately to subsystems (INCOSE 2004a). This results in a better understanding of the requirements that might require further analysis. This iterative process is referred to as the *requirements loop*.

The purpose of the *design synthesis* activity is to develop a system physical architecture that satisfies the system requirements. The *design loop* provides feedback for revisiting the architecture to ensure that the design can realize functionality and performance as defined in the system requirements.

After specifying a system's functional and physical architecture and allocating system-level requirements to subsystems, the next step of the systems engineering process is commonly referred to as *requirements flowdown* (see Figure 6.2). The flowdown activity consists of deriving requirements specifications for each element of the system architecture based on the allocated system requirements (Dorfman and Thayer 1997). The concept of requirements flowdown is a key element in many systems engineering approaches, since it supports (a) traceability and (b) recursive application of the systems engineering process to subsystems.

6.3 Systems Product Line Engineering with PLUSS+

In this section we describe a process for systems product line engineering based on our earlier work on PLUSS (Eriksson, Börstler, and Borg 2005, 2006; Eriksson et al. 2005, 2006) and FAR (Functional Architectures by use case Realizations) (Eriksson, Börstler, and Borg 2008). Although PLUSS and FAR were developed to be used together, they have so far only been described independently of each other.

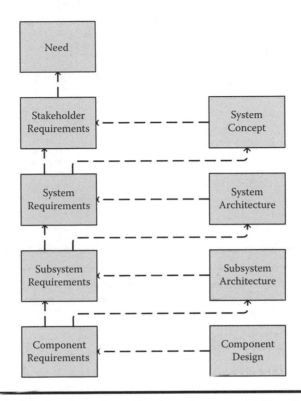

Figure 6.2 Flowdown of requirements through a system hierarchy. The arrows depict dependencies (traceability) induced by the flowdown activity.

PLUSS is an approach for variability management in whole families of products. Like FeatuRSEB (Griss, Favaro, and d'Alessandro 1998), PLUSS integrates feature modeling and use case modeling. In addition to that, it also supports (textual) parameterization of use cases. FAR is a use case–driven approach for allocating system requirements to the components (subsystems) of a system architecture. Based on these allocations, one can systematically derive requirements for each of the subsystems.

Our integrated approach, which we refer to as PLUSS+, is based on the traditional *domain engineering–application engineering* view of software product line development (Weiss and Lai 1999; van der Linden, Schmid, and Rommes 2007). The purpose of domain engineering is to develop a product line's reusable core assets to provide a production capability for products (Northrop 2002). The purpose of application engineering is to generate new systems utilizing the assets developed by domain engineering. To emphasize PLUSS+'s focus on system product lines, we refer to the application engineering activities as *systems engineering* (see Figure 6.3).

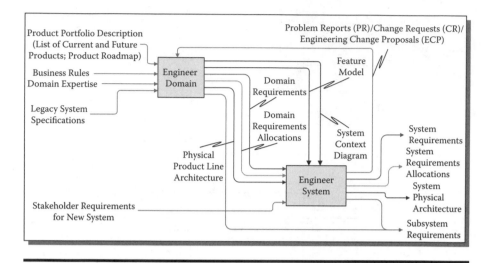

Figure 6.3 An IDEFØ diagram for PLUSS+ showing the relationship between domain engineering (*engineer domain*) and systems engineering (*engineer system*).

6.4 Underlying Models

PLUSS+ is a use case–driven approach that utilizes feature models for variability modeling. The main modeling techniques used are use cases (Adolph et al. 2003), use case realizations (Bittner and Spence 2003), change cases (Ecklund, Delcambre, and Freiling 1996), and feature models (Kang et al. 1990). Besides these modeling notations, various plain-text notations such as tables and natural-language requirements are also utilized. The following subsections will introduce the major PLUSS+ artifact types.

6.4.1 System Context Diagram

The purpose of the system-context diagram (SCD) is to clearly visualize the system of interest (ISO 2002) and its context (external interfaces and users). It defines the set of allowed entities for describing the black-box view of the system. This helps analysts maintain focus when specifying requirements and functionality. As shown in Figure 6.4, a PLUSS+ SCD contains less information than, for example, the "elaborated system context diagram" used in OOSEM (Object Oriented Systems Engineering Method) (Lykins, Friedenthal, and Meilich 2000) or an IDEFØ (integration definition for function modeling) context diagram (NIST 1993). By omitting details regarding provided services and input/output data, we improve the readability of the diagram.

We utilize the Unified Modeling Language (UML) use case actors (OMG 2007a) as a syntactic and semantic basis for the PLUSS+ SCD. An actor is some

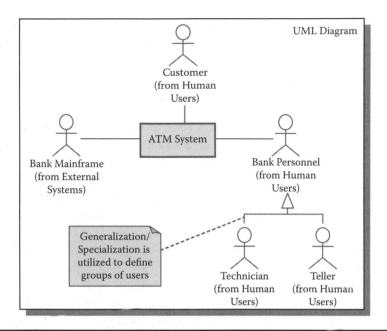

Figure 6.4   An example of a PLUSS+ system-context diagram.

type of entity, external to the system of interest, that can interact with the system by exchanging information (i.e., has an interface to the system of interest). An actor can either be a human user or an external system. Actors can have "association" relationships to use cases, specifying that they either initiate a use case or take part in the behavior defined by that use case. In the case of a PLUSS+ SCD, an association relationship to the system of interest means that the actor has an interface to the system.

Actors can also have specialization/generalization relationships to other actors. More-specialized actors inherit all association relationships from the more general actor (see technician/teller relationship to bank personnel in Figure 6.4), but they can also have association relationships to further use cases. In PLUSS+, this relation is utilized for creating groups of actors that can initiate common sets of use cases.

6.4.2 *Natural-Language Requirements*

Natural-language requirements, which are part of the *domain requirements*, the *system requirements*, and the *subsystem requirements* in Figure 6.3, can be ambiguous and therefore be misunderstood. However, in contrast to more formal descriptions, almost everyone can read natural language. For this reason, natural-language requirements specifications will continue to be used in development for the foreseeable future and are therefore an integral part of PLUSS+. For detailed guide-lines on how to develop high-quality natural-language requirement statements, we refer to Sommerville and Sawyer (1997).

6.4.3 Use Cases and Use Case Scenarios

Use cases, which are part of the *domain requirements* and the *system requirements* in Figure 6.3, provide a semiformal framework for modeling (mainly) functional requirements (Jacobsson, Griss, and Jonsson 1997). A use case can be described as something a user of a system wants to accomplish by interacting with the system. Our way of working with use cases has to a large extent been inspired by Adolph et al. (2003), in particular their *goal-oriented* approach to use case modeling. A use case must either be a complete goal of the primary actors of that use case or a sub-goal derived from another use case (see Figure 6.5). A primary actor can initiate the behavior defined by a use case; secondary actors "just" participate in the behavior (interaction with the system). In PLUSS+, the primary actors of a use case have directed associations to it (e.g., *customer* in Figure 6.5). Complete-goal use cases shall be derived from and be traceable to system requirements. Subgoal use cases typically define common behavior in several complete-goal use cases that can be factored out and "reused" (c.f. <<include>> relationship in Figure 6.5). Use cases are named as verb-phrase-goals and depicted in UML use case diagrams (OMG 2007a) as shown in Figure 6.5.

Each use case is further described by one or more scenarios. A use case scenario defines the steps of interaction between the system and its actors, with the purpose of achieving the goal stated in the use case name. Scenarios thereby distribute responsibility for performing behavior between the system and its actors. The name of a scenario should clearly describe what is unique about it. The only exception from this naming rule is the main success scenario, which is not named specifically

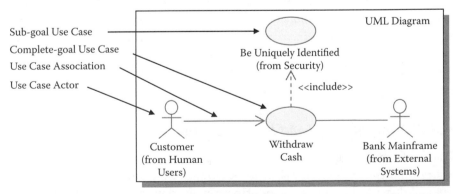

Figure 6.5   A use case decomposition example.

if the normal procedure is obvious from the scenario context or use case name. Like Adolph et al. (2003), we distinguish three types of scenarios:

- A *main success scenario*, which describes the "normal" way of achieving the goal stated in the use case name.
- *Alternative scenarios*, which describe alternative ways of achieving the goal stated in the use case name.
- *Exceptional scenarios*, which describe how different failures are detected and handled by the system.

We describe use case scenarios in a tabular natural-language notation (see Figure 6.6), since this is easier to understand when dealing with diverse sets of system stakeholders than, for example, UML/SysML interaction diagrams (OMG 2007a, 2007b). Our notation is based on the Rational Unified Process for Systems Engineering (RUP-SE) black-box flow of events (Rational 2003), which has three advantages compared with traditional textual descriptions:

Main Success Scenario *(for Use Case: Be Uniquely Identified)*

Step	Actor Action	Black-box System Response	Budgeted Req.
1	The use case begins when the **Customer** provides a Magnetic Stripe Card (MSC).	The **System** accepts the MSC and requests a PIN from the **Customer**.	Max response time 1 sec.
2	The **Customer** provides a PIN code.	The **System** accepts the PIN and requests that the **BankMainframe** validate the MSC and the PIN.	Max response time 0.5 sec.
3	The **BankMainframe** verifies that the MSC and PIN is valid.	The use case ends when the **System** presents available services to the **Customer**.	Max response time 0.5 sec.

Exceptional Scenario – Incorrect PIN, MSC captured
Preconditions
• The customer has provided an invalid PIN twice during the authentication session.

Step	Actor Action	Black-box System Response	Budgeted Req.
3	The **BankMainframe** notifies the **System** that the PIN is not valid.	The use case ends when the **System** capture the MSC and presents an error message to the **Customer**.	Max response time 0.5 sec.

Figure 6.6 Examples of use case scenarios; main success scenario (top) and exceptional scenario with preconditions (bottom).

1. The notation is slightly more formalized and therefore easier to manage the use of tools.
2. The notation has separate fields for actor actions and system responses to those actions. This simple feature forces analysts to always think about interfaces, which is a key success factor for maintaining focus in the modeling of complex systems.
3. The "black box budgeted requirements" column of the notation (rightmost in Figure 6.6) provides an intuitive way to allocate quality attributes to a use case scenario, which is lacking in traditional notations.

As illustrated in Figure 6.6, we describe alternative and exceptional scenarios as deltas to the main success scenario (so-called scenario fragments [Adolph et al. 2003]). The first step identifier of the fragment determines the position where the fragment fits into the main success scenario. A fragment can either return to the main success scenario or terminate.

Besides the actual tabular scenarios, our use case specifications also include introductory information such as context information regarding the use case goal and possible preconditions and postconditions as, for example, in the exceptional scenario in Figure 6.6.

6.4.4 Change Cases

Change cases, which are part of the *PR/CR/ECP* feedback-loop from *engineer system* to *engineer domain* in Figure 6.3, are basically use cases that specify anticipated changes to a system over its foreseeable lifetime (Ecklund, Delcambre, and Freiling 1996). Change cases are connected to regular use cases by specific "impact links." These links provide traceability to the use cases whose implementations are affected if the change case is realized. As illustrated by Figure 6.7, we model change cases as

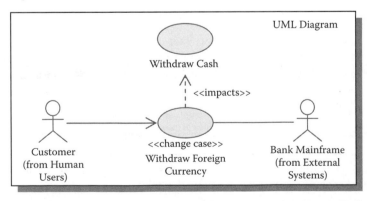

Figure 6.7   A change-case example.

use cases with the UML stereotype (OMG 2007a) <<change case>>, and we impact links as dependency relations with the stereotype <<impacts>>.

6.4.5 Use Case Realizations

Use case realizations, which are part of *domain requirements allocations* and *system requirements allocations* in Figure 6.3, describe how different design elements collaborate to perform the system tasks defined by a use case scenario. Use case realizations provide traceability between system requirements modeled as use cases and the elements of the physical system architecture.

We use a similar tabular natural-language description as for use case scenarios (see Figure 6.8) based on the RUP-SE white-box flow-of-events (Rational 2003). Each black-box step from a use case scenario is decomposed into a number of so called white-box steps, which are allocated to various subsystems of physical architecture of the system. During this process, each *black-box budgeted requirement* must also be decomposed into one or more *white-box budgeted requirements*. This usually involves trade-off analyses to evaluate different allocations, considering, for example, quality attributes such as availability, reliability, and cost.

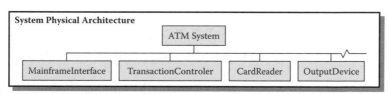

Use Case Realization *(for "Exceptional Scenario – Incorrect PIN, MSC captured")*

Step	Actor Action	Black-box System Response	Budgeted Req.	White-box Action	White-box Budgeted Req.
3	The ***Bank-Mainframe*** notifies the ***System*** that the PIN is not valid.	The use case ends when the ***System*** captures the MSC and presents an error message to the ***Customer***.	Max response time 0.5 sec.	The ***MainframeInterface*** accepts the result of the authentication attempt from the ***BankMainframe*** and notifies the ***TransactionController*** that the PIN is not valid	Max response time 0.1 sec.
				The ***TransactionController*** requests the MSC to be captured by the ***CardReader***.	Max response time 0.2 sec.
				The ***TransactionController*** requests an error message to be presented by the ***OutputDevice***.	Max response time 0.1 sec.
				The ***OutputDevice*** presents the error message to the ***Customer***.	Max response time 0.1 sec.

Figure 6.8 Example of a use case realization and its underlying *system physical architecture* (development of this architecture is beyond the scope of this chapter).

6.4.6 Feature Models

Feature models (Kang et al. 1990) are a widely used domain-analysis technique in software product line development. In feature models, system features are organized into trees of AND and OR nodes representing the commonalities and variations within a family of related systems. General features are located at the top of the tree, and more-refined features are located below. It is also possible to define feature composition rules (dependencies and incompatibilities between features) in feature models. In PLUSS+, we have slightly extended FODA (feature-oriented domain analysis) modeling (Kang et al. 1990). Among others, we introduced parametric features (see $PIN_SIZE in Figure 6.9), which are further discussed in Sections 6.5.2 and 6.5.3.

6.5 Engineer Domain

In this section, we provide a more detailed description of the PLUSS+ activity *engineer domain* from Figure 6.3. The basic idea of PLUSS+ is to manage variability in natural-language requirements, use cases, use case scenarios, and change cases by linking them to the features in a feature model, i.e., the feature model is utilized as *integrator* for all types of requirements artifacts for all products in a product line. This means that there are three distinct views available of one common underlying model:

- The *feature view* provides an overview of the common and variable requirements and functions in a product line. The feature view is also a tool for instantiating the generic product line artifacts into concrete product artifacts.
- The *natural-language requirements view* provides details regarding the product line capabilities and characteristics.
- The *use case view* provides the functional view of a product line in terms of system users, end-user goals, and usage scenarios.

Specific product views can be seen as restricted views of this common model and therefore can be easily generated by means of tools.

Figure 6.10 shows an overview of the detailed *engineer domain* activities. Note that activities are highly iterative, although feedback loops are excluded to improve readability. Identifying use cases and linking these to requirements and features, as well as identification of alternative and exceptional use case scenarios, will typically result in the identification of new or modified features in the feature model. Furthermore, while describing use case scenarios, new use cases are discovered and others are merged based on common guidelines for use case quality, like the following:

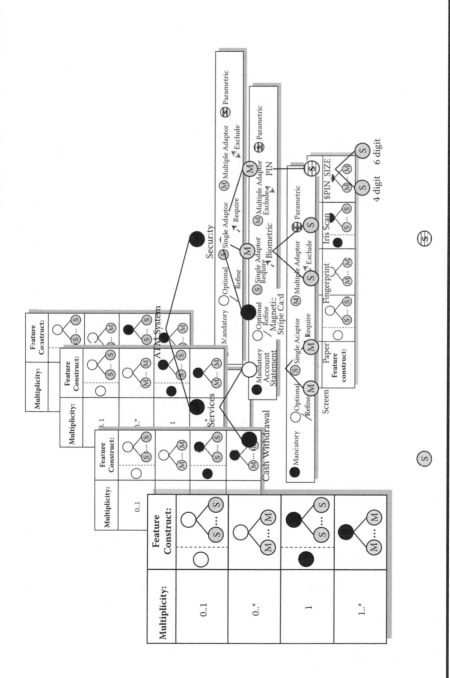

Figure 6.9   An example of a PLUSS+ feature model summarizing the notation.

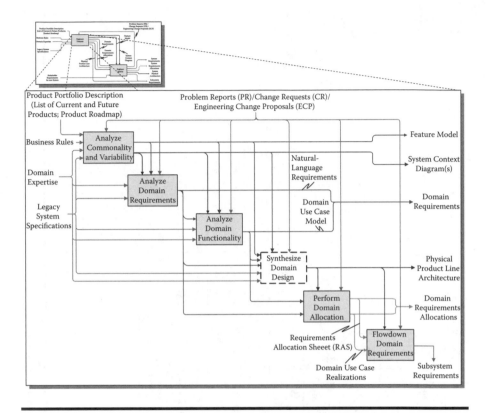

Figure 6.10 **Refinement of activity *engineer domain* from Figure 6.3 (the activity *synthesize domain design* is beyond the scope of this chapter).**

- A main success scenario should have between 3 and 10 steps.
- Common behavior should be factored out as a separate subgoal use case using UML's <<include>> relation (OMG 2007a). We avoid using the <<specialization>> relation, since its mapping to scenarios is unclear.
- Scenarios should avoid complex control structures such as (nested) loops or conditionals. If needed, the corresponding use case should rather be divided into subgoal use cases to maintain high readability.

The *PR/CR/ECP* feedback-loop from *engineer system* to *engineer domain* in Figure 6.3 may also be initiated internally from any of the domain engineering subactivities shown in Figure 6.10.

6.5.1 Analyze Commonality and Variability

The main outputs of the activity *analyze commonality and variability* are a feature model and system-context diagrams for the systems in the product line (see

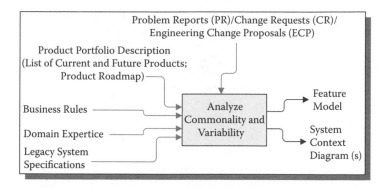

Figure 6.11 Activity *analyze commonality and variability.*

Figure 6.11). The feature model represents a set of decisions, capturing both business rules and technical constraints for a particular product in the scope of the current product line (the product portfolio description).

In our work, a combination of brainstorming session with domain experts and reverse engineering of legacy system specifications have been utilized to develop an initial feature model. This model is then continuously updated during the following analysis activities.

To develop and maintain our feature models (and other PLUSS+ artifacts), we have developed plug-ins (Eriksson et al. 2005) to the commercial requirements management tool DOORS® (registered trademark of IBM) (Telelogic 2004). For example, the plug-ins enables us to visualize feature graphs (see Figure 6.12) and to automatically verify that no contradictory rules have been defined in the feature model.

6.5.2 Analyze Domain Requirements

The main output of the activity *analyze domain requirements* is natural-language requirements for the product instances in the product line (Figure 6.13). These requirements are derived from, and traceable to, stakeholder requirements (see Figure 6.2) for the different products in the product line. These stakeholder requirements enter the activity via the *PR/CR/ECP* feedback loop from systems engineering and also via legacy system specifications. Development of these requirements is constrained by the system-context diagrams developed during commonality and variability analysis.

Variability among product line requirements is managed by linking requirements statements to appropriate features in the feature model. Natural-language requirements can either be inserted as children to their corresponding features in the feature model (see Figure 6.14) or maintained in a separate DOORS module. In the latter case, traceability is supported by explicit DOORS traceability links.

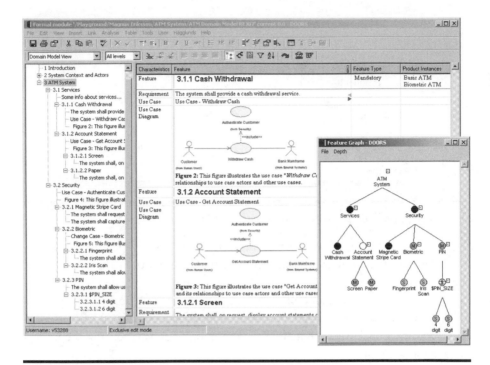

Figure 6.12   Visualizing feature graphs in DOORS.

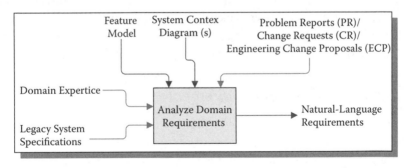

Figure 6.13   Activity *analyze domain requirements*.

As illustrated by *$PIN_SIZE* in Figure 6.14, feature models in PLUSS+ support parameters. A PLUSS+ parameter definition consists of two parts:

- A parameter nametag specifying a position in one or more requirements statements where parameters are substituted by actual values during product instantiation. A parameter nametag is a single word starting with the symbol *$*.
- A parametric feature in the feature model, with child features specifying the range of valid values for the parameter. Each unique selected value for a

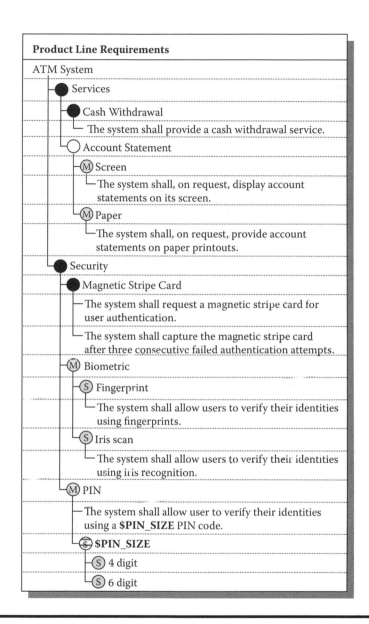

Figure 6.14 **Natural-language requirements ("shall" statements) linked to a feature model.**

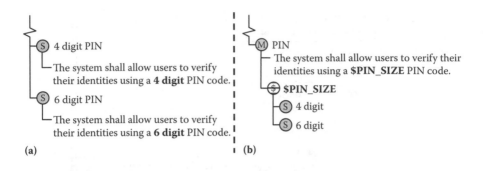

(a)

(b)

Figure 6.15 **An example of how the same requirement's variability can be modeled using (a) separate requirements statements and (b) parameters.**

parameter results in a new child feature to the parametric feature, which in turn may be included by one or more products in the product line.

PLUSS+ parameters can be either single-valued or multivalued, which is specified by selecting appropriate feature types for the child features of each parametric feature. A parametric feature can be defined on the same level of the feature tree as the requirements statement(s) using the parameter but also on any level above, i.e., they have similar scope rules as declarations in common imperative programming languages. Cross-cutting parametric features can therefore be defined on appropriate levels of the feature model and utilized in different subtrees.

In PLUSS+, some variations can be modeled using either a parameter within a single requirement statement or by using several separate and mutually exclusive requirements statements (see Figure 6.15 for an example). If the variation point is relatively small, for example consisting of a few consecutive words or a single value, parameters are usually the better choice, since it minimizes redundancy. If the variation point is larger or has structural impact on the requirements statement, it is better handled using separate and mutually exclusive requirements statements. Using parameters would lead to long and complex parameter values, which would decrease the readability of the overall model.

6.5.3 *Analyze Domain Functionality*

The main output of the activity *analyze domain functionality* is a common and complete use case model for all products in the product line (see Figure 6.16). The use cases are derived from, and traceable to, the natural-language requirements developed during domain-requirements analysis.

To be able to develop and maintain common and complete use case models for all products in the product line, effective variability management is needed. We dis-

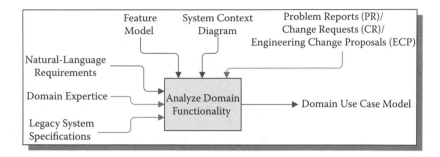

Figure 6.16 Activity *analyze domain functionality.*

tinguish four kinds of variations in use case models for product families (Eriksson, Börstler, and Borg 2006):

1. Use cases might or might not be included in a particular product.
2. Certain scenarios of an included use case might be excluded from a particular product.
3. The flow of events within an included scenario might vary.
4. Cross-cutting aspects can affect several use cases on several levels, e.g., the existence of different sets of use case actors (system users) in different products.

All such variations are managed by means of the feature model. We accomplish this by relating use cases, use case scenarios, and steps within use case scenarios to features of appropriate types in the feature model. To manage cross-cutting variability, we also include textual parameters in our use case descriptions, as described in Section 6.5.2 (see Figure 6.17).

Unlike traditional use case modeling, PLUSS+ does not utilize use case diagrams to provide an overview of the system scope. In PLUSS+, the feature model, together with the system-context diagram(s), provides a total overview over system scope and (variant) functionality. We utilize use case diagrams only to visualize relations between individual use cases and to provide an overview of the primary and secondary actors of each use case. These individual use case diagrams are then linked to their corresponding elements in the feature model, as illustrated by Figure 6.18. Furthermore, there would also be another use case diagram describing the details regarding the subgoal use case *Be uniquely identified*, which would be linked to the *security* element of the feature model, as indicated by the parentheses under the use case name. Since PLUSS+ provides an overview of the model using a feature model rather than using a use case diagram, we usually do not factor out scenarios from use cases using the UML <<extend>> relation, unless it is needed for structural reasons in the model. This strategy helps us to reduce the number of documents (use case specifications) in the model.

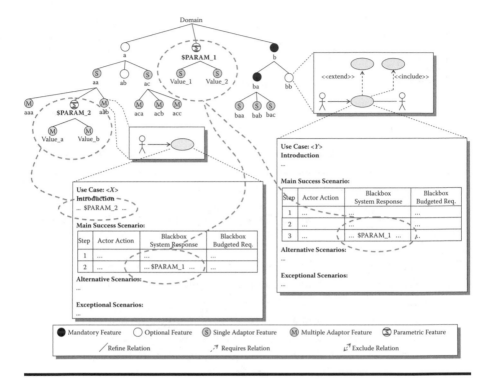

Figure 6.17   Using parametric features as use case parameters.

6.5.4 *Perform Domain Allocation*

The main outputs of the activity *perform domain allocation* are (a) a traceability report, referred to as the requirements allocation sheet (RAS), and (b) use case realizations for all use cases in the domain use case model (see Figure 6.19). Development of these allocation artifacts is constrained by the physical product line architecture developed during design synthesis, since it defines the subsystems and components to which requirements can be allocated.

The purpose of the RAS is twofold. First, as shown in Figure 6.20, we utilize it to maintain traceability between system requirements and use cases. Second, the RAS is the tool used for directly allocating those system requirements that are not suitable for use case modeling to subsystems and components. Examples of such requirements are systemwide quality attributes, like environmental constraints, legislations, standards, etc. The RAS documents which subsystems are involved in fulfilling each of these requirements. To support meaningful trade-off analyses, it is important to capture background information and rationale(s) for all allocations.

As described in Section 6.4.5, the development of PLUSS+ use case realizations involves analyzing each use case scenario step and documenting the way in which each

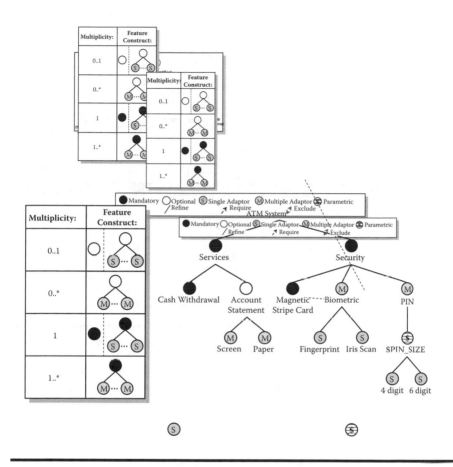

Figure 6.18 Linking individual use case diagrams (cf. Figure 6.5) to features in a feature model (cf. Figure 6.9).

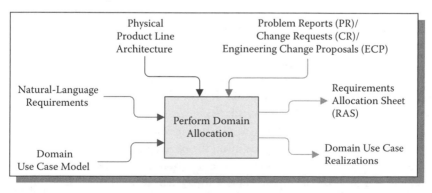

Figure 6.19 Activity *perform domain allocation*.

Req. ID	Req. Text	Use Cases					Subsystems						Allocation Rationale
		Withdraw Cash	Get Account Statement	Authenticate Customer	:	:	Mainframe Interface	Transaction Controler	Card Reader	Output Device	:	:	
Services													
SYSR867	The system shall provide a cash withdrawal service.	X											
SYSR868	The system shall provide a account statement service.		X										
...	...												
Security													
SYSR870	The system shall capture the General_ID after three consecutive failed authentication atempts.			X									
...	...												
Maintenance													
SYSR900	It shall be possible to replace any malfunctioning subsystem within 15 minutes of...						X	X	X	X	X	X	ATM customers expect 24-7 availability.

Figure 6.20   Example of a PLUSS+ requirements allocation sheet (RAS).

subsystem (defined by the architecture) participates in solving each step. Similar to how use case scenarios allocate responsibility between a system and its users for achieving an end-user goal (see Section 6.4.3), use case realizations allocate responsibility between the different subsystems to fulfill the system part of this responsibility.

6.5.5 *Flowdown Domain Requirements*

The main output of the activity *flowdown domain requirements* is natural-language requirements for the subsystems specified by the physical product line architecture. The subsystem requirements are based on the domain-requirements allocations described in the RAS and will later form the basis for detailed design within different engineering disciplines (see Figure 6.21).

Analysis of an RAS consists, to a large extent, of understanding the rationale(s) behind each allocation and the effects of particular allocations on particular subsystems. Analysis of the RAS will result in one or more subsystem requirements for each *X* in its *subsystems* part (cf. Figure 6.20). The resulting subsystem requirements are usually quality attributes constraining the development of the subsystems.

Analysis of use case realizations focuses on identifying interfaces between subsystems and allocation of responsibilities for system functionality. It is important that white-box steps are analyzed in the correct context (sequencing, preconditions, etc.). Each white-box step should be decomposed into one or more subsystem

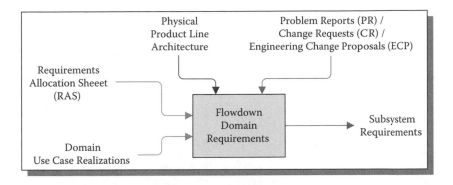

Figure 6.21 Activity *flowdown domain requirements*.

requirements. As shown in Figure 6.22, these subsystem requirements are typically of input, output, or functional character.

A problem with flowdown of domain requirements, in contrast to traditional single-system requirements, is that there is no real intuitive way to flow down parametric requirements without creating complex traceability relations. We therefore avoid developing subsystem requirements for parametric requirements during domain engineering. Instead, this activity is performed as part of the system engineering activity, once the parametric domain requirements have been instantiated for a particular product. This is another reason for avoiding parameters, if possible, as discussed in Section 6.5.2.

6.6 Engineer System

In this section, we provide a more detailed description of the activity *engineer system* from Figure 6.3. In this activity, PLUSS+ handles the specific requirements for a particular system (*stakeholder requirements for new system*, see Figure 6.23) and develops instances of the product line guided by the outputs from domain analysis. Overall, this instantiation is a two-step process. First, new requirements are analyzed, modeled, and fed back to domain engineering via the *PR/CR/ECP* loop.

White-box Action	White-box Budgeted Req.	Subsystem Requirements
The ***TransactionController*** requests the MSC to be captured by the ***CardReader***.	Max response time 0.2 sec.	The ***TransactionController*** shall produce a request to capture a MSC within 0.15 sec, if an invalid PIN have been provided three times.
		The ***CardReader*** shall accept requests to capture a MSC within 0.05 sec.
		The ***CardReader*** shall capture a MSC on request.

Figure 6.22 An example of requirements flowdown based on a use case realization.

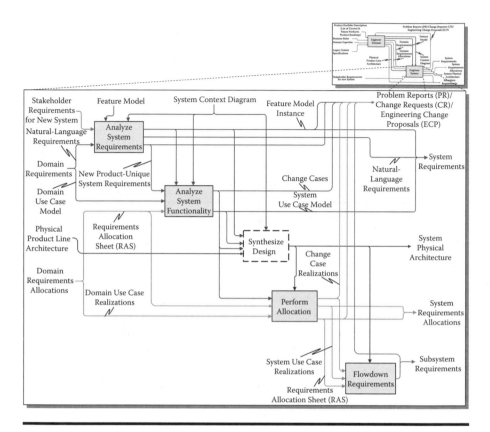

Figure 6.23 **Refinement of activity *engineer system* from Figure 6.3 (activity *synthesize design* is beyond the scope of this chapter).**

If the new requirements are accepted for inclusion in the product line by domain engineering, they are incorporated in the product line model. Then the extended product line model, now even containing the requirements for the new system, is instantiated, and product specifications are generated.

6.6.1 Analyze System Requirements

When adding a new system to a product line, there will typically be requirements unique for this particular system. They represent features or variations distinguishing it from any other systems in the current product line. The main outputs of the activity *analyze system requirements* are new natural-language requirements for the product instance in the product line (Figure 6.13) and instantiated (existing) domain requirements. These requirements are derived from, and traceable to, stakeholder requirements for the new product (Figure 6.24). Development of these requirements is constrained by the system-context diagrams developed during commonality and

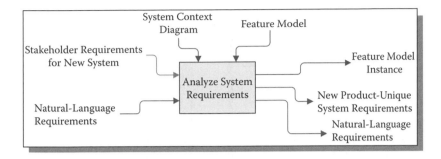

Figure 6.24 Activity *analyze system requirements.*

variability analysis. Another output of this activity is an instance of the feature model, representing the decisions made when instantiating the domain requirements.

Instantiation of the current product line model is basically done by systematically traversing the feature model and, for each feature, (a) choosing whether or not it should be included and (b) choosing appropriate values for parametric features (Figure 6.25). Instantiation results in an initial requirements specification for the new system (*feature model instance + natural-language requirements*). This instantiation is automated by means of the DOORS toolkit discussed in Section 6.5.1. The product requirements are generated from the domain requirements and saved as write-protected DOORS modules. The toolkit also provides means for verifying that a product instance does not violate any rules specified in the feature model.

Requirements unique to the new system are initially kept in a separate DOORS module and are analyzed further in the next activity. These product-unique requirements will also be part of a *PR/CR/ECP* package delivered to domain engineering as a request for adding the new system to the product line.

6.6.2 Analyze System Functionality

The main outputs of the activity *analyze system functionality* are a product instance of (a) the domain use case model for the new system (the *system use case model*) and (b) change cases modeling the new product-unique system requirements (Figure 6.26).

Instantiation of the domain use case model is performed using the same principle as instantiation of natural-language requirements described above. The feature model instance is used as a filter for extracting relevant parts of the common product line model. Also, this instantiation is automated by means of the DOORS toolkit. The system use case model (use case model survey and use case specifications) is generated from the common model and saved as write-protected DOORS modules.

The developed change cases are traceable to the new-product unique requirements and also to existing domain use cases using the <<impacts>> links described in Section 6.4.4. These change cases are also part of a *PR/CR/ECP* package delivered to domain engineering as a request for adding the new system to the product

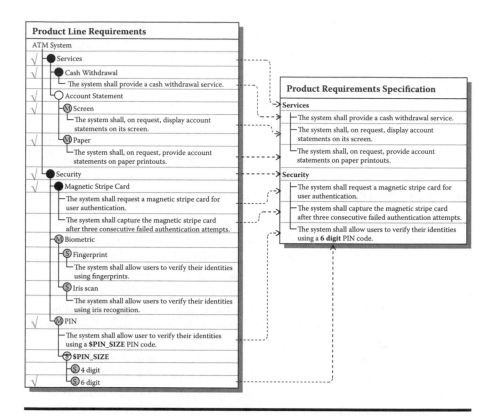

Figure 6.25 **An example of composing a product requirements specification (to the right) from product line requirements and (to the left) by means of feature selection. Selected features are check marked in the leftmost column. Features used as specification headings are underlined.**

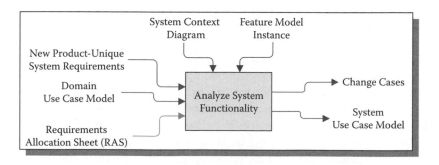

Figure 6.26 **Activity *analyze system functionality*.**

line. Once accepted for inclusion, these change cases are transformed into use cases and incorporated in the domain use case model.

6.6.3 Perform Allocation

The main outputs of the activity *perform allocation* are proposed realizations for the previously developed change cases: system use case realizations (instantiated domain use case realizations) and an RAS for the new system (see Figure 6.27). Development of these allocation artifacts is constrained by the physical system architecture, which is an instance of the physical product line architecture.

Development of change-case realizations is performed in the same way as traditional use case realizations (see Section 6.5.4). These artifacts are also part of the *PR/CR/ECP* package shown in Figure 6.23.

Besides the usage described in Sections 6.5.4 and 6.5.5, the developed RAS is also used to maintain traceability between new product unique requirements and change cases, as well as for directly allocating new requirements to subsystems. This artifact is thereby used to tie together the artifacts that compose the *PR/CR/ECP* package shown in Figure 6.23.

6.6.4 Perform System Requirements Flowdown

The main output of the activity *requirements flowdown* (Figure 6.28) is the natural-language requirements for the subsystems specified by the physical system architecture. These subsystem requirements supplement the subsystem requirements developed during the *engineer domain* activity as a basis for detailed design.

Development of these subsystem requirements follows the same principles as described in Section 6.5.5. The bases for this activity are the change-case realizations and the directly allocated requirements (in the RAS) developed in the previous activity. During this activity, subsystem requirements derived from allocations of parametric domain requirements are also developed (see discussion in Section 6.5.5).

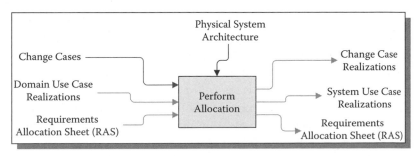

Figure 6.27 Activity *perform allocation*.

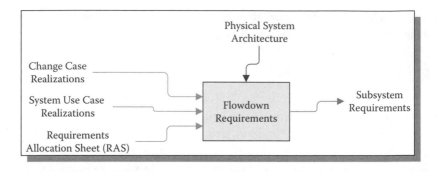

Figure 6.28 Activity *flowdown requirements*.

6.7 Lessons Learned

PLUSS+ has been developed and improved over several years of industrial application within the Swedish defense industry. Several product line efforts have been initiated using PLUSS+ and its predecessors, and a number of products have been successfully developed. PLUSS+ helped us to achieve high levels of reuse. Collecting all requirements of all products of a product line in one common model helps to reduce the total number of documents. This decreases total maintenance, but also requires strong configuration management functions. Depending on the maturity of the domain and the organization, we believe that a breakeven of the initial investment in PLUSS+ can be reached after as few as two to three successful instantiations of the product line (only counting the development effort, and not the reduced production costs due to standardization).

An important factor for the successful interaction between research and industry in developing PLUSS+ was the adoption of the "industry-as-laboratory" approach proposed by Potts (1993). According to this approach, new methods are directly applied in an industrial setting working as a real-world test environment. This allowed for a rapid evolution of PLUSS+ based on the results of continuous evaluation. The methods have evolved from the efforts of earlier research and from established practices in software and systems engineering. PLUSS+ could therefore be introduced with relative ease; a few hours of introduction is usually enough. The methods are generally experienced as straightforward, intuitive, and effective. During the initial pilot projects, we provided access to coaches or experts, which was very helpful and increased acceptance of PLUSS+. We believe that the industry-as-laboratory approach would also be an effective strategy for business improvement activities in general.

In the following subsections, we summarize a number of lessons we have learned since the introduction of system product lines.

6.7.1 The Feature Model Is a Useful and Well-Used System Reference

The feature model is a highly valued reference document and fulfills more purposes than initially envisioned. Besides providing the intended basis for an improved reuse infrastructure, it helps all kinds of stakeholders to get a good overview of the systems in a product line. Since requirements are grouped by features, it helps analysts in managing the complexity of thousands of requirements. The feature model also helps in introducing new team members to the product line and gives marketing an overview of (existing and potential) systems that could be offered to customers.

6.7.2 Use Case Realizations on System Level Might Confuse Experts

In software engineering, use case realizations are developed with the objective of identifying the (software) units that will realize some functionality. In PLUSS+, use case realizations serve a different purpose: decomposing system requirements and allocating them to existing subsystems. That is, use case realizations are utilized at a much higher level of abstraction. Even for experienced software engineers, maintaining the proper level of abstraction is a challenging aspect of PLUSS+. It is therefore important to emphasize that PLUSS+ is not a software design method, even though some aspects of it could be associated with such methods.

6.7.3 Simple Notations Support Communication

One of the most valuable characteristics of PLUSS+ is its simple notation. Its semi-formal notations—together with its structured, step-by-step approach—support communication among a broad spectrum of stakeholders. This is particularly important in the context of systems engineering. System information must not only be understood by users, customers, and developers; it must also be easily understood by people from the various engineering disciplines involved in systems development (e.g., mechanical, electrical, and software engineers) and marketing.

6.7.4 Simple Notations Might Not Be Sufficient in All Cases

Although simple notations have many advantages, there are also some disadvantages. In use case modeling, it is, for example, impossible to unambiguously define state-dependent behavior without a more formal notation.

6.7.5 Strong Configuration Management and Product Planning Functions Are Important

Our case studies have shown the importance of long-term management as well as organizational and business strategies for the implementation of product line management. Product line organizations require strong configuration management and product planning functions to be successful. Product planning must have a long-term scope and be able to span the life cycles of many releases of several products. New requirements are analyzed both from the domain-engineering and systems-engineering perspectives. Feature creep must be strictly controlled and variability must be carefully planned. Uncontrolled changes will make the common model useless. Product planning and configuration management are therefore important functions for keeping the products in line.

6.7.6 Don't Underestimate the Need for Tool Support

Tool support is essential for keeping the feature model consistent and instantiating products correctly. In PLUSS+, we have successfully used extensions to link with familiar commercially available tools. These extensions worked well, since the developers were already familiar with the tools. The tool extensions were also quite small to avoid update or maintenance problems regarding the PLUSS toolkit. On the other hand, the tools used have some limitations that we consider important for long-term success. So far they are not fully integrated with our UML modeling environment. This limitation inflicts unnecessary manual work that might lead to inconsistencies in documentation.

References

Adolph, S., P. Bramble, A. Cockburn, and A. Pols. 2003. *Patterns for effective use cases.* Boston: Addison-Wesley.

Bittner, K., and I. Spence. 2003. *Use case modeling.* Boston: Addison-Wesley.

DoD (Department of Defense). 2001. *Systems engineering fundamentals.* Fort Belvoir, VA: Defense Acquisition University Press.

Dorfman, M., and R. Thayer. 1997. *Software requirements engineering.* Los Alamitos, CA: IEEE Computer Society Press.

Ecklund, E., L. Delcambre, and M. Freiling. 1996. Change cases: Use cases that identify future requirements. In *Proceedings of the 11th ACM SIGPLAN conference on object-oriented programming, systems, languages, and applications (OOPSLA'96).* New York: ACM Press.

Eriksson, M., J. Börstler, and K. Borg. 2005. The PLUSS approach: Domain modeling with features, use cases and use case realizations. In *Proceedings of the 9th international conference on software product lines,* 33–44. Lecture Notes in Computer Science, vol. 3714. Berlin: Springer-Verlag.

Eriksson, M., J. Börstler, and K. Borg. 2006. Software product line modeling made practical: An example from the Swedish defense industry. *Communications of the ACM* 49 (12): 49–54.

Eriksson, M., J. Börstler, and K. Borg. 2008. Use cases for systems engineering: An approach and empirical evaluation. *Systems Engineering Journal* 11 (1): 39–60.

Eriksson, M., H. Morast, J. Börstler, and K. Borg. 2005. The PLUSS toolkit: Extending telelogic DOORS and IBM-rational rose to support product line use case modeling. In *Proceedings of the 20th IEEE/ACM international conference on automated software engineering*, 300–304. New York: ACM Press.

Eriksson, M., H. Morast, J. Börstler, and K. Borg. 2006. An empirical evaluation of the PLUSS toolkit. Technical report UMINF-06.31. Dept. of Computing Science, Umeå University, Sweden.

Griss, M., J. Favaro, and M. d'Alessandro. 1998. Integrating feature modeling with the RSEB. In *Proceedings of the 5th international conference on software reuse*, 76–85. Washington, DC: IEEE Computer Society.

INCOSE (International Council on Systems Engineering). 2004a. Systems engineering handbook version 2a. INCOSE-TP-2003-016-02. San Diego: INCOSE.

INCOSE (International Council on Systems Engineering). 2004b. What is systems engineering? http://www.incose.org/practice/whatissystemseng.aspx.

INCOSE (International Council on Systems Engineering). 2006. *Systems engineering handbook, version 3*. INCOSE-TP-2003-002-03. San Diego: INCOSE.

ISO/IEC. 2002. Systems engineering: System life cycle processes. International standard ISO/IEC FDIS 15288:2002(E).

Jacobsson, I., M. Griss, and P. Jonsson. 1997. *Software reuse*. Boston: Addison-Wesley.

Kang, K., S. Cohen, J. Hess, W. Novak, and A. Peterson. 1990. Feature oriented domain analysis (FODA) feasibility study. Technical report CMU/SEI-90-TR-021. Software Engineering Institute, Carnegie Mellon University, Pittsburgh.

Lykins, H., S. Friedenthal, and A. Meilich. 2000. Adapting UML for an object oriented systems engineering method (OOSEM). In *Proceedings of the 10th annual international symposium of the International Council on Systems Engineering (INCOSE'00)*. San Diego: INCOSE.

NIST (National Institute of Standards and Technology). 1993. Integration definition for function modeling (IDEF0). Federal Information Processing Standards 183.

Northrop, L. 2002. SEI's software product line tenets. *IEEE Software* 19 (4): 32–40.

OMG (Object Management Group). 2007a. Unified modeling language version 2.0. http://www.uml.org.

OMG (Object Management Group). 2007b. OMG systems modeling language: OMG SysML. http://www.omgsysml.org.

Potts, C. 1993. Software-engineering research revisited. *IEEE Software* 10 (5): 19–28.

Rational Software. 2003. The rational unified process for systems engineering. White paper ver. 1.1. ftp://ftp.software.ibm.com/software/rational/web/whitepapers/2003/TP165.pdf.

Sommerville, I., and P. Sawyer. 1997. *Requirements engineering: A good practices guide*. New York: Wiley.

Telelogic AB. 2004. DXL reference manual, DOORS 7.1. 3 May 2004.

van der Linden, F., K. Schmid, and E. Rommes. 2007. *Software product lines in action: The best industrial practice in product line engineering*. Berlin: Springer-Verlag.

Weiss, David M., Chi Tau Robert Lai. 1999. *Software product line engineering: A family-based software development process*. Boston: Addison-Wesley Longman.

Chapter 7

Adoption of Software Product Lines to Develop Autonomic Pervasive Systems

Carlos Cetina, Joan Fons, and Vicente Pelechano

Universidad Politécnica de Valencia, Spain

Contents

7.1 Introduction

Increasingly, software needs to dynamically adapt its behavior at runtime in response to changing conditions in the supporting computing infrastructure and in the surrounding physical environment (McKinley et al. 2004). Adaptability is emerging as a necessary underlying capability, particularly for highly dynamic systems. Pervasive systems are highly dynamic and fault-prone, since new kinds of entities (sensors, actuators, external software systems) can enter these systems at any time. Existing entities may fail or leave the system for a variety of reasons: hardware faults, OS errors, bugs, network faults, etc. The dynamic and fault-prone nature of these systems makes it necessary to design new techniques in order to take into account these new issues.

Pervasive computing is defined as "a technology that weaves itself into the fabric of everyday life until it is indistinguishable from it" (Weiser 1991). To be successful, the pervasive computing functioning should be transparent to the user. Such transparency is achievable if the software frees users from having to repair and reconfigure the system when faults or changes occur in the environment.

Autonomic systems (Horn 2001) configure themselves automatically in accordance with high-level policies (self-configuration) and can detect, diagnose, and repair localized problems (self-healing). In a car or an airplane, faults need to be repaired without shutting down and restarting the entire system. In a smart home, end users should be able to perform home upgrades (install new sensors or actuators) without having to reconfigure the software system. To achieve this autonomic goal, a pervasive system needs to "know itself," and its components should also possess a system identity (Ganek and Corbi 2003).

This chapter proposes the adoption of the Software Product Line (SPL) paradigm to develop autonomic pervasive systems in a methodological fashion. In particular, we argue that pervasive systems can achieve autonomic behavior by introducing SPL variability both at design and runtime. We present the extensions to the production operation of SPLs in order to transfer variability models from the SPL design to the SPL products. In addition to the selected features at design time, the final product will contain some "extra" features. These features are disabled initially but they can be enabled in a product reconfiguration. For example, a smart home can include the alarm software system that is activated when the user installs some alarm device. If the product line architecture is retargeted to the desired configuration in an autonomic way, we obtain a self-configuring system.

We illustrate this reconfiguration approach based on two adaptation scenarios that are very common in pervasive systems:

1. Evolution (a new resource is available)
2. Involution (a resource is removed)

We propose to organize the knowledge required to deal with these adaptation issues according to the specific demands (user goals) of each adaptation scenario. In involution scenarios, we extend variability models with new relationships in order to provide an autonomic response in a reduced amount of time. In evolution scenarios, we offer an advanced system response (feature dependency resolution and user participation), because we consider that evolution and involution scenarios have different requirements regarding adaptation.

7.2 Background

In this chapter, we illustrate how to apply SPLs to build autonomic pervasive systems. This section briefly provides some background information about autonomic computing and pervasive systems.

7.2.1 Autonomic Computing

In October 2001, IBM released a manifesto (Horn 2001) describing the vision of autonomic computing. The purpose is to countermeasure the complexity of software systems by making systems self-managing. The paradox has been spotted, that systems need to become even more complex to achieve this. The complexity, it is argued, can be embedded in the system infrastructure, which in turn can be automated. The similarity of the described approach to the autonomic nervous system of the body, which relieves basic control from our consciousness, gave birth to the term *autonomic computing*.

Autonomic Computing is a potential solution to the problem of increasing system complexity and costs of maintenance. It is an approach where the ultimate goal is to create computer systems that can manage themselves while hiding their complexity from the end users (Horn 2001).

Thus, by hiding and removing the low-level complexities from the realm of human control, humans can be freed from the burdens of maintenance to concentrate on achieving higher-level, business-oriented objectives.

The concept and vision behind autonomic computing is certainly a promising one. However, due to its goal-oriented approach, development in the autonomic computing field is driven by goal achievement and not by systematic engineering processes. As a result, a commonly accepted definition of autonomic computing is yet to be established, allowing any technology that exhibits behaviors of self-management to automatically be classified as "autonomic computing."

In Kephart and Chess's *The Vision of Autonomic Computing* (2003), the following four system abilities are discussed:

- Self-configuring involves automatic incorporation of new components and automatic component adjustment to new conditions.
- Self-optimizing on a system level is about automatic parameter tuning on services. A suggested method to do this is to explore, learn, and exploit.
- Self-healing from bugs and failures can be accomplished using components for detection, diagnosis, and repair.
- Self-protecting systems will prevent large-scale correlated attacks or cascading failures from permanently damaging valuable information and critical system functions. It may also act proactively to mitigate reported problems.

It is claimed that, as these aspects become properties of a general architecture, they will merge into a single self-maintenance quality. The architecture of an autonomic computing system will be a collection of components called *autonomic elements*, which encapsulate managed elements. The managed element can be hardware, application software, or an entire system. An autonomic element is an agent, managing its internal behavior and relationships with others in accordance with policies. It is driven by goals, by other elements, or by contracts established by negotiation with other elements. System self-management will arise both from interactions among agents and from agents' internal self-management.

At IBM, the autonomic computing initiative spans across all levels of computer management, from the lowest levels of hardware to the highest levels of software systems. *IBM Systems Journal* has collected some of this work. On the hardware level, systems are dynamically upgradable (Jann, Browning, and Burugula 2003). On the operating system level, active operating system code is replaced dynamically (Appavoo et al. 2003). Some work on autonomic middleware can be found at other sources (Jarvis et al. 2003; Yau et al. 2002; Blair et al. 2002). On the application level, databases self-validate optimization models (Markl, Lohman, and Raman 2003), and Web servers are dynamically reconfigured by agents to adapt service performance (Diao et al. 2003).

7.2.2 Pervasive Computing

Pervasive computing is a post-desktop model of human–computer interaction in which information processing has been thoroughly integrated into everyday objects and activities. As opposed to the desktop paradigm, in which a single user consciously engages a single device for a specialized purpose, someone "using" ubiquitous computing engages many computational devices and systems simultaneously.

> The most profound technologies are those that disappear. They weave themselves into the fabric of everyday life until they are indistinguishable from it (Weiser 1991).

This can be the summary of what Weiser stated as UBICOMP. This vision is based on the construction of computing-saturated environments properly integrated with human users. Essential to the vision is networking, for without the ability of these computing devices to communicate with one another, the functionality of such a system would be extremely limited. Weiser stated that the next-generation computing environment would be one "in which each person is continually interacting with hundreds of nearby wirelessly connected computers." At the time, such forms of wireless networking were still in their infancy, but today with wireless WiFi, WiMax, and Bluetooth, the possibilities for such dense local area networks are entering the realm of commercial reality.

Wright et al. (2005) have stated that, while researchers in the United States were working on the vision of ubiquitous computing, the European Union began promoting a similar vision for its research and development agenda. The term adopted in Europe is *ambient intelligence* (coined by Emile Aarts of Philips) which has a lot in common with Weiser's ubiquitous computing vision. This point of view is confirmed by the great number of events and research projects that are organized and/or funded in Europe under this term, the topics of which clearly match the ones that are inside the scope of the ubiquitous computing area.

Although subtle differentiations could be made between these terms according to their etymological meanings (ubiquitous does not imply intelligence, intelligence does not imply pervasiveness, etc.), in general we can state that the main idea or vision behind them is the same and, therefore, they can be equally used.

7.3 Dynamic Software Product Lines (DSPL)

The main objective of SPL is producing products where costs and time to market are reduced by an intensive reuse of commonalities and a suitable variability management. Products are commonly produced by selecting the features that are part of a product and removing those that are not part of it. To make this decision, features are selected and/or discarded at different binding times. Those features thought to be bound at runtime are kept in the final product even when they may not be used by the final product. The product must provide the mechanisms to select the suitable feature at runtime and optionally reconfigure the product. After the production, no automated activity is specified in SPL development to maintain a product in connection with the SPL, so it may not eventually benefit from feature updates.

On the other hand, DSPL development mainly intends to produce configurable products (van der Linden 2001) whose autonomy allows them to reconfigure themselves and benefit from a constant updating. In a DSPL, a configurable product (CP) is produced from a product line similar to the way that it is done in a standard SPL. However, the reconfiguration ability implies the usage of two artifacts to control it: the decision maker and the reconfigurator. The decision maker is in charge of capturing all the information in its environment that suggests a change of such information from external sensors or even from users. The analyzer must know the whole structure of a CP so that it can make a decision on which features must be activated and deactivated. The reconfigurator is responsible for executing the decision by using the standard SPL runtime binding. A CP may be considered as an extension of traditional SPL products where there are no bound features, but where the decision maker and the reconfigurator and the remaining features are bound at runtime. As a consequence, new features may be added to an existing product or even existing features may be updated at runtime.

Comparing both SPL and DSPL development, DSPL development might be considered as a particular case of SPL where the following properties are added:

- **Adaptation to changing requirements and environment:** A product is prepared to answer to the so-called adaptation triggers that alert the system of a change in the environment or the conditions in which the product is working. A user may also explicitly ask for a change in a product configuration. Both cases are analyzed and, if it is possible, the system is reconfigured to cope with the new situations.
- **Autonomic capabilities:** A CP is able to make decisions about the features that are activated and deactivated according to its environment and whenever an adaptation trigger or a user request arrives at the decision maker.
- **Product updates:** As all the features are bound at runtime, updating an existing product with new features or updates is feasible.

Several approaches for developing CP using DSPLs have been presented in the published literature. We have classified these approaches in two categories, according to the way in which product adaptation is considered:

- **Connected DSPL:** the DSPL is in charge of the product adaptation
- **Disconnected DSPL:** the CP itself is in charge of the product adaptation

We describe both connected and disconnected DSPLs from the product perspective. In this way, we study the advantages and drawbacks obtained as a result of incorporating adaptation in SPL products. The following characteristics help us to evaluate DSPLs:

- **Degree of autonomy:** This criterion addresses how much products depend on the DSPL to perform adaptation.
- **Adaptation capabilities:** This criterion addresses the adaptation level achieved by the CP.
- **Computational overload:** This criterion addresses how much computational overload is introduced by the DSPL approach in the CP execution.

Figure 7.1 shows graphically the proposals that fit in the connected and disconnected categories. They have been arranged in the order of the year in which they appeared in the literature. According to Figure 7.1, there are six DSPLs that focus their efforts on developing configurable products. Table 7.1 summarizes the specification techniques of each of these approaches as well as the infrastructure to support adaptation.

Next, we analyze the characteristics of both connected and disconnected DSPLs, and then we illustrate how product adaptation is supported.

7.3.1 Connected DSPL

Using a product line architecture, developers can create software architectures that can be rapidly retargeted from one SPL variant to another variant. In a pervasive environment, however, the retargeting of a system must happen online. When a device comes in a new context, such as the upgrade of the smart-home devices, the DSPL must quickly deduce and create a variant for the system. Connected DSPLs keep in touch with products in order to send them updates. These updates enable products to deal with the context changes. Figure 7.2 shows the steps that should be achieved to send the updates from the DSPL to the CPs.

1. The CP senses a relevant change that starts the adaptation process. Both changes in the environment and in the CP itself can trigger the adaptation process.
2. The CP sends information about the change to the SPL. Optionally, the CP can locally preprocess the information to send more specific information to the SPL.

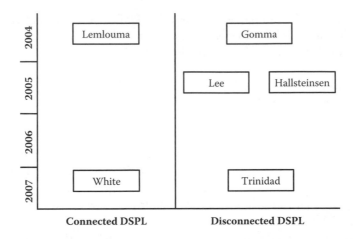

Figure 7.1 Some DSPLs that have been proposed in the last few years.

Table 7.1 DSPL Comparison

DSPL	*Variability Specification*	*Adaptation Infrastructure*
Gomaa (2004)	UML state charts	Reconfiguration patterns
Lemlouma and Layaida (2004)	Device-independent model	SOAP services
Lee and Kang (2006)	Feature model with binding units	Reconfigurable assets
Hallsteinsen et al. (2006)	UML QoS properties profile	Planning process
White et al. (2007)	Requirements specification	Variant delivery
Trinidad et al. (2007)	Feature model	Relationship components

3. The SPL incorporates the acquired information to the product requisites and then it calculates a new CP variant.

   3.1 If there is no variant that satisfies the product requisites, then the SPL notifies the CP and the adaptation process fails.

4. The SPL generates the CP update. This update can be the whole calculated variant or the difference between the old variant and the new one.

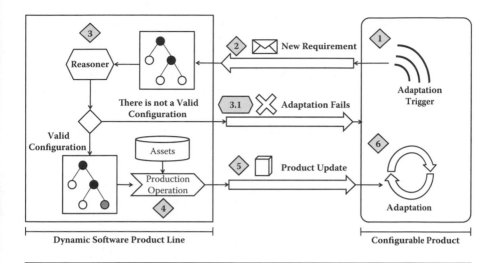

Figure 7.2   Connected DSPL overview.

5. The SPL sends the update to the CP.
6. The CP updates itself using the update information from the SPL.

According to these characteristics, we characterize a connected DSPL as follows:

- **Degree of autonomy:** The system depends on the SPL availability to get the system updates to perform the adaptation.
- **Adaptation capabilities:** To address adaptation, variability knowledge indicates the involved components. However, some of these components are not installed in the system. In this case, the system has to get these components from the SPL. Hence, a bidirectional connection between the DSPL and the CP is needed. If this connection becomes unavailable, then the adaptation cannot be performed.
- **Computational overload:** A connected DSPL approach introduces the following additional overload in the CP execution: (a) the communication with the SPL (to get system updates) and (b) the online installation of updates.

7.3.2 Disconnected DSPL

Disconnected DSPLs produce a CP that can reconfigure itself to deal with foreseen contextual changes. Disconnected DSPLs are usually applied when the number of reconfigurations is finite and can be foreseen; thus a contingency plan may be built, giving the CP an optimum response whereby it can restore itself quickly to the state where most of the services are correctly working. Unlike the case with connected DSPLs, the CP can reconfigure itself without any DSPL dependency.

CPs are augmented with variability knowledge and quiescent components in order to perform the reconfiguration, as seen in Figure 7.3:

1. The CP senses a relevant change that starts the adaptation process. Both changes in the environment and in the CP itself can trigger the adaptation process.
2. The CP calculates a new configuration to deal with the sensed change.
   2.1 If there is no configuration that satisfies the product requisites, adaptation fails.
3. The CP reconfigures itself to apply the calculated configuration. The reconfiguration operation implies (a) to start/stop components and (b) to establish connections between them.

According to these criteria, we characterize a disconnected DSPL as follows:

- **Degree of autonomy:** The CP has no dependency on the SPL to perform the adaptation because there is no need for any connection between the SPL and the CP. The adaptation depends only on CP resources. The CP reconfigures itself to perform adaptation.
- **Adaptation capabilities:** In general, the more variability knowledge the system has about itself and its variants, the more adaptive the system will be. This knowledge is captured in the variability models incorporated within the system. However, the variability models must be complemented with system components. Some components conform to the initial system configuration, while the others are used in system reconfiguration. In conclusion, the adaptation capabilities depend on the knowledge captured in

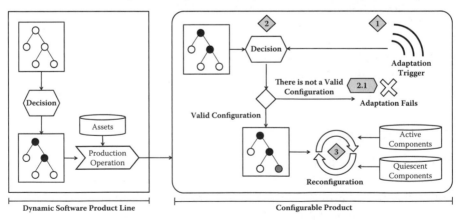

Figure 7.3 Disconnected DSPL overview.

the models and on the number of components that can be activated in system reconfiguration.

■ **Computational overload:** A disconnected DSPL approach introduces a computational overload to the system execution when the adaptation is triggered. This overload comes from (a) the model queries and (b) the execution of the reconfiguration (starting, stopping, and linking system components).

7.3.3 Conclusions

We have presented a brief analysis of the two main SPL-based approaches published in the literature that provide support for the development of adaptive systems with some autonomic degree. In this analysis, we have focused on the adaptation steps that these approaches propose. Finally, we present an analysis of their advantages and drawbacks for the development of adaptive pervasive systems. In particular, we focus on where the adaptation is performed in these approaches, whether in the SPL (connected SPL) or in the system itself (disconnected SPL).

7.4 Evolution and Involution Scenarios for Autonomic Pervasive Systems

Pervasive systems can be found in numerous and heterogeneous domains such as smart homes, health care systems, mobile devices, automotive applications, emergency situations, and urban domains. All of these application domains have different evolutionary needs, depending on the relevant evolution and involution scenarios.

In this section, we propose a categorization of pervasive systems from the evolutionary point of view—how pervasive systems respond to changes in their environment. The aim of this categorization is to establish a correlation between the knowledge required for handling in-system evolution issues and the knowledge used to design the SPLs.

SPLs for pervasive systems accomplish the construction of software systems by evolving numerous resources: sensors, actuators, and services provided by external software systems. These resources are meant to be used by the software system to achieve certain user goals (Lapouchnian et al. 2005). However, resources are very dynamic in pervasive systems. Therefore, the system must adapt dynamically according to the available resources to fulfill these goals in an autonomous way.

Since pervasive resources (R) are highly dynamic and user goals (G) can change over time, the following scenarios may arise:

1. **A resource becomes unavailable:** The software system must achieve the same goals using fewer resources ([G, R–1], see Figure 7.4, section 1). This scenario can be identified in domains such as automotive applications, mobile devices, or urban domains. A representative scenario is the Bosch Gasoline System SPL for gasoline engine control units (Tischer et al. 2007), where the system requires knowledge about how to simulate an unavailable resource by using the available resources.

2. **A new resource becomes available:** The software system can use a new resource to achieve the same user goals ([G, R+1], see Figure 7.4, section 2). This scenario can be identified in domains such us smart homes or mobile devices. A representative scenario is the SPL for home automation systems (Voelter and Groher 2007), where the system requires knowledge about how to involve the new resource to contribute in achieving the user goal.

3. **The user pursues a new goal:** The software must achieve a new user goal with the same resources ([G+1, R], see Figure 7.4, section 3). This scenario can be identified in domains such as smart homes, health care, or emergency situations. The user demands new functionality from the system that was foreseen when designing the SPL but that was not selected when producing the system. For instance, in a smart home when the users are ready to go on holidays, they may want the presence-simulation functionality, which deters thieves by acting as if there were people at home.

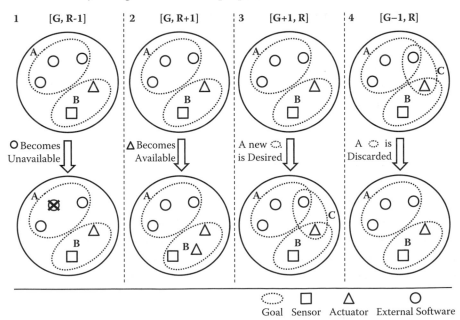

Figure 7.4 Evolution scenarios.

4. **The user discards a goal:** The software system must achieve fewer goals using the same resources ([G–1, R], see Figure 7.4, section 4). This scenario can be seen as a particular case of scenario 2 (a new resource becomes available). Discarding a goal does not always imply removing its resources. The resources associated with the discarded goal are now available to support other goals.

Through the analysis of different reconfiguration needs, we have detected several suitable reconfiguration scenarios (Cetina, Fons, and Pelechano 2008), and we have classified those reconfiguration scenarios into two groups:

- **Involution scenarios:** In scenarios of this kind, the set of active features changes, but there are no new features included. The new configuration of a system is performed by activating or deactivating the available features. These kinds of scenarios happen whenever an adaptation requirement is triggered from the system.
- **Evolution scenarios:** In scenarios of this kind, the set of features is modified by the usage of new features or the update of existing ones. The new configuration of a system can be considered as a new version.

These two kind of scenarios can impact the system in a different way. Involution scenarios involve only a change in the feature state (e.g., enable or disable a feature), so the possible combination of active features is limited in number. Thus, the number of involution scenarios is finite. However, evolution scenarios are difficult to anticipate, as an unknown number of features may appear.

Considering the time dimension, involution scenarios can occur in a more unexpected way than evolution scenarios do. Evolution scenarios are commonly related to upgrade activities. These upgrading activities can be scheduled, making evolution scenarios more predictable (users can decide when to upgrade). However, involution scenarios might arise from unpredictable events such as a device breakdown or an unavailable service. In these cases, the fastest response is needed to restore a stable state of the system where functionality is at least maintained or reduced as little as possible.

7.5 Applying SPLs to Build Autonomic Pervasive Systems

Although traditional SPL engineering recognizes that variation points are bound at different stages of development, and possibly also at runtime, it typically binds variation points before the delivery of the software. In contrast, DSPL engineers typically are not concerned with pre-runtime variation points.

However, they recognize that, in practice, mixed approaches might be feasible, where some variation points related to the environment's static properties are bound before runtime and others related to the dynamic properties are bound at runtime.

Current DSPL approaches address the design of the dynamic reconfiguration of configurable products in an ad hoc way. We believe that, to improve these approaches, it is necessary to systematically capture, by means of (feature) models, all the possible configurations of a system as a product family. These product configurations enable the system/product to automatically reconfigure the product from one configuration of the family to another. This section describes an approach for dynamic software reconfiguration in software product families based on variability management. The solution presented in this chapter allows for the automatic management of the evolution within the product family.

SPLs employ a two-life-cycle approach that separates domain and application engineering. Domain engineering involves analyzing the product line as a whole and producing any common (and reusable) variable parts. In contrast, application engineering involves creating product-specific parts and integrating all aspects of individual products. Both life cycles can rely on fundamentally different processes—for example, agile application engineering combined with plan-driven domain engineering.

To achieve the goal of dynamic reconfiguration, the system needs to know about itself and how to cope with both evolution and involution scenarios. The scope, commonality, and variability (SCV) analysis (Coplien, Hoffman, and Weiss 1998) that was made to design the SPLs (domain engineering) can contribute to this dynamical reconfiguration. To reuse the SCV analysis, it is necessary to perform the following steps to transfer the knowledge from the SPL design to the runtime system in a systematic way:

1. **Reusing the SPL reconfiguration knowledge:** Identify the useful knowledge from the SCV analysis to obtain the dynamic reconfiguration.
2. **Extend the SPL:** Extend the SPLs for pervasive systems to incorporate the relevant SCV knowledge to the pervasive system.
3. **Introduce an autonomic reconfigurator component:** Improve the pervasive system architecture by using the SCV knowledge to obtain the dynamic reconfiguration.

The aim of these steps is to translate the relevant SCV knowledge from the SPL design to the SPL output by introducing an autonomic reconfigurator component.

7.5.1 Reusing the SPL Reconfiguration Knowledge

To enable system adaptation, it is required to know about (a) the current state of the system and (b) the possible ways of changing it. In the present work, models are

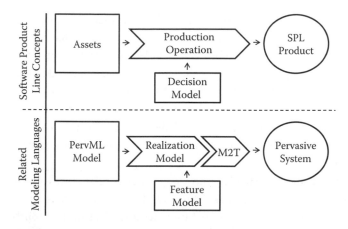

Figure 7.5   SPL following the MDD approach.

used for both purposes by querying them at runtime to perform adaptation. On the one hand, models are used for capturing the state of system components and the communication channels among them. On the other hand, the space of possible system changes is captured by means of feature modeling techniques.

The possible ways of changing a system (e.g., enabling the security feature) can be obtained by reasoning through a model that captures all the possible system features and their dependencies. This is acceptable for evolution scenarios where the system is being upgraded. However, since involution scenarios require an immediate adaptation, information required for the system reaction is precalculated in models. In this way, the effort of reasoning over the different possibilities of adaptation is avoided.

Previous works (Czarnecki et al. 2005; Schmidt, Nechypurenko, and Wuchner 2005; Trujillo, Batory, and Diaz 2007) address this same issue of applying model-driven development (MDD) to SPL development. Our work also uses MDD to transfer the knowledge from the SPL design to the SPL products. Figure 7.5 illustrates the relationship between these modeling languages and the SPL concepts. The following subsections present those modeling languages and identify the knowledge that can be reused to deal with these evolution scenarios.

7.5.1.1 The PervML Model

Pervasive Modeling Language (PervML) (Muñoz and Pelechano 2006) is a domain-specific language (DSL) for describing pervasive systems using high-level abstraction concepts. This language is focused on specifying heterogeneous services in concrete physical environments such as the services of a smart home. These services can be combined to offer more complex functionality by means of interactions. These services can also start the interaction as a reaction to changes in the environment.

The main concepts of PervML are: (a) a *service* coordinates the interaction between suppliers to accomplish specific tasks (these suppliers can be hardware or software systems); (b) a *binding provider* (BP) is a supplier adapter that embeds the issues of dealing with heterogeneous technologies; (c) an *interaction* is a description of a set of ordered invocations between services; and (d) a *trigger* is an ECA (event condition action) rule that describes how a service reacts to changes in its environment. Figure 7.6 illustrates the relationships between these concepts. This DSL has been applied to develop solutions in the smart-home domain (Muñoz, Pelechano, and Cetina 2006).

The PervML model provides knowledge that is related to the evolution scenario 2 (a new resource becomes available). The BP concept is the key element for managing new resources. The BP provides a level of indirection between the services and the resources. Resource operations interact with the environment (sensors and actuators) and provide functionality from external software systems. Services coordinate these resource operations to offer high-level functionality. If the resource operations do not match the service expectations, then a BP is used to adapt these operations. Hence, the BPs decouple services from resource operations. This property is essential for introducing extensibility to new devices and avoids having to modify existing services to support the operations presented by new devices.

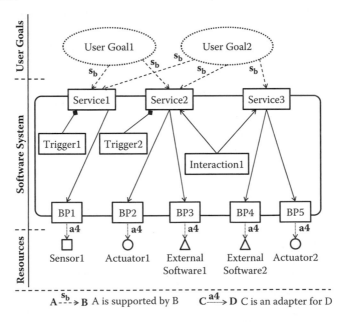

Figure 7.6   The main abstractions of a pervasive system according to the PervML language.

7.5.1.2 The FAMA Feature Model

Feature models are widely used to describe the set of products in a software product line in terms of features. In these models, features are hierarchically linked in a treelike structure and are optionally connected by cross-tree constraints. There are many proposals about the type of the relationships and the graphical representation of feature models (Schobbens et al. 2007). We have chosen the Feature Model Analyzer (FAMA) (Benavides, Cortés, and Trinidad 2005) as the modeling language because it is oriented to feature reasoning and also because it has good tool support.

The FAMA feature model allows us to introduce knowledge related to scenario 3 (the user pursues a new goal). From the point of view of the user, the goals represent his/her intentions (Lapouchnian et al. 2005). From the point of view of the system, the features represent the functionality to support the user intentions. Yu et al. (2005) present mappings from user goals to feature models. To support a new user goal, the related features must be enabled. This step implies extending the production operation to provide the required assets. The architecture must also be improved to introduce the knowledge from these models in order to dynamically integrate these assets. Thus, the goals are only limited by the available resources.

7.5.1.3 The Realization Model

The realization model is an extension that we have incorporated in the Atlas Model Weaving (AMW) model (Fabro, Bezivin, and Valduriez 2006) to relate the SPL features with the PervML elements. AMW is a model for establishing relationships between models. Our extension augments the AMW relationship with the default and alternative tags. This augmented relationship is applied between features and PervML elements (BPs and services). In the context of a BP, the default relationship means that the BP is selected for the initial configuration of the system. The alternative relationship means that the BP is considered a quiescent element that should be incorporated into the SPL product, but it does not participate in the initial configuration. Quiescent BPs provide an alternative BP to replace the default BP in case of fault. The more quiescent BPs that can be identified, the more flexible the adaptation will be.

The realization model provides knowledge related to involution scenario 1 (a resource becomes unavailable). The level of indirection introduced by the BPs facilitates the use of alternative resources, and the realization model determines the applicability of the BPs. Self-healing of the system is performed by applying a quiescent BP to a suitable resource. Quiescent elements and the realization model enable the autonomic reconfigurator to establish a dynamic binding at runtime.

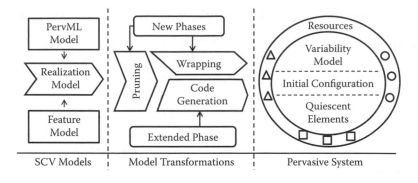

Figure 7.7   SPL extensions.

7.5.2 Extending the SPL

Once the relevant SCV knowledge has been identified, it must be transferred to the SPL product. In this step, the variability model for the relevant SCV knowledge is obtained, and the model is prepared to be deployed in the software system platform. Figure 7.7 shows the extensions incorporated in the production operation. There are two new phases (pruning and wrapping), and the code-generation phase has been enriched.

7.5.2.1 The Pruning Phase

A fundamental problem in SPL engineering is that a real product line can easily incorporate several thousands of variable features (Loesch and Ploedereder 2007). Incorporating variability models to assist the system evolution impacts the complexity and system performance. The incorporated latency is determined by (a) a model reasoner and (b) the size of the variability model. The efficiency of the model reasoner is beyond the scope of this work, and there are other works that address this problem (Benavides, Cortés, and Trinidad 2005). The size of the model can be optimized by taking care of the specific evolutionary needs of each specific domain.

The pruning phase performs model-to-model (M2M) transformations to prune the SCV models. For each one of the evolutionary scenarios that is not relevant (or interesting) in the specific domain, the pruning phase applies a set of pruning rules. These rules only prune the model elements that provide information that is related to the undesired scenarios. For example, the following algorithm describes the rules for pruning scenario 3 (the user pursues a new goal):

1. Delete the relationships (from the realization model) that are reachable from an unselected feature (FAMA feature model).
2. Delete the model elements (from the PervML model) that are not involved in a relationship (realization model).
3. Delete the features that are not selected by the user (FAMA feature model).

These rules have been implemented using the INRIA Atlas Transformation Language (ATL) and tools. They take the SCV models as input and return a pruned variability model. We have defined a set of ATL rules for each scenario, which can be applied in chain to prune more than one scenario.

7.5.2.2 The Wrapping Phase

The wrapping phase is performed after the pruning phase and has two steps. In the first step, the FAMA feature model, the realization model, and the PervML model are joined in a stand-alone XMI file (variability model). In the second step, the variability model is prepared for the specific software platform. This step depends on the deploying platform. In our case, the specific platform is OSGi (Open Services Gateway initiative) (Marples and Kriens 2001), and the model has to be wrapped in an OSGi bundle.

In summary, we can state that the SCV models describe a software system and its variants. Then, the pruning phase eliminates the variants that are related to irrelevant (or uninteresting) evolution scenarios, and the wrapping phase prepares the variability model for the deploying platform.

7.5.2.3 The Code Generation Phase

The code-generation phase translates the model elements into the implementation code. This translation is performed by applying a model-to-text (M2T) transformation to a subset of the PervML model. This subset is made up of the elements involved in a default relationship with a selected feature. The transformation takes the subset model as input and generates the OSGi bundles with the Java implementation (Cetina et al. 2007). An OSGi bundle contains all the Java classes related to only one PervML concept (service bundles, interaction bundles, trigger bundles, and BP bundles). These bundles make up the initial configuration of the system, and they are installed and started in the OSGi environment.

The extension to this phase addresses the generation of the quiescent elements. These elements are those PervML elements that, after the pruning phase, are not related to any selected feature or those elements that are related to an alternative relationship. The generated bundles represent variations to the system: They can transit from an active (operational state) to a quiescent (idle) state and the other way around. These alternative bundles are the building blocks to perform the dynamic reconfiguration. The following section describes how the system is dynamically reconfigured using these bundles and the variability model.

7.5.3 Introducing the Autonomic Reconfigurator Component

The autonomic reconfigurator component is responsible for applying the autonomic behavior to the system architecture by performing dynamic bindings, after taking the available resources and the variability model into account. This component is

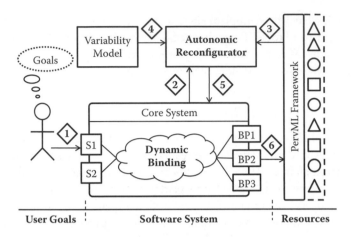

Figure 7.8   Reconfiguration strategy.

involved in the steps of resource discovery, model querying, and reconfiguration execution. Figure 7.8 shows these steps.

1. The user invokes a service of the system to achieve a specific goal.
2. The software system core asks the autonomic reconfigurator component for a dynamic binding of services and resources by using BPs.
3. The autonomic reconfigurator layer discovers the available resources by using the discovery capabilities of the PervML framework (Muñoz and Pelechano 2006).
4. The variability model is queried to perform the dynamic binding according to the available resources. The autonomic reconfigurator gets a set of relationships between services and BPs from the variability model. If this set is empty, the reconfiguration procedure is stopped and the user is informed that there are no suitable resources to fulfill the goal.
5. The autonomic reconfigurator component performs the binding of services and BPs. If there is more than one feasible binding, the bindings that involve bundles from the *default* category are preferred (versus the *alternative* ones). This step is performed by using the dynamic capabilities of the OSGi framework (Lee, Nordstedt, and Helal 2003) to install, start, restart, and uninstall services and BPs (wrapped in OSGi bundles) without restarting the entire system.
6. Once all the bindings between services and BPs are performed, the system is ready to access the available resources.

These steps are performed when the user starts the interaction using a concrete service. However, in a pervasive system, the interaction can also be started by the resources. For instance, when a presence sensor detects a person within its action range, the alarm service is started. To cope with these situations, steps 3 to 5 are performed when there is a change in the availability of any resource.

7.6 Case Study: An Autonomic Smart Home

We illustrate the proposed SPL for autonomic pervasive systems by modeling a smart-home family: a localized technology-augmented environment where people perform everyday life activities. This section presents the models of the SPL and the output smart home produced by the SPL. Then, we identify a set of adaptation scenarios to check the adaptation capabilities. Finally, we describe how the smart home reconfigures itself when adaptation tests are applied.

7.6.1 The Models of the SPL

The SPL developed for this case study addresses automated lighting, presence detection, and security functionality for the smart homes. The SPL models describe the collection of all smart homes that can be produced in this SPL. A smart home is uniquely defined by the selections on the FAMA feature model. These selected features determine (by means of the realization model) which elements of the PervML model are used for the initial configuration of the smart home.

From an adaptive point of view, the unselected features of the FAMA feature model represent variants to the selected smart home. These unselected features determine which elements of the PervML model are used to dynamically reconfigure the system. All these models are presented as follows:

1. **The FAMA feature model:** This model (see the top of Figure 7.9, evolution scenario knowledge) determines the initial and the potential features of the smart home. The grey features are the features selected to specify a member of the smart-home family. The white features represent potential variants. Initially, the smart home provides automated lighting and a security system. This security system relies on perimeter presence detection (outside the home) and a visual alarm. The system can potentially be upgraded with in-home presence detection and more alarms to enhance home security.

   As stated in Section 7.4, supporting a new user goal is translated into enabling more features. Some features can be enabled by plugging in new physical resources, while other features can be enabled because the restrictions (mandatory, excludes, or requires) are resolved. For instance, features 8 and 13 can be enabled if a volumetric detector is plugged in. Once feature 8 is enabled, the *requires* dependency from feature 2 to 8 can be fulfilled.

2. **The PervML model:** This model (see the bottom of Figure 7.9, system knowledge) describes the building blocks for the assembly of a pervasive system (Muñoz and Pelechano 2006). The grey blocks implement the functionality

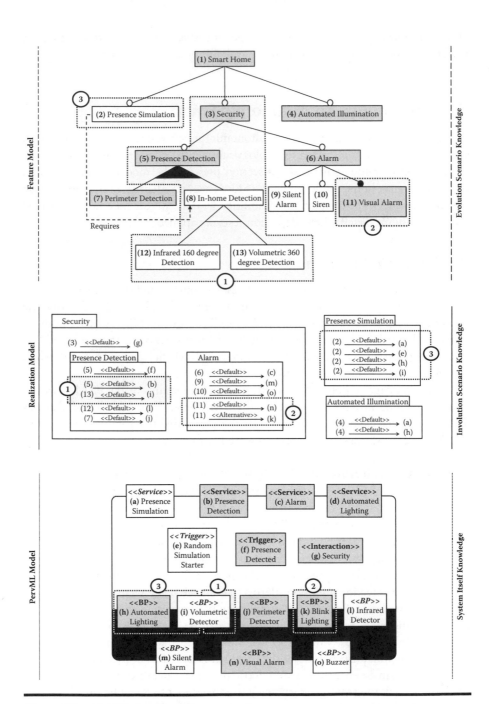

Figure 7.9 Models for the SPL.

of the selected features. The white blocks enable the reconfiguration of the system. The (a) and (e) blocks implement the functionality for the unselected presence-simulation feature. The (i), (k), (l), (m), and (o) blocks provide adapters for the new resources that can become available, as mentioned in Section 7.4. The autonomic reconfigurator prioritizes the gray blocks over the white blocks, since they are related to the original features of the system, as stated in Section 7.5.3.

3. **The realization model:** This model (see the middle of Figure 7.9, involution scenario knowledge) establishes the relationships between the features and the PervML elements. Section 7.5.1.3 introduced the alternative relationship to identify binding providers (BPs) and services that mitigate system faults. For instance, the visual alarm feature is related to a BP (n) for visual alarms, but, alternatively, it can be replaced with a BP (k) that emulates the visual alarm by using the general lighting.

7.6.2 Adaptation Scenarios

The adaptation scenarios are designed to evaluate the adaptation capabilities of a smart home. They describe changes in the physical environment or in the user intentions according to the scenarios described in Section 7.4. These adaptation scenarios are performed by using our test bed (see Figure 7.10), which features a scaled smart home driven by a bare-bones gateway, an Ultra Mobile PC (UMPC) for displaying the user interfaces, and several European InstaBus (EIB) devices. This smart home represents the physical resources for performing hot plugging tests. The bare-bones gateway runs the OSGi server, where all the services, BPs, triggers, and interactions are deployed, and it also runs the nonphysical resources, such as a weather forecaster or an instant-messaging client. Figure 7.10 shows the EIB devices related to the adaptation tests.

1. **A new resource becomes available:** The security system relies on a presence-detection service. This service integrates the functionality of several sensors. Hence, the more coverage the sensors have, the more reliable the service will be. In this adaptation scenario we improve the coverage by incorporating a new in-home volumetric sensor (see the top of Figure 7.11).

2. **A resource becomes unavailable:** In a security system, the alarm is a key element. A fault (or manipulation) of this resource can invalidate the entire security system. The aim of this resource is to alert the neighbors of an unexpected situation in the house. There are several kinds of alarms, such as visual, acoustic, or silent alarms. This adaptation scenario focuses on dynamically replacing a damaged visual alarm with another one that consists of a fast and constant blinking of all the lights in the home (see the middle of Figure 7.11).

Figure 7.10   Test bed.

3. **The user pursues a new goal:** The addition of new resources to the system reinforces the support of current goals. It can also potentially enable the system to support new goals. Achieving presence simulation involves automated lighting and an in-home-presence sensor (see Figure 7.9). The new plugged-in home sensor enables the system to offer the presence-simulation service, which was not previously supported (see the bottom of Figure 7.11).

7.6.3 Smart-Home Reconfiguration

The knowledge from the SPL models enables the autonomic reconfigurator to establish a dynamic binding between the system components. When the adaptation scenarios are applied, the system reconfigures itself as follows:

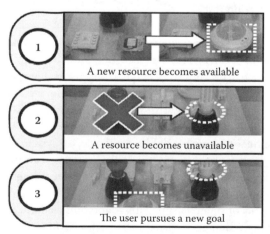

Figure 7.11   Adaptation tests.

1. **A new resource becomes available:** When a new resource is discovered by the PervML framework, it establishes a new connection with the related device. This corresponds to steps 3 to 5 of Section 7.5.3. First (step 3, Figure 7.8), the PervML framework identifies the category ID of the new resource for the autonomic reconfigurator. To identify the binding provider PervML element (BP) that is appropriate for this resource (step 4, Figure 7.8), the autonomic reconfigurator queries the PervML model with the category ID. The autonomic reconfigurator must also identify the services that have to be aware of the BP. The realization model is queried for the features related to the BP. Then, the autonomic reconfigurator navigates from these features to the first parent feature that is related to a service. The set of parent features indicates the services that have to be used. Finally, the dynamic binding between the BP and these services is performed (step 5, Figure 7.8). These bindings are implemented by using the OSGi wire class (an OSGi wire is an implementation of the publish-subscribe pattern oriented to dynamic systems). The BP for the new resource (in a quiescent state) is started and subscribed to the identified service wires.

   This behavior is tested by applying the first adaptation scenario of Section 7.6.2 (see the top of Figure 7.11). When the volumetric detector is plugged in, the presence-detection service needs to be aware of its notifications. The volumetric-detector BP is related to feature (13), and the first parent feature that is related to a service is the one labeled with a (5). Hence, the volumetric-detector BP is subscribed to the wire of the presence-detected service. The relevant model elements of this example are denoted with the number 1 in Figure 7.4.

2. **A resource becomes unavailable:** When the PervML framework detects an unavailable resource, a dynamic binding to an alternative BP is requested from the autonomic reconfigurator. Steps 2 to 5 of Section 7.5.3 are applied to perform this binding. First (step 2, Figure 7.8), the active service asks the autonomic reconfigurator for a dynamic binding with the resources. The PervML framework looks for the available resources (step 3). The autonomic framework queries the models (step 4) for the feature that represents the active service of step 2. The BPs that are related to this feature (realization model) are evaluated against the available resources. If there is no BP available with the default tag, then the first BP with the alternative tag is selected. The binding is performed by subscribing the selected BP to the wire of the active service (step 5).

   This behavior is tested by applying the second adaptation scenario of Section 7.6.2 (see the middle of Figure 7.11). When the visual alarm fails, the alarm service needs an alternative supplier. The automated lights can be adapted to simulate a visual alarm. The BP (k) is selected to adapt the behavior of the automated lights by performing a continuous blinking. The relevant model elements of this example are denoted with the number 2 in Figure 7.4.

3. **The user pursues a new goal:** Plugging in new resources can enable the system to support new user goals. The features that are related to the new resources can resolve the restrictions (mandatory, excludes, or requires) of other features. However, reasoning about feature dependencies is not a trivial task. We have implemented a prototypical reasoner within the autonomic reconfigurator using the EMF (Eclipse Modeling Framework) runtime. This is just a proof of concept; we plan to integrate the FAMA reasoner, which is based on constraint programming. This reasoner determines the new features that can be enabled. Then, the autonomic reconfigurator starts the quiescent bundles and performs the suitable subscriptions to the OSGi wires.

This behavior is tested by applying the third adaptation scenario of Section 7.6.2 (see at the bottom of Figure 7.11). The new volumetric detector involves features (13) and (8), and feature (8) resolves the require dependency of feature (2). The relevant model elements of this example are denoted with the number 3 in Figure 7.9.

7.7 Related Work

The approach presented in this chapter has been significantly influenced by several related projects on feature model reasoning and automatic variant selection. For example, Mannion (2002) presents a method for specifying product-line architecture (PLA) compositional requirements using first-order logic. The validity of a variant can be checked by determining whether (or not) a PLA satisfies a logical statement. Benavides, Cortés, and Trinidad (2005) provide a mapping from feature selection to a constraint solver problem (CSP). They deal with automated reasoning on feature models using CSP. Although both approaches treat automatic manipulation of feature models, they do not use this knowledge to improve SPL product adaptability.

Lemlouma and Layaida (2004) present a framework for adapting and customizing content before delivering it to a mobile device. Their strategy takes into account device preferences and capabilities. The Scatter tool (White et al. 2007) supports efficient online variant selection. This tool captures the requirements of a PLA and the resources of a mobile device and then quickly constructs a custom variant for the device. Although both of these approaches treat content delivery from the SPL to the devices, the SPL products must stay in touch with the SPL to perform the adaptation. Our approach proposes that SPL products perform the adaptation in an autonomic way, without any dependency on the SPL.

The MADAM approach (Hallsteinsen et al. 2006) is based on SPL techniques to build adaptive systems. This approach builds adaptive systems as component-based systems families with the variability modeled explicitly as part of the family architecture. MADAM uses property annotations on components to describe their quality of service (QoS). For example, a video-streaming component may have properties such as startup time, jitter, and frame drop. At runtime, the adaptation is performed using these properties and a utility function for selecting the component that best fits the current context. We promote decoupling system components from reconfiguration information by using models at runtime. This strategy enables updating the reconfiguration information by means of model replacements or model updates. Furthermore, since our approach uses feature models, we can benefit from current work on feature model reasoning (Benavides, Cortés, and Trinidad 2005) instead of developing ad hoc reasoners.

Trinidad et al. (2007) present a process to automatically build a component model from a feature model based on the assumption that a feature can be modeled as a component. This process focuses on enabling a dynamic SPL to dynamically change a product by activating or deactivating its features at runtime. Our approach follows these ideas by introducing the variability models at runtime. To deal with the latency introduced by reasoning on complex models, we apply the pruning phase, where M2M transformations are applied to prune variability models, as stated in Section 7.5.2.1.

Existing works on adaptive systems (e.g., context-aware and self-healing systems) propose the use of behavior models (Zhang and Cheng 2006) or ontologies (Wagelaar 2005) to dynamically adapt systems according to the operational context. The drawback of behavior models is that the quality of these models depends on the designer experience or creativity, whereas our approach promotes the fact that adaptability behavior is obtained from SPL design in a systematic way. Compared with ontology-based approaches, feature models are views over ontologies (Czarnecki, Kim, and Kalleberg 2006) that narrow these ontologies to the scope defined in the SPL. Decreasing the size of the reasoning model helps to reduce the latency introduced to the systems response, as stated in Section 7.5.2.1.

Zhang and Cheng (2006) introduce a method for constructing and verifying adaptation models using Petri nets. They address directly the verifications of the adaptation models by means of visual inspection and automated analysis. On the other hand, our approach is focused on reuse of the variability modeling of SPLs at runtime. However, our approach can benefit SPL reasoners that are tasked to check system properties (Benavides, Cortés, and Trinidad 2005). Finally, Zhang's approach separates the adaptation specification and nonadaptation specifications, as does our approach. However, our approach introduces precalculated adaptations in order to achieve a faster response in involution scenarios.

Other works on adaptive systems also propose techniques (Schilit, Adams, and Want 1994) that address recognition of current situations by analyzing data from software or hardware environments. These techniques are essential to support dynamic product reconfiguration. They provide criteria to perform the system reconfiguration. Our work uses the device notifications of PervML framework as input to perform the reconfiguration.

7.8 Conclusions and Future Work

In this chapter, we have proposed a model-driven SPL for developing autonomic pervasive systems. The process focuses on reusing the SCV (scope, commonality, and variability) knowledge from the SPL design to the SPL products. This SCV knowledge enables SPL products to deal with evolution in an autonomic way. We have described suitable scenarios where this knowledge can be applied. We have presented SPL extensions to transfer and gather all of this knowledge to the SPL products. Finally, we have made an improvement in architecture (autonomic reconfigurator) in order to be able to reuse this knowledge.

One of the main challenges of testing our approach in the context of smart homes is to simulate the evolution of end-user needs. Furthermore, testers do not usually know the technological possibilities to upgrade a smart home; their thinking is limited by what works for them and their own knowledge of technology. The adaptation scenarios presented in this chapter stimulate tester creativity by means of ideas about alternative configurations of smart homes.

Based on our experience with performing adaptation tests, it turns out that the seamless integration of services and devices presents a challenge to the upgrading of smart homes. Some of our tests fail because testers took too long to find the appropriate feature to tune the behavior of services, or they did not find it at all. This feedback suggests that end users need advanced mechanisms to manipulate feature models. In particular, testers need operations to limit the potential configurations according to a filter, and they also need operations to identify the best products according to a specific criterion.

References

Appavoo, J., K. Hui, C. A. N. Soules, et al. 2003. Enabling autonomic behavior in systems software with hot swapping. *IBM Systems Journal* 42 (1): 60–76.

Benavides, D., R. A. Cortés, and P. Trinidad. 2005. Automated reasoning on feature models. *Lecture Notes in Computer Science* 3520:491–503.

Blair, G. S., G. Coulson, L. Blair, H. Duran-Limon, P. Grace, R. Moreira, and N. Parlavantzas. 2002. Reflection, self-awareness and self-healing in OpenORB. In *Proceedings of the first workshop on self-healing systems*, 9–14. New York: ACM Press.

Cetina, C., J. Fons, and V. Pelechano. 2008. Applying software product lines to build autonomic pervasive systems. In *Proceedings of the 2008 12th international software product line conference*, 117–126. Washington, DC: IEEE Computer Society.

Cetina, C., E. Serral, J. Munoz, and V. Pelechano. 2007. Tool support for model driven development of pervasive systems. In *Proceedings of the 4th international workshop on model-based methodologies for pervasive and embedded software*, 33–44. Washington, DC: IEEE Computer Society.

Coplien, J., D. Hoffman, and D. Weiss. 1998. Commonality and variability in software engineering. *IEEE Software* 15 (6): 37–45.

Czarnecki, K., M. Antkiewicz, C. H. P. Kim, et al. 2005. Model-driven software product lines. In *OOPSLA '05: Companion to the 20th annual ACM SIGPLAN conference on object-oriented programming, systems, languages, and applications*, 126–127. New York: ACM Press.

Czarnecki, K., C. H. P. Kim, and K. T. Kalleberg. 2006. Feature models are views on ontologies. In *Proceedings of the 10th international software product line conference*, 41–51. Washington, DC: IEEE Computer Society.

Diao, Y., J. L. Hellerstein, S. Parekh, et al. 2003. Managing web server performance with autotune agents. *IBM Systems Journal* 42 (1): 136–149.

Fabro, M. D. D., J. Bézivin, and P. Valduriez. 2006. Weaving models with the eclipse AMW plugin. Paper presented at Eclipse modeling symposium, Esslingen, Germany.

Ganek, A. G., and T. A. Corbi. 2003. The dawning of the autonomic computing era. *IBM Systems Journal* 42 (1): 5–18.

Gomaa, H. 2004. *Designing software product lines with UML: From use cases to pattern-based software architectures.* Redwood City, CA: Addison-Wesley Longman.

Hallsteinsen, S., E. Stav, A. Solberg, and J. Floch. 2006. Using product line techniques to build adaptive systems. In *Proceedings of the 10th international software product line conference*, 21–24. Washington, DC: IEEE Computer Society.

Horn, P. 2001. Autonomic computing: IBM's perspective on the state of information technology. IBM, New York.

Jann, J., L. M. Browning, and R. S. Burugula. 2003. Dynamic reconfiguration: Basic building blocks for autonomic computing on IBM pSeries servers. *IBM Systems Journal* 42 (1): 29–37.

Jarvis, S. A., D. P. Spooner, H. N. L. C. Keung, J. R. D. Dyson, L. Zhao, and G. R. Nudd. 2003. Performance-based middleware services for grid computing. In *Proceedings of the autonomic computing workshop: Fifth annual international workshop on active middleware services*, 151–159. Washington, DC: IEEE Computer Society. http://www.dcs.warwick.ac.uk/~saj/papers/AHM.pdf.

Kephart, J. O., and D. M. Chess. 2003. The vision of autonomic computing. *Computer* 36 (1): 41–50.

Lapouchnian, A., S. Liaskos, J. Mylopoulos, et al. 2005. Toward requirements-driven autonomic systems design. In *DEAS '05: Proceedings of the 2005 workshop on design and evolution of autonomic application software*, 1–7. New York: ACM Press.

Lee, C., D. Nordstedt, and S. Helal. 2003. Enabling smart spaces with OSGi. *Pervasive Computing, IEEE* 2 (3): 89–94.

Lee, J., and K. C. Kang. 2006. A feature-oriented approach to developing dynamically reconfigurable products in product line engineering. In *Proceedings of the 10th international software product line conference*, 131–140. Washington, DC: IEEE Computer Society.

Lemlouma, T., and N. Layaida. 2004. Context-aware adaptation for mobile devices. In *Proceedings of the IEEE international conference on mobile data management*, 106–111. Washington, DC: IEEE Computer Society.

Loesch, F., and E. Ploedereder. 2007. Optimization of variability in software product lines. In *Proceedings of the 11th international software product line conference*, 151–162. Washington, DC: IEEE Computer Society.

Mannion, M. 2002. Using first-order logic for product line model validation. In *SPLC 2: Proceedings of the 2nd international conference on software product lines*, 176–187. Berlin/Heidelberg: Springer-Verlag.

Markl, V., G. M. Lohman, and V. Raman. 2003. Leo: An autonomic query optimizer for DB2. *IBM Systems Journal* 42 (1): 98–106.

Marples, D., and P. Kriens. 2001. The open services gateway initiative: An introductory overview. *Communications Magazine, IEEE* 39 (12): 110–114.

McKinley, P., S. Sadjadi, E. Kasten, et al. 2004. Composing adaptive software. *Computer* 37 (7): 56–64.

Muñoz, J., and V. Pelechano. 2006. Applying software factories to pervasive systems: A platform specific framework. Paper presented at the 8th international conference on enterprise information systems, 337–342. ICEIS 2006, Paphos, Cyprus.

Muñoz, J., V. Pelechano, and C. Cetina. 2006. Implementing a pervasive meeting room: A model driven approach. Paper presented at the 3rd international workshop on ubiquitous computing, 13–20. IWUC 2006, Paphos, Cyprus.

Schilit, B., N. Adams, and R. Want. 1994. Context-aware computing applications. In *Proceedings of the workshop on mobile computing systems and applications*, 85–90. Washington, DC: IEEE Computer Society.

Schmidt, D. C., A. Nechypurenko, and E. Wuchner, eds. 2005. MDD for software product lines: Fact or fiction? Paper presented at MoDELS '05 workshop 9.

Schobbens, P.-Y., P. Heymans, J.-C. Trigaux, and Y. Bontemps. 2007. Generic semantics of feature diagrams. *Computer Networks* 51 (2): 456–479.

Tischer, C., A. Muller, M. Ketterer, and L. Geyer. 2007. Why does it take that long? Establishing product lines in the automotive domain. In *Proceedings of the 11th international software product line conference*, 269–274. Berlin/Heidelberg: Springer-Verlag.

Trinidad, P., A. Ruiz-Cortés, J. Peña, and D. Benavides. 2007. Mapping feature models onto component models to build dynamic software product lines. In *Proceedings of the 11th international software product line conference* (SPLC 2007), 51–56, Kyoto, Japan.

Trujillo, S., D. Batory, and O. Diaz. 2007. Feature oriented model driven development: A case study for portlets. In *Proceedings of the 29th international conference on software engineering*, 44–53. Washington, DC: IEEE Computer Society.

van der Linden, F., ed. 2001. *4th international workshop on software product-family engineering*. Lecture Notes in Computer Science, vol. 2290. Berlin/Heidelberg: Springer.

Voelter, M., and I. Groher. 2007. Product line implementation using aspect-oriented and model-driven software development. In *Proceedings of the 11th international software product line conference* (SPLC 2007), 233–242, Kyoto, Japan.

Wagelaar, D. 2005. Towards context-aware feature modelling using ontologies. Paper presented at MoDELS 2005 workshop on MDD for software product lines: Fact or Fiction? Montego Bay, Jamaica.

Weiser, M. 1991. The computer for the 21st century. *Scientific American* 265 (3): 94–104.

White, J., D. C. Schmidt, E. Wuchner, and A. Nechypurenko. 2007. Automating product line variant selection for mobile devices. In *Proceedings of the 11th international software product line conference* (SPLC 2007), 129–140, Kyoto, Japan.

Wright, D., E. Vildjiounaite, I. Maghiros, et al. 2005. Safeguards in a world of ambient intelligence (SWAMI) deliverable D1: The brave new world of ambient intelligence: A state-of-the-art review. Report of the SWAMI consortium to the European Commission under contract 006507.

Yau, S. S., F. Karim, Y. Wang, B. Wang, and S. Gupta. 2002. Reconfigurable context-sensitive middleware for pervasive computing. *IEEE Pervasive Computing* 1 (3): 33–40.

Yu, Y., J. Mylopoulos, A. Lapouchnian, et al. 2005. From stakeholder goals to high-variability software designs. Technical report, University of Toronto. ftp://ftp.cs.toronto.edu/csrg-technical-reports/509/.

Zhang, J., and B. Cheng. 2006. Model-based development of dynamically adaptive software. In *Proceedings of the 28th international conference on software engineering* (ICSE '06), 371–380. New York: ACM Press.

Chapter 8

Development of a Software Product Line for Validation Environments

Belén Magro
Dimetronic, Madrid, Spain

Juan Garbajosa and Jennifer Pérez
Universidad Politécnica de Madrid, Spain

Contents

8.1 Introduction

One of the main issues in software development is to ensure that the final product will satisfy the requirements of the software system. As a consequence, the validation process will require an important effort and investment in cost and time during the software life cycle, not only to ensure that the code is correct, but also to be confident that the final product satisfies the requirements of the system, both functional and nonfunctional. The growing complexity of applications is resulting in an increased relevance of nonfunctional requirements and, therefore, of the validation field.

This chapter is focused on those environments that provide some level of automation for the validation process. Following the IEEE definition (IEEE Std. 610.12-1990), "Validation is the process of evaluating a system or a component during or at the end of the development process to determine whether a system component satisfies the specified requirements." This chapter is concerned with those environments that assist in the validation of the final product, often identified in the literature as *the system*. This kind of validation is often known as acceptance testing. Acceptance testing is defined by the IEEE as "formal testing conducted to determine whether or not a system satisfies its acceptance criteria and to enable the customer to determine whether or not to accept the system" (IEEE Std. 1059–1993). Acceptance testing is becoming increasingly significance in concert with some emerging life-cycle proposals. Such is the case of Agile approaches, as described by Abrahamsson et al. (2002) and Dybå and Dingsøyr (2008).

Validation environments are essential to support requirements checking, especially those requirements that are concerned with the behavior of the system. Validation environments for testing of code are used by test programmers highly skilled in conventional programming languages. In contrast, validation environments for testing the behavioral requirements of the system are used by test engineers who are experts in the final product. There is a significant gap between the concepts that an expert of the final product will make use of to describe the behavior of a system and those other concepts underlying conventional programming languages. Hence, one of the ways in which validation environments can assist the test engineer, who will perform the validation process, is reducing this gap.

Therefore, the expert of the final product of a validation environment will probably not be a programmer with a remarkable background in programming languages. A test engineer will know every detail of the System Under Test (SUT), and he/she will need to perform the testing process in a way that is close to that of the actual system operation.

Validation environments have to support a wide variability scope, since they must be able to test applications of different domains, technologies, and programming languages. For this reason, validation environments are very often highly specialized in issues such as domains, programming languages, and technologies as is the case for FIT (2009), Fitnesse (2009), Easyaccept (Sauvé, Neto, and Cirne 2006), Selenium (2009), and TestingTech (2009). As a consequence, companies have to use different validation environments for different domains, programming languages, or technologies; this means a big investment in specialized staff and tools. Therefore, it is possible to conclude that:

- The test engineer should not be required to have more than some basic programming skills to work with a validation environment.
- Validation environments, desirably, should be domain specific, in line with Cook et al. (2007) and Deursen, Klint, and Visser (2000); this way, test engineers will be able to test the system in a more friendly way.
- Validation environments should somehow be able to be self-adaptable to each SUT and support variability factors such as the test language, the programming language, and the SUT technology. The test language must change, depending on the SUT features, i.e., the commands that the validation environment provides to define tests should be specific to the SUT vocabulary.

For a number of years, we have been taking part in various projects with different partners in which domain-specific validation environments have been necessary. For that reason, we had to develop these environments or we had to integrate them with other tools. Thanks to the different scopes of these projects, such as Dobertsee (2009) and Metses (2000), we had the chance to develop validation environments for different domains and in the context of different life-cycle models. In addition, we could study and analyze the architecture of different domain-specific validation environments as in Garbajosa et al. (2000, 2001), the integration of validation environments into document-centric software engineering environments (Alarcón et al. 2004), the deployment of validation tests in automated environments (Garbajosa and Alarcón 2005), the use of test data for monitoring (Alarcón et al. 2006), and the knowledge stored in models to derive domain-specific validation environments (Yagüe and Garbajosa 2007).

From our experience, we identified that validation environments for different software systems share a set of commonalities and variabilities. As a result, we decided to leverage the invested effort defining a product line for domain-specific validation environments. All these results were materialized in a Test and Operation Environment called TOPEN, which was used for experimenting and has been maturing progressively. The main goal of this chapter is to present those results that have been obtained from the application of a software product line methodology to validation environments. Specifically, it presents the common and generic architecture as well as a set of variability points that allow us to derive different products, i.e., domain-specific validation environments for defining and executing tests on a specific platform. Some other efforts have attempted to address this problem, such as those of Rankin (2002), Sun et al. (2000), and

Williams et al. (2002), though they are more focused on techniques to build good test environments in general, rather than on validation environments. More recently, testing tools have paid attention to domain-specific languages, as in the case of Allen, Shaffer, and Watson (2005); Grant and Reza (2007); and Hartman, Katara, and Paradkar (2007).

This chapter also illustrates how the software product line approach has been applied to produce two different case studies: a digital TV decoder system and a networked slot-machines system. Both case studies developed two different products to validate the interactive services of a digital television decoder and the behavior of a network of interconnected slot machines, respectively. These products are two validation environments with different domain-specific languages for testing, programming languages, and technology platforms (Java Runtime Environment, .NET, OSGI, etc.).

The structure of the chapter is the following: Section 8.2 provides an overview of the product line definition by presenting the steps that have been followed. Section 8.3 gives an introduction to validation environments and presents how the generic architecture has been obtained. Section 8.4 shows how digital-television and slot-machines case studies are derived from the generic software architecture. Section 8.5 reviews the obtained results. Finally, conclusions and further work are presented.

8.2 Product Line Definition

This chapter presents the guiding principles for the development of the software product line for validation environments. The main goal for the development was to produce a reference architecture for validation environments. This required identifying the variability points for deriving domain-specific validation environments. The common architecture, the variability points, and the derivation process of a specific product have been developed following a set of steps. The foundation for these steps is based on previous works from Bosch (2000), D'Souza and Wills (1999), and Mili et al. (2002) as well as the first author's experience on software development of critical systems. The set of steps has been defined as follows:

▪ **Step 1:** *Definition and analysis of the domain.* The first step was to analyze the validation domain to understand whether the product line development for validation environments was feasible and advantageous. Once the advantages and the disadvantages were identified, and the feasibility of the development could be confirmed, it was possible to specify the general domain requirements and other requirements, depending on specific products. These requirements are the source for defining the commonalities and variabilities of the domain, i.e., the baseline for developing the common architecture and its variation points.

■ **Step 2:** *Product planning.* The second step considered all kinds of requirements associated with the different products that can result from the product line deployment. Therefore, this step was concerned with identifying new requirements that emerge after the product line deployment. Special attention was paid to those requirements that can become visible in the short term and that are relevant to most of the products that can be derived from the reference architecture. Another set of requirements were those that can increase the complexity of the product implementation. The main outcome of this step was a release planning.

■ **Step 3:** *Design of the architecture of reference.* The third step defined the architecture of reference. This definition comprises the identification of the architectural components as well as the design of these components and their interactions.

■ **Step 4:** *Development of the reference architecture components.* The fourth step specified in detail and broke down the components of the architecture, defined in the previous step. This step was performed using the concept of parametrical components. It is usually called a *framework.* A framework is a reusable and non-product-specific component that is partially implemented. There are parts of the framework that can change, depending on the product. As such, in this step, the common parts of the components were implemented, and the implementation needs for the variability points were clearly identified.

■ **Step 5:** *Architecture evaluation.* In the fifth step, previous steps were reviewed, and the architecture of reference was evaluated to detect problems and drawbacks. The main goal of this step was to obtain feedback from previous stages.

■ **Step 6:** *Derivation of a specific product.* Finally, the sixth step developed the variability points of the architecture of reference for the specific product. At this step, the variable parts of the architectural frameworks were specified for each specific product by introducing the specific piece of code in the framework as a parameter. Finally, the domain-specific architecture was evaluated and reviewed to provide feedback to previous stages.

8.3 Validation Environments

This section presents the main requirements of a product line for validation environments. In addition, it shows how the steps presented in Section 8.2 have been applied to develop the product line.

8.3.1 Domain Overview

Validation environments support the test engineer in his/her work of testing the behavior of the SUT. The test engineer and the SUT are the external entities of a validation environment, i.e., the entities that interact with the validation environment (see Figure 8.1).

To define the main requirements that a validation environment should provide, an analysis of a representative set of the existing validation environments was performed. This analysis started a few years ago thanks to some experience exchange carried out between the authors and a group of European Space Agency (ESA) engineers, members of the PROBA2 project team. This group had the mission of developing the common electrical ground support equipment (EGSE) system for PROBA2, a low-cost satellite, as outlined by Valera (1999). Since space systems are very complex and require an exhaustive checkout phase, this PROBA2 project allowed us to get to know how a validation activity needs to be performed and the required infrastructure for automated validation. At the same time, we were developing a validation environment for CMIP-based network systems (CMIP 1999), and we realized that the PROBA2 EGSE architecture and the architecture of our validation environment had a high number of commonalities. From this study, a set of requirements for validation environments was obtained. The objective was to get a collection of the requirements that was as complete as possible for a generic validation environment. Requirements were divided into several groups:

- *Functionality*: test definition, test execution, analysis of testing faults, test management, test planning, and test process measurement
- *Architectural properties*: portability, adaptability, reusability, maintainability, and openness for integration
- *Test engineer assistance*: this assistance had to be provided for the items under the first item number of this list, namely, functionality
- *Support for different process models*: this implied that the validation environment should not be constrained by a process model but should be used under different models and integrated with tools and environments supporting different process models
- *Interoperability*: integration with other environments; this is the case for process model support and also for test analysis or any other situation in which it is worthwhile integrating a third-party tool to achieve a new or improved functionality

These requirements were later compared to some technical publications, such as Protest II (Prolog Test Environment), TAOS (Testing with Analysis and Oracle

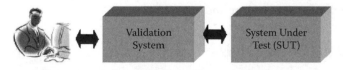

Figure 8.1 Validation environments.

Support), and CITE (CONVEX, Integrated Test Environment) (Eickelmann and Richardson 1996); RTI verified (Tufarolo et al. 1999); embedded test software (Mathur 1978); and Test Automation Framework (TAF) tools (Blackburn and Busser 2003). Table 8.1 shows which requirements (rows) are provided by each validation environment (columns).These works had some of the identified requirements in our analysis, but not all of them. Thus, the need to provide an environment that could support all of them came out.

The obtained requirements can be classified into three categories: common functional, common nonfunctional, and variable. Common requirements are those that never change. Variable requirements are those that are going to change depending on the product. Functional requirements are those that are regarded in light of the functionality of the validation environment, whereas nonfunctional requirements are not regarded in terms of their functionality. These requirements (R1, R2, etc.) are presented in detail as follows:

1. Common functional requirements of a validation environment
   - R1: To support validation, the process must include the assisted definition of test procedures and the assisted execution of test procedures.
   - R2: The state of the SUT must always be shown.
   - R3: System monitoring must be supported.
   - R4: On-line and off-line commands and test-procedure execution must be supported.
   - R5: Commands and test procedures sent to the SUT and the SUT responses must be held under control.
   - R6: The SUT information that is needed to perform the validation process must be stored.
2. Common nonfunctional requirements of a validation environment
   - R7: The reliability of the environment must not be less than 90%. A failure in one of the components must not affect the rest of the components.
   - R8: The performance of the system must not be less than 85%. The time of the execution processing and response time, from a command, must be reduced to a minimum.
   - R9: Flexibility must be provided to adapt the validation environment to new requirements.
   - R10: Maintainability must be ensured and easy to perform.
   - R11: The security of the stored information must be ensured.
3. Variable requirements of a validation environment
   - R12: One or more graphical user interfaces (GUI) of several kinds should be provided to test the SUT. They can be specific for each SUT, and can be either purely graphical or textual (formal language, natural language, etc.). It should be clarified that the term man–machine interface (MMI) is less frequent than GUI, but for some communities it is more meaningful.

Table 8.1 Analysis of Validation Environments

	Protest II	TAOS	CITE	RTI Verified	Embedded Test SW	TAF Tools
Criterion 1: Functionality						
Test execution	yes	yes	yes	yes	yes	yes
Test development	yes	yes	yes	no	yes	yes
Metrics of testing	yes	yes	yes	no	no	yes
Analysis of testing faults	no	yes	yes	yes	no	yes
Test management	no	yes	yes	yes	no	...
Test planning	no	no	no	no	no	partially
Criterion 2: Architecture Properties						
Portability, Adaptability, Reusability, Maintainability	no	reusability	reusability	maintainability	yes	reusability and maintainability
Criterion 3: Operator Support						
Test definition	...	...	...	no	...	no
Test execution	...	...	...	no	...	...

Assessment of the results	...	...	...	no	yes	yes
Criterion 4: Support of Other Process Models						
	no	yes	yes	no	no	partially
Criterion 5: Interoperability						
(Integration into others' tools)	no	no	yes	partially	no	yes

- R13: More than one operation mode to test the SUT must be provided: at least both command mode and procedural mode.
- R14: One GUI should support more than one operation mode.
- R15: Different mechanisms for controlling the test-procedure execution should be provided.
- R16: The integration of tools for analyzing the testing results must be supported.
- R17: Mechanisms for translating and generating code should be provided. They should transform procedures and commands in domain-specific test languages into commands of SUT languages and vice versa.
- R18: As the actual time for the execution of a command should be shown, low-level mechanisms that may be specific for each SUT will be required.

Domain-specific test languages could have different representations, such as graphical, natural language, or formal language. In a very early publication (Garbajosa, Tejedor, and Wolff 1994), three forms for the commands and test procedures were identified: the *external form*, a representation at user level, i.e., using natural language or pictorial resources; the *internal form*, which is highly independent from any formalism and which uses an abstract representation; and the *target form*, which uses a concrete, SUT programming language. Transformations between all of them must be supported; this transformation is called *generation* within this chapter. For instance, generation of tests from a domain-oriented language test procedure stands for transformation between this external form (domain oriented) and the internal form (SUT oriented).

From the analysis and study of the domain and its requirements it is possible to identify the elements that a validation environment is composed of. They are represented in Figure 8.2: the validation environment interface (graphical user interface, GUI), the validation environment engine, the database, and the SUT interface.

The validation environment GUI is used by the test engineer to define tests, test the system, and get and analyze results. The engine is necessary to translate the domain-specific commands of the test language to the programming language that the SUT understands, and to interpret responses from the SUT. The database is essential in the previous translation process due to the fact that the all data is stored inside it. The database is queried by the engine during the translation process to perform the transformation in a suitable way. Finally, the SW/HW SUT interface allows the environment to send commands to the SUT, which then processes their answers (see Figure 8.2).

A simple test command implies a set of communication exchanges between these elements that compose the validation environment. To understand how a validation environment works, Figure 8.3 represents a simple interaction among the elements at a high abstraction level. When the test engineer sends a command through the GUI of the validation environment (see step 1, Figure 8.3), the GUI sends the command to the engine (see step 2, Figure 8.3). The engine transforms the domain-specific

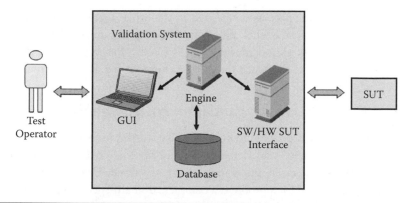

Figure 8.2 **Main elements of a validation environment.**

command into *something* that the SUT understands (see step 5, Figure 8.3). The engine queries the database during the transformation process to obtain the correspondences between the source and target languages (see steps 3 and 4, Figure 8.3). Once the engine has finished the transformation, the translated command is sent to the SUT interface (see step 6, Figure 8.3), which is the element in charge of sending the command to the SUT and to read the result of its execution (see steps 7 and

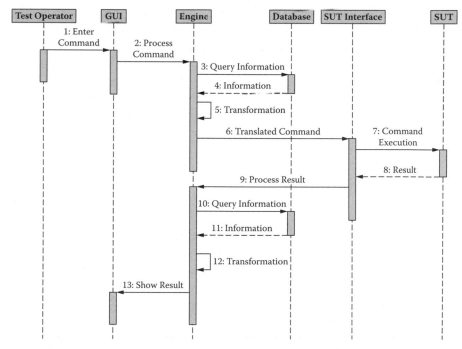

Figure 8.3 **Interaction between the elements of a validation environment.**

8, Figure 8.3). Then, the process is repeated in the other direction, i.e., the engine translates the result from the SUT programming language to the domain-specific language (see steps 9, 10, 11 and 12, Figure 8.3). Finally, the engine sends the translated result to the GUI to be shown for the test engineer in a user-friendly way.

8.3.2 A Product Line for Validation Environments

From Section 8.3.1, it is possible to conclude that all the validation environments share a set of requirements and elements. In addition, it is possible to assert that there is a specific set of variability points clearly identified. Once these variability points are particularized for a product, a complete domain-specific validation environment is provided.

In accord with all this effort, a product line for validation environments was developed taking into account the requirements analysis of the previous subsection and the steps presented in Section 8.2. In this section, steps 1 to 5 of Section 8.2 have been applied to develop the architecture of reference for validation environments.

- **Step 1:** *Definition and analysis of the domain.* The main function of a validation environment is to test the SUT in a suitable, secure, and user-friendly way. The validation environment must interact between the test engineer and the SUT to fully implement the validation process (see Figure 8.1). One of the most important features of the system is the domain-specific language that the engineer uses to test the SUT. The requirements analysis of the domain of validation environments has been provided in Section 8.3.1.

- **Step 2:** *Product planning.* It was identified that testing more than one SUT at the same time could be needed. In this way, the effort invested in testing could have a better payoff. Moreover, a facility to automatically generate tests specified using SUT models is usually required by test engineers who need not be experts in programming languages. To take a step forward in the engineer requirements, this facility could be considered as a requirement of the product line. Finally, it is important to take into account the fact that the heterogeneity of current devices and their technologies implies that validation environments should be able to interact with SUTs that manage different devices with different technologies and interface features.

  These are three requirements that can be understood as future needs. These requirements were included as variable requirements of the product line. They are variable because they are optional, i.e., they are not indispensable requirements to test a software system. Other requirements could also be included under this category. However, we only present these three requirements as an example of those requirements that can be identified in this step. As a result, the list of variable functional requirements of a validation environment is extended with these three new requirements (see Section 8.3.1).

- ■ **R19:** The validation environment should be able to test more than one SUT at the same time.
  - – **R20:** The validation environment should be able to automatically generate tests for the SUT from high-order languages driven by models of the SUT.
  - – **R21:** The validation environment should be able to be adapted to different interfaces of the SUT when it is composed of different devices.
- ■ **Step 3:** *Design of the architecture of reference.* The design of the architecture was defined by taking into account the identified elements during the analysis of the domain (see step 1, Section 8.3.2). These elements are the common main parts of a validation environment. At least one component will be necessary for each element. In this case, the elements were refined into one or more components of the architecture (see Figure 8.4). They are presented in detail in the following paragraphs.

The *GUI* of the validation environment was decomposed into three components. This decomposition was performed to separate the different functionalities that the GUI offers. This functionality separation increases the component and module cohesion facilitating the maintenance of the architecture (Pfleeger and Atlee 2005). These three components are the following:

1. The *TPPI* (test procedure panel interface) is the component that provides the interface that allows the test engineer to interact with the validation environment. It offers facilities to create, execute, and control the test procedures.
2. The *MPI* (manager panel interface) is the component that defines the interface that shows the test procedures to the test engineer.

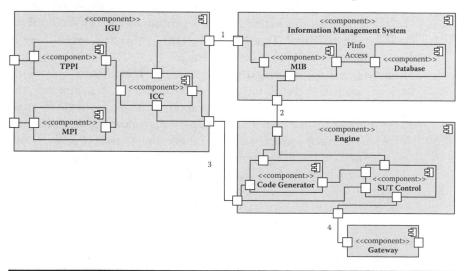

Figure 8.4   Architecture of reference.

3. The *ICC* (interface control component) is the component that manages the TPPI and MPI components and interacts with the rest of components of the architecture. It is in charge of receiving all the information about the definition, execution mode, and controlling features that the engineer introduces into the GUI. For this reason, the ICC must get this information stored into the database so that it can be available during the transformation and test execution processes.

On the other hand, the interface with the SUT was defined as a unique component called *gateway*. The gateway is responsible for sending to the SUT the execution requests of the testing commands and procedures. In addition, the gateway will receive the results from the command execution or notifications that have not been previously requested. It is important to keep in mind that the gateway is dependent on the technology used to build the SUT. This is due to the fact that the communication between the SUT and the validation environment is performed using the technology platform and programming language and the application program interface of the SUT.

The *information management system* was decomposed into two components: the database and a system to get access to data.

1. The *database* is the component that stores all information that is necessary to keep and transform or generate the testing commands and procedures, and to store meaningful results.
2. The *MIB* (mission information base) is the component that implements the business logic to access the database. This component was defined as an interface with a set of primitives to provide access to data. The objective was to prevent the communication between the database and the rest of the components from being overly dependent on the DBMS (database management system). Therefore, if the DBMS changes, the MIB is the unique component that undergoes changes.

A domain-specific validation process requires two different functionalities clearly identified: transforming and SUT controlling. Consequently, the *engine* of a domain-specific validation environment is composed of two components. Each of them is responsible for one of the following functionalities.

1. The *code generator* is responsible for transforming the test procedures and commands written in the domain-specific test language to the programming language of the SUT and vice versa.
2. The *SUT control* is the component that controls the interaction between the environment and the SUT. That is, it sends commands to the SUT and evaluates the execution outcomes.

Figure 8.4 presents the whole reference architecture of validation environments, detailing components and channels that communicate components through their ports. The information management system and the GUI must be connected so that the information related to the domain-specific interface of the validation environment (see channel 1, Figure 8.4) can be stored and retrieved. The communication between the information management system and the engine is also necessary to store the information about the transformations and the results of the testing commands and procedures. Thus, there is a communication channel between both (see channel 2, Figure 8.4).

In addition, the communication between the engine and the GUI is needed so that the results from the testing process can be shown and the test procedures and commands that the engineer wants to execute can be received (see channel 3, Figure 8.4). Finally, it is important to mention the channel that communicates between the engine and the gateway, which supports the interaction with the SUT (see channel 4, Figure 8.4).

■ **Step 4:** *Development of the reference architecture components.* Not all the components of the reference architecture have been completely implemented. Some of them are components that have been partially implemented. This is due to the fact that parts of these components are dependent on the product features. As a result, these parts are empty and are identified as variability points of the reference architecture. These partially finished components are usually called frameworks.

The variability points of a framework are traced from the requirements of the system. Each variability requirement, which was identified in Sections 8.3.1 and 8.3.2, corresponds to one or more variability points of one or more frameworks of the reference architecture. Table 8.2 defines the traceability relationship between requirements, frameworks, and variability points.

■ **Step 5:** *Architecture evaluation.* At this point, the obtained architecture of reference was reviewed to check if all the requirements had been taken into account. This evaluation provided us with important feedback to improve and amend the architecture.

An exhaustive review was performed on all the models (class diagrams, use cases, sequence diagrams, etc.) that compose the frameworks. In addition, an estimation of nonfunctional requirements was also performed at this step. This estimation was mainly based on the patterns described in Gamma et al. (1995) that were used to develop the diagram classes that frameworks are composed of.

Because of limited space, this chapter does not describe how the models that compose the frameworks were modified to improve the architecture. However, we do provide some examples that illustrate this improvement at the architectural level. An example of the reference architecture improvement, thanks to this evaluation step, is the information management system (see Figure 8.4). At the beginning of the product line development process, MIB was its unique component. This component included the database and the business logic to access the

Table 8.2 Variability Traceability: From Requirements to Architecture

Variability Requirement	Framework	Variability Point
R12: One or more graphical user interfaces (GUI) to test the SUT should be provided	GUI	**Selection:** 1. A unique view of the system, or 2. Management of different views of the system, which are based on the different roles that the test engineer can play
R13: More than one operation mode to test SUT must be provided R14: One interface can support more than one operation mode	GUI	**Selection:** 1. A unique mode of operation 2. Selection from the two predefined modes of operation: command and procedure 3. Selection from different modes of operation: the predefined in option 2, and new different modes that the test engineer can define
R15: Mechanisms for controlling the test procedure execution should be provided R16: Tools for analyzing the results must be included	Test control	**Selection:** 1. To control the test execution by the SUT 2. To control the test execution by the SUT and the correct execution of the test procedures **Addition:** Evaluation of results: Information, analysis, and data mining
R17: Mechanisms for translating and generating code should be provided	Code generator	**Selection:** The different combinations of transforming one or more domain-specific languages into one or more programming languages and vice versa **Addition:** The different combinations of adding one or more new programming languages and their correspondences to one or more predefined domain-specific languages and vice versa **Selection:** of the lexical and syntactical analysis of the programming language

R18: The actual time spent in the command execution should be shown	Test control	**Selection:** 1. Time is not considered, or 2. Adding time-counting mechanisms
R18: The actual time that command takes in its execution should be shown	Information system	**Selection:** 1. No storage of time, or 2. Storage of time
R19: The validation system should be able to test more than one SUT	Information system	**Selection:** 1. A unique session, or 2. Multisession
R20: The validation system should be able to automatically generate test from the models of the SUT	Engine	**Addition:** New component test generator
R20: The validation system should be able to automatically generate test from the models of the SUT	GUI	**Addition:** New windows for presenting the test generation facilities
R21: The validation system should be able to be adapted to different interfaces of the SUT when it is composed of different devices	Gateway	**Selection:** 1. A unique interface device, or 2. Selection of multiple interface devices

data. However, any interaction with the database was dependent on the DBMS, and the maintenance of the architecture was really difficult. The evaluation of the architecture allowed us to identify this inconvenience and to redefine the component as a complex component. It is composed of two different subcomponents, allowing the separation of data access and business logic and the solution of the problem.

Another improvement was related to the GUI. At the beginning, the GUI consisted of only one component; after the evaluation, it was decomposed into three components. Also, whereas the engine was initially created with the unique purpose of generating code, it was also improved by adding new capabilities to it. Finally, it is important to mention that the gateway was added as a new component of the architecture when we realized that its tasks were not duties of the engine.

8.4 Case Studies

In this section, step 6 presented in Section 8.2 is applied to the development of a validation tool for a specific product. The step consists of deriving a specific product from the variability points of the architecture of reference. In this case, the obtained architecture of reference (see step 3, Section 8.3.2) is applied to two different case studies: a group of networked slot machines and a system of digital TV decoders. This section introduces both products and how some variability points are derived from each product. Because of space limitations, this variability derivation is presented without entering the details of modeling and implementation, with the main objective of conveying to the reader our positive product line experience.

8.4.1 Networked Slot Machine System

The main goal of this case study is to develop a validation environment for testing networked slot machines. This SUT is characterized by being composed of a master slot machine and a set of accumulator machines connected to it (see Figure 8.5). The accumulator machines provide two different kinds of prizes: their own prize and the jackpot, which is controlled by the master and is obtained as a percentage of each of the accumulator machines.

The validation process of this system consists of certifying the machines by testing the individual accumulator machines' behavior as well as the global behavior from their interconnection. Two of the main properties that are necessary to check are average game time and the number of moves between two prizes of the same kind.

The validation tool for slot-machine systems was also obtained by deriving the variation points. This derivation process of the validation tool for slot-machine

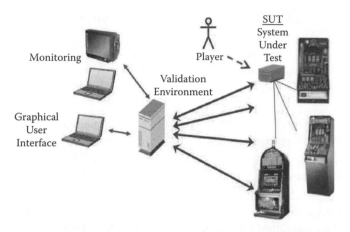

Figure 8.5   A slot-machine system.

systems is also presented at a high level of abstraction. To show how the variability points are specified for slot-machine systems, Table 8.3 presents for each variable requirement the alternative that was selected for this domain.

The selection of the variability points presented in Table 8.3 allowed us to develop a domain-specific product for validating networked slot-machine systems following a product line approach (see Figure 8.6).

8.4.2 Digital Television Decoder Systems

The main goal of this case study is to develop a validation environment for testing a digital television decoder system. This system tests the interactive services of digital television, i.e., when the user enters a TV channel button of the TV remote control, the selected TV channel must be shown in the TV. The interface of the validation tool has to provide commands that are domain-specific. For example: press the button, capture the image, etc. The system is composed of a TV remote control, a television, and a set of decoders (see Figure 8.7).

The validation tool to test digital television systems was obtained by deriving the variation points. It consisted of including a specific module (part of a class diagram, uses cases, sequence diagram, or code) that implements the variable parts of each framework. At a high abstraction level, it consists of selecting one of the alternatives presented in Table 8.2 for each variability point. To show how the variability points are specified to digital television systems, Table 8.4 presents for each variable requirement the alternative that was selected for this domain. This selection also allowed us to develop a specific validation environment for digital TV systems.

Table 8.3   Variability Selection for Slot-Machine Systems

Variability Requirement	Variability Point Selection
R12: One or more graphical user interfaces (GUI) to test the SUT should be provided	Two different views of interaction are provided to the test engineer: graphical and textual
R13: More than one operation mode to test SUT must be provided R14: One interface can support more than one operation mode	The validation environment provides the two predefined modes of operation—command and procedure—to the test the slot machines
R15: Mechanisms for controlling the test procedure execution should be provided R16: Tools for analyzing the results must be included	It is only possible to control the execution test in the SUT, and there are no evaluation mechanisms for the results
R17: Mechanisms for translating and generating code should be provided	It is possible to transform from the slot machines' domain-specific language to the Java programming language for execution on the OSGi platform; the specific language of slot machines and the correspondences between its elements and Java have been included in the validation system
R18: The actual time that command takes in its execution should be shown	The validation environment provides time-counting mechanisms The validation environment stores the execution time
R19: The validation environment should be able to test more than one SUT at the same time	The validation environment does not permit testing of more than one SUT at the same time
R20: The validation environment should be able to automatically generate test from the models of the SUT	The validation environment does not contain a test generator component
R21: The validation environment should be able to be adapted to different interfaces of the SUT when it is composed of different devices	Since all the slot machines communicate using RMI, the validation system only manages RMI mechanisms

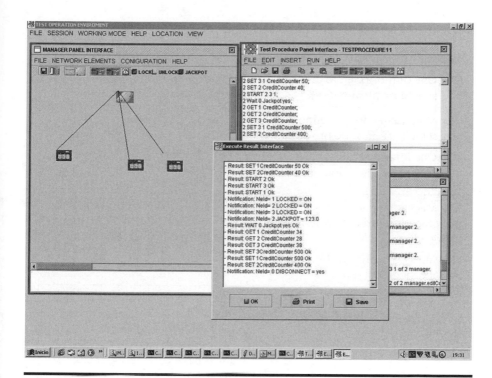

Figure 8.6 **The specific validation environment for networked slot-machine systems.**

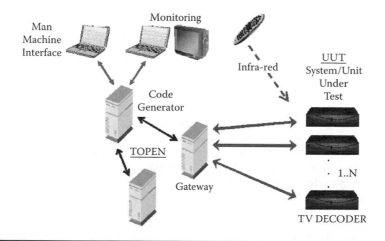

Figure 8.7 **A digital television system.**

Table 8.4   Variability Selection for Digital Television Systems

Variability Requirement	Variability Point Selection
R12: One or more GUI to test the SUT should be provided	A unique view of the system: graphical view
R13: More than one operation mode to test the SUT must be provided R14: One interface can support more than one operation mode	The validation environment provides the two predefined modes of operation (command and procedure) to test the digital TV SUT
R15: Mechanisms for controlling the test procedure execution should be provided R16: Tools for analyzing the result must be included	It is only possible to control the execution test in the SUT, and there are no evaluation mechanisms for the results
R17: Mechanisms for translating and generating code should be provided	It is possible to transform from the domain-specific languages to two programming languages, C# and C++, to be executed on the .NET platform; the correspondences between digital television and C# and C++ have been added
R18: The actual time that the command takes in its execution should be shown	The validation environment provides time-counting mechanisms The validation environment stores execution time
R19: The validation environment should be able to test more than one SUT at the same time	The validation environment enables the test engineer to test different TV systems using multisession mechanisms
R20: The validation environment should be able to automatically generate tests driven by the models of the SUT	The validation environment does not contain a test-generator component
R21: The validation environment should be able to be adapted to different interfaces of the SUT when it is composed of different devices	Since the decoder uses the same technology platform, the validation environment only manages a unique interface device

8.5 Lessons Learned

From this experience of applying the software product line approach to develop domain-specific validation environments, we have learned the following lessons:

It is possible to identify a set of commonalities and variability points in validation environments that are focused on acceptance testing. From this set of commonalities and variability points, a common architecture could be defined. This architecture can be shared by different validation environments for different products and different domains. The location of the variability points in the architecture allowed us to develop the network slot-machine validation environment for testing slot-machine systems that are programmed using Java and some of their components executed on OSGi. The TV digital validation environment was also developed just by deriving its variability points. Both products were successfully deployed. This showed us that the product line approach was suitable and advantageous for these two products.

The cost and time invested in developing the architecture of reference for the validation environment was high, probably from 4 to 8 person-years. It is difficult to estimate precisely due to the fact that it was developed in an academic environment. The investment in developing the architecture of reference was partially capitalized during the development of both products. Since the development of both products consisted of deriving the variability points of the reference architecture, the cost and time invested for developing the products was clearly lower than if they had been developed from scratch. Together with the product line definition, a test and validation environment, TOPEN (Alarcón et al. 2004), has been developed. TOPEN has been evolving following the maturation of the architecture, and it now reflects most of the aspects of the product line.

Although the design of the different architecture components was performed following the same process under the same methodology, and basically by the same core team, we came upon clearly different situations. For example, consider the case of the GUI and the engine. The design of the GUI underwent some changes rather early in the project, and its functionalities have remained unchanged since then. At the same time, our early view of the engine was too naïve. We called it the "code generator," which we considered to be its main function. However, experience showed us that *transforming* was only one of its functionalities, and we realized that *controlling* was at least as important as transforming, and far more complex to implement. This evolution can be considered dramatic. Only through the experience of deriving the architecture for different products could we get the proper understanding for the role of the engine.

8.6 Conclusions

This chapter presents our experience in applying the product line approach to develop domain-specific validation environments for acceptance testing. It describes and defines the architecture of reference as well as its variability points. It presents the application of the product line to two real case studies: a digital TV decoder and a networked slot-machine system. These case studies are presented to emphasize how the variability points have been derived to support the particularities of each product.

This experience was successful and allowed us to consolidate the development of the TOPEN environment, which was the starting point to apply the product line concept to other domains such as home automation, as described by Díaz et al. (2008). It is important to mention that this new application allowed us to demonstrate that future requirements of step 2 of the methodology have been identified as requirements for other domains. For example, in the home-automation field, it became clear that support for different platforms was needed because of the different devices that are involved in these types of systems (see R21 in Section 8.3.2). For this reason, we have already started to develop the variability of the gateway by using the product line approach presented by Díaz et al. (2008).

In the future, we also intend to formalize and improve the steps presented in this chapter to define a methodology for developing systems using the product line approach. Finally, we want to take into account the feedback provided by the application of new products to improve the product line definition and the product derivation.

Acknowledgments

This work has been partially sponsored by the projects OVAL/PM TIN2006-14840, AGMOD TIC2003-08503, DOBERTSEE ESA/ESTEC 15133/01/NL/ND, and FLEXI ITEA2 6022 FIT-340005-2007-37. The authors are indebted to Mr. Brian Melton and Mr. Serge Valera, from ESA/ESTEC, for their support of this research work, which proved to be essential right at the time it was starting; to Fundacion Labein for providing the slot-machine system case study under the project METSES, IST-2000-28583; to the Xpertia Soluciones Integrales for the support provided with the Digital TV decoder case study; and finally to all the members of team, some of whom are coauthors of some of the listed references.

References

Abrahamsson, P., O. Salo, J. Ronkainen, and J. Warsta. 2002. *Agile software development methods: Review and analysis*. Espoo, Finland: VTT Publications.

Alarcón, P. P., J. Garbajosa, A. Crespo, and B. Magro. 2004. Automated integrated support for requirements: area and validation processes related to system development. In *INDIN '04: 2nd IEEE international conference on industrial informatics*, 287–292. Washington, DC: IEEE Computer Society.

Alarcón, P. P., A. Yagüe, J. Garbajosa, and J. Díaz. 2006. TOPEN data model and analysis for system validation. *In STV '06: Fourth workshop on system testing and validation*, in conjunction with 13th annual IEEE international conference and workshop on the engineering of computer based systems (ECBS 2006). Stuttgart: Fraunhofer IRB Verlag.

Allen, N. A., C. A. Shaffer, and L. T. Watson. 2005. Building modeling tools that support verification, validation, and testing for the domain expert. In *WSC '05: Proceedings of the 37th winter simulation conference*, 419–426.

Blackburn, A. N. M., and R. Busser. 2003. Understanding the generations of the test automation. Paper presented at the Software Productivity Consortium, STAREAST Conference.

Bosch, J. 2000. *Design and use of software architecture: Adopting and evolving a product line approach*. Boston: Addison-Wesley.

CMIP (Common Management Information Protocol). 1999. X.700-series OSI systems management implementers' guide, version 7.0. May 1999.

Cook, S., G. Jones, S. Kent, and A. C. Wills. 2007. *Domain-specific development with visual studio DSL tools*. Boston: Addison-Wesley Professional.

Deursen, A. van, P. Klint, and J. Visser. 2000. Domain-specific languages: An annotated bibliography. *SIGPLAN Not.* 35 (6): 26–36.

Díaz, J., A. Yagüe, P. P. Alarcón, and J. Garbajosa. 2008. A generic gateway for testing heterogeneous components in acceptance testing tools. In *Proceedings of the 7th international conference on composition-based software systems* (ICCBSS), 110–119, Washington, DC: IEEE Computer Society.

Dobertsee Consortium. 2009. Dependable on-board embedded real-time software engineering environment (DOBERTSEE)/Low-cost on-board software development toolkit. Ref. ESA/ESTEC 15133/01/NL/ND and CCN-1.

D'Souza, D. F., and A. C. Wills. 1999. *Objects, components, and frameworks with UML: The catalysis approach*. Boston: Addison-Wesley Longman.

Dybå, T., and T. Dingsøyr. 2008. Empirical studies of agile software development: A systematic review. *Information and Software Technology* 50 (9-10): 833–859.

Eickelmann, N. S., and D. J. Richardson. 1996. An evaluation of software test environment architectures. In *ICSE '96: Proceedings of the 18th international conference on software engineering*, 353–364. Washington, DC: IEEE Computer Society.

FIT. 2009. Fit acceptance testing framework. http://fit.c2.com.

Fitnesse. 2009. http://fitnesse.org/.

Gamma, E., R. Helm, R. Johnson, and J. M. Vlissides. 1995. *Design patterns: Elements of reusable object-oriented software*. Reading, MA: Addison-Wesley.

Garbajosa, J., M. Alandes, M.-A. Mahillo, and M. Piattini. 2000. Assisting the definition and execution of test suites for complex systems. In *Proceedings of the 7th international conference on engineering of computer based systems* (ECBS00), 327–333. Washington, DC: IEEE Computer Society.

Garbajosa, J., and P. P. Alarcón. 2005. Deploying validation tests in systems development. Paper presented at 3rd International Industrial Simulation Conference (ISC'2005), Berlin, Germany, June.

Garbajosa, J., H. Garcia, M. Alandes, M.-A. Mahillo, and B. Magro. 2001. An architectural framework for a testing environment for geographically distributed teams. In *New technologies for computer control 2001* (NTCC 2001), a proceedings volume from the IFAC conference, 584. International Federation of Automatic Control by Pergamon.

Garbajosa, J., O. Tejedor, and M. Wolff. 1994. Natural language front end to test systems. *Annual Review in Automatic Programming* 19: 261–267.

Grant, E. S., and H. Reza. 2007. Towards the development of a rigorous model-driven domain-specific software engineering environment. In *ACST'07: Proceedings of the 3rd IASTED international conference: Advances in computer science and technology*, 102–107. Calgary, AB: ACTA Press.

Hartman, A., M. Katara, and A. Paradkar. 2007. Domain specific approaches to software test automation. In *ESEC-FSE '07: Proceedings of the 6th joint meeting of the European software engineering conference and the ACM SIGSOFT symposium on the foundations of software engineering*, 621–622. New York: ACM Press.

IEEE Std. 610.12-1990. IEEE standard glossary of software engineering terminology. IEEE, pub-IEEE-STD:adr, 1990.

IEEE Std. 1059-1993. IEEE guide for software verification and validation plans. IEEE, pub-IEEE-STD:adr, April 1994.

Mathur, F. 1978. Testing, testing. *Computer* 11 (4): 81–82.

Metses Consortium. 2000. Metses: Multiple-site environment for testing systems with embedded software. IST-2000-28583.

Mili, H., A. Mili, S. Yacoub, and E. Addy. 2002. *Reuse-based software engineering: Techniques, organization, and controls.* New York: Wiley-Interscience, John Wiley & Sons.

Pfleeger, S. L., and J. M. Atlee. 2005. *Software engineering*, 3rd ed. New York: Prentice Hall.

Rankin, C. 2002. The software testing automation framework. *IBM Systems Journal* 41 (1): 126–139.

Sauvé, J. P., O. L. A. Neto, and W. Cirne. 2006. Easyaccept: A tool to easily create, run and drive development with automated acceptance tests. In *AST '06: Proceedings of the 2006 international workshop on automation of software test*, 111–117. New York: ACM Press.

Selenium. 2009. http://seleniumhq.org/.

Sun, C., C. Liu, M. Jin, and M. Zhang. 2000. Architecture framework for software test tool. In *TOOLS: Proceedings of the 36th international conference on technology of object-oriented languages and systems* (TOOLS-Asia'00), 40–49. Washington, DC: IEEE Computer Society.

TestingTech. 2009. Testing Technologies IST GmbH. TTWorkbench. http://www.testingtech.com/products/ttworkbench.php.

Tufarolo, J. A., J. Nielsen, S. Symington, R. M. Weatherly, A. L. Wilson, and T. C. Hyon. 1999. Automated distributed system testing: Designing an RTI verification system. In *Proceedings of the 31st winter simulation conference: Simulation—A bridge to the future*, vol. 2, 1094–1102. New York: ACM Press.

Valera, S. 1999. EGSE and mission control system. The PROBA EGSE/SCOS2 experience. Slide presentation. ESA/ESTEC.

Williams, C., H. Sluiman, D. Pitcher, M. Slavescu, J. Spratley, M. Brodhun, J. McLean, C. Rankin, and K. Rosengren. 2002. The STCL test tools architecture. *IBM Systems Journal* 41 (1): 74–88.

Yagüe, A., and J. Garbajosa. 2007. Applying the knowledge stored in systems models to derive validation tools and environments. In *ICCI07: The 6th IEEE international conference on cognitive informatics*, 391–400. New York: IEEE Computer Society.

Chapter 9

Building a Family of Compilers

Wonseok Chae and Matthias Blume

Toyota Technological Institute at Chicago, IL

Contents

9.1 Introduction

When a new extension is added to a base compiler, we often copy the source code of the base compiler and edit it. This easy approach results in two different compilers, which then need to be maintained differently despite the fact that much of their code is duplicated and should be shared. Even if we are lucky and manage to merge new extensions back to the base compiler to have only one code base, they would quickly increase the overall complexity and make it harder to serve as a basis for further extensions. This is what we have experienced in the MLPolyR compiler project (MLPolyR 2008). From the beginning, the MLPolyR compiler was expected to serve as a foundation for teaching and for programming language research by providing the basic infrastructure. Indeed, it has served as the starting point for interesting design and implementation ideas (Blume, Acar, and Chae 2006, 2008). As the compiler grew larger, however, accumulation of code from our experimentation weakened its original purpose. It became more and more difficult to use as the starting point of new research.

One possible way of addressing this problem is to adopt the product line engineering paradigm. Product line engineering is a paradigm of developing a family of products (Kang, Lee, and Donohoe 2002; Lee, Kang, and Lee 2002; SEI 2008). A software product line is a set of software systems that share a common set of features with variations. Therefore, they are expected to be developed from a common set of software components (called *core assets*) on the same software architecture. Product line engineering encourages developers to focus on developing a set of products rather than on developing one particular product. Then, products are built from core assets rather than from scratch. Among various product line approaches, we adopted *feature-oriented product line engineering* for the following reasons. First, feature-oriented product line engineering provides adequate means to reason about commonality and variability in terms of features (Lee, Kang, and Lee 2002). Features express commonality and variability among products to the extent that they define differences (i.e., extension) between compilers. Moreover, aspects of a compiler can be investigated more deeply by comparison with similar compilers than they could be in isolation. Second, it promotes architecture-based development (Kang, Lee, and Donohoe 2002), which is a good fit for a compiler because almost all compilers have a pipe-and-filter architectural style. That is, a compiler is organized to have several batch sequential phases from parsing to generating code (Aho et al. 2006). Each phase can be implemented individually as a component. Therefore, a set of compilers can be obtained by adding new components or replacing existing components from the reference architecture. Doing so will increase transparency and reusability. In this chapter, we describe our experience of building a family of compilers based on feature-oriented product line engineering.

This work was first presented as a conference paper (Chae and Blume 2008) and has been extended to cover more engineering activities, some technical improvements, and new material on exploiting compiler generators. After brief introduction to the MLPolyR compilers (Section 9.2) and the product line engineering paradigm (Section 9.3), we show engineering activities for a family of compilers from product line analysis through product line architecture design to product line component design (Section 9.4). Then, we explain how to build a particular compiler from the core assets that are the result of the previous activities (Section 9.5).

9.2 The MLPolyR Compiler Family History

The MLPolyR language was first introduced as a classroom project in 2005 (MLPolyR 2008). As an object of study in the classroom, it was clear and simple, but it had state-of-the-art features such as a Hindley–Milner-style polymorphic-type system (Milner 1978) and record polymorphism (Rémy 1991). It was implemented in the Standard ML language (SML) (Milner et al. 1997). Soon, its concrete and simple implementation had served as a foundation for new research beyond the classroom to present some interesting new features, including a clean and simple integration of functional record update, extensible cases, and type-safe exception handling (Blume, Acar, and Chae 2006, 2008). Along with the evolution of the language itself, its compiler also has evolved to support the compilation of these new concepts. While the base compiler evolved, new research directions introduced new development lines (called *branches*), extending the base compiler (see Figure 9.1). The source code of the base compiler was copied and edited for new extensions. Some extensions were merged back into the base compiler, enabling a new version of the enhanced compiler. At these points, development paths essentially converged. However, some extensions caused diverging paths of evolution. As a result, the MLPolyR project grew up to have four major branches:

- The base MLPolyR compiler, which emits native PowerPC code (MC)
- The MLPolyR front-end compiler generating C--, which runs on Intel x86 (MM) (Jones, Ramsey, and Reig 1999)

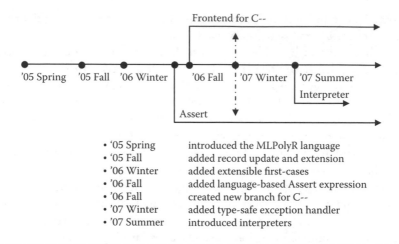

• '05 Spring   introduced the MLPolyR language
• '05 Fall   added record update and extension
• '06 Winter   added extensible first-cases
• '06 Fall   added language-based Assert expression
• '06 Fall   created new branch for C--
• '07 Winter   added type-safe exception handler
• '07 Summer   introduced interpreters

Figure 9.1   Development timeline.

■ The MLPolyR lambda interpreter, which runs as an interpreter, not as a compiler (INT)
■ The MLPolyR compiler with language-based Assert expression (AST)

Even though these branches were independent projects, they all had to be modified as the base compiler evolved, for they shared some portion of the code base. For example, we also had to modify the C-- front-end compiler when type-safe exception handling was introduced to the base language because both were assumed to logically share the front end, even though the code was not physically shared. Moreover, we often copied the source code of the base compiler and edited it when a modification was made to the base compiler. This easy approach resulted in multiple versions of compilers, which were required to be maintained separately even though much of their code was duplicated and should be shared. As a consequence of adding new features and creating multiple branches around the thousands of lines of code, the MLPolyR compiler, once having begun with a clean design and small size, became too complicated. This complexity made the compiler less desirable as a starting point of new research.

One may argue that source-code configuration tools such as CVS and Subversion could solve this problem by providing a mechanism for revisions and branches (Fogel and Bar 2001; Collins-Sussman, Fitzpatrick, and Pilato 2004). They surely support the concept of a branch (meaning a line of development that exists independently of another line) and track logical relations between branches. Suppose one branch represents a baseline of development and another branch represents an extension to it. Subversion-like tools help copying changes between branches and merging of multiple branches. Therefore, new researchers can add their extensions to a proper branch on which their work will be built. However, the approach based on branches has several limitations.

1. Different extensions usually reside in different branches, so it would be difficult to see the whole picture unless they are merged into one branch.
2. An extension, regardless of its impact, would have to introduce a new branch. For example, both a new back end and a new optimization technique introduced new branches, while the former required half of the compiler to be rewritten and the latter only replaced a few lines.
3. Two different techniques (e.g., different register allocation algorithms) cannot exist in the same branch unless they are annotated with some preprocessing macro for selective inclusion.
4. Not all branches will eventually be merged. Some features (e.g., call-by-value interpreter and call-by-name interpreter) were not intended to coexist from the beginning.
5. Even if we could manage to merge back all extensions into the base compiler, the code base would become too complicated to understand and would possibly force us to maintain complex configuration files (i.e., how to compile it and set proper flags) and sophisticated runtime options (e.g., backend PPC-call-by-value-use-optimizer-output foo.s).

As the number of branches increased and the size of the implementation grew, the MLPolyR compiler, even though its code base had been well maintained using subversion-like tools, became less attractive to be the foundation for new research. Indeed, the same problem might explain why we do not see even more research projects being based on big production-quality compilers such as SML/NJ (SML 2008) or GCC (GCC 2008). For example, the GNU Compiler Collection (GCC) started as an efficient C compiler but has evolved to officially support more than seven programming languages and a large number of target architectures. However, a variety of source languages and target architectures have resulted in a complexity that makes it difficult to do GCC development (Vichare 2008). This effect apparently even led to some rifts within the GCC developer community (Matzan 2007).

The bottom line is that we need a way of organizing both shared code and sets of extensions across a family of compilers, so that we can easily maintain multiple versions and at the same time easily construct new versions on top of the existing code base. To achieve this, we must be able to identify shared code among different branches and analyze the variations among multiple versions of compilers.

9.3 Product Line Engineering as the Family Doctor

Whenever a new extension was proposed to the base compiler, we had a tendency to focus on just this particular extended version of the compiler, at least for a while.

After accumulating a few experiments, multiple versions of the implementation started to coexist, and they quickly became so little compatible with each other that they required separate maintenance. One possible way of tackling this problem is to adopt product line engineering, which forces us to focus on a family of compilers, not on just one particular compiler. Parnas defines a set of programs to be a *program family* "if they have so much in common that it pays to study their common aspects before looking at the differentiating aspects" (Parnas 1978). A family of compilers is a more specific set of compiler programs in that they share the same architecture (i.e., overall structure of a compiler), and each of them can be built on any other by a combination of extensions and/or contractions. Due to this observation, we believed that product line engineering as a developing paradigm of a family of products would ease the problem in building a family of MLPolyR compilers.

Briefly speaking, product line engineering highlights the development of products from core assets and deemphasizes from-scratch development. Therefore, the paradigm separates the process of building core assets from the process of building an individual product, as shown in Figure 9.2. Product line asset development consists of analyzing a product line, designing reference architectures, and developing reusable components. In the product development process, a particular product is instantiated by selecting an appropriate architecture and adapting corresponding components. In our case, we adopted the feature-oriented product line approach. More information on this approach is available elsewhere (Kang, Lee, and Donohoe 2002; Lee, Kang, and Lee 2002; SEI 2008).

Although feature-oriented product line engineering is independent of implementation technologies, we decided to take full advantage of high-level programming languages such as SML not only because the MLPolyR compiler has already been implemented in SML, but also because we believed that its module system (including parameterized modules called *functors*) (Paulson 1996; Harper 2005) is powerful enough to manage variations among compilers. In the following section, we will show the applicability of this module system to product line engineering, especially for development and adaptation of reusable components.

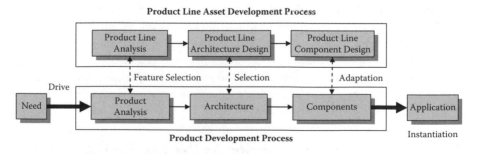

Figure 9.2 Product development process (adapted from feature-oriented product line engineering [Kang, Lee, and Donohoe 2002]).

9.4 Product Line Engineering for a Family of the MLPolyR Compilers

In this section, we discuss product line core asset development. This process is also known as *domain engineering*. After narrowing down the scope of the product line, products are analyzed to obtain a sufficiently detailed picture of their commonality and variability. This domain knowledge is represented in the feature model, which guides product line engineers to determine how features are turned into reusable core assets such as architectures and components. We will now show these product line engineering activities for our family of the MLPolyR compilers.

9.4.1 Product Line Analysis

We analyzed the commonalities and variabilities within our family of MLPolyR compilers. Because a typical compiler has phases such as parsing, type checking, and code generation, we can easily identify each conventional compilation phase as common functionality. Moreover, in our case, all the compilers began as a copy of the base compiler with extensions. Therefore, we can easily consider features in the base compiler as commonalities and exclusive features that exist only in the branch as variations. It is well known that having clear interfaces between phases allows for reuse of major components by easily replacing one phase without affecting other phases. Garlan and Shaw called this style "pipe-and-filter" (Garlan and Shaw 1994). Having this in mind, the conventional compilation phases in the base compiler are identified as common functionalities: lexer, parser, elaborator (type checker), translator, optimizer, closure converter, clusterifier, treeifier, code generator, assembler, linker, and so on (Blume, Acar, and Chac 2006).

We then analyzed the variations among family members based on a diagrammatic representation that uses boxes and dashes. Figure 9.3 shows the result of the analysis on the base compiler and three other branches. In Figure 9.3, the arrows between phases are omitted, but it should still be interpreted as a sequential process from left to right. Each box in a row represents a phase (translation step, e.g., parsing, type checking, or code generation phase). Each column represents one phase across different compilers.

Boxes and dashes represent the level of variation. Three kinds of boxes (empty box, half-filled box, and solid-filled box) represent how close each phase is when compared to the corresponding phase of the base compiler. An empty box indicates that this phase is the same as the corresponding phase of the base compiler. For example, the entire first row for MC consists of empty boxes. A half-filled box indicates that this phase is derived from the base phase but has a modification. A solid-filled box indicates that this phase is newly added only for a certain compiler. A dash indicates that some phase is not required for some compiler. For example, MM has three half-filled boxes, four dashed lines, and one solid-filled box:

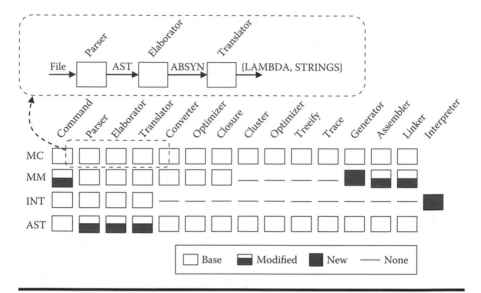

Figure 9.3   Result of the analysis on the base compiler and three other branches. MC refers to the base compiler; MM for the MLPolyR front-end compiler for C--; INT for the MLPolyR interpreter; AST for Assert compiler.

- The first half-filled box indicates that MM modifies the base compiler's command line interface (Command phase).
- The six empty boxes indicate that MM has the same front-end phases as the base compiler.
- Four dashes indicate that MM does not share some parts of the back end (e.g., it skips the Treeify phase).
- One solid-filled box indicates that MM has its own code generator, producing C--.
- The second and third half-filled boxes indicate that MM modifies the Assemble and Link phases.

This analysis leads us to observe that there are two kinds of variations in this product line. One is *architectural variation*, which captures inclusion or exclusion of certain phases. Some versions of the compiler require more sophisticated back-end phases, while others do not. In Figure 9.3, the MLPolyR interpreter (INT) excludes many back-end phases: Code generator, Assembler, and Linker. The other kind of variation is *component-level variation*, which captures something that may be implemented in different ways in different compilers. For example, the implementation of the code generator for PowerPC would be different from the one for Intelx86, while most of their front ends are the same. In Figure 9.3, the Closure phase has no variation at the level of components across all family members. Therefore, we can have just one implementation that provides the same functionality to all family members. We call such components *static components*. However, some phases such as the Code-generator phase require different implementations. We name such components *generic components*. It is here where we isolate variations that are handled later during design.

We then determined the underlying reasons for these differences at both the architectural level and the component level. For example, we can obviously tell that the choice of platform differentiates compilers. Similarly, the choice of running mode makes an impact (i.e., whether the program runs either as a compiler or as an interpreter, or supports both modes). In the case of the Assert compiler (AST), there exist two implementation choices: language-based or library-based. The language-based implementation requires modifications of the Parser, Elaborator, and Translator phases, while the library-based implementation only requires changes in the runtime system, which provides the libraries. We refer to such factors that differentiate products as *features* (Kang et al. 1998; Kang, Lee, and Donohoe 2002). Figure 9.4 shows the feature model according to our product line analysis.

Note that the Mode feature requires either the Interpreter feature or the Compiler feature or both, which is represented as a closed-triangle relationship (many-of), while the alternative choice between PowerPC and Intelx86 is represented as an open-triangle relationship (one-of) (Czarnecki and Eisenecker 2000; Lee, Kang, and Lee 2002).

9.4.2 Product Line Architecture Design

The next step is architecture design, which involves identifying components and specifying their configuration. For product line architecture, a lot of care must be taken here because different products require different components in different configurations.

During product line analysis, we already had obtained a fair amount of information about the structure of our compilers in terms of phases. Based on this analysis, we can easily define three different reference architectures, as shown in Figure 9.5, depending on the mode (i.e., the presence of the interpreter feature): (a) compiler only, (b) interpreter only, and (c) both. For each reference architecture, we simply map each compilation phase to a distinct component that performs the required tasks of this phase. The result clearly shows a pipe-and-filter architecture style. Strictly speaking, we should call it "batch sequential" style because there may not exist explicit data flow between filters (i.e., between the Assemble and Link phases), but an explicit computation order is required (i.e., the Assemble phase should be followed by the Link phase), something that is better thought of as control flow. An architecture is represented as a set of components, while a component can be one of three different kinds. A static component performs common functionality. One example for such common functionality is closure conversion. A generic component encapsulates variations when some aspect of this component varies in different compilers. The code-generator component is a typical example. An optional component (which is also either generic or static) may be excluded in some products.

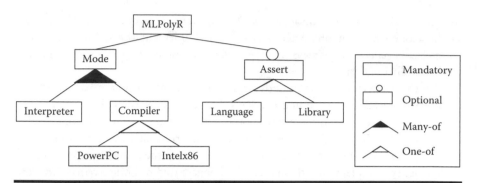

Figure 9.4 Feature model for the MLPolyR compiler.

In order to have well-defined reference architectures, we have to not only identify components, but also define interfaces between components. In order to do this more formally, we have specified architectures in textual form. In particular, we use the SML module language as an architecture description language (Allen and Garlan 1994) in order to describe both components and their interfaces. Each component in a reference architecture can be mapped to an SML program unit (called a *structure*), and interfaces among them can be specified as *signatures*. Signatures show the types of all components. Figure 9.6 shows that the signature PARSER specifies a structure that must provide a function parse, which takes a string (i.e., file name) and returns a pair of abstract syntax trees (ASTs) and source information. It captures the same information as what is described by Figure 9.3. Note that the symbol -> is SML's function type constructor and the symbol * is the type constructor representing the Cartesian product of two types. Thus, the specification says that parse takes a string and returns a pair of an AST and a source.

Then, by using those components, we can specify the overall structure of a compiler and their sequential behavior within a reference architecture. Figure 9.7 shows SML code that specifies the reference architecture in Figure 9.5a. Command.parse is the first component in this sequential chain. It takes command line options, interprets them, and passes the proper information (i.e., file names and targets) to the next phase, which is Parse.parse, and so on. Each source line corresponds to a box in the reference architecture in Figure 9.5a. Arguments represent an input to a box, while return values represent an output of a box.

Because we are using the SML programming language as an architecture description language, our reference architecture model is not just a specification but also an executable program. Moreover, we get the benefits of type checking, i.e., static checks of whether any inconsistencies exist between signatures and structures at compile time, for free. For example, the SML-type system will make sure that Parse.parse, which has a type of string -> Ast.program * Source.

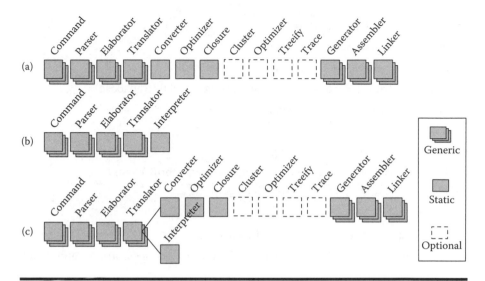

Figure 9.5   Reference architectures.

```
signature PARSER = sig

    val parse : string -> Ast.program * Source.inputSource

end
```

Figure 9.6   Signature of the parser component.

inputSource in Figure 9.6, is properly used in the architecture description such as Figure 9.7.

In sum, the product line architecture design phase produces reference architectures and defines required components and their interfaces. The next step is to implement such components.

9.4.3 Product Line Component Design

Product line component design involves realization of components whose interfaces are defined during architecture design. As already mentioned, we categorize components into different kinds (i.e., static and generic). Each category requires different implementation strategies. We will explain various abstraction mechanisms of SML in detail in order to show that variations among components can be efficiently implemented by existing high-level programming languages without relying on extra tools.

```
val (stopAt, file) = Command.parse args

val ast = Parse.parse (#org file)

val absyn = Elaborate.elaborate BaseEnv.elabBase ast

val {lambda, strings} = Translate.translate (absyn, BaseEnv.transBase)

val anf = LambdaToANF.convert lambda

val anf_op = Optimize.optimize anf

val closed = Closure.convert anf_op

val fc as {entrylabel, clusters} = FunctionClusters.clusterify closed

val clusters_cse = ValueNumbering.cse clusters

val bbt_clusters = Treeify.treeify clusters_cse

val traces = TraceSchedule.schedule bbt_clusters

val _ = (stopAt Command.ToAsm) andalso CodeGen.cg (traces, strings, entrylabel,
#asm file)

val _ = (stopAt Command.ToObj) andalso Assemble.assemble (#asm file, #obj file)

val _ = (stopAt Command.ToExe) andalso Link.link (#obj file, #exe file)
```

Figure 9.7 Architecture description in Standard ML.

9.4.3.1 Static Components

A static component would have only one implementation that satisfies its signature. Our product line analysis identifies the closure phase as a static component. Its signature CLOSURE is specified during architecture design. Component design now provides the SML structure, which implements signature CLOSURE as shown in Figure 9.8. With the implementation in place, the convert function can be accessed as Closure.convert, for example from within the architecture description such as Figure 9.7.

```
signature CLOSURE = sig

    val convert : ANF.function -> Closed.program

end


structure Closure : CLOSURE = struct

    fun convert f = (* omitted *)

end
```

Figure 9.8 Static component.

9.4.3.2 Generic Components with Structure Abbreviation

While there would be only one implementation for each static component, generic components usually have multiple implementations, each of which builds a particular feature such as PowerPC or Intelx86. All these implementations must provide all the components required by their signatures. For example, our product line analysis identifies the Assemble phase as a generic component (see Figure 9.5). Its signature ASM is specified during architecture design. Now, component design provides two structures, each of which matches signature ASM in Figure 9.9. These two structures implement the same feature in different ways.

Depending on the feature selection, either AsmPPC.assemble or Asmx86. assemble would be used in the architecture description. However, this means that we have to modify the architecture description according to the proper component name. We can do better with a *structure abbreviation* that introduces one structure identifier as an abbreviation for another as follows:

```
signature ASM = sig

    val assemble : string * string -> bool

end


structure AsmPPC : ASM = struct

  fun assemble (asmfile, objfile) =

    System.exec (concat ["as –o ", objfile, " ", asmfile])

    before System.remove asmfile

end


structure Asmx86 : ASM = struct

  fun assemble (asmfile, objfile) =

    System.exec (concat ["qc-- -c ", objfile, " ", asmfile])

    before System.remove asmfile

end
```

Figure 9.9 Structure Asm PPC and Asmx86.

```
structure Assemble = AsmPPC
```

or

```
structure Assemble = Asmx86
```

Finally, the function Assemble.assemble would be used in both architecture descriptions, regardless of their respective platform.

9.4.3.3 Generic Components with Parameterization over Components

In the previous strategy, a structure abbreviation increases readability, but it does not fully utilize the product line analysis yet. The product line analysis already reveals that the difference comes from information on the platform (see Figure 9.4). Otherwise, the AsmPPC structure and the Asmx86 structure should be identical. As we can see in Figure 9.9, both implementations duplicate most of their code. *Functorization* helps to remove such redundancy by implementing the common part once and sharing it among all instances. We factor out the parts that differentiate AsmPPC and Asmx86 structures into the signature PLATFORM with two matching structures in Figure 9.10. Simply speaking, a *functor* is a component-level function that takes a structure as an argument and yields a structure as result (Paulson 1996). Then, the functor AsmFun defines the part that is common to both AsmPPC and Asmx86. The parts that differ are given as parameters:

```
functor AsmFun (structure P : PLATFORM) : ASM = struct
 fun assemble (asmfile, objfile) =
 System.exec (concat [P.asm, objfile, " ", asmfile])
 before System.remove asmfile
end
```

The functor takes a structure satisfying signature PLATFORM and returns a structure satisfying signature ASM. In the main body of the specification, platform-specific information (i.e., P.asm) is provided in the form of arguments. Then, structure Assemble is obtained by providing these arguments to AsmFun:

```
structure Assemble =AsmFun (structure P = PowerPC)
```

or

```
structure Assemble =AsmFun (structure P = Intelx86)
```

At this point, the function Assemble.assemble can be used exactly as if it had been defined as shown before with a structure abbreviation.

```
signature PLATFORM = sig

    (* the external tools with options *)

    val asm : string

    val linker : string

    (* information on each platform *)

    val src : string option

    val asm : string option

    val obj : string option

    val exe : string option

end


structure PowerPC = struct

    (* the external tools with options *)

    val asm = "as -arch ppc -o "

    val linker = "cc -arch ppc -o "

    (* information on each platform *)

    val src = SOME "mlpr"
```

Figure 9.10A   A signature PLATFORM and two matching structures.

9.4.3.4 Generic Components with Parameterization over Types

So far, we have demonstrated how we can increase readability and decrease redundancy in component design. However, the previous implementation strategy only works well for the structures whose concrete type remains the same across all variations. This cannot always be the case. In some configurations, concrete types vary. For example, our product line analysis identifies the Generator phase as a generic component and architecture design determines that the Trace phase is followed by the Codegen phase. As a first cut, signature CODEGEN0 could be specified as follows:

```
signature CODEGEN0 = sig
 val codegen : TraceTree.entrytrace list *
               (string * Label.label) list *
               Label.label option * string -> bool
end
```

```
            val asm = SOME "s"

            val obj = SOME "o"

            val exe = NONE

        end


        structure Intelx86 = struct

            (* the external tools with options *)

            val asm = "qc-- -globals -c "

            val linker = "qc-- -globals -o "

            (* information on each platform *)

            val src = SOME "mlpr"

            val asm = SOME "c--"

            val obj = SOME "o"

            val exe = NONE

        end
```

Figure 9.10B   A signature PLATFORM and two matching structures.

This specification requires that any structure that implements this signature must provide a function codegen that takes an argument of type TraceTree.entrytrace list and returns a Boolean value. However, the Generator phase in MM follows the Closure phase, not the Trace phase (Figure 9.3), and this fact has been captured by identifying the Trace phase as an optional component (Figure 9.5a). Therefore, the Codegen component for the Intelx86 feature, which takes an argument of type Closed.program instead of TraceTree.entrytrace list, does not satisfy signature CODEGEN0. Fortunately, it is possible to postpone writing down any concrete type (i.e., either Closed.program or TraceTree.entrytrace list) in a signature definition by using a *type specification* and referring to it by name. That is, signature CODEGEN uses a type specification for type source. This makes any code depending on an instance of CODEGEN be polymorphic in that type. Concrete instances of CODEGEN must pick a concrete type for source, but there does not need to be agreement on the choice across different instances (Figure 9.11).

Signature CODEGEN specifies a function codegen whose type mentions source. A structure that implements signature CODEGEN must provide not only a value component (i.e., codegen), but also a type component (i.e., source). The

```
signature CODEGEN = sig

  type source

  val codegen : source * (string * Label.label) list * Label.label option * string -> bool

end



structure CGPPC : CODEGEN where type source = TraceTree.entrytrace list

= struct

  type source = TraceTree.entrytrace list

  fun codegen (trace, strings, entrylabel, asmfile) = ...

end



structure CGCmm : CODEGEN where type source = Closed.program

= struct

  type source = Closed.program

  fun codegen (closed, strings, entrylable, asmfile) = ...

end
```

Figure 9.11   A signature CODEGEN and two matching structures.

structure CGPPC provides TraceTree.entrytrace list as the definition of source so that function codegen takes a TraceTree.entrytrace list. On the other hand, structure CGCmm defines source to be Closed.program, so that function codegen takes an argument of type Closed.program. Note that the where clause following a signature name in a structure definition augments the signature with the additional constraints. With this setup in place, we can obtain a structure CodeGen via a structure abbreviation as follows:

```
structure CodeGen = CGPPC
```

or

```
structure CodeGen = CGCmm
```

Depending on structure bindings (i.e., either CGPPC or CGCmm), the function CodeGen.codegen varies in type. Therefore, it may seem that we have to worry about type inconsistencies among components when developing an architecture description. However, the SML type system will make sure that there will be no such inconsistency so that a reference architecture becomes easy to model.

Note that the reason we want to keep the same name for different implementations is that we want to keep the architecture description as general as possible by isolating application-specific information (i.e., changeable factors) inside a structure and hiding them by language techniques such as functor applications and polymorphism.

9.5 Product Engineering of a Family

During the product line asset development process, we obtained product line core assets such as feature models showing variation points among compilers, reference architecture models that represent architectural variations, and component models implementing component-level variations. In product engineering (also known as *application engineering*), building a product is essentially the same as instantiating a member of the family from product line core assets. First of all, a set of desired features is identified from the feature model. Then, each feature gives advice on how to select an application architecture and how to instantiate required components.

Figure 9.12 shows this overall process. The selected feature set gives advice on selection among reference architectures. At the same time, it guides us on whether optional components should be included or excluded. The feature set also shows which components need to be instantiated and how they would be instantiated at the component level. In this section, we will see those activities when building a MLPolyR front-end compiler for C--.

9.5.1 Product Analysis

The MLPolyR frontend compiler for C-- has the following properties:

- It runs in compiler-only mode.
- It runs on the Intelx86 architecture.

Based on these product requirements, a set of desired features is identified from the feature model. In this case, the set is {Mode, Compiler, Intelx86}.

9.5.2 Architecture Selection

The selected feature set gives advice on the selection among reference architectures. At same time, it tells us whether optional components should be included or excluded. For example, the reference architecture in Figure 9.5a gets selected from the three references, guided by the presence of the Compiler feature. If the Interpreter feature were also in the selected feature set, the reference architecture in

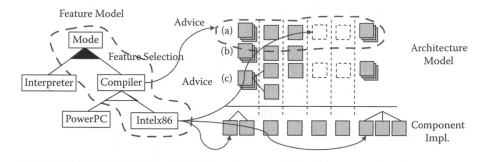

Figure 9.12   Engineering of a compiler.

Figure 9.5c would be selected instead of Figure 9.5a. The selected reference architecture may have optional components that can either be included or excluded for a certain compiler. For example, Cluster, Optimizer, Treeify, and Trace are such optional components. During product line analysis, we recognized that these optional components were only required for the PowerPC platform. Therefore, the Intelx86 feature gives advice that they are not included.

In addition to the diagrammatic notation, each reference architecture model has its own specification written in SML. In this example, Figure 9.7 shows a specification that corresponds to the diagram in Figure 9.5a. After selecting the right reference architecture, a source line representing an optional component that should be excluded according to the feature set will be deleted. Figure 9.13 shows the final architecture specification of a MLPolyR front-end compiler for C--. For the purpose of comparison with its reference architecture, the components that would be excluded are represented as being struck out (see Figure 9.7). Note that the final specification has been massaged for CodeGen.codegen to take closed (of type Closed.program) instead of traces (of type TraceTree.entrytrace list), as in the original specification of the reference architecture (Figure 9.7). Such manual modifications could be automated or avoided easily in various ways. The final architecture description in SML faithfully reflects the product line analysis and clearly highlights where two compilers differ in terms of components.

9.5.3 Component Instantiation

The feature set also shows which components need to be instantiated (only generic components can be instantiated) and how they would be instantiated at the component level. For example, Command, CodeGen, Assemble, and Link components are generic among selected components (see Figure 9.5), so they would be instantiated by choosing appropriate component implementations.

In the product line component design phase, the Assemble component was implemented as a functor that takes a structure satisfying signature PLATFORM. There

```
val (stopAt, file) = Command.parse args

val ast = Parse.parse (#org file)

val absyn = Elaborate.elaborate BaseEnv.elabBase ast

val {lambda, strings} = Translate.translate (absyn, BaseEnv.transBase)

val anf = LambdaToANF.convert lambda

val anf_op = Optimize.optimize anf

val closed = Closure.convert anf_op

val fc as {entrylabel, clusters} = FunctionClusters.clusterify closed

val clusters_cse = ValueNumbering.cse clusters

val bbt_clusters = Treeify.treeify clusters_cse

val traces = TraceSchedule.schedule bbt_clusters

val _ = (stopAt Command.ToAsm) andalso CodeGen.codegen (traces closed, strings,

NONE, #asm file)

val _ = (stopAt Command.ToObj) andalso Assemble.assemble (#asm file, #obj file)

val _ = (stopAt Command.ToExe) andalso Link.link (#obj file, #exe file)
```

Figure 9.13 Architecture selection.

were two components implementing signature PLATFORM: Intelx86 and PowerPC. The feature set provides guidance on which component should be used. In this case, the Intelx86 feature guided us to use the Intelx86 component. Similarly, the Command and Link functors also take the Intelx86 component. The CodeGen component is bound to a structure-matching signature CODEGEN. This will be either CGPPC or CGCmm, depending on the architecture platform. Again, the Intelx86 feature guides us to use CGCmm over CGPPC. So, the (almost) complete list of instantiations for generic components in the architecture description is the following:

```
structure Command = CommandFun (structure P = Intelx86)
structure CodeGen = CGCmm
structure Assemble = AsmFun (structure P = Intelx86)
structure Link = LinkFun (structure P = Intelx86)
```

(The Parser, Elaborator, and Translator components should also be instantiated properly, for they are generic, too, in Figure 9.5. We omit them for brevity.)

9.5.4 Product Instantiation

The code describing these component instantiations, combined with the architecture description, becomes a "main" file for the MLPolyR front-end compiler for C--, as shown in Figure 9.14. A few annotations had to be added to instruct how to compile this file properly. For example, the architecture description portion now becomes a function main, and everything turns into a procedure that takes command options and returns an exit code to the operating system. Note that all variations, including both architectural variations and component-level variations, are explicitly described at this same level, which increases readability and maintainability. Previously, in the original implementation, the variations were scattered all over the source code.

9.6 Discussion

9.6.1 Architecture Style

Our approach heavily relies on the property of the pipe-and-filter style: easy to add new components (filters) and easy to replace an existing component with an improved one (Garlan and Shaw 1994). Addition and replacement of components are our basic mechanisms for implementing variations. In addition, both kinds of variations are specified in the same place, e.g., the top-level program or the "main" function. This increases understandability and maintainability. Our component design fully separates common parts from variations by using several implementation strategies based on product line analysis. As a result, it is less complex than we could have managed had we used the popular macro processor-based technique, where differences are scattered between conditional statements in the component specification.

However, the pipe-and-filter style also has certain disadvantages, which limit what we have achieved so far. For example, the pure approach that decomposes the system into sequential steps makes it difficult to support an interactive system. This could be problematic in practice because many compilers, including the SML/NJ compiler, do support an interactive mode. To overcome this problem, we would have to consider a blackboard style where each phase operates on a central shared repository (Garlan and Shaw 1994).

9.6.2 Module Hierarchies

We have implemented our family of MLPolyR compilers in SML. Its module system is powerful enough to specify the pipe-and-filter style and implement variations identified by the product line analysis. So far, the pipe-and-filter architectural style results in a linear sequence of modules, but the SML module

```
(* main-c--.sml :

 * Driver routine for the MLPolyR frontend compiler for C--

 *)

structure MainCmm : sig

    val main : string * string list -> OS.Process.status

end = struct


structure Command = CommandFun (structure P = Intelx86)

structure CodeGen = CGCmm

structure Assemble = AsmFun (structure P = Intelx86)

structure Link =       LinkFun (structure P = Intelx86)


fun main (self, args) = let

    val (stopAt, file) = Command.parse args

    val ast = Parse.parse (#org file)

    val absyn = Elaborate.elaborate BaseEnv.elabBase ast

    val {lambda, strings} = Translate.translate (absyn, BaseEnv.transBase)

    val anf = LambdaToANF.convert lambda

    val anf_op = Optimize.optimize anf

    val closed = Closure.convert anf_op

    val _ = (stopAt Command.ToAsm) and also CodeGen.codegen (closed, strings, NONE,
#asm file)

        val _ = (stopAt Command.ToObj) and also Assemble.assemble (#asm file, #obj file)

        val _ = (stopAt Command.ToExe) and also Link.link (#obj file, #exe file)

    in OS.Process.success

    end
```

Figure 9.14   A main file for the MLPolyR for C- -.

language also supports *module hierarchies*, where modules are organized in tree-like configurations by grouping related phases into a subgroup. For example, we can think of a substructure Backend which combines multiple phases from the Converter phase to the Linker phase (see Figure 9.3). Depending on the specific platform, we would have two version of the Backend implementation as follows:

```
structure Backendx86 : BACKEND = struct
  structure CodeGen = CGCmm
  structure Assemble = AsmFun (structure P = Intelx86)
  structure Link = LinkFun (structure P = Intelx86)
  fun cg … = …
end
```

or

```
structure BackendPPC : BACKEND = struct
  structure CodeGen = CGPPC
  structure Assemble = AsmFun (structure P = PowerPC)
  structure Link = LinkFun (structure P = PowerPC)
  fun cg … = …
end
```

Then, the main program becomes more concise than before, as shown in Figure 9.15. This structuring mechanism is useful especially when programs grow in size and complexity (Harper 2005). However, it may also weaken the original clarity of our architecture-based approach because this tree-like structure breaks a flat pipe-and-filter style, and variations would be scattered in various layers, whereas all variations had been located at the top level in our earlier approach. That is, it could require more effort to understand variation points if anyone has to investigate deeply into a substructure.

9.6.3 Compiler Generators

Our approach helps us maintain source code where all variations, including both architectural and component-level variations, are easily identified. This clean organization provides us with the chance of utilizing features of the SML language even better. For example, because now we know which parts can be changeable, we can factor out the changeable parts and parameterize over them via functorization. Then, the main file becomes a functor, which takes variations and produces a specific compiler; that is, it becomes a *compiler generator*. Previously, in Figure 9.15, we had to maintain two different main files, one for PowerPC and one for Intelx86. The differences mostly lie in the declaration part of component instantiation. For example:

```
(* main-c--.sml :

* Driver routine for the MLPolyR frontend compiler for C--

*)

structure MainCmm : sig

    val main : string * string list -> OS.Process.status

end = struct


structure Command = CommandFun (structure P = Intelx86)

structure Backend = Backendx86


fun main (self, args) = let

    val (stopAt, file) = Command.parse args

    val ast = Parse.parse (#org file)

    val absyn = Elaborate.elaborate BaseEnv.elabBase ast

    val {lambda, strings} = Translate.translate (absyn, BaseEnv.transBase)

    val _ = Backend.cg (file, lambda, strings, stopAt)

in OS.Process.success

    end
```

Figure 9.15   Module hierarchy.

```
structure Command = CommandFun (structure P = Intelx86)
structure Backend = Backendx86
vs.
structure Command = CommandFun (structure P = PowerPC)
structure Backend = BackendPPC
```

We can parameterize over these differences and convert the structure main into the functor MainFun, which takes two structures and yields a compiler, as shown in Figure 9.16. Then, the final compiler can be obtained by functor application with specific architecture information:

```
structure Compiler = MainFun (structure P = Intelx86
 structure B = Backendx86)
or
structure Compiler = MainFun (structure P = PowerPC
 structure B = BackendPPC)
```

```
functor MainCompiler (structure P : PLATFORM

                             structure CG : CODEGEN) : COMPILER = struct

   structure Command = CmdFun (structure P = P)

   structure Backend = CG


   fun main (self, args) = let

       val (stopAt, file) = Command.parse args

       val ast = Parse.parse (#org file)

       val absyn = Elaborate.elaborate BaseEnv.elabBase ast

       val {lambda, strings} = Translate.translate (absyn, BaseEnv.transBase)

       val _  = Backend.cg (file, lambda, strings, stopAt)

   in OS.Process.success

   end

end
```

Figure 9.16 Compiler generator.

Functional programming languages have encouraged developers to write their code in this style right from the start, thereby reducing redundancy, increasing reusability, and improving flexibility. However, it is hard for even experienced programmers to predict which portion will be changeable. Product line engineering as a design paradigm can be truly helpful here in that its domain analysis acts as a systematic way of identifying commonalities and variabilities. This makes it possible to design and implement reusable and flexible software by obtaining guidance on where functorization is useful.

9.7 Related Work
9.7.1 Extensible Compilers

A lot of previous work on extensible compilers has proposed new techniques on how to easily add extensions to existing programming languages and their compilers. For example, JaCo is an extensible compiler for Java based on extensible algebraic types (Zenger and Odersky 2001a, 2001b). The Polyglot framework implements an extensible compiler where even changes of compilation phases and manipulation of internal abstract syntax trees are possible (Nystrom, Clarkson, and Myers 2003). Aspect-oriented concepts (i.e., crosscutting concerns) are also applied to extensible compiler construction (Wu et al. 2005). The MLPolyR language presents first-class cases to build extensible interpreters (Blume, Acar, and Chae 2006). However, while all this work successfully demonstrates that a base compiler can be extended easily, one rarely sees the general issues that product line engineering tackles addressed: which architecture style will be used across compilers, how commonality and variability among extensions are analyzed and utilized, and how reusable core assets will be maintained. Moreover, existing methods do not focus on sets of extensions (including relations between them), but only focus on one extension from the base compiler. However, we believe that these methods proposed by other authors in previous works could easily be extended to adopt product line engineering principles in a way similar to what we have shown in this chapter.

9.7.2 Product line Implementation

While most efforts in product line engineering have focused on principles and guidelines, some have suggested concrete means of implementing variations: macro processors (Kang et al. 1998, 2005), aspect-oriented programming (Lee et al. 2006), or C++ templates (Czarnecki and Eisenecker 2000). Our work shows that modern programming language technology such as the module system in Standard SML is a powerful tool for expressing and implementing variations identified by product line analysis. It is worth noting that the relations among features, architectures, and components in our approach are expressed only informally during the product line analysis, while other product line methods usually provide a way of expressing those relations explicitly using some form of notation provided by CASE tools. In FORM, for example, those explicit relations make it possible to automatically generate product code from specifications (Kang et al. 1998). In our approach, the specification *is* the code.

9.7.3 Product Line–Based Reengineering

Using the techniques of product line engineering, there have been efforts to reengineer legacy systems into reusable assets (Kang et al. 2005, 2006; Kim, Kim, and Kim 2007). For example, Kang et al. reengineered robot applications based on product line analysis. They provided a new, flexible architecture using components to decrease development cost and increase flexibility (Kang et al. 2005). Compared with theirs, our work can be understood as a "lightweight" reengineering effort, for we did not modify the existing overall architecture but rearranged components by refactoring source code.

9.7.4 Program Families

Parnas discussed two methods of producing program families (Parnas 1976): step-wise refinement and module specification. Our approach is very similar to module specification because "signatures" and "structures" in SML correspond to his "module specifications" and "modules," respectively. The method of module specification allows certain decisions, e.g., sequencing steps, to be postponed. This leads to a broader family when compared with stepwise refinement. However, such postponement makes it difficult to express sequencing decisions. Therefore, he suggests a "main program" that describes a sequence of operations. In our approach, sequencing decisions are not postponed, but made early during architecture design due to the choice of the pipe-and-filter style. They are specified in the architecture description in terms of components. However, our methodology in fact would allow the postponement of decisions about implementation detail as Parnas described, thus also leading to a large family.

9.8 Conclusion

Our original motivation was to provide a compiler implementation that could serve as foundation both for teaching and for research. We expected that a simple and clean design would be sufficient, but we realized that the accumulation of new extensions had quickly obscured the original goal of being the starting point of new research.

In this chapter, we explained how we adopted the product line engineering paradigm to address our problem. This paradigm encourages developers to focus on enabling a set of compilers rather than on developing one particular compiler. We have shown engineering activities for a family of compilers from product line analysis through product line architecture design to product line component design. We then explained how to build particular compilers from core assets that were the results of the previous activities.

By adopting feature-oriented product line engineering, we are able to easily identify shared code and efficiently analyze variations among multiple versions of our compilers. Therefore, we can easily construct a family of compilers. Moreover, domain analysis makes it possible to utilize the powerful SML module system in a systematic way. Our experience demonstrates that product line engineering as a developing paradigm is a very effective way to build a family of compilers, especially when combined with a high-level programming language.

References

Aho, Alfred V., Monica S. Lam, Ravi Sethi, and Jeffrey D. Ullman. 2006. *Compilers: Principles, techniques, and tools*, 2nd ed. London: Pearson Addison-Wesley.

Allen, Robert, and David Garlan. 1994. Formalizing architectural connection. In *Proceedings of the 16th international conference on software engineering*, 71–80. Los Alamitos, CA: IEEE Computer Society Press.

Blume, M., Umut A. Acar, and Wonseok Chae. 2006. Extensible programming with first-class cases. In *Proceedings of the 11th international conference on functional programming*, 239–250. New York: ACM Press.

Blume, M., Umut A. Acar, and Wonseok Chae. 2008. Exception handlers as extensible cases. In *Proceedings of the 6th ASIAN symposium on programming languages and systems*, 273–289. Berlin/Heidelberg: Springer-Verlag.

Chae, W., and Matthias Blume. 2008. Building a family of compilers. In *Proceedings of the 12th international software product line conference*, 307–316. Washington, DC: IEEE Computer Society.

Collins-Sussman, B., Brian W. Fitzpatrick, and C. Michael Pilato. 2004. *Version control with subversion*. Sebastopol, CA: O'Reilly.

Czarnecki, Krzysztof, and Ulrich W. Eisenecker. 2000. *Generative programming: Methods, tools, and applications*. New York: Addison-Wesley.

Fogel, Karl, and Moshe Bar. 2001. *Open source development with CVS*, 2nd ed. Sebastopol, CA: O'Reilly.

Garlan, David, and Mary Shaw. 1994. An introduction to software architecture. Technical report CS-94-166. Carnegie Mellon University, Pittsburgh.

GCC. 2008. The GNU compiler collection. http://gcc.gnu.org.

Harper, Robert. 2005. Programming in Standard ML. Carnegie Mellon University. Working draft. Available at http://www.cs.cmu.edu/~rwh/sml/book/.

Jones, S. P., Norman Ramsey, and Fermin Reig. 1999. C--: A portable assembly language that supports garbage collection. In *Proceedings of the international conference on principles and practice of declarative programming*, 1–28. London: Springer-Verlag.

Kang, Kyo C., Moonzoo Kim, Jaejoon Lee, and Byungkil Kim. 2005. Feature-oriented re-engineering of legacy systems into product line assets: A case study. In *Proceedings of the 9th international software product line conference*, 45–56. Berlin/Heidelberg: Springer.

Kang, Kyo C., Sajoong Kim, Jaejoon Lee, Kijoo Kim, Euiseob Shin, and Moonhang Huh. 1998. FORM: A feature-oriented reuse method with domain-specific reference architectures. In *Annals of Software Engineering*, 143–168. Red Bank, NJ: J. C. Baltzer AG Science Publishers.

Kang, Kyo C., Jaejoon Lee, and Patrick Donohoe. 2002. Feature-oriented product line engineering. *IEEE Software* 9 (4): 58–65.

Kang, Kyo C., Jaejoon Lee, Byungkil Kim, Moonzoo Kim, Chang-woo Seo, and Seung-lyeol Yu. 2006. Re-engineering a credit card authorization system for maintainability and reusability of components: a case study. In *Proceedings of the 9th international conference on software reuse: Methods, techniques, and tools*, 156–169. Berlin: Springer.

Kim, K., Hyungrok Kim, and Woomok Kim. 2007. Building software product line from the legacy systems: Experience in the digital audio and video domain. In *Proceedings of the 11th international software product line conference*, 171–180. Washington, DC: IEEE Computer Society.

Lee, K., Kyo C. Kang, and Jaejoon Lee. 2002. Concepts and guidelines of feature modeling for product line software engineering. In *Proceedings of the 7th international conference on software reuse: Methods, techniques, and tools*, 62–77. London: Springer-Verlag.

Lee, K., Kyo C. Kang, Minseong Kim, and Sooyong Park. 2006. Combining feature-oriented analysis and aspect-oriented programming for product line asset development. In *Proceedings of the 10th international software product line conference*, 103–112. Washington, DC: IEEE Computer Society.

Matzan, Jem. 2007. More on OpenBSD's new compiler. http://www.thejemreport.com/content/view/369/.

Milner, Robin. 1978. A theory of type polymorphism in programming. *Journal of Computer and System Sciences* 13 (2): 348–375.

Milner, R., Mads Tofte, Robert Harper, and David MacQueen. 1997. *The definition of Standard ML* (revised). Cambridge, MA: MIT Press.

MLPolyR. 2008. The MLPolyR project. http://ttic.uchicago.edu/~wchae/mlpolyr/.

Nystrom, N., Michael R. Clarkson, and Andrew C. Myers. 2003. Polyglot: An extensible compiler framework for Java. In *Proceedings of the 12th international conference on compiler construction*, 138–152. Berlin: Springer.

Parnas, David L. 1976. On the design and development of program families. *IEEE Transactions on Software Engineering* 2 (1): 1–9.

Parnas, David L. 1978. Designing software for ease of extension and contraction. In *Proceedings of the 3rd international conference on software engineering*, 264–277. Piscataway, NJ: IEEE Press.

Paulson, Larry C. 1996. *ML for the working programmer*. London: Cambridge University Press.

Rémy, Didier. 1991. Type inference for records in a natural extension of ML. Research report 1431. Institut National de Recherche en Informatique et Automatisme.

SEI. 2008. http://www.sei.cmu.edu/productlines/.

SML. 2008. Standard ML of New Jersey. http://smlnj.org.

Vichare, Abhijat. 2008. Basic information about GCC. Indian Institute of Technology, Bombay. http://www.cfdvs.iitb.ac.in/~amv/gcc-int-docs.

Wu, X., Suman Roychoudhury, Barrett Bryant, Jeff Gray, and Marjan Mernik. 2005. A two-dimensional separation of concerns for compiler construction. In *Proceedings of the 2005 ACM symposium on applied computing (SAC)*; Session: Programming for separation of concerns, 1365–1369. New York: ACM.

Zenger, Matthias, and Martin Odersky. 2001a. Extensible algebraic datatypes with defaults. In *Proceedings of the 6th international conference on functional programming*, 241–252. New York: ACM.

Zenger, Matthias, and Martin Odersky. 2001b. Implementing extensible compilers. Paper presented at ECOOP workshop on multiparadigm programming with object-oriented languages, Budapest, Hungary.

Chapter 10

Formal Verification and Software Product Lines

Tomoji Kishi
Waseda University, Tokyo, Japan

Natsuko Noda
NEC Corporation, Tokyo, Japan

Contents

10.1 Introduction

Advances in embedded computing technologies have made society extremely dependent on embedded software used in automobile, mobile phone, and home electronics applications, etc. Consequently, the reliability of embedded software is crucial for daily life. In the past, the development of embedded software has been implementation-centric. However, due to an increase in the size and complexity of software and a reduction in development time, it is difficult to produce reliable software using conventional techniques. Therefore, the quality of embedded software has become a matter of concern. To solve this problem, various software engineering techniques, such as analysis/design methods and reuse technologies, are currently introduced. Product line engineering is one of the most advanced software practices based on these results (Clements and Northrop 2001).

It is expected that scientific approaches such as formal verification will be introduced in addition to these engineering approaches. Unlike conventional testing, in which we run a limited number of test cases, this technique, if successful, exhaustively verifies the properties of the target system. Formal verification has a long history and has been reported to be successful in many cases. However, most of these cases belong to the hardware domain or critical software fields, such as military and avionics. Furthermore, the application of formal verification to embedded software development for civilian industries such as automobiles, communications, and consumer electronics has thus far been limited. One of the main reasons is that the techniques require a large amount of time and human resources. With this background, we examine the application of formal verification techniques in the context of software product line development (Kishi et al. 2004; Kishi, Noda, and Katayuma 2005; Kishi and Noda 2006). This is because a majority of embedded systems in civilian industries are developed as product lines, and we can expect to reduce the cost by reusing the verification schemes in the application-engineering phase. The reuse of test schemes has already been proposed (Pohl, Böckle, and van der Linden 2005), and in this chapter, we extend it to formal verification. We also apply the techniques in the domain-engineering phase, as it is desirable to verify core assets in terms of possible usage of the assets, and we can expect to exhaustively verify the assets by using formal techniques.

In Section 10.2, we introduce design testing, an application of formal verification techniques to design verification. In Sections 10.3 and 10.4, we explain how our design testing works in the application-engineering phase and the domain-engineering phase, respectively. In Section 10.5, we introduce a tool that supports design testing in the context of product line development (PLD).

10.2 Design Testing

In this section, we clarify the type of design verification that was examined and the method of applying model-checking techniques (Clarke, Grumberg, and Peled 1999) to the verification.

10.2.1 Design Verification Based on Test Scenario

In this study, we examined a family of embedded software for a car audio system (CAS) that controls audio equipment such as CD players and AM/FM tuners in response to user operations. This example is based on actual software provided by a company, but in this chapter we simplify the case for the sake of brevity.

Among the many issues that have to be verified, the main issue in the project is to check the validity of the software design based on test scenarios. A test scenario is a set of event sequences that are expected to make the target system move into a specific state; it can be defined as a quadruplet $(T, I, \{S\}, F)$, where T denotes target system, I denotes the initial state of T, $\{S\}$ denotes a set of event sequences sent to T from external entities, and F denotes the final state of T. In other words, design verification based on test scenarios (we term it *design testing*) is an activity to check whether the target design model of state I moves into state F after receiving an event sequence included in $\{S\}$.

10.2.2 Applying Model Checking Techniques

One of the most common techniques to verify the design is reviewing. Although reviewing is a useful technique, it is not effective for exhaustive checking, since it is performed manually. We can also verify the design by using tools such as design simulators and can actually execute the design model. However, it is difficult to prepare test scenarios that cover every possible situation. In order to realize more exhaustive checking, we examine the application of model checking techniques for design testing.

A model-checking technique is a formal verification technique in which we describe the target system as a finite-state model, provide some logical properties, and automatically check whether the given properties are valid (Clarke, Grumberg, and Peled 1999). Since embedded software must appropriately react to every possible combination and sequence of events occurring within its environment, it is necessary to exhaustively check its behavior. Model-checking techniques are suitable for this type of verification (Holzmann 2004; Lavazza, Quaroni, and Venturelli 2001). Further, we focus on design verification instead of code verification; this is because many bugs are embedded in the design phase, and it is important to verify the design before coding.

A typical use of model-checking techniques is to describe the target system and its environment as a state model, give some logical properties, and automatically check whether the given property holds. Based on this scheme, we develop a verification model (T, E, P) for each test scenario $(T, I, \{S\}, F)$. Here, T denotes a target model similar to the one referred to in the test scenario, E denotes the environment model that sends event sequences included in $\{S\}$ to T, and P denotes the property that expresses "if the target T in state I receives any event sequence included in $\{S\}$, eventually, it falls into state F." We can test the design model in terms of the test scenario by combining T and E and applying the model checker to verify whether the P holds.

Figure 10.1 shows an example of the verification model. Here, the target model T has EV-Hdlr (event handler) and CD-Ctrl (CD controller), and the environment model E has BTN1 (button1) and BTN2 (button2) that capture user operations, and CD (CD drive) that are controlled by this software. The property P is expressed in our extended representation of Linear Temporal Logic (LTL) formula as [] (BTN1@END_RELEASED)->(<> CD@OFF) (whenever BTN1 reaches the state END_RELEASED, CD eventually reaches the state OFF). We can check the model (combination of the target and environment models) along with the property by using a model checker. Thus, we can exhaustively check the test scenario

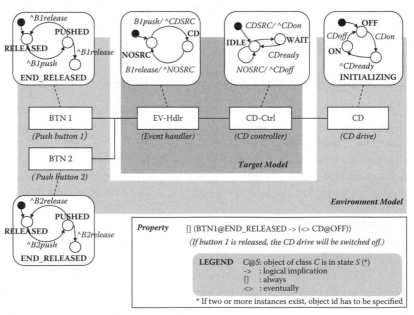

Figure 10.1   Example of the verification model.

because a model checker can handle generic test scenarios expressed in regular expressions (which is equivalent to a state model).

10.3 Verification by Reuse

10.3.1 Issues

PLD comprises two phases—developing core assets for product families (domain-engineering phase) and developing each product with the core assets (application-engineering phase) (Clements and Northrop 2001; Gomaa and Barber 2004; Pohl, Böckle, and van der Linden 2005). In this section, we examine an application of our design testing to the application-engineering phase. In other words, before actually implementing the product, we want to check whether its design correctly realizes the required features. Since products in a product family are similar, the test scenarios for each product are also similar. Therefore, similar to a reusable design model, we can develop a reusable verification model that can be applied to multiple products in a family.

Intuitively speaking, we define generic verification models, i.e., generic environment models and properties that can be applied to every product, and we reuse them throughout the PLD. If some parts of the environment model or properties differ among products, we define variation points at these points; further, we prepare variants for them. When we select a feature for a product, we identify the variants that correspond to the feature and apply the variants to the variation point in order to define the corresponding verification model.

10.3.2 Variation Points in a Verification Model

In order to examine reuse in PLD, we have classified the software design into the following three levels:

1. **Shared Architecture (SA) level:** The component structure (configuration of components) that is shared by all products. This level corresponds to the frozen spot of product line architecture (PLA). Generally, this part is developed as the core asset and should be built and verified in the domain-engineering phase. We will examine how to verify core assets in the following section.
2. **Derived Architecture (DA) level:** The component structure that may differ according to the product. In this case, "derived" implies that these structures are among the variations of PLA. Figure 10.2 shows the PLA of the CAS. Multiple BTNs capture user operations, and Ev-Hdlr interprets user operations into manipulation events to devices. CAS generally has multiple DV (devices), such as CD-player, AM/FM tuner, and liquid-crystal display (LCD). Each device is controlled by a corresponding DV-Ctrl (device

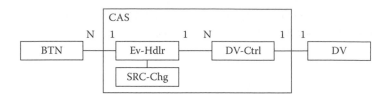

Figure 10.2   Product line architecture (static structure) of a CAS.

controller). From this PLA, we can derive a variety of architectures. In the application-engineering phase, we decide the concrete architecture for a product.

3. **Component (CO) level:** The internal structure of each component. As each product has a different component structure (in the DA level), each component has to handle different events from different components. Further, each component may have a different behavior, depending on the product. In application engineering, we need to verify whether a design realizes the intended behavior.

The upper side of Figure 10.3 shows an example of a reusable verification model. Here, overview of a CAS product family is as follows: every product has two buttons (BTN1 and BTN2), and some products have an additional button (BTN3). Every product has a CD, and some products have a TNR (tuner). Some tuners have a TI (Traffic Information) function that directly tunes the tuner to a traffic information frequency. This reusable model has BTN3 and TNR as optional components (denoted as //OPTIONAL) in the environment model, and TNR-Ctrl as an optional component in the target model. CAS also has EV-Hdler and SRC-Chg (source change) that switches audio mode (such as CD, tuner, and TI). As products may have different audio modes, SRC-Chg is defined as an alternative component (denoted as //ALTERNATIVE), with two variants: SRC-Chg-A and SRC-Chg-B (denoted as //VARIANT); in order to handle a TI function, the state diagram for SRC-Chg-B has optional transitions (denoted as //OPT).

The lower part of Figure 10.3 shows two derived verification models: The left is a verification model for a product that has two buttons and only a CD player. The right is a verification model for a product that has three buttons, a CD player, and an AM/FM TUNER. If the TUNER has no TI function, transition t1 in the state diagram for SRC-Chg-B is selected; if it has TI function, transitions t2 and t3 are selected.

In defining a reusable verification model for the CAS, we use the following modeling mechanisms:

■ **DA level:** This level is related to the variations in components and connections defined in a static model.
  – Optional component (class with //OPTIONAL stereotype)

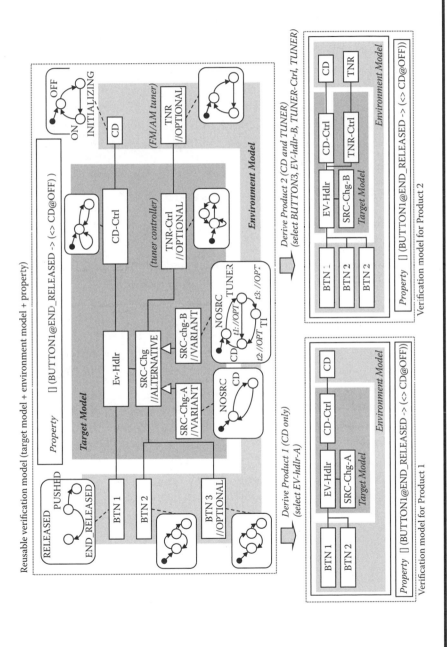

Figure 10.3   Example of a reusable verification model.

– Optional connection (association with //OPTIONAL stereotype)
■ **CO level:** This level is related to the variations in behavior of each component defined in the state model.
   – Alternative state model: prepare multiple state models for a component as variants. Strictly speaking, we define alternative components (class with //ALTERNATIVE stereotype) that have multiple components as variants (class with //VARIANT stereotype); each has its own state model. An alternative component and its variant components are associated with a generalization relationship.
   – Optional transition (transition with //OPT stereotype)
■ Alternative guard, conditions: prepare multiple guards/actions as variants (these are realized by using macros)

We also define optional and alternative parts in the properties.

10.3.3 Organizing Core Assets

In this section, we show how to organize core assets and how to manage traceability among feature models, design models, and verification models.

10.3.3.1 Feature Model and Extended Design Model

In the feature model, we hierarchically depict the features of a product family. The features can be mandatory, optional, or alternative (Kang et al. 1990). Figure 10.4 shows a part of the feature model of the CAS.

The design model is depicted in UML with some extensions in order to describe PLA as explained in Section 10.3.2; namely, we introduce an optional and alternative part into the class diagram and state diagrams. Figure 10.5 shows a part of the design model of the CAS. In this figure, optional components such as BTN3, TNR-Ctrl, and TNR are defined. SRC-Chg is defined as an alternative component and has multiple variants. We can define a different state model

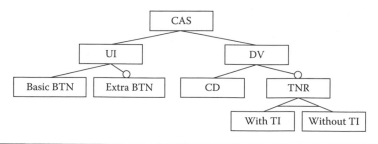

Figure 10.4   Example of a CAS feature model.

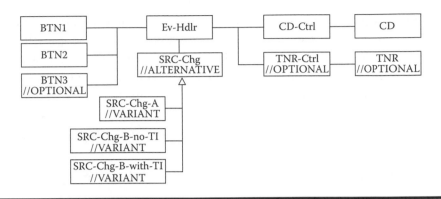

Figure 10.5   Example of a CAS design model.

for each variant and switch the behavior of alternative classes by selecting one of their variants.

The reusable verification model (target model *T* and environment model *E*) is depicted by using the same notation as the design model. The properties *P* are given by a textual description. Figure 10.6 shows a part of the verification model of the CAS. It should be noted that the configuration of target components is the same as the design model shown in Figure 10.5, and the state models for these target components are derived from the design model. On the other hand, we define the state model of the environment components in order to send event sequences included in {*S*} of the corresponding test scenario.

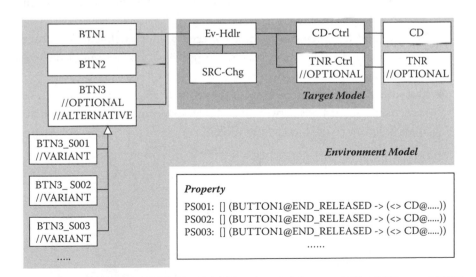

Figure 10.6   Example of a CAS verification model.

Since a target generally has multiple test scenarios, we prepare multiple verification models. Since the static structure of each verification model is generally the same, we can organize multiple verification models into one verification model utilizing the alternative notation. In Figure 10.6, the environment component BTN3 is defined as an alternative component. Each variant (such as BTN3_S001 and BTN3_S002) corresponds to a different test scenario. Descriptions such as PS001 and PS002 are properties that correspond to a test scenario.

10.3.3.2 Traceability

We define the following links among the models explained in Section 10.3.3.1 so as to systematically obtain the verification model for a specific test scenario (Figure 10.7).

■ **Product names and features:** For each product in product families, define links between the product name and its features in a feature model. Using these links, we can identify the features of a product in a product family.

■ **Features and constituents of the design model and verification model:** For each feature, define the links between the feature and components, connections, transitions/guards/actions in the design, and verification models. Using these links, we can identify a design model for the product as well as a verification model with alternative parts. (Since a product generally has multiple test scenarios, the verification model for a product has multiple variants corresponding to them.)

■ **Product and test scenario names:** For each product, define links between the product and test scenario names. Using these links, we can identify test scenario names related to the product.

■ **Test scenario names and variants in the verification model:** For each test scenario name, define links between it and the variants in the verification model. These links can be used to identify variants corresponding to the test scenario.

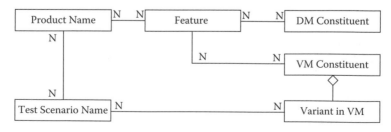

Figure 10.7   Overview of links among models.

10.4 Verification for Reuse

10.4.1 Issues

We have introduced an application of formal verification to the application-engineering phase. In this section, we examine the application of formal verification to the domain-engineering phase. In this phase, we develop core assets that can be used by many products. Therefore, these assets must be verified in terms of every possible situation in which they will be used. Here, the term *situation* implies not only the usage of the components, such as parameter values and calling sequences, but also assumptions under which the component are used, such as relative priority of components and usage of shared resources.

In an actual situation, it is unreasonable to verify the core assets in every possible situation because of the large number of situations that must be considered (Pohl, Böckle, and van der Linden 2005; Trew 2005). Even though we apply model-checking techniques that exhaustively check the properties of a given model, state explosion problems can occur, and that prevents us from checking of every possible situation. Hence, we must develop a strategy to reduce the number of situations. For testing core assets, a technique is proposed in which we can concretely assume which potential products will use the core assets and then test them from these products (Pohl, Böckle, and van der Linden 2005). We apply the technique in our formal verification. In order to apply the strategy systematically, we utilize an *assumption model*. In the next subsection, we will explain the model.

10.4.2 Assumption Model

The assumption model is a model that depicts a core asset and its environment in terms of a class diagram. The purpose of the assumption model is to define explicitly in what environment the core asset is used. We believe it is important to examine meaningful situations of the environment rather than to simply list up every possible situation or examine the environment in an ad hoc fashion.

Figure 10.8 shows another CAS-PLA. In this PLA, user operation is captured by (multiple) BTNs (buttons), and EV-Hdlr decides the necessary operation to device-controllers. SRC-Chg switches the current audio source. CD-Ctrl, CDCHG-Ctrl (CD-changer control), and TNR-Ctrl control CD, CD-CHG (CD-changer), and TNR, respectively. DSP-Ctrl (display-controller) controls LCD. LCD displays the current status based on information from EV-Hdlr. LCD also displays information from CD, such as track number. CD-Ctrl and TNR-Ctrl have two variations: one for standard model (S) and one for high-end model (H).

Assume that we make EV-Hdlr, SRC-Chg, and DispCtrl as core assets. The following are steps to develop assumption model.

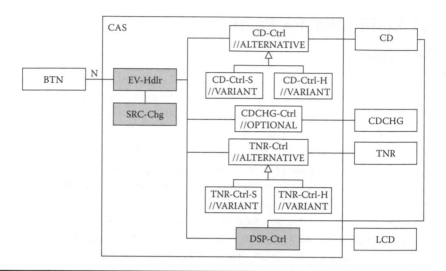

Figure 10.8 An example of a CAS core asset.

1. Clarify scope. Firstly, determine potential products. In this example, we include three products: P1 (with two BTNs, CD-Ctrl-S, TNR-Ctrl-S), P2 (with three BTNs, CD-Ctrl-H, TNR-Ctrl-H), and P3 (with three BTNs, CD-Ctrl-H, TNR-Ctrl-H, CD-Chg-Ctrl) in the scope.

2. Identify components that directly have interaction with the core asset. In this example, BTNs, CD-Ctrl (CD-Ctrl-S and CD-Ctrl-H), CDCH-Ctrl, TNR-Ctrl (TNR-Ctrl-S and TNR-Ctrl-H), and DSP-Ctrl have direct interaction.

3. Add constraints on the diagram so that only meaningful component combination are allowed. In this example, CD-Ctrl-S and TNR-Ctrl-S are selected together, and CD-Ctrl-H and TNR-Ctrl-H are selected together. Also, CD-CHG-Ctrl and CD-Ctrl-H are selected together. Hence, we add dependencies among these components.

4. Identify components that have an impact on the behavior of the above selected components. In this example, CD has an impact on the behavior of the DSP-Ctrl, and is selected.

Figure 10.9 shows the assumption model of this example. This depicts the environment in which the core asset is used under the above-mentioned assumption (usage).

10.4.3 Verification Strategy

Based on the assumption model mentioned in Section 10.4.2, we systematically verify the core asset. The following is the basic strategy:

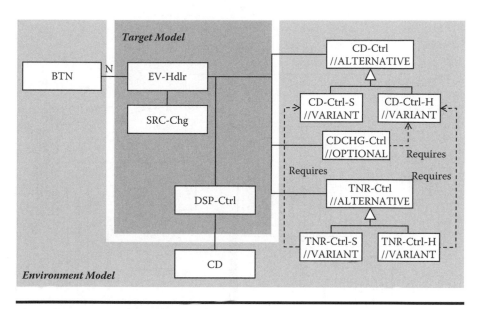

Figure 10.9   An assumption model.

1. *Examine possible component configurations*: In this example, there are three possible configurations corresponding to P1, P2, and P3.
2. *Examine possible test scenarios*: In this example, each BTN has various sets of operation sequences. Decide the test sequences to be tested.
3. *If the combination is too large, add constraints*: Generally, the number of possible configurations and test sequences (and their combinations) can become large. If it becomes too large to verify, add constraints on the assumption model to reduce the verification cost. For example, restrict some combinations, change the multiplicity (e.g., describe 1, 16, or 32 combinations instead of *N*), and reduce the number of test scenarios.

Assumption modeling helps us to explicitly examine meaningful usage of a core asset and also to explicitly model the environment. It also supports us to examine how to reduce possible usage if it becomes too large.

10.5 Support Tool

We have developed a support tool for the above-mentioned design verification (Figure 10.10) (Kishi et al. 2004; Kishi, Noda, and Katayama 2005; Kishi and Noda 2006; Noda and Kishi 2007). The tool was developed on an Eclipse platform (Eclipse Foundation 2004) and uses a SPIN model checker (Holzmann 2004). Using Modeler, users can define UML models (target and environment

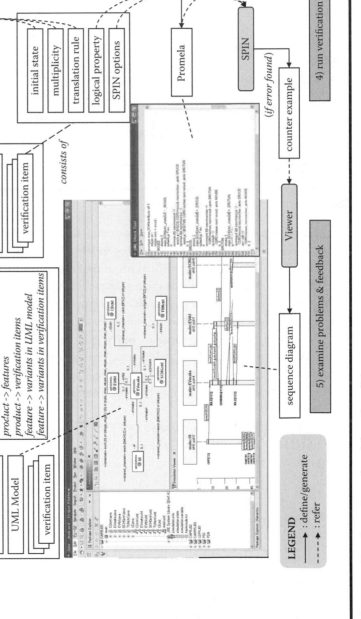

Figure 10.10 Overview of tool functionalities.

models), feature models for describing the features of a product line, and verification items and links among them. A verification item is a set of properties and other necessary information, as described later. By specifying a product, Link Manager derives verification models and necessary verification items. Translator translates the model into the input language of SPIN (Promela), and SPIN verifies the properties defined in the verification item. Since the initial state, initial value of the attribute, and translation rule (e.g., how to handle events not defined in the state model) may be different for each verification item, each test item contains this information along with SPIN options. When the verification fails, SPIN shows a counterexample (an execution trace that violates the given property). Since the counterexample is based on Promela, Viewer shows it in the form of a UML sequence diagram.

The tool has the following features to support design testing for both application engineering and domain engineering:

■ Extend UML class-diagram and state-diagram notation to be able to define variation points.
■ Support to define multiple test scenarios compactly. The tool provides a simple scenario description language to compactly define multiple scenarios and verify model in terms of defined test scenarios.
■ Derive verification model. By selecting features defined in the feature model, the system derives the verification model and a set of verification items.
■ Support to define multiple verification items and verify them in a lump. Each verification item may be based on different configurations and properties. As we have to verify various verification items derived from the assumption model, this capability makes the verification work easier.

10.6 Conclusion

One of the important objectives of product line development is the timely delivery of products. In order to achieve this goal, we must reduce the time taken for both the derivation and verification of products. We have proposed a systematic method to verify products based on formal verification techniques. Though formal verification is one of the promising techniques to develop reliable embedded software, it is expensive to apply. We will refine our verification approach to make formal verification more widely usable for embedded software development.

References

Clarke Jr., Edmund M., Orna Grumberg, and Doron A. Peled. 1999. *Model checking.* Cambridge, MA: MIT Press.

Clements, Paul, and Linda Northrop. 2001. *Software product lines: Practices and patterns.* Indianapolis: Addison-Wesley.

Eclipse Foundation. 2004. Eclipse home page. http://www.eclipse.org/.

Gomaa, Hassan, and Mayann Barber. 2004. *Designing software product lines with UML: From use cases to pattern-based software architectures.* Indianapolis: Addison-Wesley.

Holzmann, Gerard J. 2004. *The SPIN model checker: Primer and reference manual.* Indianapolis: Addison-Wesley.

Kang, Kyo C., Sholom G. Cohen, James A. Hess, William E. Novak, and A. Spencer Peterson. 1990. Feature-oriented domain analysis (FODA) feasibility study. Technical report. CMU/SEI-90-TR-21. Carnegie Mellon University, Pittsburgh.

Kishi, Tomoji, Toshiaki Aoki, Shin Nakajima, Takuya Katayama, and Natsuko Noda. 2004. Project report: High reliable object-oriented embedded software design. In *Proceedings of the 2nd IEEE workshop on software technology for embedded and ubiquitous computing systems* (WSTFEUS'04), 144–148. Washington, DC: IEEE Computer Society.

Kishi, Tomoji, Natsuko Noda, and Takuya Katayama. 2005. Design verification for product line development. *In Proceedings of software product line conference 2005* (SPLC Europe), 150–161. Berlin/Heidelberg: Springer.

Kishi, Tomoji, and Natsuko Noda. 2006. Formal verification and software product line. *Communications of the ACM* 49 (12): 73–77.

Lavazza, Luigi, Gabliele Quaroni, and Matteo Venturelli. 2001. Combining UML and formal notations for modeling real-time systems. *ACM SIGSOFT Software Engineering Notes* 16 (5): 196–206.

Noda, Natsuko, and Tomoji Kishi. 2007. Design verification tool for product line development. In *Proceedings of the 11th international software product line conference* (SPLC 2007), 147–148. Washington, DC: IEEE Computer Society.

Pohl, Klaus, Günter Böckle, and Frank van der Linden. 2005. *Software product line engineering: Foundations, principles, and techniques.* New York: Springer-Verlag.

Trew, Tim. 2005. Enabling the smooth integration of core assets: Defining and packaging architectural rules for a family of embedded products. In *Proceedings of software product line conference 2005* (SPLC Europe), 137–149. Berlin/Heidelberg: Springer.

TECHNICAL ISSUES III

Chapter 11

Multiple-View Requirements Models for Software Product Line Engineering

Hassan Gomaa and Erika Mir Olimpiew

George Mason University, Fairfax, VA

Contents

11.1 Introduction

Software applications are developed to fulfill the needs of different users in various business domains, such as the customers and operators of a banking system. Over time, a business may develop and deploy several similar applications and configure each application for a different environment, with variations in language, business rules, operating system, and hardware features. Managing variability in these applications becomes an important issue as the number of features and feature combinations increases.

A software product line (SPL) development method proactively designs a family of applications with similar characteristics in order to reuse common features across the members of an SPL and also to distinguish between the features, or requirements, that differentiate these applications. An SPL is a collection of applications that have so much in common that it is worthwhile to study and analyze the common features as well as analyzing the features that differentiate the applications (Parnas 1978; Clements and Northrop 2002; Gomaa 2005; Weiss and Lai 1999). Developing an SPL requires more time and resources than developing a single application. Over time, however, this additional investment is expected to pay off by reducing the time to market and costs of deriving and configuring new applications (Clements and Northrop 2002).

Many software specification and design methods advocate a modeling approach in which the system under development is represented by means of multiple views (Gomaa and Shin 2004). Each view presents a different perspective on the system being developed. Multiple-view modeling of SPLs faces additional challenges, namely how to model commonality and variability among the family members that constitute the SPL. Furthermore, it is important to define how the multiple views relate to each other, for example how variability in one view of the product line relates to variability in a different view and how a change to one view affects other views. This chapter describes the multiple-view requirements model of software product lines developed using an object-oriented UML-based product line modeling approach.

Managing features is an essential part of SPL development, where common features are present in every application of the SPL, optional features are present in some applications of the SPL, and alternative features are mutually exclusive with other features in the SPL. Using a feature-oriented approach in a model-based SPL development method can facilitate the representation and analysis of variability in the functional requirements models of a SPL.

This chapter describes how a feature-oriented approach is used to relate features to variability in multiple-view requirements models of an SPL, and to distinguish between coarse-grained and fine-grained functional variability in these models. The reusable-requirements models are reusable use case models, reusable feature models, reusable activity models, and reusable functional-test models. This approach is illustrated using examples from a banking system SPL case study.

11.2 Reusable Software Requirements Models

11.2.1 Multiple-View Requirements Models for Single Applications

A model of a software application is an abstraction of that application from a particular viewpoint, described with a graphical or textual notation, such as UML (Rumbaugh, Jacobson, and Booch 2005; OMG 2007). A software-modeling method describes how to develop software models using a modeling notation. Many modeling approaches use several modeling views of a software system, referred to as *multiple-view modeling* (Gomaa and Shin 2004).

Multiple-view modeling includes a functional modeling view to describe the functions of the system: a static modeling view (to provide a structural perspective of the system) and a dynamic modeling view (to provide a behavioral perspective of the system). In UML-based modeling methods, the functional view is provided through a use case model, which provides informal, narrative descriptions of interactions between the actor (application user) and application in terms of a main sequence (scenario) and alternative sequences (Jacobson et al. 1992).

Use case models can be supplemented with additional models, such as activity diagrams and decision tables, to more precisely describe an application's functional requirements. Activity diagrams formalize the logic and sequencing of activities in a use case description, and decision tables (McMullen 1984) can be used to concisely describe the conditions and activities associated with each use case scenario (Binder 2002). These models can also be used to create functional test specifications for an application derived from the SPL.

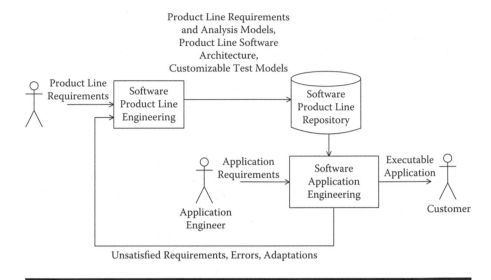

Figure 11.1   SPL development process used with PLUS.

11.2.2 Multiple-View Requirements Models for Software Product Lines

Several SPL development methods have been investigated (Kang et al. 1998; Weiss and Lai 1999; Clements and Northrop 2002; Gomaa and Webber 2004; Gomaa and Saleh 2005; Gomaa 2005). SPL development consists of SPL engineering and application engineering (Figure 11.1). SPL engineering is the development of requirements, analysis, and design models for a family of systems that comprise the application domain. During application engineering, an application configuration is derived from the SPL, which includes all the common features and selected optional and alternative features. The requirements, analysis, design, and code models are also customized based on the features selected for that application.

Product line UML-based software (PLUS) engineering is a feature-oriented UML-based design method. In the requirements phase, PLUS uses feature modeling to model variability and use case modeling to describe the SPL functional requirements (Gomaa 2005). The relationship between features and use case is explicitly modeled by means of a feature/use case dependency table.

11.3 Reusable Use Case Models

In single applications, use cases describe the functional requirements of a system; they can also serve this purpose in SPLs. Griss et al. indicated that the goal of the use case analysis is to get a good understanding of the functional requirements, whereas the goal of feature analysis is to enable reuse (Griss, Favaro, and Alessandro 1998). Use cases and features complement each other. Thus optional and alternative use cases are mapped to optional and alternative features, respectively, while use case variation points are also mapped to features (Gomaa 2005).

In an SPL, kernel use cases are required by all members of the SPL. Other use cases are optional, in that they are required by some but not all members of the SPL. Some use cases may be alternative, i.e., different versions of the use case are required by different members of the SPL. In UML, the use cases are labeled with the stereotype «kernel», «optional», or «alternative» (Gomaa 2005). In addition, variation points specify locations in the use case, where variability can be introduced (Jacobson, Griss, and Jonsson 1997; Gomaa and Webber 2004; Gomaa 2005).

Large-scale (coarse grained) variability is represented by optional and alternative use cases. Small-scale (fine grained) variability is represented by variation points within use cases. Use cases also help address variability by describing where variability is introduced in the sequence of interactions between actors and use cases.

11.3.1 Example of Use Case Model and Feature to Use Case Relationship Table

An excerpt from the banking system, SPL use case model is presented in Figure 11.2. An ATM customer can query, transfer funds, or withdraw funds from his or her account by inserting a card at an ATM. An online customer can use a Web browser to query or transfer funds from his or her account. The use cases of the banking system SPL have several variation points. Some of these variation points are a vpLanguage variation point that describes locations in a use case description that are impacted by a language variation; a vpPinFormat variation point that describes a variation in the pin format entered by the user in an ATM; and vpMaxPinAttempts, which set the maximum number of invalid pin attempts at an ATM.

11.4 Reusable Feature Models

The emphasis in feature modeling is capturing the SPL variability, as given by optional and alternative features, since these features differentiate one member of the family from the others (Kang 1990; Kang et al. 1998). Features are analyzed and categorized as common features (must be supported in all SPL members), optional features (only required in some SPL members), alternative features (a choice of features is available), and prerequisite features (dependent upon other features). There may also be dependencies among features, such as mutually exclusive features.

With PLUS, features can be incorporated into UML using the meta-class concept, in which features are modeled using the UML static-modeling notation and given stereotypes to differentiate between «common feature», «optional feature», and

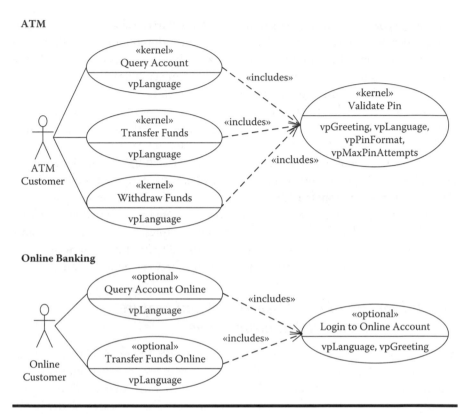

Figure 11.2   Excerpt of use case model of banking system SPL.

«alternative feature» (Gomaa 2005). Furthermore, feature groups, which place a constraint on how certain features can be selected for an SPL member, such as mutually exclusive features, are also modeled using meta-classes and given stereotypes, e.g., «zero-or-one-of feature group» or «exactly-one-of feature group» (Gomaa 2005).

The advantage of feature modeling to identify modeling variability is that features capture both large-scale and small-scale variability in a uniform way and provide a precise way of describing feature dependencies and feature constraints. Features can be determined from use cases and represented in tables that map the relationship of features to use cases (Gomaa 2005).

11.4.1 Example of Feature Model

A banking system SPL example will be used to illustrate the reusable requirements models. Figure 11.3 shows a feature model of the banking system SPL. This banking system SPL provides ATM services and optional online services to its customers. This SPL can be used to derive a configuration of a banking application that provides ATM services only, or an application that provides both ATM and online

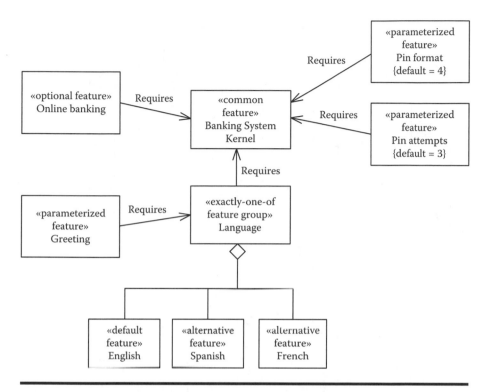

Figure 11.3   Excerpt of feature model of banking system SPL.

services. In addition, a banking application can be configured for one of three different languages, a customized greeting, a pin length, and a maximum number of pin attempts.

An excerpt of the feature to use case relationship table for the banking system SPL is shown in Table 11.1. The Banking System Kernel feature is associated with the Validate Pin, Query Account, Transfer Funds, and Withdraw Funds kernel use cases. The Online Banking feature is associated with the Login to Online Account, Query Account Online, and Transfer Funds Online optional use cases. The English, French, and Spanish alternative language features are associated with the vpLanguage variation point in all use cases of the banking system SPL. This variation point affects all display prompts of an ATM.

11.5 Reusable Activity Models

Functional models, such as activity diagrams, can be used to make the sequencing of activities in a use case description more precise for analysis and testing. A requirements analyst develops an activity diagram for each use case and explicitly models each use case scenario. Decision points identify where alternative scenarios

Table 11.1 Excerpt of Feature to Use case Relationship Table for Banking System SPL

Feature Name	Feature Category	Use case Name	Use Case/Var. Pt. (vp)	Variation Point Name
Banking System Kernel	common	Validate Pin	kernel	
		Query Account	kernel	
		Transfer Funds	kernel	
		Withdraw Funds	kernel	
Online Banking	optional	Login to Online Account	optional	
		Query Account Online	optional	
	optional	Transfer Funds Online	optional	
English	default, alternative		vp	vpLanguage
Spanish	alternative		vp	vpLanguage
French	alternative		vp	vpLanguage
Pin Attempts	parameterized	Validate Pin	vp	vpPinAttempts
Pin Format	parameterized	Validate Pin	vp	vpPinFormat

diverge from the main scenario. An activity diagram is developed from each use case description in the use case model, and then activities in the activity diagrams are associated with the features in the feature model.

However, sometimes it is not clear how to best represent and configure the variability in these models, in particular how to relate features to the activity nodes on the activity diagrams. An activity node can be used to represent different granularities of functional variations, ranging from a fine granularity of functional variation, such as a parameter in a use case step, to a coarse granularity of functional variation, such as a set of use cases. Further, fine-grained functional variations tend to be dispersed and repeated across the use case activity diagrams of an SPL, while coarse-grained variations are represented by an entire use case activity diagram or by a group of use case activity diagrams. Thus, managing fine-grained variability requires more sophisticated techniques to group related functions and to minimize redundancy. CADeT uses UML stereotypes to distinguish between different granularities of functional variability in the activity diagrams of an SPL, and uses feature conditions to relate this variability to features in the feature model.

The following stereotypes are used in an activity node to distinguish between different levels of functional abstraction:

- A «use case» activity node, which describes a use case
- An «extension use case» activity node, which describes an extension use case
- An «included use case» activity node, which describes an included use case
- An «aggregate step» activity node, which groups a sequence of activities, or events, in a use case description
- An «input step», which describes an input event from the actor to the application in a use case description
- An «output step», which describes an output event from the application to the actor in a use case description
- An «internal step», which documents an internal (nonobservable) activity in the application

An engineer uses the feature to use case relationship table of PLUS (Gomaa 2005), together with reuse stereotypes and feature conditions of CADeT, to analyze the impact of common, optional, and alternative features on the activity diagrams. A feature relationship table associates a feature with one or more use cases or variation points, where a variation point identifies one or more locations of change in the use cases (Gomaa 2005). A reuse stereotype is a UML notation that classifies a modeling element in an SPL by its reuse properties (Gomaa 2005). CADeT reuse stereotypes are applied to activity nodes rather than decision nodes as in (Reuys et al. 2005), since activity nodes can be abstracted or decomposed to represent different levels of functional granularity. CADeT contains the following reuse stereotypes to describe how an activity node is reused in the applications derived from the SPL:

- A «kernel» activity node, which corresponds to a «common» feature in the feature model
- An «optional» activity node, which corresponds to an «optional» feature in the feature model
- A «variant» activity node, which corresponds to an «alternative» feature in the feature model
- An «adaptable» activity node, which identifies an activity node that is associated with a use case variation point

For example, an «optional input step» activity node refers to an optional input event from an actor to a use case, while an «optional extension use case» activity node refers to an optional extension use case.

Besides reuse stereotypes, feature conditions are added to associate the variability in the control flow of an activity diagram with a feature in a feature model. The values of a feature condition represent possible feature selections. An optional feature in the feature model is associated with a Boolean feature condition with two possible values. An alternative feature in the feature model is associated with a feature condition that represents its feature group, where each alternative is a possible value for that feature condition. Setting the value of a feature condition enables or disables the activities associated with the feature in the activity diagram of an application derived from the SPL.

11.5.1 Example of Activity Diagram

Table 11.2 shows the feature conditions and feature selections associated with features of the banking system SPL. Figure 11.4 shows a simplified activity diagram created from the Validate Pin use case description. The Spanish, French, and English

Table 11.2   Feature Conditions of Banking System SPL

Feature Condition	Feature Selections
BankingSystemKernel	T
onlineBanking	{T, F}
language	{English, Spanish, French}
pinFormat	[3…10]
maxAttempts	[1…5]

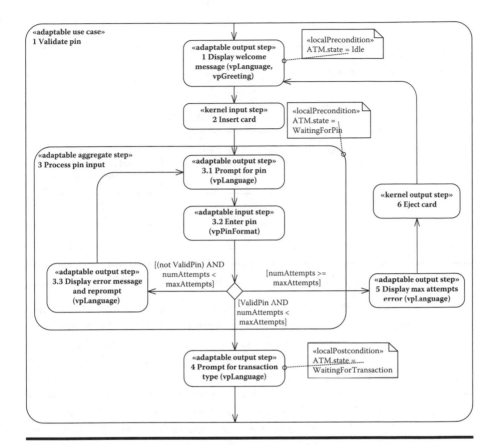

Figure 11.4   Activity diagram for Validate Pin use case.

language features correspond to the vpLanguage variation point in the feature to use case relationship table, which impacts all output steps in the activity diagram of Figure 11.4. Each of these activity nodes is stereotyped as «adaptable». The subactivity diagram in Figure 11.5 shows the feature conditions, feature condition values, and variant display prompts associated with the Spanish, French, and English language features. Since these features belong to the «exactly one of» feature group in the feature model of Figure 11.3, the language feature condition is added to the subactivity diagram with English, Spanish, and French as possible values for that condition.

11.6 Reusable Test Models

11.6.1 Model-Based Test Design for Software Product Lines

Use case-based testing methods for SPLs extend use cases, or functional models developed from these use cases, to be configurable for an application derived from

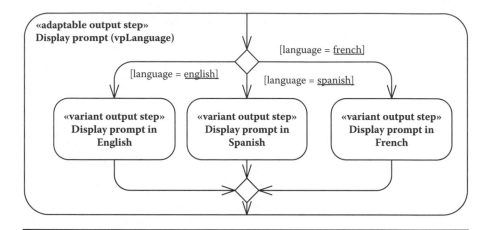

Figure 11.5   A subactivity diagram for a display prompt adaptable output step.

an SPL (Reuys et al. 2005; Kamsties, Pohl, and Reuys 2003; Bertolino and Gnesi 2003; McGregor 2001), while feature-based testing approaches for SPLs use feature models to select representative configurations to test, in situations where the set of applications derived from the SPL is not predetermined and is likely to change (Scheidemann 2006). For example, an SPL for a mobile phone may contain several optional features, which can be selected by a prospective customer. Customizable activity diagrams, decision tables and test specifications (CADeT) is a functional testing method for an SPL that creates test specifications from both the use case and feature models of an SPL. CADeT manages the relationships of common, optional, and alternative features to the use cases of an SPL by applying a feature-based coverage criterion together with a use case based coverage criterion to cover all features, all use case scenarios, and relevant feature combinations of an SPL. Managing these relationships reduces (a) the number of application configurations to test and (b) the number of reusable test specifications that need to be created to cover all use case scenarios of the SPL.

CADeT extends PLUS to create functional models that can be used to generate functional system test specifications. Figure 11.6 shows how CADeT (shaded in gray) impacts the PLUS method (Gomaa 2005). An SPL engineer develops the SPL requirement models, analysis models, and software architecture using PLUS. Then, a test engineer uses CADeT to develop customizable activity diagrams, decision tables, and test specifications from the feature and use case requirements models. An application engineer applies feature-based application derivation to derive one or more applications from the SPL, while a test engineer uses CADeT to apply feature-based test derivation to select and customize the test specifications for these applications. Any unsatisfied requirements, errors, and adaptations are sent back to the SPL engineer, who changes the reusable assets and stores them in the SPL repository. The process of updating the

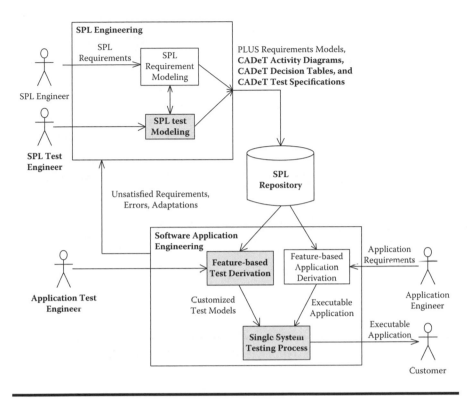

Figure 11.6   Extending PLUS with CADeT.

reusable assets, selecting features, and deriving and testing each application is repeated until the applications are ready to be delivered to the customers.

11.6.2 Meta-Modeling for Reusable Requirement Models

A meta-model describes the constructs and rules needed for creating models. Figure 11.7 is a meta-model that describes the relationships between the multiple-view requirement models of software product lines. The feature to use case relationship table in PLUS associates the features from an SPL feature model to use cases from an SPL use case model (Gomaa 2005). One feature is associated with one or more use cases, and one use case is associated with one or more features. An activity diagram and a decision table are created for each use case in the use case model. The association of features to use cases are then applied to the activity diagram and decision table created from each use case. Each feature in the feature model is associated with one or more activity diagrams, and each activity diagram is associated with one or more features. Each feature in the feature model is associated with one or more decision tables, and each decision table is associated with one or more features. Likewise, each feature in the feature model is associated with

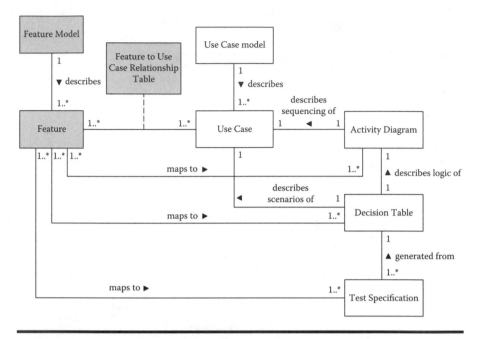

Figure 11.7   Meta-model describing relationships between multiple-view require-ments models.

one or more test specifications, and each test specification is associated with one or more features. Mapping features to the activity diagrams, decision tables, and test specifications allows these models to be selected and configured for an application derived from the SPL.

11.6.3 Decision Tables

In CADeT, decision tables are used to represent and organize the associations between features and test specifications created to cover the use case scenarios in an SPL. A decision table is created from each activity diagram in the SPL so that test specifications can be associated with each use case scenario. The pre-conditions, feature conditions, execution conditions, postconditions, and activity nodes of an activity diagram are mapped to condition rows in the decision table. Simple paths are traced from an activity diagram for each use case scenario and then mapped to a reusable test specification in a column in the decision table. A *simple path* is a sequence of unique, nonrepeating activity nodes traced from an activity diagram. A simple path begins at a precondition and ends at the next precondition or postcondition state in the activity diagram. Each simple path is mapped to a reusable test specification in a column in the decision table.

A feature can be associated with a test specification created for a use case scenario, which represents a unit of coarse-grained functionality, or a feature can be associated with a variation point in that test specification, which represents a unit of fine-grained functionality. As in an activity diagram, a variation point in a test specification in a decision table is represented using the «adaptable» stereotype.

CADeT distinguishes between the binding times of coarse-grained functional variability (feature to test specification) and fine-grained variability (feature to variation point). The feature selections of feature conditions associated with test specifications are bound during SPL engineering, while the feature selections of feature conditions associated with variation points are bound during feature-based test derivation. Delaying the binding of the fine-grained variability improves the reusability of the test specifications by reducing the number of test specifications that need to be created and maintained for an SPL.

11.6.4 Example of Decision Table

Table 11.3 shows a simplified decision table for the Validate Pin use case, which contains four test specifications that correspond to paths (columns) traced from the activity diagram in Figure 11.5 for three use case scenarios. These test specifications contain vpLanguage, vpPinFormat, and vpPinAttempts variation points. The vpLanguage variation point occurs in every test specification and is impacted by the alternative English, French, and Spanish language features. Thus, the feature selections of the language feature condition {English, French, Spanish} are entered in the intersection of each test specification with the language feature condition.

11.6.5 A Variability Mechanism to Customize Decision Tables

A *variability mechanism* is a technique that enables the automatic configuration of variability in an application's requirements, models, implementation, and test specifications. CADeT contains a tool suite that uses a parameterization variability mechanism to customize the decision tables, and then generate test specifications from these tables for an application derived from the SPL. To automate the customization of the fine-grained variability, the decision tables need to be modified to describe the variations associated with each variation point, and these variations need to be linked to features in a feature list. A feature list describes all feature conditions and possible feature selections of the SPL. A *feature condition* is a parameter variable that contains mutually exclusive feature selections, such as true/false values. Selecting the value of a feature condition selects the test specifications associated with that feature, and also customizes the fine-grained variability in the test specifications.

Table 11.3 Decision Table for Validate Pin

1 Validate Pin	«adaptable» Init sequence	«adaptable» Pin is valid	«adaptable» Pin is invalid	«adaptable» Pin is invalid max times
Feature conditions:				
BankingSystemKernel	T	T	T	T
language	{English, French, Spanish}	{English, French, Spanish}	{English, French, Spanish}	{English, French, Spanish}
pinFormat		[3...10]	[3...10]	[3...10]
maxAttempts		[1...5]	[1...5]	[1...5]
Preconditions:				
ATM	Idle	WaitingForPin	WaitingForPin	WaitingForPin
Execution conditions:				
ValidPin		T	F	F
numAttempts >= maxAttempts		F	F	T
Actions:				
1. «adaptable output step» Display welcome message (vpLanguage)	√			
2. «kernel input step» Insert card	√			

	WaitingForPin	WaitingForTransaction	WaitingForPin	Idle
3.1. «adaptable output step» Prompt for pin (vpLanguage)			√	√
3.2. «adaptable input step» Enter pin (vpPinFormat)		√	√	√
3.3. «adaptable output step» Display error message and re-prompt for pin (vpLanguage)			√	
4. «adaptable output step» Prompt for transaction type (vpLanguage)		√		
5. «adaptable output step» Display max attempts error (vpLanguage)				√
2. «kernel output step» Eject card				√
Postconditions:				
ATM	WaitingForPin	WaitingForTransaction	WaitingForPin	Idle

11.7 Configuring Reusable Test Models

A feature-based testing method for SPLs is used to customize the test specifications for SPL applications during feature-based test derivation. CADeT has tools to automate feature-based selection and customization of test specifications for each application.

First, the feature selections in the feature list of the SPL are set to correspond to the feature selections of an application derived from the SPL, which customizes the decision tables for that application. Next, CADeT's test specification generator tool is used to generate a test-specifications document from the customized decision tables for the application.

Then, CADeT's test procedure definition tool is used to create a test-procedure document for the application. The test-procedure document describes a collection of system tests, where a system test describes the order in which a sequence of test cases (test specification instances) will be executed for an application derived from the SPL. This tool applies a graph-building algorithm to construct a test-order graph from the customized decision tables during feature-based test derivation. The test-order graph sorts the test specifications by pre- and postconditions, constraining the order in which these specifications can be executed for the application. A test engineer creates system tests by tracing paths through the test-order graph and then saving these paths to a system-tests document.

11.8 Conclusions

This chapter has described a feature-oriented approach for modeling and managing variability in multiple-view requirement models of an SPL, in particular reusable feature models, reusable use case models, reusable activity models, and reusable functional test models. This approach associated features with the activity diagrams and decision tables during SPL engineering, and also distinguished between coarse-grained and fine-grained functional variability in these models. The binding time of the fine-grained variability in the test models was delayed until application derivation time in order to reduce the number of test specifications that needed to be created during SPL engineering to cover all use case scenarios and features in an SPL. A parameterization variability mechanism was applied to the decision tables, and tools were used to automatically customize these tables and generate test specifications based on the features selected for an application derived from the SPL.

Acknowledgments

Thanks to Diana Webber, who developed the initial version of the banking system SPL, and to Vinesh Vonteru, who created an SPL implementation. Thanks are also due to D. Anderson, L. Beauvais, H. Hussein, J. Pepper, and R. Rabbi for evaluating the feasibility of this method on the banking system SPL.

References

Bertolino, A., and Stefania Gnesi. 2003. PLUTO: A test methodology for product families. Paper presented at Software product-family engineering: 5th international workshop, November 4–6, 2003, Siena, Italy.

Binder, Robert. 2002. *Testing object-oriented systems: Models, patterns, and tools*. Reading, MA: Addison-Wesley.

Clements, Paul, and Linda Northrop. 2002. *Software product lines practices and patterns, SEI series in software engineering*. Boston, MA: Addison-Wesley.

Gomaa, Hassan. 2005. *Designing software product lines with UML: From use cases to pattern-based software architectures*. The Addison-Wesley Object Technology Series. London: Addison-Wesley.

Gomaa, Hassan, and Mazen Saleh. 2005. Software product line engineering for Web services and UML. Paper presented at IEEE international conference on computer systems and applications, January 2005, Cairo, Egypt.

Gomaa, Hassan, and Michael E. Shin. 2004. A multiple-view meta-modeling approach for variability management in software product lines. Paper presented at 8th international conference on software reuse, Madrid, Spain.

Gomaa, Hassan, and Diana L. Webber. 2004. Modeling adaptive and evolvable software product lines using the variation point model. Paper presented at Hawaii international conference on system sciences, January 7, 2004, Big Island, Hawaii.

Griss, M. L., J. Favaro, and M. d'Alessandro. 1998. Integrating feature modeling with the RSEB. In *International conference on software reuse*. Victoria, Canada: IEEE Computer Society.

Jacobson, I., M. Christerson, P. Jonson, and G. Overgaard. 1992. *Object-oriented software engineering: A use case driven approach*. Reading, MA: Addison-Wesley.

Jacobson, Ivar, Martin Griss, and Patrik Jonsson. 1997. *Software reuse: Architecture, process and organization for business success*. Reading, MA: Addison-Wesley.

Kamsties, Erik, Klaus Pohl, and Andreas Reuys. 2003. Supporting test case derivation in domain engineering. Paper presented at the 7th world conference on integrated design and process technology, December 2003, Austin, Texas.

Kang, K. 1990. *Feature oriented domain analysis*. Pittsburg: Software Engineering Institute.

Kang, Kyo C., Sajoong Kim, Jaejoon Lee, Kijoo Kim, Euiseob Shin, and Moonhang Huh. 1998. FORM: A feature-oriented reuse method with domain-specific reference architectures. *Annals of Software Engineering* 5: 143–168.

McGregor, John D. 2001. Testing a software product line. Technical report CMU/SEI-2001-TR-22. Software Engineering Institute, Carnegie Mellon University, Pittsburgh.

McMullen, Bill. 1984. Structured decision tables. *ACM SIGPLAN Notices* 19 (4): 34–43.

OMG. 2007. Unified modeling language: Superstructure, version 2.1. Object Management Group. http://www.omg.org/.

Parnas, D. L. 1978. Designing software for ease of extension and contraction. Paper presented at the 3rd international conference on software engineering, 1978, Atlanta, Georgia.

Reuys, A., E. Kamsties, K. Pohl, and S. Reis. 2005. Model-based testing of software product families. *Lecture Notes in Computer Science* 3520: 519–534.

Rumbaugh, J., Ivar Jacobson, and Grady Booch. 2005. *The UML reference manual*, 2nd ed. Boston, MA: Addison-Wesley.

Scheidemann, Kathrin. 2006. Optimizing the selection of representative configurations in verification of evolving product lines of distributed embedded systems. Paper presented at the 10th international software product line conference, Baltimore, MD.

Weiss, David M., and Chi Tau Robert Lai. 1999. *Software product line engineering: A family based software development process.* Reading, MA: Addison-Wesley.

Chapter 12

Managing Flexibility and Variability: A Road to Competitive Advantage

Wim Codenie, Nicolás González-Deleito,
Jeroen Deleu, and Vladimir Blagojević
Sirris, Brussels, Belgium

Pasi Kuvaja and Jouni Similä
University of Oulu, Finland

Contents

12.1 Introduction

Flexible development (flexibility) and product variability (variability) have become strategic challenges in software-intensive product development. Although they are often mixed, both are fundamentally different problems. *Flexible development* is the ability to efficiently respond to new market opportunities in an effective manner (i.e., the speed by which ideas are brought to the market). *Product variability* is the ability to offer a large number of variants to customers in an efficient manner. For many software-intensive product builders, being able to address one or even both of these challenges can result in a competitive advantage.

Given the large available state of the art in flexibility and variability management techniques, it is remarkable that implementing an effective flexibility and variability strategy still poses so many challenges to software-intensive product builders.

An empirical study conducted by Sirris at 57 software product builders in Belgium (Codenie et al. 2008) reveals two root causes for these difficulties. A first reason is that companies often neglect to interpret the flexibility and variability challenges in the scope of their specific product-development model. They apply the state of the art in flexibility and variability without much interpretation toward their specific context.

A second reason is caused by changes in the business environment and in the technological context. Not many companies remain in the same product-development model for a long period of time. Instead, they are undergoing transitions toward other development models. For these companies, choosing a flexibility and a variability approach is not a one-off decision, but a continuous activity that requires reinterpretation each time the development model changes.

The goal of this chapter is to take its readers on a journey to provide insights in the "relativity" of flexibility and variability in software product development. The core of the chapter is to present a decision framework that assists companies to reason about the static perspective of flexibility and variability (i.e., how to interpret both challenges in the applied development model) and the dynamic perspective (i.e., how to deal with changes in the development model).

This chapter is organized as follows (see Figure 12.1). Section 12.2 introduces software-intensive product development. This is followed (Section 12.3) by an overview of the four basic software product-development models used by companies: project-based development, technology platform development, customized product development, and out-of-the-box product development. Section 12.4 introduces flexibility and variability and explains why they are becoming so dominant. It also presents an overview of the state of the art in both domains. Section 12.5 introduces the static view on flexibility and variability. Section 12.6 extends this to the dynamic view by observing that many companies are facing transition between the software product-development models, resulting in different interpretations of flexibility and variability.

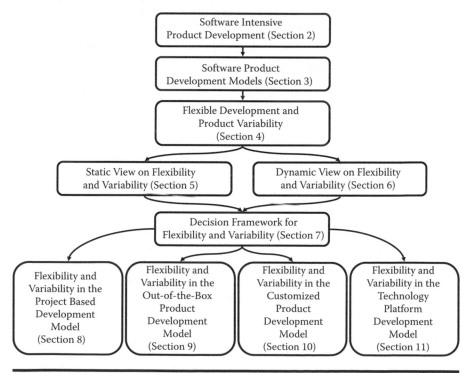

Figure 12.1   The roadmap of this chapter.

In the five following sections (Sections 12.7 through 12.11), the decision framework is introduced. Section 12.7 introduces the core of the decision framework (provides trade-offs), whereas the four remaining sections analyze both challenges in the context of each of the software product-development models.

12.2 Software-Intensive Product Development

Product development is the set of activities starting with the perception of a market opportunity and ending in the production, sale, and delivery of a product (Ulrich and Eppinger 2000). Software is playing an increasingly important role in product development (ITEA 2005), and basically two usage models can be identified for it.

In the first usage model, software has a supportive role: It is not part of an end product but rather it assists indirectly in the creation of other (not necessarily software) products and/or services. From the product builders' viewpoint, using software in this way means that software is a tool and is often considered a "necessary evil." For them, the development of the software itself is not a core activity, and in many cases the software is acquired through a buying process (COTS) (Franch and Torchiano 2005) or commissioned if it is very specific.

Software also features a second usage model in which it is made part of the end product. Because software has become a major instrument for product innovation (ITEA 2005; Rubner 2005), software is ascending the value chain of products. This is true for many sectors, including sectors that traditionally are not associated with software. An increasing number of products will become software-enabled. For example, European studies (ITEA 2005) forecast a strong global increase in the size of software development.

In this chapter we focus on companies applying the second usage model. In contrast to companies that merely use software in a supportive way, these companies are obliged to acquire a certain skill level in the domain of software engineering. Throughout this chapter, the term *software-intensive product* is used to denote a product that contains a significant software component. Companies that produce these products are called *software-intensive product builders*, and the term *software-intensive product development* is used to refer to product development as applied by software-intensive product builders.

Figure 12.2 illustrates the two usage models.* A software-intensive product builder delivers its product to three other companies. In the first two scenarios, the product is used to support the business and/or engineering processes (for a nonsoftware product builder and another software-intensive product builder). In the third scenario, the supplier relationship is different because the supplied product is a part of the product engineered by the customer. In complex supply chains, multiple nesting levels can occur.

---

* Builders can also deliver a product directly to an end user. This is not shown in the figure.

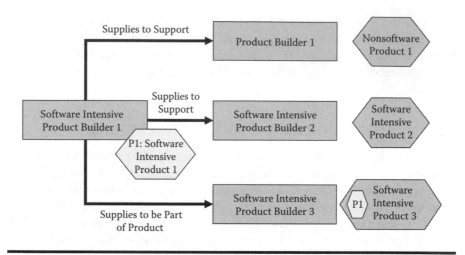

Figure 12.2 Usage models of software.

12.3 Software Product Development Models

Companies use different models for software-intensive product development. These models can be classified according to the ratio of *domain engineering* and *application engineering* they require. Domain engineering encompasses all of the engineering activities related to the development of software artifacts reusable across a set of products (i.e., activities done for groups of customers such as making a general-purpose product). Application engineering encompasses all of the engineering activities related to the development of one specific software product (i.e., all of the effort done for a single customer, such as making a tailor-made solution) (Bosch 2002; Clements and Northrop 2002; Pohl, Böckle, and van der Linden 2005).

Various product-development models are described in the literature (Bosch 2002*; Cusumano 2004†). In the context of this chapter, the following four models are considered and decomposed on the two axes of domain and application engineering (Figure 12.3):‡

1. *Project-based development (the contractors)*. This model is used when products are developed on a per-contract basis (or project basis). In this model, customers do not find the desired solution on the market and commission its development to a software-intensive product builder (the contractor).

---

* Bosch considers the following maturity levels for software product lines: independent products, standardized infrastructure, platform, software product line, configurable product base, product population, and program of product lines.
† Cusumano considers two kinds of companies: platform leaders and platform complementors.
‡ Note that the relative positions of the four models on the line of Figure 12.3 are only indicative.

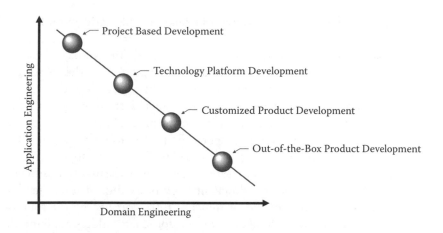

Figure 12.3   The four software product-development models.

Products developed in this model aim, therefore, at addressing a very specific demand that needs to perfectly fit in the context of the customer. Software-intensive product builders applying this model usually build these products from scratch, independently from other possibly similar products they might be developing or might have developed in the past. In some cases, excerpts from other projects might be used to build a new product. This results in ad hoc reuse between projects. In this model, the main focus is on delivering on time, within budget, and with a given quality level (Bennatan 2000). In order to be more effective and/or efficient, contractors might restrict themselves to certain markets and/or to certain technologies. For example, a contractor might be active in the financial sector and only accept Java projects.

2. *Technology platform development (the platform builders).* In this model, software-intensive product builders aim to build a dedicated platform that solves a specific technological problem (e.g., database persistence, voice recognition, facial recognition, transactional event handling, etc.). Platforms aim to be building blocks of larger products and, therefore, cannot exist on themselves. A platform can be for internal use (i.e., to be included in other products developed by a software-intensive product builder) or for external use (i.e., to be included in products developed by other companies). Companies developing a platform for internal use do it because they need the technology, but find no solution on the market. On the other hand, companies developing a platform to be used in third-party products are constantly searching for new opportunities for their technology. Once such an opportunity is found, the challenge is to integrate the platform with other products as fast and efficiently as possible. Embedding the platform in the encapsulating product typically involves

a high degree of integration activities from both the platform builder and the customer.

3. *Customized product development (the customizers).* This model is used by software-intensive product builders that develop products that need to be further adapted to suit the specific needs of customers. These companies typically operate in markets in which customers seem to have conflicting expectations. On the one hand, customers expect solutions with qualities associated with product development (e.g., proven robustness, immediate availability, proven stability, a sophisticated maintenance/support network, etc.). On the other hand, they expect solutions with qualities associated with tailor-made project development (e.g., possibility of total customer solution, every request of the customer is 100% satisfied by the solution, etc.). In order to fulfill these expectations, product builders applying this model focus on developing a common product base (e.g., some kind of "semifinished" product) that contains the core functionality shared across all the potential customers. This product base is used to derive products for customers (customization). Characteristic of the markets in which these product builders are active is that a high degree of commonalities can be found between customer needs (e.g., 80%), but at the same time, customers can have very different and opposing needs for the (smaller) remaining part (e.g., 20%). Pure out-of-the-box solutions will not work in these markets because, for a solution to be acceptable, the 20% part must also be covered. The task of deriving new products for customers from the common product base is usually done by the software-intensive product builder. It might, however, also be outsourced to external parties. In some cases, the customer can also be involved. Usually, deriving new products involves some kind of coding.

4. *Out-of-the-box product development (the box sellers).* In this model, software-intensive product builders strive to make a generic product that can suit the needs of many customers. The difference with the customized product-development model is that no customization (coding) is done by the product builder for individual customers. The assumption is that customers will be prepared to sacrifice features in favor of lower cost and product stability. For product builders applying this product-development model, finding the optimal degree of product configurability is often a challenge. Configurability can take many forms: support for different regulations (e.g., region-specific features, legislation), support for different platforms (e.g., Windows versus Linux), support for different license models (e.g., free edition, professional edition, home edition), or personalization of the product.

In the above classification, it is important to stress the difference between *customization* and *configuration*. Several definitions exist, but in this chapter the term *customization* is used to refer to the activity of changing a (generic) product into a solution satisfying the specific needs of a customer. Changing could be adding new functionality and changing or removing existing functionality. In essence, customization creates a *new* product variant that had not existed before. *Configuration* is choosing among a *predefined* set of product variants (e.g., by filling in configuration parameters).

Software-intensive product builders do not necessarily restrict themselves to only one of the above product-development models. Companies that offer a rich product portfolio can apply a different software product-development model for each product in the portfolio, depending on parameters such as market situation and product maturity.*

12.4 Flexibility and Variability in Software-Intensive Product Development

For many software-intensive product builders, resolving flexibility and/or variability is becoming a necessity to remain competitive. The section below discusses these trends and their implication on the software engineering level.

12.4.1 Product Variability: The Consequence of Embracing Customer Intimacy

Driven by customers that are increasingly cost-conscious and demanding, a large number of companies compete on the basis of giving customers exactly what they need. Customer intimacy (Treacy and Wiersema 1993) has become a business strategy that is adopted by one out of two companies (Kratochvil 2005). When applied on a large scale, customer intimacy leads to a trend called mass customization: producing in large volumes, but at the same time giving each individual customer something different. Achieving customer intimacy and mass customization leads to a large number of product variants per product base. This phenomenon is called *product variability*, the ability to offer a large number of product variants to customers.

As an increasing number of products will become software- and ICT-enabled, the variability aspects of products will be more and more situated at the software

---

* A similarity between the above models and some of the maturity levels for software product lines defined by Bosch (2002) can be observed. Unlike Bosch, the described four software product development models give no indication about maturity. For example, the out-of-the-box product development model is not necessarily more mature than the project-based development model, and vice versa. Instead, maturity must be interpreted differently for each model. For example, some companies might be very mature in applying the project-based development model while others might not.

level. This drives an increasing number of companies to raise the variability level in their software. Forecasts predict that the ability to implement an efficient and effective variability strategy will be an important prerequisite to succeed and survive as a software-intensive product builder (ITEA 2004; Kratochvil 2005). Unfortunately, many product builders do not reach the desired level of variability or fail to do so in a cost-efficient manner. This confronts software-intensive product builders with a challenging engineering paradox:

Variability paradox: How to remain efficient and effective while at the same time offer a much richer product variety to the customers?

12.4.2 Flexible Development: The Consequence of Embracing Innovation

More and more the economy is evolving from a knowledge-based economy to an economy based on creativity and innovation (Dehoff and Neely 2004; Nussbaum, Berner, and Brady 2005; Leadbeater 2008). A study by Siemens illustrates that today up to 70% of the revenue of product builders is generated by products or product features that did not exist five years ago (Rubner 2005). On top of this, 90% of the managers of companies in sectors like aviation, automotive, pharmaceuticals, and telecommunications consider innovation as essential to reach their strategic objectives (Dehoff and Neely 2004). The "innovator's dilemma" (Christensen 1997) is in many cases no longer a dilemma for companies that build products, as innovation has become an absolute necessity to deal with global challenges and trends of the future.

An important observation to make in that context is that software is increasingly being used as an instrument to realize that innovation: software as engine for innovation. This trend is not only valid within specific niche markets, it is relevant for a wide range of sectors (Glass 2006; Maiden, Robertson, and Robertson 2006; Maiden, Ncube, and Robertson 2007; Sharda 2007; Tharp 2007). Software is no longer a supporting technology, but it takes an essential role in the process of value creation.

Being "the first" is important if one wants to be innovative. Because of that, many companies are competing in a "rush to market" race. The product life cycle is shrinking at a steady pace, and few are the products today with a life cycle of one year or longer.

The principle of being first mover, the rush-to-market race, and the innovation dilemma lead to a need for flexibility. *Flexible development* is the ability to quickly respond to new market needs and customer requests. It is all about increasing the speed at which innovations and ideas are brought to the market. Companies feel the growing urge to deliver products on time.

The challenge of flexible development: Because software is "invading" in more products, flexibility is becoming a major issue in software development.

12.4.3 Flexibility and Variability Are Different

Although flexibility and variability are very different by nature, flexible development and product variability are often mixed. On the one hand, product variability is an attribute of the *product*. Increasing the degree of variability of a product corresponds to adding variation points to that product. A *variation point* is a product option. It describes a decision that can be postponed. A variation point can be fixed by making a choice between a number of options. On the other hand, flexible development is an attribute of the *engineering process*. Being flexible basically means dealing with uncertainty and with the unexpected, and being able to efficiently adapt to changes and to new contexts.

Sometimes flexibility is increased by introducing variability. In Smith (2007), for example, modularity in product architecture is put forward as an anticipation strategy to become more flexible. The reverse (increasing variability by introducing flexibility) also happens. In Extreme programming (Beck and Andres 2004), for instance, extensive upfront reasoning about future changes (with the purpose of anticipating variability) is discouraged in favor of installing a process that allows smoother software evolutions. The "extreme" view is that, if you are flexible enough, you do not need to be variable.

For some companies, only variability matters; for others, only flexibility matters; and for some others, both matter. Also, companies exist that make products for which neither variability nor flexibility matter. A study conducted by Sirris at 57 companies (Codenie et al. 2008) reveals that, for 60% of the surveyed companies, flexibility is important;* for 45% of companies, variability is important; and for 30%, both challenges are important.

The state of the art in both domains has evolved quite a bit over the past years. The domain of flexibility is dominated by agile development; in the domain of variability, a dominant position has been taken by software product lines. As for many companies, both flexibility and variability are becoming important, the combination of agile development and software product lines ("how to build a product line in an agile way") has become a major topic of interest (APLE 2006).

12.4.4 State of the Art in Product Variability

Variability can be addressed from different perspectives. From the technology perspective, object-oriented frameworks (Fayad and Schmidt 1997), design patterns (Gamma et al. 1994), and aspect-oriented development (Kiczales et al. 1996) have progressively been developed to provide better support for reuse and variability. More recently, generative techniques (Czarnecki 2005; OMG 2009) provide a

---

* Importance was rated according to five levels. In this context, important means that the company experienced difficulties managing the challenge and that it foresaw considerable optimizations if the challenge could be managed better.

different approach. They aim to generate code in an automated way from high-level specifications. Research to support this specific goal is known as *model-driven development* (Selic 2003). Some of these techniques can also be used to generate product variants from a common product.

Another relevant research area is the domain of configuration techniques. This ranges from simple configuration strategies based on parameterization (e.g., XML) up to fundamental research in configuration languages, consisting of using domain-specific languages for configuration (Mernik, Heering, and Sloane 2005). The goal is to extend products with languages to allow customers to perform more complex configurations than is possible with conventional configuration parameters.

From the engineering perspective, various modeling techniques for variability have been proposed both by academia and industry (Pohl, Böckle, and van der Linden 2005). Many of them have their roots in feature modeling (e.g., FODA), but significant contributions also have come from related areas, including configuration management, domain analysis, requirements engineering, software architecture, formal methods, and domain-specific languages.

Finally, software product lines (Clements and Northrop 2002) have received extensive attention during the last few years (ACM 2006b), and an increasing number of companies are considering adopting it. Software product line engineering has been recognized as one of the most promising software development paradigms, which substantially increases the productivity of IT-related industries, enables them to handle the diversity of global markets, and reduces time to market (Sugumaran, Park, and Kang 2006).

Despite the large available state of the art, successfully introducing variability in software-intensive products is not straightforward. A first consequence is an increased complexity in all the activities of the life cycle of a product (requirements engineering, design, implementation, testing, etc.). For example, adding a configuration parameter makes the testing phase of the product more complex, as more variants must be tested.

A second consequence is quality degradation. Evolution of the base product is often used as a strategy to create product variants. A product fulfilling certain customer needs is gradually evolved into other products by changing its design and adding features. Unfortunately, this evolution is often the cause of product quality deterioration.

A third consequence comes from discrepancy between anticipated and actual variability. Software products are often conceived in such a way that certain kinds of "changes" are easy to achieve (anticipated changes). However, in reality, actual requested changes often differ from the expected ones. This leads to the "we can't change that" syndrome (John and Bass 2003), where change requests that seem to be simple from a user's point of view turn out to require a disproportionately large amount of effort to implement.

12.4.5 State of the Art in Flexible Development

Flexible development, the ability to quickly respond to new market needs and customer requests, is typically achieved through agile development methods. These methods basically promote communication between individuals, collaboration with customers, and frequent product increments with business value (Beck, Beedle, van Bennekum 2001; Agile Alliance 2009).

Nerur and Balijepally (2007) identified some theoretical and conceptual support for validating the principles of agile methodologies. The starting point in their analysis is to see software development as a complex phenomenon with many problems, called wicked problems. They observe that the nature of traditional software development is quite similar to the development of design concepts in architecture that inspired software design patterns and reflect the evolutionary shifts in design thinking. They see that the shifts include a change in the nature of the problem from deterministic to wicked, a change of environment from stable to unpredictable, a change in the nature of learning from adaptive to generative, and a change in the goal of problem solving from optimization to responsiveness.

Examples of popular agile methods are Scrum (Schwaber 2004), Extreme programming (Beck and Andres 2004), and Lean development (Poppendieck and Poppendieck 2003). Scrum focuses mostly on agile management mechanisms. This is in contrast to Extreme programming, for example, where the focus is more on providing integrated software engineering practices. Lean development aims at improving the development process by removing any activity not providing value (waste elimination).

Although agile methods have been extensively addressed in the literature, many companies still experience challenges in introducing these techniques. These challenges may appear at the organizational level (e.g., project management), at the people level (e.g., teamwork, customer involvement), at the process level (e.g., test-driven development, continuous integration), and at the technology level (e.g., tool support for refactoring) (Nerur, Mahapatra, and Mangalaraj 2005). Becoming agile remains a challenge for many companies.

On the other hand, companies are adopting agile techniques to enhance their product delivery performance by focusing on what is really needed (waste elimination) (Poppendieck and Poppendieck 2003). Waste elimination can be very rewarding in a software engineering context, taking into account studies that have shown that almost 50% of features that are being developed are never used (Johnson 2002). Apparently, there still is a large untapped opportunity for increasing the speed of development—by simply not developing.

Experience reports show that these methods are best understood in small colocated teams, working on a single goal (Rising and Janoff 2000; Ramesh et al. 2006). Scaling agile methods to larger teams and to teams distributed among different sites are topics of ongoing research (Flexi 2009).

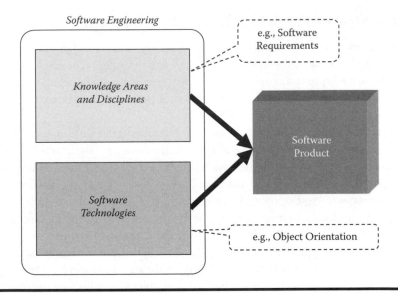

Figure 12.4 Software engineering as traditionally perceived by software-intensive product builders.

Finally, as described previously, dealing with innovation is becoming a crucial challenge for many companies. Combining innovation with agile methods is another topic of ongoing research (Flexi 2009).

12.5 A Static View on Flexible Development and Product Variability

Most software-intensive product builders consider software engineering as a broad domain that consists of a number of disciplines in which a large number of evolving software technologies can be applied (see Figure 12.4). An exhaustive overview of the software engineering knowledge areas (disciplines) is provided in SWEBOK (IEEE 2004).

Addressing the challenges of flexibility and variability is not a responsibility of a single discipline. Usually it requires well-aligned actions taken across several different disciplines at the same time. Flexibility and variability crosscut the disciplines, as illustrated in Figure 12.5. For example, introducing more variation points affects requirements engineering (one must understand what the variation points are), architecture (e.g., introduce a framework approach), as well as the testing process (to deal with the combinatorial explosion of test scenarios that are the consequence of many variation points).

In practice, the various software engineering disciplines should be interpreted differently, depending on the software product-development model. For example,

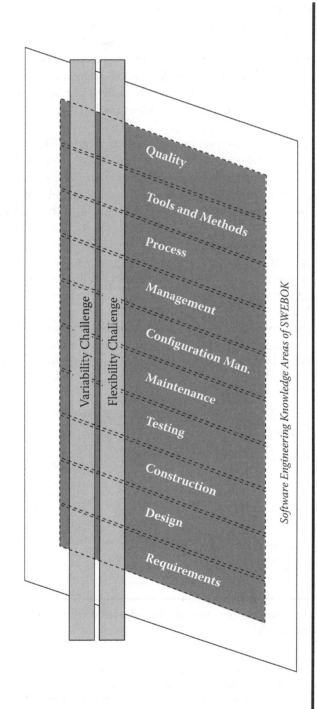

Figure 12.5 **Flexibility and variability in relation to the knowledge areas of software engineering.**

in the project-based development model, requirements engineering boils down to gathering the specific needs of a single customer (focus is on effective interviewing and understanding). In contrast, when making an out-of-the-box product, there is no direct contact with customers. Requirements engineering involves collaboration between different stakeholders to understand the domain (the focus is on decision making and conflict resolution). A similar analysis can be made for other disciplines of software engineering, such as architecture, testing, project management, etc.

Few companies are able to interpret the software-engineering disciplines in the context of their product-development model. The reason is that many companies consider "good software engineering" as a stand-alone domain. They think software engineering is independent from the product-development model and neglect to interpret the software engineering disciplines in the function of the used-software product-development model.

Understanding and dealing with the different interpretations of the software engineering disciplines in the context of a software product-development model is challenging. Software-intensive product builders should look at the domain of software-engineering through the glasses of the product-development model they apply (see Figure 12.6).*

The static perspective of flexibility and variability: Because the interpretation of the software engineering disciplines depends on the applied software product-development model, and the challenges of flexibility and variability crosscut the

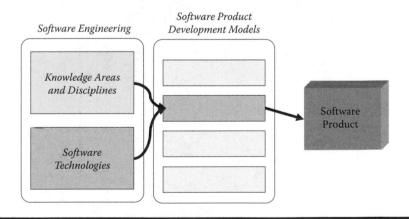

Figure 12.6 Software engineering through the glasses of the applied software product-development model.

---

* For software product lines, the Software Engineering Institute (SEI) defines a framework (SEI SPL 2009) that lists the practice areas that need to be mastered to successfully create a software product line. The practice areas explain how software engineering disciplines need to be interpreted for software product lines.

software engineering disciplines, addressing flexibility and variability is different in the context of each software product-development model.

12.6 A Dynamic View on Flexible Development and Product Variability

Companies might be in a situation where they can afford to remain in the same software product-development model for a longer period of time. Unfortunately, for many companies this is not the case. Evolutions in the business environment and the technological context can force a company to undergo a transition toward a different software product-development model (see later in this section). For these companies, choosing a flexibility and variability approach is not a one-off decision, but a recurring one.

Companies are often not globally aware of an ongoing transition, as it might be triggered by certain decisions that are taken by individuals or subdepartments of the organization (i.e., these transitions happen implicitly). Because of this (global) unawareness, companies neglect to reinterpret the software engineering disciplines in the function of the new development model, and as a consequence, they also neglect to reinterpret their flexibility and variability approaches. This explains many symptoms that companies are faced with, for example:

- Software engineering practices that seemed to work well in the past do not seem to work anymore (e.g., customer interviewing techniques that worked well in a project-based development approach are no longer efficient to define an out-of-the-box product).
- Different teams in the organization act in conflicting ways (e.g., a development team in a project-based development that invests a lot in reusable components, thereby causing frustration to a project manager who expects a "quick fix").

Deciding what the optimal model is and when to initiate the transition to that model is difficult but essential to remain effective and competitive. Several trade-offs need to be made, and sometimes remaining too long in the same model can be harmful.

In the remainder of this section, an overview is given of the business and technological phenomena that can cause companies to transition (or to consider a transition) from one software product-development model to another. These phenomena are occurring on a massive scale, as almost every company is affected by at least one of them.

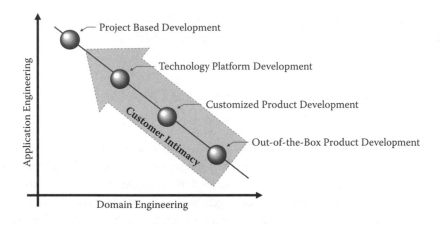

Figure 12.7 Transitions caused by an increase in customer intimacy.

12.6.1 Increasing Need for Customer Intimacy (Variability)

It seems that, for realizing variability, the project-based product-development model is ideal. It is the ultimate form of customer intimacy. Each customer wish can be realized during the projects without interference from other customers (no domain engineering, only application engineering).

Applying the strategy of customer intimacy can cause transitions toward the project-based development model (see Figure 12.7). For example, companies developing out-of-the-box products might move into other models that offer more customization opportunities.

12.6.2 Increasing Need for Bringing Innovations Faster to the Markets (Flexibility)

It seems that, for realizing flexible development, the out-of-the-box product-development model is best suited. When possible, this is a very fast way of bringing solutions to customers: customers just buy the product and start using it.

In order to increase the speed of development, companies can consider transitioning toward the out-of-the-box product-development model (see Figure 12.8). For example, a company doing project-based development might consider moving to a model in which more domain engineering is involved, so not every product has to be made from scratch.

12.6.2.1 Other Transitions Caused by Innovation

The innovation potential of software attracts many players to software engineering. Existing product builders that offer software-free products today are exploring the possibilities of software. At the same time, starting a software company requires a

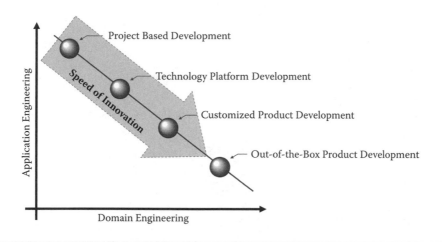

Figure 12.8   Transitions caused by an increase in the speed of innovation.

relatively small investment (a good idea is enough). Because of this software-specific phenomenon, new players appear on the market regularly, and their initial lack of legacy code can create a threat for the established products of other players. Also consider the success of open source code in this context (ITEA OSS 2004).

The relatively low threshold for entering the software market causes many new players to appear in the market. In addition, existing (nonsoftware) product builders start to adopt software in their products, hence forcing them to select an appropriate software product-development model. To respond to this dynamic, competitive environment, established players can decide, in turn, to change their development model.

12.6.3 Toward Hybrid Products: Not Too Much Product, Not Too Much Service

Cusumano (2004) observes that many organizations are shifting to hybrid models that combine services with products. Many companies that have a 100% service offering today (e.g., consultancy) consider combining these services with a product offering (e.g., a tool, a software tool, a certification program, etc.). Companies that have a 100% product offering are attempting to complement it with services (e.g., as a reaction to decreasing product license revenue). As reported by Cusumano (2007), this shift is huge. In 1990, 70% of total revenue came from products, and 30% came from services; since 2002, this has changed into a 50% share for each. Different kinds of services can be envisioned. For builders of out-of-the-box solutions, for example, an "easy" way to offer an additional service is to provide a *customization service* on top of the product. Companies that apply the project-based development model might want to leave the linear model of generating revenue (an increase in projects requires a proportional increase in

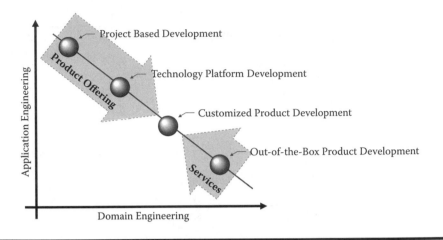

Figure 12.9   Transitions caused by combining products and services.

available resources) and partially replace it with a product offering to bring the available knowledge to the market in a less resource-intensive manner.

For builders of software-intensive products, the trend of hybrid products can result in transitions toward the customized product-development model (see Figure 12.9).

12.6.4 Transitions Induced by Technological Evolutions

New technologies also lie at the origin of many transitions. As a first example, consider Web 2.0 mashups. A mashup is a "Web application that combines data from more than one source into a single integrated tool that was not originally provided by either source."* For example, Flickrvision (2009) displays on top of Google Maps the latest photos uploaded by the user community to Flickr. By opening an API of a proprietary closed product, an entirely new range of combinations with other products becomes possible.

Due to technological evolutions, products are no longer standalone, but become "platforms" used in other products/services (mashups) (see Figure 12.10).

A second example is software as a service (SAAS). According to a McKinsey analysis, the software as a service market is rapidly growing. SAAS adoption is growing into a mature knowledge domain, and many companies are trying to understand what a transition to that model entails.

Other examples include transitions caused by the maturing process of technologies (see Figure 12.11). To successfully engineer a product, the applied technologies must be of sufficient maturity. Early-adopter companies might find themselves in a situation where this maturity level is not guaranteed by the available state of the art. As a

---

* http://www.wikipedia.com.

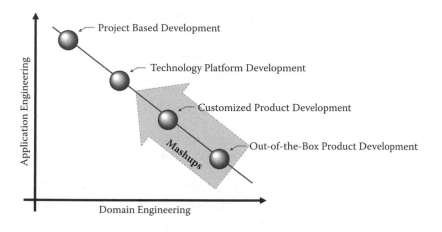

Figure 12.10 Transitions caused by products becoming platforms.

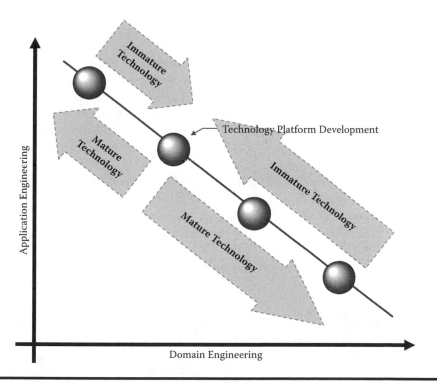

Figure 12.11 Transitions caused by technology maturation.

consequence, they might decide to invest themselves in this technology by building an in-house technology platform. Although this can be a perfectly valid strategy at the start, it can turn into a liability as soon as the state of the art is becoming sufficiently mature. After all, why invest in something that is available in the markets? As a consequence, companies might consider leaving the technology platform model and move to another model. Many examples from the past can be given, for example:

- In the 1970s, database technology was immature, and many companies designed propriety storage systems for data. Today, database technology has matured and databases are bought.
- In the 1990s, many companies invested in their own persistency layer to transform objects into relational databases. Today, an open-source standard (Hibernate 2009) that addresses that topic has emerged.

12.6.5 Transitions Induced by the Desire of Suppliers to Create Vendor Lock-In

As was discussed in Section 12.2, solutions offered by suppliers can be used to support the business and engineering processes at the customer, or they can be part of the product of the customer. In general, the latter position is more desired by suppliers. The impact they have on the customer is much higher because they are part of the product, which makes it more difficult for customers to choose a new supplier (see Figure 12.12). To achieve this, suppliers of software solutions might need to align their software product-development model with that of their customers. The consequence can be that a transition must be made toward a different software product-development model.

The dynamic perspective of flexibility and variability: Because many companies are faced with transitions between software product-development models, the challenges of flexibility and variability have to be reinterpreted in the new model each time a transition happens.

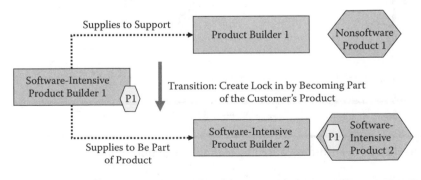

Figure 12.12 Creating product lock-in.

12.7 A Decision Framework to Improve Flexibility and Variability

Flexibility and variability have become major points of attention for many software-intensive product builders. In the previous sections, two perspectives have been analyzed. The static perspective reveals that flexibility and variability should be interpreted differently in each software product-development model. The dynamic perspective reveals that if a change in the product strategy imposes a transition toward another software product-development model, the company has to reinterpret its flexibility and variability approaches. This, of course, is only the case when the speed of innovation or customer intimacy is relevant.

To increase the levels of product variability and flexibility in the development process, two strategies can be considered.

1. Consider moving to a different software product-development model that better supports the flexibility and variability requirements. Flexibility and variability seem to push companies in opposite directions on the line of Figure 12.13. If both are important, a compromise has to be made (you can buy variability for flexibility and vice versa). In Sections 12.7.1 and 12.7.2 below, the trade-offs that need to be made are discussed.

2. Improve flexibility and/or variability within the model. Sometimes the current development model is already the optimal one (taking the product strategy and other trade-offs into account). In that case, the only option is to improve

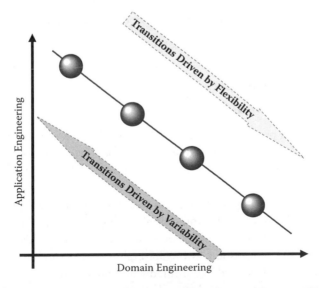

Figure 12.13   Transitions driven by flexibility and variability.

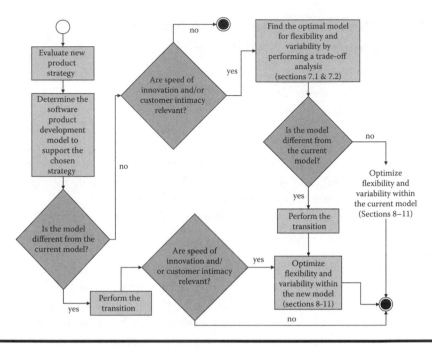

Figure 12.14 Overview of the decision framework.

flexibility and/or variability within the model. Section 12.7.3 discusses this in more detail.

Figure 12.14 shows an overview of the proposed decision framework to improve flexibility and variability.

12.7.1 Trade-Off Analysis: Choosing an Optimal Model for Variability

First, let us consider product variability. As argued in Section 12.6.1, it seems that, for realizing variability, the project-based product-development model is ideal. However, this ideal model is in many situations not feasible due to the following reasons.

▪ *Lack of expert resources.* If the human resources required to engineer the product are highly skilled IT professionals, the organization simply might not have or cannot gain access to enough resources to apply this model. Studies (Brooks 1995; Greenspun 2002) have shown that innovation in software development is generated by a limited set of individuals: the critical resources. Furthermore, studies have shown that assigning engineers to more than two projects at the same time is wasteful (Wheelwright and Clark 1992). The closer to the upper left corner in the chart of Figure 12.13, the more linear the relationship becomes between the number of developed products and the required expert resources to engineer them. The following trade-off criterion is therefore important: understanding to what extent one is prepared to pay the price for more variability in terms of assigning critical expert resources to individual customer projects.

■ *Difficulty in realizing mass customization.* Development models in the upper left corner (see Figure 12.13) require a larger amount of customer-specific development activities (application engineering), meaning that fewer customers can be served with the same amount of resources. Companies are only able to manage a certain amount of many individual "customer threads" simultaneously. Understanding this threshold is important. Companies might become a victim of their own success (e.g., increased size of customer base) if they remain in models in the upper left corner. The following trade-off criterion is therefore important: understanding to what extent one is prepared to pay the price for more variability in terms of a smaller customer base.*

■ *High time-to-market pressure.* The models situated in the upper left corner (see Figure 12.13) usually require more time to develop products. In a situation with a high pressure to deliver fast, these models might not be optimal. The following trade-off criterion is therefore important: understanding to what extent one is prepared to pay the price for more variability in terms of less flexibility.

12.7.2 Trade-Off Analysis: Choosing an Optimal Model for Flexibility

Next, let us consider flexible development. It seems that, for realizing flexibility, the out-of-the-box product-development model is best suited (Section 12.6.2). However, this ideal model is in many situations not feasible due to the following reasons:

■ *Lack of market and domain knowledge.* Mastering successfully the models in the lower right corner requires very good understanding of the domain (domain engineering) (Codenie et al. 1997). If this knowledge is not available, applying this model is risky because wrong assumptions can be made about customer needs. Companies can only increase flexibility by moving toward the lower right corner if this transition is accompanied by an acquisition of the relevant domain knowledge. The following trade-off criterion is therefore important: understanding to what extent one is prepared to pay the price for more flexibility in terms of increasing the investment involved in domain analysis.

---

* An important consideration in adoption of models in the upper left corner is profitability. For some products and markets, customers are not ready to pay the premium price for customer-specific developments that product builders need to be profitable.

■ *Increased product complexity.* Attempting to increase flexibility in the development process by adopting a product-development model closer to the lower right corner can have a (negative) side effect on the product. Increasing flexibility in this strategy is all about preparing and anticipating more flexibility in the future by introducing variation points. These variation points (often invisible to customers) are in the product architecture and add complexity to the product. For products with thousands of variation points (not an exceptional situation), the management of dependencies and interactions between these variation points might become difficult and may even result in degraded product quality. The following trade-off criterion is therefore important: understanding to what extent one is prepared to pay the price for more flexibility in terms of increasing product complexity.*

■ *Difficulty of realizing variability.* In some situations, defining a common product denominator for all these customers is difficult. Customers might require very different solutions (with even conflicting functionalities). Deriving products often requires much more than "simple" configuration. In this situation, sophisticated customization technologies are required (configuration languages, automatic code generation, etc.). The knowledge to master these technologies might not be available. In general, being adjacent to the lower right corner makes it harder to express variability. An important consideration is therefore understanding to what extent one is prepared to pay the price for more flexibility in terms of less variability.

12.7.3 *Improving Flexibility and Variability within a Software Product Development Model*

The remaining sections in this chapter provide a framework to reason about flexible development and product variability in the scope of the four software product-development models. The description includes a rationale, an overview of the typical challenges encountered, and some recommendations to consider. The information provided in these sections can be used to interpret what it means to be flexible and variable in each model. In addition, it can also be used to reinterpret this meaning in the case of transitions.

The results as presented here are a consolidation of an empirical study that has been performed at 57 software-intensive product builders in Belgium (Codenie et al. 2008), complemented with the input received from several industrial partners in the European research project Flexi (2009). For the sake of brevity, only a selection of the top challenges and recommendations has been selected for this chapter.

---

* Note that, alternatively, increasing flexibility by adopting an agile method does not suffer from the complexity problem. Only the process is affected, not the product.

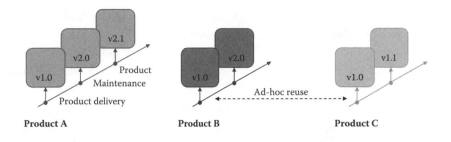

Figure 12.15   Products developed within the project-based development model.

12.8 Flexibility and Variability in the Project-Based Development Model

In the project-based development model (see Figure 12.15), products are developed during projects that address specific needs of the customers. Roughly, two development activities relevant for all products developed within this model can be identified: *product delivery* and *product maintenance*. In the former, the product is shaped and is finally delivered to the customer. In the latter, possible defects present in the product are fixed, and product updates are delivered to the customer.

Products evolve independently from one another. However, ad hoc reuse between products may exist, possibly leading to code duplication, code inconsistency, and code being used in a context different from the one initially intended.

12.8.1 Flexibility

12.8.1.1 Flexibility in Product Delivery

Companies using this model pay a lot of attention to good project management because slips in time and budget imply less profitable projects. Flexibility is important because delivering projects is the major source for generating revenue.

12.8.1.1.1 Challenges

A recurring challenge is involving customers during the development of the project, to better understand their needs, to better serve them, and to reduce the risk of dealing with customers that are uncertain about their requirements.

12.8.1.1.2 Recommendations

Adoption of agile methods can be considered for the following reasons:

- Agile methods offer project-management techniques that reduce the risk of project slips (time and budget) and allow incremental delivery of software products. The use of agile methods is sometimes kept hidden from customers, while in other cases it is made explicit and is used as a selling argument to attract customers.
- Some agile methods provide instruments for collecting early customer feedback and dealing with uncertain customers. For example, Extreme programming (Beck and Andres 2004) even goes as far as promoting the concept of "onsite customer."

Sufficient attention should be paid to the agile adoption process (Nerur, Mahapatra, and Mangalaraj 2005) and to the integration of agile methods with the plan-driven approaches traditionally associated with good project management (Boehm and Turner 2004).

12.8.1.2 Flexibility in Product Maintenance

In some cases, the contractor will have to set up a very flexible maintenance organization. This is especially the case when the delivered solution is critical to the customer.

12.8.1.2.1 Challenges

A common challenge to realize flexibility during maintenance is dealing with the team disintegration that occurs after the project has been delivered. A characteristic of this model is that employees "hop" from project to project. Flexibility during the maintenance phase might be very dependent on the ability to get access to the resources that actually developed the project. In an environment with scarce IT resources, this can be difficult to achieve.

12.8.1.2.2 Recommendations

Applying agile techniques during the maintenance phase is not straightforward because the original team is not always available after the delivery of the project. Therefore, investing in up-to-date documentation, a simple architecture, and regression testing might speed up the delivery of maintenance releases.

Having access to the original development team members can sometimes be important for the maintenance team. However, usually these resources are allocated to other projects. The organization should consider how it deals with "interrupts" generated toward resources during maintenance of already finished projects.

12.8.2 Variability

The choice of this product-development model can be driven by variability criteria (Section 12.6.1). After all, this model offers many possibilities to engineer very different variants for customers because there is low coupling between the projects (variants are independent products).

Although the product is not developed for a large customer base, the delivered end product may have high variability constraints (as requested by the customer).

12.8.2.1 Challenges

If the delivered product has high variability constraints, a typical challenge for the contractor is to understand the variability requirements of its customer. Important in that context is having insights into the usage model the customer foresees for the delivered software product: Is it used as a supportive solution (e.g., variability comes from different end users), or is it a part of a product that the customer engineers (e.g., variability comes from customers' customers)?

Another challenge is the issue of ad hoc reuse between projects. This can lead to code duplication, code inconsistency, and code being used in a context different from the one initially intended.

12.8.2.2 Recommendations

To understand the variability constraints of customers, contractors can consider involving customers during the development of the solution. In addition, they can apply the decision framework presented in this chapter to the context of the customers. This may be of particular importance if the delivered product is part of another product engineered by the customer.

To avoid problems related to ad hoc reuse, a contractor might consider installing a more structured reuse organization. Examples include deploying a reuse-competence center (Goldberg and Rubin 1995) or creating shared infrastructure between projects (Bosch 2002) in the form component libraries, etc. Note that this might trigger a transition toward the technology platform development model.

12.9 Flexibility and Variability in the Out-of-the-Box Product Development Model

In the out-of-the-box development model (see Figure 12.16), products are built for a large audience of customers. No customer-specific customizations are performed, but instead products can be made highly configurable (if desired) to allow customers to make their own variants. Two major kinds of activities can be identified in this model: *product evolution*, which brings new releases to the market (e.g., with

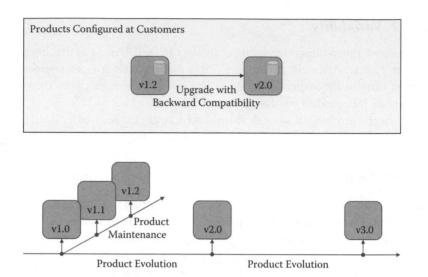

Figure 12.16 The out-of-the-box development model.

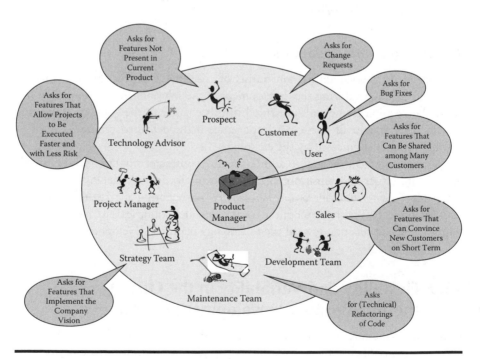

Figure 12.17 The product manager's dilemma.

new product features), and *product maintenance*, which brings maintenance releases to customers (e.g., with bug fixes).

12.9.1 Flexibility

12.9.1.1 Flexibility in Product Evolution

When out-of-the-box products are created for dynamic markets where being the first with innovations is an absolute priority, flexibility of product evolution becomes an essential challenge to master.

12.9.1.1.1 Challenges

A first challenge is the definition of a new release. From a market point of view, there is a strong demand for offering "ultimate" customer satisfaction. On the one hand, software-intensive product builders in this model are confronted with a large number of potential requirements and ideas originating from different stakeholders (see Figure 12.17). Implementing all these wishes at once is impossible because of limited available resources, time restrictions, or conflicts in the wishes formulated by the stakeholders. Choices have to be made and priorities have to be set. Release definition (in particular the definition of upcoming releases in a product roadmap) therefore fulfills a strategic role and is considered a challenging activity for many product builders (Codenie et al. 2007). Although agile methods address the importance of incremental development, most of them do not really address the decision-making problems. For example, Scrum (Schwaber 2004) stresses the importance of managing a sprint backlog containing items with the most business value but gives little insights into the decision criteria to populate this backlog.

A second challenge is the scalability of the product-development team. To achieve more flexibility, many companies are increasing the size of their development teams, either by hiring more people or by considering partnerships. In this model, the development team develops a single artifact: the out-of-the-box product. Therefore, increasing the size of the team is difficult. In many cases, the gain in flexibility is not in proportion to the growth of the teams. This is especially true for agile development techniques, which are well understood in specific contexts (e.g., small teams working closely together), but are difficult to scale up to larger teams and distributed development (Olson and Olson 2000; ACM 2006a; Duarte and Snyder 2006).

A third challenge is managing innovation. In contrast to project-based development that centralizes the role of the customer, product innovations in the out-of-the-box product development are initiated by a larger group of stakeholders. To increase flexibility, the speed with which these innovations are detected must be increased. Agile development methods do not always focus on this aspect and need to be complemented with instruments to stimulate innovation and creativity.

12.9.1.1.2 Recommendations

To improve flexibility in product evolution, product builders may consider adopting agile development, taking into account its limitations in dealing with the challenges described above (challenges of release definition, scalability, and innovation) (Flexi 2009).

Speed and flexibility in product evolution can also be increased by focusing the implementation efforts on the most valuable features (Poppendieck and Poppendieck 2003). Understanding the value of the features (taking into consideration the point of view of different stakeholders) is an essential activity. Companies in this model might consider introducing techniques for prioritizing requirements (Karlsson 2006).

To increase the innovation capabilities, companies in this model might consider defining strategies for stimulating customer involvement during the product definition. Customers are a rich source for product innovations and can, therefore, contribute to defining a better product (Perks and Sedley 2008). Examples are the lead-user concept to involve users in product innovation (von Hippel 2004), innovation games (Fraser 2005; Hohmann 2007), and specific innovation processes for software development (Highsmith 2004).

12.9.1.2 Flexibility in Product Maintenance

If the delivered product is on a critical position in the value chain of customers, installing a highly flexible maintenance organization can be a necessity.

12.9.1.2.1 Challenges

A first challenge is choosing between what is considered maintenance and what is considered product evolution. Because of customer pressure, one might be tempted to incorporate new functionalities as maintenance updates. This can introduce a lot of risk when these releases are deployed toward all customers (e.g., regression bugs introduced through upgrades).

A second challenge is ensuring backward compatibility, i.e., remaining compatible with the specific configurations done by each customer when upgrading to a newer version of the product.

12.9.1.2.2 Recommendations

To be flexible in this activity, maintenance releases should be as lightweight as possible. If possible, any demand should be postponed to a "regular" product release. Companies in this model should consider installing a reference frame and a process for "triaging" customer requests and complaints (to distinguish bugs from feature requests). Making clear to customers what they can expect from the

product may result in fewer complaints and, therefore, a more flexible maintenance process.

Companies making out-of-the-box products often have a large customer base.
In this case, companies can consider investing in an optimized (e.g., automated)
upgrade process. An alternative to consider is the SAAS model, wherein large customer bases receive a new release through a single upgrade action.

12.9.2 Variability

The consequence of choosing this software product-development model is that variability is made a concern of the customers. Almost every product builder applying
this model is making its products configurable in some way. The motivations to
introduce variability in this model can be very different: support for different languages, time zones, look and feel, etc.

12.9.2.1 Challenges

A common pitfall in this model is that the delivered product can grow into an
overconfigurable general-purpose "monster." Introducing a variation point should
be considered very carefully. The cost of introducing a variation point is often not
situated at the time of creation. The hidden costs are often revealed much later. For
example, the development cost for adding one single configuration flag might be
negligible; but if hundreds of these flags are present in a product, the testing cost to
ensure that all the combinations work can be huge.

12.9.2.2 Recommendations

Depending on the needs, straightforward models for configuration can be sufficient
(e.g., a configuration XML file). In many cases, more sophisticated configuration
strategies will have to be mastered by the product builder:

- Development of configuration wizards and configurators
- Configuration by designing a domain-specific language that is part of
  the product
- Exploring generative techniques
- Publishing an API so that third-party products can be integrated

In addition, companies also can consider installing a process to detect and
remove variation points that are never used by the customers.

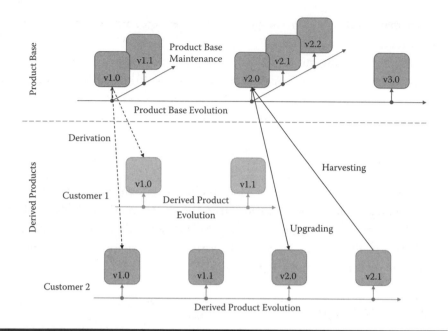

Figure 12.18 The customizable product-development model.

12.10 Flexibility and Variability in the Customized Product Development Model

Products developed within this model (see Figure 12.18) are built from a product base, a semifinished product that captures the commonalities shared by all of them. Within regular intervals, new versions of the product base can become available (through *product-base evolution*). The release frequency depends on the context (e.g., market). Each release might in itself be subject to a series of minor changes (referred to as *product-base maintenance*).

To create a new product for a customer, a derivation is made from an available version of the product base (through the *derivation* activity). Different derivations can be made from the same version of the product base, and each derived product can have its own life cycle (*derived product evolution* activity). If new versions of the product base become available, upgrades at existing customers may have to be performed (through the *upgrading* activity). In some cases, features from the derived products can be promoted to the product base (through the *harvesting* activity).

12.10.1 Flexibility

12.10.1.1 Flexibility in Product Base Evolution and Maintenance

During product base evolution, new versions are created to add new functionality or remove depreciated functionality from the product base. Depending on the context, flexibility might or might not be relevant. For example, in the situation where the product base is immature, a high need for flexibility can be required.

12.10.1.1.1 Challenges

The challenges are similar to those from the out-of-the-box product-development model.

An additional challenge occurs in the case where the product base is made incrementally together with the derived products. Teams working on derived products while also being responsible for the product base are faced with conflicting goals: on the one hand satisfying the customer needs, and on the other hand ensuring reusability for other customers.

12.10.1.1.2 Recommendations

To increase flexibility, adoption of agile methods might be considered. However, it should be taken into account that many agile development techniques are not optimized to deal with situations in which a team is working on multiple goals (e.g., delivering a product base increment together with a customer solution). Extreme programming (Beck and Andres 2004), for example, promotes simplicity in architecture and discourages anticipation on the level of the architecture.

Companies might consider an organizational structure that separates application engineering and domain engineering (Goldberg and Rubin 1995). However, this split can reduce flexibility because it requires the management of the rendezvous points between these two teams.

12.10.1.2 Flexibility in Derivation

Sometimes the issue is not to install a flexible process for the evolution of the product base, but rather to be very flexible in deriving products from this product base. This situation can occur when a company is confronted with an increase in the size of its customer base and/or when the customizations are labor intensive. Some companies also exploit this flexibility as a competitive advantage to quickly win a customer and create a lock-in. In this scenario, customers are attracted because of excellent delivery capacity.

12.10.1.2.1 Challenges

A common challenge in performing this activity is optimizing the collaboration between the team responsible for deriving new products and the team responsible for the evolution of the product base. Often these are different or even distributed teams.

12.10.1.2.2 Recommendations

Companies should consider keeping the product base as simple as possible to allow the derivation team (possibly a third party) to derive a new product as quickly as possible. Companies might also consider automating part of their derivation processes.

12.10.1.3 Flexibility in Upgrading

If the product base is subject to many evolutions, the derived products may become based on older versions of the product base. Being able to swiftly upgrade to newer versions of the product base can then be important to (a) allow customers to benefit from new functionalities and (b) to reduce the complexity of the release management.

12.10.1.3.1 Challenges

A recurring challenge of this activity is dealing with backwards compatibility. Customizations done for the customers in the past must be compatible with the new version of the product base. In some situations, customizations need to be adapted to be compatible with the new version. This can be a very tedious operation, especially if the amount of customization code is large or the customizations are (partly) done by the customers.

12.10.1.3.2 Recommendations

To enable efficient upgrades and to avoid backward-compatibility problems, companies in this model can consider putting in place very strict guidelines for refactoring the product base to ensure that the potential problems when upgrading certain clients are better understood.

An important consideration is also the definition of the upgrade strategy. Different possibilities exist. For example, will the upgrades be pushed to customers (e.g., customers are "forced" to accept upgrades), or can customers decide autonomously whether they accept a new release or not?

12.10.1.4 Flexibility in Harvesting

Harvesting is the activity of "productizing" custom-developed functionalities scattered across various derived products into the product base. Some functionality developed for the specific customers can have a high value for the product. For example, if innovative features have been developed for an atypical customer, bringing these functionalities to the product base might offer new market opportunities.

12.10.1.4.1 Challenges

A typical challenge of this activity is deciding whether a feature is relevant enough to be promoted into the product base. A trade-off has to be made between the value and the cost.

Another challenge is to consolidate similar features present in different derived products into one generic feature for inclusion in the product base.

12.10.1.4.2 Recommendations

Companies can choose from two strategies:

- *Up-front analysis.* Companies can consider increasing customer involvement during product base development (Keil and Carmel 1995). Shifting the decision to an earlier point in the development life cycle can reduce the amount of harvesting activities.
- *After-the-fact analysis.* Companies can also decide to not do too much up-front analysis and only promote functionality to the product base if enough customer cases have been found.

12.10.1.5 Flexibility in Derived Product Evolution

This situation is similar to the project-based development model. However, there are additional constraints imposed by the upgrade and the harvesting activities.

12.10.1.5.1 Challenges

A common challenge in this activity is ensuring that the flexibility gained during the evolution of the derived product is not paid back by decreased flexibility during upgrades to a newer version of the product base.

Another challenge is deciding whether a customer request will be considered as a specific development for the customer or as an evolution of the product base. For flexibility reasons, one might be tempted to develop it as a specific feature, thereby potentially impacting the harvesting activities.

12.10.1.5.2 Recommendations

Care should be taken with allowing too much customization. Companies might consider informing customers about the costs of having too much customer-specific customizations (future upgrades can be difficult and expensive, etc.).

12.10.2 Variability

Companies adopt the customizable product-development model to efficiently offer tailored solutions to customers. Customers benefit from a proven product base deployed at other customer sites.

12.10.2.1 Challenges

A critical challenge in this model is to define an architectural design supporting the development of a product base and a series of products derived from that product base.

Another challenge is to decide who is responsible for making the derived products. It can be the product builder itself, it can be the customer, or it can be a third party. The last two scenarios have as a consequence that the product builder is not always aware of the exact details of the customizations.

12.10.2.2 Recommendations

Companies often follow a software product line approach in order to adopt the customizable product-development model. Companies transitioning toward this model might thus consider looking at adoption models for software product lines.

Companies adhering to this model should have a sophisticated upgrade- and release-management strategy. As a consequence, the version management and configuration management are essential to them, as they have to manage different customer variants and different product variants.

12.11 Flexibility and Variability in the Technology Platform Development Model

Products (platforms) built using the technology platform development model are encapsulated into larger products (see Figure 12.19). Apart from evolving and maintaining the platform, two other activities are relevant in this model: encapsulating the platform into other products (i.e., *encapsulation*) and incorporating the feedback obtained from using the platform for engineering new versions of the platform (i.e., *feedback*).

12.11.1 Flexibility

12.11.1.1 Flexibility in Platform Evolution and Maintenance

These activities are very similar to the corresponding activities in the models for out-of-the-box product development and for customizable product development.

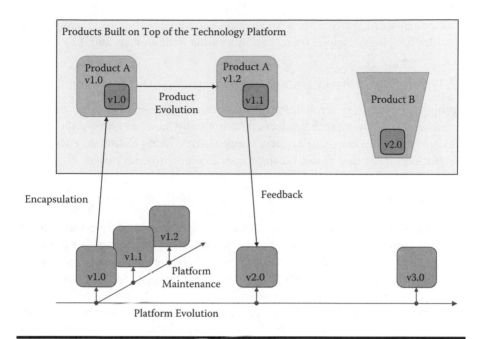

Figure 12.19   The technology platform development model.

Flexibility can be essential to bring innovations in the technological domain as fast as possible to the market. Flexibility can also be imposed by the customer. Because the platform is part of a larger product, the flexibility needs of the customer can ripple through to the builder of the platform.

12.11.1.1.1 Challenges

A specific challenge in this activity might be dealing with the differences in development life cycles of the technology platform and the encapsulating products. For example, the releases need to be synchronized, and the platform builder has to take into account all the constraints on the level of the development life cycles imposed by its customers.

12.11.1.1.2 Recommendations

To increase flexibility, adoption of agile methods might be considered for evolution of the platform itself, but synchronization with the encapsulating product life cycle remains a difficult challenge.

Companies might consider acquiring the technological know-how from external parties to speed up the evolution of the technology platform.

Companies in search of new application domains for their technology might consider applying principles from open innovation (Chesbrough 2003).

12.11.1.2 Flexibility in Encapsulation

Technology platforms are solutions that offer a high value for other products. Companies developing such products do not usually focus on one specific market and are constantly searching for new opportunities. Being flexible to encapsulate the platform into other products can provide a competitive advantage.

12.11.1.2.1 Challenges

The encapsulation can be a joined development effort between the platform builder and the customer. To achieve flexibility, both teams have to work together smoothly, realizing that flexibility is not always controlled solely by the platform builder. For example, critical resources from the (encapsulating) product company required for encapsulation may not be available when needed.

Another challenge is acquiring an optimal level of understanding of the domain of the product in which the platform will be encapsulated and used. Without that knowledge, flexibility is difficult to achieve.

12.11.1.2.2 Recommendations

In this activity, companies may benefit from strategic partnerships to increase their flexibility. Companies may search for partners that have the knowledge to bring solutions to niche markets in which their technology is used.

To increase flexibility, companies in this model may consider applying agile methodologies for encapsulating; however, it might be difficult because it requires a team composed of members from different organizations.

12.11.1.3 Flexibility in Feedback

The experiences in encapsulating the platform into products may result in useful information that platform builders can use to improve their products. For example, this feedback can allow the platform to become more open and enable it to be encapsulated into products for a new market. Gathering and incorporating the feedback is similar to "feature harvesting," as described previously for the customized product-development model.

12.11.2 Variability

Many variability considerations described for the customized product-development model also apply to the present model. With respect to variability, a recurring theme for builders of technology platforms is "openness." As the platform is not a stand-alone solution, it has to be made as open as possible.

12.11.2.1 Challenges

Platform builders may need to adapt their platforms to the different (perhaps even conflicting) nonfunctional requirements originating from the encapsulating products. For example, some products may have different performance requirements, different robustness requirements, different safety requirements, etc.

A second challenge is finding the optimal degree of openness and choosing the best approach to implement this.

12.11.2.2 Recommendations

Companies in this model can benefit from understanding different relevant open standards. They might consider building skills in the domains of APIs and interface definition and even consider the development of a software development kit (SDK) that accompanies the platform.

12.12 Conclusion

This chapter discusses the relativity of flexibility and variability in the context of four popular software product-development models (project-based development, technology platform development, customized product development, and out-of-the-box product development). Both challenges can be interpreted differently in the context of each model, and they should be reinterpreted each time a transition occurs to another development model.

A decision framework is presented that supports companies in improving their flexibility and variability approaches. Basically, this can be done by changing the software development model and/or by improving the flexibility and variability within the model. This chapter provides an overview of the interpretation of flexibility and variability in the four software product-development models.

With respect to future research, an interesting research topic seems to be the study of the transitions between software development models. In many cases they occur very implicitly, and research to define instruments for companies to better understand when they are in transition or when they should consider a transition seems to be of high industrial relevance.

Another interesting research topic is studying the interactions between the software product-development models. In most cases, companies use combinations of the four models. Understanding the intricate relationships between these models is still not always well understood.

Acknowledgments

The authors from Sirris would like to thank ISRIB (Institute for the Encouragement of Scientific Research and Innovation of Brussels), IWT (Institute for the Promotion of Innovation by Science and Technology in Flanders), and the Brussels-Capital Region for the support they provided for this research and publication. They would also like to thank their colleagues for the useful remarks provided on earlier versions of this document.

References

ACM. 2006a. Flexible and distributed software processes (special issue). *Communications of the ACM* 49 (10).

ACM. 2006b. Software product line engineering (special issue). *Communications of the ACM* 49 (12).

Agile Alliance. 2009. http://www.agilealliance.org/.

APLE. 2006. 1st international workshop on agile product line engineering. http://www.lsi.upc.edu/events/aple/.

Beck, K., and C. Andres. 2004. *Extreme programming explained: Embrace change*, 2nd ed. Reading, MA: Addison-Wesley.

Beck, K., M. Beedle, A. van Bennekum, et al. 2001. Manifesto for agile software development. http://www.agilemanifesto.org/.

Bennatan, E. M. 2000. *On time within budget: Software project management practices and techniques*, 3rd ed. New York: Wiley.

Boehm, B., and R. Turner. 2004. *Balancing agility and discipline: A guide for the perplexed*. Reading, MA: Addison-Wesley.

Bosch, J. 2002. Maturity and evolution in software product lines: Approaches, artefacts and organization. In *Proceedings of the 2nd software product line conference* (SPLC2). Lecture Notes in Computer Science, vol. 2379, 257–271. Berlin/Heidelberg: Springer-Verlag.

Brooks, F. P. 1995. *The mythical man-month: Essays on software engineering*, anniversary edition (2nd ed.) Reading, MA: Addison-Wesley Professional.

Chesbrough, H. W. 2003. *Open innovation: The new imperative for creating and profiting from technology*. Boston: Harvard Business School Press.

Christensen, C. M. 1997. *The innovator's dilemma: When new technologies cause great firms to fail*. Boston: Harvard Business School Press.

Clements, P., and L. Northrop. 2002. *Software product lines: Practices and patterns*. Upper Saddle River, NJ: Addison-Wesley.

Codenie, W., O. Biot, V. Blagojević, N. González-Deleito, T. Tourwé, and J. Deleu. 2008. Cruising the Bermuda Triangle of software development. Manuscript submitted for publication and available from the authors.

Codenie, W., K. De Hondt, P. Steyaert, and A. Vercammen. 1997. From custom applications to domain-specific frameworks. *Communications of the ACM* 40 (10): 70–77.

Codenie, W., T. Tourwé, C. Van Lock, et al. 2007. The product manager's dilemma. *Flexi Newsletter* 1: 12–13.

Cusumano, M. A. 2004. *The business of software: What every manager, programmer, and entrepreneur must know to thrive and survive in good times and bad*. New York: Free Press.

Cusumano, M. A. 2007. Continuing the debate on products vs. services: Which is the better business model, in software and other industries? Talk given at the 2007 MIT Europe conference: Achieving growth through strategic innovation II, Brussels, Belgium.

Czarnecki, K. 2005. Overview of generative software development. In *Proceedings of unconventional programming paradigms* (UPP). Lecture Notes in Computer Science, vol. 3566, 313–328. Berlin/Heidelberg: Springer-Verlag.

Dehoff, K., and D. Neely. 2004. Innovation and product development: Clearing the new performance bar. Booz Allen Hamilton. http://www.boozallen.com/media/file/138077.pdf.

Duarte, D. L., and N. T. Snyder. 2006. *Mastering virtual teams: Strategies, tools, and techniques that succeed*, 3rd ed. San Francisco: Jossey-Bass.

Fayad, M., and D. C. Schmidt. 1997. Object-oriented application frameworks. *Communications of the ACM* 40 (10): 32–38.

Flexi. 2009. Flexible integration in global product development. http://flexi-itea2.org/.

Flickrvision. 2009. http://flickrvision.com/.

Franch, X., and M. Torchiano. 2005. Towards a reference framework for COTS-based development: A proposal. *ACM SIGSOFT Software Engineering Notes* 30 (4): 1–4.

Fraser, J. 2005. Inspired innovation: How Corel is drawing upon employees' ideas for user focused innovation. In *Proceedings of the 2005 conference on designing for user experience*, vol. 135. New York: American Institute of Graphic Arts.

Gamma, E., R. Helm, R. Johnson, and J. M. Vlissides. 1994. *Design patterns: Elements of reusable object-oriented software*. Reading, MA: Addison-Wesley.

Glass, R. I. 2006. *Software creativity 2.0*. developer.* Books. http://www.developerdotstar.com.

Goldberg, A., and K. S. Rubin. 1995. *Succeeding with objects: Decision frameworks for project management*. Reading, MA: Addison-Wesley.

Greenspun, P. 2002. Managing software engineers. http://philip.greenspun.com/ancient-history/managing-software-engineers.

Hibernate. 2009. http://www.hibernate.org/.

Highsmith, J. 2004. *Agile project management*. Reading, MA: Addison-Wesley.

Hohmann, L. 2007. *Innovation games: Creating breakthrough products through collaborative play*. Upper Saddle River, NJ: Addison-Wesley.

IEEE. 2004. Guide to the SWEBOK (software engineering body of knowledge). http://www.swebok.org/.

ITEA. 2004. *ITEA technology roadmap for software-intensive systems*, 2nd ed. http://www.itea2.org/itea_roadmap_2.

ITEA. 2005. ITEA blue book: European leadership in software-intensive systems and services: The case for ITEA 2. 2009. http://www.itea2.org/itea_2_blue_book.

ITEA OSS. 2004. Report on Open Source Software. http://www.itea2.org/itea_report_on_oss.

John, B. E., and L. Bass. 2003. Avoiding "We can't change that!": Software architecture & usability. CHI 2003 tutorial, Carnegie Mellon University, Pittsburgh.

Johnson, J. 2002. Standish Group, keynote speech at XP 2002 Conference, Sardinia, Italy.

Karlsson, L. 2006. Requirements prioritisation and retrospective analysis for release planning process improvement. PhD thesis, Lund University.

Keil, M., and E. Carmel. 1995. Customer-developer links in software development. *Communications of the ACM* 38 (5): 33–44.

Kiczales, G., J. Irwin, J. Lamping, J.-M. Loingtier, C. Videria Lopes, C. Maeda, and A. Mendhekar. 1996. Aspect-oriented programming. *ACM Computing Surveys* 28 (4es): 154.

Kratochvil, M. 2005. *Growing modular: Mass customization of complex products, services and software*. Berlin: Springer.

Leadbeater, C. 2008. *We-think: Mass innovation, not mass production*. London: Profile Books.

Maiden, N., S. Robertson, and J. Robertson. 2006. Creative requirements: Invention and its role in requirements engineering. In *Proceedings of the 28th international conference on software engineering* (ICSE'06), 1073–1074. New York: ACM.

Maiden, N., C. Ncube, and S. Robertson. 2007. Can requirements be creative? Experiences with an enhanced air space management system. In *Proceedings of the 29th international conference on software engineering*, 632–641. Washington, DC: IEEE Computer Society.

McKinsey Quarterly. 2006. *Delivering software as a service.* http://www.mckinseyquarterly.com/Delivering_software_as_a_service_2006.

Mernik, M., J. Heering, and A. M. Sloane. 2005. When and how to develop domain-specific languages. *ACM Computing Surveys* 37 (4): 316–344.

Nerur, S., and V. Balijepally. 2007. Theoretical reflections on agile development methodologies. *Communications of the ACM* 50 (3): 79–83.

Nerur, S., R. Mahapatra, and G. Mangalaraj. 2005. Challenges of migrating to agile methodologies. *Communications of the ACM* 48 (5): 72–78.

Nussbaum, B., R. Berner, and D. Brady. 2005. Get creative! How to build innovative companies. *Business Week*, August 1. http://www.businessweek.com/magazine/content/05_31/b3945401.htm.

Olson, G. M., and J. S. Olson. 2000. Distance matters. *Human Computer Interaction* 15 (2): 139–178.

OMG (Object Management Group). 2009. Model driven architecture. http://www.omg.org/mda/.

Perks, M., and R. Sedley. 2008. *Winners and losers in a troubled economy*. London: cScape.

Pohl, K., G. Böckle, and F. van der Linden. 2005. *Software product line engineering: Foundations, principles, and techniques*. New York: Springer-Verlag.

Poppendieck, M., and T. Poppendieck. 2003. *Lean software development: An agile toolkit*. Addison-Wesley Professional (online).

Ramesh, B., L. Cao, K. Mohan, and P. Xu. 2006. Can distributed software development be agile? *Communications of the ACM* 49 (10): 41–46.

Rising, L., and N. S. Janoff. 2000. The Scrum software development process for small teams. *IEEE Software* 17 (4): 26–32.

Rubner, J. 2005. Tuned in to today's megatrends. In Siemens's *Pictures of the future*, 90–91. http://w1.siemens.com/innovation/pool/en/publikationen/publications_pof/pof_fall_2005/corporate_technology/interview_with_claus_weyrich/pof205_editorial_1326165.pdf.

Schwaber, K. 2004. *Agile project management with Scrum*. Redmond, WA: Microsoft Press.

SEI SPL. 2009. Software product lines framework. Software Engineering Institute (SEI), Carnegie Mellon University, Pittsburgh. http://www.sei.cmu.edu/productlines/framework.html.

Selic, B. 2003. The pragmatics of model-driven development. *IEEE Software* 20 (5): 19–25.

Sharda, N. K. 2007. Creating innovative new media programs: Need, challenges, and development framework. In *Proceedings of the international workshop on educational multimedia and multimedia education* (EMME'07), 77–86. New York: ACM.

Smith, P. G. 2007. *Flexible product development: Building agility for changing markets*. San Francisco: Jossey-Bass.

Sugumaran, V., S. Park, and K. C. Kang. 2006. Software product line engineering. *Communications of the ACM* 49 (12): 28–32.

Tharp, A. L. 2007. Innovating: The importance of right brain skills for computer science graduates. *ACM SIGCSE Bulletin* 39 (3): 126–130.

Treacy, M., and F. Wiersema. 1993. Customer Intimacy and Other Value Disciplines. *Harvard Business Review*.

Ulrich, K. T., and S. D. Eppinger. 2000. *Product design and development*, 2nd ed. New York: McGraw-Hill. http://www.ulrich-eppinger.net/.

von Hippel, E. 2004. *The sources of innovation*. Oxford: Oxford University Press.

Wheelwright, S. C., and K. B. Clark. 1992. *Revolutionizing product development: Quantum leaps in speed, efficiency, and quality*. New York: Free Press.

Chapter 13

Feature Oriented Analysis and Design for Dynamically Reconfigurable Product Lines

Jaejoon Lee
Lancaster University

Dirk Muthig
Fraunhofer Institute for Experimental Software Engineering

Contents

13.1 Introduction

Dynamic product reconfiguration refers to making changes to a deployed product configuration at runtime. Dynamic addition, deletion, or modification of product features, or dynamic changes of architectural structures (Gomaa and Hussein, 2004; Kramer and Magee, 1990) are examples of dynamic reconfiguration. Dynamic product reconfiguration has been studied in various research areas such as self-healing systems (Garlan and Schmerl, 2002; Ganek and Corbi, 2003; Oreizy et al., 1999), context-aware computing (Yau et al., 2002; (Schilit et al., 1994) software component deployment (Mikic-Rakic and Medvidovic, 2002; (van der Hoek and Wolf, 2003; Hall et al.. 1999), and ubiquitous computing (Sousa and Garlan, 2002; Banavar and Bernstein, 2002). When a change in the operational context is detected, it may trigger product reconfiguration to provide context-relevant services or to meet quality requirements (e.g., performance).

Different from statically configured products, dynamically reconfigurable products should be able to:

■ monitor the current situation (i.e., the operational context) of a product
■ validate a reconfiguration request with consideration of change impacts and available resources
■ determine strategies to handle currently active services during reconfiguration
■ perform dynamic reconfiguration while maintaining system integrity

Dynamic reconfiguration approaches in the literature have mainly focused so far on reconfiguration of a single product, on mechanisms for detecting changes and trigger reconfigurations, and on techniques for correctly reconfiguring the product technically at runtime. The dynamically realized adaptations of a single product correspond to a set of statically configured variants of the same product. This set of variations however is only a subset of all variations needed when organizations look at families of systems.

Product line engineering is an approach that organizations choose when aiming at an efficient development of families of products with high quality (Clements and Northrop, 2002; Weiss and Lai, 1999; Kang et al., 2002). Product line engineering thus has to deal with all variations within the scope of a family; the binding times of these variations generally may range from core asset development time to runtime. The binding time of particular variations may even change during the evolution of a product line. Hence, product line methods aim at a unified approach for managing variability covering all possible binding times—explicitly including runtime. Consequently, we have been addressing these issues for developing reusable core assets that supports dynamic product reconfiguration (Lee and Kang, 2006; Lee and Muthig, 2006; Lee and Muthig 2008) in the context of our product line research activities.

In this chapter, we integrate our proposed techniques and guidelines that address the core issues of dynamic product reconfiguration and show how these pieces fit together to construct such a reuse infrastructure. The presented approach consists of two phases.

The first phase is a feature analysis that enriches feature models by feature binding units (FBUs). A FBU is thereby defined as a set of features whose variability aspects are strongly related to each other. In section 13.2, we first discuss our view on feature orientation and introduce feature oriented analysis and specification of dynamic reconfiguration in section 3.

The second phase takes the analysis results to guide the design of a product line. That is, product line architects consider variability on at the level of FBUs rather than on the level of single features. Hence, the design achieves more easily the exact degree of the required configurability. When products need to change their configuration during runtime, the knowledge captured by defining the FBU in the feature model is exactly the one to be evaluated at runtime. In section 13.4, we propose architecture design guidelines to achieve the goal and demonstrate how the guidelines can be applied. Finally, section 13.5 concludes this chapter.

13.2 Feature Orientation

The idea of feature orientation for analyzing commonality and variability of a product line appeals to many product line engineers as features are effective "media" supporting communication among diverse stakeholders of a product line. Therefore, it is natural and intuitive for people to express commonality and variability of product lines in terms of features.

Feature orientation, as such, has been used extensively for product line engineering both in industry and academia, after the Software Engineering Institute (SEI) first introduced Feature-Oriented Domain Analysis (FODA) (Kang et al., 1990) as early as in 1990. For example, Organization Domain Modeling (ODM) (Simos, 1995) builds on both the faceted classification approach and FODA, and FeatuRSEB (Jacobson et al., 1997) incorporated the FODA's feature model as a catalogue of commonality and variability captured in models (e.g., use case and object models). Feature Oriented Reuse Method (FORM) (Kang et al,. 2002) also extended the original FODA to address the issues of reference architecture development and object-oriented component engineering. Moreover, a feature model is used in conjunction with aspect-oriented programming (Lee et al., 2006), generative programming (Czarnecki and Eisenecker, 2000), formal methods (Batory, 2005), and reengineering of legacy systems (Ferber et al., 2005).

Feature modeling is the activity of identifying externally visible characteristics of products in a product line and organizing them into a feature model. Feature can be services (e.g., call forwarding in the telephony product line), operations (e.g., dialing in the telephony product line), nonfunctional characteristics (e.g., performance), and technologies (e.g., navigation methods in the avionics product line) of a product line.

Common features among different products are modeled as mandatory features, while different features among them may be optional or alternative. Optional features represent selectable features for products of a given product line and alternative features indicate that no more than one feature can be selected for a product. A feature diagram, a graphical AND/OR hierarchy of features, organizes identified features by using three types of relationships: *composed-of, generalization/specialization, and implemented-by.* Composition rules supplement the feature model with mutual dependency and mutual exclusion relationships which are used to constrain the selection from optional or alternative features.

For example, Figure 13.1 shows a feature model of a Virtual Office of the Future (VOF) product line, which provides various office services (e.g., printing, organizing a meeting, planning a business trip, etc.) to a user virtually anywhere in an office building whenever the user requests (VOF 2000). The VOF product line includes service features (e.g., *Virtual Printer, Follow Me, Smart Fax,* etc.), operational features (e.g., *Log-on, User Localize,* etc.), and technology features (e.g., *User Positioning Method*).

A feature model can then be further analyzed to capture feature binding units (FBUs) (Lee and Kang, 2004); An FBU is defined as a set of features that are related to each other by the relationships in a feature model. (See Figure 13.1 for the identified FBUs. Please note that we only identified three FBUs in Figure 13.1.) Features that belong to the same FBU work for a common service and, therefore, they have to exist together for correct operation of the service. This grouping reduces complexity in managing variations of product configuration, thus helping engineers to analyze change impacts of a feature selection. Also, binding dependency between variation points can be identified and managed efficiently with mappings to FBUs.

Feature binding unit identification starts with identification of independently configurable service features. (For short, we will label these as service features in the remainder of this chapter.) A service feature represents a major functionality of a system and may be added or removed as a service unit. In VOF, *Virtual Printer, Smart Fax,* and *Follow Me* features are examples of service features.

A service feature uses other features (e.g., operational, environmental, and implementation features) to function properly and the constituents of a binding unit can be found by traversing the feature model along the feature relationships and composition rules. For

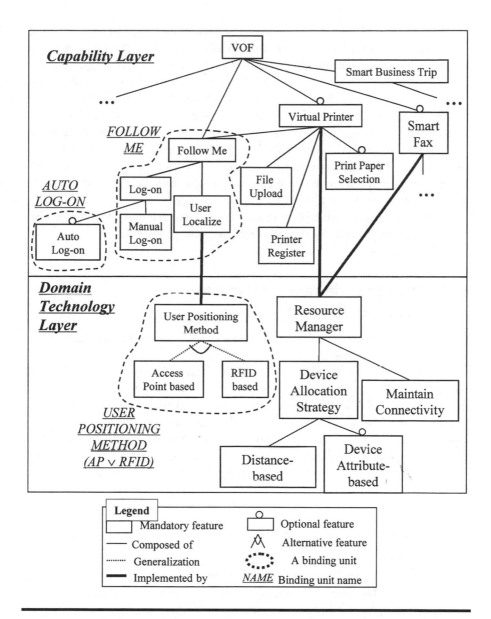

Figure 13.1 Feature model of VOF product line. (*Source:* Adapted from Lee, J. and D. Muthig. 2006. Feature oriented variability management in product line engineering, *Communications of ACM*, 49: 55–59.)

example, as we start from the *Follow Me* service feature, *Log-on*, *Manual Log-on*, *Auto Log-on*, *User Localize*, and *User Positioning Method* features can be identified. All of these features are needed to provide the follow me service.

Within a feature binding unit, there may exist optional or alternative features that should be selected based on customer's needs. These features impose variations on the component design and, therefore, they have to be identified as separate feature binding units. For example, only one of the subfeatures of *User Positioning Method* can be selected based on the device type that a customer may choose. (See the *User Positioning Method* feature at the domain technology layer in Figure 13.1.)

After all feature binding units are identified, a name is assigned to each feature binding unit; the feature name that represents a binding unit is given to the corresponding feature binding unit but the name is written in upper case letters to distinguish it from the name of the feature. (See the dotted circles and the names of binding units in Figure 13.1.)

In the next section, we explain extensions that are made to address new challenges originating from a dynamically reconfigurable product line.

13.3 Feature Oriented Analysis for Dynamic Reconfiguration

Recently, there have been increasing demands for the postponement of decisions on product variations to runtime to provide an operating-context relevant service. It means that features can be selected and/or parameterized at runtime by a user or by a product when a certain contextual change is recognized. For example, the service features of VOF should be dynamically reconfigured to provide context relevant services as users' physical locations and available resources change dynamically. To support such demands, a feature model is further enhanced with a feature binding graph, which is a labeled digraph without cycles and captures feature binding units and their binding relations with preconditions. (See Figure 13.2 for a feature binding graph of VOF.)

13.3.1 Feature Binding Graph

In a feature binding graph, each node corresponds to an FBU identified through the feature binding analysis and the relation between two FBUs is either static or dynamic. With the feature binding graph, we can provide an intuitive and visual description of dynamically changing product configuration. Also, we can explore appropriate binding techniques based on this information.

In the following, we define features, FBUs, and a feature binding graph.

Definition 1 (feature)

A feature is defined as a 2-tuple <*FName, C*>, where

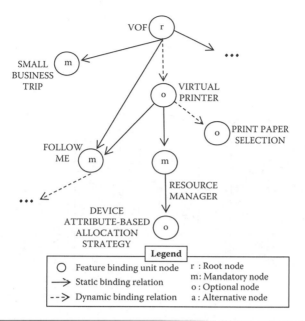

Figure 13.2 **Feature binding graph.** (*Source:* Adapted from Lee, J. and D. Muthig. 2006. **Feature oriented variability management in product line engineering,** *Communications of ACM,* **49: 55–59.**)

- *FName*: the name of a feature.
- *C*: the commonality of a feature, which is one of mandatory, optional, or alternative.

Definition 2 (feature binding unit)

An FBU is defined as a 3-tuple <*FBUName, C, CF*>, where

- *FBUName*: the name of a feature binding unit.
- *C*: the commonality of a feature binding unit, which is one of mandatory, optional, or alternative.
- *CF*: a set of features that constitute a feature binding unit.

Definition 3 (feature binding graph)

A feature binding graph *G* is defined as a labeled digraph without cycles, where:

- Each vertex is a feature binding unit and V(*G*) is the vertex set.
- *G* has a unique root vertex r, which represents a system.
- The vertex types *m*, *o*, and *a* represent mandatory, optional, and alternative feature binding units, respectively.

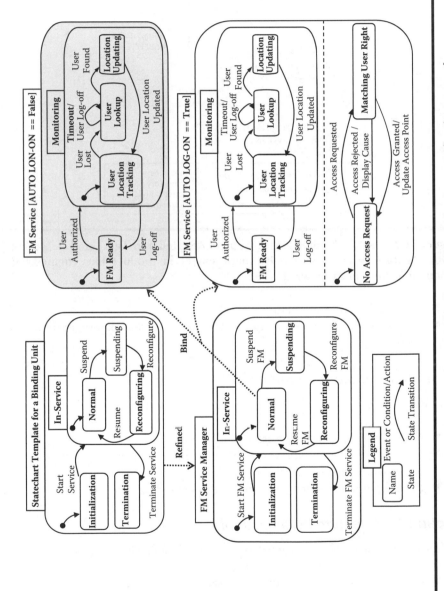

Figure 13.3 Statechart template for FBU behavior specification and FM behavior specification example.

- Each label of a vertex is the name of a feature binding unit.
- Each edge indicates a binding relation of two feature binding units and the binding relation is either static or dynamic binding. $E(G)$ is the edge set.
- Two vertices cannot have multiple relations.

In our approach, the dynamic reconfiguration is specified through four subactivities: behavior and data flow specifications of FBUs, reconfiguration context analysis and specification, reconfiguration strategy specification, and confirmation of consistency rules between specifications. Each of these activities is explained with examples in the following.

13.3.2 Behavior and Data Flow Specifications of FBUs

Different from statically configured products, a dynamically reconfigurable product should be able to handle requests to change its current configuration. In this chapter, a Statechart template, which defines a common behavior required for dynamic reconfiguration, is proposed. (See the upper left portion of Figure 13.3.)

At the top level of the Statechart, three states exist: *Initialization, Termination*, and *In-Service*. The *Initialization* and *Termination* states are for the specification of tasks t required at the initialization and termination time of a binding unit (e.g., a device initialization and shutting-down). The *In-Service* state is further refined into the *Normal, Suspending*, and *Reconfiguring* states. The *Normal* state is used to specify service behavior of a FBU. The *Suspending* state specifies necessary behaviors before starting dynamic reconfiguration (e.g., current service state saving, current active service completing, etc). Reconfiguration actions of a feature binding unit are performed at the *Reconfiguring* state (e.g., changing service behaviors).

This Statechart template is refined for FBUs of service features. For example, Figure 13.3 shows Statechart specifications for *FOLLOW ME (FM)*, which provides user localization related services. In Figure 13.3, two variants of the *Normal* state of *FM* are presented: when *AUTO LOG-ON* is requested at runtime, the Statechart at right-lower portion of Figure 13.3 is bound to the *Normal* state during reconfiguration.

Of these states in the template, the *Suspending* state defines a strategy on how to handle currently active services. The strategy can be either one of the following:

1. Suspending immediately without saving current states
2. Suspending after saving current states for state recovery
3. Suspending after finishing current active services
4. No suspending (i.e., seamless provision of services during reconfiguration). For example, *FM* is specified to keep providing a user localization service during product reconfiguration (strategy 4) by replicating its service behavior into *Suspending* and *Reconfiguring* states.

Once we specify behaviors of feature binding units, functionalities of each binding unit are analyzed and specified. In our approach, the functionality of a feature binding unit is specified using data flow diagrams (DFD). DFD shows data and control flows between processes, and processes in DFD are controlled by a Statechart specification. For example, the processes in Figure 13.4 are controlled by the *FM* Statechart.

To present variants in a DFD, a stereotype, <<v>> is used. For example, the *FOLLOW ME* Service Controller in Figure 13.4 has a Boolean guard (*[AUTO LOG-ON == True]*), which means that all elements of this DFD are selected when the *AUTO LOG-ON* binding unit is selected. If it is not selected, the variant processes *Auto Log-On Computation* and its data/control flows are removed from this DFD.

13.3.3 Context Analysis and Specification

The context analysis starts with identifying *contextual parameters* of a product line. A contextual parameter is defined as an environmental element that has a piece of information about a system's context (e.g., current location of a user, battery remaining time, etc.). Once contextual parameters are identified, we refine them by defining attributes of each parameter. The attributes may include data type, sampling

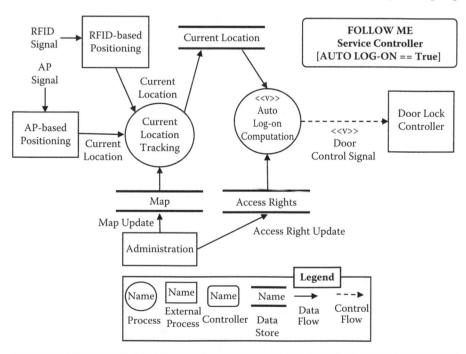

Figure 13.4   DFD specification of FM.

rates, and validity conditions. (See Table 13.1 for a part of dynamic parameter definitions for *VOF.*) In the *Type* column, the types of contextual parameter values are defined. The *Sampling Rate* defines how often the contextual parameters should be checked. A contextual parameter may be valid only if its value is within a predefined range or a set of values: such conditions are defined in the *Validity* column. The validity conditions of each contextual parameter should be satisfied before a contextual parameter is used to detect contextual changes.

Then, reconfiguration situations are specified as a logical expression of dynamic parameters. A reconfiguration situation is an event that triggers a dynamic reconfiguration. For instance, a *Director in Move* situation is true when *Privilege Level (P)* is *Director* and the *User in Move (UM)* is true. For this situation, the *AUTO LOG-ON* FBU is bound and activated.

Next, a reconfiguration strategy specification for each reconfiguration situation is explained.

13.3.4 Specification of Reconfiguration Strategies

A dynamic reconfiguration strategy is about "how" to perform dynamic reconfiguration and is specified for each reconfiguration situation with considerations of binding dependencies (i.e., require and exclude), change impact to other binding units, and required resources (e.g., components). Therefore, the action specification should include information on:

■ Pre/post-conditions for reconfiguration (e.g., required binding units or hardware resources),

Table 13.1
Contextual Parameter Definition

Attributes of Contextual Parameters	Type	Sampling Rate	Validity[a] (a valid range of value or a set of valid values)
Privilege level (P)	String	Log-in time	P = Director; D = head, manager, scientist, visitor, administrator
Locations (L)	String	30 seconds	L = Entry; D = office, meeting room 1, meeting room 2
User in move (UM)	Boolean	60 seconds	UM = True if L ? L' UM = False if L = L'

[a] Valid range of values or set of valid values.

Source: Lee, J. and D. Muthig. 2008. In *ICSR2008: Lecture Notes in Computer Science,* Vol. 5030, Mei, H., Ed., Springer, Berlin, pp. 154–165.

■ Identification of FBUs that are involved in reconfiguration (e.g., binding units to be added, removed, or substituted), and
■ Ways to handle currently active services (e.g., stop, suspend, or keep providing current active services).

For the specification of first two items, we adopt a graph transformation (Corradini et al., 1996), which is explained in the following.

Definition 4 (graph transformation) (Corradini et al., 1996)

A graph transformation is defined as a production p: $L \rightarrow R$, where,

■ Feature binding graphs L and R are called the left- and the right-hand side, respectively.
■ p is a schematic description of direct derivations.
■ A production p defines a partial correspondence between the elements of L and R, determining which vertices and edges of L should be preserved, deleted, and created at R by an application of p.

In this chapter, L_u is a *pre-image graph* for the binding of an FBU u and R_u is a *resulting graph* after the binding of u. The pre-image graph L_u of u is specified with the consideration of "require" and "exclude" dependencies of u. For the formal definition of a pre-image graph, the following sets are used.

Definition 5 (dangling vertex)

■ The degree d of a vertex v is the number of edges connected to v. If $d(v) = 0$, the vertex v is called a dangling vertex.

Definition 6 (require set for feature binding of u)

■ Require(u): A set of feature binding units that must be present in a current configuration for the binding of an FBU u.

Definition 7 (exclude set for feature binding of u)

■ Exclude(u): A set of feature binding units that must not be present in a current configuration for the binding of u.

Definition 8 (pre-image graph of u)

A pre-image graph L_u of an FBU u is a feature binding graph, where

- A root vertex $r \in$ Require(u)
- $\forall \ bu \in$ Require(u) • there exists a path from the root vertex r to bu
- $\forall \ bu \in$ Exclude(u) • d(bu) = 0
- Require(u) $\cap$ Exclude(u) = $\varnothing$
- $\forall \ bu \in$ V(L_u) • $bu \in$ Require(u) $\vee$ $bu \in$ Exclude(u)

As the definition 8 shows, L_u has the *require* vertices of u as a connected graph from r and has the *exclude* vertex of u as a dangling vertex. For example, *VOF, FM*, and *USER POSITIONING METHOD (RFID)* (*UPM(RFID)* in short) are the *require* vertices to bind *AUTO LOG-ON*, and the *exclude* vertex is the dangling vertex *UMP(AP)*. This means that *AUTO LOG-ON* requires its parent FBU bound in a current configuration and the user position method should be *RFID based*, not *AP based*. Like this, we can explicitly specify pre-conditions for the binding of FBUs.

A pre-image graph is specified for each FBU and used to determine whether or not a binding request is acceptable under a current configuration of a product. To check the acceptability, the following rules are used.

Rule 1 (inclusion of require binding units)

Let C be a feature binding graph that presents a current configuration of a product at runtime. Let L_u be a pre-image graph of an FBU u. For binding of u, C must include the binding units in Require (u). This rule is formally defined as

- $\forall \ bu \in$ Require(u) • $bu \in$ V(C)

Rule 2 (absence of exclude binding units)

Let C be a feature binding graph that presents a current configuration of a product at runtime. Let L_u be a pre-image graph of a binding unit u. For the binding of u, C must not include the binding units in Exclude (u). This rule is formally defined as

- $\forall \ bu \in$ Exclude(u) • $bu \notin$ V(C)

These two rules are checked as a pre-condition for binding of a binding unit. In addition, the following rule is checked as a post-condition.

Rule 3 (inclusion of a resulting binding graph)

Let H be a feature binding graph that presents a current configuration after a reconfiguration at runtime. Let R_u be a resulting graph of a binding unit u. After binding of u, H must include the binding graph R_u as its sub-graph. This rule is formally defined as

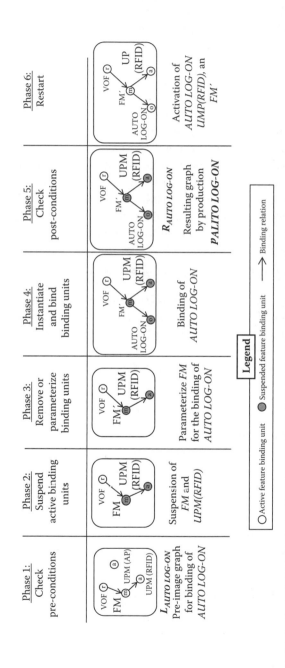

Figure 13.5 Six phases for dynamic reconfiguration. (*Source:* Lee, J. and D. Muthig. 2008. In *ICSR2008: Lecture Notes in Computer Science*, Vol. 5030, Mei, H., Ed., Springer, Berlin, pp. 154–165.)

- ▪ $\forall\ bu \in V(R_u) \bullet bu \in V(H)$
- ▪ $\forall\ e \in E(R_u) \bullet e \in E(H)$

Next, six phases of reconfiguration are specified with the consideration of feature binding units to be reconfigured and impacts to other binding units. (See Figure 13.5.) The six phases are 1) check pre-condition, 2) suspend active binding units that are involved in reconfiguration, 3) remove or parameterize binding units that have to be deleted or have to change their behaviors, 4) instantiate and bind binding units that are newly added, 5) check post-conditions, and 6) activate new or suspended binding units. By "active" we mean that the state of a binding unit is in the normal operational state.

The first and fifth phases, which check pre/post-conditions of a reconfiguration, are performed based on the rules 1, 2, and 3. At the second phase, we determine whether an involved FBU should be suspended or should provide services continuously during reconfiguration. For example, the *FM* FBU at *Phase 2* in Figure 13.5 is suspended for reconfiguration. This means that *FM* finishes its current service and prepares reconfiguration. However, *VOF* coordinates other services (e.g., *VIRTUAL PRINTER*) continuously during reconfiguration: *VOF* is notified that *FM* is being reconfigured and should not request a service to *FM* during reconfiguration.

At the third phase, FBUs that are no longer needed in the product configuration are removed. If an FBU's behavior can be changed through parameterization instead of removing and newly instantiating the FBU, relevant parameters for a new configuration are sent to the FBU. For example, the behavior of *FM* is changed from the one that does not include *AUTO LOG-ON* to the one with *AUTO LOG-ON*. At the fourth phase, binding units to be newly added to a current configuration are instantiated and bound to a product. Finally, FBUs are activated, after checking the post-condition of the reconfiguration.

In the following section, consistency rules for dynamic reconfiguration specification are introduced.

13.3.5 Confirmation of Consistency Rules

In this section, two categories of consistency rules are introduced: consistency between FBUs and consistency between reconfiguration strategy specification and behavior specification of FBUs. When more than two FBUs are reconfigured, we have to check the dependency between pre/post-conditions of binding units. These are sequential and parallel dependencies, and their definitions are as follows:

Definition 9 (Sequential Dependency)

- ▪ Given two reconfigurations p_1 and p_2 such that $G \overset{p_1}{\Rightarrow} H_1 \overset{p_2}{\Rightarrow} H_2$, p_2 is sequentially dependent on p_1, if and only if at least one of "require" vertices (say v_r)

of p_2 such that $v_r \notin G$ is added to the graph G by p_1 and H_1 satisfies the precondition of p_2.

This dependency means that the reconfiguration p_2 can only be performed after the reconfiguration p_1. For example, *AUTO LOG-ON* can be bound only when its parent binding unit *FM* is bound beforehand.

Definition 9 (Parallel Dependency)

◾ Two alternative reconfigurations p_1 and p_2 such that $H_1 \overset{p_1}{\Rightarrow} G \overset{p_2}{\Rightarrow} H_2$ are parallel dependent, if and only if at least one of "exclude" vertices (say v_{e2}) of p_2 such that $v_{e2} \notin G$ is added to the graph G by p_1, and at least one of "exclude" vertices (say v_{e1}) of p_1 such that $v_{e1} \notin G$ is added to the graph G by p_2.

This dependency means that only one of the reconfigurations p_1 and p_2 can be performed. Suppose, for example, that *AUTO LOG-ON* and *VP* may require two distinct variants of the *USER POSITIONING METHOD* FBU (i.e., *AP- based* or *RFID-based*). Then, only one of *AUTO LOG-ON* and *VP* can be bound to a product configuration at the same time.

Next, we should consider the consistency between reconfiguration strategy specification and behavior specification of FBUs. During reconfiguration, some events (e.g., *Suspend*, *Terminate*, or *Resume* events) are sent to FBUs to control their behavior for reconfiguration. To maintain system integrity, we have to be sure that these events are processed correctly at each FBU. That is, the behavior specification of each FBU should be able to handle the received events and to generate corresponding responses (e.g., an acknowledging message for a successful process of the *Suspend* event) so that the phases of reconfiguration strategy can be proceeded. The consistency between the two specifications can be checked by tracing events and state transitions.

13.4 Architecture Design for Dynamic Reconfiguration

To develop dynamically reconfigurable core assets, commonality and variability of a product line must be analyzed first and then the analysis results must be used to guide the development of core assets. That is, variability design is the activity of constructing and evolving a reuse infrastructure, which realizes all variability requirements specified in a feature model and dynamic reconfiguration specifications. One of the key factors to achieve the goal is designing an architecture in such a way to support dynamic reconfiguration. In this section, we present architecture design guidelines and their applying result as an example.

13.4.1 Guidelines for Designing Dynamically Reconfigurable Architectures

In the following, we propose four engineering guidelines for architecture design. The guidelines are to enhance visibility and traceability of dynamic reconfiguration using feature based specifications. In the following, proposed architecture design guidelines are explained.

Guideline one: Separation of control components from data components. In the product line analysis phase, we specify behaviors and data flows of each binding unit using Statechart and DFD, respectively. These two analysis results have distinct characteristics: behavior analysis for the identification of control data that determine behavior of a feature binding unit, and data flow analysis for the identification of functionalities that are required to provide services.

By separating these two concerns in an architecture model, we can establish mappings from feature binding units to architectural components more clearly. Behaviors are allocated to the control plane, which contains control components, and functionalities are allocated to the data plane, which contains data/computational components. With this separation, feature based dynamic product reconfiguration can be made more visible and manageable in an architecture model, since we can easily trace related architectural components of a configuration.

Guideline two: Separation of global behavior from local behavior. In our approach, we propose to classify control components into two categories: local behavior control components and global behavior control components. Each feature binding unit may have its own states (local behavior) to provide required services and they are allocated to a local behavior control component. To maintain integrity of a system as a whole, global system behavior must be defined (e.g., safety critical user commands should override currently active services), and local behavior control components must behave in coordination with the global behavior (e.g., system mode). The global behavior is allocated to a global behavior control component. With this separation, we can clearly specify and validate feature interaction behaviors, which are critical for maintaining system integrity before and after a reconfiguration.

Guideline three: Identification of architectural components in correspondence with feature binding units. Identification of "right" architectural components with "right" granularity is critical for designing dynamically reconfigurable product line architecture. Suppose, for example, that a variant architectural component is added or removed at runtime. Then, all components included in that component should also be added or removed as well. Therefore, architectural components and their variations should be determined carefully so that their addition or removal would not create any undesirable side effects such as addition of unnecessary components, or removal of required components.

This guideline proposes that architectural components should be identified based on feature binding units, and explicit mappings between feature binding units and architectural components should be established. By complying to this guideline, we can reduce change impacts and improve traceability between configurations. If there is difficulty establishing mappings, the related architectural components should be examined for further decomposition, refinement, or restructuring.

Guideline four: Separation of context from content. As pointed out in (Gomaa and Jussein, 2004; Kramer and Magee, 1990), the separation of product service concerns (content) from product reconfiguration concerns (context) is important to reduce the complexity of dynamic reconfiguration. That is, the product service concern should focus on interactions and computations of components to provide services, while the product reconfiguration concern should focus on monitoring current product situations and reconfiguration transactions. Thus, the separation of these two concerns can clarify responsibilities of architectural components.

In the following section, how these guidelines can be used to design a dynamically reconfigurable product line architecture is demonstrated with VOF.

13.4.2 Example: VOF Architecture

For a case study, we adopted the C2 architecture style (Medvidovic et al., 1999; Medvidovic and Taylor, 1997) for the development of VOF architecture model as shown in Figure 13.6. The C2 style provides flexibility through its layered structure and modular components, which are called "bricks." A brick can send/receive

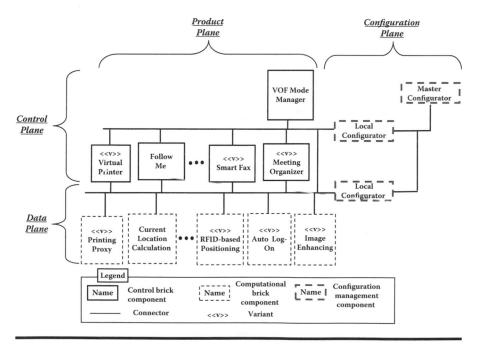

Figure 13.6   Architecture model for VOF product line.

messages to/from other bricks through its top and bottom ports, and bus-style connectors connecting ports.

Though the C2 style is flexible for changes, the style itself does not provide design guidelines such as how one can identify bricks and layers, and how functionalities should be allocated to them. In this section, we explain how the style is refined and extended to accommodate runtime flexibility. As we apply the proposed engineering guidelines, we divide the C2 style into different planes. First, the architecture model is divided into configuration and product planes, and the product plane is further refined into control and data planes. In the following, each of these planes is explained.

Control plane of product plane (related guidelines: one, two, and three): Bricks in the control plane control behaviors of the system. Each of local behavior control bricks (e.g., the *Virtual Printer* brick in Figure 13.6) defines behavior of a feature binding unit and it can be executed and tested independently from other control bricks. The global behavior control brick (e.g., the *VOF Mode Manager* brick in Figure 13.6) defines system modes (e.g., initialization, termination, and power saving modes) and an interaction policy (e.g., priority, concurrency) of local control bricks.

Data plane of product plane (related guidelines: one): The data plane consists of computational bricks, which read input data from sensors and process them to make outputs such as events and temporary data. Event data are sent to *VOF Mode Manager* to determine global states of a system. Temporary data are sent to other computational bricks as inputs.

Functionalities that are allocated to the bricks in the data plane can be found in the DFD specifications of feature binding units. This means that an explicit mapping between feature binding units and bricks in the data plane can also be established. Therefore, change effects from addition or removal of a feature binding unit can also be traced clearly in the data plane. For instance, dynamic binding of *AUTO LOG-ON* should result in the binding the *Auto Log-on* brick, as the brick is used by *AUTO LOG-ON*.

Configuration plane (related guideline: four): The configuration plane is in charge of detecting contextual changes, determining and validating a reconfiguration strategy, and executing reconfiguration. The plane consists of two types of components: *Master Configurator* and *Local Configurator*. *Master Configurator* collects information from *Local Configurators* and/or external probes to detect contextual changes. If a contextual change that requires product reconfiguration is detected, *Master Configurator* processes a relevant reconfiguration transaction to change the current product configuration. Each *Local Configurator* is connected to a connector, and monitors the product by inspecting messages between bricks.

As we applied the guidelines for architecture design, mappings between feature binding units and architectural components could be established easily and clearly, and interactions of feature binding units became visible and manageable. Also, separation of reconfiguration concerns from product service concerns could alleviate complexity of component behavior specifications, as the role of each component became simple and clear.

In the next section, we discuss and conclude this chapter.

13.5 Conclusions

Most efforts in product line engineering have focused on core asset development with variation points for *static configuration* of products: identification and specification of variation points, consistency management among them, and techniques for product code generation. Recently, Reconfigurable Product Line UML Based SE Environment (RPLUSEE) (Gomaa and Hussein, 2004) is proposed and its specialty is the provision of software dynamic reconfiguration patterns. Depending on the location of dynamic reconfiguration information, these patterns are classified into master-slave, centralized, client-server, and decentralized. This method also provides reconfiguration Statechart and reconfiguration transaction models for the dynamic reconfiguration. This approach focuses on high-level specifications of dynamic reconfigurable units; however, it does not describe techniques and guidelines for reconfigurable component identification, design, and implementation in detail.

On the other hand, most efforts in dynamic product reconfiguration (e.g., context-aware and self-healing systems) have focused on specific problems in each application area: behavior models to adapt dynamic changes of operational context (Kramer and Magee, 1990), recognition of current situations by analyzing data from software or hardware environments (Yau et al.,; 2002; Schilit et al., 1994; Mikic-Rakic and Medvidovic, 2002), and autonomous management of product configurations and software component versions (Garlan and Schmerl, 2002; Ganek and Corbi, 2003; Oreizy et al., 1999; van der Hoek and Wolf, 2003; Hall et al., 1999). These techniques are essential to support dynamic product reconfiguration; however, how these techniques can be organized to support product line variations has not been addressed. That is, a support for static and dynamic variations of product configurations, which may differ from one product to other, has not been considered in the fields of dynamic reconfigurations.

The chapter has presented techniques that enable the explicit modeling and management of product line variability across the life cycle from problem to solution space. The combination of feature modeling and variability design provides the basic mechanisms needed to implement feature-oriented variability management.

We have realized the presented approach several times in diverse industry contexts. Its implementations are already practically useful; however, we also uncovered several technical challenges that clearly require further research. Our approach needs to be extended to address other issues such as a formal base for analyzing consistency between various artifacts (e.g., behavior specifications, architecture models) and a support for controlling and evolving variability information consistently along the evolution of a product line infrastructure. Especially managing and modeling varying non-functional or quality properties of products in a product line is not fully possible with available technologies.

References

Gomaa, H. and M. Hussein 2004. Dynamic software reconfiguration in software product families. In *Software Product Family Engineering, Lecture Notes in Computer Science, Vol. 3014*, ed. F. van der Linden, 435-444. Springer-Verlag, Berlin Heidelberg.

Kramer, J. and J. Magee 1990. The evolving philosophers problem: dynamic change management. *Transaction on Software Engineering* 16(11):1293-1306.

Garlan, D. and B. Schmerl 2002. Model-based adaptation for self-healing systems. In *Proceeding of the Workshop on Self-Healing Systems* (WOSS'02), Nov.18-19:27-32.

Ganek, A.G. and T.A. Corbi 2003. The drawing of the autonomic computing era. *IBM Systems Journal*, 42(1):5-18.

Oreizy, P., M. M. Gorlick, R. N. Taylor, et al. 1999. An architecture-based approach to self-adaptive software. *IEEE Intelligent Systems*, May/June:54-62.

Yau, S. S., F. Karim, Y. Wang, et al. 2002. Reconfigurable context-sensitive middleware for pervasive computing. *Pervasive Computing*, July/September:33-40.

Schilit, B., N. Adams and R. Want 1994. Context-aware computing applications, *Proceedings of IEEE Workshop Mobile Computing Systems and Applications*, 85-90. IEEE CS Press, Los Alamitos, Calf.

Mikic-Rakic, M. and N. Medvidovic 2002. Architecture-level support for software component deployment in resource constrained environments. *Proceedings of First International IFIP/ACM Working Conference on Component Deployment*, Berlin, Germany:31-50.

van der Hoek, A. and A.L. Wolf 2003. Software release management for component-based software, *Software-Practice and Experience*, 33:77-98.

Hall, R. S., D. M. Heimbigner, and A. L. Wolf 1999. A cooperative approach to support software deployment using the software dock, *Proceedings of the 1999 International Conference on Software Engineering*, 174-183. ACM Press: New York, NY.

Sousa, J. P. and D. Garlan 2002. Aura: an architectural framework for user mobility in ubiquitous computing environments, *Proceeding of the 3rd Working IEEE/IFIP Conference on Software Architecture*, 29-43. Kluwer Academic Publishers.

Banavar, G. and A. Bernstein 2002. Software infrastructure and design challenges for ubiquitous computing applications, *Communications of ACM*, 45(12):92-96.

Clements, P. and L. Northrop 2002. *Software product lines: Practices and Pattern*. Addison Wesley, Upper Saddle River, NJ.

Weiss, D. M. and C. T. R Lai 1999. *Software product-line engineering: a family-based software development process*. Reading, MA: Addison Wesley Longman, Inc.

Kang, K., J. Lee, and P. Donohoe 2002. Feature-oriented product line engineering, *IEEE Software*, 19(4):58-65.

Lee, J. and K. Kang 2006. A feature-oriented approach for developing dynamically reconfigurable products in product line engineering, *Proceedings of the 10th International Software Product Line Conference*, 131-140. IEEE CS Press, Los Alamitos, CA.

Lee, J. and D. Muthig 2006. Feature-oriented variability management in product line engineering, *Communications of ACM*, 49(12):55-59.

Lee, J. and D. Muthig 2008. Feature-oriented analysis and specification of dynamic product reconfiguration. In *ICSR2008. Lecture Notes in Computer Science, Vol. 5030*. ed. H. Mei, 154-165. Springer-Verlag, Berlin Heidelberg.

Kang, K., S. Cohen, J. Hess, et al. 1990. Feature-oriented domain analysis (FODA) feasibility study. *Technical Report CMU/SEI-90-TR-21*, Pittsburgh, PA, Software Engineering Institute, Carnegie Mellon University.

Simos, M. A. 1995. Organization domain modeling (ODM): formalizing the core domain modeling life cycle. *ACM SIGSOFT Software Engineering Notes* 20(S1):196-205.

Jacobson, I., M. Griss, and P. Jonsson 1997. *Software Reuse: Architecture, Process and Organization for Business Success*. Addison-Wesley, New York.

Lee, K., K. C. Kang, M. Kim, et al. 2006. Combining feature-oriented analysis and aspect-oriented programming for product line asset development. *Proceedings of the 10th International on Software Product Line Conference* (SPLC 2006), 103-112. Baltimore, Maryland.

Czarnecki, K. and U. Eisenecker 2000. *Generative programming: methods, tools, and applications*, Addison-Wesley, New York.

Batory, D. 2005. Feature models, grammars, and propositional formulas. In *Software Product Lines. LNCS, Vol. 3714*, ed. H. Obbink and P. Klaus. 7-20. Springer-Verlag, Berlin Heidelberg.

S. Ferber, et al. 2005. Feature interaction and dependencies: modeling features for reengineering a legacy product line. In *Software Product Lines. LNCS, Vol. 2319*, ed. G.J. Chastek, 235-256. Springer-Verlag, Berlin Heidelberg.

VOF 2000.Virtual Office of the Future, http://www.iese.fraunhofer.de/research/vof/vof.jsp

Lee, J. and K. Kang 2004. Feature binding analysis for product line component development. In *Software Product Family Engineering, Lecture Notes in Computer Science, Vol. 3014*, ed. F. van der Linden, 266-276. Springer-Verlag, Berlin Heidelberg.

Corradini, A., et al. 1996. Algebraic approaches to graph transformation, Part I: basic concepts and double pushout approach. Technical Report TR-96-17, Pisa, Italy, Universita Di Pisa.

Medvidovic, N., D. S. Rosenblum and R. N. Taylor 1999. A language and environment for architecture-based software development and evolution. *Proceedings of the 21st International Conference on Software Engineering*, 44-53. ACM Press: New York, NY.

Medvidovic, N. and R. N. Taylor 1997. Exploiting architectural style to develop a family of applications. *Software Engineering, IEE Proceeding*, 144(5-6):237-248.

Chapter 14

Separating Application and Security Concerns in Modeling Software Product Lines

Michael E. Shin
Texas Tech University, Lubbock, TX

Hassan Gomaa
George Mason University, Fairfax, VA

Contents

14.1 Introduction

There are many potential threats to distributed application systems, such as electronic commerce and banking systems. Some of the potential threats (Ford and Baum 1997; Pfleeger 1997) are:

- *System penetration.* An unauthorized person tries to gain access to an application system and execute unauthorized transactions.
- *Authorization violation.* A person authorized to use an application system misuses or abuses it.
- *Confidentiality disclosure.* Secret information such as card numbers and bank accounts are disclosed to an unauthorized person.
- *Integrity compromise.* An unauthorized person changes application data in database or communication data.
- *Repudiation.* A person who performs some transaction or communication activity later falsely denies that the transaction or activity occurred.
- *Denial of service.* Legitimate access to application systems is deliberately disturbed.

Security requirements are often considered to be nonfunctional requirements. However, they eventually lead to functional requirements for security when developed in more detail (Sommerville 2001). Several approaches (Shin and Ahn 2000; Cysneiros and Leite 2001; Ahn and Shin 2001) address modeling security requirements as functional requirements. In one approach (Cysneiros and Leite 2001), operations in the class model are classified using stereotypes as operations for security requirements and for the application's functional requirements. Another approach (Shin and Ahn 2000) models role-based access control (RBAC) (Sandhu et al. 1996) using the Unified Modeling Language (UML) notation (Fowler and Scott 1997; Gomaa 2000; Rumbaugh, Booch, and Jacobson 2004; Booch, Rumbaugh, and Jacobson 2005), while a related paper (Ahn and

Shin 2001) specifies RBAC constraints using the Object Constraint Language (Warmer and Kleppe 1999).

This chapter describes how to model security requirements and designs (Gomaa and Shin 2004) for software product lines using the UML notation. This chapter describes an approach for modeling security requirements and designs separately from the application's business requirements and designs. Security concerns address-protecting application systems from potential threats, whereas business concerns address business requirements in application systems, such as electronic commerce or banking systems. An earlier paper described separation of application and security concerns for single systems (Gomaa and Shin 2004). This chapter greatly expands on these concepts by applying them to software product lines.

By careful separation of concerns, security concerns and business concerns of software product lines are captured separately. Security concerns are captured in security use cases and are encapsulated in security objects using the UML notation in the requirements modeling of a secure software product line. In the design, security concerns are encapsulated in security components separately from the application components as well. Separation of security concerns from business concerns can make a secure software product line more maintainable, such that there is minimal impact on the application requirements and design when changes are made to the requirements and design of security function- ality, and vice versa. The security use cases, objects, and components can also be reused in different software product lines. With UML, the system is viewed through multiple views: A functional requirements view is achieved through use case modeling; a static view is achieved using class modeling; and a dynamic view is achieved through both object collaboration modeling and statechart modeling (Gomaa 2000; Rumbaugh, Booch, and Jacobson 2004; Booch, Rumbaugh, and Jacobson 2005).

This chapter begins by describing security services/requirements for application systems in Section 14.2. Section 14.3 describes security requirements modeling of software product lines with use cases. Section 14.4 describes modeling the static aspects of systems. Section 14.5 describes modeling the dynamic view of systems. Section 14.6 describes component-based software architecture for secure software product lines. Examples are given from an electronic commerce (e-commerce) software product line that supports business-to-business (B2B) and business-to- customer (B2C) systems, which has been simplified for this chapter. The e-com- merce example was originally used to illustrate how to develop software product lines with a UML-based design method (Gomaa 2000). The approach for model- ing security concerns separately from application concerns is illustrated by extend- ing the e-commerce example in (Gomaa, 2000) to address security concerns.

14.2 Security Services for Application Systems

Potential threats to distributed application systems can be protected by the following security services/requirements (Chapman and Zwicky 1995; Ford and Baum 1997; Pfleeger 1997):

- *Authentication service.* Authentication services allow an entity (a user or system) to identify itself positively to another entity. When a cardholder, a merchant, a bank, or a credit card company claims to be a certain identity, an authentication service confirms the validity of this claim. This is an essential requirement of all security services because reliable authentication is necessary to enforce access control and accountability, and to achieve nonrepudiation. Authentication methods can be realized via password, personal identification number (PIN), challenge/response, digital certificate, smart card, or biometrics.
- *Access control service.* Based on security policies, access control services protect against unauthorized access to resources. In a business-to-business (B2B) application system, a person in an organization may only place orders authorized to him/her. For example, a software engineer in a construction company who is authorized to order only computer equipment and software would not be permitted to place an order for steel. Access control policies include mandatory access control (MAC) and discretionary access control (DAC).
- *Confidentiality service.* Confidentiality services protect against information being disclosed or revealed to any unauthorized entity by utilizing encryption. For example, secure e-commerce is needed to make sure confidential information about a customer credit card, bank account, or payment instructions is not disclosed to others. The means of achieving confidentiality include secret key cryptosystem, public key cryptosystem, secure socket layer (SSL), and secure electronic transaction (SET).
- *Integrity service.* Integrity services protect against unauthorized changes to data. Changing data in e-commerce includes adding, deleting, or modifying data such as credit card and bank account numbers, payment instructions, and order data. Unauthorized changes can be protected through a hash function, message digest (MD), or message authentication code (MAC).
- *Nonrepudiation service.* Nonrepudiation services protect against one party to a transaction or communication activity later falsely denying that the transaction or activity occurred. It is possible to authenticate an entity without nonrepudiation, but nonrepudiation is more than just authentication. Nonrepudiation is the ability to prove to a third party that a specific communication was submitted by, or was delivered to, a certain party. For example, in an e-commerce application, a legitimate customer purchases a product from a merchant's Web site and later may want to deny that he bought the product from the site. Without a nonrepudiation

service, the merchant would have difficulty in providing strong evidence to resolve such a disagreement. This repudiation can be resolved using a digital signature.

■ *Availability service (denial of service).* Denial of service occurs when an authorized party is prevented from accessing a system to which he or she has legitimate access. For example, a service access port is deliberately and heavily used so that service to other users is impeded. Another example is an Internet address flooded with packets. This denial of services can be detected by analysis of network data.

This chapter assumes that:

1. Key management is outside the scope of this chapter. It is assumed that keys associated with cryptosystems are provided.
2. The database is secure. Therefore, encryption or integrity checks for data to be stored in the database are not needed.
3. To simplify the requirements and design, security requirements and design are modeled independently from specific security techniques or algorithms.
4. Denial of service is outside the scope of this chapter.

14.3 Security Requirements Modeling of Software Product Lines

Security requirements of a software product line can be modeled in UML through use case modeling. The use case model describes the functional view for a software product line.

14.3.1 Use Case Modeling for Software Product Lines

The functional requirements of a software product line are defined in terms of use cases and actors (Jacobson, Griss, and Jonsson 1997; Gomaa 2004; Booch, Rumbaugh, and Jacobson 2005). An actor is a user type. A use case describes the sequence of interactions between the actor and the system, which is considered as a black box.

To capture the commonality and variability of a software product line, use cases are categorized as kernel, optional, or alternative use cases. Kernel use cases are those use cases required by all members of the software product line. Optional use cases are those use cases required by some but not all members of the software product line. Some use cases may be alternative use cases, such that different versions of the use case are required by different members of the software product line.

The alternative use cases are often mutually exclusive (Gomaa 2004). The use case categorization is depicted using the UML stereotype notation, e.g., «kernel».

The use case modeling approach advocated in this chapter is to model a software product line's functional requirements by means of nonsecure business use cases and to separately model the security requirements by means of security use cases. With this modeling approach, security use cases are categorized as optional use cases that may be required by only secure members of a software product line. When the software product line requires security services, the security use cases are extended from the nonsecure business use cases at extension points. An extension point (Jacobson, Griss, and Jonsson 1997; Rumbaugh, Booch, and Jacobson 2004) is a location where a use case extends another use case if the proper condition holds. The business use cases specify the functionality of software product lines. A business use case can provide an extension point where a security use case would extend the business use case, if the appropriate security requirement condition holds. Security requirements are considered to be optional features, meaning that if the security feature is required in a given software product line, then the appropriate security requirement condition is set to true; otherwise, it is set to false.

14.3.2 Separation of Concerns in Use Case Modeling

By careful separation of concerns, the security use cases for software product lines are specified separately from the business use cases. The security use cases can have parameters whose values are passed from the business use cases that they extend. Parameterized security use cases can be reused to allow other software product lines to provide security services. The parameterized security use cases needed for security services are outlined below and described in more detail in Section 14.3.3. In all cases, reference is made to a software product line system, which is a member of the software product line.

- Authentication Service determines whether a subject is a valid user of the software product line system.
  Authenticate (Subject) use case. The software product line system authenticates that a subject, such as a customer or supplier, is a legitimate user. The subject is a parameter of the Authenticate use case.
- Access Control Service determines whether a subject is allowed to access an object.
  Access Control (Subject, Object) use case. The software product line system authorizes a subject to access an object. The subject and object are parameters of the Access Control use case.
- Confidentiality Service. A sender encrypts a plaintext for confidentiality and a receiver decrypts the ciphertext.

Encrypt (Plaintext) use case. The software product line system encrypts a plaintext with a key agreed upon by a sender and a receiver. The plaintext is a parameter of the Encrypt use case.

Decrypt (Ciphertext) use case. The software product line system decrypts the ciphertext from the sender with a key. The ciphertext is a parameter of the Decrypt use case.

■ Integrity Service generates an integrity check value for a plaintext and checks for the unauthorized change to the plaintext using the value.

Generate Integrity Check Value (Plaintext) use case. The software product line system generates a value for plaintext integrity check, which will be checked by a receiver. The plaintext is a parameter of the Generate Integrity Check Value use case.

Check Integrity (Plaintext, Value) use case. The software product line system generates an integrity check value from the plaintext and compares it with the integrity check value received. The plaintext and value are parameters of the Check Integrity use case.

■ Nonrepudiation Service generates a signature for plaintext nonrepudiation and checks for validity of the signature.

Provide Nonrepudiation (Plaintext) use case. The software product line system generates a signature for nonrepudiation of a plaintext that will be verified by a receiver. The plaintext is a parameter of the Provide Nonrepudiation use case.

Check Nonrepudiation (Plaintext, Signature) use case. The software product line system checks nonrepudiation of the plaintext and maintains the evidence. The plaintext and signature are parameters of the Check Nonrepudiation use case.

These security services are described at a general level, independently from specific security techniques or algorithms. Each security service described in this chapter can be specialized to a unique security technique or algorithm. For example, access control service can be realized by RBAC (Sandhu et al. 1996), although how to model each security service in detail (Shin and Ahn 2000; Ahn and Shin 2001) is outside the scope of this chapter.

14.3.3 Examples of Separation of Concerns in Use Case Modeling

An example of the separation of business and security use cases in an electronic commerce software product line is shown in a UML use case diagram (Figure 14.1). In the kernel use case for Browse Catalog required by all members of the electronic commerce software product line, a customer browses through various WWW catalogs and views various catalog items from a given supplier's

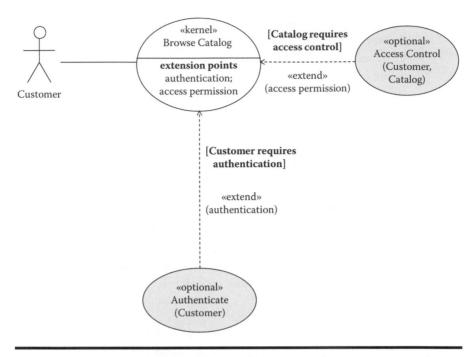

Figure 14.1 Browse Catalog with Security use case in e-commerce software product line.

catalog. The Browse Catalog business use case is extended by the Authenticate and Access Control security use cases, shaded in gray. A customer may need to get authentication before browsing a catalog. The customer may also need permission to access a specific catalog. These security concerns are captured in separate security use cases: Authenticate (Customer) and Access Control (Customer, Catalog). Authenticate (Customer), a parameterized use case, extends Browse Catalog at an extension point called Authentication, if a given system requires an authentication service for the customer. In a similar manner, a parameterized use case, Access Control (Customer, Catalog), extends Browse Catalog at an extension point, Access Permission, if the software product line needs to control access to catalogs. These security use cases are categorized as optional use cases, which are selected by some member systems of an electronic commerce software product line when authentication and/or access control security requirements are needed for secure systems. These security use cases can be reused by providing them as extension use cases to the business use cases of different software product lines when authentication and access control security services are needed elsewhere.

The following example describes specifications for a Browse Catalog business use case and for Authenticate and Access Control security use cases.

Use Case Name: Browse Catalog
Summary: Customer chooses a catalog to browse.
Actor: Customer
Precondition: System is ready.
Description (Base use case):
1. <authentication>
2. Customer chooses to view a catalog index.
3. System displays catalog index.
4. User requests to view a specific catalog.
5. <access permission>
6. System reads the catalog and displays it.
Postcondition: Customer has browsed a catalog.

In the above example, for a nonsecure software product line where the security condition [Customer Requires Authentication] is set to false, step 1 above is a null function. For a secure software product line where the security condition [Customer Requires Authentication] is set to true, at step 1 above the statement <authentication> is replaced by the following Authenticate extension use case:

Use Case Name: Authenticate (Subject)
Summary: System authenticates that a subject, such as customer or supplier, is a legitimate user of system.
Dependency: Extension use case for several use cases
Actor: {Subject}
Precondition: A subject has not been authenticated.
Description:
1. {Subject} enters input for identity authentication.
2. System checks the {subject} identity.
3. System stores {subject} identity information for its access control.
Alternatives:
1. If the system does not recognize the input, it displays a message to {subject} asking for another input to authenticate.
2. If the {subject} is not valid, system displays Access Denied message.
Postcondition: System has authenticated a {subject}.

Similarly, for a nonsecure software product line where the security condition [Catalog Requires Access Control] is false, step 5 in the Browse Catalog use case is a null function. For a secure software product line where the security condition [Catalog Requires Access Control] is true, step 5 <access permission> in Browse Catalog is replaced by the following Access Control extension use case:

Use Case Name: Access Control (Subject, Object)
Summary: System authorizes subject access to object.
Dependency: Extension use case for several use cases
Actor: {Subject}
Precondition: {Subject} is authenticated as a legitimate user.
Description:

    1. Using {subject} identity information, the system checks whether {subject} has permission to access {object}.
    2. If {subject} has permission, system permits {subject} to gain access to {object}.

Alternatives:
    1. If {subject} does not have permission to access {object}, the system displays Access Denied message.

Postcondition: System has authorized {subject} to gain access to {object}.

Security use cases can also describe alternative scenarios. In the Authenticate (Subject) use case, if the software product line does not recognize the subject identity, it displays a message asking for another identity to authenticate. In the Access Control (Subject, Object) use case, if the subject is not granted access permission, the software product line displays the Access Denied message.

Another example of a security use case extension is shown in Figure 14.2, which depicts the Send Purchase Request and Receive Purchase Request kernel use cases. A customer wanting to pay by credit card sends a purchase request to a supplier, expecting it to maintain confidentiality and integrity. The supplier, who requests the customer bank to check the customer payment status, may want to prevent the customer from repudiating his purchase request, which could cause trouble later on. To avoid this, the supplier needs a nonrepudiation security service. These security concerns can be captured in separate security use cases:

Encrypt (Purchase Request)
Generate Integrity Check Value (Purchase Request)
Provide Nonrepudiation (Purchase Request)

These security use cases extend the Send Purchase Request use case when the software product line requires confidentiality, integrity, or nonrepudiation security services. The Encrypt (Purchase Request) use case encrypts the customer purchase request with a key agreed upon by the customer and supplier. This optional security use case extends Send Purchase Request use case at an extension point "encryption." The other two use cases are alternative use cases:

Generate Integrity Check Value (Purchase Request), which extends Send Purchase Request at the extension point "integrity," creating a value for checking integrity of the customer purchase request.
Provide Nonrepudiation (Purchase Request), which extends Send Purchase Request at the extension point "nonrepudiation," makes a signature with a customer purchase request that will be verified by the supplier.

These security use cases can be used individually for each security service. However, if they are used together to extend a nonsecure business use case, they need to be applied in a given order. First, one of the following extension use cases

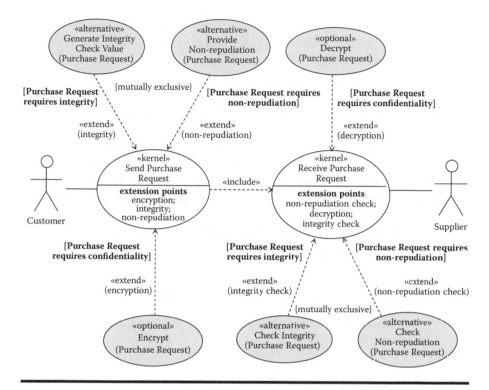

Figure 14.2   Send Purchase Request and Receive Purchase Request use cases.

may be applied, Generate Integrity Check Value (Purchase Request) or Provide Nonrepudiation (Purchase Request) use case, followed by the Encrypt (Purchase Request) use case. This is because the Encrypt (Purchase Request) use case not only protects against revealing the confidential data (i.e., the Purchase Request) to unauthorized persons, but also the fact that either Generate Integrity Check Value (Purchase Request) or Provide Nonrepudiation (Purchase Request) has been applied to the Purchase Request data.

In some situations, there may be some restrictions on extending a business use case with security use cases. For example, two security use cases might be mutually exclusive. Security constraints are used to define relationships between security use cases. Use cases can be depicted as being mutually exclusive in UML by using the constraint notation {mutually exclusive}, as shown in Figure 14.2. However, this constraint can be shown more formally using the Object Constraint Language (OCL) (Warmer and Kleppe 1999) to specify the security constraints. OCL is a formal language that is used to describe constraints on object-oriented models. In Figure 14.2, the Generate Integrity Check Value (Purchase Request) use case can have a mutually exclusive (zero or one) relationship with Provide Nonrepudiation (Purchase Request) because the digital signature for providing the nonrepudiation security service can be implemented using a hash function (Pfleeger 1997), which also provides an integrity service. This constraint is specified using OCL as follows (Gomaa and Shin 2002; Shin 2002):

$$(su1 \; \textbf{xor} \; su2) \; \textbf{or} \; (\textbf{not} \; (su1 \; \textbf{and} \; su2))$$

where su1 is Generate Integrity Check Value (Purchase Request) use case, and su2 is Provide Nonrepudiation (Purchase Request) use case.

This OCL constraint is true if only one of su1 and su2 is true, or if both su1 and su2 are false. (su1 **xor** su2) is true if either su1 or su2 is true, but not both. (**not** (su1 **and** su2)) is true if both su1 and su2 are false. This means that the application can choose to have neither security use case; alternatively, it can choose to have one or the other.

The following examples describe specifications for Send Purchase Request, Encrypt, Generate Integrity Check Value, and Provide Nonrepudiation use cases.

> **Use Case Name:** Send Purchase Request
> **Summary:** Customer sends a purchase request to supplier.
> **Actor:** Customer
> **Precondition:** Customer has selected items to be purchased.
> **Description**: (Base use case)
>   1. <nonrepudiation> or <integrity>
>   2. <encryption>
>   3. Customer sends a purchase request to supplier.
> **Postcondition:** Customer has sent a purchase request to supplier.

At step 1 in the above use case, either the nonrepudiation extension use case or the integrity extension use case can be inserted. However, if neither is required, then it is also possible for this to be a null step. Thus, the Provide Nonrepudiation (Purchase Request) extension use case is inserted at the <nonrepudiation> extension point of step 1 if the [Purchase Request requires nonrepudiation] condition is true. Alternatively, the Generate Integrity Check Value (Purchase Request) extension use case is inserted at the <integrity> extension point of step 1 if the [Purchase Request requires integrity] condition is true. At step 2, the Encrypt (Purchase Request) extension use case is inserted at the <encryption> extension point if the condition [Purchase Request requires confidentiality] is true.

> **Use Case Name:** Encrypt (Data)
> **Summary:** System encrypts data with a key.
> **Actor:** Base use case actor
> **Dependency:** Extension use case for several use cases
> **Precondition:** Data is ready to be encrypted.
> **Description:**
>   1. System gets a key to be used for encryption.
>   2. System encrypts {data} with the key.
> **Postcondition:** System has encrypted {data} with a key.

Use Case Name: Generate Integrity Check Value (Data)
Summary: System generates a value for data integrity check.
Actor: Base use case actor
Dependency: Extension use case for several use cases
Precondition: Data is ready for integrity check.
Description:
1. System computes an integrity check value for {data}.
2. System attaches the integrity check value to the original {data}.
Postcondition: System has generated a value for integrity check of data.

Use Case Name: Provide Nonrepudiation (Data)
Summary: System generates a signature for nonrepudiation of data.
Actor: Base use case actor
Dependency: Extension use case for several use cases
Precondition: Data is ready for nonrepudiation.
Description:
1. System signs {data} with a key to get a signature.
2. System attaches the signature to the original {data}.
Postcondition: System has generated a signature for {data}.

The following examples describe specifications for Receive Purchase Request, Decrypt, Check Integrity, and Check Nonrepudiation use cases.

Use Case Name: Receive Purchase Request
Summary: Supplier receives a purchase request and stores it in database.
Actor: Supplier
Precondition: Customer sent a purchase request to supplier.
Description:
1. <decryption>
2. <integrity check> or <nonrepudiation check>
3. System checks for validity of purchase request.
4. System stores purchase request in database.
5. System displays the status of purchase request to supplier.
Postcondition: Supplier has received a purchase request.

In the above use case, a Decrypt (Purchase Request) extension use case is inserted at <decryption> insertion point in step 1 if the extension point condition [Purchase Request requires confidentiality] is true. Thus the same extension point condition determines whether the Encrypt and Decrypt extension use cases are both provided or neither provided. Either Check Integrity (Purchase Request) extension use case is inserted at <integrity check> in step 2 or Check Nonrepudiation (Purchase Request) extension use case is inserted at <nonrepudiation check> in step 2, or neither. As with the Encrypt/Decrypt use cases, the integrity and nonrepudiation use cases are provided in pairs.

Use Case Name: Decrypt (Data)
Summary: System decrypts data with a key.
Actor: Base use case actor
Dependency: Extension use case for several use cases
Precondition: Data is ready to be decrypted.
Description:
  1. System retrieves a key.
  2. System decrypts {data} with the key.
Alternatives:
Postcondition: System has decrypted {data} with a key.

Use Case Name: Check Integrity (Data)
Summary: System generates an integrity check value from data and compares it with the integrity value received.
Actor: Base use case actor
Dependency: Extension use case for several use cases
Precondition: Data is ready for integrity check.
Description:
  1. System computes an integrity check value using {data} and compares it with the integrity check value sent by sender.
  2. If the two values match correctly, system permits data to be stored.
Alternatives:
  1. If the two values do not match, system displays Integrity Compromised message.
Postcondition: System has checked {data} integrity.

Use Case Name: Check Nonrepudiation (Data)
Summary: System checks nonrepudiation of data and saves the evidence.
Actor: Base use case actor
Dependency: Extension use case for several use cases
Precondition: A signature is ready to be checked for nonrepudiation of data.
Description:
  1. System verifies {data} with customer public key.
  2. If the signature is valid, system saves nonrepudiation evidence.
Postcondition: System has verified customer signature and saved the nonrepudiation evidence for {data}.

14.4 Static Modeling of Software Product Line Application and Security Concerns

Static modeling is used in UML to depict the static structural aspects of a software product line by modeling classes. The static model defines the classes in the software product line, their attributes, and the relationships between classes. There are three types of relationships among classes: associations, composition/aggregation relationships, and generalization/specialization relationships (Gomaa 2000).

Classes in a software product line class model can be categorized according to two orthogonal perspectives, the software product line reuse perspective and the application role perspective. A class can be categorized as a kernel, optional, or variant class to describe commonality and variability of classes in the software product line. From an application perspective, a class is categorized depending on the role it plays, such as control, algorithm, entity, or interface (Gomaa 2000). The class categorization is depicted using separate UML reuse and role stereotypes such as «optional» and «user interface». As with optional security use cases for software product lines, each security class is categorized as an optional class that may be required by only some members of a software product line.

The relationship between a software product line nonsecure business class (i.e., a class that does not provide access to a security service) and a software product line secure business class (i.e., a class that provides access to a security service) is modeled by means of a generalization/specialization hierarchy. The nonsecure business class and the secure business class are specialized from a generalized superclass using the inheritance mechanism. The secure business class inherits the generalized properties, such as attributes and operations, from the superclass and then adds attributes and operations to provide access to the security services.

Figures 14.3 and 14.4 depict generalization/specialization hierarchies for the Customer Interface and Customer Agent classes in the e-commerce software product line. Customers interact with the Customer Interface to place a product order. The Customer Interface is specialized to the Non-Secure Customer Interface and Secure Customer Interface classes. The Secure Customer Interface provides business services as well as access to an authentication security service (authenticate operation of Secure Customer Interface class in Figure 14.3). The Customer Agent (in Figure 14.4) acts on behalf of the human customer. It is specialized to the Non-Secure Customer Agent, which provides a nonsecure business service, and the Secure Customer Agent, which provides secure services by communicating with security objects in the security layer. The Secure Customer Agent class provides the following secure operations:

- RequestAuthentication operation. This operation requests for authenticating customers or suppliers from security objects.
- RequestAuthorizedCatalog operation. This operation requests for authorizing customer access to catalogs based upon customer right from security objects.
- RequestOrder operation. This operation requests a purchase order that may need to be secure by security service from security objects. A parameter "securityCondition" in this operation indicates security services required for a purchase request.

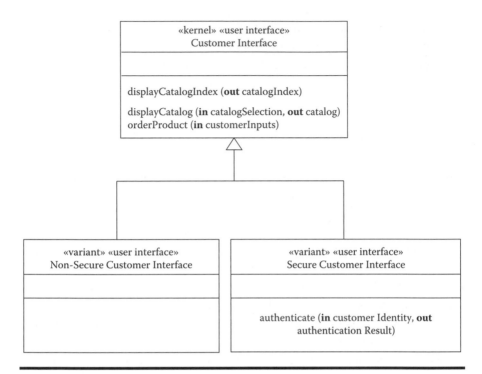

Figure 14.3 Generalization/specialization hierarchy for Customer Interface class.

14.4.1 Separation of Concerns in Static Modeling

Separation of concerns is achieved in software product line static modeling by structuring the business classes, which contain the application functionality and business concerns, separately from the security service classes, which provide security services. Applying a layered hierarchy, the business classes are structured into the software product line application layer, and the security service classes are structured into the software product line security layer, respectively.

Figure 14.5 depicts the e-commerce software product line application layer and e-commerce security layer, and the relationship between them. The e-commerce software product line application layer contains only business classes, which provide business services, while the security layer includes security service classes and database wrapper classes. Security service classes provide services for the business classes in the e-commerce software product line application layer.

The security service classes can be reused in other software product lines that need security services. Using the UML notation, each class in Figure 14.5 is depicted with two stereotypes—the software product line reuse perspective and the application role perspective—e.g., «optional» and «business logic», the former depicting the reuse perspective and the latter the role perspective (Gomaa 2000). In the

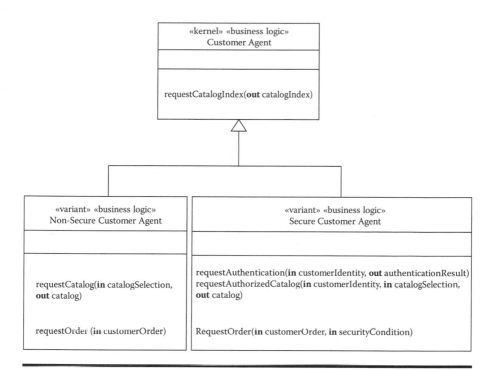

Figure 14.4 Generalization/specialization hierarchy for Customer Agent class.

e-commerce software product line application layer, the Catalog Server, and Delivery Order Agent classes are common to both business-to-business (B2B) and business-to-customer (B2C) systems, and consequently these classes are categorized as kernel classes. The Non-Secure Customer Interface, Non-Secure Customer Agent, Secure Customer Agent, and Secure Customer Interface classes are variants of kernel classes, as depicted in Figures 14.3 and 14.4. The business logic classes in the application layer encapsulate the business rules of the application. The security service classes and database wrapper classes of the security layer are optional classes because they are only needed if a software product line member needs secure services. A security service class contains either security logic or a security algorithm, whereas a database wrapper class encapsulates how the data stored in a database is accessed.

14.5 Dynamic Modeling of Secure Software Product Lines

The dynamic aspects of a software product line are described by means of the collaboration model and the statechart model. The collaboration model addresses the sequence of messages passed between objects, whereas the statechart model

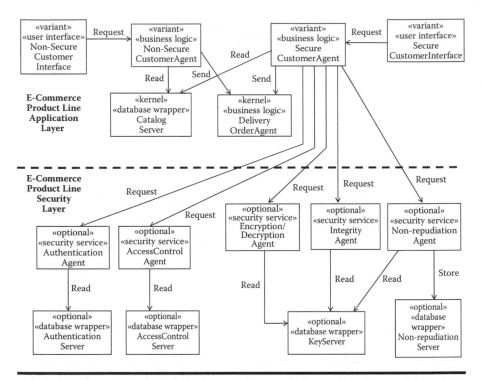

Figure 14.5 Relationships between Non-Secure classes and Security Service classes.

defines states and transitions between states to model dynamic aspects of a software product line.

14.5.1 Separation of Concerns in Collaboration Modeling

The dynamic views of a software product line are captured in the collaboration model through objects and the messages between objects. The collaboration model is used to depict the objects that participate in each use case for the software product line and the sequence of messages passed between them (Gomaa 2000; Booch, Rumbaugh, and Jacobson 2005). Once the use cases have been determined, the collaboration diagrams can be developed.

A dynamic model for the security extension of a software product line is represented through an alternative message sequence in the collaboration model that is taken if the proper security condition holds. As before, objects in the collaboration model are divided into the software product line application layer and security layer. Security concerns are separated from the software product line's business concerns by modeling software product line business objects separately from security objects. Security concerns captured in separate use cases are encapsulated in separate security objects. If a security requirement condition is true, meaning that the software product line needs to be secure, business logic objects in the software product line application layer communicate with security objects in the software product line security layer (following an alternative message sequence on the collaboration diagram) that provide security services. The alternative message sequence for the security scenario is only selected when the proper security condition holds. It should be noted that the same security condition is used in both the use case model and the dynamic model, thereby providing traceability from one model to the other.

Figure 14.6 depicts the collaboration diagram for Browse Catalog with security use case (Section 14.3.1) for situations when the software product line requires both authentication and access control security for catalogs. If the security requirement condition [Customer requires authentication] is true, Secure Customer Agent (in the e-commerce software product line application layer) requests Authentication Agent (in the e-commerce software product line security layer) to verify the customer using authentication data maintained by the Authentication Server. The authentication security service is provided by the Authentication Agent and Authentication Server objects separately from the application layer objects. Authentication Agent is a security service object that verifies a subject's identity based on security techniques (to implement authentication services) such as password, challenge response, or digital certificate, whereas Authentication

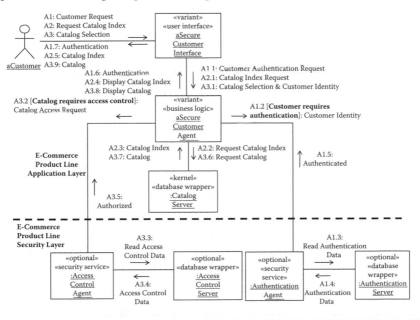

Figure 14.6 Collaboration diagram for Browse Catalog with Security use case.

Server maintains authentication data for the subjects. If Catalog requires access control, Secure Customer Agent also requests Access Control Agent to authorize customer access to a specific catalog. Access Control security service is provided by the Access Control Agent and Access Control Server objects. Depending on an organization's access control policy, such as mandatory access control (MAC), Access Control Agent authorizes a subject access to an object using access control data stored in Access Control Server. As these objects are instances of the product line classes in the static model, the Customer Interface, Secure Customer Agent, and Catalog Server objects are placed in the e-commerce software product line application layer, whereas the Authentication Agent, Authentication Server, Access Control Agent, and Access Control Server are located in the e-commerce software product line security layer. Each object in Figure 14.6 is modeled using two stereotypes, one to depict the software product line reuse perspective and the other to depict the application role perspective (Figure 14.5).

Figure 14.7 depicts a collaboration diagram for Send Purchase Request use case in the electronic commerce software product line with nonrepudiation and encryption security services when the software product line requires both these services for purchase requests. If Purchase Request requires both nonrepudiation

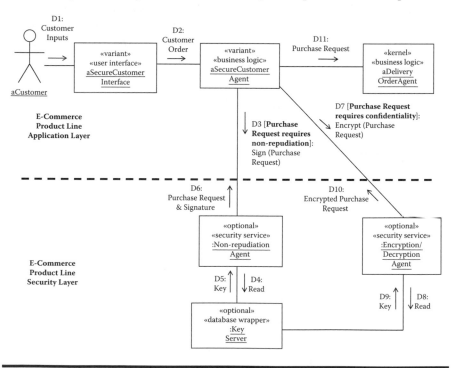

Figure 14.7   Collaboration diagram for Send Purchase Request use case: nonrepudiation and encryption.

and confidentiality, Secure Customer Agent requests Nonrepudiation Agent, which is a security service object, to sign the purchase request with a key from Key Server. Then it sends the signed purchase request to Encryption/Decryption Agent, which is a security service object, to encrypt the secret data with a key before sending it to Delivery Order Agent. As with Figure 14.6, objects in Figure 14.7 are depicted in terms of the software product line reuse and application role perspectives.

14.5.2 Separation of Concerns in Statechart Modeling

The statechart model, along with the collaboration model, addresses the dynamic aspects of a software product line. A statechart (Harel and Gary 1996) is developed for each state-dependent object in the collaboration model, including kernel, optional, and variant objects. Each state-dependent object in a collaboration diagram is specified by means of a statechart consisting of states and transitions between states.

The statechart model describes the security aspects of software product lines through alternative state transitions that are triggered if the appropriate security conditions are satisfied. Each statechart diagram describes the behavior of state-dependent use case whose corresponding collaboration diagram contains state-dependent objects. As a software product line nonsecure use case is extended to provide security, the corresponding statechart model captures the change in use case behavior by using an alternative state transition when the security condition holds.

Figure 14.8 depicts the statechart model for Secure Customer Agent object in the Browse Catalog use case (Figure 14.1), in which alternative state transitions for Authenticate (Customer) and Access Control (Customer, Catalog) security use cases are shaded in gray. If the customer requires authentication, then the state chart transitions from an Idle state to an Authenticating Customer state. When the software product line requires authorization of access to a secure file, e.g., to access a secure catalog, the statechart makes an alternative state transition from the Selecting Catalog state to the Authorizing Catalog Access state. Similarly, Figure 14.9 shows the statechart for modeling the behavior of the Secure Customer Agent object in the Send Purchase Request use case (Figure 14.2) when Purchase Request requires nonrepudiation and/or Purchase Request requires confidentiality. The sequence numbers shown on the statecharts correspond to the sequence numbers shown on the collaboration diagrams.

14.6 Component-Based Software Architecture for Secure Software Product Lines

The software architecture for a software product line describes the commonality and variability of the overall structure of the software product line. A software

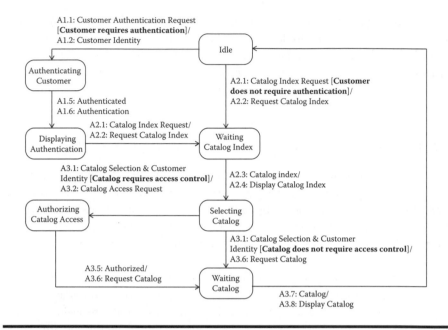

Figure 14.8   Statechart for Secure Customer Agent object.

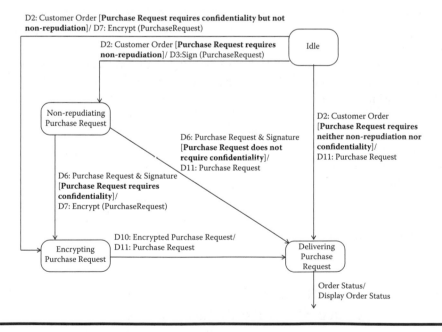

Figure 14.9   Statechart for Secure Customer Agent object.

product line is designed to components, and the interfaces between the components are defined. The software architecture of a software product line contains kernel, optional, and variant components in order to capture the commonality and variability of the software product line (Gomaa 2004). Each component is designed such that its interface is explicitly defined in terms of the operations it provides as well as the operations it requires. The static view of the software architecture for a software product line is represented using the composite structure diagram in UML (Gomaa and Shin 2002), whereas the dynamic view is modeled using the concurrent communication diagram (Gomaa 2004).

Figure 14.10 depicts the application components in software architecture for an e-commerce software product line. The business classes in Section 14.4 are encapsulated in application components in the software architecture, which provide application functionality. Each component is modeled using concurrent component notation in UML. The application components in an e-commerce software product line are defined as follows:

1. Non-Secure Customer Interface component. Nonsecure functions for customer interface are provided by this component.

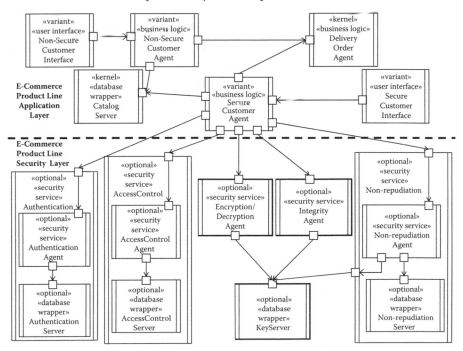

Figure 14.10   Software architecture for e-commerce software product line.

2. Secure Customer Interface component. This component provides secure functions for customer interface.
3. Non-Secure Customer Agent component. Acting on behalf of the human customer, this component provides nonsecure business services.
4. Secure Customer Agent component. This component provides a secure service by communicating with security objects. This component acts on behalf of the human customer.
5. Catalog Server component. The Catalog Server component maintains catalogs.
6. Delivery Order Agent component. The Delivery Order Agent component handles purchase requests from customers.

14.6.1 Separation of Concerns in Component- Based Software Architecture Modeling

Separation of concerns in the software architecture is achieved by a layered software architecture, in which the security layer is separated from the application layer. The security layer contains only security components, whereas the application layer contains only application components. Security classes in Section 14.4.1 are encapsulated in security components, which are designed separately from application components in the application layer. In a software product line software architecture, where the security components are optional, the security components are selected when a given software product line member needs security services. Security components (Figure 14.10) are defined as follows:

1. Authentication component. This component is a composite component that contains both Authentication Agent component and Authentication Server component.
2. Authentication Agent component. This component verifies a subject using the data from Authentication Server component.
3. Authentication Server component. This component maintains authentication data for subjects.
4. Access Control component. This component is a composite component that contains both Access Control Agent component and Access Control Server component.
5. Access Control Agent component. This component authorizes a subject's access to objects based on the policy.
6. Access Control Server component. This component contains access control policy for an organization.
7. Encryption/Decryption Agent component. This component contains cryptographic algorithms for encrypting and decrypting secret data.

8. Integrity Agent component. This component provides integrity security service against unauthorized changes to data.

9. Nonrepudiation component. This component is a composite component that contains both Nonrepudiation Agent and Nonrepudiation Server components.

10. Nonrepudiation Agent component. This component provides a security service that prevents one party from falsely denying that a business transaction occurred.

11. Nonrepudiation Server component. This component maintains the evidence of nonrepudiation of business transactions.

12. Key Server component. This component maintains keys that are used in confidentiality, integrity, and nonrepudiation security services.

Figure 14.11 depicts the ports with provided and required interfaces for Secure Customer Agent, Access Control Agent, and Authentication Agent components. The name of a component's required port starts with the letter R to emphasize that the component has a required port. The name of a component's provided port starts with the letter P to emphasize the component has a provided port. The Secure Customer Agent component has seven ports with required interfaces (RAuthentication, RAccessControl, REncryptionDecryption, RIntegrity,

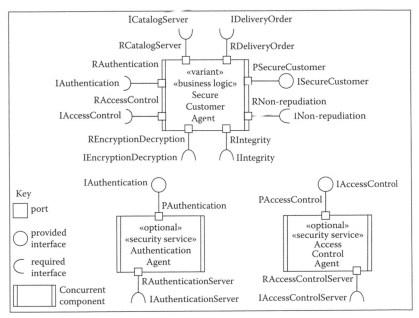

Figure 14.11   Ports with required and provided interfaces for Secure Customer Agent, Authentication Agent, and Access Control Agent components.

RNonrepudiation, RDeliveryOrder, and RCatalogServer) and one port with a provided interface (PSecureCustomer). The Authentication Agent component has a port with a required interface (RAuthenticationServer) and a port with a provided interface (PAuthentication). The Access Control Agent component has a port with a required interface (RAccessControlServer) and a port with a provided interface (PAccessControl). Figure 14.12 depicts the definition of the interfaces of the ports of Secure Customer Agent, Authentication Agent, and Access Control Agent components.

Figure 14.13 depicts the concurrent communication diagram for Browse Catalog with security components, which describes the dynamic view of the software architecture for an e-commerce software product line. Security components in the security layer are selected only if the security condition is true. Security conditions are used for software product line nonsecure business use cases to be extended by security use cases in Section 14.3.1 and for nonsecure business objects to communicate with security objects that provide security services in Section 14.5. For security component selection, the security conditions are used to determine which security components are needed in a software product line. In Figure 14.13, security components in the security layer are required by the Secure Customer Agent application component in the application layer when the software product line requires a specific security service, i.e., when a security

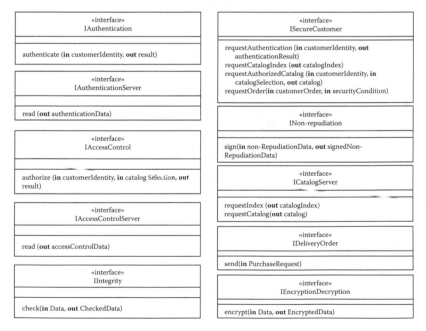

Figure 14.12 Component interfaces for Secure Customer Agent, Authentication Agent, and Access Control Agent.

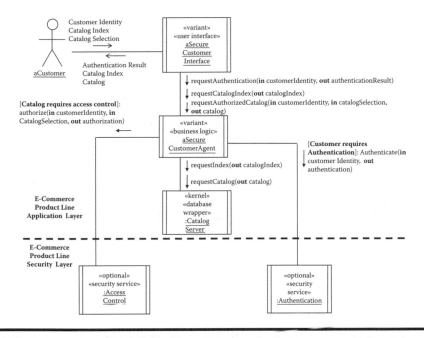

Figure 14.13 Concurrent communication diagram for Browse Catalog with security components.

condition is true. Authentication Agent and Access Control Agent security components in the security layer are needed by the Secure Customer Agent application component in the application layer when the security conditions, [Customer requires authentication] and [Catalog requires access control], are set to true, respectively.

Figure 14.14 depicts the concurrent communication diagram for Purchase Request with security components. The Secure Customer Agent application component in the application layer requires the Encryption/Decryption security component in the security layer if the security condition [Purchase request requires confidentiality] is true, whereas it needs the Integrity security component if the security condition [Purchase request requires Integrity] holds. Nonrepudiation security service in the security layer is selected by the Secure Customer Agent application in the application component only when the security condition [Purchase request requires nonrepudiation] is satisfied.

Using OCL, security constraints can be also defined to restrict accessibility to security components. For example, an integrity security service can be realized by either Integrity Agent or Nonrepudiation security component if a digital signature in the Nonrepudiation security component is realized through a hash function. In this case, these security components have a mutually exclusive relationship with each other. This constraint for an integrity security service can be expressed using OCL as follows:

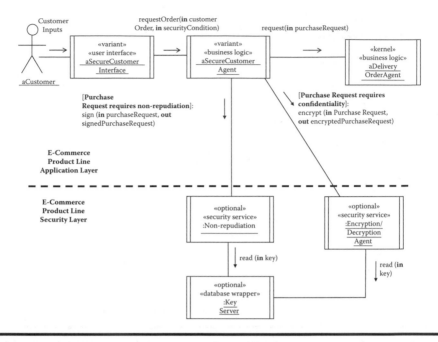

Figure 14.14 Concurrent communication diagram for Send Purchase Request with security components.

```
(Integrity Agent component xor Nonrepudiation component) or
(not (Integrity Agent component and Nonrepudiation component))
```

Similar to the constraint between use cases in Section 14.3.1, this OCL constraint is true if only one of Integrity or Nonrepudiation security condition is true, or if both the Integrity and Nonrepudiation security conditions are false.

14.7 Conclusions

This chapter has described how to model a software product line's security concerns separately from the application business concerns. Security concerns are separated from business concerns to reduce the complexity of requirements and designs. The security concerns are captured in separate use cases and encapsulated in separate objects. Security use cases can extend business use cases from different software product lines. By this means, security objects are used to provide secure services for different software product lines. This chapter has also described how the security requirements can be mapped to a layered component-based secure software architecture, in which the application components are stored at the application layer and optionally use security services provided by security components at the security layer.

The security requirements can also be validated using executable models such as Rational Rose Real-Time or colored Petri nets. The approach is to deploy the secure software architecture to executable models, which can be used to execute secure and nonsecure applications derived from the software product line architecture and compare them from both the logic and performance perspectives.

References

Ahn, G. J., and M. E. Shin. 2001. Role-based authorization constraints specification using object constraint language, 157–162. In *Proceedings of the 10th IEEE international workshops on enabling technologies: Infrastructure for collaborative enterprises.* Washington, DC: IEEE Computer Society.

Booch, G., J. Rumbaugh, and I. Jacobson. 2005. *The unified modeling language user guide,* 2nd ed. Reading, MA: Addison-Wesley.

Chapman, B., and E. Zwicky. 1995. *Building internet firewalls.* Sebastopol, CA: O'Reilly and Associates.

Cysneiros, L. M., and J. C. S. P. Leite. 2001. Using UML to reflect non-functional requirements. In *Proceedings of the 2001 conference of the center for the advanced studies on collaborative research* (CASCON). IBM Press.

Ford, W., and M. S. Baum. 1997. *Secure electronic commerce: Building the infrastructure for digital signatures and encryption.* Upper Saddle River, NJ: Prentice Hall PRT.

Fowler, M., and K. Scott. 1997. *UML distilled: Applying the standard object modeling language.* Reading, MA: Addison-Wesley.

Gomaa, H. 2000. *Designing concurrent, distributed, and real-time applications with UML.* Reading, MA: Addison-Wesley.

Gomaa, H. 2004. *Designing software product lines with UML.* Reading, MA: Addison-Wesley.

Gomaa, H., and M. E. Shin. 2002. Multiple-view meta-modeling of software product lines. In *Proceedings of the 8th IEEE international conference on engineering of complex computer systems,* 238. Washington, DC: IEEE Computer Society.

Gomaa, H., and M. E. Shin. 2004. Modeling complex systems by separating application and security concerns. In *Proceedings of the 9th IEEE international conference on engineering of complex computer systems navigating complexity in the e-engineering age,* 19–28. Washington, DC: IEEE Computer Society.

Harel, D., and E. Gary. 1996. Executable object modeling with statecharts. In *Proceedings of the 18th international conference on software engineering,* 246–257. Washington, DC: IEEE Computer Society.

Jacobson, I., M. Griss, and P. Jonsson. 1997. *Software reuse: Architecture, process and organization for business success.* Reading, MA: Addison-Wesley.

Pfleeger, C. P. 1997. *Security in computing,* 2nd ed. New York: Prentice Hall.

Rumbaugh, J., G. Booch, and I. Jacobson. 2004. *The unified modeling language reference manual,* 2nd ed. Reading, MA: Addison-Wesley.

Sandhu, R. S., E. J. Coyne, H. L. Feinstein, and C. E. Youman. 1996. Role-based access control models. *IEEE Computer* 29 (2): 38–47.

Shin, M. E. 2002. Evolution in multiple-view models in software product families. Ph.D. dissertation, George Mason University.

Shin, M. E., and G. J. Ahn. 2000. UML-based representation of role-based access control. In *Proceedings of the 9th IEEE international workshop on enabling technologies: Infrastructure for collaborative enterprises*, 195–200. Washington, DC: IEEE Computer Society.

Sommerville, I. 2001. *Software engineering*, 6th ed. Reading, MA: Addison-Wesley.

Warmer, J., and A. Kleppe. 1999. *The object constraint language: Precise modeling with UML*. Boston: Addison-Wesley Longman.

Chapter 15

Architecture as Language

Markus Voelter

Independent consultant, Stuttgart, Germany

Contents

15.1 Introduction

Architecture is typically either a very intangible, conceptual aspect of a software system that can primarily be found in Word documents, or it is entirely driven by technology ("we use an XML architecture"). Both are bad: the former makes it hard to work with, and the latter hides architectural concepts behind technology hype. This is especially problematic for platforms and product lines where a well-defined architecture is crucial for making sure the products can be maintained over the (typically long) lifetime of the product line.

What can be done? As you develop the architecture, evolve a language that allows you to describe systems based on this architecture. Based on my experience in a number of real-world projects, this makes the architecture tangible and provides an unambiguous description of the architectural building blocks as well as the concrete system while still staying away from technology decisions (which then can be made consciously in a separate step). Based on this language, you can also describe variants in the context of a product line.

This chapter starts out illustrating the idea using a real-world story. We build a language to express systems in a flight management system product line. We then discuss what we did and provide some of the rationales for the approach.

15.2 A Story

15.2.1 *System Background*

So I was with a customer for one of my regular consulting gigs. The customer decided they wanted to build a new flight management system. Airlines use systems like these to track and publish information about whether airplanes have landed at a given airport, whether they are late, the technical status of the aircraft, etc. The system also populates the online tracking system on the Internet and information monitors at airports, etc. This system is in many ways a typically distributed system, consisting of many machines running different parts of the overall system. There is a central data center to do some of the heavy number crunching, but there are additional machines distributed over relatively large areas.

My customer had been building systems like these for many years and they were planning to introduce a new generation of this system. The new system had to be able to evolve over a 15–20 year time frame. It was clear from this requirement alone that they needed some kind of technology abstraction, because technology probably goes through eight hype cycles over 15–20 years. Another good reason for abstracting technology is that different parts of the system will be built with different technologies: Java, C++, C#. This is not an atypical requirement for large distributed systems, either. Often you use Java technology for the back end, and use .NET technology for a Windows front end.

Because of the distributed nature of the system, it is impossible to update all parts of the system at the same time. This resulted in a requirement for being able to evolve the system piece by piece, in turn resulting in requirements for versioning of the various system components (to make sure component A could still talk to component B after B had been upgraded to a new version).

Finally, it is worth noting that the there will not actually be *one* system. Rather, what we build is a product line of flight management systems. Different customers will buy, install, and operate different variants of the system.

15.2.2 *The Starting Point*

When I arrived at the project, they had already decided that the backbone of the system would be a messaging infrastructure (which is a good decision for this kind of system), and they were evaluating different messaging backbones for performance and throughput. They had also already decided they would go with a systemwide business object model to describe the data that the system works with. (This is actually not a very good decision for systems like these, but it's not important to the punch line of this story.)

So when I arrived, they briefed me about all the details of the system and the architectural decisions they had already made, and then basically asked me whether all this makes sense. It turned out quickly that, while they knew many of the requirements and had made pinpoint decisions about certain architectural aspects, they didn't have what I'd call a *consistent architecture*: a definition of the building blocks (types of things) from which the actual system will be built. They had no *language* to talk about the system.

This is actually a very common observation when I arrive at projects to help out. And of course this is something that I think is a *huge* problem: If you don't know the *kinds of things* of which your system will be composed, it is very hard to actually talk about, describe, and, of course, build the system consistently. You need to define a language.

15.2.3 Background: What Is a Language?

You know you have a consistent architecture when you have a *language* to talk about the system from an architectural perspective.* So what is a language? Obviously, it is first and foremost a set of well-defined terms. *Well defined* means primarily that all stakeholders agree on the meanings of the terms. If you look at languages from an informal point of view, terms and their meanings are probably already enough to define *language*.

However—and that might come as a surprise here—I am advocating a *formal* language for architecture description. To define a formal language, you need more than terms and meanings. You need a grammar on how to build "sentences" (or models) from those terms, and you need a concrete syntax to express them.†

Using a formal language for describing your architecture provides several benefits that will become clear from the rest of the story. I will also recap toward the end of the chapter.

15.2.4 Developing a Language for Describing Architecture

So let's continue our story. My customer and I agreed that it might be worthwhile to spend a day going through some technical requirements and building a formal language for an architecture that could realize those requirements. We would actually build the grammar, some constraints, and an editor (using the Xtext tool [oAW 2009]), as we discussed the architecture.

---

* Eric Evans (2003) talks about a domain language that provides a language for the domain, for the business functionality of the system. This is of course also important, but in this chapter I discuss a language for the architecture.

† You also need some kind of tool for writing sentences in the language. More on that later.

15.2.4.1 Getting Started

We started with the notion of a component. At that point, the notion of *components* was defined relatively loosely. It's simply the smallest architecturally relevant building block, a piece of encapsulated application functionality. We also assumed that components can be instantiated, making components the architectural equivalent to classes in OO programming. So here's an initial example model we built based on the initial grammar we defined:

```
component DelayCalculator {}
component InfoScreen {}
component AircraftModule {}
```

Note how we did two things here: We defined that the concept of a *component* exists (making a component a building block for the system we're about to build), and we also decided (preliminarily) that there are the three components: DelayCalculator, InfoScreen, and AircraftModule. We refer to the set of building blocks for an architecture as the *conceptual architecture* and to the set of concrete exemplars of those building blocks as the *application architecture,* or the *product architecture* in the context of product lines.

15.2.4.2 Interfaces

Of course the above notion of a component is more or less useless because components cannot interact. It is clear from the domain that the DelayCalculator would have to receive information from the AircraftModules, calculate the delay status for flights, and then forward the results to InfoScreens. We knew that they would somehow exchange messages (remember: the messaging decision had already been made). But we decided to not introduce messages yet, but rather abstract a set of related messages into interfaces.*

```
component DelayCalculator implements IDelayCalculator {}
component InfoScreen implements IInfoScreen {}
component AircraftModule implements IAircraftModule {}
interface IDelayCalculator {}
interface IInfoScreen {}
interface IAircraftModule {}
```

The above code, we realized, looks quite a bit like Java code. This is not surprising, since my customer had a Java background, and the primary target language for the system was Java. It is therefore likely that the well-known concepts from

---

* Coming up with the concrete set of components, their responsibilities, and consequently, their interfaces is not necessarily trivial either. Techniques like CRC cards (Brummond 1996) can help here.

the language they were used to working with trickled into our own languages. However, we quickly noticed that this is not very useful: We could not express that a component *uses* a certain interface (as opposed to providing it). Knowing about the interface requirements of a component is important, because we want to be able to understand (and, later, analyze with a tool) the dependencies a component has. This is important for any system, but especially important for the versioning requirement mentioned above. Also, if you want to compose different products from a set of (pre-defined) components, knowing about the dependency graph is essential.

So we changed the grammar somewhat, supporting the following:

```
component DelayCalculator {
 provides IDelayCalculator
 requires IInfoScreen
}
component InfoScreen {
 provides IInfoScreen
}
component AircraftModule {
 provides IAircraftModule
 requires IDelayCalculator
}
interface IDelayCalculator {}
interface IInfoScreen {}
interface IAircraftModule {}
```

15.2.4.3 Describing Systems

We then looked at how those components would be used. It became clear very quickly that the components needed to be instantiable. Obviously, there are many aircraft, each of them running an AircraftModule component, and there are even more InfoScreens. It was not entirely clear whether we'd have many DelayCalculators or not, but we decided to postpone this discussion and go with the instantiation idea.

So we need to be able to express instances of components.

```
instance screen1: InfoScreen
instance screen2: InfoScreen
...
```

We were then discussing how to "wire" the system: How to express that a certain InfoScreen talks to a certain DelayCalculator? Somehow we would have to express a relationship between instances. The types, respectively, already had "compatible" interfaces; a DelayCalculator could talk to an InfoScreen. But this "talk to" relationship was hard to grasp as of yet. We also noticed that *one* DelayCalculator instance typically talks to *many* InfoScreen instances. So cardinalities had to get into the language, somehow.

After some tinkering around, I introduced the concept of *ports* (this is actually a well-known concept in component technology and also UML, but was relatively new to my customer). A port is a communication endpoint defined on a component type that is instantiated whenever the owning component is instantiated. So we refactored the component description language to allow us to express the ports. Ports are defined with the *provides* and *requires* keywords, followed by the port name and cardinality, a colon, and the port's associated interface.

```
component DelayCalculator {
 provides default: IDelayCalculator
 requires screens[0..n]: IInfoScreen
}
component InfoScreen {
 provides default: IInfoScreen
}
component AircraftModule {
 provides default: IAircraftModule
 requires calculator[1]: IDelayCalculator
}
```

The above model expresses that any DelayCalculator instance has a connection to many InfoScreens. From the perspective of the DelayCalculator implementation code, this set of InfoScreens can be addressed via the *screens* port. The AircraftModule has to talk to *exactly one* DelayCalculator, which is what the *[1]* expresses.

This new notion of interfaces inspired my customers to change the IDelayCalculator, because they noticed that there should be different interfaces (and hence, ports) for different communication partners. We changed the example application architecture to this:

```
component DelayCalculator {
 provides aircraft: IAircraftStatus
 provides managementConsole: IManagementConsole
 requires screens[0..n]: IInfoScreen
}
component Manager {
 requires backend[1]: IManagementConsole
}
component InfoScreen {
 provides default: IInfoScreen
}
component AircraftModule {
 requires calculator[1]: IAircraftStatus
}
```

Notice how the introduction of ports led to better application architecture, because we now have role-specific interfaces (IAircraftStatus, IManagementConsole).

Now that we had ports, we could *name* communication endpoints. This allowed us to easily describe systems: connected instances of components. Note the new *connect* construct. As we will see later, these "wirings" will change for different products in the product line.

```
instance dc: DelayCalculator
instance screen1: InfoScreen
instance screen2: InfoScreen
connect dc.screens to (screen1.default, screen2.default)
```

15.2.4.4 Keeping the Overview

Of course at some point it became clear that, in order to not get lost in all the components, instances, and connectors, we need to introduce some kind of namespace concept. And of course we can distribute things to different files (the tool support makes sure that *go to definition* and *find references* still work).

```
namespace com.mycompany {
 namespace datacenter {
  component DelayCalculator {
   provides aircraft: IAircraftStatus
   provides managementConsole: IManagementConsole
   requires screens[0..n]: IInfoScreen
  }
  component Manager {
   requires backend[1]: IManagementConsole
  }
 }
 namespace mobile {
  component InfoScreen {
   provides default: IInfoScreen
  }
  component AircraftModule {
   requires calculator[1]: IAircraftStatus
  }
 }
}
```

Of course it is a good idea to keep component and interface definitions (essentially, type definitions) separate from system definitions (connected instances), so here we define a system:

```
namespace com.mycompany.test {
 system testSystem {
```

```
  instance dc: DelayCalculator
  instance screen1: InfoScreen
  instance screen2: InfoScreen
  connect dc.screens to (screen1.default, screen2.default)
  }
}
```

It should be clear from this description that one way to build different products (i.e., different applications) is simply to reuse the same components and build different *systems*, with different instances and different connections. However, there are other, more fine-grained possibilities, as explained later.

Of course in a real system, the DelayCalculator would have to dynamically discover all the available InfoScreens at runtime. There is not much point in manually describing those connections. So, here we go. We specify a query that is executed at runtime against some kind of naming/trader/lookup/registry infrastructure. It is reexecuted every 60 seconds to find InfoScreens that had just come online.

```
namespace com.mycompany.production {
  instance dc: DelayCalculator
  // InfoScreen instances are created and
  // started in other configurations
  dynamic connect dc.screens every 60 query {
    type = IInfoScreen
    status = active
  }
}
```

A similar approach can be used to realize load balancing or fault tolerance. A static connector can point to a primary as well as a backup instance. Or a dynamic query can be reexecuted when the currently used system becomes unavailable.

To support registration of instances, we add additional syntax to their definition. A *registered* instance automatically registers itself with the registry, using its name (qualified through the namespace) and all provided interfaces. Additional parameters can be specified. The following example registers a primary and a backup instance for the DelayCalculator:

```
namespace com.mycompany.datacenter {
  registered instance dc1: DelayCalculator {
    registration parameters {role = primary}
  }
  registered instance dc2: DelayCalculator {
    registration parameters {role = backup}
  }
}
```

15.2.4.5 Interfaces, Part II

Until now we didn't really define what an interface was. We knew that we'd like to build the system based on a messaging infrastructure, so it was clear that an interface had to be defined as a collection of messages. Here's our first idea: a collection of messages, where each message has a name and a list of typed parameters.

```
interface IInfoScreen {
 message expectedAircraftArrivalUpdate(id: ID, time: Time)
 message flightCancelled(flightID: ID)
 ...
}
```

Of course this also requires the ability to define data structures. So we added that:

```
typedef long ID
struct Time {
 hour: int
 min: int
 seconds: int
}
```

Now, after discussing this interface thing for a while, we noticed that it's not enough to simply define an interface as a set of messages. The minimal thing we want to do is to be able to define the direction of a message: Does it flow *in* or *out* of the port? More generally, which kinds of message interaction patterns are there? We identified several: here are examples of one-way and request-reply:

```
interface IAircraftStatus {
 oneway message reportPosition(aircraft: ID, pos: Position )
 request-reply message reportProblem {
  request (aircraft: ID, problem: Problem, comment: String)
  reply (repairProcedure: ID)
 }
}
```

15.2.4.6 Are They Really Messages?

We talked a long time about various message interaction patterns. After a while it turned out that one of the core use cases for messages is to push status updates of various assets out to various interested parties. For example, if a flight is delayed because of a technical problem with an aircraft, then this information has to be pushed out to all the InfoScreens in the system. We prototyped several of the messages necessary for "broadcasting" complete updates of a certain status item, incremental updates, invalidations, etc.

And at some point it hit us: We were working with the wrong abstraction! While messaging is a suitable transport abstraction for these things, we're really talking about *replicated data structures*. It basically works the same way for all of those structures:

- You define a data structure (such as *FlightInfo*).
- The system then keeps track of a collection of such data structures.
- This collection is updated by a few components and is typically read by many other components.
- The update strategies from publisher to receiver always included full update of all items in the collection, incremental updates of just one or several items, invalidations, etc.

Of course, once we understood that in addition to messages there's this additional core abstraction in the system, we added this to our architecture language and were able to write something like the following. We define data structures and replicated items. Components can then publish or consume those replicated data structures.

```
struct FlightInfo {
 from: Airport
 to: Airport
 scheduled: Time
 expected: Time
 ...
}
replicated singleton flights {
 flights: FlightInfo[]
}
component DelayCalculator {
 publishes flights
}
component InfoScreen {
 consumes flights
}
```

This is, of course, much more concise compared with a description based on messages. The system can automatically derive the kinds of messages needed for full update, incremental update, invalidation, etc. This description also reflects the actual architectural intent much more clearly: This description expresses better *what* we want to do (replicate state) compared with a lower level description of *how* we want to do it (sending around state update messages).

Of course it does not stop there. Now that we have state replication as a first-class citizen, we can add more information to its specification:

```
component DelayCalculator {
 publishes flights { publication = onchange }
}
component InfoScreen {
 consumes flights { init = all update = every(60) }
}
```

We describe that the publisher publishes the replicated data whenever something changes in the underlying data structure. However, the InfoScreen only needs an update every 60 seconds (as well as a full load of data when it is started up). Based on that information, we can derive all the required messages and also an update schedule for the participants.

15.2.5 Variability

As I mentioned in the introduction, my customer will be deploying the system to many customers of theirs. Those various systems will contain system-specific components, and they will also reuse existing, standardized components. In addition, they will also need to define variants of their components and systems. As a consequence, we needed to address variability in our models.

15.2.5.1 Background: Variability with Feature Models

Variability management is a well-known activity in product line engineering (Software Engineering Institute 2009). A best practice is to manage the variability with formal variability models. For example, feature modeling (Czarnecki and Eisenecker 2000) is a good formalism to do this. Figure 15.1 shows a part of the overall feature model for the kind of system we've been describing in the first part of this chapter:

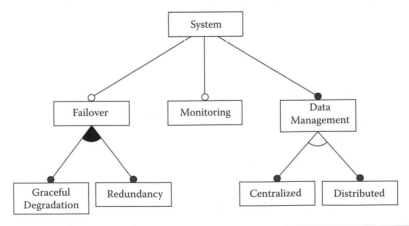

Figure 15.1   Feature model.

Let us look at the meaning of the notation. The notation describes a system (in the sense of the previous sections). It has an optional feature Monitoring (optional is described using the outlined circle). It has mandatory feature Data Management (mandatory is shown via the filled circle), which can either be Centralized or Distributed (either/or is represented via the arc between the lines with the filled circles). Finally, Failover can include Graceful Degradation or Redundancy or both (the filled arc represents *n-of-m*).

This notation is useful because it only shows the features and their conceptual relationship. The diagram says nothing about how the features are implemented. However, based on this notation you can easily define combinations of features that describe a valid system. For example, a system that includes Failover via Graceful Degradation and Centralized Data Management is valid. Another valid example would be a system with Monitoring as well as Distributed Data Management.

Expressing the variability on a conceptual level is one thing. However, we also need to be able to connect the architectural artifacts to those conceptual features. We have two kinds of implementation artifacts: the models expressed via the architecture DSL as well as the manually written implementation code. The next two sections look at connecting those to the conceptual variability models.

15.2.5.2 Negative Variability in the Models

Negative variability describes an approach to variability where optional parts are removed from a superset if configuration features are not selected.

As we've learned above, applications are described with a textual DSL that is specific to our architecture. If we want to express parts that are only present in case a certain feature is selected, we can simply extend our grammar accordingly:

```
component DelayCalculator {
 provides default: IDelayCalculator
 requires screens[0..n]: IInfoScreen
 provides mon: IMonitoring feature monitoring
}
```

This notation describes that the component DelayCalculator only provides the IMonitoring interface via the *mon* port if the feature *monitoring* is selected in the configuration model. The idea behind this is that we can extend the grammar to support the optional addition of a feature dependency for more or less any grammar element.

Let us look at the next example, where we mark up a region of the model to be dependent on the *monitoring* feature. This is of course much more useful where several aspects of the overall systems depend on certain features.

```
feature testing {
 component MonitoringConsole {
  requires devices:[*]: IMonitor
 }
 instance monitor: MonitoringConsole
  dynamic connect monitor.devices query {
   type = IMonitor
 }
}
```

We noticed subsequently that instead of having separate *feature* sections, you could reuse namespaces for this:

```
namespace com.mycompany {
 namespace datacenter {
 // … as before …
  namespace monitoting feature testing {
   component MonitoringConsole {
    requires devices:[*]: IMonitor
   }
   instance monitor: MonitoringConsole
   dynamic connect monitor.devices query {
    type = IMonitor
   }
  }
 }
}
```

15.2.5.3 Positive Variability in the Models

In positive variability, we add optional parts to a minimal core if a certain configuration feature is selected. To be able to do that, we need a way to address the "place" to where we add something in the core. Aspect orientation (AOSD 2009), with its joinpoints and pointcuts, is a good approach to achieve this.

Consider again the example above. The monitoring feature can be modularized for the MonitoringConsole component and the *monitor* instance, as well as the connector. However, there's also a crosscutting concern, where each component should provide a port called *mon* associated with the IMonitoring interface. We can also modularize this concern using AO technology:

```
feature testing {
 component MonitoringConsole …
 instance monitor: …
 dynamic connect monitor.devices …
 aspect (*) component {
  provides mon: IMonitoring
 }
}
```

The component aspect queries for all components in the system (hence the asterisk) and adds a new provided port to them, of course only if the feature *monitoring* is selected in the product configuration. The asterisk is a pointcut that selects all instances of a component. Instead of selecting all, you can also select by name or via tags, as is shown in the next example.

We want to optionally include graceful degradation policies in the system. Let us look at the following piece of model code:

```
component InfoScreen tags (degrade) {
  ...
}
aspect (tag=degrade) component feature gracefuldegradation {
 provides shutdown: IShutdown
 requires health: IHealthStatus
}
```

In this example, we add the required port *health* through which a component can report local or systemwide health issues to a global system coordinator. Through the provided port *shutdown*, the component instance can be told to shut down. Note how the aspect works here: It applies only to components that have the *degrade* tag, and it is only applied to the system if the feature *gracefuldegradation* is selected in the product configuration.

15.2.5.4 Variability in Manually Written Code

Since our systems are completely described via the DSL as well as manually written code, we need to think about expressing variability in those two artifacts.

In manually written code, we use special comments to delineate areas of the text file that are only present if a specific feature is present. This approach is also used by product line tools such as pure::variants (pure systems 2009) or Gears (BigLever 2009).

Note that since only some aspects of the overall business logic are written manually, the amount of programming language code that needs to be "marked up" like this is limited. All the technical code is generated, as seen in the next section.

15.3 Recap and Benefits

15.3.1 What We Did in a Nutshell

The approach includes the definition of a formal language for your product line's conceptual architecture. You develop the language as the understanding of your architecture grows. The language therefore always resembles the complete understanding about your architecture in a clear and unambiguous way. As we enhance the language, we also describe the application architecture using that language, as well as the variability between the various products in the product line.

15.3.2 Domain-Specific Languages

The language we built above is a DSL, a domain-specific language. Here is how I like to define DSLs:

> A DSL is a focused, processable language for describing a specific concern when building a system in a specific domain. The abstractions and notations used are tailored to the stakeholders who specify that particular concern.

DSLs can be used to specify any aspect of a software system. The big hype is around using a DSL to describe the business functionality (for example, calculation rules in an insurance system). While this is a very worthwhile use of DSL, it is also worthwhile to use DSLs to describe software architecture; this is what we do here.

So the architecture language built above—and the approach I am generally advocating in this chapter—is to use DSL technology to define a DSL that expresses your architecture.

15.3.3 The Importance of Viewpoints

Viewpoints capture the idea of describing systems from several perspectives. Each perspective is relevant for a certain group of stakeholders. When building a system, they execute certain activities with a suitable tool (here, DSL) and produce implementation artifacts based on some technology. Figure 15.2 (adapted from a slide by Steve Cook, and based on the IEEE 1471 standard) illustrates this.

A good DSL will have different parts, each describing a specific viewpoint of the system (alternatively you can say that there are several, combinable DSLs that as a group describe the system). Note that you need to carefully manage the dependencies between the viewpoints and make sure you clearly define their "connection points."

In the example we've seen two viewpoints, both expressed as part of the single DSL: a type definition viewpoint (components, interfaces, messages, data structures) and an instantiation viewpoint (instances, wirings). I consider those two viewpoints the bare minimum for real-world systems. In most cases you'll have additional viewpoints, such as deployment (how to distribute instances onto nodes, specifying all kinds of technology mappings for the stuff in the type and instance viewpoints) or persistence (how to map data structures to a persistent, typical relational database).

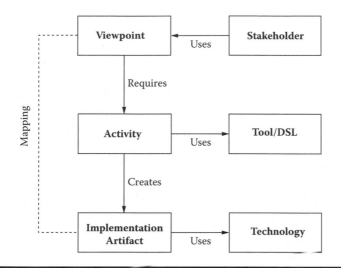

Figure 15.2 Viewpoints. (Adapted from a slide by Steve Cook. With permission.)

15.3.4 Benefits

Everybody involved will have a clear understanding of the concepts used to describe the system. There is a clear and unambiguous vocabulary to describe applications or products. The created models can be analyzed and used as a basis for code generation (see below). The architecture is freed from implementation details, or in other words: conceptual architecture and technology decisions are decoupled, making both easier to evolve. We can express variations directly, connected to feature models. We can also define a clear programming model based on the conceptual architecture (how to model and code components using all the architectural features defined above). Last but not least, the architect can now contribute directly to the project by building (or helping to build) an artifact that the rest of the team can actually use.

15.3.5 Why Textual?

Or, why not use a graphical notation? Textual DSLs have several advantages. Here are some of them:

- First of all, languages as well as nice editors are much easier to build compared with custom graphical editors (e.g., those built with Eclipse GMF).
- Textual artifacts integrate much better with the existing developer tooling than graphical models based on some kind of repository. You can use the well-known diff/merge tools, and it is much easier to version/tag/branch *models and code together*.

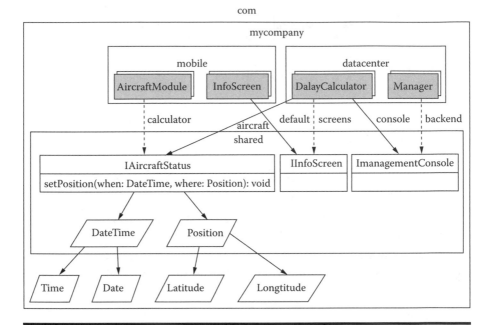

Figure 15.3 Graphviz.

■ Model evolution (i.e., the adaptation of the models in cases where the DSL evolves over time, something you'll *always* have in practice) is much simpler. While you can use the standard approach—a model-to-model transformation from the old version to the new version—you can always use search/replace or grep as a fallback, a technology familiar to basically anybody.

■ Lastly, textual DSLs are often more appreciated by developers, since "real developers don't draw pictures."

For aspects of the system where a graphical notation is useful to see relationships between architectural elements, you can use tools like Graphviz (2009) or Prefuse (2009). Since the model contains the relevant data in a clear and unpolluted form, you can easily export the model data in a form that tools like Graphviz or Prefuse can read.

Figure 15.3 is an example of a Graphviz-generated diagram. It shows namespaces, components, interface, and data types as well as the dependencies between those.

15.3.6 Tooling

15.3.6.1 DSLs and Editors

To make the approach introduced above feasible, you need tooling that supports the efficient definition of DSLs. We use openArchitectureWare's Xtext [oAW]. Xtext does the following things for you:

- It provides a way of specifying grammars.
- From this grammar, the tool generates an ANTLR (Another Tool for Language Recognition) grammar to do the actual parsing.
- It also generates an EMF Ecore metamodel; the generated parser instantiates this metamodel from sentences of the language. You can then use all EMF-based tools to process the model.
- You can also specify constraints based on the generated Ecore model. Constraints are specified using oAW's Check language (essentially a streamlined OCL).
- Finally, the tool also generates a powerful editor for your DSL that provides code folding, syntax coloring, and customizable code completion as well as an outline view and cross-file *go-to-definition* and *find references*. It also evaluates your language constraints in real time and outputs error messages.

After a little bit of practice, Xtext gets out of your way and really allows you to specify the language as you understand architectural details and make architectural decisions. Customizing code completion might take a little bit longer, but you can do that when the language exploration phase has reached a plateau.

Compared with the tooling described in the first part of this chapter, where Xtext was sufficient to describe the grammar and generate meta models and editors, we now need additional tooling.

15.3.6.2 Describing Feature Models and Configurations

First of all, we need a tool to describe the feature models as well as the configurations defined based on them. There are several tools available (feature modeling plug-in [FMP 2009], XFeature [PNP Software 2009], and pure::variants [Pure Systems 2009]). While the tooling can be built based on any of them, we would probably choose pure::variants because it is the most mature and the most scalable, and it also integrates nicely with an EMF world (Section 15.3.6.3). Figure 15.4 is the feature model shown above represented by pure::variants. They do not use the graphical notation shown above (because it does not scale very well), but they use the same constraints: *mandatory*, *optional*, *1-of-m*, and *n-of-m*.

Once you have defined your feature model, you can change to another mode and create any number of configurations. For example, Figure 15.5 shows the *Failover* via *Graceful Degradation* and *Centralized Data Management* product configuration. Note that it is, of course, not possible to create invalid configurations, as the constraints expressed in the feature model are enforced by the configuration editor. It is also possible in pure variants to express nonlocal constraints between features and to associate configuration values with them (strings, integers).

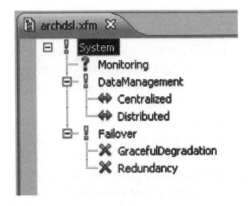

Figure 15.4 XFM.

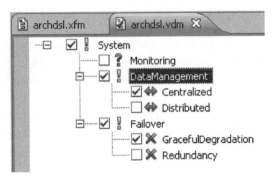

Figure 15.5 VDM.

15.3.6.3 Feature Model Integration

The *feature* clauses in the textual model obviously have to mention features that exist in the feature model. You cannot make a piece of model depend on features that don't even exist. This mandates two kinds of integration:

1. A constraint check needs to be put in place to validate that feature names that are mentioned in feature clauses do actually exist in the feature model. Xtext supports the validation of such constraints in real time as the user is editing the model.
2. You also want to provide code completion for the architecture model. The proposals should only be those features available in the feature model.

Luckily, the pure::variants tool provides an automatic EMF export whenever you change something in a feature model. Based on this export, the implementation of the constraint checks and the code completion takes only a matter of hours and, hence, the export is available in the tooling.

It is also easily possible to get support for the other way around: selecting a feature and showing all the locations in the DSL files (and the manually written code) that depend on that feature. The pure::variants tool provides an extension point where you can easily plug in to achieve this goal.

15.3.6.4 Feature Clauses

The *feature* clauses are a way of expressing negative variability. Negative variability means that you code the overall artifact and then selectively remove those parts whose associated features are not selected for a given product. So the challenge is to implement the actual removal. This is technically very easy: You simply grab all the model elements that result from *feature* clauses. Then we check whether their associated feature is selected and, if not, we delete the node that owns the feature clause, including all its children.

15.3.6.5 Aspect Weaving

The aspect language is, of course, specific to the DSL itself; hence, you cannot write a generic aspect weaver. However, writing, a DSL-specific weaver is trivial, since you define the granularity of the joinpoint model and the expressiveness of the pointcut expressions. In any case, the weaving happens on the level of the EMF model that is parsed from the textual source. Implementing a custom weaver there is a matter of a couple of tens of lines of transformation code.

15.3.7 Validating the Model

If we want to describe an application or product architecture formally and correctly, we need to put validation rules into place that constrain the model even further than what can be expressed via the grammar. Simple examples include the typical name-uniqueness constraints, type checks, or non-nullness. Expressing such (relatively) local constraints is straightforward using OCL or OCL-like languages.

However, we also want to verify more complex and less local constraints. For example, in the context of our story above, the constraints check that new versions of components and interfaces are actually compatible with their predecessors and hence can be used in the same context. To be able to implement such nontrivial constraints, two preconditions are necessary:

1. The constraint itself must actually be formally describable, i.e., there must be some kind of algorithm that determines whether the constraint holds or not. Once you know the algorithm, you can implement it in whatever constraint language your tooling supports (in our case here, the OCL-like Xtend or Java)

2. The data that is needed to run the defined constraint-checking algorithm must actually be available in the model. For example, if you want to verify whether a certain deployment scheme is feasible, you might have to put the available network bandwidth and the timings of certain messages—as well as the size of primitive date types—into the model.* However, while capturing those data sounds like a burden, this is actually an advantage, since this is core architectural knowledge.

15.3.8 Generating Code

It should be clear from this chapter that the primary benefit of developing the DSL architecture (and using it) is the ability to understand concepts by removing any ambiguity and defining them formally. The DSL architecture helps you to understand your system and get rid of unwanted technology interference. But of course, now that we have a formal model of the conceptual architecture (the language) and a formal description of the system(s) we're building (the sentences [or models] defined using the language), we might as well use it to do more good:

■ We generate an API against which the implementation is coded. That API can be nontrivial, taking into account the various messaging paradigms, replicated state, etc. The generated API allows developers to code the implementation in a way that does not depend on any technological decisions: The generated API hides those from the component implementation code. We call this generated API and the set of idioms to use it the *programming model*.

■ Remember that we expect some kind of component container or middleware platform to run the components. So we also generate the code that is necessary to run the components (including their technology-neutral implementation) on the implementation technology of choice. We call this layer of code the technology-mapping code (or glue code). It typically also contains a whole bunch of configuration files for the various platforms involved. Sometimes this requires additional "mix in models" that specify configuration details for the platform. As a side effect, the generators capture best practices in working with the technologies you've decided to use.

It is, of course, completely feasible to generate APIs for several target languages (supporting component implementation in various languages) and/or generating glue code for several target platforms (supporting the execution of the same component on different middleware platforms). This nicely supports potential multiplat-

---

* You might actually want to put them into a different file, so this aspect does not pollute the core models. But this is a tooling issue.

form requirements in a product line, and also provides a way to scale or evolve the infrastructure over time.

Another note worth making is that you typically generate in several phases. A first phase uses type definitions (components, data structures, interfaces) to generate the API code so you can code the implementation. A second phase generates the glue code and the system configuration code. As a consequence, it is often sensible to separate type definitions from system definitions in models; they are used at different times in the overall process, and they are also often created, modified, and processed by different people.

In summary, the generated code supports an efficient and technology-independent implementation, and it hides much of the underlying technological complexity, making development more efficient.

15.3.8.1 Variability in the Transformations and Code Generators

When building product lines based on model-driven technologies and domain-specific languages, it is often not enough to be able to express variability in the models. In addition, it is very helpful if we can define variants of transformations or code generators. Although I don't want to go into much detail about this in this chapter, it is worth mentioning that the openArchitectureWare tooling supports those features:

- From within a model transformation or code generation template, you can query a configuration model about whether a feature is selected. This boils down to a kind of feature-dependent *#ifdef* for transformers and generators. It is an example of negative variability.
- It is also possible to define aspects for transformations and templates. Those can be before, after, and around (instead of) existing transformations/templates, allowing you to noninvasively customize an existing transformer/generator. Of course, the decision of whether such an aspect should actually be woven or not can be tied to the selection of a feature in the configuration model.

15.3.9 Standards, ADLs, and UML

Describing architecture with formal languages is not a new idea. Various communities recommend using Architecture Description Languages (ADLs) or the Unified Modeling Language (UML) for describing architecture. Some even (try to) generate code from the resulting models. However, all of those approaches advocate using existing generic languages for documenting the architecture (although some of them, including the UML, can be customized). However (as you probably can tell from the story above), this completely misses the point!

I don't see much benefit in shoehorning your architecture description into the (typically very limited) constructs provided by predefined/standardized languages. One of the core activities of the approach explained in this chapter is the process of actually building your own language to capture your system's conceptual architecture. Adapting your architecture to the few concepts provided by the ADLs or UML is not very helpful.

So this raises the general question about standards. Are they important? Where? And when? To use any architecture modeling language successfully, people must first and foremost understand the architectural concepts they are dealing with. Even if the UML standard is used to do this, people will still have to understand the concepts and map them to the language. In the case of using UML, that would be an architecture-specific profile. Of course, then, the question is whether such a profiled UML is still rightfully called a *standard*. And it is not like I am proposing to not use *any* standard. The tools I propose are built on MOF/EMOF, which is an OMG standard, just like the UML, just on a different meta level.

A specific note on UML and profiles: Yes, you could use the approach explained above with UML, building a profile as opposed to a textual language. I have done this in several projects, and my conclusion is that it doesn't work well in most environments. Here are some of the reasons:

■ Instead of thinking about your architectural concepts, working with UML requires you to think more about how you can use UML's existing constructs to more or less sensibly express your intentions. That's the wrong focus!

■ Also, UML tools typically don't integrate very well with your existing development infrastructure (editors, CVS/SVN, diff/merge). That's not much of a problem when you use UML during some kind of analysis or design phase, but once you use your models as source code (they accurately reflect the architecture of your system, and you generate real code from them), this becomes a big issue.

■ Finally, UML tools are often quite heavyweight and complex, and are often perceived as "bloatware" or "drawing tools" by "real" developers. Using a nice textual language can be a much lower acceptance hurdle.

15.3.10 What about Reuse?

The approach described in this chapter suggests the development of a specific language for each system, platform, or product line. This of course raises the question of whether or not certain aspects of the language can be reused between systems. Here are a couple of points of interest.

There is a minimal set of concepts that can be reused in each of these specific architecture description languages. Among them are namespaces and associated visibility/import facilities, feature dependencies, and the aspect/weaver facilities. These abstractions and tools can be provided as a starting point. Components, ports, and interfaces are probably also generic enough so that they can be made available for reuse.

However, one can even go one step further. Based on my experience of years of doing architecture modeling, there is a large set of reusable architectural abstractions: components, interfaces, messages, operations, exceptions, data replication, events, subsystems, etc. Of course, not every system uses every one of them. However, to be able to create system-specific architecture DSLs, the following approach is feasible:

Using negative variability (feature-dependencies) for the language, editor, and tooling itself, you can build a "configurable language" that can be tailored via feature model configuration to your system's needs. Of course, it must be possible to add system-specific abstractions to the configured language.

We're currently working on a proof of concept for this approach.

15.3.11 Why Not Simply Use a Programming Language?

Architectural abstractions, such as messages or components, are not first-class citizens in today's 3GL programming languages. Of course, you can use classes to represent all of them. Using annotations (also called attributes), you can even associate metadata to classes and some of their contents (operations, fields). Consequently, you can express quite a lot with a 3GL, somehow. But this approach has problems:

- Just like in the case of UML explained above, this approach forces you to shoehorn clear domain-specific concepts into prebuilt abstractions. In many ways, annotations/attributes are comparable to UML stereotypes and tagged values, and you will experience similar problems.
- Analyzability of the model is limited. While there are tools like Spoon for Java, there is nothing easier to work with and process than a formal model.
- Finally, expressing things with "architecture-enhanced Java or C#" also means that you are tempted to mix architectural concerns with implementation concerns. This blurs the clear distinction, and potentially sacrifices technology independence.

15.3.12 My Notions of Components

There are many (more or less formal) definitions of what a components is. They range from "a building block of software systems," to "something with explicitly defined context dependencies," to "something that contains business logic and is run inside a container."

My understanding (notice I am not saying I have a real definition) is that a component is the smallest architecture building block. When defining a system's architecture, you don't look *inside* components. Components have to specify all of their architecturally relevant properties declaratively (either in metadata or models). As a consequence, components become analyzable and composable by tools. Typically, they do run inside a container that serves as a framework to act on the runtime-relevant parts of the metadata. The component boundary is the level at which the container can provide technical services such as logging, monitoring, or failover.

I don't have any specific requirements regarding what metadata a component actually contains (and hence, which properties are described). I think that the concrete notion of components has to be defined for each (system/platform/product line) architecture. And this is exactly what we do with the language approach introduced in this chapter.

15.3.13 Component Implementation

By default, component implementation happens manually. The implementation code is written against the generated API code introduced in the previous section. Developers add manually written code to the component skeleton, either by adding the code directly to the generated class, or—a much better approach—by using other means of composition such as inheritance or partial classes. However, there are other alternatives for component implementation that do not use a 3GL programming language for component implementation, but instead use formalisms that are specific to the kind of behavior that should be specified.

- Behavior that is very regular can be implemented using the generator, after parameterizing it in the model by setting a small number of well-defined variability points. Feature models are good at expressing the variabilities that need to be decided so that an implementation can be generated.
- For state-based behavior, state machines can be used.
- For things such as business rules, you can define a DSL that directly expresses these rules and uses a rules engine to evaluate them. Several rules engines are available off the shelf.
- For domain-specific calculations, such as those common in the insurance domain, you might want to provide a specific notation that supports the mathematical operations required for the domain directly. Such languages are often interpreted; the component implementation technically consists of an interpreter that is parameterized with the program it should run.

There is also the alternative of using Action Semantics Languages (ASLs). However, it is important to point out that they don't provide domain-specific abstractions; they are generic in the same way as, for example, UML is a generic modeling language. However, even if you use more-specific notations, there might still be a need to specify small snippets of behavior generically. A good example of this is the actions in state machines.

To combine the various ways of specifying behavior with the notion of components, it is useful to define various kinds of components, using subtyping at the

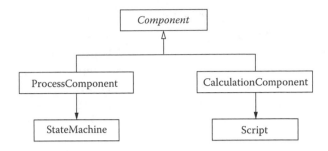

Figure 15.6 Submetaclasses.

meta level, that each have their own notation for specifying behavior. Figure 15.6 illustrates the idea. Since component implementation is about behavior, technically, it is often useful to use an interpreter encapsulated inside the component.

As a final note, be aware that the discussion in this section is only really relevant for application-specific behavior, not for all implementation code. Huge amounts of implementation code are related to the technical infrastructure—remoting, persistence, workflow, and so on—of an application, and such code can be derived from the architectural models.

15.3.14 The Role of Patterns

Patterns are an important part of today's software engineering practice. They are a proven way of capturing working solutions to recurring problems, including their applicability, trade-offs, and consequences. So how do patterns factor into the approach described above?

- Architecture patterns and pattern languages describe blueprints for architectures that have been used successfully. They can serve as an inspiration for building your own system's architecture. Once you have decided on using a pattern (and have adapted it to your specific context), you can make concepts defined in the pattern first-class citizens of your DSL. In other words, patterns influence the architecture, and hence the grammar of the DSL.
- Design patterns, as their name implies, are more concrete, more implementation-specific than architectural patterns. It is unlikely that they will end up being central concepts in your architecture DSL. However, when generating code from the models, your code generator will typically generate code that resembles the solution structure of a number of patterns. Note, however, that the generator cannot decide on whether a pattern should be used: This is a trade-off the (generator) developer has to make manually.

When talking about DSLs, generation, and patterns, it is important to mention that you cannot completely automate patterns. A pattern doesn't just consist of the solution's UML diagram! Significant parts of a pattern explain which forces affect the pattern's solution, when a pattern can be applied, and when it cannot, as well as the consequences of using the pattern. Moreover, a pattern often documents many variations of itself that may all have different advantages and disadvantages. A pattern that has been implemented in the context of a transformation does not account for these aspects. The developer of the transformations must take them into account, assess them, and make decisions accordingly.

15.3.15 What Needs to Be Documented?

I advertise the approach presented here as a way to formally describe your system's conceptual and application architecture. So, this means it serves as some kind of documentation, right?

Right, but it does not mean that you don't have to document anything else. Here's a bunch of things you still need to document:

Rationales/architectural decisions: the DSLs describe *what* your architecture(s) look like, but it does not explain *why*. You still need to document the rationales for your architectural and technological decisions. Typically, you should refer back to your (nonfunctional) requirements here. Note that the grammar is a really good baseline. Each of the constructs in your architecture DSL grammar results from a number of architectural decisions. So if you explain for each grammar element why it is there (and maybe why certain other alternatives have not been chosen), you are well on your way to documenting the important architectural decisions. A similar approach can be used for the application architecture, i.e., the instances of the DSL.

User guides: A language grammar can serve as a well-defined and formal way of capturing an architecture, but it is not a good teaching tool. So you need to create tutorials for your users (i.e., the application programmers) on how to use the architecture. This includes what and how to model (using your DSL), how to generate code, and how to use the programming model (how to fill in the implementation code into the generated skeletons).

Variations: If you use the approach for product lines, expressing variability in the system using *feature* clauses and aspects, you need to describe the variants, why they exist, and which effects the selection of a feature has on the application.

There are more aspects of an architecture that might be worth documenting, but the above three are the most important.

15.4 Summary

I consider this approach for software architecture very useful. It makes software architecture very concrete while remaining technology independent. Using code generation, the architectural intentions can be generated into API code and glue code.

For product line architecture specifically, the approach is powerful. It raises the abstraction level for variation points from the (low level and detailed) implementation code up to (domain-specific and more expressive) models. However, it does so while still using textual notations; this has a lot of advantages regarding integration with existing developer tooling (CVS/SVN, diff/merge).

Acknowledgments

I would like to thank (in no particular order) Iris Groher, Alex Chatziparaskewas, Axel Uhl, Michael Kircher, Tom Quas, and Stefan Tilkov for their very useful comments on previous versions.

References

AOSD. 2009. Aspect-oriented software development. http://aosd.net/.

BigLever Software. 2009. BigLever Software Gears. http://www.biglever.com/solution/product.html.

Brummond, N. 1996. CRC cards tutorial. http://users.csc.calpoly.edu/~dbutler/tutorials/winter96/crc_b/.

Czarnecki, K., and U. Eisenecker. 2000. *Generative programming*. Reading, MA: Addison-Wesley.

Evans, E. 2003. *Domain driven design*. Reading, MA: Addison-Wesley.

FMP. 2009. Feature modeling plug-in. University of Waterloo, Generative Software Development Lab. http://gsd.uwaterloo.ca/projects/fmp-plugin/.

Graphviz. 2009. Graphic visualization software. http://graphviz.org.

oAW. 2009. openArchitectureWare. http://www.openarchitectureware.org.

PNP Software. 2009. XFeature modeling tool. http://www.pnp-software.com/XFeature/.

Prefuse. 2009. Prefuse visualization toolkit. http://prefuse.org.

Pure Systems GmbH. 2009. pure::variants. Variant management. http://www.pure-systems.com/Variant_Management.49.0.html.

Software Engineering Institute. 2009. Software product lines. http://www.sei.cmu.edu/productlines/.

INDUSTRY EXPERIENCES AND CASE STUDIES

Chapter 16

Management and Financial Controls of a Software Product Line Adoption

Yoshihiro Matsumoto

The ASTEM Research Institute of Kyoto, Japan

Contents

16.1 Introduction

This chapter summarizes the practices actually applied in the Toshiba Software Factory, in which a series of software product lines for the domain of electric power generation, EPG-SPL, has been developed and adopted since 1962. In September 2008, the EPG-SPL was chosen as a member of the Software Product Line Hall of Fame at Carnegie Mellon University.

The first part of the chapter presents how EPG-SPL was developed, adopted, and managed in the software factory. In the latter part, the chapter presents a guide used to periodically monitor the shortage of return on investment and to help achieve successful adoptions of SPL.

The phrase "software engineering" was coined for the first time in the NATO Software Engineering Conference held in Garmisch (Germany) on October 7–11 in 1968. Then the concept "software factory" was introduced (McIlroy 1969). Afterward, a number of industries tried to implement software factories (Cusumano 1991). The software factory is a concept to commit long-term integrated efforts to apply software engineering and practices over multiple projects to increase productivity using standardized tools, computer-based interface, and a database with historical data for financial management and controls (Aaen, Botcher, and Mathiassen 1997).

Toshiba created a large-scale reuse-based software factory at Fuchu (Toshiba Software Factory [TSF]) in 1977 (Matsumoto 1987, 1990, 1994) that specialized in the domains of electric power, steel, traffic control, and factory automation, linking productivity and reusability. TSF housed approximately 2,300 employees when it started its first operation. In TSF, many projects for different application domains ran in concurrence, utilizing domain-specific reusable series of product assets. The concept of "software product line" (SPL) (Clements and Northrop 2002), now popular, was not known then. However, TSF's idea in domain-specific implementation of reusable product assets was almost the same as that of modern SPLs.

In the following Sections 16.2, 16.3, 16.4, 16.5, and 16.6, the facts about and experiences that we had in TSF are described. Section 16.7 focuses our view on the financial aspects and presents a guide useful for the management and control of SPL adoption. Sections 16.8 and 16.9 describe related works and future work.

16.2 Organizational Setup

In the early 1950s, James D. Watson and Francis Crick discovered DNA and the principle called "Watson–Crick complementary." Motivated by those achievements in another world, we came to believe that even when user requirements were very complex and versatile, there should be some simple common computing rules and fundamental components that will play a pivotal role for solving target applications. In the early 1960s, the domain preparation teams were organized for realizing this belief, especially in applications of electric power generation, electric power dispatch control, and hot/cold strip mill control in steel industries, which were then being undertaken in the factory.

Organizational functions for supporting these team activities, and for improving the productivity and quality of the factory products by systematic software reuse were explored. Then the following functions were identified:*

- *Function 1*: The function to collect reusable software products and components and reuse feedback from real acting projects
  Outcome: software products and components, reuse reports, and reuse feedback
- *Function 2*: The domain-engineering activities and tasks to conduct domain analysis, domain design, asset development, asset provision, and asset maintenance
  Outcome: domain models, domain architectures, boundaries of the target domain, and assets such as software architecture, domain-specific languages, code-generators, and program modules
- *Function 3*: The function to serve asset storage/retrieval mechanism, asset management, and asset control
  Outcome: asset classification, asset storage and retrieval mechanism, control of asset changes, and change notification
- *Function 4*: The function to establish and commit the scope and boundary of the target domain, and the function to coordinate and to promote activities of reuse programs
  Outcome: assessment of reuse capability, assessment of reuse potential, reuse strategy, and reuse proposals

In 1977, when TSF started operations, the organizational setup shown in Figure 16.1† was realized, and each of the above functions that fit this setup was customized and implemented for each application domain in the factory. The organizational elements identified and organized at that time are shown below:

- *Element 1*: The group of project facilitators (sometimes called project secretaries or assistants), who were involved in the real ongoing commercial projects, shown in the left-hand side of Figure 16.1, played Function 1.
- *Element 2*: The parts manufacturing department, shown in the right-hand side of Figure 16.1, was responsible for Function 2.
- *Element 3*: The parts center, shown in the lower center part of Figure 16.1, was responsible for Function 3.
- *Element 4*: The software parts steering committee, shown in the upper center of Figure 16.1, played the role of Function 4.

---

* The terminology used in this manuscript is based on ISO/IEC FCD 12207 (2006-12-17).
† This figure was first published in Matsumoto 1987.

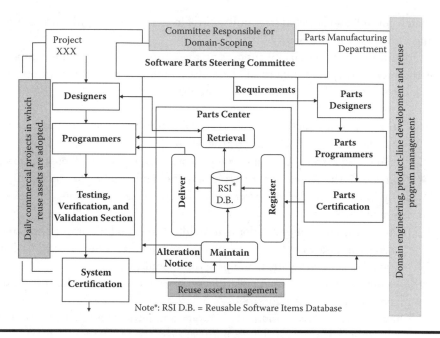

Figure 16.1 Major organizational components implemented in Toshiba Software Factory. (From Matsumoto 2007. ©2007 IEEE. With permission.)

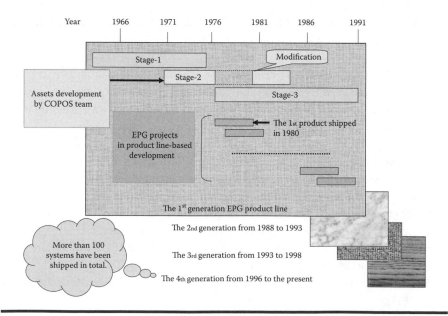

Figure 16.2 Transition to SPL-based paradigm in the first generation EPG-SPL. (From Matsumoto 2007. ©2007 IEEE. With permission.)

In TSF, several SPL adoption plans for different domains were conducted in concurrence. The SPL for the domain of electric power generation (EPG) was one of those. The organizational transition from the so-called one-off development paradigm to the SPL-based development in the EPG domain was conducted step by step through the three interleaved stages shown in Figure 16.2:

- *Stage 1*: The software steering committee defined the EPG domain and its boundary for the development of the EPG-SPL. Following after the EPG domain-preparation team, the EPG-SPL development team (called COPOS* team) was organized in 1971. Using all software products shipped to the customers of the EPG domain before 1971 and during the years from 1971 to 1976, the reusability of all software products and components ever produced for the EPG domain, including specifications, manuals, design patterns, architecture patterns, code modules, and test cases, were assessed by the COPOS team. The software parts steering committee convened periodically to bridge the activities of Element 1 to the COPOS team's activities.

- *Stage 2*: The COPOS team conducted domain analysis and designed a domain model and a domain architecture. Then the team developed a software architecture and the fill-in-the-blank-format type DSL (domain-specific languages) explained in Section 16.4. The tabular formats filled with descriptions in DSL were called *plant tables*. Plant tables were put into the code generators, which generate automatically the data and interpretive codes that are to be read or interpreted in the objective system (see Figure 16.12). The outcomes from the COPOS team were reviewed and certified until the results were accepted by the related organizational elements.

- *Stage 3*: In 1976, the COPOS team submitted to the parts center all core assets and components, including code generators and documents. Project mangers of ongoing EPG commercial projects were required to plan, establish, manage, control, and monitor their reuse programs and to systematically exploit reuse opportunities. During this stage, the COPOS team and the parts center supported the promotion of active reuse programs.

Figure 16.2 shows the schedule followed by the organizations of the EPG domain in TSF from the early 1960s to 1986. In Stage 1, approximately 10 of the current EPGs supplied software products and components that were thought to be reusable to the parts manufacturing department. Average EPG project was the one responsible for the customers' orders of software-centric control systems† to be embedded in from 125-MW to 600-MW fossil-fuel- or crude-oil-type electric power generation plants. The software products and components supplied during Stage 1 were passed over to the COPOS team to

---

* Computerized Optimum Plant Operation System.
† Source lines of code numbered approximately 1.6 million (data codes not included).

develop the EPG-SPL in Stage 2. About 5 years were spent for the development of the first generation EPG-SPL that embedded so-called COPOS assets. The product line paradigm was applied to two to three EPG projects per year, started after 1976 and completed before 1986. After 1986, all assets of the first generation SPL were inherited by the second-, third-, and fourth-generation EPG-SPLs. At present, the fourth-generation EPG-SPL provides active services. More than 150 systems in total have been developed, and shipped through these four generations.

16.3 Problem and Solution Features

In the domain analysis conducted by the COPOS team, the problem features (Kang et al. 1990) F1, F2, F3, F4, and F5, listed in Figure 16.3, were identified from the viewpoint of systems engineering. Then, the 11 solution features that are the features created from the software engineer's point of view (Greenfield and Short 2004), listed in Figure 16.4, were defined. The review on the results of domain analysis was conducted by domain experts, software developers, and asset managers. The products and solution features were analyzed, and then the mapping from problem features to solution features, shown in Figure 16.5, was created, reviewed, evaluated, and validated. Next, the dependencies between solution features were analyzed and identified, which resulted in the diagrams exemplified in Figure 16.6. The symbols and values described in the six kinds of fill-in-the-blank formats, which are Plant Master Status table (PMS), Macro Status

> • Problem features ("Problem" is the view created by customers and users.)
>   – Confirm all necessary entities (F1)
>   • Physical entities, Logical entities, Abstract entities and Actors
>   – Keep the plant in safe conditions (F2)
>   • Periodic monitoring, and on-demand monitoring
>   – Safe and reliable operation (F3)
>   • Supervisory, Control, Analysis, and Maintenance
>   – Labor saving (F4)
>   • Automatic start-stop control, Regulatory control, Fail-safe control, Recovery control
>   – Productivity and quality improvement (F5)
>   • Assistance for Failure/fault analysis and Equipment-performance analysis and management, Operational guidance, and Maintenance guidance

Figure 16.3 Key problem features from the viewpoint of EPG systems engineering. (From Matsumoto 2007. ©2007 IEEE. With permission.)

> - Solution features
>   - Data
>   - Plant data management (S1), Input/output data management (S2)
>   - Plant monitor
>   - Communication in/out monitoring agent (S4), Plant in/out monitoring agent (S5)
>   - Operators interactions control
>   - Alarm agent (S6), Operator input/output agent (S7), Graphic user interface management agent (S8)
>   - Automatic control (S3)
>   - Automatic control agent
>   - Operation timing definitions, Combinatory condition definitions, Operation administration, Operational logical sequences, Operational action details, Monitoring administration, Monitoring logical sequences, Monitoring action details, Display administration, Display logical sequences, Display action details
>   - Performance computation and operator supports
>   - Maintenance support agent (S9), Plant performance management agent (S10), Failure/fault analysis and operational guidance agent (S11)

Figure 16.4   Key solution features from the viewpoint of EPG software engineering. (From Matsumoto 2007. ©2007 IEEE. With permission.)

Determiner (MSD), Master Control Sequencer definitions (MCS), input/output List (I-O List), Alarm Group definitions (ALG), and Operation Block definitions (OB), provide common (fixed) and variability data. The description of these formats is open and is taught using Customer Training Textbook No. PG-606A, edited by Toshiba Fuchu Engineering School (Kaneda et al. 1984). The framework that implements and executes the EPG functions on the objective systems by reading and interpreting the codes generated from those formalized definitions was patented (Japanese patent no. 1063709-81.9.22, no. 1063717-81.9.22, and no. P1122909-82.11.12).

16.4 Domain-Specific Language

The six kinds of fill-in-the-blank formats can be filled based upon the syntax and semantics defined in EPG-DSL. An average EPG project produced more than 5,000 sheets of plant tables (completed formats) per project. The plant tables were usually produced by Toshiba members; however, advanced customers occasionally produced almost 60% of the sheets by themselves. The notion of the EPG-DSL is summarized below using a very simple example: water storage level control. Let us assume that we have an entity ENT. ENT changes its state when an action

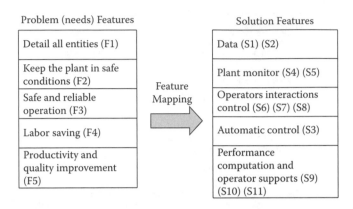

Figure 16.5 Mapping from problem features to solution features. (From Matsumoto 2007. ©2007 IEEE. With permission.)

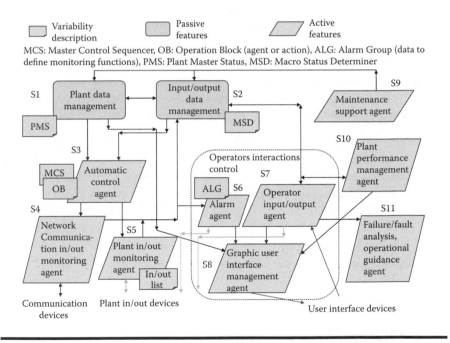

Figure 16.6 Diagram to show dependencies between solution features and variability formats. (From Matsumoto 2007. ©2007 IEEE. With permission.)

is observed in the defined channel. For example, ENT can be an electric power generating station that will encompass a series of concatenated states: SLEEPING, PREPARATION, START-UP, RATED-OPERATION, and SHUT-DOWN, where each of those states might be further refined to numerous substates. The transitions of the ENT state will be caused by the observed actions, which will include human operations. ENT can also be decomposed into numerous subsidiaries. Let us assume that CTL (controller) is one of those subsidiaries.

We will model the behaviors of CTL using CCS (Calculus of Communication Systems) (Milner 1980). Let us assume in Figure 16.7 that S is a CCS agent (or process) to model the behavior of a CTL. When an action "a" is observed in the channel created by S, S changes its state and replaces itself, also named S. The action prefix S=a:S denotes this behavior. S might be further refined, for example, S = a:(b:NIL+c:d:S), where a, b, c, and d are actions; NIL is an undefined other agent. Many CCS agents may run in concurrence in the controller. A CTL is allowed to start when the logical conjunction

```
{<timing condition TC is true>∧<precondition PC is
true>∧<trap-condition TP is false>∧<trigger-condition TG is
true>∧<interrupt-condition IR is false>}
```

is true. The active CTL will be aborted and returns to the trap-handling system whenever TP becomes true. TP in false presents the condition that can keep CTL alive, for example, the power supply to CTL is on. When CTL successfully stops activity, postcondition PS must become true. TG can be described using a regular expression*. The active CTL is interrupted if IR becomes true (does some other things and then resumes the most recent state). If postcondition PS is incomplete when the action finishes, it is notified. The conditions TP, PS, and IR are presented by logical expressions or event-expressions. TG and IR can be guarded by other conditions. An event is a logical message received through channels to signify an important occurrence in ENT, and the value of the event will be a logical value. For example, the true value of event X-TEMP-OVERHEAT means that the measured value of the x-temperature is equal or higher than the predetermined limit value.

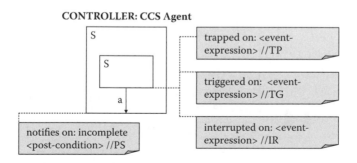

Figure 16.7 CCS model for controller. (From Matsumoto 2007. ©2007 IEEE. With permission.)

---

* A classical expression to describe behavior of the finite automata.

An event-expression is a logical expression that consists of logical variables of which each represents an event.

MCS is the table to define a logical product between multiple conditions. (A condition is a logical value to present a state of an atomic entity.) PMS is the table to define timing conditions. MSD is the table to define composite conditions where conditions are related to one another using logical products or logical sums. OB is the table that defines actions in relation to corresponding timing events, trigger events, preconditions, traps, interrupts, postconditions, and guard conditions. ALG is the table that defines periodic monitoring and alarming actions in relation to corresponding timing events, trigger events, preconditions, traps, interrupts, postconditions, and guard conditions.

How to use these tables is explained using a water storage level control. The water level controller opens or closes the inlet valve V1 and the outlet valve V2 so as to keep the water level in state S1, S2, or S3 shown in Figure 16.8. In response to the controller activities, the water level changes its state. The state transitions of the water level are shown in Figure 16.9. The transitions take place when the event, which announces the change of on/off state of the level switch, arrives. The states and state transitions of the controller are shown in Figure 16.10. The state transitions of both water level and controller run in concurrence, but both interact with each other. While the water level stays in state Si (i = 1, 2, or 3), the controller is in state Ci. The controller performs the activity shown in Figure 16.10, which results in the state of the water level moving from Si to the adjacent state. If the state of water level is moved to outside of S1, S2, and S3, it is in the failure state S-fail. If the controller moves to outside of state C1, C2, and C3, it is in the failure state C-fail. The controller Cont.1521can be activated or deactivated by the result of logical

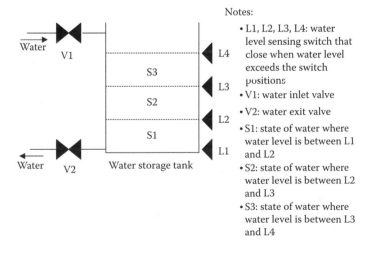

Notes:
- L1, L2, L3, L4: water level sensing switch that close when water level exceeds the switch positions
- V1: water inlet valve
- V2: water exit valve
- S1: state of water where water level is between L1 and L2
- S2: state of water where water level is between L2 and L3
- S3: state of water where water level is between L3 and L4

Figure 16.8 Diagram to explain water level control.

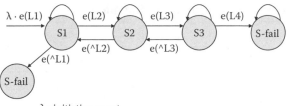

λ : initiation event
e(Li): event that Li is closed where i=1,2,3,4.
e(^Li): event that Li is opened where i=1,2,3,4.

Figure 16.9   Water level states and state transitions.

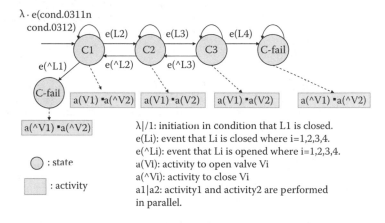

λ|/1: initiation in condition that L1 is closed.
e(Li): event that Li is closed where i=1,2,3,4.
e(^Li): event that Li is opened where i=1,2,3,4.
a(Vi): activity to open valve Vi
a(^Vi): activity to close Vi
a1|a2: activity1 and activity2 are performed
in parallel.

○ : state

▭ : activity

Figure 16.10   Controller states and state transitions.

conjunction between condition Cond.0311 and Cond.0312, shown in Table 16.1. The activities to be performed by Cont.1521 are defined in Table 16.2.

The activity in rule1, for example, opens V1 and closes V2 in parallel. This activity can take place at the moment that timing event, trigger event, and precondition, defined in Table 16.2, are all true. When the activity successfully stops, the defined postcondition should become true. If trap condition, defined in Table 16.2, becomes true while the activity is performed, the activity should be aborted and the controller resumes the default state. PMS is equivalent to Table 16.1. OB and ALG are the realization of Table 16.2, where OB is used for defining control activities, and ALG is used for defining alarm/display activities. MSD is used for defining trap conditions. The relationships between conditions, event, and an activity are shown in Figure 16.11. The activity in the bottom line of the figure can be activated at the time when (1) the timing condition is true, (2) the trap condition is false, (3) the precondition is true. If the trap condition becomes true while the activity is active, the activity is aborted. If the activity finishes and stops successfully, the postcondition must be true.

Table 16.1　Conditions for Controller Initiation

	Variable ID	Rules			
		1	2	3	...
Conditions:	Condition 0311 (Water source is ready)	true	false	true	false
	Condition 0312 (Water can be supplied from the storage)	true	false	false	true
Controls:	Control 1521 (Water storage level controls)	activates	deactivates	activates	activates

Table 16.2　Definition of Controller Activities

Activities of Control 1521	Rules	
	1	2
Timing event (in regular expression)	$\lambda \times e(\text{cond.0311 cond.0312})$	$\lambda \times e(\text{cond.0311 cond.0312})$
Trigger event	$e(^\wedge L1)$	$e(^\wedge L2)$
Precondition	$^\wedge V1 \cap \times {^\wedge}V2$	$^\wedge V1 \cap {^\wedge}V2$
Trap (exit) condition	$^\wedge(L1 \cap {^\wedge}L2)$	$^\wedge(L1 \cap {^\wedge}L2)$
Activity	$a(V1)\ a(^\wedge V2)$	$a(V1) \times a(^\wedge V2)$
Postcondition	$L1 \cap {^\wedge}L2 \cap V1 \cap {^\wedge}V2$	$L1 \cap {^\wedge}L2 \cap V1 \cap {^\wedge}V2$

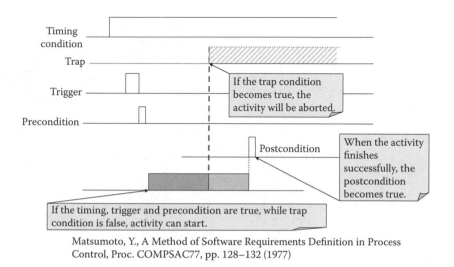

Matsumoto, Y., A Method of Software Requirements Definition in Process Control, Proc. COMPSAC77, pp. 128–132 (1977)

Figure 16.11   Timing chart.

16.5 Code Generation

Figure 16.12 illustrates how (1) inputs and outputs (described in I/O List), (2) relationships between timing/trigger-events, pre-/trap/post-conditions (described in PMS, MCS, and MSD) and control/alarm-activities (in OB or ALG), and (3) control logic representations (in OB) are transformed to the codes by the converter. The codes generated by the converter are interpretive codes, except the codes that are converted from I/O List. The codes converted from I/O List are database codes. The interpreter is invoked by the primitives provided by the primitives processor. The mediation of the primitives processor enables the converter (code-generator) independent from the platform that consists of operating systems, utilities (middleware), and hardware. Frequently, the installed codes were changed or updated at users' sites with the purposes of functional improvements and enhancements. The changes made at customers' sites were quickly reflected to the plant tables using the inverter. The plant tables were always kept updated automatically so as to match the updated codes. EPG-SPL accommodates DSL, code converter/inverter as its core assets, together with all plant-tables/runtime-utilities and codes deployed in all objective systems being operated at current customers' sites. Related documents and specifications have also been accommodated. Maintenance, configuration control, and version control of EPG-SPL have been conducted. The fundamental core of the DSL grammar and fill-in-the-blank formats has never been changed throughout all four EPG-SPL generations illustrated in Figure 16.2.

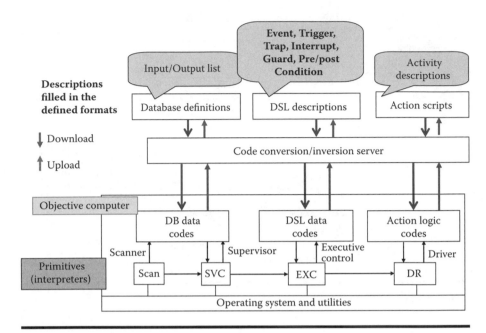

Figure 16.12 Software configuration. (From Matsumoto 2007. ©2007 IEEE. With permission.)

16.6 Experiences

While we were in Stage 1, the length of the EPG-SPL life span including Stages 2 and 3, the number of customers' orders that we will be able to obtain, and the minimum cash flow that we will be able to bear during the SPL life span were estimated. Using these results, PV (present value*) was calculated. Consequently, the upper bounds to be allowed for spending in Stage 2 were determined. In Stage 2, the COPOS team spent approximately five years, from 1971 to 1976. The cost of the COPOS team was controlled and suppressed below these bounds. After EPG-SPL was ready for the usage in around 1976, Stage 3 was made to start. While we were in the middle of Stage 3, we found that the accumulation of PV (present value) was less than the initial investment that we expended in Stages 1 and 2. As a result, we modified EPG-SPL and the adoption plan. The modification started in 1981. While the modification was planned, the following activities were conducted:

- The initial EPG-SPL was reexamined in 1981, and the product lines for the two subsidiary EPG domains, which were nuclear power generation and private in-house power generation, were developed and added to the original EGP-SPL. The dependencies between these three product lines (conventional,

---

* See Figure 16.7 and row 18 of Table 16.3.

nuclear, and private in-house) were defined. It was not necessary to change the syntactic and semantic structure of the DSL. However, program modules related to the plant equipment, such the devices for driving actuators and controllers, had to be changed.

■ The cost of the development for those additional subdomain product lines was estimated.

■ The total life span of the EPG-SPL series—which means a set of product lines including conventional EPG product line, nuclear power generation product line, and private in-house power generation product line—was estimated, and then the value of the investment to be allowed was revised.

■ The reuse program covering the adoption of whole EPG-SPL series was revised and activated.

The time schedule shown in Figure 16.2 only shows the first generation EPG-SPL. Around 1986, we had to replace hardware and platforms, including operating systems and programming languages. The second-generation EPG-SPL program was made available in 1986, where Stages 1, 2, and 3 were conducted again in the same way as they were conducted in the first generation EPG-SPL.

16.7 A Guide for Management and Controls

One of the serious problems that we encountered was that the amount paid by customers sometimes covered only the cost spent for the development of newly built functions or codes. This caused the problem that we were not able to disinvest the cost spent for the development and maintenance of SPL. To cope with this problem, we found that some guidance was necessary for the management and control of the SPL development and adoption program, which might include instructions to teach organizational managers how to measure cash flows, how to monitor accumulated PV (present value) at the end of every fiscal year, how to use those for the control of the ongoing SPL adoption program, and how to talk with customers concerning the usefulness of reuse plans. Net present value (NPV), a concept developed almost 50 years ago (Fischer 1965; Hirschleifer 1958), which can be computed using the following equation, was helpful:

$$NPV = CF(1)/(1+c) + CF(2)/(1+c)^2 + \ldots + CF(N)/(1+c)^N - I$$

where

c = the standard interest rate (SIR)

$CF(t)$ = cash flow at the fiscal year of which the ordinal number is t

I = initial investment

t = ordinal number of the fiscal year that is set as 1 for the year when the SPL is first adopted

N = ordinal number of the fiscal year at present

It is assumed that the costs to be spent at Stage 1 and Stage 2 can be funded by the corporate budget of the company, and these should be disinvested by the accumulated cash flows to be obtained during Stage 3. The guidance recommends that the measurement of cash flows, variable costs, and fixed costs at every fiscal year should start in Stage 3. Let us assume that we are in ith fiscal year in Stage 3, where the first fiscal year corresponds to the first fiscal year of Stage 3.

1. The cash flow should be measured at the end of the ith fiscal year.
2. The variable and fixed cost should also be measured at the end of the ith fiscal year.
3. The measured result should be used to calculate the ith PV (present value), or PV(i).
4. The accumulation of PVs or the sum of PV(i) from i = 1 to i should be calculated.
5. The investment to SPL during Stage 1 and Stage 2 subtracted by the accumulated PV gives the ROI shortage or the shortage of return.
6. If the ROI shortage is thought dissolvable within residual years of Stage 3, we can continue the current adoption plan.
7. If the ROI shortage will be thought hard to be dissolved, we have to revise the contents of the current SPL and adoption plan.

Tables 16.3, 16.4, and 16.5 show the forms that are used for the calculation of the ROI shortage at the ith fiscal year. The ordinal numbers shown in the top of the tables identify the sequential order of the fiscal years in Stage 3. Usually, the corporate level of the company defines the values such as standard interest rate (cost of capital), the tax rate, and the depreciation in advance. The number of shipments in fiscal year i, or n(i), means the number of systems released and installed within that fiscal year developed in SPL paradigm. The sales amount S(i) means the sum of customers' payment within fiscal year i. The breakdowns of variable cost and fixed cost are listed, respectively, in Tables 16.4 and 16.5. The explanations for every symbolized item are noted in the rightmost columns. In Table 16.4, the cost of maintenance, enhancement, and configuration management required for running installed systems should also be included in TC(i). The costs of activities, such as development of new items necessary to satisfy individual customer's requirements, development of additional assets, improvement of the existing assets, the development of subdomain product lines, and modification efforts (such as development of subdomain SPL, and modification of SPL adoption programs), should be included in TC(i). In Table 16.5, the organizational costs necessary for keeping the fixed activities and tasks, such as the ones conducted by the fixed organizational element, Elements 2, 3, and 4 (explained in Section 16.2), should be included in department expense DX(i). Using VC(i) and FC(i) calculated in Tables 16.4 and 16.5, the shortage of the return SR(i) should be calculated using the equation in the bottom row of Table 16.3. This

Table 16.3   ROI Calculation Form

No.	Item	Symbol	Notes
1	Ordinal number	i	The i of the fiscal year when the product line is first adopted is set 1
2	Standard interest rate (unit value)	SIR	SIR is the value that is internal to the company; SIR corresponds to cost of capital, and its value is defined a little higher than the cost of capital
3	Tax rate (unit value)	T	
4	Number of shipment	$n(i)$	
5	Sales amount ($)	$S(i)$	
6	Variable cost ($)	$VC(i)$	The cost breakdown is shown in Table 16.4
7	Marginal profit ($)	$MP(i)$	$MP(i) = S(i)\ VC(i)$
8	Fixed cost ($)	$FC(i)$	The cost breakdown is shown in Table 16.5
9	Profit ($)	$P(i)$	$P(i) = MP(i) - FC(i)$
10	Profit after taxes ($)	$PAT(i)$	$PAT(i) = P(i) * (1-T)$
11	Depreciation ($)	$DP(i)$	
12	Cash in ($)	$CI(i)$	$CI(i) = PAT(i) + DP(i) + RV(i)$
13	Additional investment (for software) ($)	$IS(i)$	The cost breakdown is shown in Tables 16.4 and 16.5
14	Additional investment (for hardware) ($)	$IH(i)$	The cost breakdown is shown in Tables 16.4 and 16.5
15	Cash out ($)	$CO(i)$	$CO(i) = IS(i) + IH(i)$
16	Cash flow ($)	$CF(i)$	$CF(i) = CI(i) - CO(i)$
17	Discount rate (unit value)	$DR(i)$	$DR(i) = 1/(1 + SIR)**i$
18	Present value of cash flow ($)	$PV(i)$	$PV(i) = CF(i) * DR(i)$
19	Shortage of return ($)	$SR(i)$	$SR(i) = $ (initial investment) $-$ (sum of $PV(1),\dots,$ and $PV(i)$)

Source: From Matsumoto 2007. ©2007 IEEE. With permission.

Table 16.4   Calculation of Variable Cost

No.	Item	Symbol	Notes
1	Ordinal number of fiscal year	I	
2	Cost spent for acquiring products from outside vendors ($)	AC(*i*)	
3	Cost spent for product outsourcing ($)	OC(*i*)	
4	Cost spent by the domain-engineering team ($)	TC(*i*)	Develop additional assets, improve the existing assets, and develop subdomain product lines
5	Variable cost ($)	VC(*i*)	VC(*i*) = AC(*i*) + OC(*i*) + TC(*i*)

Source: From Matsumoto 2007. ©2007 IEEE. With permission.

suggests the value to be returned before the end of SPL life span. These tables can also be used for estimating NPV and the upper bound of initial investment in the following way:

1. Time estimation: At the beginning or in the early part of Stage 1, the length of SPL life and the time length to be consumed at each following stage should be estimated first of all. For every fiscal year of Stage 3, its ordinal number i ($i = 1$ at the first year of Stage 3) can be identified and entered in the tables.
2. PV estimation: Expected cash flows, variable costs, fixed costs, and the PV at every fiscal year in Stage 3 should be predicted.
3. NPV estimation: Then, the sum of the PVs for all fiscal years included in Stage 3 will be obtainable, from which NPV could be derived. This gives the upper bound of cost to be allowed during Stage 1 and Stage 2.

16.8 Related Works

The idea with which EGP-SPL was developed was to promote reusable software from the viewpoint of higher abstract levels than was presented by Matsumoto (1984). The development with domain specialization and scoping was supported by Freeman (1987) at the time. Cusumano (1991) described a survey on

Table 16.5 Calculation of Fixed Cost

No.	Item	Symbol	Notes
1	Depreciation ($)	DP(i)	
2	Personnel cost ($)	PC(i)	
3	Operative overheads ($)	OO(i)	
4	Department expense ($)	DX(i)	
5	Fixed cost ($)	FC(i)	FC(i) = DP(i) + PC(i) + OO(i) + DX(i)

Source: From Matsumoto 2007. ©2007 IEEE. With permission.

the first generation TSF, which introduced the organizational setup described in Figure 16.1. The activities itemized in ISO/IEC FCD12207 (2006-12-17), Software Life Cycle Processes–7.3 "Software Reuse Processes," were worthwhile for brushing up our organizational functions described in Section 16.2. The concept of "features" on which our work relied has been derived from conceptual properties described by Smith and Medin (1981) and Fisher (1965). FODA (Kang et al. 1990) had also provided us a good guidance for the promotion of SPL adoptions. The COPOS code generator, which generates interpretive codes, but not objective codes, was totally hand-coded. There are many XML-based code generators available now. However, we do not feel a need to move to the XML-based code generation, because: (a) the basic structure and ontology that underlie our domains do not change very often and (b) the time efficiency of code generation strongly favors hand-coding. A number of ROI-based discussions on SPL adoption have been published. However, business practitioners from our financial sector favor the comparison between NPV and cash flows just from a practical point of view, rather than the usage of various equations presented in the SPL community, for example those by Böckle et al. (2004). Recent systematic approaches such as "product lines" (Clements and Northrop 2002), "product families" (van der Linden 1998), and "Microsoft's software factories" (Greenfield and Short 2004) are all closely related to our work.

16.9 Future Work

Enterprises, or electric utility companies in the case of EPG applications, usually acquire software products from different software factories of different vendors. Enterprises and vendors are looking forward to the day when the services for the product development and maintenance will be provided at different distributed workplaces. For example, services for describing input/output lists, DSL descriptions, and action scripts (see Figure 16.12) are expected to be available at the plant sites. Figure 16.13 shows a presumptive style of software factory accompanied by a service factory. Software products developed or maintained by a software factory under the EPG contract agreements may be classified into agile products and reusable products. While the former will be supplied directly to the enterprise from the software factory, the latter will be transferred to its service factory, where the reusable software products will be converted to services and supplied to the enterprise through service environments. For example, these services may include means to complete DSL descriptions, generate the codes, test programs, and download the codes to the computers in EPG plants. The code conversion/inversion server, shown in Figure 16.12, will be included in the service environments, so that the codes to/from objective computers can be supplied or maintained at the distributed workplaces.

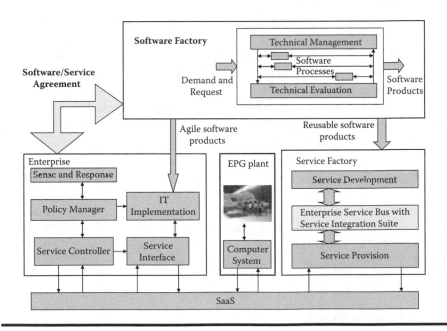

Figure 16.13 A future style of EPG software/service factory.

References

Aaen, I., P. Botcher, L. Mathiassen. 1997. The software factory: Contributions and illusions. In *Proceedings of the 20th information systems research seminar in Scandinavia*. Institutt for Informatikk, Oslo.

Böckle, G., P. Clements, J. D. McGregor, D. Muthig, and K. Schmid. 2004. Calculating ROI for software product lines. *IEEE Software* 21 (3): 23–31.

Clements, P., and L. Northrop. 2002. *Software product lines*. Reading, MA: Addison-Wesley.

Cusumano, M. A. 1991. *Japan's software factories*. New York: Oxford University Press.

Fisher, I. 1965. *The theory of interest*. New York: Augustus M. Kelly Publishers.

Freeman, P. 1987. A conceptual analysis of the Draco approach to constructing software systems. *IEEE Trans. on Software Engineering* 13 (7): 830–844.

Greenfield, J., and K. Short. 2004. *Software factories*. New York: Wiley Publishing.

Hirschleifer, J. 1958. On the theory of optimal investment decision. *Journal of Political Economy* 66 (4): 329–352.

Kaneda, M., et al. 1984. Nuclear power plant monitoring and control system software. In *Proc. AIEA/IAEA Meeting*, Communication N' 21, Saclay, France.

Kang, K., S. Cohen, J. Hess, W. Novak, and A. Peterson. 1990. Feature-oriented domain analysis (FODA) feasibility study. Technical report CMU/SEI-90-TR-021. Software Engineering Institute, Carnegie-Mellon University, Pittsburgh.

Matsumoto, Y. 1977. A method of software requirements definition in process control. In *Proceedings of COMPSAC77*, 128–132. Washington, DC: IEEE Computer Society.

Matsumoto, Y. 1984. Some experiences in promoting reusable software: Presentation in higher abstract levels. *IEEE Trans. Software Engineering* 10 (5): 502–513.

Matsumoto, Y. 1987. A software factory: An overall approach to software production. In *Software reusability*, ed. P. Freeman, 155–178. Washington, DC: IEEE Computer Society.

Matsumoto, Y. 1990. Toshiba software factory. In *Modern software engineering*, ed. P. A. Ng and R. T. Yeh, 479–501. New York: Van Nostrand Reinhold.

Matsumoto, Y. 1994. Japanese software factory. In *The encyclopedia of software engineering*, ed. J. J. Marciniak, 1st ed., 593–605. New York: John Wiley & Sons.

Matsumoto, Y. 2007. A guide for management and financial controls of product lines. In *Proceedings of the 11th international software product line conference*, 163–170. Washington, DC: IEEE Computer Society.

McIlroy, M. D. 1969. Mass-produced software components. In *Software engineering reports*, distributed at a software engineering conference sponsored by the NATO Science Committee, Brussels.

Milner, R. 1980. *A calculus of communication systems*. Lecture Notes in Computer Science, vol. 92. Berlin/Heidelberg: Springer-Verlag.

Smith, E. E., and D. L. Medin. 1981. *Categories and concepts*. Cambridge, MA: Harvard University Press.

Van der Linden, F., ed. 1998. *Development and evolution of software architectures for product families*. Lecture Notes in Computer Science, vol. 1429. New York: Springer-Verlag.

Chapter 17

Efficient Scoping with CaVE: A Case Study

Isabel John and Jens Knodel

Fraunhofer Institute for Experimental Software Engineering (IESE), Kaiserslautern, Germany

Torsten Schulz

IBS AG, Höhr-Grenzhausen, Germany

Contents

17.1 Introduction

Introducing product line engineering is a major investment that has to be planned for. This investment comprises also an investment into the scoping activities (Boeckle et al. 2004). Scoping (Schmid 2003) builds a solid basis for the decision about where and what to invest in reuse. Scoping, as we propose it in our product line engineering methodology Fraunhofer PuLSE™* (Bayer et al. 1999; John et al. 2006) but also in other approaches, is a very knowledge-intensive activity. The basis of scoping is the domain knowledge of domain experts. This is supported by the fact that one of the key practices in SEI's Product Line Practice framework (Clements and Northrop 2001) is the understanding of relevant domains. Scoping plans for the product line investment by deciding which features the products of the product line should have and by finding out about reuse potential in different subdomains of the product line. But scoping itself is also an investment. We have to invest the time and effort of the product line engineers and of the domain experts. Domain experts can be architects, developers, project managers, testers, etc.; they are part of the development organization of the product line to be built. Domain experts have a deep understanding of the application domain of the envisioned product line. In existing product line engineering and scoping approaches, the information is elicited interactively from domain experts, which is an effort-intensive task due to the large number of experts that are involved (typically 3–10 experts per subdomain with about 80–150 features) and the time needed for workshops and interviews.

When doing scoping in the context of the introduction of PuLSE, we often had the experience that planning the interviews and especially the workshops is almost impossible because of the high workload that domain experts have (Knauber et al. 2000). Additionally, in the times of increasing distributed development, we need methods that can be applied concurrently. To make product line engineering possible in distributed development scenarios, we cannot solely rely on interactive workshops when introducing product line engineering; we need techniques that are

---

* PuLSE™ is a registered trademark of Fraunhofer IESE. The acronym PuLSE stands for Product Line Software Engineering.

independent of space or time, techniques that can be applied anytime, anywhere, by almost every person without domain knowledge.

In this chapter we present an industrial case study of the CaVE approach (commonality and variability extraction), which we have already introduced in a number of publications where we described the initial method, an academic case study, and an experiment with students (Fantechi et al. 2004; John 2006). The case study that we present here shows that the approach is applicable in the context of large industrial companies and shows the completeness and correctness of the results produced with the approach. So we shortly describe the approach here, demonstrate it with data from the case study, and show the concrete and measurable use of the results in scoping. We also compare the results of the case study presented here with the first industrial case study presented in a work by John (2006). The approach supports structured gathering of information for scoping from user documentation. It assists the introduction of product line engineering in a development organization by systematically eliciting information relevant for scoping from documents. The approach supports the gaining of domain knowledge from existing documentation instead of building all information up interactively. We show that, with the CaVE approach, the expert load of the domain experts can be reduced by several hours per subdomain; in the case study we had a reduction of more than 50% (5 of 14 hours and 3 of 5.8 hours for all experts). We also show in this case study that we have an overall time reduction if we sum up expert time and nonexpert time. The case study also shows that the results produced by the approach achieve a correctness of over 79%.

This chapter is structured as follows: In Section 17.2 we briefly describe the scoping process as we apply it and compare the information needed for different scoping approaches. Then we present the elicitation approach in Section 17.3. In Section 17.4 we describe the case study, its context, planning, and performance, and we analyze the results and the threads to the validity. We also give relations to other empirical studies we performed as validation steps of the CaVE approach.

17.2 Scoping

Scoping is the planning instrument for successful introduction of product line engineering (Boeckle et al. 2004; Schmid 2003). It aims to dispel doubts and uncertainty in the decisions about which products will become part of the product line and whether or not to invest into reuse (i.e., gain advantages from commonalities). Scoping drives the data collection on the domain and subdomains, the planned and existing products of the product line, and their common and variable features.

17.2.1 The Scoping Process

Effective scoping approaches capture crucial information to support all later phases of product line engineering. They start the modeling of the product line infrastructure, which, once architected and implemented, supports the derivation of product line instances. Wrong decisions, missing information sources, or incomplete data in the scoping phase heavily affect the overall product line success. In short, scoping is planning for product-centered reuse.

Product line scoping has its base in the areas of domain-specific reuse, economic modeling in reuse, marketing science, and mainly in product line engineering. The first scoping approach that was extensively described in the literature is the PuLSE-Eco approach (Schmid 2003). PuLSE-Eco consists of a feature-oriented product line mapping step, where products, features, and domains are identified, and a domain potential assessment step, which investigates the reuse potential of the identified domains and a reuse infrastructure scoping. Figure 17.1 gives an overview on the scoping process and the artifacts produced. Scoping in PuLSE-Eco mainly consists of two phases:

1. *Product line mapping* identifies products and features of an envisioned product line. The main output is the product-feature matrix, which is the central artifact for subsequent steps. Product line mapping provides an overview on domains, features, and their distribution in the products.
2. *Domain potential assessment* evaluates the (sub-) domains of the envisioned product line for their product line potential. This phase quantifies the reuse potential and recommends the high-potential areas where later activities (like architecting) should be focused.

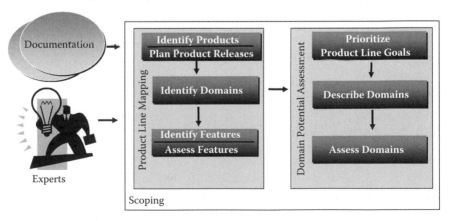

Figure 17.1   The scoping process.

There is also a third phase called *reuse infrastructure scoping* (Schmid 2003), but it is out of focus for the case study and this chapter, so we concentrate on the two phases: product line mapping and domain potential assessment. The main roles in the scoping process are the *domain experts* with technical or marketing knowledge, next to *scoping experts* and the *product line manager* (Schmid 2003). The domain experts provide their knowledge on the products and the application domain from the technical or marketing side. The product line manager provides an overview on the product line, its goals, and embedding in the organizational environment. The scoping experts perform the scoping.

17.2.2 Product Line Mapping

The goal of product line mapping is to identify the planned products in the product line and to identify their features. Additionally, domains are identified and the features distributed in the domains. This is done in one or more workshops or interviews by the scoping experts and the domain experts. In product line mapping, the technical view is brought together with the marketing view. The minimal duration of a product line mapping is five to eight hours; in complex settings it can take a few days (John et al. 2006).

Product line mapping starts with *product identification* (see Figure 17.1). The goal is to find appropriate products for the product line and describe their potential market, their high-level features, and the rough release plan. The output of this step is a one-page product description for each of the planned products. The participation of a scoping expert, domain experts with a marketing as well as a technical background, and of the product line manager is needed. For this activity at least one hour should be scheduled.

The activity *plan product releases* uses the product descriptions to produce an overview of the releases scheduled for the products. The output of this step is a product release plan as part of the product description, which is a graphical representation of the release dates of the products as well as their interdependencies. At least the product line manager should be involved in this activity. The planning minimally takes a half hour.

The next step is the activity *identify domains*. The goal is to find internal and external subdomains of the product line domain. A domain is a conceptual unit (as opposed to, for example, components that describe realization units) that describes functionalities that are generally used together in the product line. The feature list and the product description are used as input for the activity. Output is a domain list that will be refined to domain descriptions in the domain potential assessment phase. The identification and description of the domains are often done together, so the two activities or process parts overlap. In this activity at least the available domain experts with technical knowledge should be involved. For domain identification we schedule at least one hour. In complex domains the conduction of the activity itself is more difficult and more time-consuming.

The product description is also used as an input to the activity *identify features*. The goal of this activity is to refine the high-level features that were already captured in the product description and to identify innovative functionality for the products of the future. The required input artifact for this activity is the product description; other optional artifacts can be used.

The output is a feature list that can already be organized by products. A scoping expert and domain experts have to be involved in this activity, usually taking about one hour. In the activity *specify product-feature matrix*, the results of the preceding activities are combined to a first version of the product map. The features are distributed to the identified domains and assigned to the products. With this matrix we can identify common and variable features and get a first guess of variations in the domains and between the products. At least the product line manager should be involved in the activity, with a duration between one and two hours.

The guess regarding possible variations is refined in the activity *assess features*. The features and domains are weighted to find a prioritization for the realization of the features. The prioritization can be done with a modification of the Kano Model, which is part of quality function deployment (QFD) (Cohen 1995) or with a customized QFD (Herzwurm, Schockert, and Helferich 2005). Further, the feature distribution in the different products (product portfolio scoping) can be optimized by using marketing-oriented models like those described by Robertson and Ulrich (1998). Input for the activity is the product-feature matrix. The result is a prioritized and optimized product map. In this prioritization and optimization, all available domain experts with technical or marketing knowledge should be involved. The assessment takes at least one hour.

Our experience showed that it is more important to go over all steps than to produce complete results only for some steps. Partially filled assets can be filled by single experts after the workshop or just left incomplete for later additions.

17.2..3 Domain Potential Assessment

The goal of domain potential assessment is to give recommendations for a product line strategy in the different subdomains. The process is strongly influenced by process assessments as they are done in SPICE (El Emam, Drouin, and Melo 1998). The assessment is normally performed in the form of a briefing workshop, several interviews with one or two interviewees, and a closing workshop, but it can also be performed differently according to different customizations. The results of this scoping process phase are reuse recommendations for all subdomains of the application domain, generally bundled in an assessment report. A domain potential assessment (see Figure 17.1) typically is performed in one to three days, depending on the number of subdomains interviewed. For each interview, we need one to two hours; some hours for planning, interview preparation, and goal identification; and at least half a day for reporting.

The first step in domain potential assessment is the *domain description*, if not already done during the product line mapping activity *identify domains*. The domain list serves as input, and the domains are described more in depth with their requirements, existing assets, etc. Output is the domain description. This activity lasts at least one hour more plus 15 minutes per domain.

To assess the described domains, first the *product line goals* have to be identified. The goal of this step is to find the organizational goals for institutionalizing the product line based on a standardized list. The list contains goals like decrease time to market, increase quality, reduce cost, etc. Output is a selection of goals from the standardized list extended with goals specified by the product line manager.

Subsequently, the goals are prioritized. The activity *prioritize product line goals* leads to a customization of the successive assessments. Based on the prioritized product line goals and the domain description, the activity *assess domains* is performed as mentioned via interviews. The subdomains are assessed against a selection of nine dimensions (Schmid 2000, 2003) by using a different interview guideline for each dimension. The nine dimensions are maturity, stability, resource constraints, organizational constraints, external market potential, internal market potential, commonality and variability, coupling and cohesion, and existing assets.

The selection of the dimensions is customized with the product line goals (e.g., if the development of a new market is the main goal, the market potential and the existing assets are in focus). The results of the interviews/workshops are analyzed and documented in a *domain assessment report* subdivided in the subdomains. The content of the report depends on the customization but normally consists of the product-feature matrix from product line mapping, the domain description, a profile of the subdomain according to the assessed dimensions, and recommendations for investing in building reusable components for the domain when starting the product line. Additionally, general pros and cons and recommendations for improvement are obtained as a result of the interviews.

17.2.4 Information Need in Scoping

We now analyze which data and information are needed and required by scoping. The need is caused by the objective of capturing and managing variability and commonality in the envisioned product line. The information need of the scoping approach formulates what a scoping approach has to deliver and elicit from the domain experts. Being aware of this information need, it is possible to systematically identify the parts of the approach that can be supported by extracting information from user documentation in order to reduce the workload of the domain experts.

Input to our analysis included the following scoping approaches: PuLSE-Eco, described in Section 17.2.1 (John et al. 2006; Schmid 2003); scoping as proposed in the SEI product line practice framework (Clements and Northrop 2001);

QFD-PPP (Herzwurm, Schockert, and Helferich 2005); the release matrix (Taborda 2004); the approach by Thiel and Peruzzi (2000); and the approach by van Zyl and Walker (2000). The common information need can be identified as follows (see Table 17.1):

In a *product description*, the planned products of the product line are described. To build a product description, high-level information on the planned and existing products (like features, general capabilities, and distinguishing characteristics to other products) is needed. For a *subdomain description,* information about functional areas of the products is also needed. The subdomain description should describe the system from an outside, conceptual point of view, so we need conceptual information here (and not realization information, as it can, for example, be found in the code or the architecture). A *feature* can be defined as a user-visible functional or nonfunctional capability of the system in focus (Kang et al. 1990). The features of a product describe the system from an outside point of view. So, if we want to find features we need information on the user-visible functionalities

Table 17.1   Mapping of Information Need to User Documentation

Artifact	Information Need	Can Be Found in User Documentation
Product description	Information on the planned and existing products	Feature lists, product overview in the user documentation, table of contents
Subdomain description	Information on the functional areas of the products	Main sections of the user documentation, general overview
Feature	Information on the functionalities of the planned and existing products	Feature lists, table of contents, text of user documentation
Product line goals	Strategic information on the product line	—
Commonality	Things that are common to all products	Common sentences in different documentations
Variability	Different capabilities of the products in the product line	Varying or left-out sentences in different documentations
Decision	Causes for different capabilities in the products	—

of the planned and existing products. For scoping and planning the product line strategy, the *product line goals* are also important. For this task we need strategic and planning information on the product line.

One of the main peculiarities of product line engineering is the modeling of commonality and variability. To be able to work with commonality and variability in the different product line phases, we need knowledge about the *commonalities* and *variabilities* among the products. Additionally, knowledge on domain concepts and relations in different manifestations and representations (like features for scoping, use cases for requirements engineering, or scenarios for architecture) has to be built up by domain experts and product line engineers with the available information. The underlying *decisions* give causes for these commonalities and variabilities and help in deciding on a certain variant during application engineering. In existing processes, all this information is elicited interactively in workshops and interviews with high domain expert involvement. There is no systematic use of documentation.

Experience from introducing product lines with PuLSE (Bayer et al. 1999) showed that, especially in small and medium enterprises (SMEs), there are almost no requirements specifications or design documents, and if there are some, they are outdated. This experience is confirmed by Olsson and Runeson (2002); Lethbridge, Singer, and Forward (2003); and Melchisedech (1998). The only documentation assets that can be found almost always that are rather up to date are user manuals (John, Muthig, and Schmettow 2004). As we want to build an approach that is applicable everywhere, we decided to concentrate on user documentation in our further analysis. In our case, user documentation describes the system in use from an outside point of view and consists of the complete set of documents describing the system in use (Sommerville 2000).

We can fulfill a large part of the information need that we have in scoping by looking at user documentation (see Figure 17.2). Information on different scoping artifacts can be identified in different parts of the user documentation. For

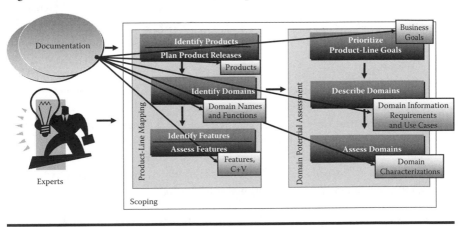

Figure 17.2 **Information provided by user documentation.**

example, can features be found in feature lists, as lists in the table of contents of a user documentation, or distributed in the text of the user documentation? Apart from these rather syntactical characterizations, there are also more semantic items like variabilities that can be found by comparing different user documentations. Figure 17.2 shows how the information need in scoping can be fulfilled through user documentation: User documentation is now an additional input/output of CaVE (a validated or unvalidated product map), which is used as an alternative (and much better and more structured input) for the product line mapping step. So the product map does not have to be built from scratch any more, but only has to be validated.

Subdomain descriptions can be identified as main sections of the documentation or they can be found in the general overview. Features can be found in feature lists or technical descriptions, but they can also be distributed in the text of the user documentation. Commonality and variability that are essential for product line engineering can be found by comparing documentation for similar systems. Elements that are common in different documentations relate to common information; elements that can only be found in parts of the documentation relate to variable (alternative or optional) information.

The only information that cannot be found in user documentation are the product line goals and information on underlying decisions. This information still has to be elicited interactively with domain experts.

17.3 CaVE

PuLSE-CaVE (commonality and variability extraction) is a pattern-based approach for structured and controlled information extraction from user documentation of existing systems. With CaVE, common and variable features, domains and subdomains, and product descriptions can be elicited. The approach was extensively described by John (2006). We give only a short sketch of the approach here to be able to describe the case study. The approach consists of the following three steps (see Figure 17.3):

1. *Preparation*: The product line engineer prepares the user documentation and selects the appropriate extraction patterns.
2. *Search*: The product line engineer analyzes the documents with the selected extraction patterns and marks the elements found. The selected elements are put together into a partial product line artifact like a product map.
3. *Validation*: The unvalidated artifact is presented to the expert, who can change elements and add additional information.

The first two steps of the approach can be performed by persons who just have a slight domain understanding; they do not have to be domain experts. The third step

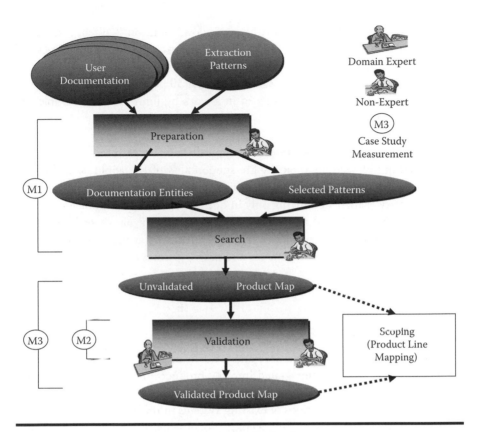

Figure 17.3   An outline of the extraction approach.

requires involvement of domain experts. We can perform the validation step with one or two experts before the scoping step, or we can integrate the validation step into the product line mapping phase of scoping (see Figure 17.3). Figure 17.3 also shows the measurement points of the case study. We will come to this in Section 17.4. We will first describe the patterns that form the basis of the approach and afterwards the three steps.

17.3.1 Patterns

The extraction patterns describe a transition between document elements and product line elements as they are needed in scoping and as they are described in Table 17.1. They form heuristics or rules of thumb that are not applicable in all situations but describe typical cases where information on product line artifacts can be found in documentation. Although the information in the documentation is domain dependent, the patterns can be generally applied because they are based on general layout information (like being a heading in a text or being a list element) or use general keywords or phrases (like "window," "button," "often," "security," etc.). We built up patterns for features and subdomains and for commonalities and variabilities. In an earlier version of the approach, we also had patterns for use case elements and requirements. There exist more than 30 patterns so far. The patterns are described in a template that is given in a work by John (2006). Examples for patterns are as follows:

- Headings of sections or subsections typically contain features.
- Headings of sections typically are subdomains of the application domain. The subheadings can then be the features for the domain.
- Arbitrary elements occurring only in one user manual are optional elements
- Headings or subheadings that have slightly different names or headings or subheadings that have different names, but that are at the same place in the table of contents, can be hints for alternative features.

We will now describe the steps of the approach that uses the patterns.

17.3.2 Preparation

During preparation, the product line analyst collects all user documentations for the systems that should be integrated into the product line and for those systems that are related in order to have all potential information sources available. For analysis, all user documentations of existing systems in the domain should be considered. After selecting about three typical documents, the product line analyst divides them into manageable and comparable parts. Experience has shown that 3–10 pages (e.g., comparable subchapters) are a suitable size for the parts to compare. Then for each of those manageable parts (or for a subset of those parts that includes typical subdomains), the product line analyst browses through them in order to decide the amount of variability in them. If the documents differ in more than one-third of the text, the product line analyst then processes them one after another in the second step and chooses the biggest document as the document to start with the analysis. If the difference of the documents is less than one third of the text, the product line analyst compares the documents in parallel. In the pattern selection step, the patterns to be applied are selected.

17.3.3 Search

In the search step, the elements that should be identified when applying the approach are marked in the documents and tagged. With the help of the subset of extraction patterns that were selected, which are not complete but help in finding a relevant part of the features, commonalities, and variabilities, the user documents should be marked.

> **Planning, Optimization and Control of the Logistics Chain** S
>
> IBS systems help OEMs simplify complex logistics
>
> processes on the inter- and intra-company level.
>
> They permit real-time process control thanks to
> F
> Internet-based processes in dynamic networks
>
> with all supply chain partners.
>
> **Manufacturing** S
>
> IBS software solutions integrate all supply chain.
>
> logistics and customer service processes in the
> F   F
> sense of a MES system. IBM solutions offer the
>
> complete range of functions for integral quality
>
> management precise manufacturing planning and
> F   F
> control as well as selective data creation for the
> F   F
> executive management.

Figure 17.4   Marked user documentation from IBS AG.

Figure 17.4 shows how the elements can be marked. Two potential subdomains of the IBS product line are marked with *S*, and the features within the subdomains are marked with *F*. The marked documentation entities are an intermediate artifact of the search step.

The elements, which should be sized from one word to at most five to six lines, that were identified to be useful can be marked only in the document and presented to the expert, but they can also be extracted from the document and put together in an artifact like a partially filled unvalidated product map.

17.3.4 Validation

In the last step, the unvalidated artifacts have to be validated and changed by one or more domain experts. For instance, not all text excerpts marked as possible features really are features, and not all elements marked as optional in the user documentation will really be optional in the new product line. So the domain experts have to judge whether the extracted elements should be used for scoping. The result of the method is a validated artifact like a product map consisting of common and variable features, subdomains, etc., that can be extended during scoping (e.g., with new and innovative features that cannot be found in the user documentation). If it is not possible to involve a domain expert in advance, the validation step can also be performed during scoping, when the unvalidated product map can be validated and extended by the whole expert group.

17.4 Case Study

In this section we describe a case study we performed to partially validate the CaVE approach. The goals of this case study were the following:

- To give measures for correctness and completeness of the results that were found with CaVE
- To show that there is expert-load reduction when applying the method
- To analyze whether or not the application of the approach has an influence on the results, i.e., to determine whether there is a method bias.

In the following section, we will further detail the study goals, describe and analyze the case study, and compare the results with the results of the other empirical studies we performed (another case study and an experiment, described by John [2006]).

17.4.1 Case Study Context and Goals

The case study was performed in the context of the project LifeCycleQM, a publicly funded applied research project with strong industrial participation. The goal of the project was to develop a systematic and tool-supported approach and model for optimizing the combined usage of different quality techniques in the life cycle of reusable software. The study was performed as part of the scoping activities that were done at IBS AG, which has been offering its software solutions and services for industrial productivity management worldwide since 1982. In keeping with the company philosophy, "the productivity advantage," IBS AG has set itself the task of developing and implementing solutions for different application domains that play a part in optimizing the business processes of its customers and increasing corporate productivity. The company today consists of six subsidiaries in Germany, the United States, Lithuania, and China. It employs about 185 employees.

The goal of the scoping activities at IBS was to apply PuLSE-ECO to find out about product line potential. Then a product line could be built up with PuLSE within the project. The case study was designed as an embedded single-case case study (Yin 2003) and was planned as follows:

Our task was to find information on three subdomains of the IBS AG product line in the documentation by applying the CaVE approach. So, before the scoping activities started, user documentation of all products was provided by the IBS AG. With the identified (sub)subdomains, features, and commonality and variability information, a product-feature matrix could initially be filled for each of the subdomains. The results of the analysis could then be presented at the scoping workshop and the matrices corrected and completed. The three subdomains were selected during the planning phase of the scoping activities without knowledge of the documentation, so there was no influence of the size or complexity of the documentation there. There were three case study goals.

1. *First case study goal*: Obtain values for completeness and correctness. To obtain measures for our case study goal, we needed to collect different values. To obtain values for correctness, completeness, and expert-load reduction of the results, we had to count the correct and wrong features and so compare the unvalidated product map with the validated product map (Figure 17.3, measurement point 3). We also needed the number of experts and nonexperts involved in the different stages of the case study. Furthermore, we had to track the time needed for preparation and search (the nonexpert time, see Figure 17.3, measurement point 1) as well as for the selection step (Figure 17.3, measurement point 2). With this quantitative data, we were able to calculate the correctness and completeness of the approach. For us, a correct feature is a feature that was validated by the expert group, so we can obtain data on correctness and completeness by comparing the unvalidated product map produced by CaVE with the validated product map validated by the experts (measurement point M3 in Figure 17.3). As finding information from documents is an information-retrieval task, we can use measures from information retrieval here (Alves et al. 2008; Baeza-Yates and Ribeiro-Neto 1999). Following the formulas for recall and the precision of an information retrieval approach (Baeza-Yates and Ribeiro-Neto 1999), we can calculate correctness and completeness as:

Completeness (features) = [number of correct features identified by CaVE]/ [number of correct features in the final and corrected product-feature matrix] (17.1)

Correctness (features) = [number of correct features identified by CaVE]/ [number of all features identified by CaVE] (17.2)

We can also use these formulas to calculate completeness and correctness of the commonalities and variabilities found. An information-retrieval approach provides good results if it has a high correctness/precision and completeness/recall. Having a high correctness has a higher importance than having a high completeness in our case. Producing false results that have to be deleted manually is not acceptable in most cases, as the deletion of false positives during a workshop is very tedious work.

2. *Second case study goal*: Show that the approach reduces the expert load. The domain experts in our case were the scoping-workshop participants from IBS AG. The participants were seven experts from different business units, all being technical or marketing experts in the production-management domain. The case study was performed by three nondomain experts of Fraunhofer IESE; one person did the CaVE analysis, and two persons led the workshop. When we define *expert load* as the time that a domain expert has to spend on finding a product-feature matrix, we can calculate expert load with the following formula:

$$\text{Expert load} = [\text{time to find a new feature}] \times$$
$$[\text{number of involved experts}] \qquad (17.3)$$

$$\text{Expert-load reduction} = [\text{time to find a new feature}] \times$$
$$[\text{number of involved experts}] \times$$
$$[\text{number of correct features found with CaVE}] \qquad (17.4)$$

Expert-load reduction is the time that the experts save through having the CaVE results. We can calculate this by giving the time that all experts have to spend in the workshop to find one feature (without having a basic product map) and multiply it with the maximum number of features that can be found with CaVE (for all other features that cannot be found by CaVE, expert involvement is needed in any case).

3. *Third case study goal*: Investigate whether the application method has biased or influenced the results. We compared potentially biased results (under the influence of CaVE) with unbiased results (found without CaVE). We planned beforehand to present one complete matrix and only parts of the other two matrices, and then to have parts of the features identified from scratch by the domain experts. By comparing the correctness of the results of the domain with the prepared matrices and the one that was only partially filled, we learned something about the influence the method has on the results. The hypothesis that we had (and that we wanted to reject) was that the correctness of the results produced by CaVE were influenced by the method, as people tend to accept things that they see written down instead of changing them when they are not exactly right.

17.4.2 Case Study Performance

As planned, the three domains *IBS general* (the overview or high-level features of the product line), *reporting* (everything concerning the structured output of information), and *user management* (the domain concerned with access rights of different users and the structuring of user groups) were analyzed with the CaVE method by one person who did not participate in the workshop (see measurement point M1 in Figure 17.3). The documentation was browsed, and relevant documentation parts for the three subdomains were identified. For *IBS general*, 62 pages were analyzed; for *reporting*, 48 pages were analyzed; and for *user management*, 33 pages were analyzed. The patterns for features, commonalities, and variabilities were selected from the pattern list. Then the patterns were applied by marking potential features in the documentation. Afterwards, an initial product map was filled for each domain. In parallel, duplicate and apparently wrong features were deleted because they were not relevant (e.g., the heading "introduction" is not a feature, although it is identified by the heading-to-feature pattern). In this step we identified 67 features in the domain *IBS general*, 51 in *reporting*, and 53 in *user management*. The nonexpert needed 210 minutes for the analysis in the domain *IBS general* (measurement point 1 in Figure 17.3, comprising the preparation and search steps of the CaVE method).

The scoping workshop served as the selection step of the CaVE method (measurement point 2 in Figure 17.3). The workshop was performed as a one-day workshop for product line mapping. The workshop was led by two persons from Fraunhofer IESE that were not familiar with the CaVE method and did not know the results of the CaVE analysis before. Seven domain experts from IBS AG were present at the workshop. During the workshop, there was a focus shift. The two domains *user management* and *reporting* could not be analyzed, and the domain *masterdata* was analyzed instead. So a product map for the domain *masterdata* (the domain concerned with relatively static data characterizing the user of the software and the company context) was built from scratch instead because it fit better into the product line strategy. This decision was taken by all workshop participants together, as the general goal (getting appropriate results for scoping) was more important for the workshop than the case study results. The product map for *IBS general* was corrected and extended in the workshop. Table 17.2 shows an excerpt of the product map. The product map for the domain *masterdata* was filled from scratch. In order to still fit into our case study goal, the domain *masterdata* was analyzed with CaVE after the workshop (85 pages of documentation were analyzed; the nonexpert needed 50 minutes for the analysis of the documentation and preparation of the unvalidated product map), so we still had two domains where we could compare completeness and correctness and get some data on method bias.

17.4.3 Case Study Results

The results of the case study are shown in Table 17.3. For correctness and completeness, we compared the unvalidated product map with the validated product map (see Figure 17.3, measurement point 3). In the first domain we analyzed, *IBS general*, we found 67 features with the CaVE analysis of the user documentation. Of these features, 60 of 67 were approved by the experts in the workshop, and 7 features were rejected. In addition, there were 102 new features found in the workshop. So we can calculate the completeness of the CaVE results with the formulas given in Section 17.4.1 as 37% and a correctness of almost 90%.

The commonalities and variabilities in the features can be analyzed similarly: If we count an "X" or a " " in the product map as a commonality or variability between the products, we come to a maximum number of 300 commonalities and variabilities that could be found with CaVE (60 correct features × 5 existing products). Nearly all of the elements (290 of 300) were assigned (10 were marked as unclear), but 4 of these unclear elements stayed after the validation, so we had a total of 296 validated elements. CaVE correctly assigned 264 of them, and 32 were

Table 17.2 Excerpt of the Product Map of the Domain "IBS General"

Subdomain	No.	Feature	Automotive	LIMS	PRISMA	Professional	Future Products
Configuration	76	Web interface	X			X	
	77	Unicode					
	78	Language configuration					X
	79	.....					
Analysis	85	LIMS-report		X			
Reporting	86	Printing	X	X	X	X	X
	87	Data warehouse	X	X			

Table 17.3   Case Study Results

IBS General Domain	Features	C+V		Masterdata Domain	Features	C+V
Number of elements found with CaVE	67	290		Number of elements found with CaVE	97	391
Number of correct elements CaVE	60	264		Number of correct elements CaVE	79	310
Number of elements after validation	162	296		Number of elements after validation	93	395
Completeness/Recall	**37.0%**	**89.2%**		**Completeness/Recall**	**84.9%**	**78.5%**
Correctness/Precision	**89.6%**	**91.0%**		**Correctness/Precision**	**81.4%**	**79.3%**
IBS General Domain	*CaVE*	*Workshop*		*Masterdata Domain*	*CaVE*	*Workshop*
Duration (analysis/ workshop) [min]	210	120		Duration (analysis/ workshop) [min]	50	30
Time/feature per person [min]	3.56	0.74		Time/feature per person [min]	0.51	0.32
Overall expert-load reduction [h]		**5.18**		**Potential expert-load reduction [h]**		**2.95**

Note: C+V represents commonalities and variabilities.

changed during the workshop. So we obtained correctness and completeness values of 89.2% correctness and 91.0% completeness for commonalities and variabilities.

When we calculated expert load and expert-load reduction, we came to the following results. When we used the time that was needed to find or validate a feature (time spent with the product map/number of features), we came to the value of 120/162 = 0.74 minutes per feature, with a workshop duration of 120 minutes and 162 correct features found (see Table 17.3). As validating an existing feature is surely less time-consuming than finding a new one, this is a conservative guess for the time to find a new feature. With this value we came to an expert-load reduction of 0.74 minutes × 7 (experts) × 60 (correct features found with CaVE) = 5.18 hours of total expert-load reduction, so we have almost one hour less effort per expert in this case.

In the second domain, *masterdata*, we found 97 features with the CaVE analysis of the user documentation. When comparing the features we found in the documentation with the features found in the workshop, 79 features were identical, and all in all 93 features were identified in the workshop (so 18 features found with CaVE could not be mapped to correct IBS features). So we obtained the completeness of the CaVE results of 84.9% and a correctness of 81.4%. When following the procedure to evaluate commonalities and variabilities in this section, we obtained the values given in Table 17.3: 78.5% correctness and 79.3% completeness.

In this domain we can only speak of a potential expert-load reduction, as the CaVE results and the workshop results were built up independently. When using the values for duration and the number of correct features, we come to 0.32 minutes × 7 (experts) × 79 (correct features) = 2.95 hours of (potential) expert-load reduction that we could have reached with a CaVE analysis and a presentation of a partially filled product-feature matrix in a workshop.

17.4.4 Case Study Analysis

When analyzing the case study results we can make the following observations:

Correctness: The correctness of the CaVE results was quite high in both domains, with almost 90% and 81%, respectively. This high correctness is very important, as it is essential to not have too many false positives and thus have many rejections of suggested features during the workshop. With a high correctness, all participants can trust in the method and its results.

Completeness of features: There was quite a large difference in completeness of features in both domains. In the general domain we only had a completeness of 37%, and in the *masterdata* domain we had a high completeness of almost 85%. When analyzing the features that the CaVE analysis missed, we could identify two reasons:

1. Many of the features added at the workshop were features that were put into different subdomains/different parts of the product map by the CaVE analysis. In parallel, parts of the respective documentation were not selected in the browsing phase of the CaVE analysis, and so some of the features were left out. For example, there were more than 40 features that were assigned to the subdomain *masterdata* of the *IBS general* domain that were identified as subdomain features in the later CaVE analysis and not overview features of the *IBS general* domain.
2. There were 46 features that were purely innovative features. So these features will only occur in future products. Of course these features cannot be found in existing documentation, so this reason is inherent to the method. But having the basic features already present helps in concentrating on the interesting new features.

Nevertheless, the completeness of commonalities and variabilities was quite high in both domains with, 91% and 79.3%, respectively.

Analysis speed: In the domain *masterdata*, the analysis speed was quite high (0.32 minutes to find a feature), although there was no predefined product map present. During a part of the workshop, the experts used a table in the user documentation for one system themselves to list parts of the *masterdata* features. So they followed parts of the strategy proposed by CaVE themselves, without knowing about the CaVE approach. But this live analysis is only possible if the information is already in the form of a list or table and not if the features are scattered around hundreds of pages of documentation.

Expert-load reduction: In both domains a certain amount of expert-load reduction could be shown. If we calculate expert-load reduction with the formula given in Section 17.4.1, we come to an expert-load reduction of 5.18 hours in the case of the *IBS general* domain. It can be expected that the duration of the workshop would have been 44 minutes longer (5.18 hours expert-load reduction/7) had we not had the CaVE results present (or fewer features would have been identified), so we have an expert-load reduction of 37% (44 minutes/2 hours). In the *masterdata* domain, the already fast analysis could have been speeded up by prepared results (see Table 17.3).

Overall reduction of analysis time: If we compare the absolute time for an analysis, we do not only come to expert-load reduction, but to an overall reduction of analysis time with CaVE. In the domain *IBS general*, the nonexpert needed 210 minutes for the preparation and analysis of the documentation, and the experts needed 840 minutes (120 × 7 experts), or, if we add the time of the two product line analysts, even 1080 minutes. So with CaVE we found 0.29 correct features/minute (60 correct features/210 minutes), while during the workshop only 1.35 features per minute were found (162 correct features/120 minutes). In the domain *masterdata* we found 1.58 correct features/minute (79 correct features/50 minutes), while during the workshop only

0.44 features per minute were found (93 correct features/[30 × 7] minutes). So in both domains, CaVE worked faster than the experts if we sum up all the expert time. But nevertheless, the expert time is still needed to a certain extent for clarifications and discussions of features and for finding innovative functionality. With CaVE it is possible to focus on these issues and not repeat the boring standard features over and over again.

Method bias: Our initial plan for identifying the method bias was foiled by the changing domain focus during the workshop. But when we compare the correctness of the two domains, we see that both values are comparable (for features: 89.6% for changing results that were prepared with CaVE vs. 81.4% for results that were won independently; for commonalities and variabilities: 91.0% compared to 79.3%). We cannot give any significance for this two-value set, but the high completeness in all cases gives hope that there is no strong method bias, so that the workshop participants do not tend to just accept the CaVE results even though they might be wrong. Nevertheless, there is a difference of about 10% when comparing the commonalities and variabilities, so if one wants to be sure of having no method bias, it would be a possibility to only present the features in the product map—but not the commonalities and variabilities—as prepared X's in the product map.

17.4.5 Threats to Validity

Additionally, we identified the following three threads to the validity of our analysis:

1. There surely exist different domain types. Domains can be well known or unknown; they can be cohesive or scattered (Schmid 2003). The influence of the domain type on the results is unclear, and with only two data points we cannot give any values for the influence.
2. Both analyses were part of a one-day workshop. It is unclear if there is either (a) an influence of fatigue that results in potentially more correct and complete results during the first analysis at the beginning of the workshop or (b) a learning effect (e.g., learning about the structure of the product map, getting familiar with the workshop atmosphere) that led to more correct and complete results during the second analysis.
3. The experimenter bias—the influence that a method developer naturally has in presenting his or her method in a positive light and to get good results—was eliminated by using staff that was not familiar with the method when performing the workshop. Nevertheless, the patterns were applied by the method developer, so there still might be some form of bias. Especially when comparing the overall reduction of analysis time, the fact that the nonexpert was very familiar with the method and the patterns surely speeded up the CaVE analysis.

17.4.6 Comparison to Other Studies

As this was not the first study we performed, we can compare the results of this study to the other study described by John (2006). The case study was performed in a small company and had the goals to show correctness and completeness of CaVE and to give a value for expert-load reduction. There was only one overview domain analyzed. The completeness of the CaVE results was 87%, and the correctness was 95%. So the value for correctness was comparable to the value in this case study. The value for completeness was higher than in the *IBS general* domain, probably because the goal of the scoping workshop was not to identify innovative, not-yet-existing features, but to find features for a small product derived from the existing product line. Additionally, the documentation was smaller (only 28 pages for each product) and was analyzed completely, so there was no problem with the selection of the right documentation part. For expert-load reduction, the domain experts were asked in a questionnaire for how many hours they would assess the analysis; their average estimate was 16 hours. In this case study, the total time for the analysis was 9.6 hours. Of these 9.6 hours, 3.3 hours were expert hours, and 6.3 hours were nonexpert (product line analyst) hours, so we have an estimated expert-load reduction of 12.6 hours.

In the experiment we performed we had a group of 45 students that performed a CaVE analysis on different documentation. For finding features we came to a correctness value of 96% accompanied by a completeness of only 13%. The low completeness was a result of very strict time restrictions, so no student had enough time to complete the analysis of the whole documentation. The correctness nevertheless is comparable to the results that we found in the IBS case study and in the earlier case study. So we can recapitulate that CaVE produces correct results (between 81.4% in the domain *masterdata* and 96% in the experiment) in different contexts and different domains.

17.5 Conclusions

In this chapter we showed how information for scoping can be extracted from user documentation. We presented the CaVE approach for structured elicitation and validated the approach in a case study. The case study shows that the correctness of the results provided by the approach lies over 85% and that the completeness of the results is between 37% and 84.9%. We also showed that, using this approach, the expert load of the domain experts can be reduced by several hours per subdomain. Although not all information that is needed for scoping can be found in documents (for example, business goals cannot be found in user documentation), a significant part of the information that is needed can be extracted from documents, and so the expert time can be spent for other tasks.

Comparison with other case studies where the same approach was applied showed that the completeness and correctness of the results is comparable over different domains and that the correctness of the results especially is on a high level, with at least 79%.

With the scoping activities at IBS, detailed recommendations for a product line introduction strategy in different areas (e.g., overall product line potential, establishment of family engineering, development of overlapping domain expertise, and development of generic reusable components) could be given. The results of the scoping activities are currently under review by IBS AG and will be used in defining a product line strategy for future product developments based on .NET technology.

For the CaVE approach, the following extensions are planned:

- Further patterns for scoping artifacts
- Partial automation in a tool using information retrieval techniques like the Vector Space Model (Alves et al. 2008)
- Additional analysis of graphical elements (e.g., models)

Acknowledgments

This work was partially supported by the Project "LifeCycleQM," funded by German Ministry of Education and Research (BMBF) under grant number 01 IS E05.

References

Alves, V., C. Schwanninger, L. Barbosa, et al. 2008. An exploratory study of information retrieval techniques in domain analysis. In *Proceedings of the 12th international software product line conference* (SPLC 2008), 67–76. Washington, DC: IEEE Computer Society.

Baeza-Yates, R., and B. Ribeiro-Neto. 1999. *Modern information retrieval.* Harlow, England: Addison-Wesley.

Bayer, J., O. Flege, P. Knauber, et al. 1999. PuLSE: A methodology to develop software product lines. In *Proceedings of the symposium on software reusability* (SSR '99), 122–131. New York: ACM.

Boeckle, G., P. Clements, J. McGregor, D. Muthig, and K. Schmid. 2004. Calculating ROI for software product lines. *IEEE Software* 21 (3): 23–31.

Clements, P., and L. Northrop. 2001. *Software product lines: Practices and patterns.* Reading, MA: Addison-Wesley.

Cohen, L. 1995. *Quality function deployment.* Reading, MA: Addison-Wesley.

El Emam, K., J. N. Drouin, and W. Melo. 1998. *SPICE: The theory and practice of software process improvement and capability determination.* Washington, DC: IEEE Computer Society.

Fantechi, A., S. Gnesi, I. John, G. Lami, and J. Dörr. 2004. Elicitation of use cases for product lines. In *Proceedings of the fifth workshop on product family engineering* (PFE5), 152–167. Lecture Notes in Computer Science, vol. 3014. Berlin/Heidelberg: Springer.

Herzwurm, G., S. Schockert, and A. Helferich. 2005. QFD-PPP: Product line portfolio planning using quality function deployment. In *Proceedings of the 2005 software product line conference* (SPLC 2005), 162–173. Lecture Notes in Computer Science, vol. 3154. Berlin/Heidelberg: Springer.

John, I. 2006. Capturing product line information from legacy user documentation. In *Software product lines: Research issues in engineering and management*, ed. T. Käkölä and J. C. Dueñas. Berlin/Heidelberg: Springer.

John, I., J. Knodel, T. Lehner, and D. Muthig. 2006 . A practical guide to product line scoping. In *Proceedings of the 10th international software product line conference* (SPLC 2006), 3–12. Washington, DC: IEEE Computer Society.

John, I., D. Muthig, and M. Schmettow. 2004. The state of the practice of systematic software development/product line development in Germany. IESE-Report, 071.04/E. Fraunhofer IESE.

Kang, K., S. Cohen, J. Hess, W. Novak, and S. Peterson. 1990. Feature-oriented domain analysis (FODA) feasibility study. Technical report CMU/SEI-90-TR-21, Carnegie Mellon University, Pittsburgh.

Knauber, P., D. Muthig, K. Schmid, and T. Widen. 2000. Applying product line concepts in small and medium-sized companies. *IEEE Software* 17 (5): 88–95.

Lethbridge, T. C., J. Singer, and A. Forward. 2003. How software engineers use documentation: The state of the practice. *IEEE Software* 20 (6): 35–39.

Melchisedech, R. 1998. Investigation of requirements documents written in natural language. *Requirements Engineering* 3 (2): 91–97.

Olsson, T., and P. Runeson. 2002. Document use in software development: A qualitative survey. In *Proceedings of the second conference on software engineering research and practise in Sweden* (SERPS'02).

Robertson, D., and K. Ulrich. 1998. Planning for product platforms. *Sloan Management Review* 39 (4): 19–31.

Schmid, K. 2000. A method for scoping software product lines from a functional point of view. IESE-Report 041.00/E, Fraunhofer IESE.

Schmid, K. 2003. Planning software reuse: A disciplined scoping approach for software product lines. PhD thesis in experimental software engineering, Fraunhofer IRB.

Sommerville, I. 2000. *Software engineering*, 6th ed. Reading, MA: Addison-Wesley.

Taborda, L. 2004. Generalized release planning for product line architectures. In *Proceedings of the third software product line conference* (SPLC 2004), 238–254. Lecture Notes in Computer Science, vol. 3154. Berlin/Heidelberg: Springer.

Thiel, S., and F. Peruzzi. 2000. Starting a product line approach for an envisioned market. In *Proceedings of the first software product line conference: Experience and research directions* (SPLC1), 495–512. Norwell, MA: Kluwer.

Yin, R. 2003. *Case study research: Design and methods*, 3rd ed. Newbury Park, CA: Sage Publications.

Van Zyl, J., and A. J. Walker. 2000. Strategic product development. In *Proceedings of the first software product line conference: Experience and research directions* (SPLC1), 85–110. Norwell, MA: Kluwer.

Chapter 18

Model-Driven, Aspect-Oriented Product Line Engineering: An Industrial Case Study

Iris Groher
Johannes Kepler University Linz, Austria

Christa Schwanninger
Siemens AG, Erlangen, Germany

Markus Voelter
Independent consultant, Goeppingen, Germany

Contents

18.1 Introduction and Motivation

Software product line engineering (SPLE) (Pohl et al. 2005; Clements and Northrop 2001) aims to reduce development time, effort, cost, and complexity by taking advantage of the commonalities within a portfolio of similar products. Most high-tech companies provide products for a specific market. Those products usually tend to have many things in common. An increasing number of these companies realize that product line development fosters strategic reuse at all stages of the life cycle, shortens development time, and helps staying competitive.

Commonalities between products in the portfolio as well as the flexibility to adapt to different product requirements are captured in so-called core assets. Those reusable assets are created during *domain engineering*. During *application engineering*, products are either automatically or manually assembled using the core assets and completed with product-specific artifacts.

The effectiveness of a software product line approach directly depends on how well feature variability within the portfolio is managed from early analysis to implementation and through maintenance and evolution. Though software product lines aim to simplify software development and improve reuse by managing variations of a software across different operational contexts, they themselves tend to become quite complex. Variations often have widespread impact on multiple artifacts in multiple life-cycle stages, making their effective management a predominant engineering challenge in SPLE. For example, variations in the persistence or security policies employed by products in a product line can have a widespread impact on

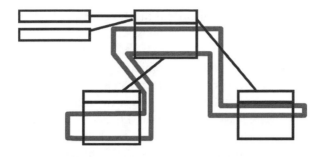

Figure 18.1 The effect of crosscutting.

the different kinds of artifacts, from requirements to test specifications. They are also spread over multiple assets within one artifact type, i.e., they *crosscut* various requirements documents, designs, code, and test artifacts. Figure 18.1 illustrates the effect of crosscutting. The red line represents a feature that is scattered across many different modules.

Another important pitfall is that features and architecture are often derived from requirements in a nonsystematic, ad hoc way without documenting the reasoning behind architectural decisions (Grünbacher et al. 2004). For software product lines, it is essential to know the relationships between requirements, the derived architecture, the design, and the implementation artifacts, since all artifacts have to be reusable and evolvable over time. Without knowing the relationships among these artifacts, product line evolution becomes unmanageable. Consequently, a systematic way to group requirements into features that are then related to architectural entities and seamless tracing of requirements throughout the whole life cycle is necessary. This is a difficult task, as variability tends to crosscut multiple regions within artifacts as well as different artifacts in the software development life cycle.

Especially, the mapping between *problem space* and *solution space* is not trivial. The problem space is concerned with end-user understandable concepts representing the business domain of the product line. The solution space deals with the elements necessary for implementing the solution, typically IT-relevant artifacts. There is a many-to-many relationship between entities in the problem space (requirements and features) to entities in the solution space (software components). This causes a strong need for a formally defined mapping between problem and solution space rather than an ad hoc definition of a product line architecture based on domain requirements.

Moreover, the effects of variability and, in particular, new variations brought on by evolution, tend to propagate in ways that cannot be easily modeled or managed. New requirements may necessitate changes to code, design, documentation, and user manuals, amongst many other artifacts and assets that go into making a product line. Ensuring the traceability of requirements and their variations throughout the software life cycle is key for successful software development in general and a successful product line in particular.

Based on these deficiencies in current SPLE practice, we identify the following challenges:

- An improved modularization of variability is necessary to deal with the often crosscutting characteristics of feature implementations in the solution space.
- A systematic treatment of variability across the software life cycle is vital for successful software mass customization. Efficient reuse requires a systematic derivation of a product line architecture from domain requirements. Based on a flexible architecture, the subsequent implementation of reusable domain artifacts needs to be clearly reasoned and documented.
- Advanced maintenance of (forward and backward) traceability of variations is needed to avoid an unmanageable propagation of variability brought by evolution. This is vitally important, as the number of variation points typically increases during the life cycle of a product line.

Model-driven software development (MDSD) (Stahl and Voelter 2006; Greenfield et al. 2004) and aspect-oriented software development (AOSD) (Filman et al. 2004; Kiczales et al. 1997) are two promising technologies for improving the modularity, composability, evolvability, and reusability of software systems, which are complementary in nature. AOSD can improve the way in which software is modularized, localizing its variability in independent aspects, while MDSD can help to raise the level of abstraction and to manage traceability from model to model.

Our model-driven, aspect-oriented SPLE approach (Voelter and Groher 2007a) targets the aforementioned challenges by providing concepts and tools to facilitate variability implementation, management, and tracing from requirements modeling to implementation of product lines. In this chapter we present an industrial case study conducted at Siemens AG that shows how our approach effectively supports the development of a product line during domain engineering and a systematic product derivation during application engineering.

The remainder of this chapter is organized as follows: Section 18.2 provides an overview of the approach we propose. Section 18.3 presents the industrial case study of a home-automation product line. In Section 18.4 our approach is evaluated by analyzing the results of the case study. We conclude with a discussion of related work and a summary in Sections 18.5 and 18.6.

18.2 Integrating Models and Aspects into Product Line Engineering

Our approach uses models to describe product lines. Transformations generate products as members of the product line. Aspect-oriented (AO) techniques are used to help define the variants in the models as well as in the transformers and generators. There is a similarity to the concept of join points in aspect-orientation and variation points in SPLE. In AO, join points are those elements of the programming language semantics with which the aspects coordinate. In product lines, variation points represent variability subjects within domain artifacts (Pohl et al. 2005). Domain artifacts include all kinds of development artifacts, such as requirements, architecture, design, code, and tests. This similarity in the concept of a variation point and a join point makes AO a well-suited candidate for implementing variability.

We distinguish between structural and configurative variability. Languages describing configurative variability support the configuration of the system to be built basically by choosing from a number of options. Feature modeling languages, for example, describe configurative variability. Languages that describe structural variability allow users to creatively instantiate and connect language elements. They are typically more complex than configuration languages but provide the most flexibility. The Unified Modeling Language (UML), for example, is a language that allows users to create any kind of model that conforms to the UML metamodel.

An overview of our approach[*] is given in Figure 18.2. Variable domain requirements are captured in a problem-space metamodel. Based on product requirements, a problem-space model is created that is an instance of the problem-space metamodel. The problem-space metamodel defines the vocabulary and grammar, i.e., the abstract syntax, used to build the problem-space model. The model itself is built using a Domain Specific Language (DSL) (Stahl and Voelter 2006). A DSL is a formalism for building models. It encompasses a metamodel (in this case the problem-space metamodel) as well as a definition of a concrete syntax that is used to represent the model. The concrete syntax can be textual, graphical, or expressed in tables, trees, or dialogs. It is essential that the concrete syntax can sensibly represent the concepts of the domain the DSL is built for. A suitable editor has to be provided that supports the creation of models using the DSL. This DSL captures the structural variability of the product line, i.e., how the different domain entities are composed and interlinked. Using the DSL, an infinite number of valid models can be created. It is important to understand that the problem-space model only deals with domain concepts and does not contain anything concerned with the actual implementation of those concepts.

Both problem-space metamodels and problem-space models can be configured using AO on a model level by adding optional model parts to a minimal core. Figure 18.3 illustrates the concept of model weaving. A given base model (M A) and an aspect model (M Aspect) are composed. The aspect model consists of pointcut definitions that capture the points where, in the base model, additional model elements should be added. The aspect element A* that contains the pointcut definition is marked with a dotted box. In addition to the pointcut definitions, the aspect

---

[*] Our tool suite is part of openArchitectureWare 4.3 and can be downloaded from http://www. openarchitectureware.org/.

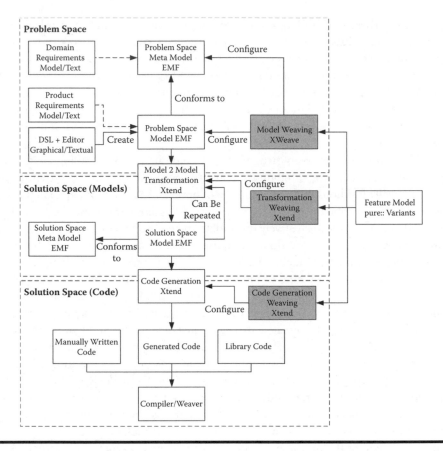

Figure 18.2   Model-driven aspect-oriented product line engineering.

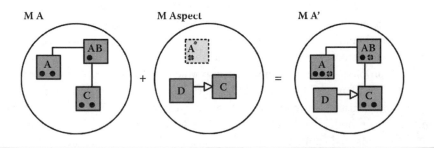

Figure 18.3   Model weaving.

model contains advices that represent the elements to be added. The aspect model uses both name matching and pointcut expressions to select the desired join points. In the example, the model element D of the aspect model M Aspect that is derived from element C is added to the result model. The weaving rule applied here is simple name matching. The elements named C in both models correspond, so both elements are combined. This results in C having a new child D in the result model. The aspect element A* specifies that the dotted gray element within A* should be added to all base elements whose name starts with A, in this case element A and element AB. This is an example of a pointcut expression. After the weaving process, a result model (M A') is created that contains all the original base model elements plus the aspect elements added at the desired join points.

The solution space describes the implementation of the product using software technologies. An architectural metamodel is created (or an existing metamodel is used) that supports the definition of a concrete system architecture. The architecture metamodel defines the terms we can use for defining architecture models. The solution-space metamodel can be platform independent or platform specific.

A formal mapping is defined between the problem-space metamodel and the solution-space metamodel that allows for an automatic transformation of a problem-space model into a corresponding solution-space model. The mapping need not be done in one single step, but can be modularized into a sequence of transformations. For example, one could first map the problem-space metamodel to a platform-independent solution-space metamodel and map this metamodel to a platform-specific metamodel. This separation makes it possible to easily support different platform technologies. An important advantage of using model transformations is that a clean separation between the models and also between the metamodels can be achieved. Additionally, the problem-space metamodel and the various solution-space metamodels can evolve independently.

Model transformations can be configured using AO on a transformation level. The transformation of model elements can, for example, be configured based on the presence or absence of nonfunctional requirements. The transformation language Xtend (openArchitectureWare 2008) has been extended with support for aspects. Aspects can be linked to features, which allows us to capture variable parts of transformations in transformation aspects. If and only if a certain feature is part of a configuration, the transformation advice is executed. Figure 18.4 illustrates how this is realized. A transformation script contains a set of transformation steps. An advice defined within a transformation aspect can intercept the execution of such a step and add additional transformation behavior to it. The original transformation is called within the workflow. Depending on whether a certain feature is selected in the current configuration, the transformation aspect is activated in the workflow. In the case that the transformation aspect is activated, the advice adds additional transformation behavior to the original transformation. Using aspects allows for a clear separation between common and variable parts of model transformations. The core transformation only contains the transformation steps common to all

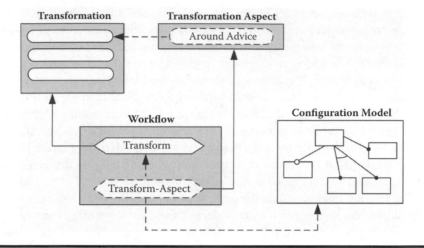

Figure 18.4   Variability in model transformations.

products of the product line. Optional parts of the transformation are captured in transformation aspects.

To be able to link features defined in a feature model to aspects, the variant management tool pure::variants (pure systems GmbH 2006) has been integrated into our tool suite (Groher et al. 2007). Within our tooling, a pure::variants variant model is used to describe the global configuration of the product line. Such a global configuration model can be queried and, hence, MDSD activities can be performed based on the selection of features. Workflow components, model transformations, and code-generation templates can be linked to features. Their execution then depends on the presence or absence of features in the configuration model.

To create a running system, code is generated from the solution-space model. This step can also be configured using AO on a code-generation template level. The template language Xpand (openArchitectureWare 2008) provides support for template aspects (Voelter and Groher 2007b). Again, the adaptation of code-generation templates is only required in the case that the respective features are selected in the current configuration. As with model-transformation aspects, the dependency between template aspects and features is specified in the workflow. Figure 18.5 illustrates how this is realized. A code-generation template file contains a set of templates. An advice defined within a template aspect can intercept the execution of such a template and add additional generation behavior to it. The original template is called within the workflow. Depending on whether a certain feature is selected in the current configuration, the template aspect is activated in the workflow. In the case that the template aspect is activated, the advice adds additional behavior to the original generator. Aspect-orientation on a code-generation template level allows us to selectively adapt code generators. Aspects can be linked to features, which allows us to capture variable parts of the generator in generation aspects.

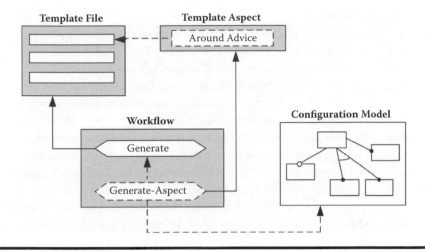

Figure 18.5   Variability in code-generation templates.

As a 100% code generation is not realistic, manually written code has to be integrated with the generated code in well-defined ways. Also, it might be necessary to integrate prebuilt reusable components into the generated system. Due to the fact that in our approach all artifacts have representations on a model level, we can process them using model transformations. Based on the information in the models, we can determine whether a given component (either manually written or prebuilt) is part of a product and thus has to be integrated.

Due to the fact that in real-world product lines it is necessary to include manually written code for customer-specific requirements into a product, variability on source code level is an issue. We use aspect-oriented programming (AOP) (Kiczales et al. 1997) to implement variability on the code level.

18.3 Industrial Case Study

This section illustrates the case study we conducted at Siemens AG, a home-automation system called *Smart Home*. The main challenge of such a product line is the large amount of both structural and configurative variability that has to be implemented in domain engineering and then bound to concrete variants in application engineering. We demonstrate how our approach and the tool suite we provide were used to solve this challenge.

18.3.1 Home Automation Domain

In homes there are a wide range of electrical and electronic devices such as lights, thermostats, electric blinds, fire and smoke detection sensors, white goods such as washing machines, as well as entertainment equipment. Smart Home connects those devices and enables inhabitants to monitor and control them from a common user interface. The home network also allows the devices to coordinate their behavior in order to fulfill complex tasks without human intervention.

Sensors are devices that measure physical properties of the environment and make them available to Smart Home. Controllers activate devices whose state can be monitored and changed. All installed devices are part of the Smart Home network. The status of devices can either be changed by inhabitants via the user interface or by the system using predefined policies. Policies let the system act autonomously in the case of certain events. For example, in the case of smoke detection, windows get closed automatically and the fire brigade is called.

Varying types of houses, different customer demands, the need for a short time to market, and the desire to reduce costs drive the need for a Smart Home product line and are the main causes for variability. When building a home-automation product line, dealing with structural variability is a challenge. Device controllers can be implemented once and reused in many places, and higher level features such as heating control can also be easily encapsulated in a software module. But the different kinds, number, and distribution of devices within a home, including their specific wiring, varies considerably. Without appropriate support, software developers have to manually implement the logic that instantiates the correct number of devices, wires them, and initializes the higher level features appropriately. The subsequent sections illustrate how our approach uses models and aspects to automate the product-instantiation process.

18.3.2 Problem Space Modeling

To support building architects in specifying which devices should be installed where in the home and how those devices are connected, we developed a domain-specific language (DSL) that uses problem space, i.e., home automation, terminology. For this purpose, a metamodel is defined that contains entities of the home-automation domain. Figure 18.6 shows parts of the problem-space metamodel of Smart Home. Buildings contain floors and floors contain rooms. Staircases connect the different floors in the house. Different kinds of devices are located in rooms. Note that this model does not contain anything concerned with software or computing hardware. It formally describes domain requirements.

Using this metamodel, a DSL is built that supports modeling Smart Home systems from the perspective of a building architect or a home owner. The syntax is semigraphical, and a customized tree view is developed using the Eclipse plugin Exeed (Eclipse 2008). Figure 18.7 shows an example of a house that is modeled using the DSL. It contains one floor, the cellar, two rooms (cellar corridor and stockroom), and several devices located in those rooms. The DSL is a creative construction DSL. Alternatively, the building data could also be extracted from a CAD drawing.

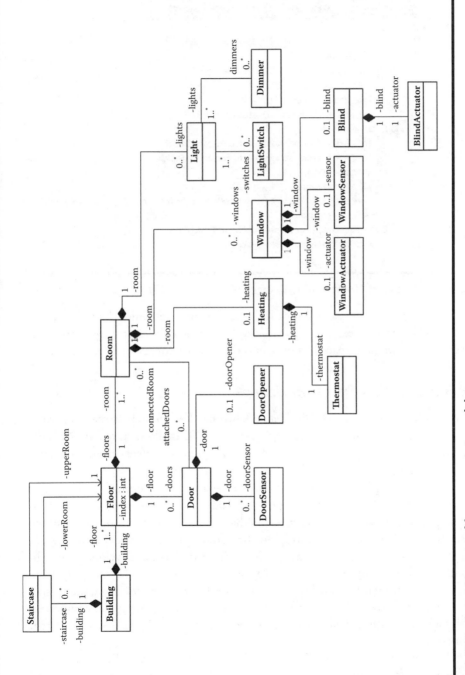

Figure 18.6   Smart Home problem-space metamodel.

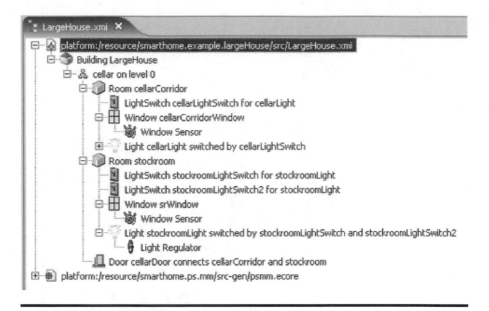

Figure 18.7   Smart Home problem-space model.

We consider the development of the problem-space metamodel a manual task performed by domain experts as part of the *Domain Requirements Engineering* process step. The problem-space metamodel is the primary input to our approach.

18.3.3 Solution-Space Modeling

Once the problem-space DSL is defined, we need to provide a mapping from problem-space elements to solution-space elements. This allows us to automatically instantiate solution-space artifacts such as software components from a concrete problem description created with the problem-space DSL.

The solution space comprises a component-based architecture. We first create a platform-neutral component metamodel and, in a second step, create a platform-specific metamodel. This separation has several benefits. First, the mapping from the problem-space metamodel to the component metamodel is simpler, as no platform-specific concerns have to be considered. Second, developers can efficiently implement several different platforms by redefining the mapping from the component metamodel to the platform-specific metamodel. No domain-specific concerns have to be considered here. Also, mappings from the component metamodel to different platform metamodels can easily be reused in different domains.

The component metamodel defines what a component actually is. We divide the metamodel into different viewpoints that each describe a certain concern of the overall metamodel. There is no need to provide a sophisticated concrete syntax for

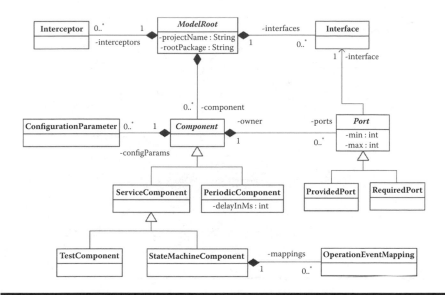

Figure 18.8 Solution-space metamodel: types viewpoint.

solution-space models, since the models are created automatically by model transformations from problem-space models.

Figure 18.8 shows the *types viewpoint* of the component metamodel. It describes component types and interfaces. Data structures, operations, and properties are specified in separate metamodels. Components can either be service components or periodic components. Service components offer services to other components, whereas periodic components consume services and are activated automatically after a specific period of time. Also, components own ports. A port can either be provided or required. A system can define a number of interceptors. Generally, a component model can either describe a concrete system or a library of reusable components.

There are three additional viewpoints, namely the *testing viewpoint*, the *channels viewpoint*, and the *configuration viewpoint*. The testing viewpoint is concerned with testing issues and the channels viewpoint addresses data replication between components. The configuration viewpoint describes component instances and how they are connected. Those are not described here as the illustrated viewpoints are sufficient for understanding the case study.

18.3.4 Solution-Space Implementation

The platform-independent component metamodel demonstrated in the previous section has to be mapped to a platform-specific metamodel. We decided to use OSGi (OSGi Alliance 2008) as the target platform, as it is the state-of-the-art platform in the home-automation domain.

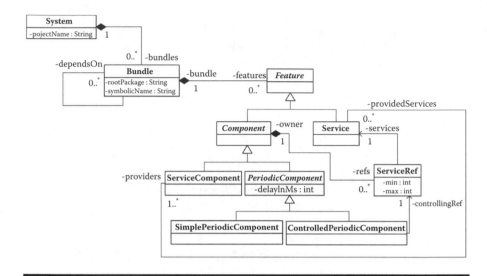

Figure 18.9   OSGi metamodel.

Figure 18.9 shows the OSGi metamodel we developed. Similar to the component metamodel, the OSGi metamodel contains service components and periodic components. Service components provide services and periodic components consume services. A system consists of a set of bundles that can depend on each other. Bundles contain a set of features that can either be services or components. Concrete components are service components, simple periodic components, or controlled periodic components. For controlled periodic components, the lookup process within the OSGi runtime can be controlled.

18.3.5 Mapping from Problem Space to Solution Space

We develop mappings from the problem-space metamodel to the component metamodel and from there to the OSGi metamodel. These mappings allow us to automatically transform the model provided by the building architect to an OSGi-specific component model.

In the last step, we generate code from the OSGi model. We therefore develop a code generator based on the OSGi metamodel. We distinguish between two kinds of generated code, namely platform-independent code and platform-dependent code. Platform-agnostic Java code is generated wherever possible. This part is completely independent of the target platform. Manually written code, i.e., business logic code, only depends on the platform-independent code. This is important to guarantee that the same manually written code can be used within different runtime platforms. The generated platform-independent code basically comprises base classes, interfaces, and Java Beans as well as a number of technical interfaces that are subsequently implemented by the OSGi generation layer.

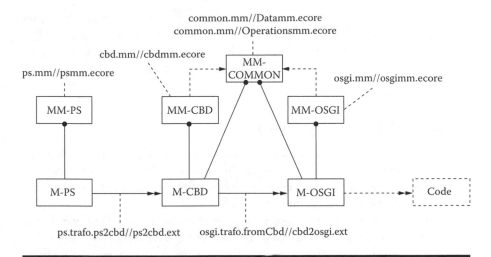

Figure 18.10   Smart Home models and transformations overview.

Figure 18.10 illustrates the metamodels, models, and transformation steps of the Smart Home product line. The problem-space model (M-PS) that conforms to the problem-space metamodel (MM-PS) is transformed into a platform-independent component model (M-CBD). This model is transformed into an OSGi model (M-OSGI). Component model and OSGi model conform to their respective metamodels (MM-CBD and MM-OSGI). Operations and data types are common to those metamodels and are therefore modeled in separate metamodels (MM-COMMON). The separate metamodels are integrated using XJoin (openArchitectureWare 2008). Finally, code is generated from the OSGi model.

18.3.6 Smart Home Component Library

To a large extent, Smart Home systems consist of a specific arrangement of prebuilt sensors and actuators (although a specific system can have custom devices). It therefore makes sense to keep a library of software components that control certain types of hardware. We use a combination of manually written code and models to represent these components in order to be able to use them to define a given system. Based on the problem-space model, the transformation instantiates, wires, and deploys those library software components.

In the Smart Home product line, library component code is partly generated and partly handwritten. It does not depend on the concrete implementation technology (such as OSGi). Base classes (and other skeleton artifacts) are generated, and the manually written business logic code is integrated in well-defined ways.

Code that is specific to the concrete component container technology (in this case OSGi) is completely generated. It wraps or uses the platform-independent code and adapts it to the concrete platform technology.

The Smart Home library contains prebuilt components, interfaces, and data types that are needed for building Smart Home systems. Interfaces and data types are model only, whereas components are model/code mixed, because they contain manually written code parts. The library comes with a model file as well as a source code directory.

18.3.7 Orthogonal Variability

With what we provide so far, a building architect can easily specify which kinds of devices should go where in a home and how those devices are interconnected. Developers can model different instances of houses and automatically generate the appropriate implementation from them.

However, there exists another form of variability that is hard to solve with the means presented so far. This kind of variability typically incorporates features that are *orthogonal* to the house structure. By orthogonal we mean variability that affects multiple domain entities and their subsequent processing (i.e., transformation and generation) steps. For example, building architects often want to deploy automation scenarios onto the house such as intrusion control where all available glass-break sensors, cameras, and movement sensors are involved together with sirens and flashing lights.

We use a global feature model to incorporate such features. This configurative variability is realized using AO at the appropriate levels. The variant management tool pure::variants (pure systems GmbH 2006) is used for feature modeling. Figure 18.11 shows the feature model of Smart Home. We use the feature modeling notation introduced by Czarnecki and Eisenecker (1999). It provides several automation features that let the house act autonomously according to defined policies. Additionally, it provides debugging and testing features and several alternatives with respect to deployment.

18.3.7.1 Automatic Windows

The Automatic Windows feature automatically opens the windows if the temperature in a room raises above a certain threshold and closes them if the temperature falls below a certain threshold. For this feature to be included in a configuration, the necessary devices have to be woven into the building model.

Figure 18.12 shows the aspect model that is responsible for weaving the respective devices into the example house shown in Figure 18.7. It weaves a thermometer in every room that has at least one window and adds a window actuator to the windows. The pointcut expressions used in the aspect model are shown in Listing 18.1. The expression rooms in Listing 18.1 returns all rooms that have windows. This pointcut expression is referenced with %rooms in the aspect model. The % sign is used because the expression *rooms* returns a set of elements. To all of them a thermometer should be added, and thermoName is a helper function that creates

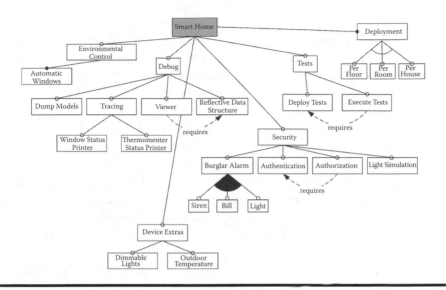

Figure 18.11 Smart Home feature model.

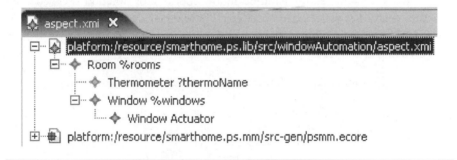

Figure 18.12 Window automation aspect.

a sensible name for this thermometer. The thermoName expression is referenced with ?thermoName in the aspect model. The ? sign is used because the thermoName expression returns a String expression. The expression *windows* returns all windows of these rooms and a window actuator is added to them. The windows expression is referenced with %windows in the aspect model. The % sign is used because the expression windows returns a set of elements.

Listing 18.1. Window automation pointcut expressions

```
rooms(Building this) : floors.rooms.select(e|e.windows.size>0);
windows(Building this) : rooms().windows;
thermoName(Thermometer this) : ((Room)eContainer.name.
toFirstLower() +
 "Thermometer";
```

The resulting (woven) model has a thermometer in each room to measure the current temperature and a window actuator for each window to be able to automatically open or close it. If the Automatic Windows feature is present in the configuration model, XWeave (Groher and Voelter 2007) weaves the content of the aspect model into the house model. This dependency is specified in the workflow.

The additional devices have to be transformed into platform-independent components. Also, the component that includes the business logic (i.e., the logic that periodically checks the temperature and triggers the opening and closing of the windows) has to be taken from the library and added to the platform-independent component model. These additional transformation steps are implemented as a model transformation aspect. Parts of the transformation aspect and the original transformation function are shown in Listing 18.2. The function createConfig transforms a floor into an object of type Configuration. The around advice first calls the original function (cf. ctx.proceed()) and then handles the additional devices. It creates an instance of a window actuator and adds it to the list of component instances owned by the configuration. If a room has at least one window and at least one thermometer, the handleWindowCoordinator function is called. This function establishes a connection between windows and thermometers.

There is no need to change the code generator, as the variability is purely handled on a model and transformator level.

Listing 18.2. Window automation transformation advice

```
around ps2cbd::createConfig( Floor f ):
    let config = (Configuration)ctx.proceed():
          config.instances.addAll(
                  f.rooms.windows.actuator.
createInstance()) ->
          (f.rooms.windows.size > 0 &&
                  f.rooms.devices.typeSelect(Thermometer).
size > 0 )?
                  config.handleWindowCoordinator(f) : null ->
          config;
create Configuration createConfig( Floor f ):
    createTrace( f, "floor2configuration" ) ->
    setName( f.name+"FloorConfiguration" );
```

The business logic of the Automatic Windows feature (the actual opening or closing of the windows in the case that the temperature reaches or falls below a certain threshold) is prebuilt in the form of a library component and included into the final product in case the feature is selected. Since all prebuilt components have representations on the model level, we can process them using model transformations (cf. the handling of the window coordinator in Listing 18.2). Based on the information in the models, it is possible to determine whether the window automation component is part of a product or not.

18.3.7.2 Reflective Data Structures

In order to debug and control Smart Home systems, we can run a graphical user interface (GUI) with the generated application. The GUI itself is not generated. It is part of the platform and accesses the system using reflection. For this to work, certain parts of the system need to include a specific reflection layer that is used by that GUI. Specifically, if component instance states should be inspected, the data structures representing the state need to be "reflective" and, upon system startup, the state objects of each instance need to be registered with the GUI.

Of course, since this functionality is for debugging purposes only, it is optional, i.e., it depends on whether the Debug feature is selected or not.

In the following, we will only show the code-generator aspect that is used to add the reflection layer to the state data structures. The code generator for the data structures contains the following templates: typeClass generates a Java class that represents the state data structure (basically a bean with getters and setters). That template in turn calls the imports and body templates. Listing 18.3 shows the templates that will be adviced by the template aspect.

Listing 18.3. Data structure templates

```
<<DEFINE typeClass FOR ComplexType>>
    <<FILE fileName()>>
            package <<implClassPackage()>>;
            <<EXPAND imports>>
            public class <<className()>> { <<EXPAND body>> }
    <<ENDFILE>>
<<ENDDEFINE>>
<<DEFINE imports FOR ComplexType>> ... <<ENDDEFINE>>
<<DEFINE body FOR ComplexType>> ... <<ENDDEFINE>>
```

The piece of Xpand code in Listing 18.4 is the template aspect that adds the reflection layer to the generated data structures. Note how the AROUND declarations reference existing DEFINEs in order to advice them. targetDef.proceed() calls the original template.

Listing 18.4. Reflection layer template aspect

```
<<AROUND data::api::data::body FOR ComplexType>>
    <<targetDef.proceed()>>
    <<EXPAND reflectionImplementation>>
<<ENDAROUND>>
<<AROUND data::api::data::imports FOR ComplexType>>
```

```
        <<targetDef.proceed()>>
        import smarthome.common.platform.MemberMeta;
        import smarthome.common.platform.ComplexTypeMeta;
<<ENDAROUND>>
<<DEFINE reflectionImplementation FOR ComplexType>>
        private transient ComplexTypeMeta _meta = null;
        public ComplexTypeMeta _metaObject() { ... }
        public void _metaSet( MemberMeta member, Object value )
{ ... }
        public Object _metaGet( MemberMeta member ) { ... }
<<ENDDEFINE>>
```

Of course, to make this work as desired, we have to couple the aspect with the configuration model. This dependency is specified in the workflow. The template aspect is only woven in the case that the Reflective Data Structure feature is selected in the current configuration.

18.3.7.3 Burglar Detection

The Burglar Detection feature should prevent burglars from breaking into the house by providing different forms of alarm devices that inhabitants can choose. Users can install a siren, a bell, or a light, or a combination of the three.

We provide a library of components necessary for implementing the Burglar Detection feature. It includes several service components for dealing with the different types of alarm devices. It also includes a state machine that allows for defining the burglar detection algorithm.

Figure 18.13 illustrates the state machine for the Burglar Detection feature. The state machine consists of a start state, a stop state, and four simple states. The burglar detection system can be either in off, armed, attention, or alarm state. Triggered by different types of events, the state machine changes its state. Also, entry and exit actions for states are specified. Based on the state-machine model, code is generated that implements the desired algorithm.

If the Burglar Detection feature is to be included, the additional components have to be added to the platform-independent component model. This is realized by a model transformation aspect that is woven in the case that the feature is part of the current configuration. Listing 18.5 shows parts of this aspect. Within the transformation function handleBurglarAlarm, the global feature model is queried, and the respective alarm devices are transformed.

Listing 18.5. Burglar detection transformation advice

```
handleBurglarAlarm( System this ):
    let conf = createBurglarConfig(): (
            ...
        isFeatureSelected( "siren" ) ? (
```

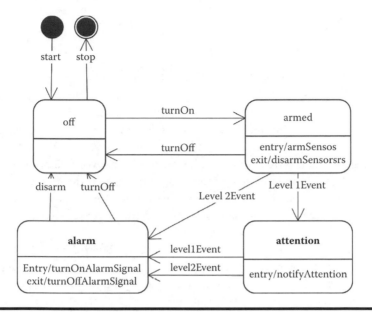

Figure 18.13   Burglar detection state machine.

```
                    let siren = conf.
addAlarmDevice("AlarmSiren"):
                          siren.configParamValues.add(
                            siren.
createConfigParamForLevel() )
          ) : null ->
          isFeatureSelected( "bell" ) ?
              conf.addAlarmDevice("AlarmBell") : null ->
          isFeatureSelected( "light" ) ?
              conf.addAlarmDevice("AlarmLight") : null
);
```

18.3.8 Application Engineering

All of the aforementioned tasks are performed during domain engineering. During application engineering, a model of the system to be built is created using the DSLs. Product requirements serve as input to this task. Furthermore, a configuration model is created by selecting a valid set of features from the feature model.

The product is automatically generated based on the system model and the configuration model. In the case that functionality not supported by the product line architecture needs to be implemented, aspect-oriented programming languages such as AspectJ (Kiczales et al. 2001) can be used. Features are implemented as code-level aspects to deliver the product in time, but these should be refactored and integrated into the product line architecture afterwards.

18.4 Evaluation

18.4.1 Challenges Revisited

In Section 18.1 we identified key challenges in current SPLE practice. The current state of the art shows that there is a lack of support for modularizing crosscutting feature implementations. Features tend to have a widespread impact on the product line artifacts and are thus hard to encapsulate in currently used programming paradigms.

Further, variability is mainly handled at the code level. We observed that in some cases feature models are used to model variability in the problem space, but there is a lack of a holistic treatment of variability from problem-space to solution-space artifacts. At best, features defined in a feature model are somehow linked to code-level artifacts.

Features and the corresponding architecture are often derived from requirements in a nonsystematic, ad hoc way without documenting the reasoning behind architectural decisions. This is an important pitfall in current SPLE practice, as it is absolutely necessary to know the relationships between requirements, the derived architecture, the design, and the implementation artifacts. Experience in industry shows that this information is necessary not only for finding artifacts that can be reused, but also for impact analysis in both directions and for requirements changes, as well as for changes in design and code artifacts.

When integrating MDSD and AOSD into SPLE, the identified deficiencies can be overcome. Our approach starts with modeling the varying parts of the problem space of the product line, i.e., with creating a metamodel of the variable domain requirements. Thus, the variation in domain requirements is formally described and can be mapped to solution-space artifacts. By creating a DSL including an appropriate editor, product requirements can be captured in a problem-space model. As the DSL reflects the domain concepts, domain experts who are not familiar with software terminology can specify the system to be built.

After the target architecture of the product line is defined, an architectural metamodel is created. It is easily possible to separate the solution-space metamodels into platform-neutral and platform-specific metamodels. As the solution-space metamodels are created, a formal mapping is defined from the problem-space metamodel to the solution-space metamodel. This allows for systematically linking variation points in the problem space to variation points in the solution space. In this way, we can ensure that solution-space variability is bound according to the corresponding variability in the problem space, i.e., that the resulting systems fulfills its requirements. This also makes the derivation of the product line architecture from requirements more systematic, as the mapping has to be well understood to be able to define the transformation. Finally, a code generator is implemented that transforms the final solution-space model to executable code. Again, in order to define the transformation to code, the mapping has to be thought through.

All variability with respect to the structure of the system can be handled by the model-driven part of our approach. We clearly separate structural variability from configurative variability, as the two are orthogonal. By integrating MDSD into SPLE, creative construction DSLs can handle variability with respect to the structure or behavior the DSL intends to model. A DSL allows creating models that are instances of a defined metamodel, which models variability using the terminology of the domain. Variability with respect to domain entities and their relations can be efficiently handled using the model-driven part of our approach.

In SPLE, configurative variability is an important issue as well. This kind of variability is typically expressed in feature models and tends to crosscut the structure expressed in the creative construction DSL. Thus, advanced modularization mechanisms are required that are able to capture crosscutting variability.

We use AO concepts and techniques on model, transformator, generator, and code level to handle the so-called orthogonal variability. We use a feature model to describe the configurative variability of the product line and realize the features using AO at the appropriate levels. Features can thus be localized in aspects and combined with the core as desired.

We argue that, due to the fact that models are more abstract and less detailed than code, variability on the model level is inherently less scattered and therefore simpler to manage. As shown in Figure 18.14, the higher the abstraction level is, the fewer variations points exist. In the Smart Home product line, this assumption has proven to be valid. For the implementation of the features, we needed at most two different aspects, but in most cases only one aspect was required. The pointcuts defined in these aspects matched, at most, three join points. If we compare the matched join points that represent variation points with variation points required to implement the features in Java, the number of variation points in our solution is significantly lower. For example, the Reflective Data Structures feature that we implemented in Smart Home (cf. Section 18.3.7) is captured in a single template aspect that matches two join points. A Java-based implementation would require

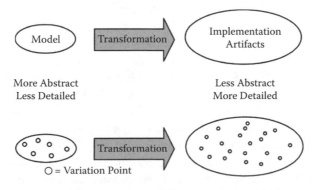

Figure 18.14 Mapping abstract models to detailed implementations.

adding the required members (one attribute and three methods) to every class that should be reflective. Typically, every actuator and every sensor-driver class should be reflective; this means that every component implementing a driver would have to be changed. In Smart Home, this would be 13 classes.

Given the observation that a higher level of abstraction reduces the number of variation points, features expressed on a model level are inherently simpler and easier to manage than features expressed on a generator level. We therefore argue to always express features on the highest possible level.

In the home-automation example we were able to implement all desired cross-cutting features using AO techniques at the model, transformator, generator, and code level. In most cases we needed only one aspect (in some cases two) to implement the desired functionality. The features are well modularized, as their implementation is localized in a single aspect. This reduces the number of trace links and improves understandability and maintainability. Generally, AO techniques provide efficient means for modularizing variability that crosscuts the structure that the creative construction DSL intends to model.

Our approach supports the highest level of product line maturity (Bosch 2002), namely the configurable product base. In such cases, the effort shifts dramatically to domain engineering, making application engineering a task that can be handled solely by domain experts. For domains that are not mature enough or that evolve too swiftly to effectively maintain such a product derivation infrastructure, it is often possible to identify subdomains that can be automated.

18.4.2 Threats to Validity

Threats to validity are known as factors that can lead to incorrect conclusions about relationships in our observations. These can be distinguished between *internal* and *external* validity. Internal validity tackles the question of whether, if we assume that there is a relationship in the application example, the relationship is causal. External validity answers the question of whether, if we assume that there is a causal relationship in this application example between the constructs of the cause and the effect, we can generalize the effect to other applications.

A possible threat to internal validity is that one could argue that the features we implemented in the example have been selected to fit well into the concepts of our approach. The Smart Home application example has been picked by Siemens AG to validate our approach in an industrial setting. Also, the chosen features are very different in their nature. There are some that implement automation capabilities of Smart Home, some that deal with different deployment options, and some that are related to the GUI. To ensure a broad spectrum, we implemented business features as well as technical features. Furthermore, the high consistency of the results of the example gives evidence to consider the findings of the application example valid.

In the case of external validity, the question is whether we can generalize the positive effect of our approach in our industrial example to other domains. We believe that this is possible, as we provide the means to deal with both structural and configurative variability. Even if only one of them is applicable in a certain domain, our approach can still be used. Further, there might be domains where only partial automation makes sense. Even in this case, the benefits of our approach can be exploited. According to Stahl and Voelter (2006), MDSD always brings a benefit to projects, as productivity and quality are already improved during the first model-driven project. Also, the implementation effort can be reduced up to 50% compared with manual programming.

18.5 Related Work

This section discusses work that is related to our model-driven, aspect-oriented product line engineering approach. To the best of our knowledge, there is no other approach that provides a systematic treatment of variability from problem space to solution space using aspect-oriented and model-driven techniques. On the other hand, there is existing research that is related to parts of our approach.

18.5.1 Aspects on the Model Level

The Atlas Model Weaver (AMW) (Fabro and Valduriez 2007) is a tool created as part of the Atlas Model Management Architecture. Its primary goal is to establish relationships between elements of different models that are stored in a so-called weaving model. This process can be done manually or semiautomatically. Based on the weaving model, one can generate model transformations that merge models. AMW is similar to XWeave, as both tools can weave or merge models. There is, however, an important difference. AMW does not support a join-point model. It provides an interactive tool to build weaving models, whereas XWeave uses name correspondence or pointcut expressions to quantify over join points.

C-SAW (Gray et al. 2006) is a general transformation engine for manipulating models based on aspect specifications using Embedded Constraint Language (ECL), a variant of Object Constraint Language (OCL). The weaver traverses the model and selects a set of elements to which the aspects should be applied. The advice then modifies the selected element in some way, for example by adding a precondition or changing the element's structure. C-SAW has been developed to tackle the challenge of evolving large models in a consistent way. Instead of applying a set of changes manually, one merely writes an aspect that applies the changes to all selected elements in the model. Comparing it to XWeave reveals that C-SAW does not weave models (in the sense of merging them) as XWeave does. Rather, it efficiently applies (crosscutting) changes to a collection of elements in a large model.

The Motorola WEAVR (Cottenier et al. 2007) is a model weaver developed as a plugin for Telelogic TAU. It supports weaving of UML statecharts that include action semantics and are thus executable. There are two different types of join points: action and transition join points. Advices are encapsulated in a construct called *connector*. Similar to XWeave, the Motorola WEAVR weaves aspects based on pointcut specifications. The main difference between the two approaches is that XWeave provides a generic Eclipse Modeling Framework (EMF)-based solution that can weave arbitrary models and metamodels. The Motorola WEAVR only supports weaving of UML statecharts.

General Aspect Oriented Modeling (AOM) approaches are also related to XWeave. Theme/UML (Baniassad and Clarke 2004), for example, provides an extension to UML that supports concern modeling and composition. Most AOM techniques are based on UML, which is an important difference to XWeave. Also, most approaches lack tool support, which is essential for a successful application of the technique in an industrial product line context.

18.5.2 Aspects on Transformator Level

In Oldevik and Haugen (2007), higher-order transformations are presented. They include an aspect-oriented extension to a model-to-text transformation language. Those so-called higher-order transformations can be used to represent variability in product line engineering. This approach, which is similar to our approach as an existing transformation language, has been extended with support for aspects. An important difference is that our approach supports linking these aspects to features defined in a feature model.

Lengyel et al. (2006) presented an approach called *Global Constraint Weaver* that supports the weaving of crosscutting constraints in graph-transformation steps. An aspect-oriented solution is provided that propagates aspect-oriented constraints to graph-transformation steps. Constraint aspects are added to the transformation steps at the appropriate locations. The approach is similar to our approach in that it supports AO on the model-transformation level. However, our approach allows us to capture transformation steps in aspects that are applied to transformation functions as desired. The weaver presented by Lengyel et al. (2006) only supports weaving of OCL constraints.

18.5.3 Aspects on Generator Level

In Loughran and Rashid (2004), a generative approach called *Framed Aspects* is proposed. Framed Aspects combines AOP with frame technology, a template-based generator approach, to modularize crosscutting feature implementations and improve evolution of product lines. In contrast, in our approach, code-generation templates are extended with aspect-oriented capabilities to incorporate features into the code-generation process. The approach presented in Loughran and Rashid (2004) only parameterizes aspects.

The transformation engine of ArcStyler, CARAT (Interactive objects 2008), supports the specialization of cartridges. It allows one to override template code specified in a supercartridge, which is also possible with our approach. However, our approach is more generic because it also supports quantification—the ability to select a set of join points using a pointcut to add generator behavior in several places at once.

18.6 Conclusions

We integrated parts of MDSD and AOSD into SPLE to overcome deficiencies identified in current SPLE practice. The result of this integration is a new approach for model-driven, aspect-oriented software product line engineering.

Our approach supports the specification of the problem-space variability using appropriate DSLs that are based on domain concepts. Based on a defined product line architecture, architectural metamodels are created. We recommend dividing the solution-space metamodels into platform-neutral and platform-specific metamodels. The transformations from problem-space models to solution-space models are implemented as model-to-model transformations. Finally, code is generated from the final solution-space model. This part of our approach deals with the handling of structural variability, i.e., how the elements of the system are arranged and interlinked.

To handle configurative variability, we provide AO concepts and tools that allow us to efficiently integrate feature functionality into the system. Metamodels, models, model transformations, code generators, and code can be enhanced by weaving in aspects at the appropriate locations. AO techniques are used to realize variability within MDSD artifacts. Further, we integrate the variant-management tool pure::variants (pure systems GmbH 2006) into the tool suite to support querying of configuration models from within MDSD artifacts.

To validate our approach, we present an industrial case study that was conducted at Siemens AG. The home-automation product line that we developed proved our hypotheses. The number of variation points is significantly reduced at higher levels of abstraction. All desired features could be implemented using the concepts and tools we provide, resulting in well-modularized feature implementations. Based on two input models, a model created with the DSLs and a configuration model, members of the product line could be generated. Automation was maximized to a point where no manual coding was required to derive a customized product from the domain artifacts.

References

Baniassad, E., and S. Clarke. 2004. Theme: An approach for aspect-oriented analysis and design. In *Proceedings of the 26th international conference on software engineering*. Washington, DC: IEEE Computer Society.

Bosch, J. 2002. Maturity and evolution in software product lines: Approaches, artefacts and organization. In *Proceedings of the 2nd international conference on software product lines*, 257–271. New York: Springer.

Clements, P., and L. Northrop. 2001. *Software product lines: Practices and patterns*. SEI Series in Software Engineering. Reading, MA: Addison-Wesley.

Cottenier, T., A. v. d. Berg, et al. 2007. Joinpoint inference from behavioral specification to implementation. In *Proceedings of the 21st European conference on object-oriented programming*. New York: Springer.

Czarnecki, K., and U. W. Eisenecker. 1999. *Generative programming: Methods, techniques, and applications*. Reading, MA: Addison-Wesley.

Eclipse. 2008. Epsilon. http://www.eclipse.org/gmt/epsilon/.

Fabro, M. D. D., and P. Valduriez. 2007. Semi-automatic model integration using matching transformations and weaving models. In *Proceedings of the 2007 ACM symposium on applied computing*, 963–970. New York: ACM.

Filman, R. E., T. Elrad, et al. 2004. *Aspect-oriented software development*. Reading, MA: Addison-Wesley Longman.

Gray, J., Y. Lin, et al. 2006. Automating change evolution in model-driven engineering. *IEEE Computer* 39 (2): 51–58.

Greenfield, J., K. Short, et al. 2004. *Software factories: Assembling applications with patterns, models, frameworks, and tools*. New York: Wiley & Sons.

Groher, I., H. Papajewski, et al. 2007. Integrating model-driven development and software product line engineering. Paper presented at Eclipse Summit '07: Proceedings of the Eclipse modeling symposium. Ludwigsburg, Germany.

Groher, I., and M. Voelter. 2007. XWeave: Models and aspects in concert. In *Proceedings of the 10th international workshop on Aspect-oriented modeling*, 35–40. New York: ACM Press.

Grünbacher, P., A. Egyed, et al. 2004. Reconciling software requirements and architectures with intermediate models. *Journal for Software and Systems Modeling (SoSyM)* 3 (3): 235–253.

Interactive objects. 2008. ArcStyler. http://www.interactive-objects.com/.

Kiczales, G., E. Hilsdale, et al. 2001. An overview of AspectJ. In *Proceedings of the 15th European conference on object-oriented programming*. Berlin/Heidelberg: Springer.

Kiczales, G., J. Lamping, et al. 1997. Aspect-oriented programming. In *Proceedings of the 11th European conference on object-oriented programming*. Berlin: Springer-Verlag.

Lengyel, L., T. Levendovszky, et al. 2006. Metamodel-based model transformation with aspect-oriented constraints. *Electronic Notes on Theoretical Computer Science* 152: 111–123.

Loughran, N., and A. Rashid. 2004. Framed aspects: Supporting variability and configurability for AOP. In *Proceedings of the 8th international conference on software reuse: Methods, techniques and tools*. New York: Springer.

Oldevik, J., and O. Haugen. 2007. Higher-order transformations for product lines. In *Proceedings of the 11th international software product line conference*. Washington, DC: IEEE Computer Society.

openArchitectureWare. 2008. http://www.openarchitectureware.org.

OSGi Alliance. 2008. OSGi Framework. http://www.osgi.org/.

Pohl, K., G. Böckle, et al. 2005. *Software product line engineering: Foundations, principles, and techniques.* New York: Springer.

pure systems GmbH. 2006. Variant management with pure::variants. Technical white paper. http://www.pure-systems.com/fileadmin/downloads/pv-whitepaper-en-04.pdf.

Stahl, T., and M. Voelter. 2006. *Model-driven software development: Technology, engineering, management.* New York: Wiley & Sons.

Voelter, M., and I. Groher. 2007a. Handling variability in model transformations and generators. Paper presented at DSM '07: 7th OOPSLA workshop on domain-specific modeling, Montreal.

Voelter, M., and I. Groher. 2007b. Product line implementation using aspect-oriented and model-driven software development. Paper presented at 11th international software product line conference (SPLC 2007), Kyoto, Japan, IEEE CS.

Chapter 19

Evaluation of Design Options in Embedded Automotive Product Lines

Håkan Gustavsson
Scania CV AB and Mälardalen University, Västerås, Sweden

Jakob Axelsson
Volvo Car Corporation and Mälardalen University, Västerås, Sweden

Contents

19.1 Introduction

In many industries, complex embedded product lines are designed. In theory, this follows a structured and well-organized process, where a set of given requirements is transformed step by step into an optimal product. However, in reality the complexity of the products and markets often lead to much less stringent ways of working. Let us consider a fictional, but not atypical, scenario.

> Improvements of the existing product are debated during coffee breaks and in the hallways. Ideas are discussed and eventually a new function is developed. The new function is not part of any project, and no budget exists. Instead it is the creation of highly motivated developers and their ambition to improve the product.
>
> To implement this new functionality they need management support, which is created through prototype demonstrations. From this point in time everything moves very rapidly. Customers are invited to workshops, and it turns out that they are willing to pay for the functionality, but it will probably only be sold in low volumes to a high-end segment. The decision is made to introduce the function as fast as possible based on very uncertain information. The function that has been demonstrated is developed using components made for an experimental environment. However, that does not fit in the current system architecture and is not suitable for production. Management stresses that time to market is important, and it is assured that the quality of the product will not be affected if implemented as is. Therefore, the decision is made to integrate the function rapidly, even if the chosen solution does not follow the common design rationale and removes many degrees of freedom for the future evolution of the system.

This was system development as a short fictive story. It is hopefully not too common in practice, but it still includes many of the issues that most system developers have experienced in various projects. The chosen solution solves the problem today, but could cause difficulties in the future (a situation referred to as "technical debt" by Cunningham [1992]).

The developers did not have the methods available to evaluate and show the economical value of a longer term solution. Such methods would be very useful early in the design process when uncertainty is high. Functions developed in this fashion are likely to be innovative and will meet the demands of the customer but could severely impact the future flexibility and adaptability of the system. A valuation of the resources early in the design process could remedy this problem and reduce the life-cycle cost of the system. If designs are made in a structured manner, the design decision will be traceable, and continuous improvements are more likely to occur.

This chapter discusses how to deal with scenarios as previous presented by putting a value on flexibility in the system solution. Thereby, it becomes clearer when to focus on short-term solutions and when to keep the long-term evolution of a product line in mind. The approach taken is to evaluate flexibility using a concept called Real Options. The method is motivated and described by using as an example an industrial area where very complex product lines occur, namely automotive embedded systems. To improve the usability of the method, a structured evaluation process is defined to aid practitioners such as developers and architects. The evaluation process provides a way of valuing system designs and enables the practitioner to think about the future in a systematic manner. The value of a flexible design can thereby be quantified, and the proposed process shows how it can be accepted by practitioners within the automotive industry.

In the next section, an overview of automotive electronics and software is given. Then the concept of Real Options is introduced, followed by a discussion of how it can be used in embedded system design. The following two sections present a step-by-step approach to evaluating flexibility in embedded systems, first as a theoretical process and then applied to a case from automotive electronics. The final two sections discuss related work and summarize the conclusions of the chapter.

19.2 Automotive Embedded Systems

Today, most innovations made within the automotive domain are driven by electronics. According to a study made by Hoch et al. (2006), the total value of electronics in automobiles is expected to rise from the current 25% to 40% in 2010. The automotive customers demand new functionality with every new product release, and the time to market is constantly shortened.

An example of new functions is Advanced Driver Assistance Systems (ADAS) that help the customer to drive the vehicle safety. Those systems typically use information about the surroundings to increase road safety. This is done by using sensors to identify nearby objects or through communication with other vehicles or infrastructure to attain more information. The increased interaction between various components and the wider boundaries of the system increase the complexity and demand flexibility to be easily integrated.

There are many other new functions that are about to be introduced or are already introduced that have a large impact on the electrical system of automotive vehicles. To cope with this continuous change, the system needs to be designed with the right amount of flexibility. It is crucial that each of those functions can be implemented without causing large systemwide changes.

Further complexity is added by the fact that vehicle developers strive to use a product line approach, where the same embedded system is used in a wide range of vehicles. The base system thus needs to be able to evolve over a long time and be adaptable to very different surroundings.

19.2.1 System Architecture

The building blocks of an automotive electrical and electronic (E/E) system consist of electronic control units (ECUs) executing software modules that implement functionality. ECUs are connected to communication networks. As shown in Figure 19.1, the communication networks are usually divided into subnetworks, and the communication between those is made through gateway ECUs connected to a backbone. Different sensors and actuators are connected to the ECUs, depending on the function allocated to the ECU.

Most design decisions in automotive E/E architectures are made during the early phases. Often, the E/E architecture needs to support a full product line of vehicles or vehicle variants that are released over a number of years. They must allow a large degree of variability to cope with the demands of different customers. The long life cycle of automotive products demands that changes to the product can be made with as little impact to the different components as possible.

To be able to satisfy the growing demand on functionality, the original equipment manufacturer (OEM) needs to develop architectures that can evolve throughout its lifetime without forcing premature architectural changes. Similar products in

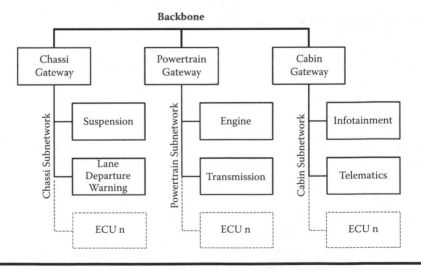

Figure 19.1 A typical vehicle communication network.

some other industries solve this problem by simply adding extra resources to cope with future demands. The cost-sensitive automotive industry has to optimize the use of the system's limited resources, but in the meantime also be flexible. Design decisions are usually based on many factors that pull in different directions, such as maintenance, portability, usability, etc. The complexity of the system and the many uncertain factors create a need to define methods that can provide guidance in the design process.

19.2.2 Decision Levels

Architectural decisions are made when selecting components and allocating them to subsystems, which then are combined into a system. The decisions can be made on different levels, which have various impacts and predictability. Florentz and Huhn (2007) group the decisions into three levels: top level, high level, and low level (Figure 19.2). Top-level decisions concern the quality and function attributes and have the largest impact. Choosing architectural patterns and technologies are found to be high-level decisions. The most predictable decisions are those concerning the hardware architecture and function mapping. The impact of the decision will vary, depending on how decoupled the software is from the hardware. This work has been focused on the low-level decisions concerning function and communication mapping.

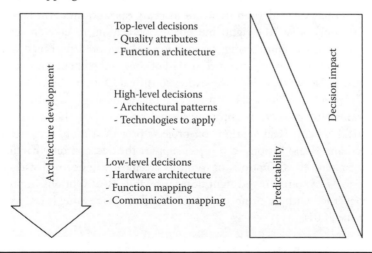

Figure 19.2 Decisions made during the development of the architecture will have a different impact and the outcome will be more or less predictable (Florentz and Huhn 2007).

19.3 Introducing Real Options

In this section, the concept and background of options in general and real options in particular is introduced.

19.3.1 Financial Options

Using options theory is one approach for dealing with the high level of uncertainty when making design decisions in the early phases. The theory derives from finance, where an option is the right but not the obligation to exercise a feature of a contract at a future date (Hull 1993). A typical example is a stock option that gives the right but not the obligation to buy a certain stock at a given price on a predefined date. An option has a value because it gives its owner the possibility to decide in the future whether or not to pay the strike price for an asset whose future value is not known today. An option therefore provides a right to make the costly decision after receiving more information.

There are two different types of options, American and European. A European option may only be exercised on the predefined exercise day, whereas an American option can be exercised any time until the exercise date.

19.3.2 Real Options

Since the 1990s, options theory has become more widely utilized within the field of engineering. It is called Real Options and was developed to manage the risk of uncertain design decisions. Real Options could be seen as an extension of financial option theory to options on real (nonfinancial) assets. Copeland and Antikarov (2001) define a real option as: "the right, but not the obligation, to take an action (e.g., deferring, expanding, contracting, or abandoning) at a predetermined cost called the exercise price, for a predetermined period of time—the life of the option."

In 2001 de Neufville coined the expressions Real Options "in" and "on" projects. Real Options "on" projects treat the enabling technology as a black box, while Real Options "in" projects are options created by changing the actual design of the technical system. Real Options on projects provide a more accurate value of the project, and Real Options in projects support the decision on what amount of flexibility to add. "Real Options on projects are mostly concerned with an accurate value to assist sound investment decisions, while Real Options in projects are mostly concerned with go or no go decisions and an exact value is less important" (de Neufville 2001).

19.3.3 Social Considerations

The Real Options approach does not only provide a way of valuing system designs, but it also forces the developer to think about the future in a systematic manner.

By giving future flexibility a value, it assists the developing organization in making decisions and also enables a way of predicting the growth of the complete system (Larses 2005). Leslie and Michaels (1997) conclude the article, "The real power of Real Options" with the following: "The final, and perhaps greatest, benefit of Real Option thinking is precisely that—thinking." The possibility of changing the way people think might also be the hardest part in bringing acceptance to new methods such as using Real Options. The new method must not only be better than the one it is replacing, it should also be triable, observable, and have low complexity (Copeland and Antikarov 2001).

19.3.4 Valuing Real Options

One of the advantages with Real Options compared with many other architecture evaluation methods is the possibility to value different system designs and thereby to find the most economically sound investment. This is probably the most complicated part of using Real Options, and over the years several approaches to calculating its value have been proposed. They all have various assumptions, and in this section we will evaluate the most appropriate for our case. Amram and Kulatilaka (1999) propose three general solution methods:

- *Black–Scholes–Merton model.* This method calculates the option value by solving a partial differential equation including the value of a replicating portfolio.
- *Binomial model.* The dynamic programming approach lays out the possible future outcomes and folds back the value of an optimal future strategy.
- *Monte Carlo simulation.* The simulation approach averages the value of the optimal strategy at the decision date for thousands of possible outcomes.

We will now present the first two models in more detail, whereas the third model is beyond the scope of this study. (It should be pointed out that the method described later in this chapter does not require the practicing engineer to understand, or even be aware of, the calculation method.)

19.3.4.1 Black–Scholes–Merton Model

The Black–Scholes–Merton (BSM) model, for which they later received the Nobel Prize, was created by Black and Scholes in 1973 and is widely used on financial options. The BSM model makes two major assumptions that concern our case: It demands a replicating portfolio, and it only supports European options.

A replicating portfolio contains assets with a value matching those of the target asset. The replicating portfolio of financial options can easily be found on the stock exchange as the stock value, but when looking at Real Options that are not traded, it can be very difficult to find.

Considering our case, it seems very unlikely that the assets needed are exercised at a predefined time. Sullivan et al. (1999) discuss the assumptions made and write: "They will not hold for some, perhaps many, software design decisions." More recently, Copeland and Antikarov (2001) argue: "There are valuation methodologies that effectively capture the complexities and the iterative nature of managerial decisions, and the Black–Scholes–Merton model is not the only, or even the most appropriate, way to value Real Options." Also Amram and Kulatilaka (1999), who provide a four-step solution using BSM, state: "The Black–Scholes solution is appropriate for fewer Real Options applications, but when appropriate it provides a simple solution and a quick answer." The conclusion is that the BSM model is suitable for financial options, but hard to use in our case.

19.3.4.2 Binomial Model

The binomial model does not need a replicating portfolio (Banerjee 2004) and also supports American options. The initial value of the asset, A, changes with each time interval and either goes up with the probability p to A_u or down to A_d until its final date (Amram and Kulatilaka 1999). The value of the asset (A) at each decision point is given through Equation (19.1), with r being the risk-free interest rate, σ being the volatility, and the time period being Δt.

$$A = (pA_u + (1-p)A_d)e^{-r\Delta t} \tag{19.1}$$

Assuming that the underlying asset has a symmetric up-and-down movement u = 1 / d, then the up and down factors are given through:

$$u = e^{\sigma\sqrt{\Delta t}} \tag{19.2}$$

$$d = e^{-\sigma\sqrt{\Delta t}} \tag{19.3}$$

The probability of an up movement is then:

$$p = \frac{e^{r\Delta t} - d}{u - d} \tag{19.4}$$

Looking back at our case, the value of the flexibility option would change during the development stages (see Figure 19.3).

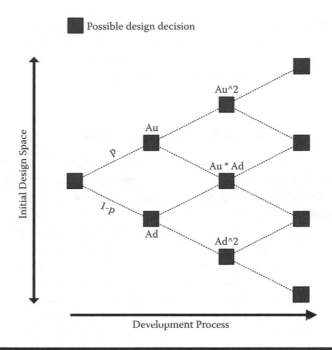

<figure>
■ Possible design decision
</figure>

Figure 19.3 The decisions made narrow the initial design space.

19.4 Real Options in Embedded System Design

There are as many Real Options in embedded system design projects as in any other engineering project. Those systems contain a large amount of design variables and parameters that can be valued as Real Options in projects.

19.4.1 Suitability of Real Options

To find out if Real Options would be a support in embedded system design, one needs to clarify the characteristics of this domain. As stated earlier (Hoch et al. 2006), the large volume and cost of the product make errors in the design very expensive. Also, conflicting requirements found late in the development phase cause a high cost. At the same time, there is a very high level of uncertainty during this design phase, and important decisions are made by a small group of engineers (Axelsson 2006). The automotive embedded systems are characterized by being mechatronic systems, which adds complexity. The systems are often resource-constrained, and trade-offs between the system behavior and the resources required are of great importance (Larses 2005).

When to use Real Options is explained by many authors. Copeland and Antikarov (2001) state that "it is making the tough decisions—those where the Net Present Value is close to zero—that the additional value of flexibility makes a big difference." This is, in our case, true when developing a new functionality where the market demand is very uncertain. If the design includes a real option to abandon or change course, the risk taken could be minimized. Under these conditions, the difference between real option valuation and other decision tools is substantial.

19.4.2 Real Options in Automotive Systems

There are many new functions that are about to be introduced or are already introduced that have a large impact on the electrical system of automotive vehicles. Using Real Options as a method to evaluate alternative solutions gives the possibility to value the flexibility of the technical solution. A solution that is more likely to withstand change due to future demands therefore has a higher value when evaluated using real options compared with traditional evaluation methods. To enable the possibility of future reuse, the system needs to be designed with interfaces between components (both SW and HW) that are prepared for future needs.

The design will be different, depending on how long the system is planned to withstand future change. To evaluate what level of flexibility is appropriate, one must therefore first provide the rough requirements of future needs. Given the estimated value of the future functionality, a Real Options analysis will then show what amount of flexibility should be added to make the investment adequate. Current and future technical demands of the system, together with economical and organizational demands, call for a systematic evaluation process.

19.5 Evaluation Process

To improve usability, we have defined an evaluation process that can aid practitioners such as developers and architects of embedded automotive systems. Practitioners working with embedded systems are often not used to evaluate design alternatives with economic valuation methods. To make the practitioners utilize and trust the method, it is important to present a step-by-step process for carrying out the valuation. During the evaluation process, the different stakeholders will have to specify their gut feelings in figures and consider whether flexibility has an added value. The evaluation process presented in Figure 19.4 consists of eight steps with a description and some concrete advice. (In the next section, the steps will be exemplified in a small case study.)

Step 1: Describe the design alternatives
Each valid design alternative is described to identify what resources are used. This can be simplified by reusing patterns from previous designs.
Step 2: Perform traditional valuation

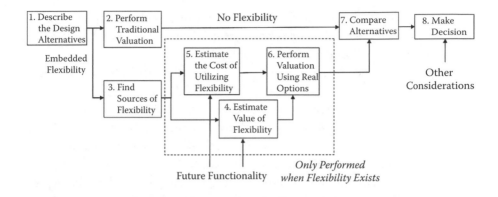

Figure 19.4 The data flow of the evaluation process.

The traditional method to derive the value of an investment is by calculating its net present value (NPV), taking into account the value today of cash received or paid in the future. To calculate NPV, a discount rate is used, often corresponding to the current interest rate.

Step 3: Find sources of flexibility

It would not be wise to analyze all the real options available. When designing a function distributed over a communication network, there are some assets that are generic and can easily be used by other functions. Those represent the source of flexibility or Real Options. Commonly they are hardware assets such as inputs, outputs, or communication capacity. If there is such an asset, the difference in NPV could be due to the cost of designing for flexibility. If there is no source of flexibility, the result given through the valuation in Step 2 is true, and the evaluation is completed.

Step 4: Estimate value of flexibility

Each resource is analyzed to distinguish whether it has a future value. When available, it provides an increased amount of flexibility or available design space and thereby an added value. The value will often be due to the revenue of future functions that represent the underlying asset (S) and can be calculated through a simplified model, as seen in Equation (19.5). The product cost is the estimated costs during the system life cycle.

$$S = \text{volume} \times (\text{customer price} - \text{product cost}) \tag{19.5}$$

Of course, a more elaborate model can also be used if more detailed information is available.

Step 5: Estimate the cost of utilizing flexibility

Utilizing the flexibility is usually a question of implementing a future function or extension of an existing function. The price to be paid is therefore the added cost of implementing this future functionality. Figure 19.5

illustrates how the added cost (the exercise price of the real option) will be paid later in the life cycle of the system when the flexibility is utilized.

Step 6: Perform valuation using Real Options

The value of the flexibility can be calculated using Real Option valuation. The quantitative data needed, shown in Table 19.1, to perform a Real Option valuation should be extracted for the design concepts as follows:

- The planned lifetime of the platform needs to be estimated. If the function has not been implemented before the expiration date, the value of the real option is considered to be lost.
- The current value of implementing flexibility is calculated in Step 4.
- The cost of utilizing the flexibility is given from Step 5.
- The volatility is a measure of the annual up or down movement of the option value and often represents the uncertainty of future customer demands. This can be estimated through historical data or expert assessment.

By using the binomial model, the value of the option premium can be calculated.

Step 7: Compare the alternatives

Real Option theory provides an extension to the traditional NPV valuation by adding the value of flexibility. The so-called expanded NPV is the sum of the static NPV and the value of the option premium (Trigeorgis 1988):

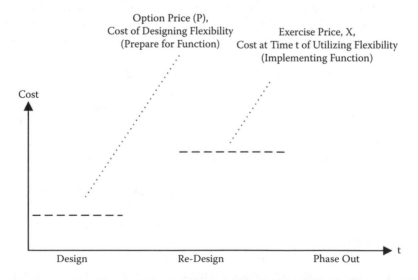

Figure 19.5 The price and exercise price of the option provide a communication interface that can be used by external suppliers.

Table 19.1 Factors Affecting the Value of an Option

Option on Stock	Real Options in Embedded Systems
Option value (V)	The value of designing flexibility
Option price (C)	Cost of designing for flexibility
Exercise price (X)	Cost of utilizing flexibility
Underlying asset value (S)	Current value of implementing flexibility
Volatility (σ)	Uncertainty of customer demand
Time to exercise (t)	Time when the option is exercised
Time to expiration (T)	Lifetime of the current system

$$\text{Expanded NPV} = \text{Static NPV} + \text{Option premium} \qquad (19.6)$$

The best investment is therefore to choose the design alternative with the highest Expanded NPV.

Step 8: Make decision

Real Options provide the opportunity to analyze the cost of designing for future growth of a platform, based on the estimated value of the future functionality. It is important to stress that decisions are often based on factors that are not valued using the presented evaluation process. Other factors that influence the decision are the choice of supplier, time to market, project priority, or organization. The last step is therefore to make the decision based on the trade-off between all influencing factors.

19.6 Case Study: Network Usage

To analyze the process and its usefulness, it is applied in a real case taken from the automotive industry. The problem is how to integrate a new feature implemented in software into an existing E/E architecture. A key element of the problem is in which ECU the new functionality should be implemented.

Step 1: Describe the design alternatives

A prestudy has found two alternative ways to provide this feature (Figure 19.6). Design alternative 1 provides this feature by connecting the external communication link directly to the current cabin gateway ECU through an existing but unused bus interface, and the advantage is a low development cost. Design alternative 2 uses a new ECU to create the external communication. The new ECU connects to the cabin gateway using an already implemented internal network. Alternative 2 is more expensive in development cost and component cost, but it does not utilize the last available communication link in the cabin gateway.

Step 2: Perform traditional valuation

The development activities required for Alternative 1 are not extensive because an existing ECU is being used. The development cost of Alternative 1 is therefore considered to be zero. For Alternative 2, a new ECU needs to be developed. Using data from previous similar projects, the development cost is estimated to be SEK 5 million (Swedish crowns) for Alternative 2. The cash flow of alternative 1 is higher due to its low component cost. The results of the calculation are shown in Table 19.2. The difference in NPV between the two alternatives is SEK 6.9 million given the annual discount rate of 11%. The analysis of the valuation tells us to choose Alternative 1, but this does not take the value of flexibility into account.

Step 3: Find sources of flexibility

The communication link is a limited resource that can be of interest to a large number of functionalities, but those functionalities cannot be safely mixed with an external device. Alternative 2 thus gives a higher flexibility for future functionality than Alternative 1.

Step 4: Estimate value of flexibility

Network communication is a limited resource within the automotive industry. Each network has a predefined maximum capacity, and the utilization is also dependent on the physical location of the network cable. There is a growing market demand to monitor and control different vehicle functions through the use of external devices. To meet this requirement, one must provide a way to connect external communication devices to the vehicle.

The expected value of the future function (underlying asset, S) is estimated to be SEK 10 million using the simplified model in Equation (19.5).

Step 5: Estimate the price of flexibility

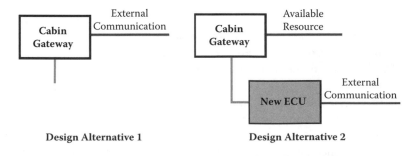

Figure 19.6 Two design alternatives that differ in their use of communication links to provide the demanded feature.

Table 19.2   The Calculated NPV of the Two Design Alternatives (million SEK)

		Alternative 1	*Alternative 2*
	Development cost:	0	−5
Cash flow:	1st year	15.5	15
	2nd year	15.5	15
	3rd year	15.5	15
	4th year	15.5	15
	5th year	15.5	15
	NPV	57.3	50.4
	Difference:	6.9	

The exercise price of SEK 2.9 million of finally implementing the function is an average of the potential functions found in the product portfolio. The exercise price includes the cost of ECU, sensors, cables, and developing application software.

Step 6: Perform valuation using Real Options

The communication link provides flexibility to the system, and its value can be calculated using Real Options valuation. The product portfolio gives us a set of functionalities that could require the use of the communication link. The data needed is provided through an internal prestudy. The planned lifetime of the platform is 5 years.

The minimum goal of the investment in the alternative is to exceed the interest gained from the company's risk-free interest rate (5%). The volatility is predicted to be 25%, mainly due to the uncertainty of future demand. The up and down factors are given using Equations (19.2) and (19.3).

$$u = e^{0.25} = 1.28$$

$$d = e^{-0.25} = 0.78$$

The risk-neutral probability can then be calculated using Equation (19.4).

$$p = \frac{e^{0.05} - 0.78}{0.5} = 0.542$$

Given the underlying asset value (SEK 10 million) from the previous step, the values can be calculated as shown in Figure 19.3. Inserting the values into Equation (19.1) calculates the current value of the option to SEK 7.7 million (see Figure 19.7).

$$A = (p \cdot 10.4 + (1 - p) \cdot 5.4)e^{-0.05} = 7.7$$

Step 7: Compare the alternatives

Alternative 2 would be a sound investment if the value of the option premium is higher than the calculated difference (SEK 6.9 million) in Table 19.1. The option premium was calculated to SEK 7.7 million, which means that adding the flexibility is a good investment compared with the alternative without flexibility.

Step 8: Make decision

The results show that the future option value increases with the number of requirements implemented (Figure 19.7). If only a low number of requirements will be demanded, the value of the option will be lost. Figure 19.7 also shows how the risk changes with the probability. This risk could be eliminated by not implementing the possibility to support a certain requirement. This would lead to a limited design space where an improved functionality cannot be implemented without a redesign of the system.

19.6.1 Discussion

The results show that investing in a flexible design would most likely be a sound investment if a large part of the future requirements were implemented during the system life cycle. The diversity of the proposed functionality makes it very uncertain what functionality will be implemented, which also is the reason why flexibility has a value. The prediction of the volatility and the value of the underlying asset are crucial to the results. One of the strengths when using Real Options valuation is that the uncertainty is taken into account and not left out of the calculation. It also provides a valuation method that can be used to analyze different future scenarios. Similar analyses can be done to estimate the value of future functions by iteration of sales volumes, customer price, etc.

19.7 Related Work

Real Options is far from being the only method developed for valuing architectures. There are, however, only a few methods that can make economic consideration, CBAM (Kazman, Asundi, and Klein 2002) being an exception. Real Options is

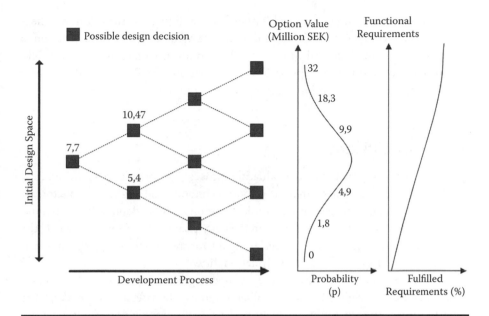

Figure 19.7 **The future option value increases with the number of requirements implemented.**

unique by also considering the flexibility and the architectural evolution over time (Bahsoon, Emmerich, and Macke 2005). Our literature survey has found three research contributions that involve the usage of Real Options in system design involving software or hardware. None of them addresses embedded systems or the automotive domain explicitly.

Browning and Engel (2006) extend Real Options "in" projects to architecture options and present a theoretical example where stakeholder overall value increases by 15% by designing the system for the right amount of adaptability. The framework presented shows a way to implement the optimal degree of flexibility. The initial research proposes using the model of Black and Scholes to calculate the value of the Real Options, but does not present a case. Browning and Engel show that architecture options provide the information to better predict the need for system upgrades and thereby increasing the lifetime value of the system.

Bahsoon and Emmerich (2003) use the concept of ArchOptions to value the stability and scalability of software architectures. ArchOptions are valued using the model of Black and Scholes, and a replicating portfolio is therefore needed. The portfolio is valued by the requirements it supports during the operation of the software system.

Banerjee (2004) argues the need for flexibility and presents the solution of flexibility options compared with a fixed design. The value of the flexibility option is calculated using the binomial model, which does not need a replicating portfolio and also supports American-type options. The work done by Banerjee (2004) seems to be what best meets our prior stated problem definition.

19.8 Conclusions

This chapter has presented an evaluation process for practitioners using Real Options theory that enables analysis of both economic and engineering factors. It presents a possibility to put an economic value on system adaptability and could therefore support the design decisions in the early phases. Real Options provide the opportunity to analyze the cost of designing for future growth of a platform, based on the estimated value of the future functionality.

When developing an embedded system using Real Options, each function would first buy the right but not the obligation to use the asset at a future date. The Real Option approach could, when fully developed, provide not only evaluation but also prediction of future needs.

References

Amram, M., and N. Kulatilaka. 1999. *Real options*. Boston, MA: Harvard Business School Press.

Axelsson, J. 2006. Cost models with explicit uncertainties for electronic architecture trade-off and risk analysis. In *Proceedings of the 16th international symposium of the international council on systems engineering*, Orlando, Florida, July.

Bahsoon, R., and W. Emmerich. 2003. ArchOptions: A real options-based model for predicting the stability of software architecture. In *Proceedings of the 5th ICSE workshop on economics-driven software engineering research* (EDSER 5), Orlando, Florida.

Bahsoon, R., W. Emmerich, and J. Macke. 2005. Using ArchOptions to select stable middleware-induced architectures. In *IEE Proceedings on Software, IEE Press* 152 (4): 176–186.

Banerjee, P. 2004. Describing, assessing and embedding flexibility in system architectures with application to wireless terrestrial networks and handset processors. M.Sc. thesis, Massachusetts Institute of Technology, System Design and Management Program.

Browning, T. R., and A. Engel. 2006. Designing systems for adaptability by means of architecture options. In *Proceedings of the 16th international symposium of the international council on systems engineering*, Orlando, Florida.

Copeland, T., and V. Antikarov. 2001. *Real options: A practitioner's guide*. New York: TEXERE Publishing Ltd.

Cunningham, W. 1992. The WyCash portfolio management system. In *Proceedings of the conference on object oriented programming systems languages and applications*, 29–30. New York: ACM Press.

Florentz, B., and M. Huhn. 2007. Architecture potential analysis: A closer look inside architecture evaluation. *Journal of Software* 2 (4): 43–56.

Hoch, D., W. Huhn, U. Naher, and A. Zielke. 2006. The race to master automotive embedded systems development. McKinsey Company, Germany, Automotive and assembly sector business technology office.

Hull, J. C. 1993. *Options, futures, and other derivative securities*, 2nd ed. Englewood Cliffs, NJ: Prentice Hall International Editions.

Kazman, R., J. Asundi, and M. Klein. 2002. Making architecture design decisions: An economic approach. Technical report CMU/SEI-2002-TR-035. Software Engineering Institute, Carnegie Mellon University, Pittsburgh.

Larses, O. 2005. Architecting and modeling automotive embedded systems. PhD thesis, Dept. of Machine Design, KTH, Stockholm.

Leslie, K. J., and M. P. Michaels. 1997. The real power of real options. *The McKinsey Quarterly*, no. 3:4–22 (McKinsey & Company Inc.).

de Neufville, R. 2001. Real options: Dealing with uncertainty in systems planning and design. Paper presented at the 5th international conference on technology policy and innovation, Technical University of Delft, Netherlands.

Sullivan, K. J., P. Chalasani, S. Jha, and V. Sazawal. 1999. Software design as an investment activity: A real options perspective. In *Real options and business strategy: Applications to decision making*, ed. L. Trigeorgis. London: Risk Books.

Trigeorgis, L. 1988. A conceptual options framework for capital budgeting. *Advances in Futures and Options Research* 3:145–167.

Chapter 20

Product Line in the Business Process Management Domain

Marcelo Fantinato
University of São Paulo, Brazil

Itana Maria de Souza Gimenes
State University of Maringá, Brazil

Maria Beatriz Felgar de Toledo
State University of Campinas, Brazil

Contents

20.1 Introduction

A business process consists of a set of tasks undertaken in a specific sequence to achieve a business goal (Weske 2007). Business processes can be seen as significant assets of organizations that can reveal their maturity level and competitiveness degree. Business process management (BPM) includes activities that enable the modeling, execution, and analysis of business processes. It is currently common for organizations to concentrate efforts on their main business and subcontract services from partners. This scenario is well known for off-line transactions. However, the Internet and the service-oriented computing (SOC) paradigm (Papazoglou and Georgakopoulos 2003) have made the electronic interchange of services possible and broadened the BPM scope from intraorganizational service interchange to interorganizational cooperation.

The current BPM scenario includes one or more organizations, electronic services (e-services) provision and consumption, electronic contracts (e-contracts) negotiation and establishment, quality of services (QoS) agreements, and e-services monitoring. To support the activities involved in this scenario, it is necessary to conceive a proper structure for BPM that includes support for: e-service description, negotiation, and customization; e-contract establishment; e-contract, process, and e-service reuse; and process auditing and monitoring. BPM can benefit from reuse techniques at several stages of business process modeling, execution, and monitoring. Current BPM techniques take little advantage of reuse. Some are limited to the reuse of e-contract templates (Griffel et al. 1998; Hoffner et al. 2001; Chiu, Cheung, and Till 2003; Berry and Milosevic 2005; Farrel et al. 2005; Hoffner and Field 2005; Kabilan and Johannesson 2003).

Product Line (PL) techniques have been successful in providing systematic reuse in several domains (Bass, Clements, and Kazman 1998; Linden, Schmid, and Rommes 2007; Software Engineering Institute 2008). BPM is one of the potential domains to which PL concepts and techniques can be applied. This chapter discusses the challenges of applying PL to the BPM domain and presents a PL structure for BPM. It focuses on one of the possible PL applications: the support of e-contract negotiation and establishment based on feature modeling. It also extends the examples previously presented in Gimenes, Fantinato, and Toledo (2008) and Fantinato, Toledo, and Gimenes (2008). Feature modeling, one of the most widely used techniques to represent common points and the variabilities in PL, allows the representation of generic e-services and possible levels for QoS attributes, which are mapped to an e-contract template. The e-contract negotiation and establishment process is oriented by the feature model and its possible configurations. The generic contracted e-services are mapped to the correspondent Web services (Alonso et al. 2003) that implement them. These Web services are referred to in the resulting e-contract.

The chapter is organized as follows. Section 20.2 introduces the BPM domain. Section 20.3 gives an overview of the PL structure for BPM. Section 20.4 presents details about the process to establish an e-contract based on feature modeling. Section 20.5 presents the application of this approach on a Telecom business process. Section 20.6 discusses the results achieved. Finally, Section 20.7 presents conclusions and future work.

20.2 The BPM Domain

The BPM domain involves several activities that range from (a) modeling the business process, (b) instantiating business process models to specific organizations, (c) supporting business process execution, (d) monitoring and auditing process execution, and (e) analysis of process execution. The SOC paradigm brought about new resources that can be used to improve BPM interchange of services within the interorganizational scope. In the SOC paradigm, e-services are elements of distributed applications that enable fast development and cost reduction. E-services are autonomous and platform independent, and can also be composed from lower granularity e-services. SOC allows e-services to be described, published, located, and invoked in a distributed system context. The Web technology, together with SOC, facilitates interorganizational application integration, as it permits the publication of e-service functionalities according to Internet standards. A Web service is a specific kind of e-service that uses standards such as XML (Bray et al. 2008), WSDL (Chinnici et al. 2007), SOAP (Gudgin et al. 2007), and UDDI (Clement et al. 2008).

The flexibility of business processes, in this wider context, brings a new scenario and additional requirements, as illustrated in Figure 20.1. In this scenario there are stakeholders that provide and consume e-services. The consumers compose Web services into business processes that are regulated by WS-contracts (e-contracts for Web services). A contract is an agreement between two or more parties interested in creating mutual relationships on business or legal obligations. It defines an activity set to be carried out by each party, which must satisfy a set of terms and conditions: the contractual clauses. A WS-contract is an electronic document (Marjanovic and Milosevic 2001) used to represent an agreement between organization partners

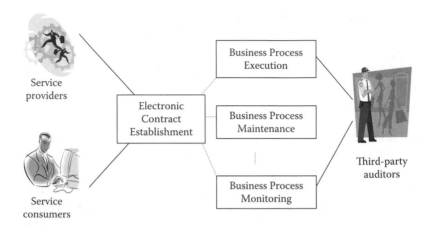

Figure 20.1 Business process scenario. (From Gimenes, Fantinato, and Toledo 2008. With permission.)

carrying out business using the Internet. The negotiated services are e-services, implemented as Web services. They contain details of the business process to be executed in a cooperative way by the organizations. The business process monitoring is supported by QoS levels defined in the WS-contract. Business processes can be specified in terms of Web services using languages such as WS-BPEL (Barreto et al. 2007). In addition, languages such as WS-Agreement (Andrieux et al. 2005) can be used to specify QoS attributes. Third-party auditors can collect information throughout the business process execution to measure the QoS and eventually apply fines according to established contractual clauses.

The parties involved in a WS-contract and the languages used to represent them are shown in Figure 20.2. A WS-contract is composed of involved parties, Web services representing the activities, and contractual clauses. Web services are composed to produce a business process between the parties. Contractual clauses represent three different types of constraints on Web services: prohibitions, permissions, and obligations. These constraints are described in this context by QoS attributes and levels. In terms of specification languages, a WS-contract is composed of three sections: a WSDL section, describing the Web services; a WS-BPEL section, describing the involved parties and the business process; and a WS-Agreement section, describing the QoS attributes and levels.

A WS-contract would be necessary, for instance, for travel agency organizations, as they may use e-services, implemented as Web services, from partner organizations such as airline or car rental companies. The travel agency system offers Web services to its customers, which require Web services provided by other company systems, thus creating an interorganizational business process. Each party provides a set of Web services to be used by any of the other parties. A WS-contract is established to define the details about the business agreement. An airline company

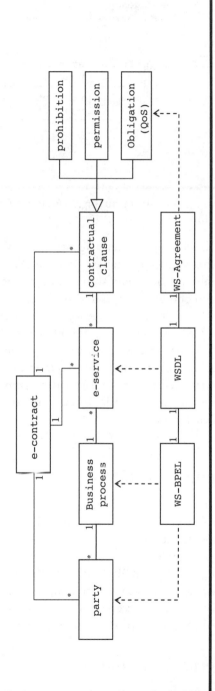

Figure 20.2   E-contract metamodel.

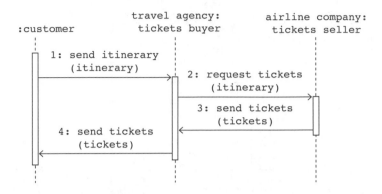

Figure 20.3 Business process for "ticket buying." (Adapted from Leymann and Roller 2002. With permission.)

can provide a series of Web services to a travel agency, such as timetable queries, flight booking, ticket purchase, itinerary changes, and seat selection. On the other hand, a travel agency can also provide some Web services to the airline company, such as customer notification of flight changes and advertisement of special offers. A possible business process involving a travel agency, its customers, and an airline company is presented, as a UML sequence diagram, in Figure 20.3, adapted from Leymann and Roller (2002). After receiving an **itinerary** from a **customer**, the **travel agency**, performing the **ticket buyer** role, **requests tickets** to the **airline company**, forwarding the received **itinerary**. The **airline company**, performing the **ticket seller** role, after issuing them, **sends tickets** to the **travel agency**, which forwards the **tickets** to its **customer**.

20.3 The PL Structure for BPM

The analysis of the scenario illustrated in Figure 20.1 as well as the example in Figure 20.3 brings several opportunities to apply PL to the BPM domain. E-contract issues, e-services functionalities, e-contracts, and business processes can be reused to reduce the complexity of e-contract negotiation, establishment, execution, and monitoring. The PL for BPM aims at offering support to model variability in business processes and Web services, and to monitor WS-contract throughout the process execution. This section presents an overview of the BPM execution environment and the process proposed to develop the PL for BPM.

20.3.1 The BPM Execution Environment

The execution of a business process according to the scenario described in Section 20.2 requires interorganizational cooperation and dynamic exchange of e-services.

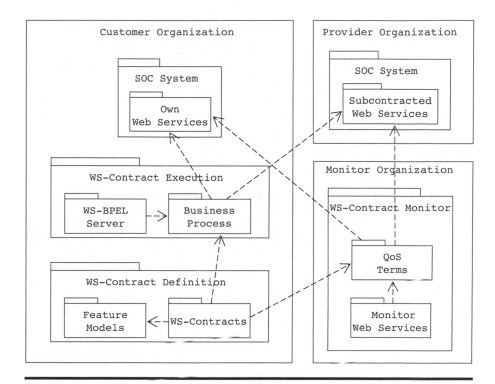

Figure 20.4 BPM execution environment architecture.

Figure 20.4 presents the elements involved in this execution environment comprising three organizations: a customer, a provider, and a monitor. The Customer Organization has the most complex structure, including (a) a structure for WS-Contract Definition, which supports WS-contract negotiation and establishment based on feature modeling, and (b) a structure for WS-Contract Execution to support the execution of business processes specified in WS-BPEL. In addition, a SOC System is necessary in the customer organization if its own Web services are required as part of the business processes to be executed. On the Provider Organization side, the SOC System controls the Web services subcontracted by the consumer organization to be executed as part of the business process involving both organizations. A third party, named the Monitor Organization, has a WS-Contract Monitor structure used to control the execution of the business process, and hence the composed Web services, by using a set of monitor Web services and the QoS terms contained in the WS-contract as a reference.

During the execution of a business process in the customer organization side, it invokes Web services, which can be local or subcontracted. For each Web service invoked, the monitor organization identifies if there are QoS terms associated to it in the WS-contract. Having one or more, the Monitor Web Services will follow up the respective Web-services execution to ensure that the contracted QoS levels are satisfied.

If they are not satisfied, actions can be undertaken, according to the WS-contractual clauses, such as process cancellation, penalty application, and contract renegotiation.

Two prototypes have already been developed to work according to this execution environment: the FeatureContract toolkit, developed to support the WS-Contract Definition structure, and the AspectMonitor tool, developed to support the WS-Contract Monitor structure based on the Aspect-oriented paradigm (Kiczales et al. 1997). This chapter focuses on the FeatureContract toolkit based on PL concepts and the feature modeling technique (described in Section 20.4).

20.3.2 The PL for BPM Development Process

The PL for BPM is designed to model the artifacts involved in the negotiation between organizations willing to establish a common WS-contract to regulate their cooperation. Although the generic approach can consider several parties involved in an e-contract, this specific approach is designed for only two parties. It can also be used for renegotiations when a previously agreed WS-contract could not be executed as planned and the parties desire to keep the cooperation by readjusting the previous contract. Thus, this PL has a core asset that contains related artifacts necessary to execute business processes according to the execution environment presented earlier. This core asset is modeled considering the variabilities involved in business processes, WS-contracts, and Web services.

The stages of this process were conceived based on the FORM method (feature-oriented reuse method) (Kang et al. 1998), which extends the FODA (feature-oriented domain analysis) method (Kang et al. 1990). Moreover, the process adopts Czarnecki's cardinality-based feature metamodel (Czarnecki, Helsen, and Eisenecker 2005). The process consists of five stages, grouped in two life-cycle models. The process is presented in Figure 20.5 and is described as follows:

1. **Contract Template Development** from scratch or from existing templates:
   Stage 1: *E-services feature model elaboration.* Two feature models are elaborated to represent the e-services and QoS attributes from the two organizations willing to establish WS-contracts.
   Stage 2: *WS-contract template creation.* Having the two e-services feature models as the basis, a WS-contract template is created. It will contain basic information that can be used in any WS-contract to be established from these models.
   Stage 3: *Web services development and publication.* Web services that implement the e-services to be electronically contracted must be developed and published to be available during WS-contract establishment.
2. **Contract Instance Development** from templates elaborated in item 1 above:

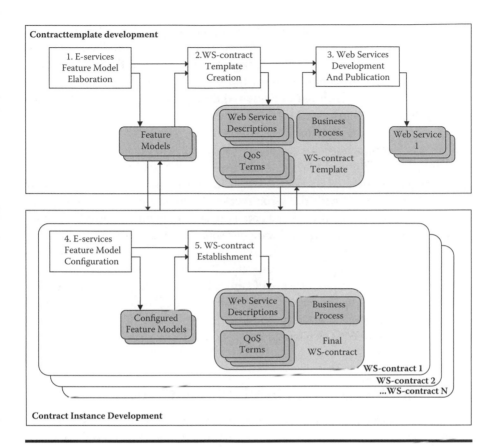

Figure 20.5 E-contract establishment process. (Adapted from Fantinato, Toledo, and Gimenes 2008. With permission.)

> Stage 4: *E-services feature model configuration.* The two e-services feature models are then configured to represent the exact e-services and QoS levels for a particular business process between two organizations.
>
> Stage 5: *WS-contract establishment.* A WS-contract is produced by refining the template based on the previously defined pair of feature model configurations.

These two life-cycle models are equivalent to the Domain Engineering and Application Engineering of Software PL approaches. Whereas the Contract Template Development model groups the activities related to the development of the base artifacts of the WS-contract, the Contract Instance Development model groups the activities related to the development of specific WS-contracts as a result of the WS-contract template instantiation. The WS-contract template is the most important artifact of the PL for BPM development process, in the same way that the Software PL architecture is the most important artifact of the Software PL.

The Web services used to compose a business process in the BPM domain can be seen as the software components used to compose a software product, both classified as independent units. In both PL types being compared, the feature models are used to identify the common points and the variabilities of the final products represented by them, which must be resolved during the Application Engineering or, here, the Contract Instance Development model.

This work takes into account a series of significant differences between software and BPM or e-contracts, such as (a) the dynamic nature of the software, which can be changed more frequently than e-contracts—mainly after its establishment and agreement of the involved parties, and (b) the higher complexity in the software development compared with the e-contract establishment process. Despite these differences, the BPM area also needs a better domain comprehension and a time-to-market reduction as well as the software development area, justifying the application of Software PL concepts into the BPM area. Both similarities and differences are considered in the proposed process, detailed in the next section. An important difference between classical Software PL and this PL for BPM is that, whereas the former produces a unique software (composed by a set of components) as the final result, the latter produces a set of specific artifacts that must cooperate in a dynamic environment (described in Section 20.3.1).

20.4 The WS-Contract Establishment Process

Two scenarios can be identified for a particular WS-contract domain, as illustrated in Figure 20.6: (a) the same pair of organizations (A and B) can establish variations of similar WS-contracts, or (b) an organization (A) that has already established WS-contracts with a certain organization (B) can now establish new similar WS-contracts with another organization (C), using at least a part of the artifacts already used in previous WS-contracts (i.e., the WS-contract template).

The process starts by assuming that the two organizations involved in the business process are known. All the stages, except possibly Stage 1, are carried out aiming at a particular partnership. Stages 1, 2, and 3 are carried out entirely for a WS-contract domain involving the same pair of organizations. Stages 4 and 5

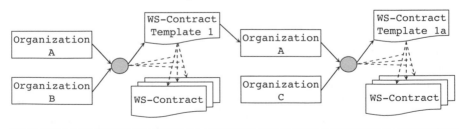

Figure 20.6   Reuse scenarios.

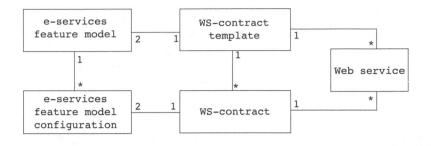

Figure 20.7 Artifacts and its relationships. (From Fantinato, Toledo, and Gimenes 2008. With permission.)

are carried out entirely for each new WS-contract instance. During the execution of Stages 4 and 5, there might be iterations with Stages 1, 2, or 3 to manage further information not treated previously. This iteration is necessary when one of the originally involved organizations is to establish a new WS-contract instance, for the same WS-contract domain, with another organization. Thus, it will need to reuse, at least partially, the artifacts already produced.

Figure 20.7 represents, as a class diagram, the artifacts produced throughout the described stages. The e-services feature model is the primary artifact from which a unique WS-contract template is generated and one or more e-services feature model configurations are derived. For each e-services feature model configuration, a particular WS-contract is established. Several WS-contracts can be established from the same template. Each Web service implementing an e-service is referred to by the WS-contract template.

Table 20.1 summarizes the organization's roles in a WS-contract establishment, acting as Web service supplier or consumer. Each stage has one organization that is responsible for the activities, driving them (Main role); whereas the other

Table 20.1 Organization Roles

Process Stage	Performance Type	Organization Responsibility	
		Consumer	Supplier
Stage 1	Individual	Support	Main
Stage 2	Collaborative	Main	Support
Stage 3	Individual	Support	Main
Stage 4	Collaborative	Main	Support
Stage 5	Collaborative	Main	Support

Source: Fantinato, Toledo, and Gimenes 2008.

provides information needed to elaborate the involved artifacts (Support role). The performance type of the organizations can be either Individual or Collaborative. In Stages 1 and 3, each organization works individually to provide the needed artifacts, but in both cases the supplier organization has the main role; in Stages 2, 4, and 5, organizations work in cooperation to provide the artifacts, and in the three cases the consumer organization has the main role.

This process is intended to be used by different teams within the organizations. For business teams, e-services feature models are useful at the e-negotiation process due to their high level of abstraction. The structured view of e-services will enhance the understanding of each party. At a lower level of abstraction, feature models and their configurations will be used by the system integration architects to refine the details of the e-services to be produced. Moreover, Web services providers can take profit from the structured view of e-services to improve planning, analysis, and design of contracted Web services before development is carried out.

The FeatureContract toolkit was developed to support this approach. Its architecture is presented in Figure 20.8. The toolkit consists of six components, which are mainly Eclipse plug-ins (Eclipse Foundation 2008). Some of them were reused from other research groups: FeaturePlugin (Generative Software Development Lab 2008), WSDL Editor (Eclipse WTP Project 2008), XML Editor (Eclipse WTP Project 2008), and ActiveBpel Designer (Active endpoints 2008). Two components were developed within our work: (a) XSLTransformer, which supports the automatic transformation from a pair of e-services feature models to an initial version of a WS-contract template, and (b) WS-Contract Factory, which supports the automatic WS-contract instantiation, based on the WS-contract template and on the pair of e-services feature model configurations.

In the next subsections, each stage of the process for WS-Contract Establishment is detailed. Parties of artifacts generated to the Travel Agency scenario (presented

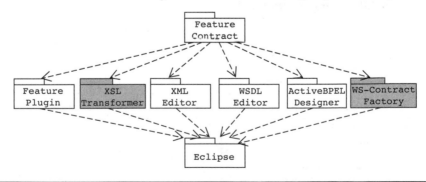

Figure 20.8 FeatureContract architecture. (From Fantinato, Toledo, and Gimenes 2008. With permission.)

in Section 20.2) are used as examples. A more complete set of artifacts, generated within a case study in the Telecom area, is presented in Section 20.5. Stage 3 is not included in either section, as development and publication of Web services are beyond the scope of this chapter.

20.4.1 E-Services Feature Model Elaboration

At Stage 1, each organization involved in a business process must provide a feature diagram representing the capabilities of its system. When the consumer organization does not use its own Web services, a feature diagram is not provided for it. In this case, the business process involving them will only use Web services from the supplier organization but not the opposite. The e-services and QoS attributes are treated as common points and variabilities in the feature models. They can be specified by mandatory, alternative, and optional features.

The inherent flexibility of the feature metamodel allows the definition of e-services and QoS attributes in many ways. Thus, a customized diagram structure for e-services and QoS attributes representation was developed, as shown in Figure 20.9.

1. Each e-services feature diagram consists of two subtrees, identified by the following prenamed root features:
   - **e-services** subtree: contains the features representing the e-services provided by an organization
   - **qos-attributes** subtree: contains the features representing the QoS attributes that can be associated to the e-services
2. Features under **e-services** subtree can be:
   - service group: represents a group or subgroup of e-services in the e-services hierarchy

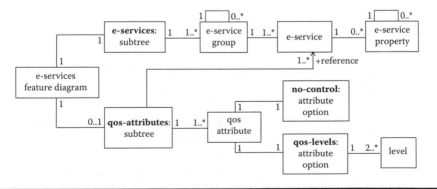

Figure 20.9 Customized feature diagram structure for e-services and QoS attributes. (From Gimenes, Fantinato, and Toledo 2008. With permission.)

- e-service: represents an e-service that corresponds to actions such as business rules, process management, or queries
- service property: represents additional information of an e-service, needed to better describe its aspects

3. Features under **qos-attributes** subtree can be:
   - qos attribute: represents a QoS attribute that must be set by the e-services; the qos attribute features must have a feature group that contains only two grouped features representing two possible attribute options
   - **no-control** attribute option: represents the option in which a QoS attribute may be undefined for a specific e-service feature
   - **qos-levels** attribute option: contains the possible levels that can be defined for a QoS attribute of a specific e-service; a **qos-levels** attribute option must have a feature group to contain its QoS levels; it represents a particular QoS level that can be defined for one QoS attribute

4. The **qos-attributes** subtree must be referred to by all the features of the e-service feature type of **e-services** subtree, using the modularization mechanism

The original cardinality-based feature metamodel (Czarnecki, Helsen, and Eisenecker 2005) was extended to include an attribute that identifies the feature types listed above. They are not graphically represented in the feature diagram by the FeaturePlugin tool, but they are presented in an additional properties panel. The names given to features may suggest their type.

Figure 20.10 presents one of the feature models elaborated for the Travel Agency scenario, following the rules defined previously in this subsection. This feature model was elaborated for the system used by the Airline Company organization. A similar feature model was also elaborated for the system used by the Travel Agency system, but the first model is enough to show the model elaboration using FeaturePlugin. Mandatory, Optional, and Alternative features are represented according to the graphical elements defined by the FeaturePlugin tool, as well as the root, solitary, and grouped features. Examples of the specific types of features in the model are in the feature diagram: both subtrees **e-services** (Figure 20.10a) and **qos-attributes** (Figure 20.10b) are present. For the **e-services** subtree, **flight-services** is an e-service group type of feature; **flight-booking** is an e-service type of feature; and no e-service property type of feature is present. For the **qos-attributes** subtree, **reply-time** is a qos attribute type of feature, with its two grouped attribute option type of features **no-control** and **qos-levels**, the latter with its grouped level type of features **60**, **120**, **360**, and **Other**. The **qos-attributes** subtree is referred to by all the e-service types of feature of the **e-services** subtree.

The additional feature constraints provided by the Czarnecki feature approach (Czarnecki, Helsen, and Eisenecker 2005) can also be used in e-services feature models. Examples of such constraints are presented, together with the artifact examples, in the next section. These additional feature constraints can force par-

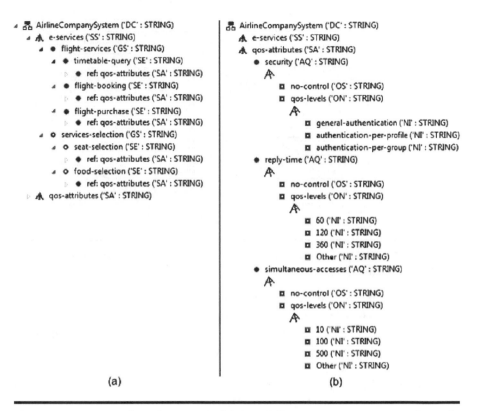

| (a) | (b) |

Figure 20.10   E-services feature model for Airline Company. (a) e-services; (b) QoS attributes.

ticular combined choices during feature model configuration and WS-contract establishment, Stages 4 and 5, respectively.

20.4.2 WS-Contract Template Creation

Stage 2 creates a WS-contract template for the two organizations involved in the business process. It uses the two e-services feature models produced in the previous stage (for example, the feature model presented in Figure 20.10 for the Airline Company system and its complementary model for the Travel Agency system). The produced WS-contract template must encompass all the required information for the resulting WS-contract. Mandatory information from the template is directly incorporated in the WS-contract, whereas the presence of alternative or optional information will be postponed to the e-negotiation time.

A WS-contract metamodel was defined to represent rules to create both WS-contracts and WS-contract templates. The metamodel includes concepts related to (a) Web services, described by the WSDL language (Chinnici et al. 2007); (b) business processes involving Web services, described by the WS-BPEL language

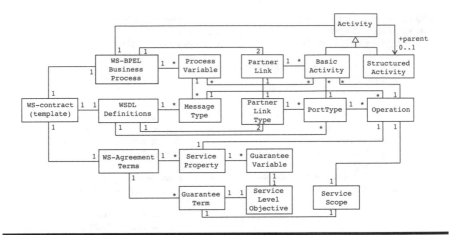

Figure 20.11 WS-contract metamodel. (From Fantinato, Toledo, and Gimenes 2008. With permission.)

(Barreto et al. 2007); and (c) QoS of Web services, described by WS-Agreement language (Andrieux et al. 2005). The metamodel is presented in Figure 20.11.

A WS-contract (template) is composed of three sections: WSDL definitions, WS-BPEL Business Process, and WS-Agreement, as follows:

1. *WSDL definitions section*: contains the base elements used to describe the Web services; these elements are used in the next sections
2. *WS-BPEL Business Process section*: used to describe the business process that composes the Web services
3. *WS-Agreement section*: describes the QoS attributes regarding the involved Web services

The creation of the WS-contract template is carried out in two steps: (a) the WSDL Definitions and the WS-Agreement terms are created directly from the two e-services feature models, where there is a mapping from elements of the feature metamodel to elements of the WS-contract metamodel; (b) the WS-BPEL Business Process is created from WSDL Definitions. The rules for the metamodels mapping are not presented here, since they depend on domain technical information.

Figures 20.12 to 20.14 show parties of the WS-contract template created from the two e-services feature models elaborated at Stage 1. They represent partial information of WS-contract sections, which correspond to elements of the WS-contract metamodel.

The information presented in Figure 20.12 comes from the WSDL section for the Airline Company system. It was automatically generated from the feature model in Figure 20.10a; thus the one-to-one relationship between their elements is noticeable. For example, from the e-service group feature **flight-services** and its three e-service features—**timetable-query**, **flight-booking**, and **flight-purchase**—the

① flight-servicesPT		
❀ timetable-queryOP		
▶] input	☞ timetable-query-Request-MSG-PART	☰ string
◀] output	☞ timetable-query-Response-MSG-PART	☰ string
❀ flight-bookingOP		
▶] input	☞ flight-booking-Request-MSG-PART	☰ string
◀] output	☞ flight-booking-Response-MSG-PART	☰ string
❀ flight-purchaseOP		
▶] input	☞ flight-purchase-Request-MSG-PART	☰ string
◀] output	☞ flight-purchase-Response-MSG-PART	☰ string

① services-selectionPT		
❀ seat-selectionOP		
▶] input	☞ seat-selection-Request-MSG-PART	☰ string
◀] output	☞ seat-selection-Response-MSG-PART	☰ string
❀ food-selectionOP		
▶] input	☞ food-selection-Request-MSG-PART	☰ string
◀] output	☞ food-selection-Response-MSG-PART	☰ string

Figure 20.12   WSDL Definitions of WS-contract template for Airline Company.

WSDL port-type **flight-servicesPT** was generated along with its three operations: **timetable-queryOP, flight-bookingOP,** and **flight-purchaseOP.** Similar WSDL definitions were also generated for the system used by the Travel Agency system from its feature model.

The information presented in Figure 20.13 comes from the WS-Agreement section for the Airline Company system. It was automatically generated from the feature model in Figure 20.10b, which also had a one-to-one relationship between the elements of the two figures. In Figure 20.13, there are several WS-Agreement definitions, five Service Properties (Figure 20.13a), and 15 Guarantee Terms (Figure 20.13b), derived from the QoS attributes and levels in Figure 20.10 (but only some definitions are expanded in the diagram). For example, from the QoS attributes **security, reply-time,** and **simultaneous-accesses**—for e-service **flight-booking**—the WS-Agreement ServiceProperty **flight-bookingSP** and the VariableSets **SecurityVAR, reply-timeVAR,** and **simultaneous-accesses-VAR** were generated. And, from the QoS levels **no-control, 60, 120, 360,** and **Other**—for the QoS attribute **reply-time** and the e-service **flight-booking**—one WS-Agreement GuaranteeTerm whose ServiceLevelObjective is formed by **reply-**

(a)

◢ ⓔ wsag:Terms	
ⓐ xmlns:wsag	http://schemas.ggf.org/graap
▷ ⓔ wsag:ServiceProperties	
◢ ⓔ wsag:ServiceProperties	
ⓐ wsag:Name	flight-bookingSP
ⓐ wsag:ServiceName	flight-bookingOP
◢ ⓔ wsag:VariableSet	
◢ ⓔ wsag:Variable	
ⓐ wsag:Name	securityVAR
ⓐ wsag:Metric	authentication-type
▷ ⓔ wsag:Location	
◢ ⓔ wsag:Variable	
ⓐ wsag:Name	reply-timeVAR
ⓐ wsag:Metric	second
▷ ⓔ wsag:Location	
◢ ⓔ wsag:Variable	
ⓐ wsag:Name	simultaneous-accessesVAR
ⓐ wsag:Metric	user
▷ ⓔ wsag:Location	
▷ ⓔ wsag:ServiceProperties	
▷ ⓔ wsag:ServiceProperties	
▷ ⓔ wsag:ServiceProperties	

(b)

▷ ⓔ wsag:GuaranteeTerm	
▷ ⓔ wsag:GuaranteeTerm	
▷ ⓔ wsag:GuaranteeTerm	
▷ ⓔ wsag:GuaranteeTerm	
◢ ⓔ wsag:GuaranteeTerm	
ⓐ Obligated	
▷ ⓔ wsag:ServiceScope	
ⓐ wsag:ServiceName	flight-bookingOP
▷ ⓔ wsag:QualifyingCondition	
◢ ⓔ wsag:ServiceLevelObjective	
ⓔ wsag:Variable	reply-timeVAR
ⓔ wsag:Operator	IS-LESS-INCLUSIVE
ⓔ wsag:Value	no-control
ⓔ wsag:Value	60
ⓔ wsag:Value	120
ⓔ wsag:Value	360
ⓔ wsag:Value	Other
▷ ⓔ wsag:BusinessValueList	
▷ ⓔ wsag:GuaranteeTerm	
▷ ⓔ wsag:GuaranteeTerm	
▷ ⓔ wsag:GuaranteeTerm	
▷ ⓔ wsag:GuaranteeTerm	
▷ ⓔ wsag:GuaranteeTerm	
▷ ⓔ wsag:GuaranteeTerm	
▷ ⓔ wsag:GuaranteeTerm	
▷ ⓔ wsag:GuaranteeTerm	
▷ ⓔ wsag:GuaranteeTerm	

Figure 20.13 **WS-Agreements Definitions of WS-contract template for Airline Company.**

timeVAR (Variable), **IS-LESS-INCLUSIVE** (Operator), and **no-control**, **60**, **120**, **360**, and **Other** (Value) was generated. Similar WS-Agreement definitions were also generated for the system used by the Travel Agency system.

The information presented in Figure 20.14 comes from the WS-BPEL section for the cooperation between both organizations, in which the Travel Agency system performs the customer role and Airline Company system performs the supplier role. This business process was not automatically generated, but elaborated based on information from the WSDL sections. Examples of activities to be performed in this business process are **book-flight**, which invokes the operation **flight-bookingOP** in the port type **flight-servicesPT**, and **select-seat**, which invokes the operation **seat-selectionOP** in the port type **services-selectionPT**.

The features in the e-services feature models are considered when creating the WS-contract template. Hence, some parties of the template will also be identified as mandatory, optional, or alternative, depending on the feature used to create each part of the template. As a result, a generic template will be created, in which several integration types between the organizations are considered. This generic template will be specialized during a new WS-contract establishment, according to the respective feature model configurations. It is possible to begin with a basic version of the template and evolve while it is being used.

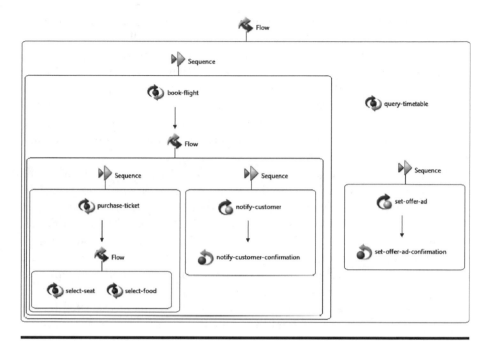

Figure 20.14   WS-BPEL Definitions of WS-contract template for Travel Agency scenario.

As both types of artifacts—the e-services feature models and the WS-contract template—are XML-based documents, the mapping between them can be carried out automatically by using the XSL Transformations (XSLT) (Clark 1999) document processor. To keep the traceability between the source and the target documents, annotations are created in the template. The annotations are created as XML comments on the WS-contract template, linking the e-services feature model elements by a feature identifier to the derived template elements. From such linking, it is possible to track, for example, whether an element in the WS-contract template is mandatory, optional, or alternative. Even the template elements created after the XSLT transformation must be annotated to point to the related e-services feature model elements.

20.4.3 E-Services Feature Model Configuration

The configuration of the two e-services feature models, carried out during Stage 4 (i.e., the feature model presented in Figure 20.10 for the Airline Company system and its complementary model for the Travel Agency system), corresponds to the main negotiation phase in which e-services, QoS attributes, and levels are chosen. The pair of feature model configurations resulting from this stage represent the information to be really used in the business process being contracted. This information includes the e-services being contracted and the specific level of the QoS attributes for these e-services.

This step uses only the e-services feature models, as the WS-contract template is not needed at this moment. Negotiation between the involved parties is carried out according to configuration techniques for feature modeling (Czarnecki, Helsen, and Eisenecker 2005). Thus, features representing mandatory e-services and/or QoS attributes are kept, whereas optional and alternative features are chosen to reflect negotiation. Both cardinality restrictions and additional-feature constraints must be satisfied.

Figure 20.15 presents a possible configuration of the feature model for the Airline Company system, based on the feature model in Figure 20.10. Similarly, a configuration for the feature model elaborated for the Travel Agency system must also be done at this stage. Examples of choices done for the configuration presented in Figure 20.15 are: all the mandatory e-services features, e.g., **flight-booking**, were automatically selected, but only the optional feature **seat-selection** was selected, whereas the optional feature **food-selection** was not; regarding features related to QoS attributes, **no-control** was defined for the QoS attribute **security**, whereas the level **120** seconds was selected for the QoS attribute **reply-time** (both taking into account the choices made for e-service **flight-booking**).

20.4.4 WS-Contract Establishment

During Stage 5, the WS-contract template is refined considering the two e-services feature models configured in the previous stage (i.e., the feature model configuration in Figure 20.15 for the Airline Company system and its complementary model for the Travel Agency system). Pending details are defined, and information not required is removed from the WS-contract. As the template elements are related to each other and to the e-services feature models via annotations, the feature model configurations are used by a parser in a removal process. In this process, all the template elements associated to mandatory features or to alternative and/or optional features that have been selected are kept in the resulting WS-contract. On the other hand, all the template elements associated to alternative or optional features not selected are removed from the WS-contract.

Figure 20.16 presents the final WSDL section for the Airline Company system: The entire **flight-bookinPT** port type was kept, since the feature **flight-booking** and all its tree subfeatures were selected; but for the **services-selectionPT** port type, only the **seat-selectionOP** operation was kept, since only the subfeature **seat-selection** was selected for the feature **services-selection**, whereas the subfeature **food-selection** was not.

Figure 20.17 presents the final WS-Agreement section for the same Airline Company system: The last ServiceProperty (Figure 20.17a), which was associated to the last e-service **food-selection** (from Figure 20.16), was completely removed,

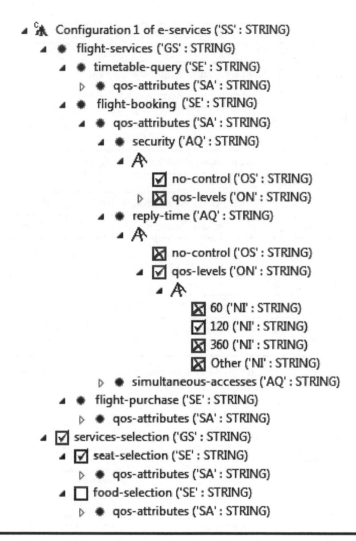

Figure 20.15   E-services feature model configuration for Airline Company.

since that feature was not selected in the respective feature model configuration, but all the other ServiceProperties were kept due to the opposite reason; similarly, the last three GuaranteeTerms were also removed, whereas all the other 15 ones were kept, but adjusted. For example, for the operation **flight-bookingOP** and Variable **reply-timeVAR**, only the Value **120** was kept, whereas the other ones were removed, according to the chosen configurations within the respective feature model.

Figure 20.18 presents the final WS-BPEL section for the cooperation between both organizations. From the whole business process in the WS-contract template, the following activities were removed: **select-food** and the sequence **set-offer-ad**

❶ flight-servicesPT		
✿ timetable-queryOP		
▷] input	⧼ timetable-query-Request-MSG-PART	= string
◁] output	⧼ timetable-query-Response-MSG-PART	= string
✿ flight-bookingOP		
▷] input	⧼ flight-booking-Request-MSG-PART	= string
◁] output	⧼ flight-booking-Response-MSG-PART	= string
✿ flight-purchaseOP		
▷] input	⧼ flight-purchase-Request-MSG-PART	= string
◁] output	⧼ flight-purchase-Response-MSG-PART	= string

❶ services-selectionPT		
✿ seat-selectionOP		
▷] input	⧼ seat-selection-Request-MSG-PART	= string
◁] output	⧼ seat-selection-Response-MSG-PART	= string

Figure 20.16   WSDL Definitions of WS-contract for Airline Company.

(a)

▲ e wsag:Terms	
ⓐ xmlns:wsag	http://schemas.ggf.org/graap
▷ e wsag:ServiceProperties	
▲ e wsag:ServiceProperties	
ⓐ wsag:Name	flight-bookingSP
ⓐ wsag:ServiceName	flight-bookingOP
▲ e wsag:VariableSet	
▲ e wsag:Variable	
ⓐ wsag:Name	securityVAR
ⓐ wsag:Metric	authentication-type
▷ e wsag:Location	
▲ e wsag:Variable	
ⓐ wsag:Name	reply-timeVAR
ⓐ wsag:Metric	second
▷ e wsag:Location	
▲ e wsag:Variable	
ⓐ wsag:Name	simultaneous-accessesVAR
ⓐ wsag:Metric	user
▷ e wsag:Location	
▷ e wsag:ServiceProperties	
▷ e wsag:ServiceProperties	

(b)

▷ e wsag:GuaranteeTerm	
▷ e wsag:GuaranteeTerm	
▷ e wsag:GuaranteeTerm	
▷ e wsag:GuaranteeTerm	
▲ e wsag:GuaranteeTerm	
ⓐ Obligated	
▷ e wsag:ServiceScope	
ⓐ wsag:ServiceName	flight-bookingOP
▷ e wsag:QualifyingCondition	
▲ e wsag:ServiceLevelObjective	
ⓐ wsag:Variable	reply-timeVAR
ⓐ wsag:Operator	IS-LESS-INCLUSIVE
ⓐ wsag:Value	120
▷ e wsag:BusinessValueList	
▷ e wsag:GuaranteeTerm	
▷ e wsag:GuaranteeTerm	
▷ e wsag:GuaranteeTerm	
▷ e wsag:GuaranteeTerm	
▷ e wsag:GuaranteeTerm	
▷ e wsag:GuaranteeTerm	

Figure 20.17   WS-Agreements Definitions of WS-contract for Airline Company.

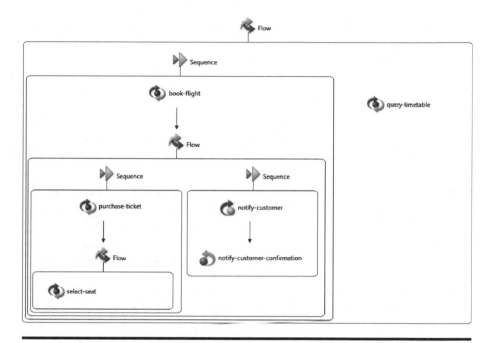

Figure 20.18   WS-BPEL Definitions of WS-contract for Travel Agency scenario.

and **set-offer-ad-confirmation**, as they were associated with features not selected at Stage 4. All the other activities in the business process are associated to WSDL definition and features selected.

During WS-contract establishments, unforeseen information such as new e-services, QoS attributes, or business process activities might be required. In this case, artifacts used in the establishment of WS-contracts (e-services feature models and WS-contract template) can be updated to include new information. This facility allows reuse during the establishment of other WS-contracts. After the last stage, the established WS-contract can be released to be used.

20.5 An Application of the WS-Contract Establishment Process in Telecom Context

This section presents the application of the WS-contract establishment process to a pseudo-scenario in a Telecom company. The systems involved are real ones. The requirements of the business process were acquired from the analysts responsible for the systems; however, they were adapted to include Web services. This application was carried out by one of the authors of this chapter, since he worked in the company.

The following subsections present the systems domain, excerpts of produced artifacts, and a brief data analysis. Again, Stage 3 is not included, as development and publication of Web services are beyond the scope of this chapter.

20.5.1 Systems Domain

The application is concerned with the integration between two Business and Operation Support Systems (BOSS) (Terplan 2001) in the telecom context (Hunger and Thiebaud 2003):

- *Customer Relationship Management* (CRM): system that manages the relationship between customers and a telecom company. E-services provided by a CRM system can include selling products and services to customers; creating products/services contracts for customers; registering, consulting, and cancelling of service orders; managing and updating customer information; and sending communications to customers;
- *Dunning*: system that supports customer debit charging. E-services provided by a dunning system can include applying, updating, and cancelling charge actions and charge-action reversions; adding and removing irregular check records; parceling and cancelling customer debits; cancelling duties; and granting discounts.

The application has considered that the Telecom company operating the CRM system outsourced the charging activities to another company that operates the Dunning system. This creates an interorganizational business process. Each system provides a set of e-services, deployed as Web services, to be used by the other. A WS-contract is established to define the details about the business agreement.

20.5.2 Produced Artifacts

Excerpts of some of the produced artifacts are presented here. Additional examples of the artifacts produced for this application can be seen in a work by Fantinato, Toledo, and Gimenes (2008). In this section, the examples are presented for each of the process stages:

Stage 1: Figures 20.19 and 20.20 show the e-services features models elaborated for the Dunning system. They represent partial information about the capabilities related to e-services and QoS attributes, respectively. Examples of the e-services in Figure 20.19 are the e-service group **Charge Actions**, consisting of three e-services: **Action Application, Action State Update**, and **Action Cancellation**. The **Charge Action Types** has subfeatures regarding e-service properties. Examples of QoS features in Figure 20.20 are **Reply Time**, as a qos-attribute feature, with level options **5, 15, 30 seconds**, and **Other** (**Integer**).

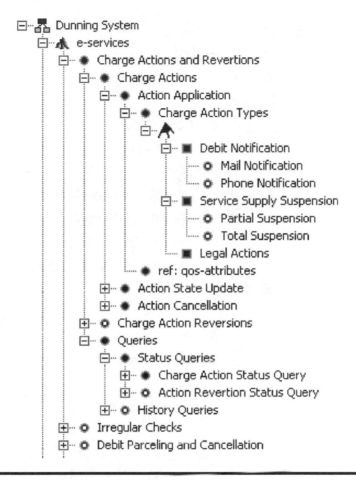

Figure 20.19 E-services feature models for Dunning System (e-services). (From Fantinato, Toledo, and Gimenes 2008. With permission.)

Stage 2: Figures 20.21 and 20.22 show parties of the WS-contract template created from the two e-services feature models. They represent partial information of WS-contract sections, which correspond to elements of the WS-contract metamodel. The information in Figure 20.21 comes from the WSDL section. It was automatically generated from the feature model in Figure 20.19; thus the one-to-one relationship between their elements is noticeable. For example, from the e-service group feature **Charge Actions**, and its three e-service features, the WSDL port type **charge-actionsPT** and its three operations were generated. A similar relationship exists between the WS-Agreement section and the feature model in Figure 20.20, omitted here for space reasons. Figure 20.22 contains part of the business process involving both organizations, taken from elements of the WSDL Definitions section. Examples of

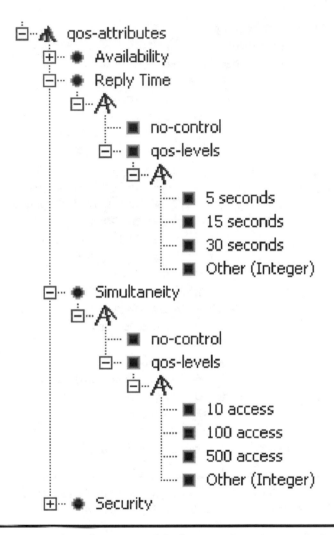

Figure 20.20 E-services feature models for Dunning System (QoS attributes). (From Fantinato, Toledo, and Gimenes, 2008. With permission.)

elements from the Dunning system are: (a) **Apply-CA**, which invokes the operation **action-applicationOP** in the port type **charge-actionsPT**, and (b) **Revert-CA**, which invokes the operation **action-reversion-applicationOP** in the port type **charge-action-reversionsPT**.

Stage 4: Examples of selected configurations (see Figure 20.19) for this application are the mandatory feature **Action Application** automatically selected and some features below **Charge Action Types** selected as they correspond to the optional/ alternative types of charging actions contracted; in contrast, the optional feature **Charge Action Reversions** and its subfeatures were not selected.

ⓘ charge-actionsPT		
❈ action-applicationOP		
▷] input	⯅ action-application-Request-MSG-PART	▤ string
	⯅ action-application-MSG-PART	▤ string
◁] output	⯅ action-application-Response-MSG-PART	▤ string
❈ action-state-updateOP		
▷] input	⯅ action-state-update-Request-MSG-PART	▤ string
◁] output	⯅ action-state-update-Response-MSG-PART	▤ string
❈ action-cancellationOP		
▷] input	⯅ action-cancellation-Request-MSG-PART	▤ string
◁] output	⯅ action-cancellation-Response-MSG-PART	▤ string

ⓘ charge-action-reverstionsPT		
❈ action-reversion-applicationOP		
▷] input	⯅ action-reversion-application-Request-MSG-PART	▤ string
◁] output	⯅ action-reversion-application-Response-MSG-PART	▤ string
❈ action-reversion-state-updateOP		
▷] input	⯅ action-reversion-state-update-Request-MSG-PART	▤ string
◁] output	⯅ action-reversion-state-update-Response-MSG-PART	▤ string
❈ action-reversion-cancellationOP		
▷] input	⯅ action-reversion-cancellation-Request-MSG-PART	▤ string
◁] output	⯅ action-reversion-cancellation-Response-MSG-PART	▤ string

Figure 20.21   WSDL Definitions of WS-contract template for Dunning e-services. (From Fantinato, Toledo, and Gimenes 2008. With permission.)

Stage 5: Regarding the application presented here, the following decisions were taken: (a) as shown in Figure 20.21, the **charge-actionsPT** port type was kept, since the feature **Action Application** was selected, but all the **charge-action-reversionsPT** port type was removed, since the feature **Charge Action Reversions** was not selected; (b) as shown in Figure 20.22, the business process sequence started with **Apply-CA** operation was kept, but all of the sequence started with **Revert-CA** was removed.

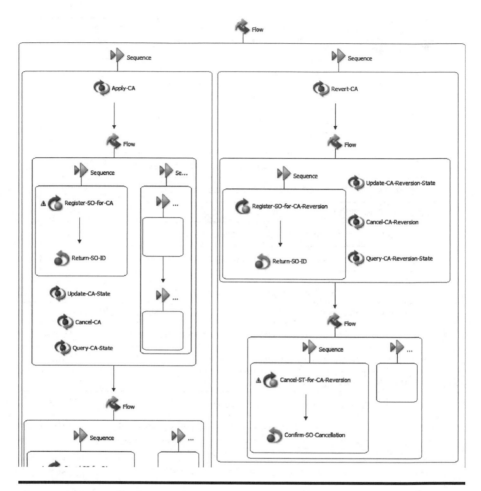

Figure 20.22 WS-BPEL Definitions of WS-contract template for CRM and Dunning cooperation. (From Fantinato, Toledo, and Gimenes 2008. With permission.)

20.5.3 Variability Degree Analysis

Aiming at characterizing the potential effectiveness of the proposed approach for e-contract establishment, this section presents a brief analysis of the variability degree (i.e., the amount of possible configurations from a feature model) obtained by this specific application. This analysis was originally presented by Fantinato, Toledo, and Gimenes (2008), but it is important to reproduce it here for a better understanding of this approach and the benefits that can be achieved by using it.

Two related metrics are presented in Table 20.2: the number of mandatory and optional/alternative features and the number of possible configurations that can be derived during feature model configuration (values provided by the

Table 20.2   Variability Metrics

E-Service Feature Diagram	Feature Types	Possible Configurations	
	Mandatory	*Optional/Alternative*	
Dunning system / e-services	19	23	288,360
CRM system / e-services	11	4	20
Dunning system / QoS attributes	6	35	12,500
CRM system / QoS attributes	3	17	100
Total	39	79	300,980

Source: Fantinato, Toledo, and Gimenes 2008.

FeaturePlugin tool). The numbers are grouped by e-services and QoS attributes for both systems.

Although these metrics cannot be seen as statistical data, since they were obtained from a unique sample space, they offer indications of the approach's effectiveness. These metrics show the potential of this proposal for a WS-contract domain having several variability points and, consequently, leading to a large number of different possible configurations. As the systems involved in this case study have well-defined roles in business cooperation, they presented differences in the analyzed metrics. As the CRM system is playing the consumer role, it is natural that it presents a smaller relative number of optional/alternative features—regarding its total number of features—than the Dunning system, which is playing the provider role.

In addition to the existing differences in the individual metrics, the accumulated amount shows that this type of WS-contract domain can present a great variability degree. Hence, the proposed approach in which the variability points are exploited, mainly to improve the information reuse among similar WS-contracts, can be very useful and effective. As the other existing approaches to establish WS-contracts do not exploit the commonalities and variabilities of a particular WS-contract domain, it is not possible to compare their results with the ones produced by the approach proposed in this chapter.

20.6 Discussion

This section presents a discussion about our experience of applying PL and feature modeling principles on the BPM context.

▪ *E-services representation by feature models*: The feature modeling technique has been considered suitable for the representation of e-services and QoS attributes.

The metamodel flexibility has allowed the use of particular rules for e-services specification. Modularization facilities have been particularly useful for QoS attributes specification. Even if the produced artifacts are not reused, the modeling of e-services as feature models allows structured representation of the optional and mandatory WS-contract elements—what is already useful per se. With the supporting tool, it has been possible to add new properties to the feature model and extend the metamodel used in the application example.

■ *Variability degree at BPM context*: An analysis of the variability degree obtained from the application example has shown that PL principles are effective for the BPM domain. Two related metrics were acquired and evaluated: (a) the number of mandatory and optional/alternative features and (b) the number of possible configurations that can be derived during the feature model configuration. The metrics values were obtained from the FeatureContract toolkit. The acquired values show that this type of WS-contract domain can present a high variability degree. For example, the Dunning system has 288,360 possible configurations. The e-services subtree has 19 mandatory features and 23 optional/alternative ones. Although the collected metrics (not presented here due to space restrictions) cannot be seen as statistical data, since they were obtained from a unique sample space, they offer indications of the approach's effectiveness.

■ *WS-contract metamodel*: The defined WS-contract metamodel includes the most relevant items required in a WS-contract. Its well-defined structure shows the potential reuse in this application domain. This shows that the feature modeling supports the WS-contract negotiation, making it easier for the stakeholders to negotiate and reuse Web services. WS-BPEL and WS-Agreement have been considered rather complete and consistent, simplifying the WS-contract template creation. An important intermediary benefit of this work is to present a unique and original WS-contract metamodel integrating the common and the different concepts existing in both WS-BPEL and WS-Agreement, which have not been presented yet. This approach is also useful in the establishment of complex WS-contracts, since the feature metamodel used to represent e-services can be easily partitioned. Therefore, a complex WS-contract can be inherently established from a series of small e-services feature models grouped in only two feature models using the modularization mechanism.

■ *Metamodels mapping*: It was possible to identify a direct mapping between elements in the e-services feature metamodel and the WS-contract metamodel. Such mapping has been facilitated, as both metamodels are based on XML. Some rules have been defined to map the different types of features representing e-services information to elements in WS-contract sections. These rules have proved to be suitable. This shows that the road for automatic generation of WS-contract and business processes is a benefit gained from the application of PL principles.

20.7 Related Work

Few projects tackle reuse in e-contract establishment or other BPM contexts. Existing solutions are based either on e-contract metamodels or templates (Griffel et al. 1998; Hoffner et al. 2001; Chiu, Cheung, and Till 2003; Berry and Milosevic 2005; Farrel et al. 2005; Hoffner and Field 2005; Kabilan and Johannesson 2003). The COSMOS project (Griffel et al. 1998) is one of the precursor projects to treat e-contracts systematically through templates. It introduced basic concepts that are still in practice, mainly concerned with the e-contract structure in terms of sections. The CrossFlow project (Hoffner et al. 2001) is possibly the most comprehensive project in the BPM area. It allows template creation from preexisting e-contracts available for several business domains. Its reuse approach allows that fields with variable values are kept blank, to be filled later for each particular e-contract. Chiu, Cheung, and Till (2003) treat templates as entities in e-contract metamodels that can contain variables whose values are defined during e-contract establishment.

More recently, Berry and Milosevic (2005) explored the community template concept, a type of domain template. It is a partially specified e-contract in which parameterized values are bound at or before e-contract activation time. Farrell et al. (2005) use event calculus for tracking the normative state of e-contracts, also using templates. Hoffner and Field (2005) develop a work on transforming agreements into e-contracts based on templates. The matchmaking process consists of selecting the right template and then populating the variable fields of the template with information from an agreement description.

A different approach, based on computational ontology, is presented by the UCM (Unified Contract Management) framework (Kabilan and Johannesson 2003). It provides support for all the e-contract life-cycle phases through a conceptual model formed by three hierarchical ontology layers for e-contracts. The lowest layer represents the e-contract template ontology, which is formed by a template library, and the upper ontology layers contain more generic information related to e-contracts.

Domain analysis concepts have been applied to service-based systems (Gruler, Harhurin, and Hartmann 2007; Lalanda and Marin 2007), but they do not model the whole BPM domain aiming at generating e-contract and process instances.

The limitations found in previous work are: (a) Templates are normally treated as just partially filled e-contracts that have empty fields to be fulfilled with some value from a predefined list; and (b) usually there is no support for the representation and selection of optional or alternative e-contract parties. The introduction of feature modeling in e-contract establishment aims at achieving a better reuse in a similar way as the software PL does.

Another category of related work is considered by Czarnecki and Antkiewicz (2005). They present a similar approach to this work, which is not specifically applied to a unique domain such as BPM. It is a general template-based approach for mapping feature models to concise representations of variability in different models. Whereas the work presented here uses feature models to parameterize particularly WS-contracts specified using WS-Agreement and WS-BPEL, their approach uses feature models to parameterize any model in a general way, although the approach has been applied so far only to UML 2.0 activity and class models. Aiming at a more particular target—WS-contract establishment—the approach presented in this chapter can address some types of specific problems not considered in their work. Moreover, the use of XSLT language to automate the transformation between the feature models and the target artifact is not used in their approach, which is based on a manually strategy.

20.8 Conclusions

This chapter has presented the benefits of applying PL principles to the BPM domain. In particular, a feature-based approach to support WS-contract negotiation and establishment was presented. The approach includes a metamodel for WS-contracts representation, a mechanism for mapping WS-contracts to business processes, and a support toolkit to enable this process automation.

The example of the process application has demonstrated that the use of feature models during the establishment of WS-contracts makes them easier to understand, simpler, and more systematic. The approach improves information and artifact reuse, and it allows quicker establishment of WS-contracts. Common points and variabilities provided by feature modeling represent e-services in a controlled and structured way. Distinct stakeholders, at different levels, can benefit from this approach. The e-services feature model can be understood as a WS-contract configuration space; depending on the choices made during feature model configurations, different and particular WS-contracts are established.

Some limitations of the approach lead to required improvements such as (a) extending the range of basic elements covered by the feature model to fulfill the demands of the BPM domain; (b) providing support for agreements between more than two parties; (c) considering the characteristics of dynamic binding of Web services; and (d) improving the FeatureContract toolkit.

This process is within a research project that aims at providing a structure for modeling and automation support of BPM. In addition to overcoming the previously mentioned limitations, ongoing working includes reuse of business processes; monitoring of WS-contracts based on aspects and production of experimental data; and discovery of Web services using semantic information.

References

Active endpoints. 2008. ActiveVOS. http://www.active-endpoints.com/.

Alonso, G., F. Casati, H. Kuno, and V. Machiraju. 2003. *Web services: Concepts, architectures, and applications.* Berlin: Springer.

Andrieux, A., K. Czajkowski, A. Dan, et al. 2005. Web services agreement specification (WS-Agreement). http://www.ogf.org/Public_Comment_Docs/Documents/Oct-2005/WS-AgreementSpecificationDraft050920.pdf.

Barreto, C., V. Bullard, T. Erl, et al. 2007. Web services business process execution language version 2.0. http://docs.oasis-open.org/wsbpel/2.0/Primer/wsbpel-v2.0-Primer.pdf.

Bass, L., P. Clements, and R. Kazman. 1998. *Software architecture in practice.* Boston: Addison-Wesley Longman.

Berry, A., and Z. Milosevic. 2005. Extending choreography with business contract constraints. *International Journal of Cooperative Information Systems* 14 (2/3): 131–179.

Bray, T., J. Paoli, C. M. Sperberg-McQueen, E. Maler, and F. Yergeau. 2008. Extensible markup language (XML) 1.0 (Fifth Edition). http://www.w3.org/TR/REC-xml/.

Chinnici, R., J.-J. Moreau, A. Ryman, and S. Weerawarana. 2007. Web services description language (WSDL) Version 2.0 Part 1: Core Language. http://www.w3.org/TR/wsdl20/.

Chiu, D. K. W., S.-C. Cheung, and S. Till. 2003. A three layer architecture for e-contract enforcement in an e-service environment. In *Proceedings of the 36th annual Hawaii international conference on system sciences,* 74. Washington, DC: IEEE Computer Society.

Clark, J. 1999. XSL transformations (XSLT) Version 1.0. http://www.w3.org/TR/xslt.

Clement, L., A. Hately, C. von Riegen, and T. Rogers. 2008. UDDI version 3.0.2. http://www.oasis-open.org/committees/uddi-spec/doc/spec/v3/uddi-v3.0.2-20041019.htm.

Czarnecki, K., and M. Antkiewicz. 2005. Mapping features to models: A template approach based on superimposed variants. In *Proceedings of the 4th international conference on generative programming and component engineering,* ed. R. Glück and M. R. Lowry, 422-437. Berlin: Springer.

Czarnecki, K., S. Helsen, and U. Eisenecker. 2005. Staged configuration through specialization and multi-level configuration of feature models. *Software Process: Improvement and Practice* 10 (2): 143–169.

Eclipse Foundation. 2008. Eclipse. http://www.eclipse.org/.

Eclipse WTP Project. 2008. Web tools platform. http://www.eclipse.org/webtools/.

Fantinato, M., M. B. F. Toledo, and I. M. S. Gimenes. 2008. WS-contract establishment with QoS: An approach based on feature modeling. *International Journal on Cooperative Information Systems* 17 (3): 373–407.

Farrell, A. D. H., M. Sergot, M. Salle, and C. Bartolini. 2005. Using the event calculus for tracking the normative state of contracts. *International Journal of Cooperative Information Systems* 14 (2/3): 131–179.

Generative Software Development Lab. 2008. Feature modeling plug-in. http://gsd.uwaterloo.ca/projects/fmp-plugin/.

Gimenes, I. M. S., M. Fantinato, and M. B. F. Toledo. 2008. A product line for business process management. In *Proceedings of the 12th international software product line conference,* 265–274. Washington, DC: IEEE Computer Society.

Griffel, F., M. Boger, H. Weinreich, W. Lamersdorf, and M. Merz. 1998. Electronic contracting with COSMOS: How to establish, negotiate and execute electronic contracts on the Internet. In *Proceedings of the 2nd international workshop on enterprise distributed object computing,* ed. C. Kobryn, 46–55. Washington, DC: IEEE Computer Society.

Gruler, A., A. Harhurin, and J. Hartmann. 2007. Development and configuration of service-based product lines. In *Proceedings of the 11th international software product line conference,* 107–116. Washington, DC: IEEE Computer Society.

Gudgin, M., M. Hadley, N. Mendelssohn, et al. 2007. SOAP version 1.2 part 1: Messaging framework (second edition). http://www.w3.org/TR/soap12-part1/.

Hoffner, Y., and S. Field. 2005. Transforming agreements into contracts. *International Journal of Cooperative Information Systems* 14 (2/3): 131–179.

Hoffner, Y., S. Field, P. Grefen, and H. Ludwig. 2001. Contract-driven creation and operation of virtual enterprises. *Computer Networks* 37: 111–136.

Hunger, J., and M. Thiebaud. 2003. *Telecommunications billing systems: Implementing and upgrading for profitability.* New York: McGraw-Hill.

Kabilan, V., and P. Johannesson. 2003. Semantic representation of contract knowledge using multi-tier ontology. In *Proceedings of the 1st international workshop on semantic web and databases,* ed. I. F. Cruz, V. Kashyap, S. Decker, and R. Eckstein, 395–414. Berlin: Springer.

Kang, K. C., S. Cohen, J. Hess, W. Novak, and A. Peterson. 1990. Feature-oriented domain analysis (FODA) feasibility study. Technical report CMU/SEI-90-TR-021. Software Engineering Institute, Carnegie Mellon University, Pittsburgh.

Kang, K. C., S. Kim, J. Lee, K. Kim, E. Shin, and M. Huh. 1998. FORM: A feature-oriented reuse method with domain-specific reference architectures. *Annals of Software Engineering* 5: 143–168.

Kiczales, G., J. Lamping, A. Mendhekar, et al. 1997. Aspect-oriented programming. In *Proceedings of the 11th European conference on object-oriented programming,* ed. M. Aksit and S. Matsuoka, 220–242. Berlin: Springer.

Lalanda, P., and C. Marin. 2007. A domain-configurable development environment for service-oriented applications. *IEEE Software* 24 (6): 31–38.

Leymann, F., and D. Roller. 2002. Business processes in a Web services world. http://www.ibm.com/developerworks/webservices/library/ws-bpelwp/.

Linden, F. van der, K. Schmid, and E. Rommes. 2007. *Software product lines in action: The best industrial practice in product line engineering.* Berlin: Springer.

Marjanovic, O., and Z. Milosevic. 2001. Towards formal modeling of e-contracts. In *Proceedings of the 5th international enterprise distributed object computing conference,* 59–68. Washington, DC: IEEE Computer Society.

Papazoglou, M., and D. Georgakopoulos. 2003. Serviceoriented computing. *Communications of the ACM* 46 (10): 24–28.

Software Engineering Institute. 2008. Software product lines. http://www.sei.cmu.edu/productlines/plp_hof.html.

Terplan, K. 2001. *OSS essentials: Support system solutions for service providers.* New York: John Wiley & Sons.

Weske, M. 2007. *Business process management: Concepts, languages, architecture.* Berlin: Springer.

Index